REPAIR & TUNE-UP GUIDE

FORD PICK-UPS 1965-86

All U.S. and Canadian models of F-100 • F-150 • F-250 • F-300 • F-350 • 2 and 4-wheel drive, gasoline and diesel engines

President LAWRENCE A. FORNASIERI
Vice President and General Manager JOHN P. KUSHNERICK
Executive Editor KERRY A. FREEMAN, S.A.E.
Senior Editor RICHARD J. RIVELE, S.A.E.
Editor RON WEBB

CHILTON BOOK COMPANY
Radnor, Pennsylvania
19089

SAFETY NOTICE

Proper service and repair procedures are vital to the safe, reliable operation of all motor vehicles, as well as the personal safety of those performing repairs. This book outlines procedures for servicing and repairing vehicles using safe, effective methods. The procedures contain many NOTES, CAUTIONS and WARNINGS which should be followed along with standard safety procedures to eliminate the possibility of personal injury or improper service which could damage the vehicle or compromise its safety.

It is important to note that repair procedures and techniques, tools and parts for servicing motor vehicles, as well as the skill and experience of the individual performing the work vary widely. It is not possible to anticipate all of the conceivable ways or conditions under which vehicles may be serviced, or to provide cautions as to all of the possible hazards that may result. Standard and accepted safety precautions and equipment should be used when handling toxic or flammable fluids, and safety goggles or other protection should be used during cutting, grinding, chiseling, prying, or any other process that can cause material removal or projectiles.

Some procedures require the use of tools specially designed for a specific purpose. Before substituting another tool or procedure, you must be completely satisfied that neither your personal safety, nor the performance of the vehicle will be endangered.

Although information in this guide is based on industry sources and is as complete as possible at the time of publication, the possibility exists that the manufacturer made later changes which could not be included here. While striving for total accuracy, Chilton Book Company cannot assume responsibility for any errors, changes, or omissions that may occur in the compilation of this data.

PART NUMBERS

Part numbers listed in this reference are not recommendations by Chilton for any product by brand name. They are references that can be used with interchange manuals and aftermarket supplier catalogs to locate each brand supplier's discrete part number.

SPECIAL TOOLS

Special tools are recommended by the vehicle manufacturer to perform their specific job. Use has been kept to a minimum, but where absolutely necessary, they are referred to in the text by the part number of the tool maufacturer. These tools can be purchased, under the appropriate part number, from Owatonna Tool Company, Owatonna, MN 55060 or an equivalent tool can be purchased locally from a tool supplier or parts outlet. Before substituting any tool for the one recommended, read the SAFETY NOTICE at the top of this page.

ACKNOWLEDGMENTS

The Chilton Book Company expresses appreciation to the Ford Motor Company; Ford Parts and Service Division, Service Technical Communications Department, Dearborn, Michigan for their generous assistance.

Published in Radnor, Pennsylvania 19089 by Chilton Book Company

Manufactured in the United States of America
1234567890 5432109876

Chilton's Repair & Tune-Up Guide: Ford Pick-Ups 1965–86
ISBN 0-8019-7662-6 pbk.
Library of Congress Catalog Card No. 85-47463

CONTENTS

Quick Reference Specifications For Your Vehicle

Fill in this chart with the most commonly used specifications for your vehicle. Specifications can be found in Chapters 1 through 3 or on the tune-up decal under the hood of the vehicle.

Tune-Up

Firing Order

Spark Plugs:

Type

Gap (in.)

Torque (ft. lbs.)

Idle Speed (rpm)

Ignition Timing (°)

Vacuum or Electronic Advance (Connected/Disconnected)

Valve Clearance (in.)

Intake Exhaust

Capacities

Engine Oil Type (API Rating)

With Filter Change (qts)

Without Filter Change (qts)

Cooling System (qts)

Manual Transmission (pts)

Type

Automatic Transmission (pts)

Type

Front Differential (pts)

Type

Rear Differential (pts)

Type

Transfer Case (pts)

Type

FREQUENTLY REPLACED PARTS

Use these spaces to record the part numbers of frequently replaced parts.

PCV VALVE	OIL FILTER	AIR FILTER	FUEL FILTER
Type	Type	Type	Type
Part No.	Part No.	Part No.	Part No.

General Information and Maintenance

1

HOW TO USE THIS BOOK

Chilton's Repair & Tune-Up Guide for Ford Pick-ups is intended to help you learn more about the inner workings of your vehicle and save you money on its upkeep and operation.

The first two chapters will be the most used, since they contain maintenance and tune-up information and procedures. Studies have shown that a properly tuned and maintained truck can get at least 10% better gas mileage than an out-of-tune truck. The other chapters deal with the more complex systems of your truck. Operating systems from engine through brakes are covered to the extent that the average do-it-yourselfer becomes mechanically involved. This book will not explain such things as rebuilding the differential for the simple reason that the expertise required and the investment in special tools make this task uneconomical. It will give you detailed instructions to help you change your own brake pads and shoes, replace points and plugs, and do many more jobs that will save you money, give you personal satisfaction, and help you avoid expensive problems.

A secondary purpose of this book is a reference for owners who want to understand their truck and/or their mechanics better. In this case, no tools at all are required.

Before removing any bolts, read through the entire procedure. This will give you the overall view of what tools and supplies will be required. There is nothing more frustrating than having to walk to the bus stop on Monday morning because you were short one bolt on Sunday afternoon. So read ahead and plan ahead. Each operation should be approached logically and all procedures thoroughly understood before attempting any work.

All chapters contain adjustments, maintenance, removal and installation procedures, and repair or overhaul procedures. When repair is not considered practical, we tell you how to remove the part and then how to install the new or rebuilt replacement. In this way, you at least save the labor costs. Backyard repair of such components as the alternator is just not practical.

Two basic mechanic's rules should be mentioned here. One, whenever the left side of the truck or engine is referred to, it is meant to specify the driver's side of the truck. Conversely, the right side of the truck means the passenger's side. Secondly, most screws and bolts are removed by turning counterclockwise, and tightened by turning clockwise.

Safety is always the most important rule. Constantly be aware of the dangers involved in working on an automobile and take the proper precautions. (See the section in this chapter "Servicing Your Vehicle Safely" and the SAFETY NOTICE on the acknowledgement page.)

Pay attention to the instructions provided. There are 3 common mistakes in mechanical work:

1. Incorrect order of assembly, disassembly or adjustment. When taking something apart or putting it together, doing things in the wrong order usually justs costs you extra time; however, it CAN break something. Read the entire procedure before beginning disassembly. Do everything in the order in which the instructions say you should do it, even if you can't immediately see a reason for it. When you're taking apart something that is very intricate (for example, a carburetor), you might want to draw a picture of how it looks when assembled at one point in order to make sure you get everything back in its proper position. (We will supply exploded view whenever possible). When making adjustments, especially tune-up adjustments, do them in order; often, one adjustment affects another, and you cannot expect even satisfactory results unless each adjust-

ment is made only when it cannot be changed by any other.

2. Overtorquing (or undertorquing). While it is more common for overtorquing to cause damage, undertorquing can cause a fastener to vibrate loose causing serious damage. Especially when dealing with aluminum parts, pay attention to torque specifications and utilize a torque wrench in assembly. If a torque figure is not available, remember that if you are using the right tool to do the job, you will probably not have to strain yourself to get a fastener tight enough. The pitch of most threads is so slight that the tension you put on the wrench will be multiplied many, many times in actual force on what you are tightening. A good example of how critical torque is can be seen in the case of spark plug installation, especially where you are putting the plug into an aluminium cylinder head. Too little torque can fail to crush the gasket, causing leakage of combustion gases and consequent overheating of the plug and engine parts. Too much torque can damage the threads, or distort the plug, which changes the spark gap.

There are many commercial products available for ensuring that fasteners won't come loose, even if they are not torqued just right (a very common brand is "Loctite®"). If you're worried about getting something together tight enough to hold, but loose enough to avoid mechanical damage during assembly, one of these products might offer substantial insurance. Read the label on the package and make sure the product is compatible with the materials, fluids, etc. involved before choosing one.

3. Crossthreading. This occurs when a part such as a bolt is screwed into a nut or casting at the wrong angle and forced. Cross threading is more likely to occur if access is difficult. It helps to clean and lubricate fasteners, and to start threading with the part to be installed going straight in. Then, start the bolt, spark plug, etc. with your fingers. If you encounter resistance, unscrew the part and start over again at a different angle until it can be inserted and turned several turns without much effort. Keep in mind that many parts, especially spark plugs, used tapered threads so that gentle turning will automatically bring the part you're threading to the proper angle if you don't force it or resist a change in angle. Don't put a wrench on the part until it's been turned a couple of turns by hand. If you suddenly encounter resistance, and the part has not seated fully, don't force it. Pull it back out and make sure it's clean and threading properly.

Always take your time and be patient; once you have some experience, working on your truck will become an enjoyable hobby.

TOOLS AND EQUIPMENT

Naturally, without the proper tools and equipment it is impossible to properly service your vehicle. It would be impossible to catalog each tool that you would need to perform each or any operation in this book. It would also be unwise for the amateur to rush out and buy an expensive set of tools on the theory that he may need one or more of them at sometime.

The best approach is to proceed slowly, gathering together a good quality set of those tools that are used most frequently. Don't be misled by the low cost of bargain tools. It is far better to spend a little more for better quality. Forged wrenches, 10 or 12 point sockets and fine tooth ratchets are by far preferable to their less expensive counterparts. As any good mechanic can tell you, there are few worse experiences than trying to work on a car or truck with bad tools. Your monetary savings will be far outweighed by frustration and mangled knuckles.

Begin accumulating those tools that are used most frequently; those associated with routine maintenance and tune-up.

In addition to the normal assortment of screwdrivers and pliers you should have the following tools for routine maintenance jobs:

1. SAE (or Metric) or SAE/Metric wrenches—sockets and combination open end/box end wrenches in sizes from ⅛ in. (3 mm) to ¾ in. (19 mm) and a spark plug socket (13⁄16 or ⅝ in. depending on plug type);

If possible, buy various length socket drive extensions. One break in this department is that the metric sockets available in the U.S. will all fit the ratchet handles and extensions you may already have (¼, ⅜, and ½ in. drive.)

2. Jackstands—for support;
3. Oil filter wrench;
4. Oil filler spout—for pouring oil;
5. Grease gun—for chassis lubrication;
6. Hydrometer—for checking the battery;
7. A container for draining oil;
8. Many rags for wiping up the inevitable mess.

In addition to the above items there are several others that are not absolutely necessary, but handy to have around. These include oil dry, a transmission funnel and the usual supply of lubricants, antifreeze and fluids, although these can be purchased as needed. This is a basic list for routine maintenance, but only your personal needs and desire can accurately determine your list of tools.

The second list of tools is for tune-ups. While the tools involved here are slightly more sophisticated, they need not be outrageously ex-

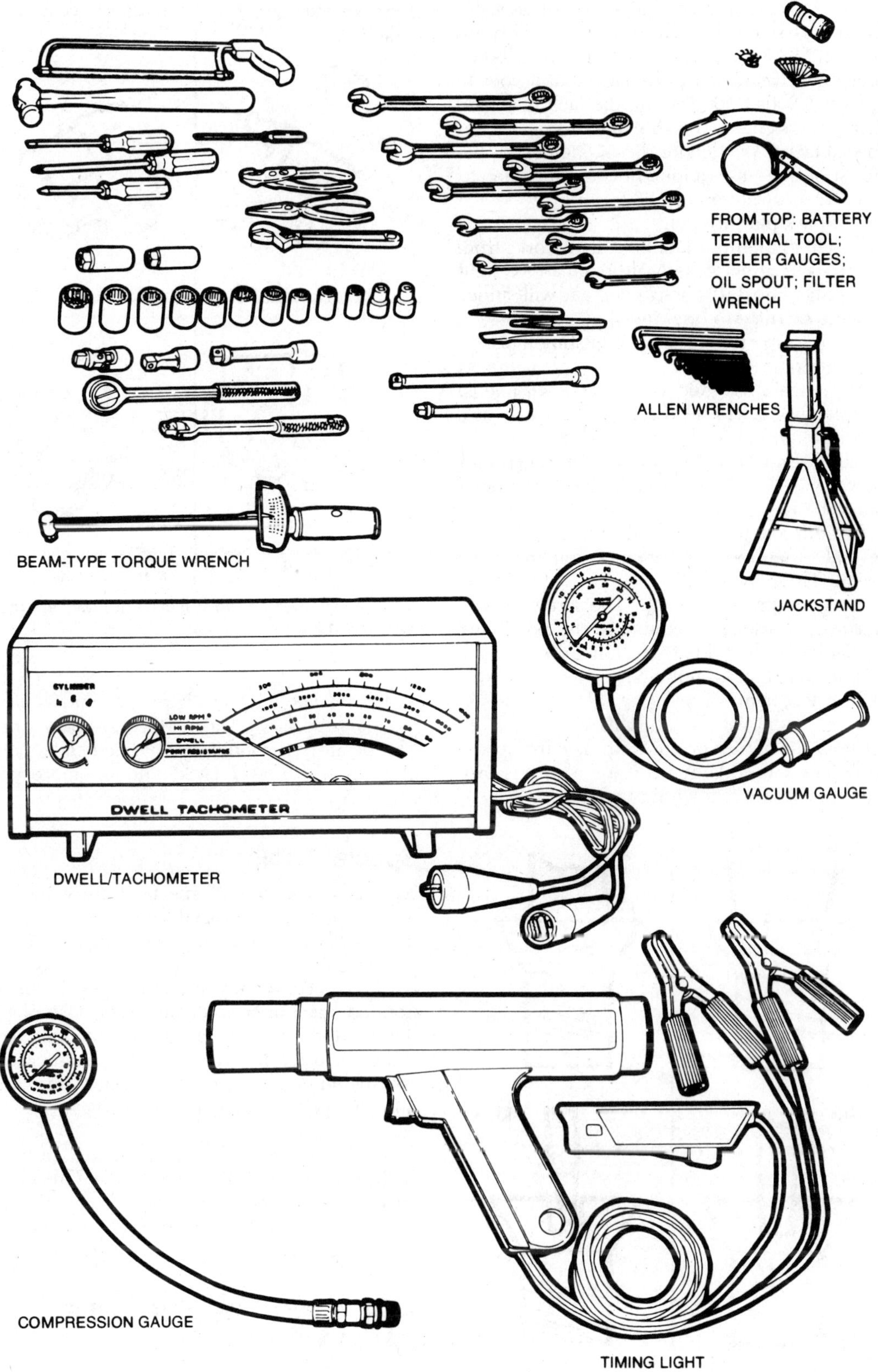

This basic collection of tools and test instruments is all you need for most maintenance on your truck

pensive. There are several inexpensive tach-dwell meters on the market that are every bit as good for the average mechanic as a $100.00 professional model. Just be sure that it goes to at least 1,200–1,500 rpm on the tach scale and that it works on 4, 6 or 8 cylinder engines. (A special tach is needed for diesel engines). A basic list of tune-up equipment could include:

1. Tach-dwell meter;
2. Spark plug wrench;
3. Timing light (a DC light that works from the truck's battery is best, although an AC light that plugs into 110V house current will suffice at some sacrifice in brightness);
4. Wire spark plug gauge/adjusting tools;
5. Set of feeler blades.

Here again, be guided by your own needs. A feeler blade will set the points as easily as a dwell meter will read well, but slightly less accurately. And since you will need a tachometer anyway . . . well, make make your own decision.

In addition to these basic tools, there are several other tools and gauges you may find useful. These include:

1. A compression gauge. The screw-in type is slower to use, but eliminates the possibility of a faulty reading due to escaping pressure;
2. A manifold vacuum gauge;
3. A test light;
4. An induction meter. This is used for determining whether or not there is current in a wire. These are handy for use if a wire is broken somewhere in a wiring harness.

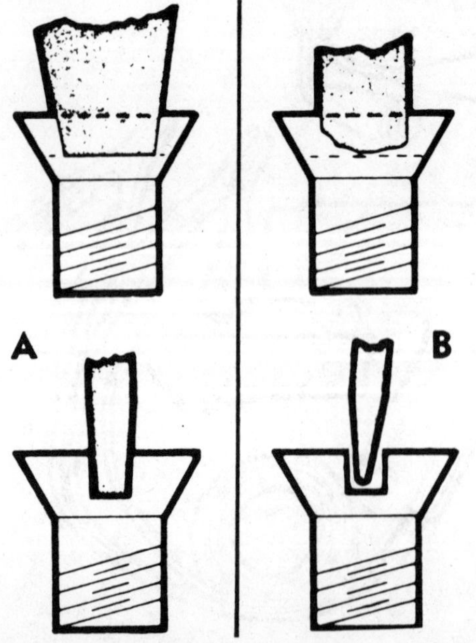

Keep screwdriver blades in good shape. They should fit the slot as shown in "A". If they look like those in "B", they need grinding or replacing

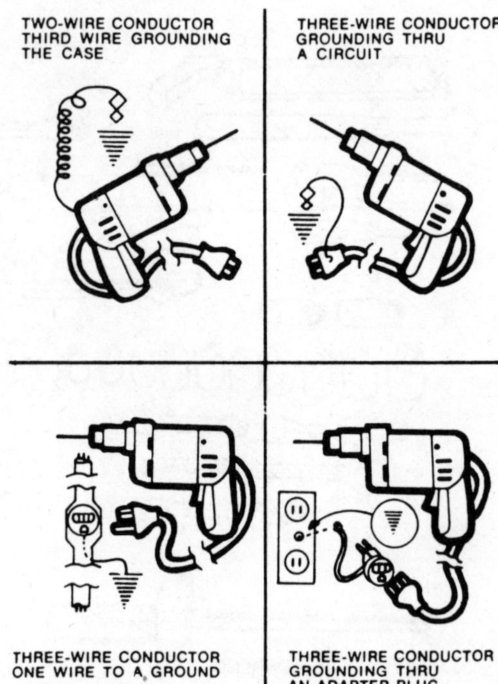

When using electric tools, make sure they are properly grounded

As a final note, you will probably find a torque wrench necessary for all but the most basic work. The beam type models are perfectly adequate, although the newer click type are more precise.

Special Tools

Normally, the use of special factory tools is avoided for repair procedures, since these are not readily available for the do-it-yourself mechanic. When it is possible to perform the job with more commonly available tools, it will be pointed out, but occasionally, a special tool was designed to perform a specific function and should be used. Before substituting another tool, you should be convinced that neither your safety nor the performance of the vehicle will be compromised.

Some special tools are available commercially from major tool manufacturers. Others can be purchased from your Ford dealer or from the Owatonna Tool Company, Owatonna, Minnesota 55060.

SERVICING YOUR VEHICLE SAFELY

It is virtually impossible to anticipate all of the hazards involved with automotive maintenance and service but care and common sense will prevent most accidents.

The rules of safety for mechanics range from "don't smoke around gasoline," to "use the proper tool for the job." The trick to avoiding injuries is to develop safe work habits and take every possible precaution.

Do's

• Do keep a fire extinguisher and first aid kit within easy reach.

• Do wear safety glasses or goggles when cutting, drilling, grinding or prying, even if you have 20-20 vision. If you wear glasses for the sake of vision, then they should be made of hardened glass that can serve also as safety glasses, or wear safety goggles over your regular glasses.

• Do shield your eyes whenever you work around the battery. Batteries contain sulphuric acid; in case of contact with the eyes or skin, flush the area with water or a mixture of water and baking soda and get medical attention immediately.

• Do use safety stands for any undertruck service. Jacks are for raising vehicles; safety stands are for making sure the vehicle stays raised until you want it to come down. Whenever the vehicle is raised, block the wheels remaining on the ground and set the parking brake.

• Do use adequate ventilation when working with any chemicals. Like carbon monoxide, the asbestos dust resulting from brake lining wear can be poisonous in sufficient quantities.

• Do disconnect the negative battery cable when working on the electrical system. The primary ignition system can contain up to 40,000 volts.

• Do follow manufacturer's directions whenever working with potentially hazardous materials. Both brake fluid and antifreeze are poisonous if taken internally.

• Do properly maintain your tools. Loose hammerheads, mushroomed punches and chisels, frayed or poorly grounded electrical cords, excessively worn screwdrivers, spread wrenches (open end), cracked sockets, slipping ratchets, or faulty droplight sockets can cause accidents.

• Do use the proper size and type of tool for the job being done.

• Do when possible, pull on a wrench handle rather than push on it, and adjust your stance to prevent a fall.

• Do be sure that adjustable wrenches are tightly adjusted on the nut or bolt and pulled so that the face is on the side of the fixed jaw.

• Do select a wrench or socket that fits the nut or bolt. The wrench or socket should sit straight, not cocked.

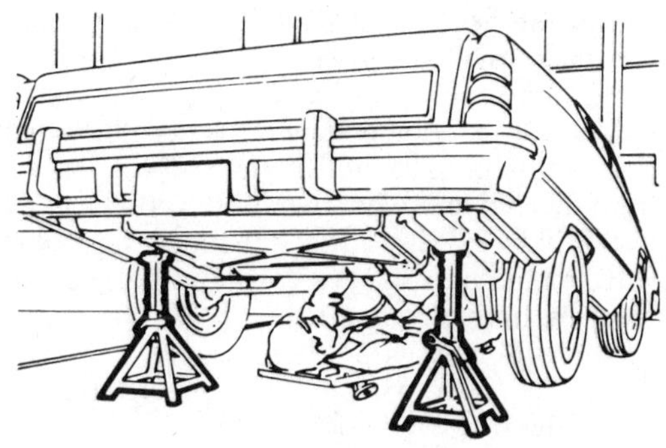

Always use jackstands when working under your truck

• Do strike squarely with a hammer—avoid glancing blows.

• Do set the parking brake and block the drive wheels if the work requires that the engine be running.

Dont's

• Don't run an engine in a garage or anywhere else without proper ventilation—EVER! Carbon monoxide is poisonous; it takes a long time to leave the human body and you can build up a deadly supply of it in your system by simply breathing in a little every day. You may not realize you are slowly poisoning yourself. Always use power vents, windows, fans or open the garage doors.

• Don't work around moving parts while wearing a necktie or other loose clothing. Short sleeves are much safer than long, loose sleeves and hard-toed shoes with neoprene soles protect your toes and give a better grip on slippery surfaces. Jewelry such as watches, fancy belt buckles, beads or body adornment of any kind is not safe working around a truck. Long hair should be hidden under a hat or cap.

• Don't use pockets for toolboxes. A fall or bump can drive a screwdriver deep into your body. Even a wiping cloth hanging from the back pocket can wrap around a spinning shaft or fan.

• Don't smoke when working around gasoline, cleaning solvent or other flammable material.

• Don't smoke when working around the battery. When the battery is being charged, it gives off explosive hydrogen gas.

• Don't use gasoline to wash your hands; there are excellent soaps available. Gasoline may contain lead, and lead can enter the body through a cut, accumulating in the body until you are very ill. Gasoline also removes all the natural oils from the skin so that bone dry hands will suck up oil and grease.

• Don't service the air conditioning system unless you are equipped with the necessary tools and training. The refrigerant, R-12, is extremely cold and when exposed to the air, will instantly freeze any surface it comes in contact with, including your eyes. Although the refrigerant is normally non-toxic, R-12 becomes a deadly poisonous gas in the presence of an open flame. One good whiff of the vapors from burning refrigerant can be fatal.

• Don't ever use a bumper jack (the jack that comes with the vehicle) for anything other than changing tires! If you are serious about maintaining your truck yourself, invest in a hydraulic floor jack of *at least* 1½ ton capacity. It will pay for itself many times over through the years.

SERIAL NUMBER IDENTIFICATION

Vehicle

The vehicle identification plate is located on the right-side of the cowl top panel under the hood. There are three lines of information on the plate, which consists of arrangements of letters and numbers.

The first line from the top is the warranty number, which is a code that identifies the series of vehicle, the engine, the assembly plant, and the numerical sequence in which the vehicle was built.

The second line of numbers contains codes that identify the wheelbase (in.), color, model code, trim code, body type code, transmission code and the rear axle code.

The third line gives the maximum gross vehicle weight (GVW) in lbs, the certified net horsepower @ rpm, and the D.S.O. number, which is the district to which the vehicle was delivered and if applicable, specially-ordered, factory-installed equipment.

VIN codes prior to 1981 are comprised of 13 digits and letters. The code was changed for 1981 and later years, and now includes 17 digits and letters. The tenth position within the VIN is the model year; "B" denotes 1981, "C" 1982, "D" 1983, etc.

Engine

The engine identification tag identifies the cubic inch displacement of the engine, the model year, the year and month in which the engine was built, where it was built and the change level number. The change level is usually the number one (1), unless there are parts on the engine that will not be completely interchangeable and will require minor modification.

The engine identification tag is located under the ignition coil attaching bolt on all engines except the 6.9L diesel. The diesel engine I.D. number is stamped on the front of the block in front of the left cylinder head.

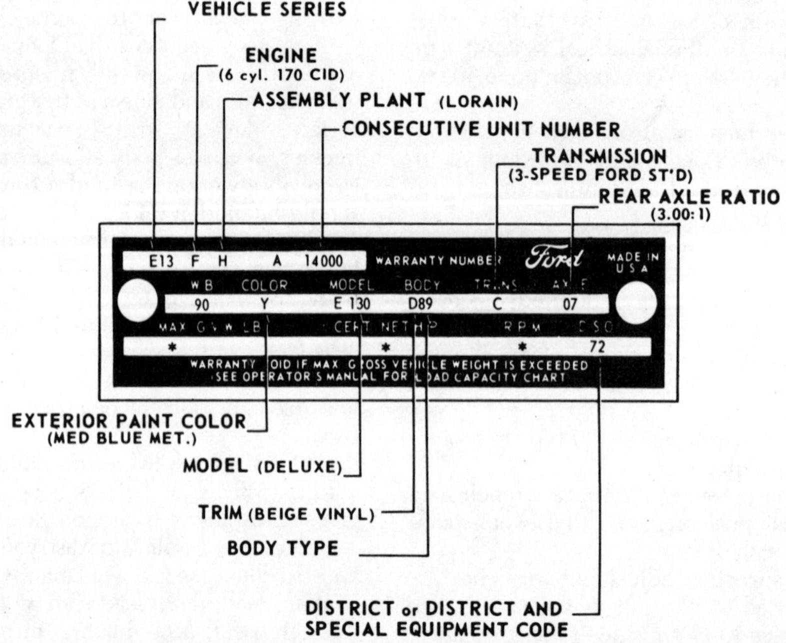

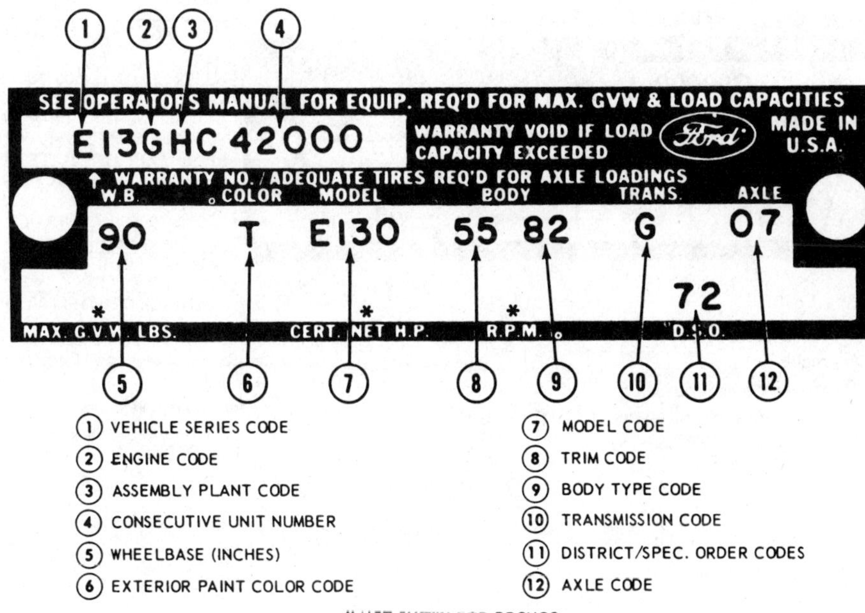

1969 VIN plate

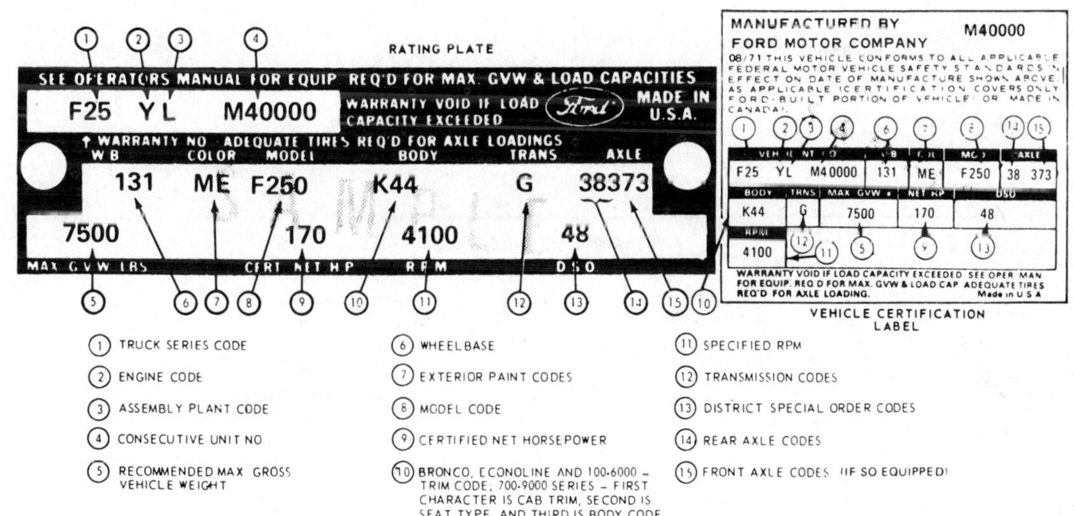

1970–72 VIN plate

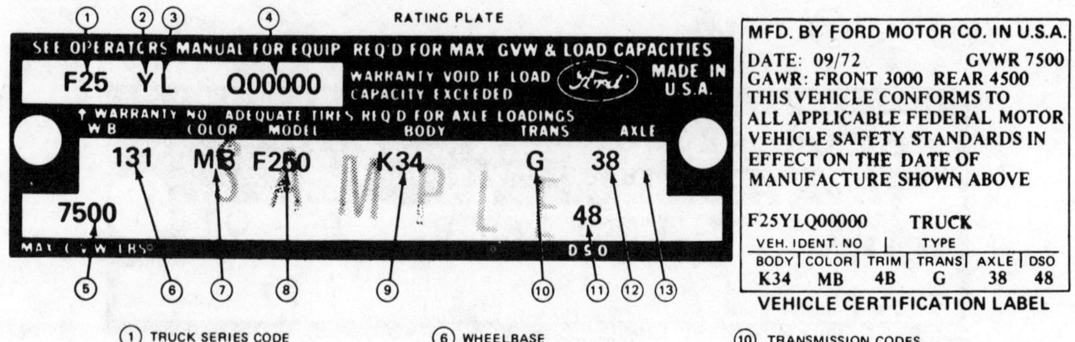

1. TRUCK SERIES CODE
2. ENGINE CODE
3. ASSEMBLY PLANT CODE
4. CONSECUTIVE UNIT NO.
5. RECOMMENDED MAX. GROSS VEHICLE WEIGHT
6. WHEELBASE
7. EXTERIOR PAINT CODES
8. MODEL CODE
9. BRONCO, ECONOLINE AND 100-6000 – TRIM CODE; 700-9000 SERIES – FIRST CHARACTER IS CAB TRIM, SECOND IS SEAT TYPE, AND THIRD IS BODY CODE
10. TRANSMISSION CODES
11. DISTRICT/SPECIAL ORDER CODES
12. REAR AXLE CODES
13. FRONT AXLE CODES (IF SO EQUIPPED)

1973–77 VIN plate

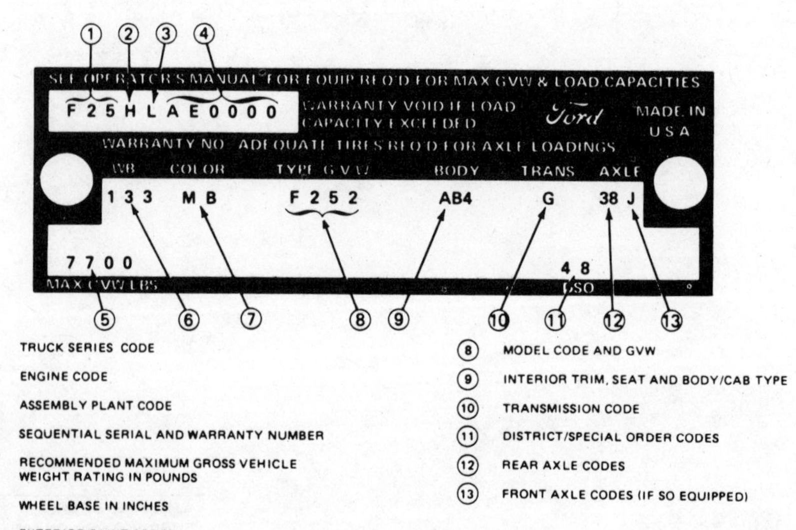

1. TRUCK SERIES CODE
2. ENGINE CODE
3. ASSEMBLY PLANT CODE
4. SEQUENTIAL SERIAL AND WARRANTY NUMBER
5. RECOMMENDED MAXIMUM GROSS VEHICLE WEIGHT RATING IN POUNDS
6. WHEEL BASE IN INCHES
7. EXTERIOR PAINT CODES
8. MODEL CODE AND GVW
9. INTERIOR TRIM, SEAT AND BODY/CAB TYPE
10. TRANSMISSION CODE
11. DISTRICT/SPECIAL ORDER CODES
12. REAR AXLE CODES
13. FRONT AXLE CODES (IF SO EQUIPPED)

1978–80 VIN plate

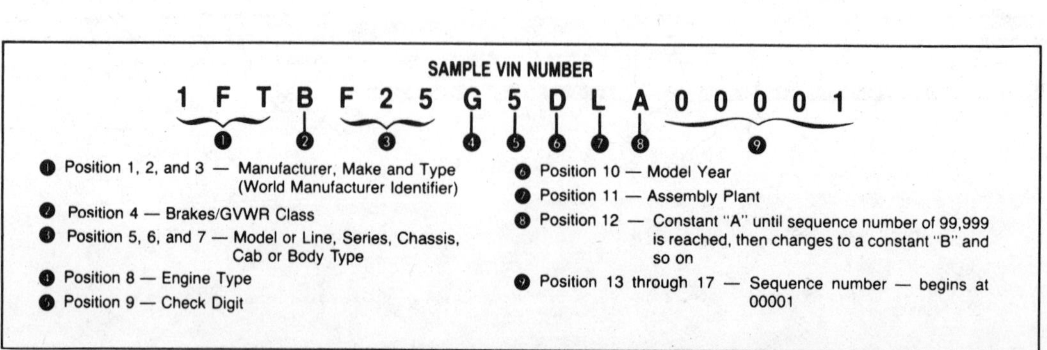

1. Position 1, 2, and 3 — Manufacturer, Make and Type (World Manufacturer Identifier)
2. Position 4 — Brakes/GVWR Class
3. Position 5, 6, and 7 — Model or Line, Series, Chassis, Cab or Body Type
4. Position 8 — Engine Type
5. Position 9 — Check Digit
6. Position 10 — Model Year
7. Position 11 — Assembly Plant
8. Position 12 — Constant "A" until sequence number of 99,999 is reached, then changes to a constant "B" and so on
9. Position 13 through 17 — Sequence number — begins at 00001

1981 and later 17-digit VIN. "D" model year denotes 1983

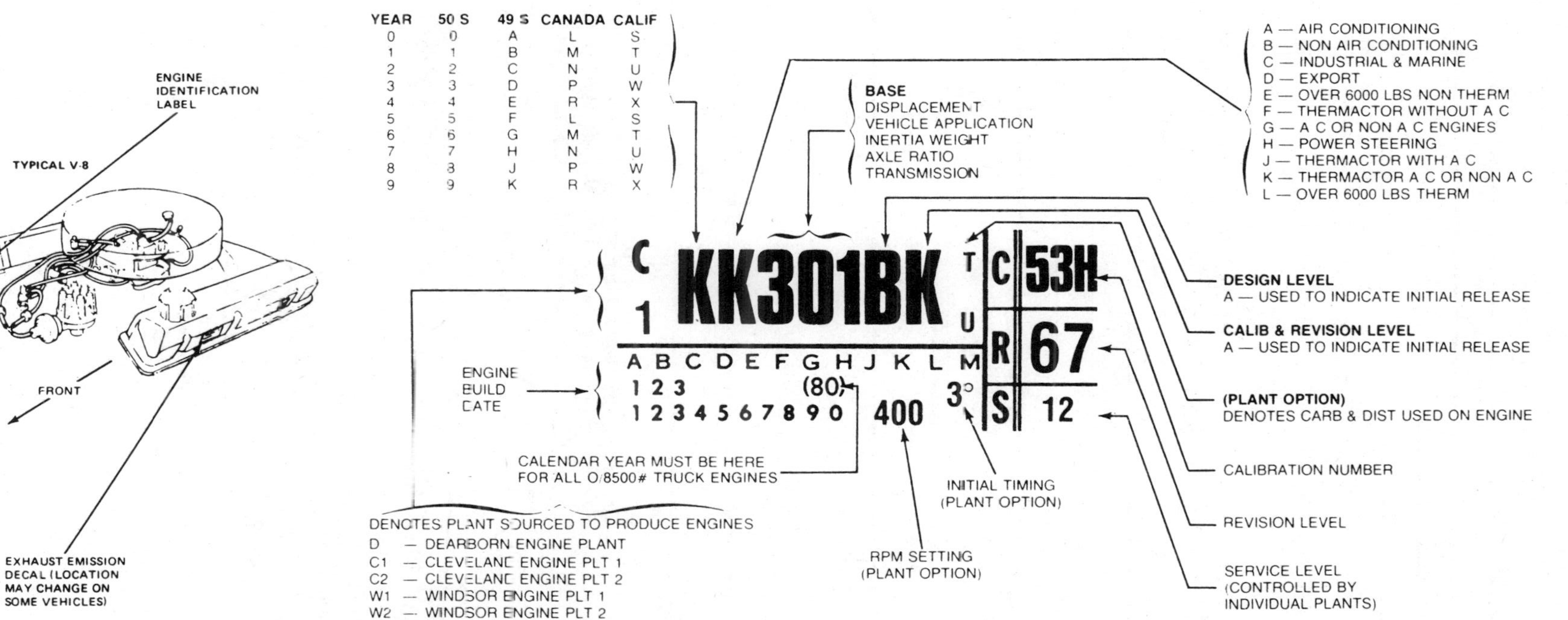

Engine identification label, 1980 shown. Label found on front of valve cover on 6 cyl. engines, on front of right valve cover on V8s

Engine Codes

Engine	65–67	68	69	70–72	73	74	75	76	77	78	79	80	81	82	83	84–86
V6-232														3	3	
6-240			A	A	A	A										
V8-255														D		
6-300							B	B	B	B	B	E	E	E	9,Y ②	Y
6-300HD											K					
V8-302			G	G	G	G					G	F	F	F	F	F
V8-351W							H	H	H	H	H	G	W	W	G	G ③
V8-351M									H	H	H					
V8-352	D															
V8-360				Y	Y	Y	Y	Y								
V8-361	E	E	E													
V8-390		H	H	H												
V8-391	F	F	F													
V8-400										S	S	S	Z			
V8-420 ①															1	I
V8-460								A	A	A	A	A				

① International-Harvester built Diesel
② 9 code set up for LP gas
③ 1985–86: H

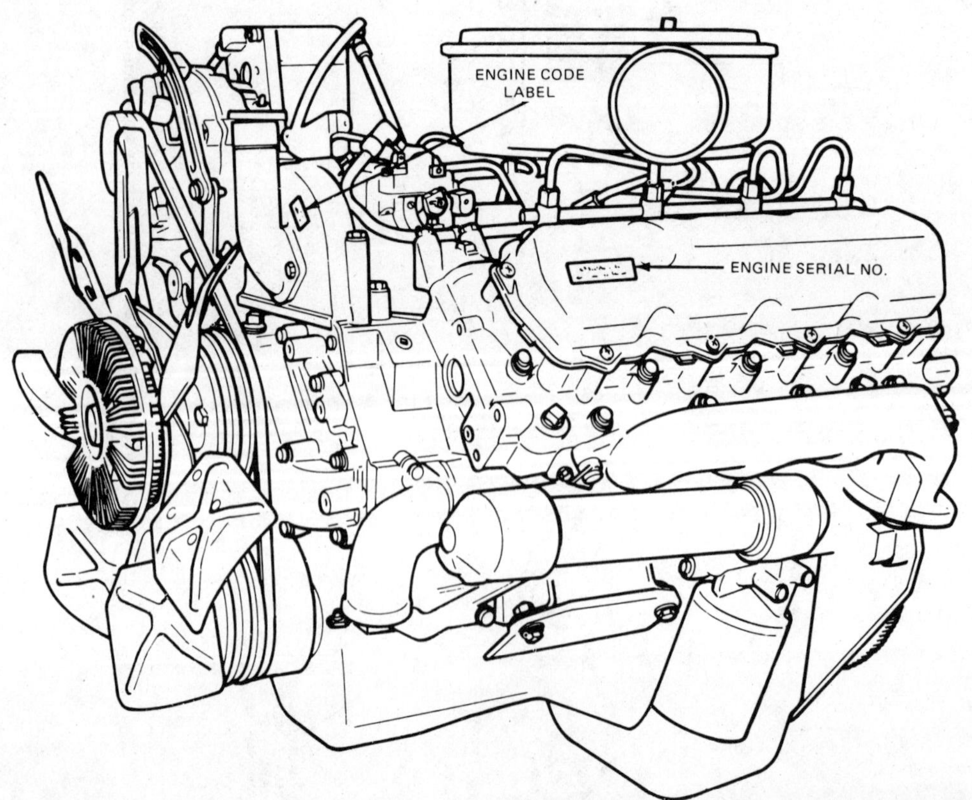

6.9L diesel engine serial and I.D. locations. The 6.9L diesel is built for Ford by International Harvester

Rear Axle Codes and Ratios

Read Ratios Across

Codes	Years																	
	65	66	67/68	69	70	71	72	73	74	75	76	77	78	79	80–82	83	84	85
01	3.50	3.50	3.50															
02	4.00	4.00	4.00					3.00	3.00	3.00	3.00	3.00						
03	4.11							4.11										
04	4.55							4.57										
07		3.00	3.00															
11		3.50c	3.50					3.50	3.50	4.11								
12		4.11	4.11					3.70	3.70	3.70								
13		4.56	4.56													2.75		4.11
A7		3.00	3.00															
B1		3.50	3.50													3.00		
B2		4.11	4.11														4.10	4.10
B3		4.57	4.57													3.54	3.54	3.54
08				3.50	3.50	3.50	3.50	3.50	3.50	3.50	3.50	3.50						
05				4.11	4.11	4.11	4.11	4.11	4.11	4.11	4.11	4.11						
17				3.25	3.25	3.25	3.25	3.25	3.25	3.25	3.25	3.25				2.47	2.47	2.47
09				3.70	3.70	3.70	3.70	3.70	3.70	3.70	3.70	3.70						
71				3.54	3.54	3.54	3.54	3.54	3.54	3.54	3.54	3.54						
72				3.73	3.73	3.73	3.73	3.73	3.73	3.73	3.73	3.73					4.10	4.10
73				4.10	4.10	4.10	4.10	4.10	4.10	4.10	4.10	4.10					3.54	3.54
G1				3.54	3.54	3.54	3.54	3.54	3.54									
G3				4.10	4.10	4.10	4.10	4.10	4.10								3.54	3.54
06						4.57												
31						3.54										3.07	3.07	3.07
33						3.73										3.54	3.54	3.54

Rear Axle Codes and Ratios (cont.)

Read Ratios Across

Codes	Years 65	66	67/68	69	70	71	72	73	74	75	76	77	78	79	80–82	83	84	85
35						4.10												
36						4.56												
C1						3.54												
C3						3.73										3.54	3.54	3.54
C5						4.10												
B4								4.10	4.10	4.10	4.10	4.10					3.73	3.73
C7								3.54										
C8								3.73	3.73	3.73	3.73	3.73	3.73					
D7								4.10	4.10	4.10	4.10	4.10	4.10	4.10	4.10			
10								3.25	3.25									
18								3.50								3.08	3.08	3.08
22								4.88									4.10	4.10
14										3.00						3.00		3.00
15										3.25						2.73		
16										3.50						3.50		3.50
23								3.31	3.31	3.31	3.31	3.31	3.31	3.31	3.31	3.54	3.54	3.54
24								4.10	4.10	4.10	4.10	4.10	4.10	4.10	4.10	3.73	3.73	3.73
25								3.31										
26								3.54	3.54							3.55	3.55	3.55
38										3.73	3.73	3.73	3.73					
B5								3.31	3.31									
D6								3.73	3.73	3.73	3.73	3.73						

H2	3.50	3.50	3.50	3.50	3.50	3.50	3.50	3.50			
H3	4.11	4.11	4.11	4.11	4.11						4.11
H4	3.25	3.25	3.25	3.25	3.25	3.25	3.25	3.25	3.00		3.00
H5			3.70	3.70	3.70				2.73		
H7							3.00	3.00			
H9						4.11	4.11	4.11	3.55	3.55	3.55
19									3.55	3.55	3.55
H8									3.08	3.08	3.08
32									4.10	4.10	4.10
34									3.73	3.73	3.73
42									4.10	4.10	4.10
43									3.54	3.54	3.54
52									4.10	4.10	4.10
53									3.59	3.54	3.54
62									4.10	4.10	4.10
65									4.56	4.56	
B6									3.55	3.55	
C2									4.10	4.10	4.10
D2									4.10	4.10	4.10
D3									3.54	3.54	3.54
21									3.00		
E2									4.10	4.10	4.10
E3										3.54	3.54
G2										4.10	4.10
H6											3.50
63											3.54

Transmission

The transmission identification letter is located on a metal tag or plate attached to the case or it is stamped directly on the transmission case.

Transmission Code Chart

Code	Description
A (1965)	Ford-Manual-3 Speed
B (1965–78)	Warner T-85-3 Speed
C	Ford-Manual-3 Speed
D	Warner T-89-3 Speed
E	Warner T-87-3 Speed
F	Warner T-18-4 Speed
N (1965)	New Process 435-4 Speed
A (1966–86)	New Process 435-4 Speed
P	Warner T-19-4 Speed
B (1979–86)	Clark-4 Speed O.D.
G	Automatic C4
W	Automatic C5
P	Automatic C6 thru 1977
K	Automatic C6 1978–86
J	Automatic FMX
T	Automatic Overdrive

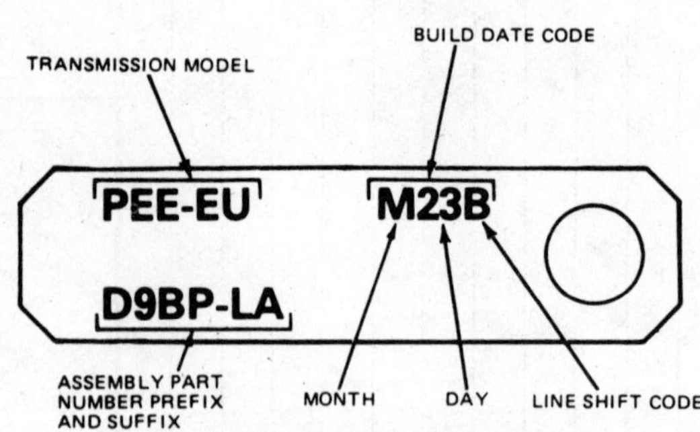

C-4 automatic transmission I.D. tag

ROUTINE MAINTENANCE

NOTE: *All maintenance procedures included in this chapter refer to both gasoline and diesel engines except where noted.*

Air Cleaner

The air cleaner is a paper element type with an oil bath type having been optional on some engines.

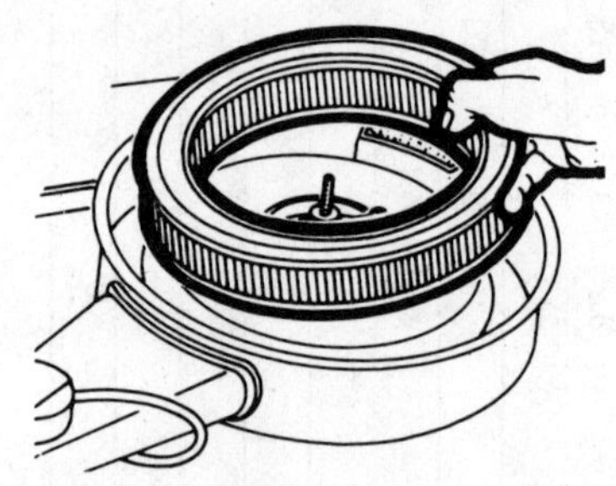

Removing the air cleaner element

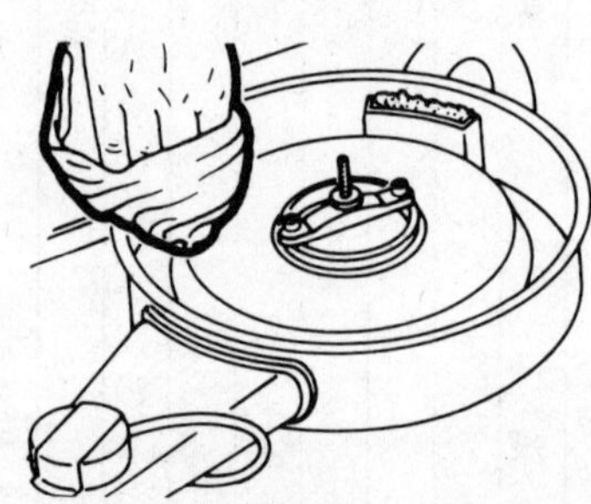

Clean out the air cleaner body before installing the new filter

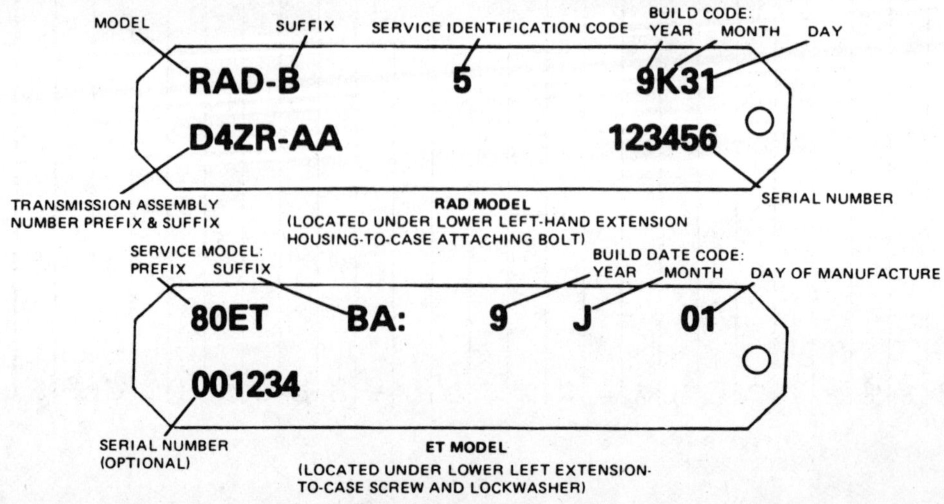

Manual transmission I.D. tag

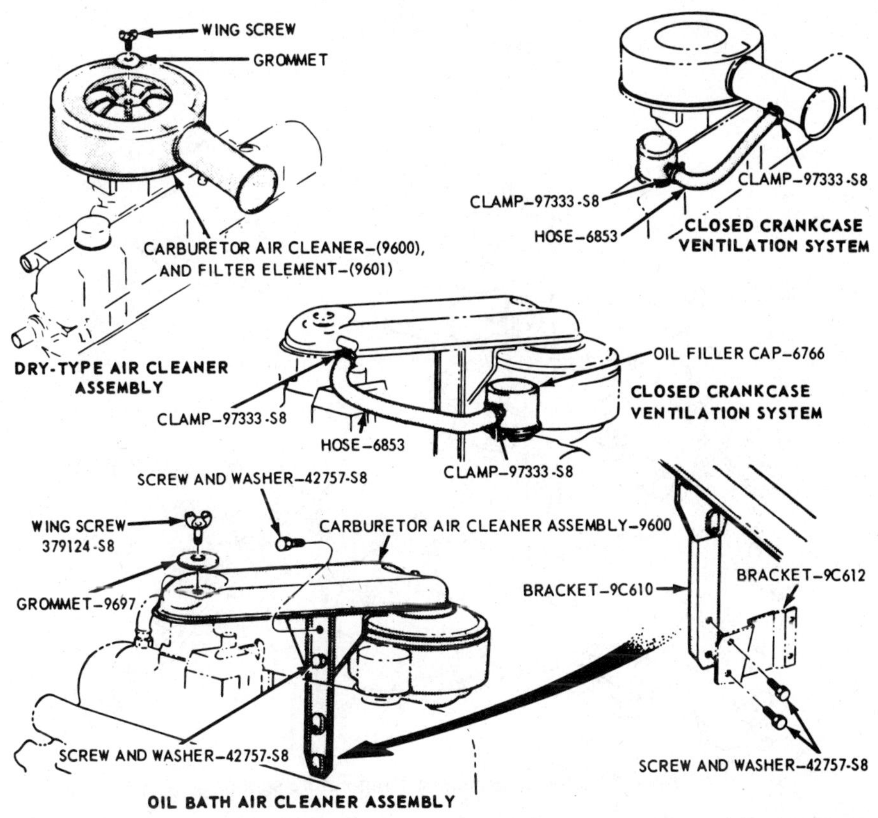

Some models may have an oil-bath air cleaner, which is emptied out, cleaned thoroughly with a rag, then filled with clean oil to the "FULL" line

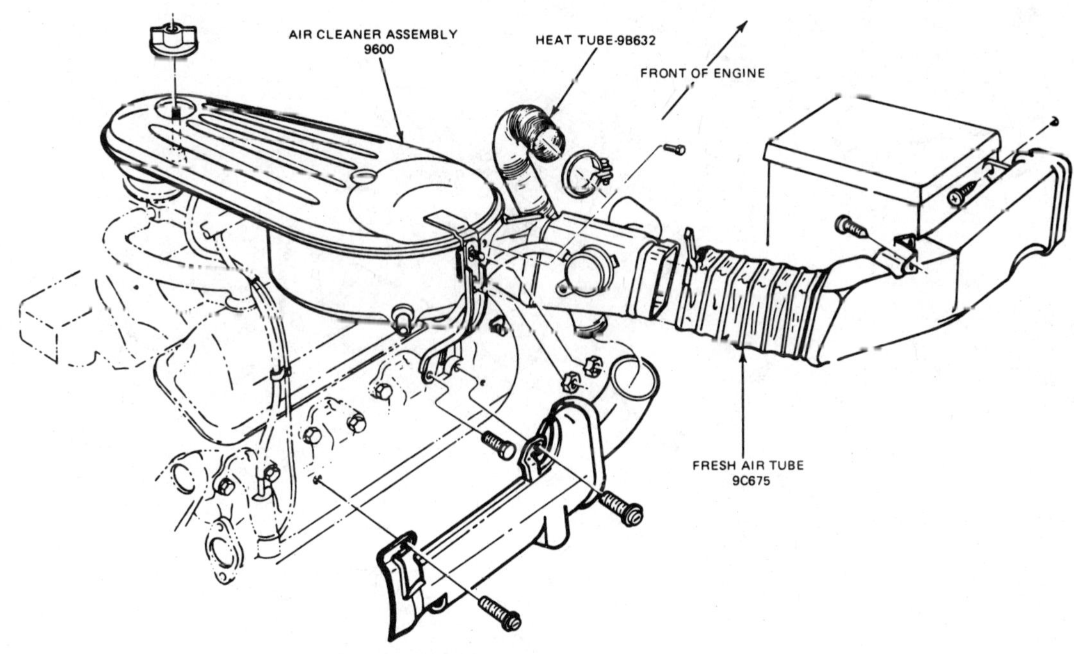

302 V8 air cleaner assembly, through 1977

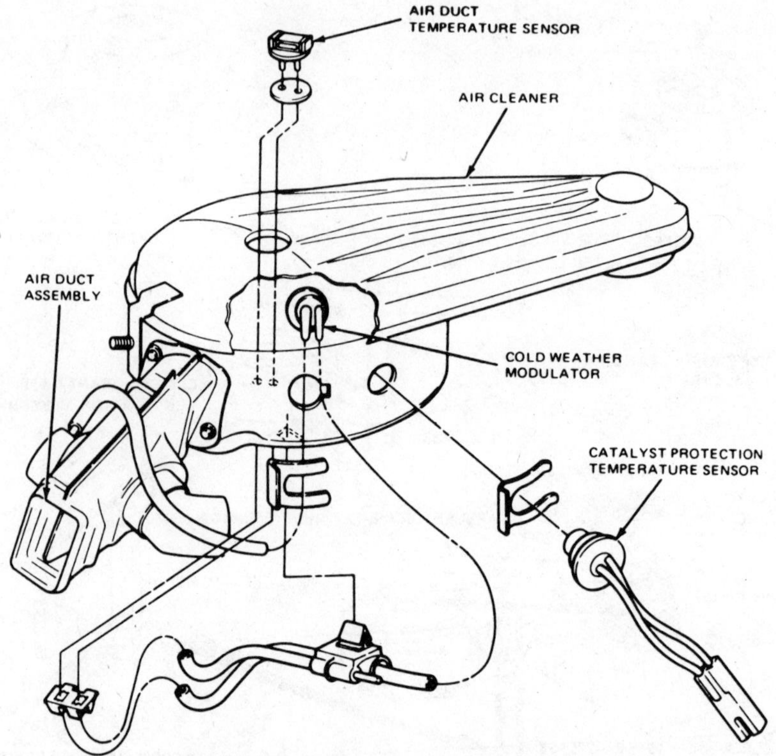

1975–77 catalyst protection temperature sensor

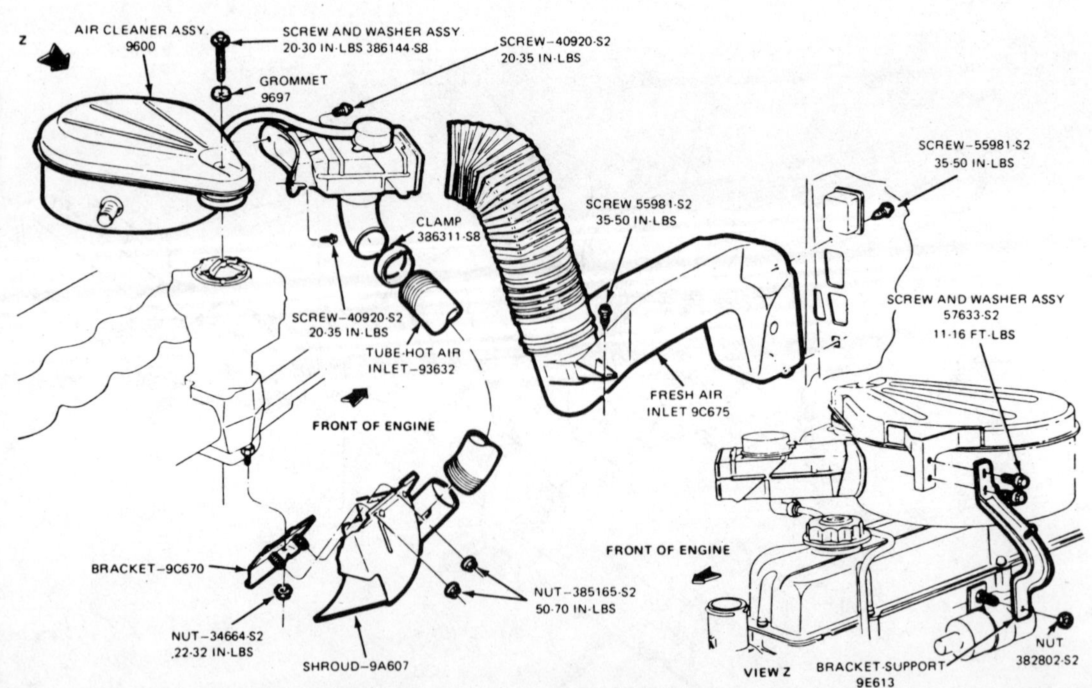

300 inline six cylinder air cleaner

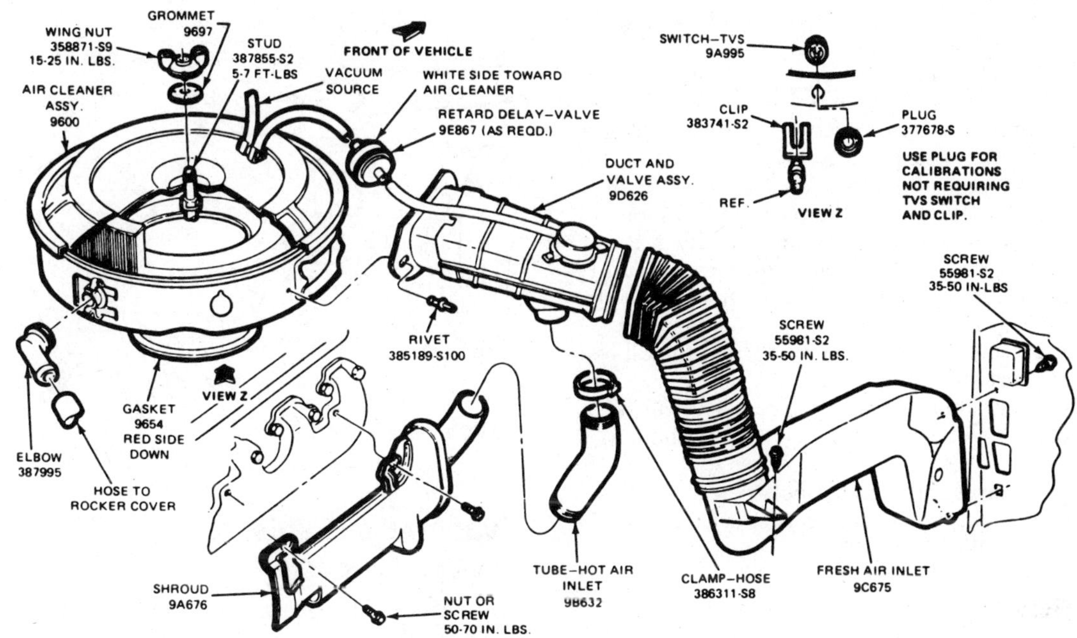

Typical V8 air cleaner, 1978 and later

The paper cartridge should be replaced according to the Preventive Maintenance Schedule at the end of this chapter.

NOTE: *Check the air filter more often if the vehicle is operated under severe dusty conditions and replace or clean it as necessary.*

The procedure for replacing the air cleaner element is as follows:

1. Open the engine compartment hood.
2. Remove the wing nut holding the air cleaner assembly to the top of the carburetor.
3. Disconnect the crankcase ventilation hose at the air cleaner and remove the entire air cleaner assembly from the carburetor.

NOTE: *When servicing the 6.9L diesel air filter element, remove the entire air cleaner assembly as one piece to prevent dirt from falling into the engine air intake.*

4. Remove and discard the old filter element, and inspect the condition of the air cleaner mounting gasket. Replace the gasket as necessary.

NOTE: *On later gasoline models a crankcase ventilation filter is located in the side of the air cleaner body. The filter should be replaced rather than cleaned. Simply pull the old filter out of the body every 20,000 miles (or more frequently if the vehicle has been used in extremely dusty conditions) and push a new filter into place.*

5. Install the air cleaner body on the carburetor so that the word FRONT faces toward the front of the vehicle.
6. Place the new filter element in the air cleaner body and install the cover and tighten the wing nut. If the word TOP appears on the element, make sure that the side the word appears on is facing up when the element is in place.
7. Connect the crankcase ventilation hose to the air cleaner.

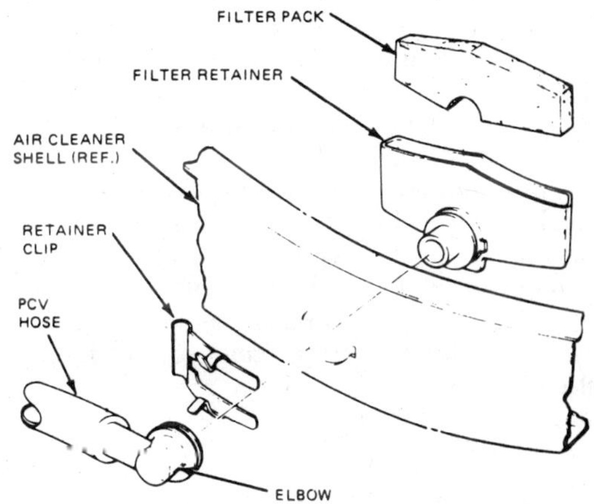

Crankcase ventilation filter in air cleaner housing

On vehicles equipped with the optional oil bath air cleaner, the air cleaner should be cleaned periodically. Replace the gasket if it looks like it can't form a good seal.

1. Saturate the filter element with clean engine oil.
2. Fill the oil reservoir to the full mark with the proper weight oil. In general, the same oil is used in the air cleaner as is being used in the engine at that particular time (about 32°F—SAE 30; below 32° F—SAE 20).

3. Replace the air cleaner assembly onto the carburetor and tighten the wing nuts.

NOTE: *Check the air air filter more often if the vehicle is operated under severe dusty conditions and replace or clean the air filter as is necessary.*

The procedure for cleaning an oil bath air cleaner and refilling the reservoir is as follows:

1. Remove the wing nuts holding the air cleaner to the carburetor and engine, and remove the air cleaner assembly from the carburetor.
2. Remove the cover and drain the oil from the reservoir. Wash all of the air cleaner parts in a suitable cleaning solvent. Dry all of the parts with compressed air, or allow them to air dry.
3. Inspect the gasket between the oil reservoir chamber and the air cleaner body.

PCV Valve

Gasoline Engines Only

Check the PCV valve according to the Preventive Maintenance Schedule at the end of this chapter to see if it is free and not gummed up, stuck or blocked. To check the valve, remove it from the engine and work the valve by sticking a screwdriver in the crankcase side of the valve. It should move. It is possible to clean the PCV valve by soaking it in a solvent and blowing it out with compressed air. This can restore the valve to some level of operating order. This should be used only as an emergency measure. Otherwise the valve should be replaced.

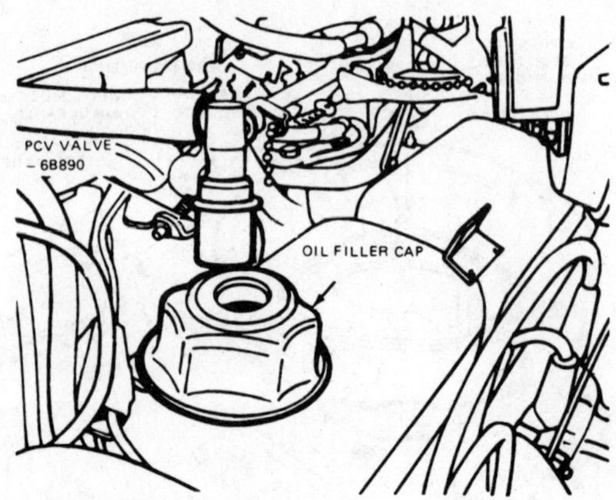

V8 PCV valve location

Evaporative Canister

Gasoline Engines Only

The fuel evaporative emission control canister should be inspected for damage or leaks at the hose fittings every 24,000 miles. Repair or replace any old or cracked hoses. Replace the canister if it is damaged in any way. The canister is located under the hood, to the right of the engine.

Battery

Loose, dirty, or corroded battery terminals are a major cause of "no-start." Every 3 months or so, remove the battery terminals and clean them, giving them a light coating of petroleum jelly when you are finished. This will help to retard corrosion.

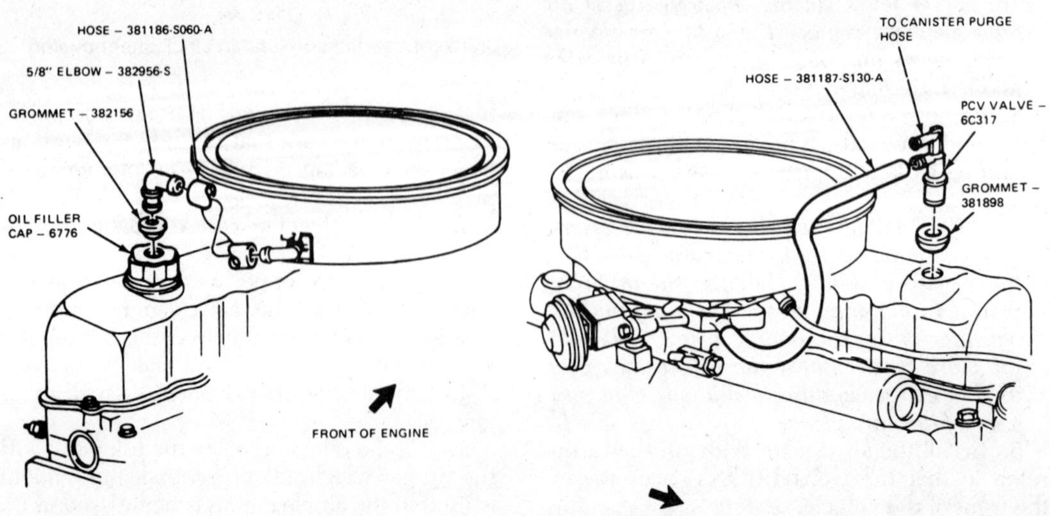

Inline six cylinder PCV valve location

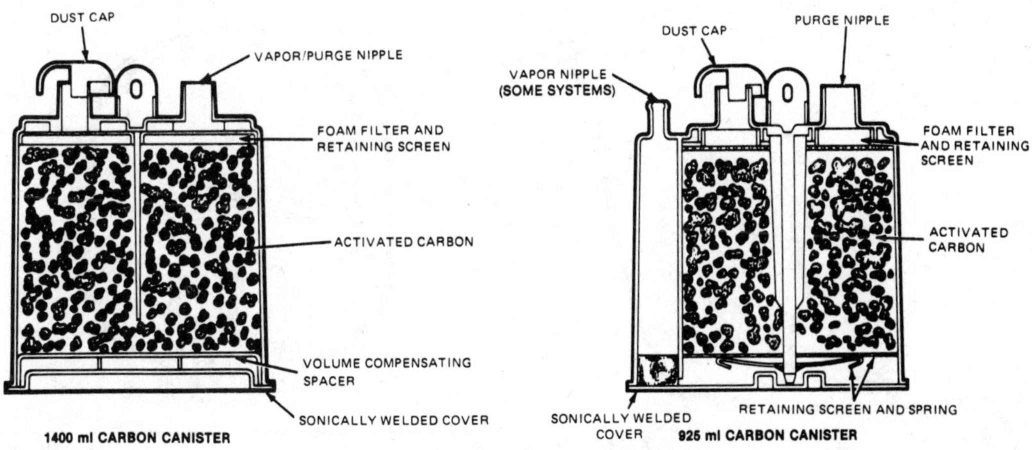

Carbon canister cross-sections

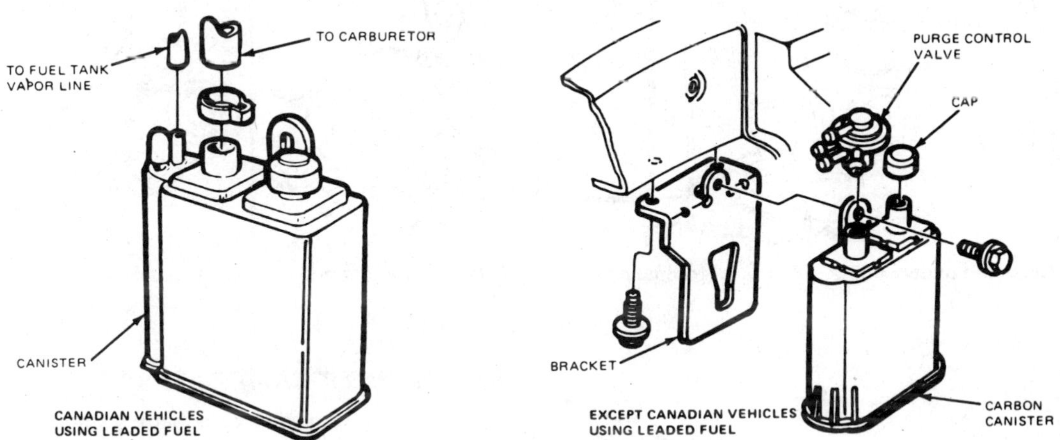

Carbon canisters are mounted on the inner fender

Check the battery cables for signs of wear or chafing and replace any cable or terminal that looks marginal. Battery terminals can be easily cleaned and inexpensive terminal cleaning tools are an excellent investment that will pay for themselves many times over. They can usually be purchased from any well-equipped auto store or parts department. Side terminal batteries require a different tool to clean the threads in the battery case. The accumulated white powder and corrosion can be cleaned from the top of the battery with an old toothbrush and a solution of baking soda and water.

Unless you have a "maintenance-free" battery, check the electrolyte level (see Battery under Fluid Level Checks in this chapter) and check the specific gravity of each cell. Be sure that the vent holes in each cell cap are not blocked by grease or dirt. The vent holes allow hydrogen gas, formed by the chemical reaction in the battery, to escape safely.

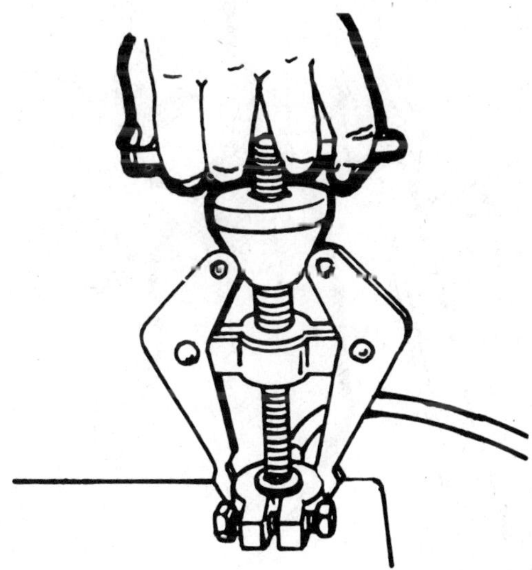
Top terminal battery cables are easily removed with this inexpensive puller

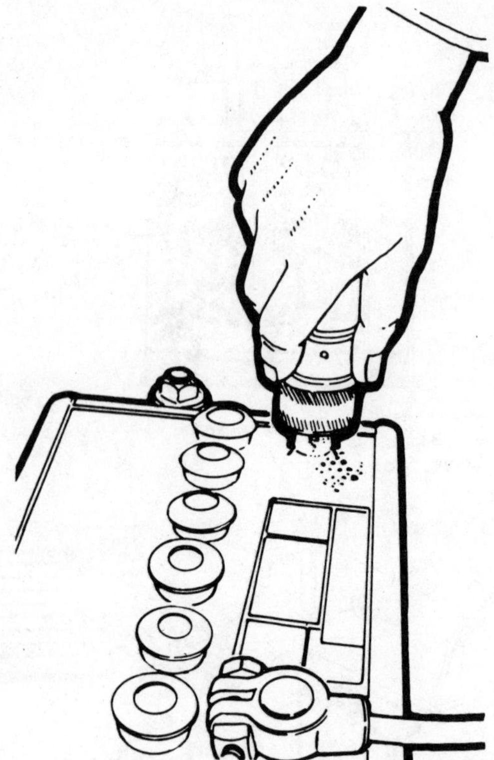

Clean the battery posts with a wire terminal cleaner

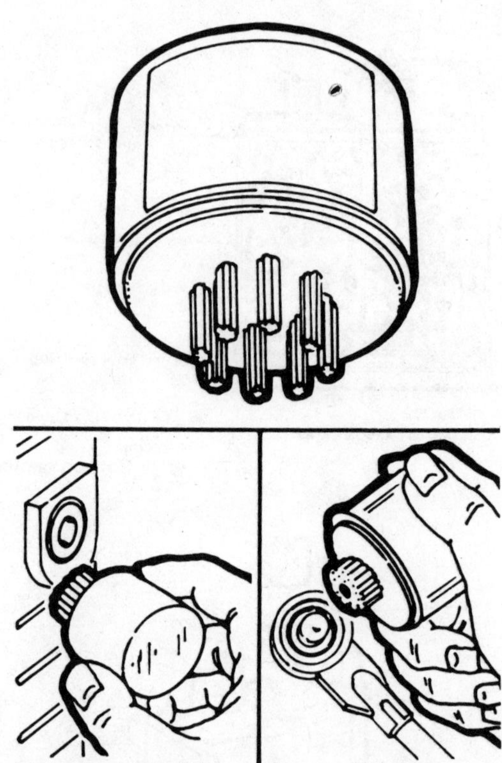

Side terminal batteries require a special wire brush for cleaning

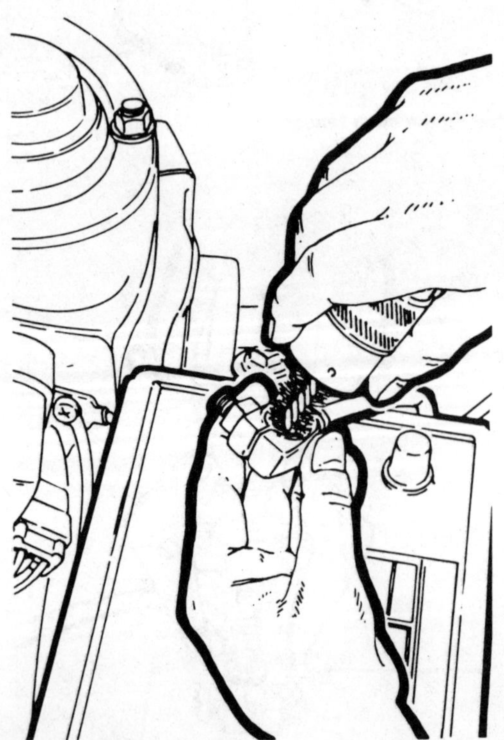

Clean the cable ends with a stiff cable cleaning tool (male end)

REPLACEMENT BATTERIES

The cold power rating of a battery measures battery starting performance and provides an approximate relationship between battery size and engine size. The cold power rating of a replacement battery should match or exceed your engine size in cubic inches.

Exhaust Control Valve (Heat Riser)

Gasoline Engines Only

An exhaust control valve used on some models from 1965–69 should be periodically checked for free operation. A valve frozen in either the open or closed position can cause poor engine performance. Unless the valve is very corrosive or damaged it can be kept in good operating condition by lubricating with a silicone base spray lubricant at regular intervals.

TEST

Rapidly accelerate and decelerate the engine while the engine is cold. The valve should momentarily open and then return to the closed position. As the engine warms up the valve

SPECIFIC GRAVITY (@ 80°F.) AND CHARGE Specific Gravity Reading (use the minimum figure for testing)	
Minimum	**Battery Charge**
1.260	100% Charged
1.230	75% Charged
1.200	50% Charged
1.170	25% Charged
1.140	Very Little Power Left
1.110	Completely Discharged

Battery specific gravity. Some testers have colored balls which correspond to the numerical values in the left column

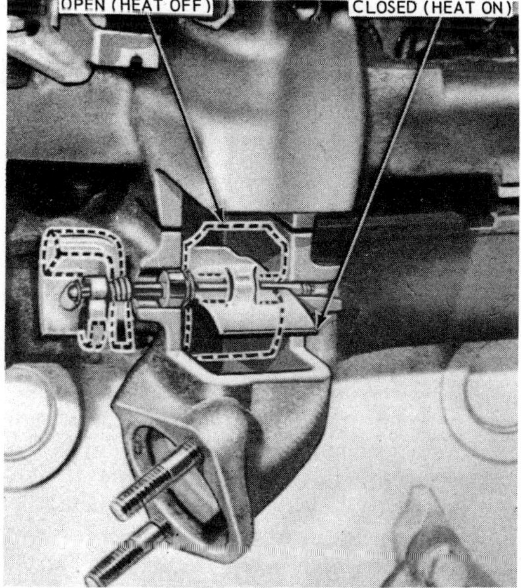

Six-cylinder exhaust control valve—typical

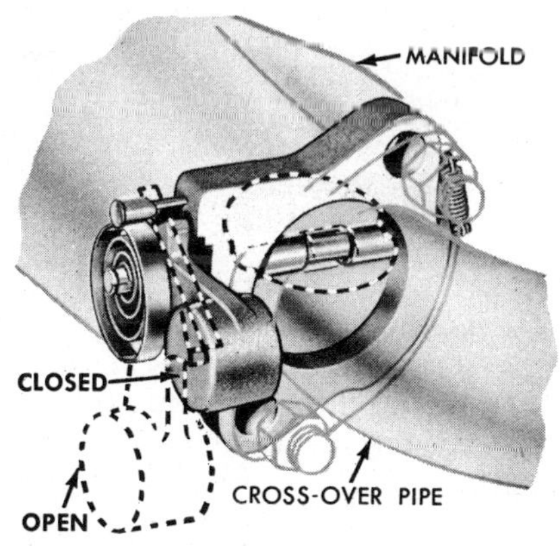

V8 exhaust control valve—typical

should gradually open, until it is fully open at normal operating temperature.

Belts

TENSION CHECKING AND ADJUSTING

Accessory drive belts should be checked for proper tension according to the Preventive Maintenance Schedule at the end of this chapter. The tension can be checked by pressing in on the belt midway between the longest run between two pulleys. As a general rule, the belt should not deflect any more than ½ in. It is recommended that in order to gain an accurate belt tension reading, a belt checking tool be used.

The belt tension as read by the tool should be as follows:

- ¼ in. wide belt, used—60 lbs; new—80 lbs
- ⅜ in., wide belts, used—110 lbs; new—140 lbs 15⁄32 in.
- ½ in. wide belt, used—110 lbs; new—140 lbs

NOTE: *A belt is considered used after it has been operated for 10 minutes or more.*

To adjust drive belt tension, loosen the accessory adjusting and mounting bolts and move the accessory toward or away from the engine as necessary to gain the proper tension. It will be necessary, in most cases, to use some sort of leverage to get the belt tight enough. Exercise caution as to where you place the lever. Do not pry on the cast housing of an alternator; it can be cracked easily. Pry only on the alternator front housing. On power steering pumps, do not pry on the reservoir portion of the pump. After the proper belt tension has been reached, tighten the adjustment bolt and the remaining attaching bolts.

HOW TO SPOT WORN V-BELTS

V-Belts are vital to efficient engine operation—they drive the fan, water pump and other accessories. They require little maintenance (occasional tightening) but they will not last forever. Slipping or failure of the V-belt will lead to overheating. If your V-belt looks like any of these, it should be replaced.

Cracking or weathering

This belt has deep cracks, which cause it to flex. Too much flexing leads to heat build-up and premature failure. These cracks can be caused by using the belt on a pulley that is too small. Notched belts are available for small diameter pulleys.

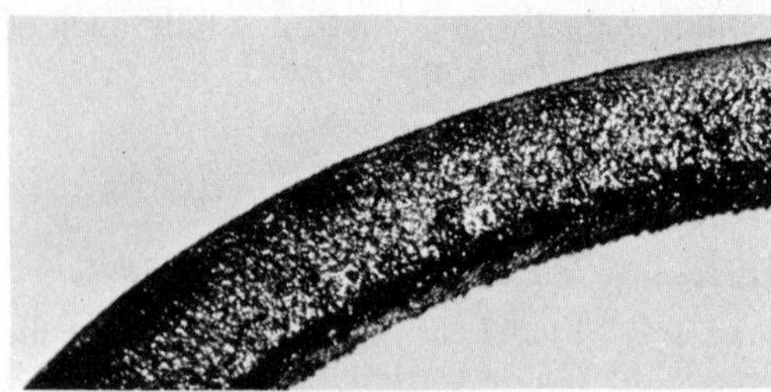

Softening (grease and oil)

Oil and grease on a belt can cause the belt's rubber compounds to soften and separate from the reinforcing cords that hold the belt together. The belt will first slip, then finally fail altogether.

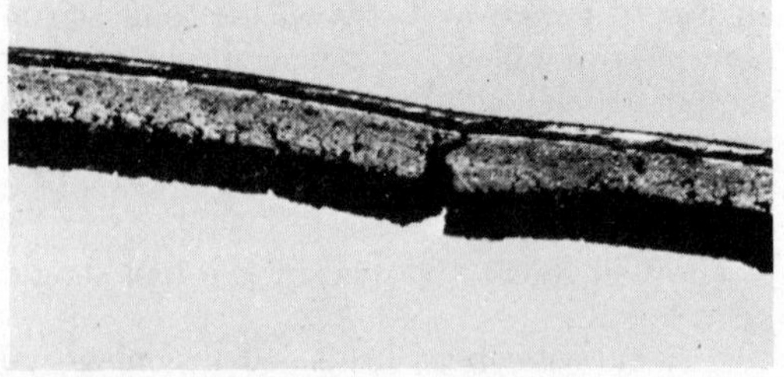

Glazing

Glazing is caused by a belt that is slipping. A slipping belt can cause a run-down battery, erratic power steering, overheating or poor accessory performance. The more the belt slips, the more glazing will be built up on the surface of the belt. The more the belt is glazed, the more it will slip. If the glazing is light, tighten the belt.

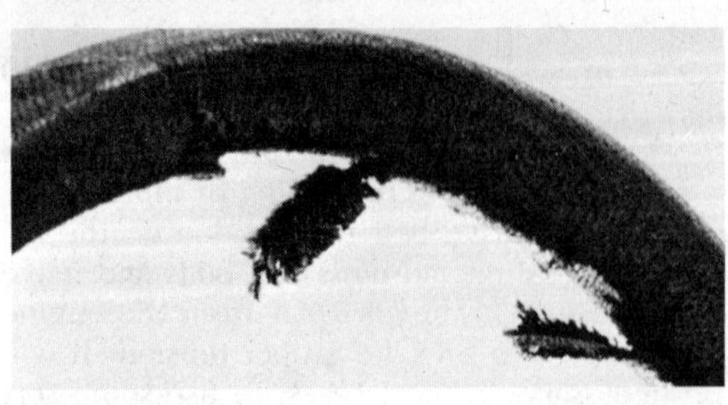

Worn cover

The cover of this belt is worn off and is peeling away. The reinforcing cords will begin to wear and the belt will shortly break. When the belt cover wears in spots or has a rough jagged appearance, check the pulley grooves for roughness.

Separation

This belt is on the verge of breaking and leaving you stranded. The layers of the belt are separating and the reinforcing cords are exposed. It's just a matter of time before it breaks completely.

HOW TO SPOT BAD HOSES

Both the upper and lower radiator hoses are called upon to perform difficult jobs in an inhospitable environment. They are subject to nearly 18 psi at under hood temperatures often over 280°F., and must circulate nearly 7500 gallons of coolant an hour—3 good reasons to have good hoses.

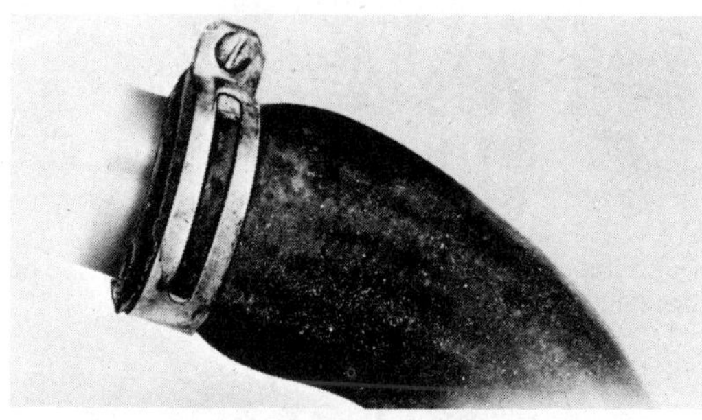

Swollen hose

A good test for any hose is to feel it for soft or spongy spots. Frequently these will appear as swollen areas of the hose. The most likely cause is oil soaking. This hose could burst at any time, when hot or under pressure.

Cracked hose

Cracked hoses can usually be seen but feel the hoses to be sure they have not hardened; a prime cause of cracking. This hose has cracked down to the reinforcing cords and could split at any of the cracks.

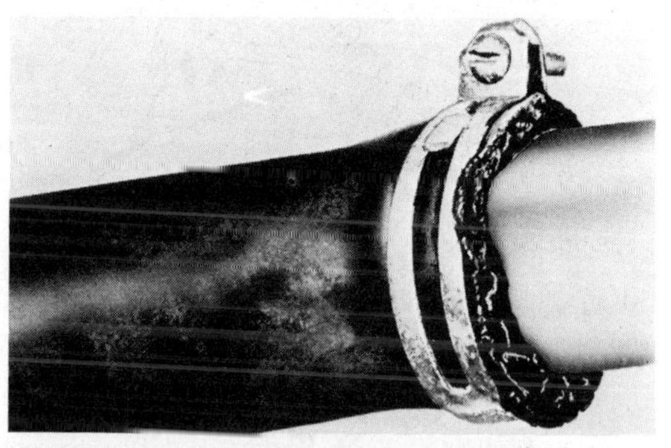

Frayed hose end (due to weak clamp)

Weakened clamps frequently are the cause of hose and cooling system failure. The connection between the pipe and hose has deteriorated enough to allow coolant to escape when the engine is hot.

Debris in cooling system

Debris, rust and scale in the cooling system can cause the inside of a hose to weaken. This can usually be felt on the outside of the hose as soft or thinner areas.

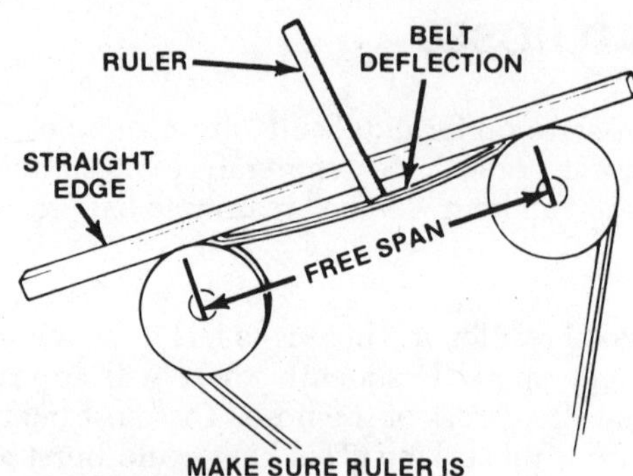

Measuring belt deflection

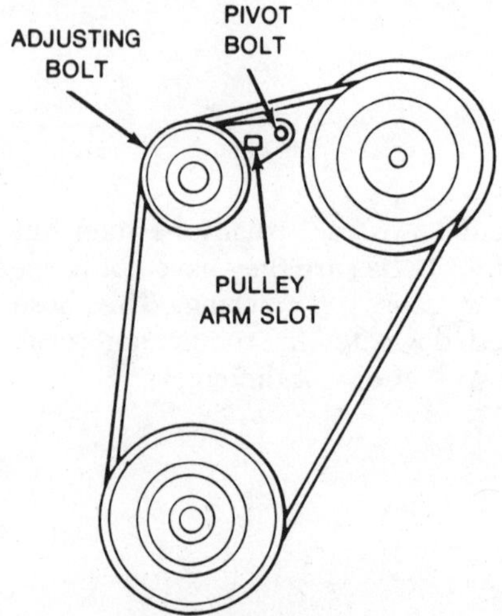

Some pulleys have a rectangular slot to aid in moving the accessory to be tightened

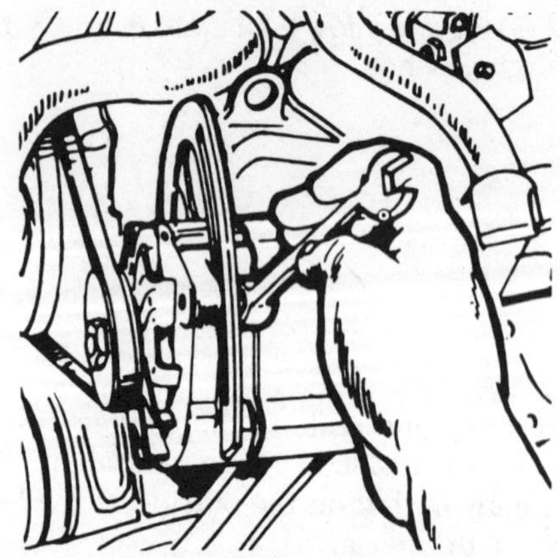

To adjust belt tension or to change belts, first loosen the component's mounting and adjusting bolts slightly

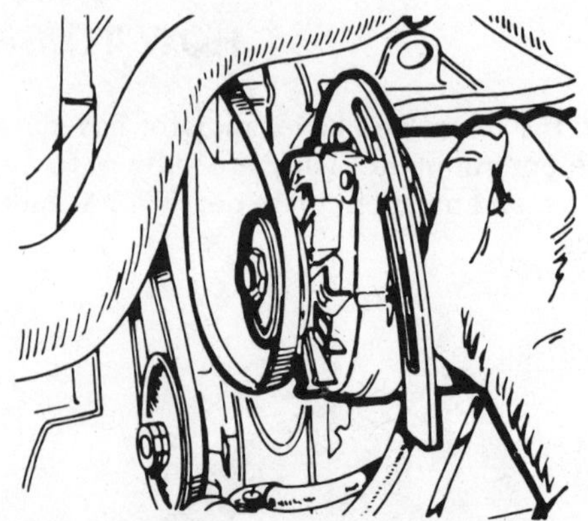

Push the component towards the engine and slip off the belt.

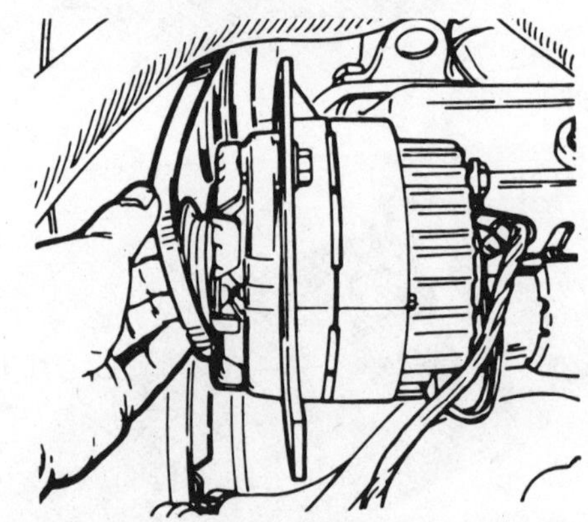

Slip the new belt over the pulley

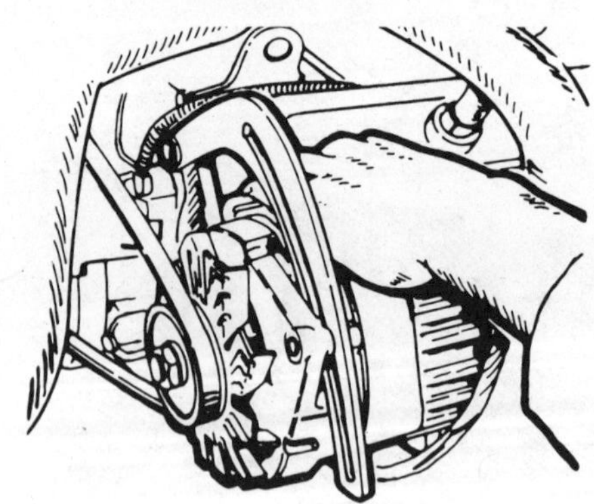

Pull outward on the component and tighten the mounting bolts

Cooling System

CAUTION: *Never remove the radiator cap under any conditions while the engine is running. Failure to follow these instructions could result in damage to the cooling system or engine and/or personal injury. To avoid having scalding hot coolant or steam blow out of the radiator, use extreme care when removing the radiator cap from a hot radiator. Wait until the engine has cooled, then wrap a thick cloth around the radiator cap and turn it slowly to the first stop. Step back while the pressure is released from the cooling system. When you are sure the pressure has been released, press down on the radia-*

tor cap (still have the cloth in position) turn and remove the radiator cap.

At least once every 2 years, the engine cooling system should be inspected, flushed, and refilled with fresh coolant. If the coolant is left in the system too long, it loses its ability to prevent rust and corrosion. If the coolant has too much water, it won't protect against freezing.

The pressure cap should be looked at for signs of age or deterioration. Fan belt and other drive belts should be inspected and adjusted to the proper tension. (See checking belt tension).

Hose clamps should be tightened, and soft or cracked hoses replaced. Damp spots, or accumulations of rust or dye near hoses, water pump or other areas, indicate possible leakage, which must be corrected before filling the system with fresh coolant.

CHECK THE RADIATOR CAP

While you are checking the coolant level, check the radiator cap for a worn or cracked gasket. If the cap doesn't seal properly, fluid will be lost and the engine will overheat.

Worn caps should be replaced with a new one.

CLEAN RADIATOR OF DEBRIS

Periodically clean any debris—leaves, paper, insects, etc.—from the radiator fins. Pick the large pieces off by hand. The smaller pieces can be washed away with water pressure from a hose.

Carefully straighten any bent radiator fins with a pair of needle nose pliers. Be careful—the fins are very soft. Don't wiggle the fins back and forth too much. Straighten them once and try not to move them again.

DRAIN AND REFILL THE COOLING SYSTEM

Completely draining and refilling the cooling system every two years at least will remove accumulated rust, scale and other deposits. Coolant in late model cars is a 50-50 mixture of ethylene glycol and water for year round use. Use a good quality antifreeze with water pump lubricants, rust inhibitors and other corrosion inhibitors along with acid neutralizers.

1. Drain the existing antifreeze and coolant. Open the radiator and engine drain petcocks, or disconnect the bottom radiator hose, at the radiator outlet.

NOTE: *Before opening the radiator petcock, spray it with some penetrating lubricant.*

2. Close the petcock or re-connect the lower hose and fill the system with water.
3. Add a can of quality radiator flush.
4. Idle the engine until the upper radiator hose gets hot.
5. Drain the system again.
6. Repeat this process until the drained water is clear and free of scale.
7. Close all petcocks and connect all the hoses.
8. If equipped with a coolant recovery system, flush the reservoir with water and leave empty.
9. Determine the capacity of your coolant

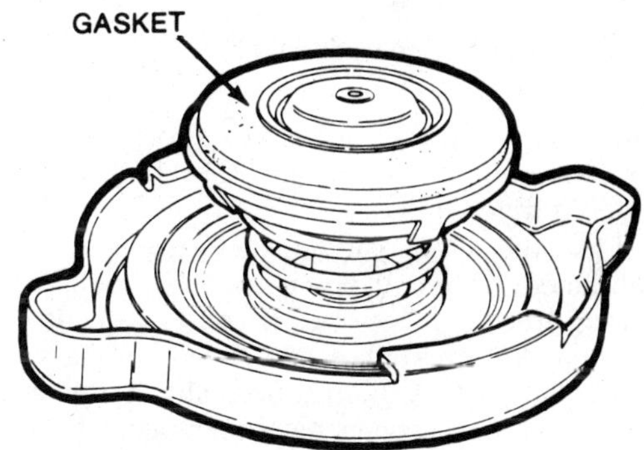

Check the radiator cap gasket for cracks or wear

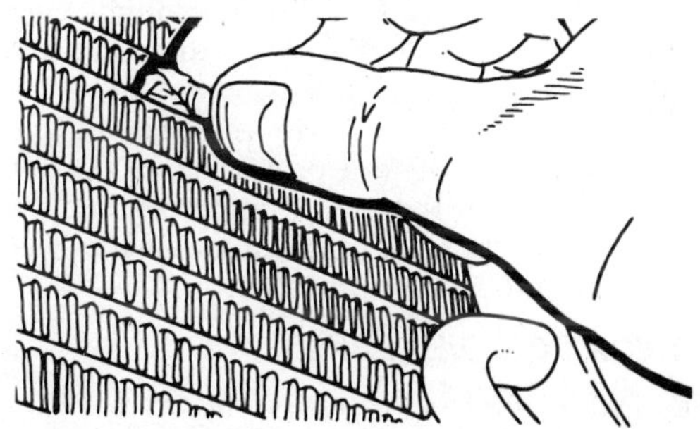

Keep the radiator fins clear of debris for maximum cooling

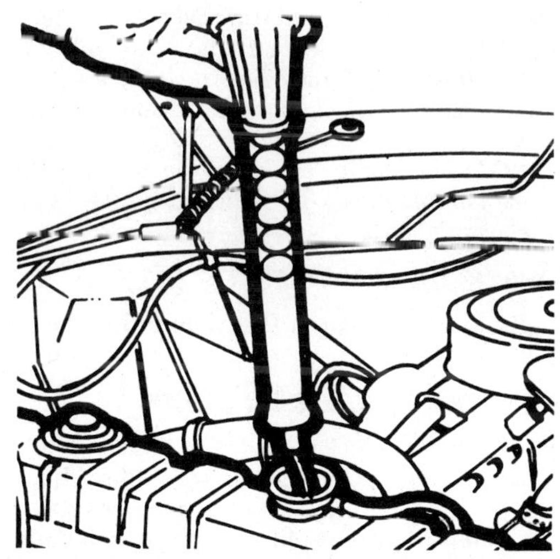

Check anti-freeze protection with an inexpensive tester

system (see capacities specifications). Add a 50/50 mix of quality antifreeze (ethylene glycol) and water to provide the desired protection.

10. Run the engine to operating temperature.

11. Stop the engine and check the coolant level.

12. Check the level of protection with an antifreeze tester, replace the cap and check for leaks.

Air Conditioning

AIR-CONDITIONING SAFETY PRECAUTIONS

There are two particular hazards associated with air conditioning systems and they both relate to the refrigerant gas.

First, the refrigerant gas is an extremely cold substance. When exposed to air, it will instantly freeze any surface it comes in contact with, including your eyes. The other hazard relates to fire. Although normally non-toxic, refrigerant gas becomes highly poisonous in the presence of an open flame. One good whiff of the vapor formed by burning refrigerant can be fatal. Keep all forms of fire (including cigarettes) well clear of the air-conditioning system.

Any repair work to an air conditioning system should be left to a professional. Do not, under any circumstances, attempt to loosen or tighten any fittings or perform any work other than that outlined here.

CHECK FOR OIL LEAKS

Refrigerant leaks show up as oily areas on the various components because the compressor oil is transported around the entire system along with the refrigerant. Look for oily spots on all the hoses and lines, and especially on the hose and tubing connections. If there are oily deposits, the system may have a leak, and you should have it checked by a qualified repairman.

NOTE: *A small area of oil on the front of the compressor is normal and no cause for alarm.*

CHECK THE COMPRESSOR BELT

Refer to the section in this chapter on "Drive Belts."

KEEP THE CONDENSER CLEAR

Periodically inspect the front of the condenser for bent fins or foreign material (dirt, bugs, leaves, etc.) If any cooling fins are bent, straighten them carefully with needlenosed pliers. You can remove any debris with a stiff bristle brush or hose.

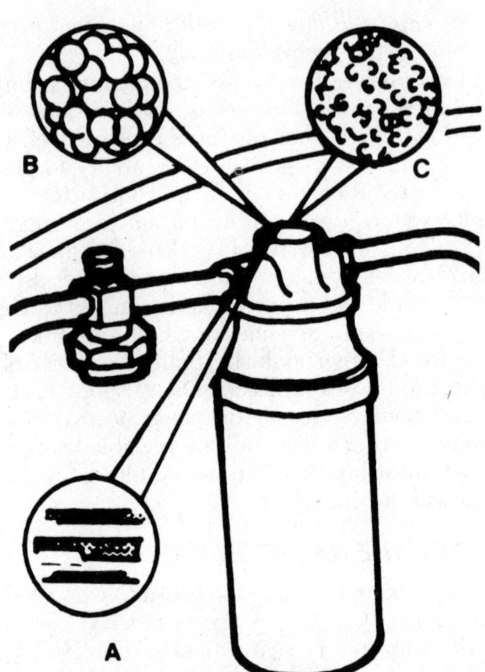

Oil streaks (A), constant bubbles (B) or foam (C) indicate there is not enough refrigerant in the system. Occasional bubbles during initial operation is normal. A clear sight glass indicates a proper charge of refrigerant or no refrigerant at all, which can be determined by the presence of cold air at the outlets in the car. If the glass is clouded with a milky white substance, have the receiver/drier checked professionally.

OPERATE THE A/C SYSTEM PERIODICALLY

A lot of A/C problems can be avoided by simply running the air conditioner at least once a week, regardless of the season. Simply let the system run for at least 5 minutes a week (even in the winter), and you'll keep the internal parts lubricated as well as preventing the hoses from hardening.

REFRIGERANT LEVEL CHECK

There are two ways to check refrigerant level, depending on how your model is equipped.

With Sight Glass

The first order of business when checking the sight glass is to find the sight glass. It will either be in the head of the receiver/drier, or in one of the metal lines leading from the top of the receiver/drier. Once you've found it, wipe it clean and proceed as follows:

1. With the engine and the air conditioning system running, look for the flow of refrigerant through the sight glass. If the air conditioner is working properly, you'll be able to see a con-

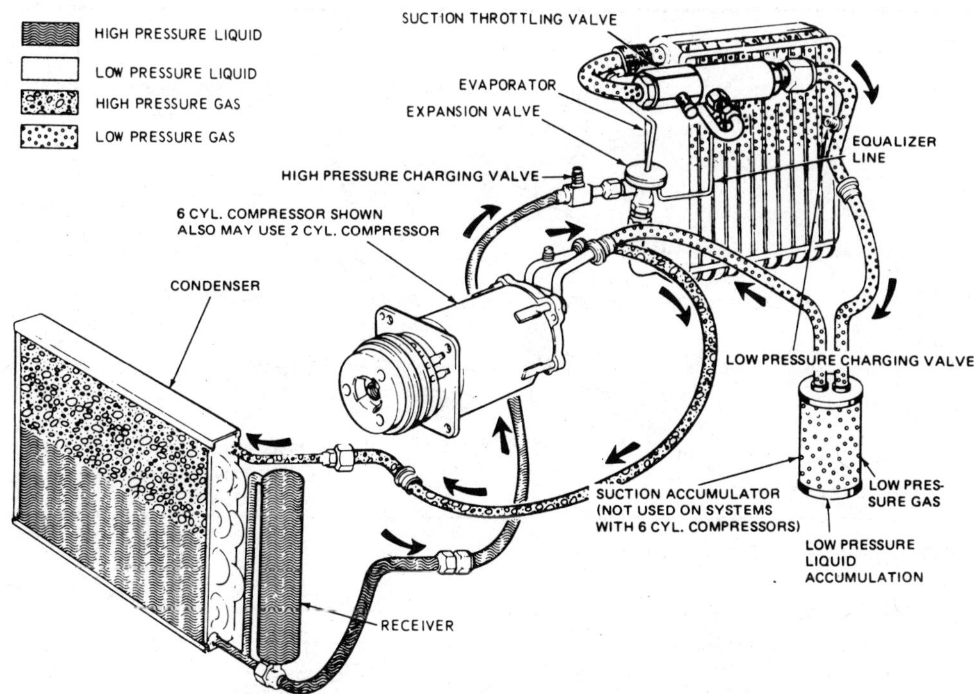

Flow diagram of a typical air conditioning system

tinuous flow of clear refrigerant through the sight glass, with perhaps an occasional bubble at very high temperatures.

2. Cycle the air conditioner on and off to make sure what you are seeing is clear refrigerant. Since the refrigerant is clear, it is possible to mistake a completely discharged system for one that is fully charged. Turn the system off and watch the sight glass. If there is refrigerant in the system, you'll see bubbles during the off cycle. If you observe no bubbles when the system is running, and the air flow from the unit in the car is delivering cold air, everything is OK.

3. If you observe bubbles in the sight glass while the system is operating, the system is low on refrigerant. Have it checked by a professional.

4. Oil streaks in the sight glass are an indication of trouble. Most of the time, if you see oil in the sight glass, it will appear as a series of streaks, although occasionally it may be a solid stream of oil. In either case, it means that part of the charge has been lost.

Some sight glasses are in the A/C lines

Without Sight Glass

On vehicles that are not equipped with sight glasses, it is necessary to feel the temperature difference in the inlet and outlet lines at the receiver/drier to gauge the refrigerant level. Use the following procedure:

1. Locate the receiver/drier. It will generally be up front near the condenser. It is shaped like a small fire extinguisher and will always have two lines connected to it. One line goes to the expansion valve and the other goes to the condenser.

2. With the engine and the air conditioner running, hold a line in each hand and gauge their relative temperatures. If they are both the same approximate temperature, the system is correctly charged.

3. If the line from the expansion valve to the receiver/drier is a lot colder than the line from the receiver/drier to the condenser, then the system is overcharged. It should be noted that this is an extremely rare condition.

4. If the line that leads from the receiver/drier to the condenser is a lot colder than the other line, the system is undercharged.

5. If the system is undercharged or over-

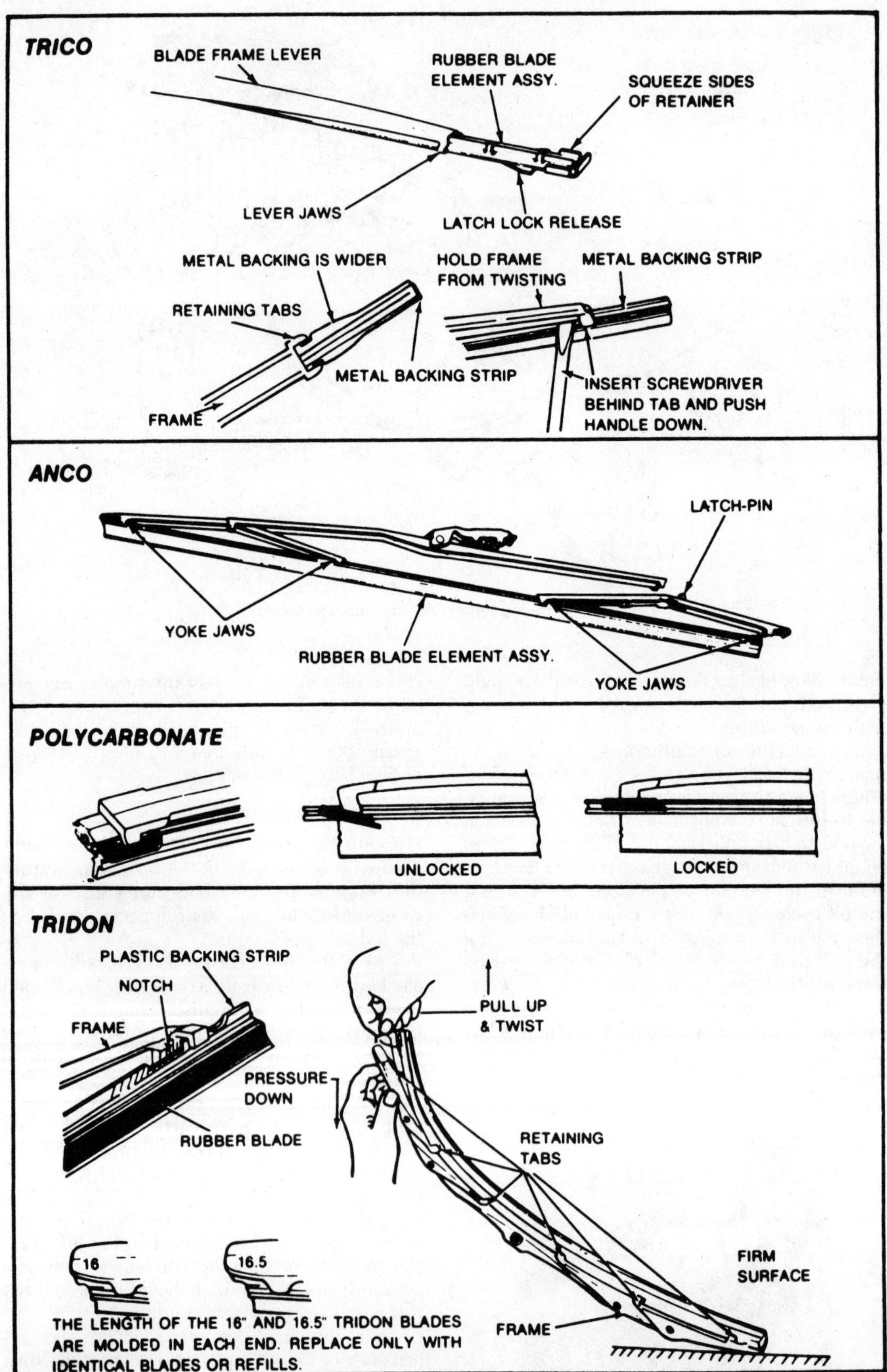

Popular styles of wiper refills

charged, have it checked by a professional air conditioning mechanic.

Windshield Wipers

Intense heat from the sun, snow and ice, road oils and the chemicals used in windshield washer solvents combine to deteriorate the rubber wiper refills. The refills should be replaced about twice a year or whenever the blades begin to streak or chatter.

WIPER REFILL REPLACEMENT

Normally, if the wipers are not cleaning the windshield properly, only the refill has to be replaced. The blade and arm usually require replacement only in the event of damage. It is not necessary (except on new Tridon refills) to remove the arm or the blade to replace the refill (rubber part), though you may have to position the arm higher on the glass. You can do this turning the ignition switch on and operating the wipers. When they are positioned where they are accessible, turn the ignition switch off.

There are several types of refills and your vehicle could have any kind, since aftermarket blades and arms may not use exactly the same type refill as the original equipment.

Most Anco styles use a release button that is pushed down to allow the refill to slide out of the yoke jaws. The new refill slides in and locks in place.

Some Trico refills are removed by locating where the metal backing strip or the refill is wider. Insert a small screwdriver blade between the frame and metal backing strip. Press down to release the refill from the retaining tab.

Other Trico blades are unlocked at one end by squeezing 2 metal tabs, and the refill is slid out of the framejaws. When the new refill is installed, the tabs will click into place, locking the refill.

The polycarbonate type is held in place by a locking lever that is pushed downward out of the groove in the arm to free the refill. When the new refill is installed, it will lock in place automatically.

The Tridon refill has a plastic backing strip with a notch about an inch from the end. Hold the blade (frame) on a hard surface so that the frame is tightly bowed. Grip the tip of the backing strip and pull up while twisting counterclockwise. The backing strip will snap out of the retaining tab. Do this for the remaining tabs until the refill is free of the arm. The length of these refills is molded into the end and they should be replaced with identical types.

No matter which type of refill you use, be sure that all of the frame claws engage the refill. Before operating the wipers, be sure that no part of the metal frame is contacting the windshield.

Fluid Level Checks

ENGINE OIL

Check the engine oil level every time you fill the gas tank. The oil level should be above the ADD mark and not above the FULL mark on the dipstick. Make sure that the distick is inserted into the crankcase as far as possible and that the vehicle is resting on level ground.

TRANSMISSION

Manual

The manual transmission level should be checked according ot the Preventive Maintenance Schedule at the end of this chapter, or daily if the vehicle has been operated in deep water. If water is noticed in the lubricant, the lubricant should be changed immediately.

Typical I-6

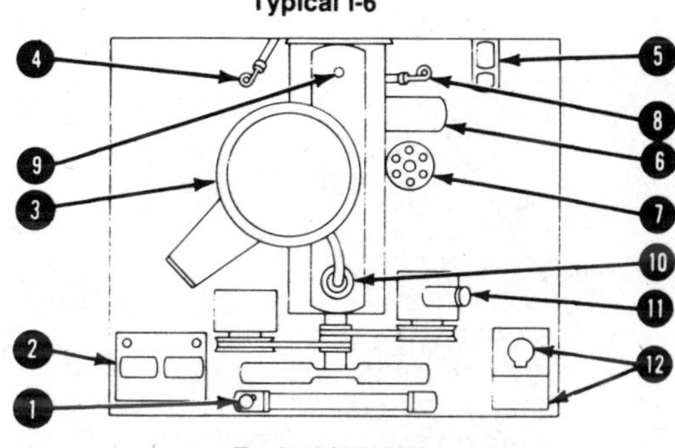

Typical V-6, V-8

1. Radiator filler cap
2. Battery
3. Air cleaner
4. Automatic transmission dipstick
5. Brake master cylinder
6. Engine oil filter
7. Distributor
8. Engine oil dipstick
9. PCV valve
10. Engine oil filler cap
11. Power steering reservoir
12. Windshield washer reservoir and radiator overflow bottle

Engine compartment service points

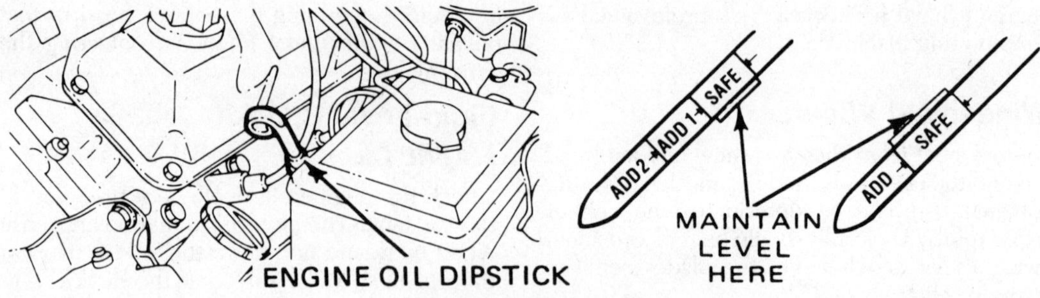

Checking engine oil level

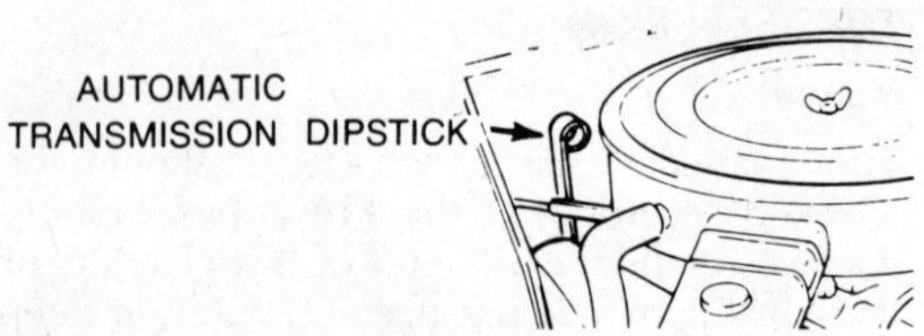

Automatic transmission dipstick is found towards the rear of the engine

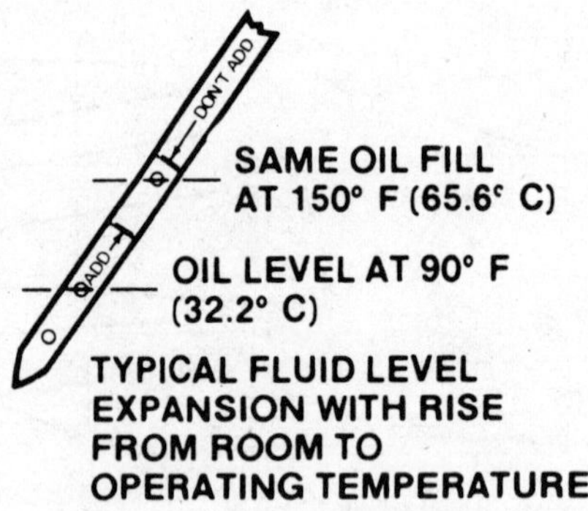

Checking automatic transmission fluid level. Check transmission when it is warmed to operating temperature

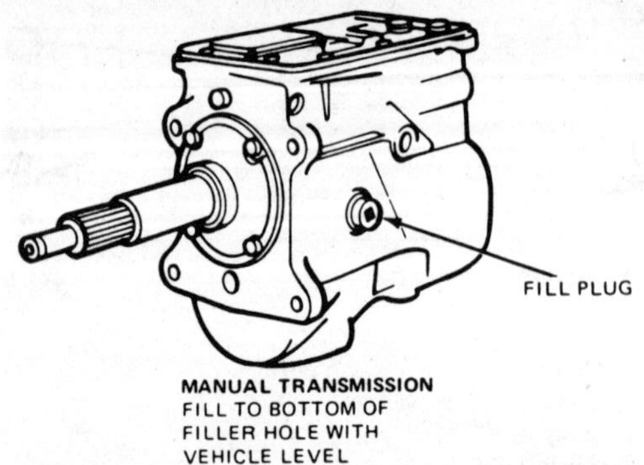

Typical manual trans filler location

Before checking the lubricant level in the transmission, make sure that the vehicle is on level ground. Remove the fill plug from the right-side of the transmission. Remove the plug slowly when it starts to reach the end of the threads on the plug. Hold the plug up against the hole and move it away slowly. This is so as to minimize the loss of lubricant through the fill hole. The level of the lubricant should be up to the bottom of the fill hole. If lubricant is not present at the bottom of the fill hole, add SAE 90 or 80 transmission lube until it reaches the proper level. A suction gun or kitchen-type baster is used to fill a manual transmission with lubricant.

Automatic Transmission

The fluid level in an automatic transmission is checked when the transmission is at operating temperature. If the vehicle has been sitting and is cold, drive it at highway speeds for at least 20 minutes to warm the transmission.

CAUTION: *Use the proper type transmission fluid when adding or changing: C4 transmission through 1979—Type F. C4 transmission 1980 and later—Dexron II. C6 transmission through 1976—Type F. C6 transmission 1977 and later—Dextron II. All C5 transmissions—Type H. All AOD transmissions—Dextron II.*

1. With the transmission in Park, the engine running at idle speed, the foot brakes applied and the vehicle resting on level ground, move the transmission gear selector through each of the gear positions, including Reverse, allowing time for the transmission to engage. Return the shift selector to the Park position and apply the parking brake. Do not turn the engine off; leave it running at idle speed.
2. Clean all dirt from around the transmission dipstick cap and the end of the filler tube.
3. Pull the dipstick out of the tube, wipe it off with a clean cloth, and push it back into the tube all the way, making sure that it seats completely.
4. Pull the dipstick out of the tube again and read the level of the fluid on the stick. The level should be between the ADD mark and the FULL mark. If fluid must be added, add enough fluid through the tube to raise the level up to between the ADD and FULL marks. Do not

Capacities Chart

CRANKCASE AND COOLING SYSTEM (QTS)

Year	Engine	Crankcase Oil and Filter Change	Cooling System					
			Standard System		Extra Cooling			
			Man Trans	Auto Trans	Man Trans	Auto Trans	With A/C	Super Cooling
1965	240	6.0	19.0	19.0	—	—	—	—
	300	6.0	19.0	19.0	—	—	—	—
	352	6.0	27.0	27.0	—	—	—	—
	361	9.0	24.0	24.0	—	—	—	—
1966–67	240, 300 eng., F-100/250 2 x 4	5.0	13.0	13.0	—	—	—	—
	F-100/250 4 x 4	6.0	14.0	14.0	—	—	—	—
	F-350	6.0	18.0	18.0	—	—	—	—
	352 eng., F-100/250	6.0	21.0	21.0	—	—	—	—
	F-350	6.0	24.0	24.0	—	—	—	—
1968	240, 300LD eng., F-100/250 2 x 4	5.0	13.0	13.0	—	—	—	—
	F-100/250 4 x 4	6.0	14.0	14.0	—	—	—	—
	F-350	6.0	18.0	18.0	—	—	—	—
	300HD eng., F-100/250	6.0	21.0	21.0	—	—	—	—
	F-350	6.0	24.0	24.0	—	—	—	—
1969	240 eng., F-100/250 4 x 2	5.0	13.0	14.5	—	—	17.0	—
	F-100/250 4 x	6.0	12.0	12.0	—	—	18.2	—
	F-350 SRW	6.0	12.0	14.5	—	—	18.2	—
	F-350 DRW	6.0	17.0	17.0	—	—	18.2	—
	300 eng., F-100/250 2 x 4, 4 x 4	6.0	14.5	14.5	—	—	17.0	—
	F-350 SRW	6.0	14.5	17.0	—	—	18.2	—
	F-350 DRW	6.0	17.0	17.0	—	—	18.2	—
	361 eng., F-100/250 2 x 4	6.0	22.0	22.0	—	—	22.2	—
	F-100/250 4 x 4	6.0	22.2	22.2	—	—	24.0	—
	F-350 DRW, SRW	6.0	22.2	22.2	—	—	24.0	—
	391 eng., F-100/250 2 x 4	6.0	22.2	22.2	—	—	—	—
	F-350 SRW, DRW	6.0	22.2	22.2	—	—	24.0	—
1970–71	240 eng., F-100/250 4 x 2	5.0	13.0	14.5	13.0	—	—	—
	F-100/250 4 x 4	6.0	14.5	—	—	—	18.25	—
	F-350 SRW	6.0	14.5	17.0	17.0	18.0	18.25	—
	F-350 DRW	6.0	17.0	17.0	18.25	18.25	18.25	—
	300 eng., F-100/250 4 x 2	6.0	13.2	14.4	16.7	16.7	16.7	—
	F-350 SRW	6.0	14.4	16.6	16.6	18.25	18.25	—
	F-350 DRW	6.0	16.6	16.6	18.25	18.25	18.25	—
	302 eng., F-100/250 4 x 2	6.0	17.1	17.1	17.5	17.5	17.5	—
	360 eng., F-100/250 4 x 2	6.0	21.9	21.9	22.2	22.2	22.2	—
	F-100/250 4 x 4	6.0	21.9	21.9	22.2	22.2	22.2	—
	F-350 SRW	6.0	22.2	22.2	23.9	23.9	23.9	—

Capacities Chart (cont.)

CRANKCASE AND COOLING SYSTEM (QTS)

			Cooling System					
			Standard System		Extra Cooling			
Year	Engine	Crankcase Oil and Filter Change	Man Trans	Auto Trans	Man Trans	Auto Trans	With A/C	Super Cooling
1970–71	F-350 DRW	6.0	22.2	22.2	23.9	23.9	23.9	—
	390 eng., F-100/250 4 x 2	6.0	21.9	21.9	22.2	22.2	22.2	—
	F-350 SRW	6.0	22.2	22.2	23.9	23.9	23.9	—
	F-350 DRW	6.0	22.2	22.2	23.9	23.9	23.9	—
1972–73	240 eng., F-100/250/350 2 x 4	5.0	14.0	14.5	14.5	17.0	17.0	—
	300 eng., F-100/250 4 x 4, 2 x 4	5.0 ①	14.5	17.0	17.0	17.0	17.0	—
	F-350	6.0	14.5	17.0	17.0	17.0	17.0	—
	F-350 DRW	6.0	17.0	17.0	18.5	18.5	—	—
	302 eng., F-100 4 x 2	6.0	17.0	17.0	17.5	17.5	17.5	—
	360 eng., F-100/250 4 x 2	6.0	22.0	22.0	22.5	22.5	22.5	—
	F-100/250 4 x 4	6.0	22.5	22.5	22.5	22.5	22.5	—
	F-350	6.0	22.5	22.5	24.0	24.0	24.0	—
	390 eng., F-100/250 4 x 2	6.0	22.0	22.0	22.5	22.5	22.5	—
	F-350	6.0	22.5	22.5	24.0	24.0	24.0	—
1974	240 eng., 4 x 2	6.0	14.1	14.4	14.4	16.3	16.3	—
	4 x 4	6.0	14.4	—	16.7	—	16.7	—
	300 eng., 4 x 2	6.0	14.4	14.4	16.3	16.3	16.3	—
	4 x 4	6.0	14.4	—	16.7	—	16.7	—
	302 eng.	6.0	14.8	14.8	17.1	17.5	17.5	—
	360 eng., 4 x 2	6.0	19.6	19.6	21.9	22.3	22.3	23.9
	4 x 4	6.0	22.3	22.3	22.3	22.3	23.9	23.9
	390 eng.	6.0	19.6	19.6	22.3	23.9	23.9	23.9
	460 eng.	6.0	—	21.0	—	21.0	22.6	23.2
1975	300 eng. F-100 4 x 2	6.0	14.4	14.4	16.3	16.3	—	—
	F-100/250 4 x 4	6.0	14.4	—	16.3	—	—	—
	F-150/250 4 x 2	6.0	14.4	14.4	16.7	16.7	—	—
	F-350	6.0	14.4	16.7	16.7	18.3	—	—
	302 eng., F-100 4 x 2	6.0	14.8	14.8	14.8	17.5	—	—
	360 eng., F-100 4 x 2	6.0	19.6	21.9	21.9	22.3	22.3	23.9
	F-150/250 4 x 2	6.0	19.6	19.6	21.9	22.9	22.3	23.9
	F-100/250 4 x 4	6.0	22.3	22.3	22.3	22.3	23.9	23.9
	F-350	6.0	22.3	22.3	23.9	23.9	23.9	23.9
	390 eng., F-100/150/250 4 x 2	6.0	22.3	22.3	22.3	22.3	23.9	24.6
	F-350	6.0	22.3	22.3	24.6	23.9	24.6	24.6
	460 eng., F-150/250	6.0	—	22.5	—	22.5	22.5	23.2
	F-350	6.0	—	22.5	—	22.5	23.2	—
1976	300 eng., F-100 4 x 2	6.0	12.5	14.5	14.5	14.5	—	—
	F-150/250 4 x 4	6.0	14.5	14.5	16.5	16.5	—	—

Capacities Chart (cont.)

CRANKCASE AND COOLING SYSTEM (QTS)

Year	Engine	Crankcase Oil and Filter Change	Cooling System: Standard System Man Trans	Cooling System: Standard System Auto Trans	Cooling System: Extra Cooling Man Trans	Cooling System: Extra Cooling Auto Trans	Cooling System: With A/C	Cooling System: Super Cooling
1976	F-150/250 4 x 2	6.0	12.5	12.5	14.5	14.5	—	—
	F-350	6.0	14.5	14.5	14.5	14.5	14.5	—
	302 eng., F-100 4 x 2	6.0	15.0	15.0	17.5	17.5	17.5	—
	360 eng., F-100 4 x 2	6.0	19.5	22.0	22.5	22.5	24.0	24.0
	F-150/250 4 x 2	6.0	19.5	19.5	22.0	22.5	24.0	24.0
	F-100/150 4 x 4	6.0	16.5	16.5	16.5	16.5	16.5	—
	F-250 4 x 4	6.0	16.5	16.5	16.5	16.5	16.5	18.5
	F-350	6.0	22.5	22.5	24.0	24.0	24.0	—
1977	300 eng., F-100/150/250 4 x 2	6.0	12.5	14.5	14.5	14.5	—	—
	F-150/250 4 x 4	6.0	14.5	14.5	14.5	14.5	—	—
	F-350	6.0	14.5	14.5	14.5	14.5	—	—
	302 eng., F-100 4 x 2	6.0	15.5	17.5	15.5	17.5	17.5	—
	351 eng., F-100 4 x 2	6.0	19.5	22.0	19.5	19.5	22.0	24.0
	F-150/250 4 x 2	6.0	19.5	19.5	19.5	19.5	22.0	24.0
	F-150/250 4 x 4	6.0	22.0	22.0	22.0	22.0	22.0	24.0
	F-350	6.0	22.0	22.0	22.0	22.0	22.0	—
	400 eng., F-100/150/250/350	6.0	22.0	22.0	22.0	22.0	22.0	24.0
	460 eng., F-150/250/350	6.0	22.5	22.5	22.5	22.5	22.5	—
1978–86	300 eng., F-100/250/350	6.0	13.0	14.0	13.0	14.0	17.0	14
	232, 255, 302 eng., F-100/150	6.0	15.0 ②	15.0 ②	15.0	18.0	18.0	11
	351 eng., F-100, F-150/350	6.0	17.0	—	17.0	—	—	16
	400 eng., F/250/350	6.0	18.0	—	18.0		18.0	24.0
	460 eng., 150/350, 250	6.0	24.0 ③	24.0 ③	24.0 ③	24.0 ③	24.0 ③	24.0 ③
	420 Diesel, All	10.0	29.0	29.0	29.0	29.0	29.0	29.0

SRW—Single rear wheels
DRW—Dual rear wheels
① 6.0 4 x 4
② 10.0 qts 1983 and later
③ 18 qts 1983 and later

Transmission and Transfer Case

Year	Model	Type	Capacity (pints)
1965	F-100/250	Ford 3-sp	3.5
	F-350	Warner T-87, 3-sp	5.5
	F-100/250	Warner T-89, 4-sp	3.3
	F-100/250/350	New Process 435, 4-sp	6.75
	F-250	Warner T-18, 4-sp	6.5
	F-100	Transfer case	1.75
	F-250	Transfer case	4.5
	F-100/250	C-4 Automatic	20.0

Transmission and Transfer Case (cont.)

Year	Model	Type	Capacity (pints)
1966	F-100/250	Ford 3-sp	3.5
	F-100	Warner T-85, 3-sp	4.0
	F-250 (4WD)	Warner T-89, 3-sp	3.3
	F-350	Warner T-87, 3-sp	5.5
	F-100/250 (4WD)	New Process 4-sp(435)	6.75
	F-100/250/350	New Process 4-sp(435)	6.75
	F-100/250	Warner T-18, 4-sp	6.5
	F-100	Transfer case	1.75
	F-250	Transfer case	4.5
	F-100/250	C-4 Automatic	20.0
1967	F-100/250	Ford 3-sp	3.5
	F-100	Warner T-85, 3-sp	4.0
	F-100/250	New Process 435, 4-sp	6.75
	F-100/250/350	Warner T-18, 4-sp	6.5
	F-100/250	C-4 Automatic	20.0
	F-100	Transfer case	1.75
	F-250	Transfer case	4.5
1968–69	F-100/250/350	Ford 3-sp	3.5
	F-100	Warner T-85, 3-sp	4.0
	F-100/250/350	New Process 435, 4-sp	6.75
	F-100/250/350	Warner T-18, 4-sp	6.5
	F-100	Transfer case	1.75
	F-250	Transfer case	4.5
	F-100/250	C-4 Automatic	20.0
1970–73	F-100/250	Ford 3.03, 3-sp	3.5
	F-100 (4 x 2)	Warner T-85N, O.D	4.0
	F-100/250/F-350 (4 x 2)	Warner T-18, 4-sp	6.5
	F-100/250/350	New Process 435, 4-sp	6.5
	F-100/250	C-4	20.5
	F-100/250/350	C-6	25.5
	F-350 (1973)	FMX	22.0
	F-100 (4 x 4)	Dana 21, 1-sp Transfer Case	1.25
	F-250 (4 x 4)	Dana 24, 2-sp Transfer Case	4.5
1974	F-100/250	Ford 3.03, 3-sp	3.5
	F-100/250/350 (4 x 2)	Warner T-18, 4-sp	7.0
	F-100/250/350	New Process 435, 4-sp with extension without extension	 7.0 6.5
	F-100/250	C-4	20.5
	F-100/350	FMX	22.0
	F-100/250 (4 x 2)	C-6	28.0
	F-100/250 (4 x 4)	C-6	26.5

Transmission and Transfer Case (cont.)

Year	Model	Type	Capacity (pints)
1974	F-350	C-6	25.0
	F-100 (4 x 4)	Dana 21, 1-sp Transfer Case	1.25
	F-100/250 (4 x 4)	New Process 205, Transfer Case	4.0
1975–76	F-100/150/250	Ford 3.03, 3-sp	3.5
	F-100/250/350 (4 x 2)	Warner T-18, 4-sp	7.0
	F-100/150/250/350	New Process 435, 4-sp with extension without extension	 7.0 6.5
	F-100/150/250	C-4 w/300 cid eng w/302 cid eng	20.5 17.5
	F-100	FMX	22.0
	F-100/150/250/350	C-6 4 x 2 w/360, 390 cid eng 4 x 2 w/460 cid eng 4 x 4	24.5 27.5 27.5
	F-100 (4 x 4)	Dana 21, 1-sp Transfer Case	1.25
	F-100/250	New Process 205, 2-sp Transfer Case	4.5
	F-100/150/250	New Process 203, Full Time Transfer Case	9.0
1977–78	F-100/150/250	Ford 3.03, 3-sp	3.5
	F-100/150/250 (4 x 2) F-250 (4 x 4) F-350	Warner T-18, 4-sp	6.5
	F-100/150/250/350	New Process 435, 4-sp with extension without extension	 7.0 6.5
	F-100/150/250	C-4 w/300 cid eng w/302 cid eng	20.0 17.5
	F-100/150/250/350	C-6 4 x 2 4 x 2	24.5 27.5
	F-150/250 (4 x 4)	New Process 205, 2-sp Transfer Case	4.0
	F-150/250 (4 x 4)	New Process 203, Full Time Transfer Case	9.0
1979–86	F-100/250	Ford 3.03, 3-sp	3.5
	F-150/250/350	Warner T-18 & T19B, 4-sp	7.0
	F-100/150/250/350	New Process 435, 4-sp with extension without extension	 7.0 6.5
	All F Series	Clark 4-sp Overdrive	5.0
	F-100/150 F-150/350	C-4 Automatic	20.0
	F-250 (4 x 4)	C-6 Automatic 351, 400, 460 engs. All others	 26.75 23.5
	F-150/250 (4 x 4)	New Process 205, 2-sp Transfer Case	4.5
	F-150/250/350 (4 x 4)	New Process 203, Full Time Transfer Case	9.0
	F-150/250 F-250/350	New Process 208, Transfer Case Borg Warner 1345, Transfer Case	7.0 6.5
	F-100/150 (4 x 2) F-250/350 (4 x 2)	C-5 Automatic	22
	All models	Automatic Overdrive (AOD)	24

Drive Axles

Year	Model	Type	Capacity (pints)
1965	F-100	Ford 3300	4.5
	F-100	Spicer 44	4.5
	F-100	Spicer 60-2	6.0
	F-250	Spicer 60	6.0
	F-350	Spicer 70	6.0
	F-100/250 (4 x 4)	Spicer 2559 Front axle	3.5
1966–68	F-100 (4 x 2)	Ford 3300	4.5 ①
	F-100 (4 x 2)	Spicer (Dana) 44-3	3.75
	F-100 (4 x 4), (4 x 2)	Spicer (Dana) 60-3	5.0
	F-250 (4 x 4), (4 x 2)	Dana 60	5.0 ②
	F-350	Dana 70	5.0 ②
	F-100	Spicer 44-7F Front axle	4.5
	F-250	Spicer 44-6F Front axle	3.75
1969	F-100	Ford 3300	6.5
	F-100 (4 x 4), (4 x 2)	Dana 60-3	6.0
	F-250 (4 x 4), (4 x 2)	Dana 60	6.0
	F-350	Dana 70	6.0
	F-100 (4 x 4)	Dana 44-7F Front axle	3.75
	F-250 (4 x 4)	Dana 44-6BF Front axle	3.75*
	F-250 (4 x 4)	Dana 44-6BF Front axle	3.75*
1970–71	F-100	Ford 3300	6.5
	F-100	Dana 60-3	6.0
	F-250	Dana 60	6.0
	F-350	Dana 70	6.0
	F-100/250	Dana 44F Front axle	3.75
	F-250	Dana 44F HD Front axle	5.75
1972–73	F-100	Ford 3300	6.5
	F-250	Dana 60	6.0
	F-350	Dana 70	6.0
	F-100	Dana 44-7F Front axle	4.75
	F-250	Dana 44-6CF Front axle	4.0
1974–75	F-100	Ford 3300	6.5
	F-100	Ford 3600, 3750	6.5
	F-250	Dana 60, 61	6.0
	F-350	Dana 70	6.0
	F-100	Dana 44-7F Front axle	4.75
	F-250	Dana 44-6CF Front axle	4.6
	F-250	Dana 44-6CF HD Front axle	5.9
	F-250	Dana 60F Front axle	6.0
1976–78	F-100/150	Ford 3300, 3750	6.5
	F-250	Dana 60, 61	6.0

Drive Axles (cont.)

Year	Model	Type	Capacity (pints)
1976–78	F-250	Dana 60, 61	6.0
	F-350	Dana-70	6.0
	F-150	Dana 44-7F Front axle	4.75
	F-250	Dana 44-6CF HD Front axle	4.0
	F-250	Dana 60F Front axle	5.5
1979–82	F-100/150	Ford	6.0
	F-250 (4 x 2) F-250/350 (4 x 4)	Dana 60-2	7.0
1979–86	F-250	Dana 61-2	6.0
	F-350	Dana 70	7.0
	F-150/250 (4 x 4)	Dana 44-9F (Front axle)	3.5†
	F-250/350 (4 x 4)	Dana 60-7F (Front axle)	6.0
	F-250/350 (4 x 4) HD	Dana 50-IFS	4.1
	F-250/350 SRW	Dana 61-1 (Rear)	6.0
	F-350 DRW	Dana 70 HD (Rear)	7.4
	F-250 (4 x 2) F-250 (4 x 4)	Dana 44 IFS (Front Axle)	3.8

*Add 1 pint for each steering knuckle
†4.0—with New Process 205 2 spd transfer case
① 5.0 pt.—1968
② 6.0 pt.—1967–68
SRW—Single Rear Wheels
DRW—Dual Real Wheels

Fuel Tank

Year	Model	Standard	Optional
1965	F-100	18.0	—
	F-250/350	17.0	—
1966–69	F-100 (Cab)	19.5	—
	F-100/250/350 (Cowl)	17.0	—
1970	F-100/250/350 Cab exc Calif	20.0	24.0
	F-100/250/350 Chassis	17.0	—
	F-100 Calif cab	18.5	—
1971–72	F-100	18.5	21.5
	F-250/350 chassis-cowl	17.0	—
	F-250/350 chassis-cab	19.5	25.0
1973–74	F-100	19.2	20.2 4 x 2 frame mount 17.2 in-cab
	F-250 (4 x 2)	19.2	22.5 frame mount 19.3 in-cab
	F-250 (4 x 2)	19.3 exc Calif 17.5 Calif	—
	F-350	19.3 exc Calif 17.5	—
1975–76	F-100	19.2	20.2 4 x 2 frame mount 17.5 in-cab

Fuel Tank (cont.)

Year	Model	Standard	Optional
1975–76	F-150/250 (4 x 2)	19.2	22.5 frame mount exc Calif 20.2 frame mount Calif 19.3 in-cab exc Calif 17.5 in-cab Calif
	F-250 (4 x 4)	19.3 exc Calif 17.5	—
	F-350	19.3	22.5 midship
	All Supercab	19.2	19.0 frame mount
1977–78	F-100	19.2	20.2 frame mount
	F-150 (4 x 2), (4 x 4), F-250 (4 x 2)	19.2 exc Calif 20.2 Calif	22.5 frame mount 19.3 in-cab 17.5 in-cab
	F-250 (4 x 4) and Crew Cab	22.5 exc Calif 20.2 Calif	—
	F-350	20.2	21.0 Aft./Axle
	All Supercab	19.5 frame mount	—
1979–82	F-100/250/350 (4 x 2) (Reg Cab)	19.2	20.2 Aft./Axle
	F-250 (4 x 4) (Reg Cab)	19.2	—
	F-250/350 (4 x 2) (Crew Cab)	20.2	—
	Super Cab	19.2	19.5 Aft./Axle
	F-350 (4 x 2) (Reg Cab)	20.2	19.0 Aft./Axle
	F-250/350 (4 x 4) (Reg Cab)	26.0	19.2 Aft./Axle
1983–86	F-100 (4 x 2) (Reg Cab)	16.5	19.0 Aft./Axle
	F-150 (4 x 2) (Crew Cab)	16.5	19.0 Aft./Axle
	F-150 (4 x 4) (Reg Cab)	16.5	19.0 Aft./Axle
	F-250 (4 x 2) (Crew Cab)	16.5	19.0 Aft./Axle
	F-150 (4 x 2) (Reg Cab)	19.0	19.0 Aft./Axle
	F-150 (4 x 4) (Reg Cab)	19.0	19.0 Aft./Axle
	F-150 (4 x 2) (Crew Cab)	19.0	19.0 Aft./Axle
	F-150 (4 x 4) (Crew Cab)	19.0	19.0 Aft./Axle
	F-250 (4 x 2) (Reg Cab)	19.0	19.0 Aft./Axle
	F-250 (4 x 2) (Crew Cab)	19.0	19.0 Aft./Axle
	F-250 (4 x 4) All	19.0	19.0 Aft./Axle
	F-350 (4 x 2) (Reg Cab)	19.0	19.0 Aft./Axle
	F-350 (4 x 2) (Super Cab)	19.0	19.0 Aft./Axle
	F-350 (4 x 2) (Cab Chassis)	19.0 ①	19.0 ① Aft./Axle

Aft./Axle—After Rear Axle
① Mounted on right outboard side of frame; 20.0 gal. tank optional

overfill the transmission because this will cause foaming, loss of fluid through the vent, and malfunctioning of the transmission.

BRAKE MASTER CYLINDER

The master cylinder reservoir is located under the hood, on the left side firewall. Before removing the master cylinder reservoir cap, make sure the vehicle is resting on level ground and clean all dirt away from the top of the master cylinder. Pry off the retaining clip or unscrew the hold-down bolt and remove the cap. The brake fluid level should be within ¼ in. of the top of the reservoir.

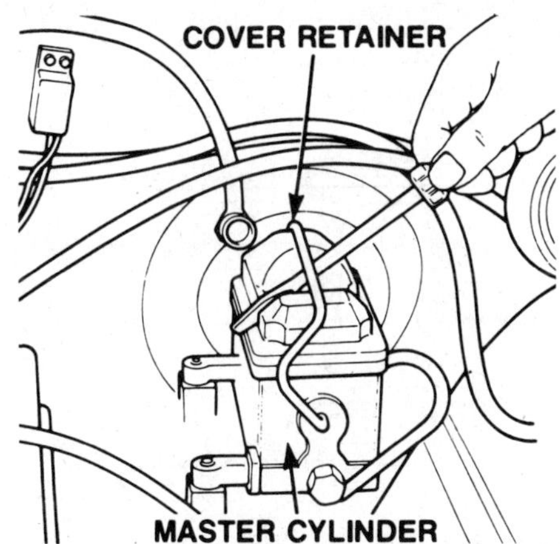

Prying off the master cylinder retaining wire

If the level of the brake fluid is less than half the volume of the reservoir, it is advised that you check the brake system for leaks. Leaks in a hydraulic brake system most commonly occur at the wheel cylinder.

There is a rubber diaphragm in the top of the master cylinder cap. As the fluid level lowers in the reservoir due to normal brake shoe wear or leakage, the diaphragm takes up the space. This is to prevent the loss of brake fluid out the vented cap and contamination by dirt. After filling the master cylinder to the proper level with heavy duty brake fluid, but before replacing the cap, fold the rubber diaphragm up into the cap, then replace the cap on the reservoir and tighten the retaining bolt or snap the retaining clip into place.

HYDRAULIC CLUTCH RESERVOIR

The 1983 and later diesel models and the 1984 and later gasoline models are equipped with hydraulic clutch systems. The hydraulic fluid reservoirs on these systems are mounted on the firewall. Fluid level checks are performed like those on the brake hydraulic system. The proper fluid level is indicated by a step on the reservoir. Keep the reservoir topped up with Ford Heavy-Duty Brake fluid or equivalent; *do not overfill.*

CAUTION: *Carefully clean the top and sides of the reservoir before opening, to prevent contamination of the system with dirt, etc. Remove the reservoir diaphragm before adding fluid, and replace after filling.*

See the illustration of the hydraulic clutch assembly in Chapter 6.

COOLANT

The coolant level should be maintained at 2 in. below the bottom of the radiator filler neck when the engine is at ambient temperatures and 1 in. below the bottom of the filler neck when the engine is hot.

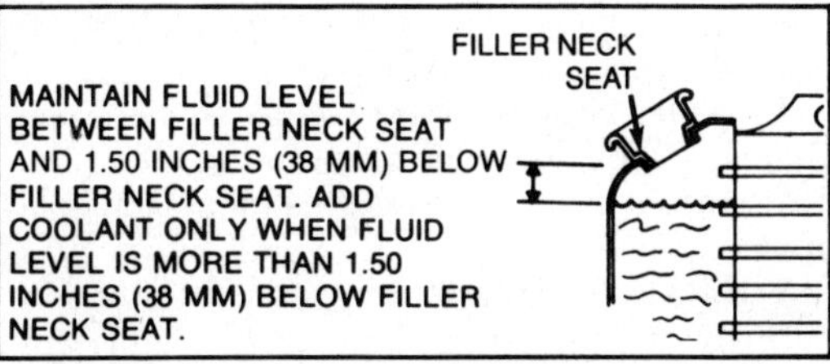

Coolant level check

For best protection against freezing and overheating, maintain an approximate 50% water and 50% antifreeze mixture in the cooling system. Do not mix brands of antifreeze so as to avoid possible chemical damage to the cooling system.

Avoid using water that is known to have a high alkaline content or is very hard, except in emergency cases. Drain and flush the cooling system as soon as possible after using such water.

CAUTION: *Cover the radiator cap with a thick cloth before removing it from a radiator in a vehicle that is hot. Turn the cap counterclockwise slowly until pressure can be heard escaping. Allow all pressure to escape from the radiator before completely removing the radiator cap.*

FRONT (4WD) AND REAR AXLE

Clean the area around the fill plug, which is located in the housing cover, before removing the plug. The lubricant level should be maintained to the bottom of the fill hole with the axle in its normal running position. If lubricant does not appear at the hole when the plug is removed, additional lubricant should be added. Use hypoid gear lubricant SAE 80 or 90.

NOTE: *If the differential is of the limited slip type, be sure and use special limited slip differential additive.*

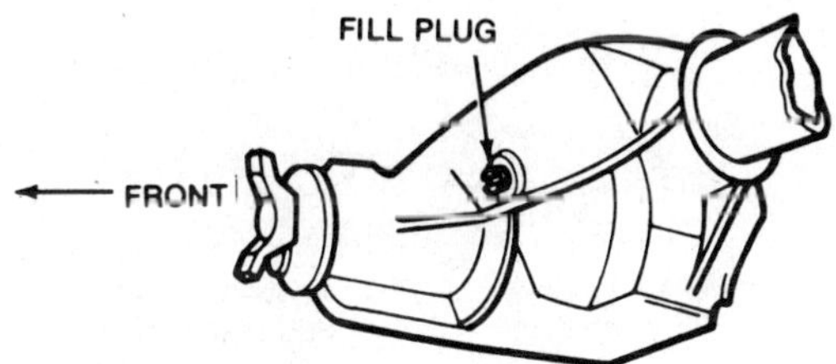

Differential fill plug location, 2-wheel drive shown. 4 × 4 front axle similar.

STEERING GEAR

2WD

1. Center the steering wheel.
2. Remove the steering gear housing filler plug.

3. Remove the lower cover-to-housing attaching bolt.
4. With a clean punch or similar object, clean out or push the loose lubricant in the filler plug hole and cover-to-housing attaching bolt hole inward.
5. Slowly turn the steering wheel to the left until the linkage reaches its stop. Lubricant should rise within the cover lower bolt hole.
6. Slowly turn the steering wheel to the right until the linkage reaches its stop. Lubricant should rise within the filler plug hole.
7. If lubricant does not rise in both of the holes, add steering gear lubricant until it comes out both the holes during the check.
8. Install the lower cover-to-housing attaching bolt and the filler plug.

4WD

1. Remove the filler plug from the sector shaft cover.
2. Check to see if the lubricant level is visible in the filler plug tower. If the lubricant is visible, install the filler plug. If the lubricant is not visible, add steering gear lubricant until the lubricant is visible about 1 in. from the top of the hole in the filler plug tower.
3. Replace the filler plug.

POWER STEERING RESERVOIR

Position the vehicle on level ground. Run the engine until the fluid is at normal operating temperature. Turn the steering wheel all the way to the left and right several times. Position the wheels in the straight ahead position, then shut off the engine. Check the fluid level on the dipstick which is attached to the reservoir cap. The level should be between the ADD and FULL marks on the dipstick. Add fluid accordingly. Do not overfill. Use power steering fluid.

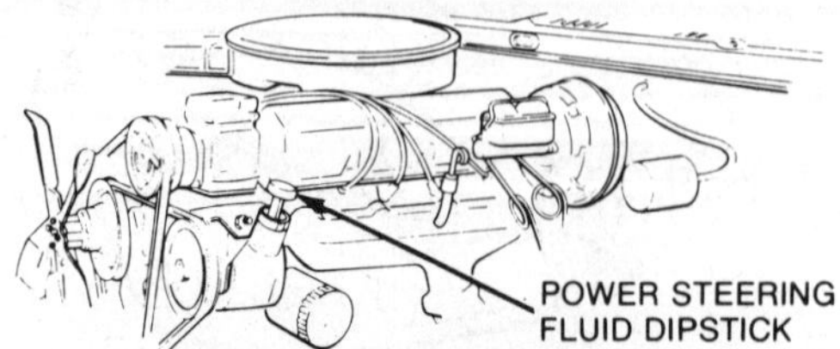

To avoid contamination of the power steering fluid, be sure the dipstick is installed with the lock tabs in the groove—then rotate the dipstick clockwise until the lock tabs contact the stop in the pump filler.

BATTERY

Check the fluid level in the battery about once a month and more often in hot and dry weather. The level should be at the bottom of the filler hole. Electrolyte should at least cover the plates.

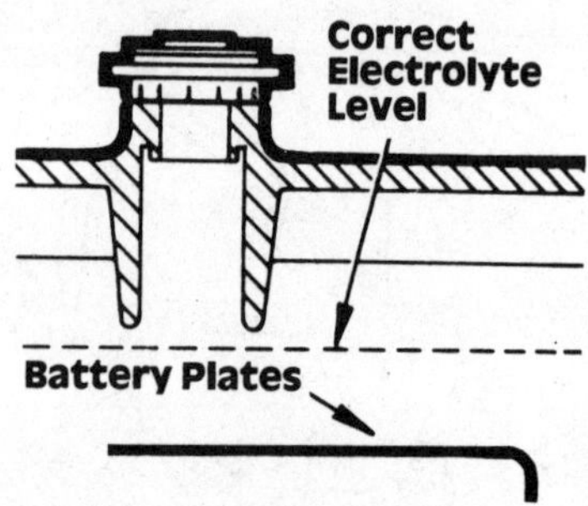

Proper battery electrolyte level

Always use distilled water to top up the battery. Tap water, in most areas, is usually too high in mineral and/or alkali content and can cause damage to the battery plates over an extended period. Distilled water is widely available in supermarkets and drug stores, usually in gallon jugs.

Keep in mind that in cold weather the efficiency of the battery is reduced. If you add water to the battery during freezing weather, drive the vehicle for several miles to mix the water with the battery electrolyte.

TRANSFER CASE

Position the vehicle on level ground. Remove the transfer case fill plug located on the left side of the transfer case. The fluid level should be up to the fill hole. If lubricant doesn't run out when the plug is removed, add lubricant until it does run out and then replace the fill plug. Use SAE 50 lubricant when the air temperature averages above 10° F and SAE 30 lubricant when the air temperature averages below 10° F.

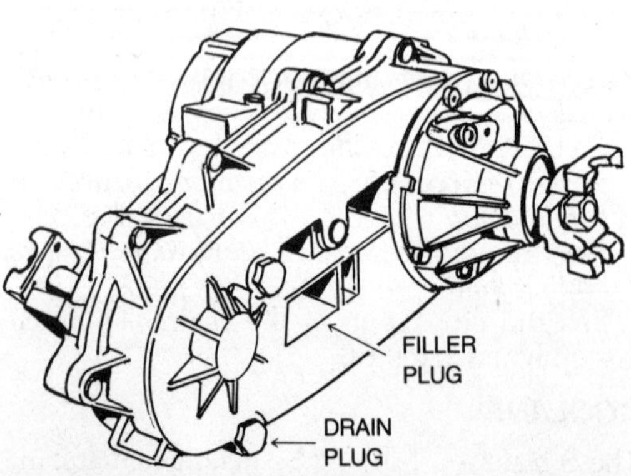

Typical transfer case filler and drain plug locations (New Process case shown)

Tires

INFLATION PRESSURE

Tire inflation is the most ignored item of auto maintenance. Gasoline mileage can drop as much as .8% for every 1 pound per square inch (psi) of under inflation.

Two items should be a permanent fixture in every glove compartment; a tire pressure gauge and a tread depth gauge. Check the tire air pressure (including the spare) regularly with a pocket type gauge. Kicking the tires won't tell you a thing, and the gauge on the service station air hose is notoriously inaccurate.

The tire pressures recommended for your truck are usually found on the glove box door or in the owners manual. Ideally, inflation pressure should be checked when the tires are cool. When the air becomes heated it expands and the pressure increases. Every 10° rise (or drop) in temperature means a difference of 1 psi, which also explains why the tire appears to lose air on a very cold night. When it is impossible to check the tires "cold", allow for pressure build-up due to heat. If the "hot" pressure exceeds the "cold" pressure by more than 15 psi, reduce your speed, load or both. Otherwise internal heat is created in the tire. When the heat approaches the temperature at which the tire was cured, during manufacture, the tread can separate from the body.

CAUTION: *Never counteract excessive pressure build-up by bleeding off air pressure (letting some air out). This will only further raise the tire operating temperature.*

Before starting a long trip with lots of luggage, you can add about 2–4 psi to the tires to make them run cooler, but never exceed the maximum inflation pressure on the side of the tire.

TREAD DEPTH

All tires made since 1968, have 8 built-in tread wear indicator bars that show up as ½″ wide smooth bands across the tire when ¹⁄₁₆″ of tread remains. The appearance of tread wear indicators means that the tires should be replaced. In fact, many states have laws prohibiting the use of tires with less than ¹⁄₁₆″ tread.

You can check your own tread depth with an inexpensive gauge or by using a Lincoln head penny. Slip the Lincoln penny into several tread grooves. If you can see the top of Lincoln's head in 2 adjacent grooves, the tires have less than ¹⁄₁₆″ tread left and should be replaced. You can measure snow tires in the same manner by using the "tails" side of the Lincoln penny. If you can see the top of the Lincoln memorial, it's time to replace the snow tires.

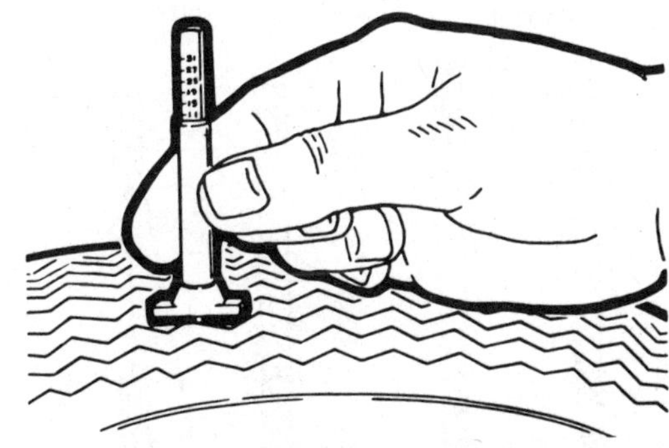

Checking tread depth with an inexpensive depth gauge

Tread wear indicators are built into all new tires. When they appear, it's time to trash that old rubber for some new skins

TIRE ROTATION

Tire wear can be equalized by switching the position of the tires about every 6000 miles. Including a conventional spare in the rotation pattern can give up to 20% more tire life.

There are certain exceptions to tire rotation, however. Studded snow tires should not be rotated, and radials should be kept on the same side of the truck (maintain the same direction of rotation). The belts on radial tires get set in a pattern. If the direction of rotation is reversed, it can cause rough ride and vibration.

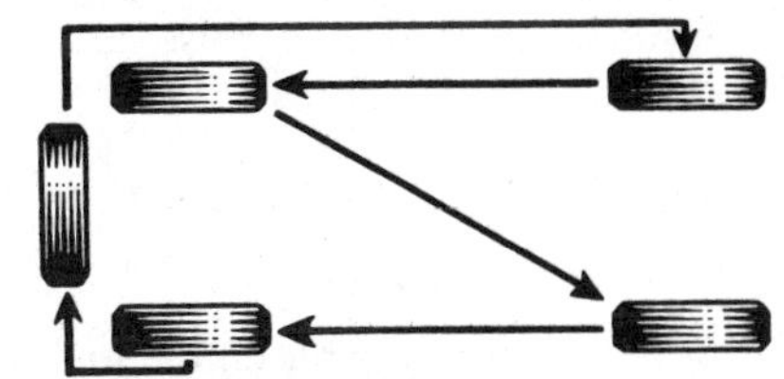

Bias-ply tire rotation diagram

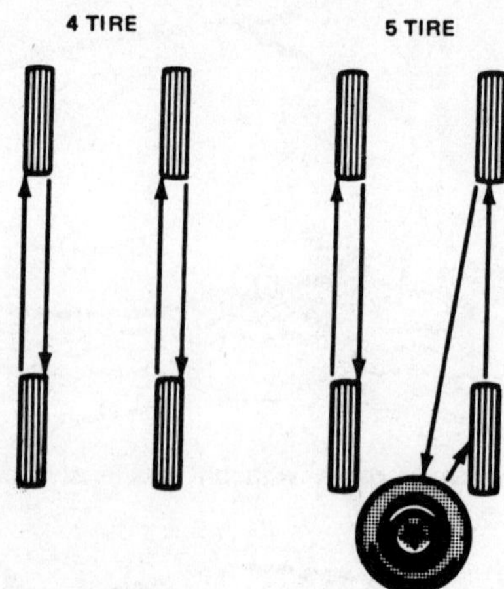

Radial-ply tire rotation diagram

NOTE: *When radials or studded snows are taken off the truck, mark them, so you can maintain the same direction of rotation.*

TIRE STORAGE

Store the tires at proper inflation pressures if they are mounted on wheels. All tires should be kept in a cool, dry place. If they are stored in the garage or basement, do not let them stand on a concrete floor; set them on strips of wood.

Fuel Filter

REMOVAL AND INSTALLATION

Gasoline Engines

The fuel filter should be replaced according to the Preventive Maintenance Schedule at the end of this chapter. The in-line filter is of one-piece construction and cannot be cleaned.

CHASSIS MOUNTED

1. Raise the hood and remove the air cleaner.
2. Loosen the retaining clamp securing the fuel inlet hose to the fuel filter.
3. Unscrew the fuel filter from the carburetor and discard the gasket. Disconnect the fuel filter from the hose and discard the retaining clamp.
4. Install a new clamp on the inlet hose and connect the hose to the filter. Place a new gasket on the new fuel filter and screw the filter into the carburetor inlet port. Tighten the filter.
5. Position the fuel line hose clamp and tighten the clamp securely.
6. Start the engine and check for fuel leaks.
7. Install the air cleaner. Close the hood.

MOUNTED IN FUEL PUMP

On those models with a filter on the fuel pump, simply unscrew the filter housing and replace the filter element and gasket.

IN LINE TYPE—1979 WITH 460 ENGINE

1. Remove the fuel line at the carburetor by placing a wrench on the fuel filter retaining nut and holding in place while loosening the fuel line nut and removing the fuel line. If possible use a flare nut wrench on the fuel line nut because it is very easy to round off the nut.
2. Remove the fuel filter retaining nut and remove gasket, filter gasket, filter and spring.
3. Install the new filter and gasket and replace the retaining nut and fuel line.

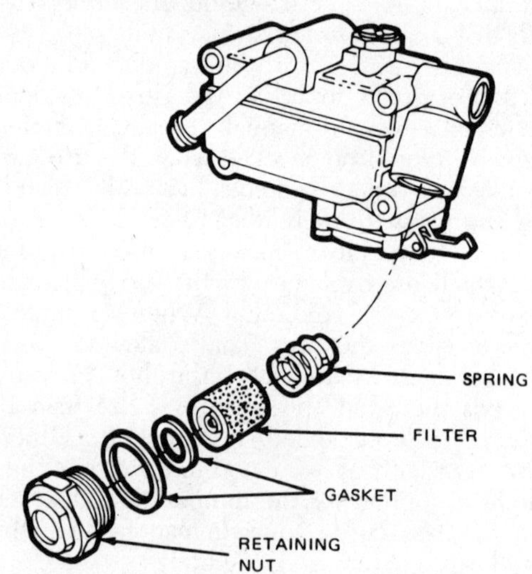

Fuel filter—Holley model 4180C 4BBl

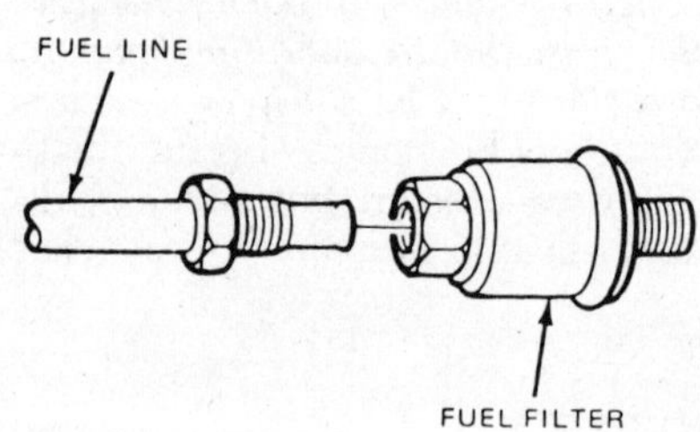

Some models have the screw-in type fuel filter which threads into the carburetor

Diesel Engines

The 6.9L diesel engine uses a one-piece spin-on fuel filter. Do not add fuel to the new fuel filter. Allow the engine to draw fuel through the filter.

1. Remove the spin-on filter by unscrewing it counterclockwise with your hands or a strap wrench.
2. Clean the filter mounting surface.
3. Coat the gasket or the replacement filter with clean diesel fuel. This helps ensure a good seal.
4. Tighten the filter by hand until the gasket touches the filter mounting surface.

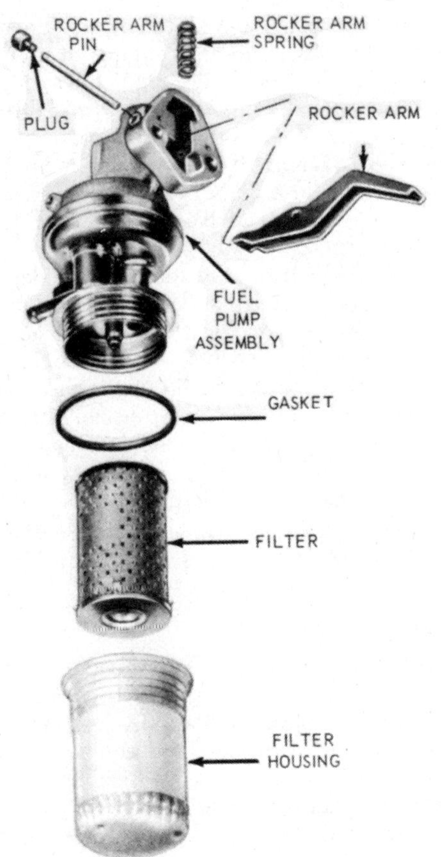

Fuel pump and filter installed on the sixes and 360 and 390 V8s

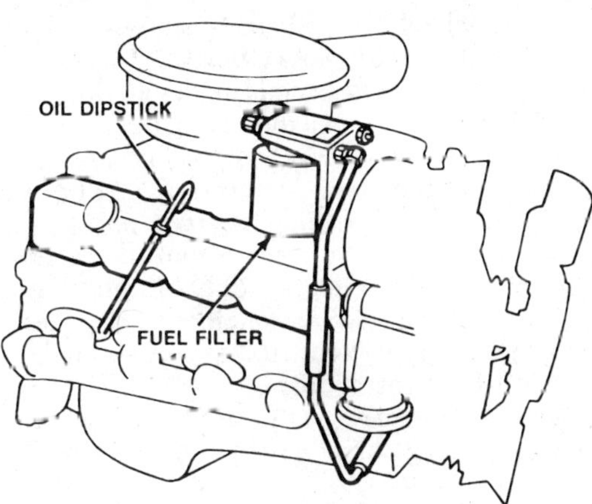

Diesel fuel filter location; filter screws on

5. Tighten the filter an additional ½ turn.

NOTE: *After changing the fuel tilter, the engine will purge the trapped air as it runs. The engine may run roughly and smoke excessively until the air is cleared from the system.*

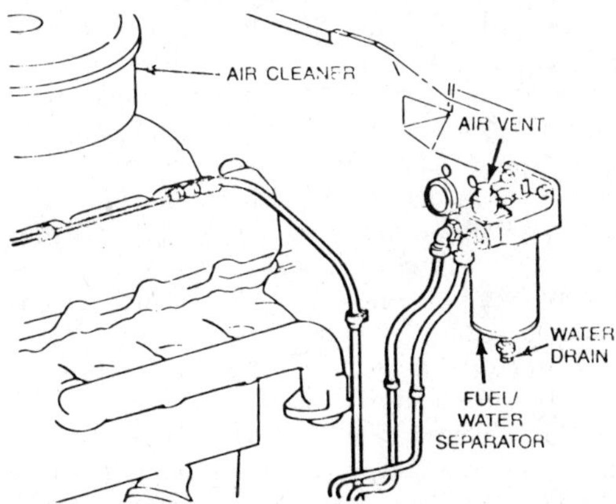

Open the drain screw on the bottom of the water separator to drain

Fuel/Water Separator

Diesel Engines

The 6.9L diesel engine is equipped with a fuel/water separator in the fuel supply line. A "Water in Fuel" indicator light is provided on the instrument panel to alert the driver. The light should glow when the ignition switch is in the "Start" position to indicate proper light and water sensor function. If the light glows continuously while the engine is running, the water must be drained from the separator as soon as possible to prevent damage to the fuel injection system.

1. Shut off the engine. Failure to shut the engine off before draining the separator will cause air to enter the system.
2. Unscrew the vent on the top center of the separator unit 2½ to 3 turns.
3. Unscrew the drain screw on the bottom of the separator 1½ to 2 turns and drain the water into an appropriate container.
4. After the water is completely drained, close the water drain fingertight.
5. Tighten the vent until snug, then turn it an additional ¼ turn.
6. Start the engine and check the "Water in Fuel" indicator light; it should not be lit. If it is lit and continues to stay so, there is a problem somewhere else in the fuel system.

NOTE: *All but very early production models have a drain hose connected to the separator which allows water to drain directly into a container placed underneath the vehicle.*

LUBRICATION

Oil and Fuel Recommendations

Gasoline Engines

All Ford Pickups not equipped with converters are designed to operate on regular grade gasoline. If the vehicle is being used for heavy-duty service, do not use lead-free gas (pre-1975 models). If your vehicle pings or knocks, use a higher octane fuel or retard the ignition timing of the engine, but not more than three degrees from the setting required for normal operations. This is recommended only for an emergency situation until you can get some higher octane fuel. A little knocking at low speeds is acceptable, but continued knock at high speeds is damaging to the engine.

Late model pickups equipped with converters must use lead-free gasoline.

The recommended oil viscosities for sustained temperatures ranging from below o°F to above 32°F are listed in this chapter. They are broken down into multiviscosities and single viscosities. Multiviscosity oils are recommended because of their wider range of acceptable temperatures and driving conditions.

When adding oil to the crankcase or changing the oil or filter, it is important that oil of an equal quality to original equipment be used in your truck. The use of inferior oils may void the warranty, damage your engine, or both.

The SAE (Society of Automotive Engineers) grade number of oil indicates the viscosity of the oil (its ability to lubricate at a given temperature). The lower the SAE number, the lighter the oil; the lower the viscosity, the easier it is to crank the engine in cold weather but the less the oil will lubricate and protect the engine at high temperatures. Thus number is marked on every oil container.

Oil viscosities should be chosen from those oils recommended for the *lowest anticipated temperatures during the oil change interval.* Due to the need for an oil that embodies both good lubrication at high temperatures and easy cranking in cold weather, multigrade oils have been developed. Basically, a multigrade oil is thinner at low temperatures and thicker at high temperatures. For example, a 10W-40 oil (the W stands for winter) exhibits the characteristics of a 10 weight (SAE 10) oil when the truck is first started and the oil is cold. Its lighter weight allows it to travel to the lubricating surfaces quicker and offer less resistance to starter motor cranking than, say, a straight 30 weight (SAE 30) oil. But after the engine reaches operating temperature, the 10W-40 oil begins acting like straight 40 weight (SAE 40) oil, its heavier weight providing greater lubrication with less chance of foaming than a straight 30 weight oil.

NOTE: *Single-grade ("straight weight") oils such as SAE 30 are more satisfactory than multi-viscosity oils for highway driving in diesel engines.*

The API (American Petroleum Institute) designation, also found on the oil container, indicates the classification of engine oil used under certain given operating conditions. Only oils designated for use "Service SE", or "SF heavy duty detergent" should be used in your truck. Oils of the SE and SF type perform many functions inside the engine besides their basic lubrication. Through a balanced system of metallic detergents and polymeric dispersants, the oil prevents high and low temperature deposits and also keeps sludge and dirt particles in suspension. Acids, particularly sulphuric acid, as well as other by-products of engine combustion are neutralized by the oil. If these acids are allowed to concentrate, they can cause corrosion and rapid wear of the internal engine parts.

CAUTION: *Non-detergent or "straight" mineral oils should not be used in your Ford engine.*

Diesel Engines

Diesel engines require different engine oil from those used in gasoline engines. Besides doing the things gasoline engine oil does, diesel oil must also deal with increased engine heat and the diesel blow-by gases, which create sulphuric acid, a high corrosive.

Under the American Petroleum Institute (API) classifications, gasoline engine oil codes begin with an "S", and diesel engine oil codes begin with a "C." This first letter designation is followed by a second letter code which explains what type of service (heavy, moderate, light) the oil is meant for. For example, the top of a typical oil can will include: "API SERVICES SC, SD, SE, CA, CB, CC." This means the oil in the can is a good, moderate duty engine oil when used in a diesel engine.

It should be noted here that the further down the alphabet the second letter of the API classification is, the greater the oil's protective qualities are (CD is the severest duty diesel engine oil, CA is the lightest duty oil, etc.) The same is true for gasoline engine oil classifications (SF is the severest duty gasoline engine oil, SA is the lightest duty oil, etc.).

Many diesel manufacturers recommend an oil with both gasoline and diesel engine API classifications.

NOTE: *Ford specifies the use of an engine oil conforming to API service categories of both SF and CD. DO NOT use oils labeled as only SF or only CD as they could cause engine damage.*

FUEL

Fuel makers produce two grades of diesel fuel, No. 1 and No. 2, for use in automotive diesel engines. Generally speaking, No. 2 fuel is recommended over No. 1 for driving in temperatures above 20°F. In fact, in many areas, No. 2 diesel is the only fuel available. By comparison, No. 2 diesel fuel is less volatile than No. 1 fuel, and gives better fuel economy. No. 2 fuel is also a better injection pump lubricant.

Two important characteristics of diesel fuel are its cetane number and its viscosity.

The cetane number of a diesel fuel refers to the ease with which a diesel fuel ignites. High cetane numbers mean that the fuel will ignite with relative ease or that it ignites well at low temperatures. Naturally, the lower the cetane number, the higher the temperature must be to ignite the fuel. Most commercial fuels have cetane numbers that range from 35 to 65. No. 1 diesel fuel generally has a higher cetane rating than No. 2 fuel.

Viscosity is the ability of a liquid, in this case diesel fuel, to flow. Using straight No. 2 diesel fuel below 20°F can cause problems, because this fuel tends to become cloudy, meaning wax crystals begin forming in the fuel (20°F is often called the "cloud point" for No. 2 fuel). In extreme cold weather, No. 2 fuel can stop flowing altogether. In either case, fuel flow is restricted, which can result in a "no start" condition or poor engine performance. Fuel manufacturers often "winterize" No. 2 diesel fuel by using various fuel additives and blends (no. 1 diesel fuel, kerosene, etc.) to lower its winter-time viscosity. Generally speaking, though, No. 1 diesel fuel is more satisfactory in extremely cold weather.

NOTE: *No. 1 and No. 2 diesel fuels will mix and burn with no ill effects, although the engine manufacturer will undoubtedly recommend one or the other. Consult the owner's manual for information.*

Depending on local climate, most fuel manufacturers make winterized No. 2 fuel available seasonally.

Many automobile manufacturers publish pamphlets giving the locations of diesel fuel stations nationwide. Contact the local dealer for information.

Do not substitute home heating oil for automotive diesel fuel. While in some cases, home heating oil refinement levels equal those of diesel fuel, many times they are far below diesel engine requirements. The result of using "dirty" home heating oil will be a clogged fuel system, in which case the entire system may have to be dismantled and cleaned.

One more word on diesel fuels. *Don't thin diesel fuel with gasoline in cold weather.* The lighter gasoline, which is more explosive, will cause rough running at the very least, and may cause extensive damage to the fuel system if enough is used.

Lubricant Changes

Engine Oil

The engine oil and filter are to be changed according to the schedule in the Preventive Maintenance Chart at the end of this chapter.

The oil should be changed more frequently if the vehicle is being operated in very dusty areas. Before draining the oil, make sure that the engine is at operating temperature. Hot oil will hold more impurities in suspension and will flow better, allowing the removal of more oil and dirt.

Loosen the drain plug with a wrench, then, unscrew the plug with your fingers, using a rag to shield your fingers from the heat. Push in on the plug as you unscrew it so you can feel when all of the screw threads are out of the hole. You can then remove the plug quickly with the minimum amount of oil running down your arm and you will also have the plug in your hand

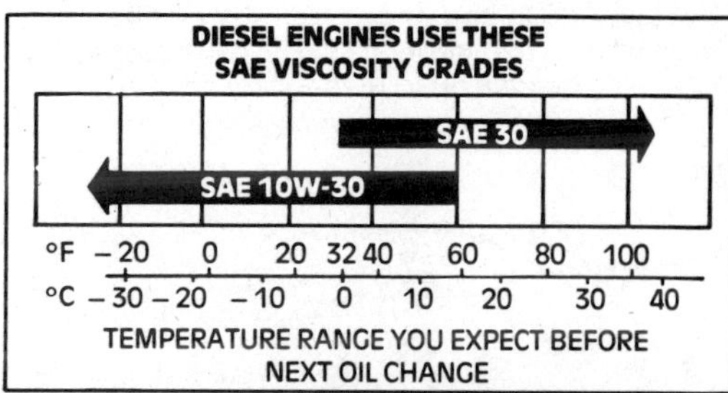

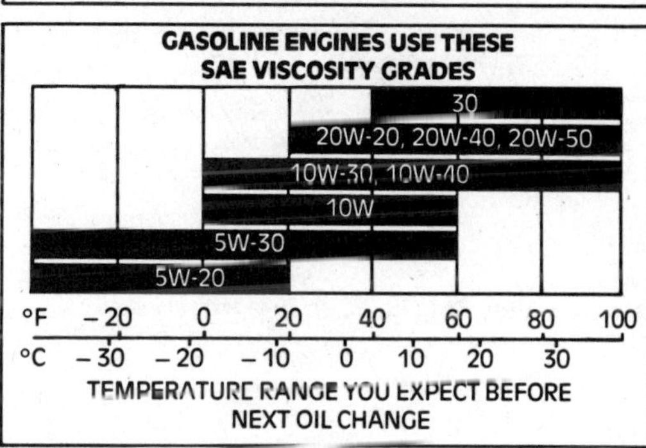

Engine oil viscosities

Loosen, but do not remove, the drain plug on the bottom of the oil pan. Get your drain pan ready

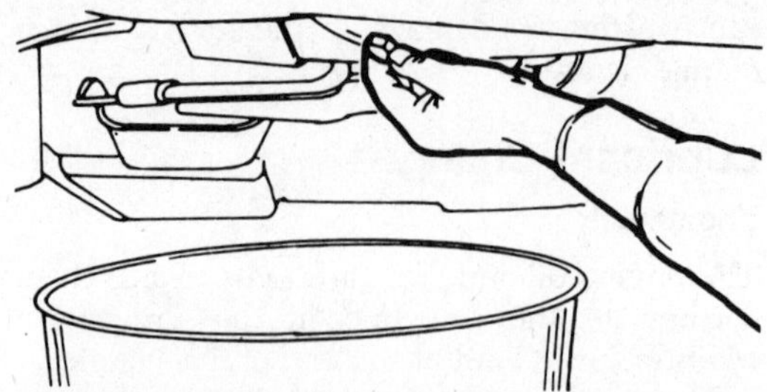

Unscrew the plug by hand. Keep an inward pressure on the plug as you unscrew it, so the oil won't escape until you pull the plug away

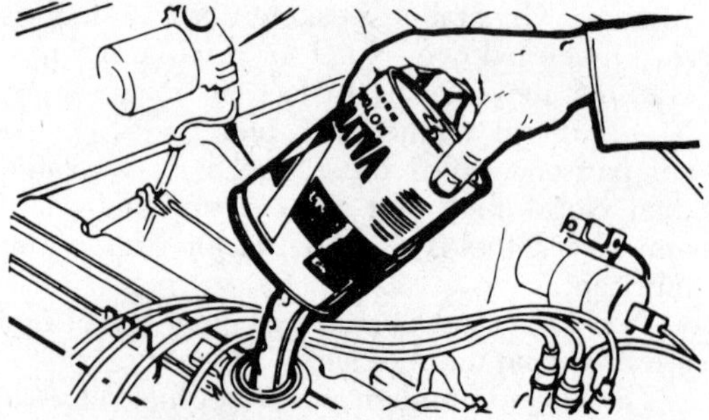

Don't forget to install the drain plug before refilling the engine with fresh oil.

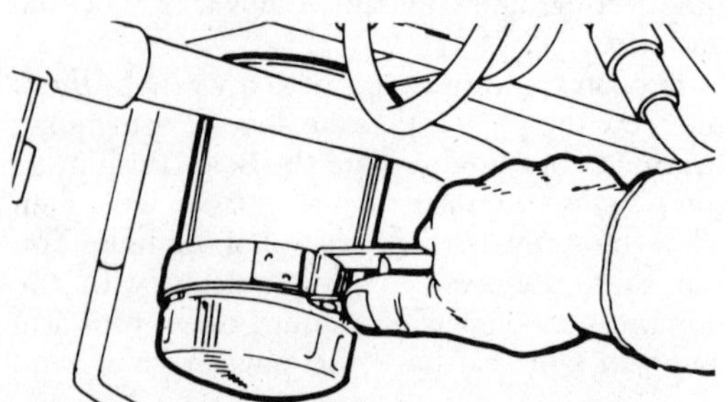

Move the drain pan underneath the oil filter. Use a strap wrench to remove the filter—remember it is still filled with about a quart of hot, dirty oil.

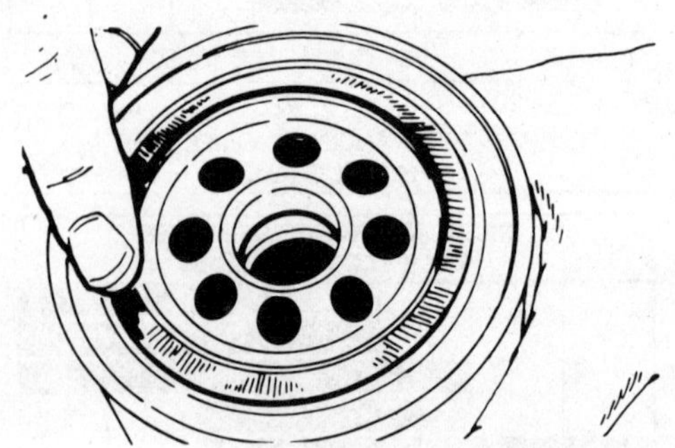

Wipe clean engine oil around the rubber gasket on the new filter. This helps ensure a good seal

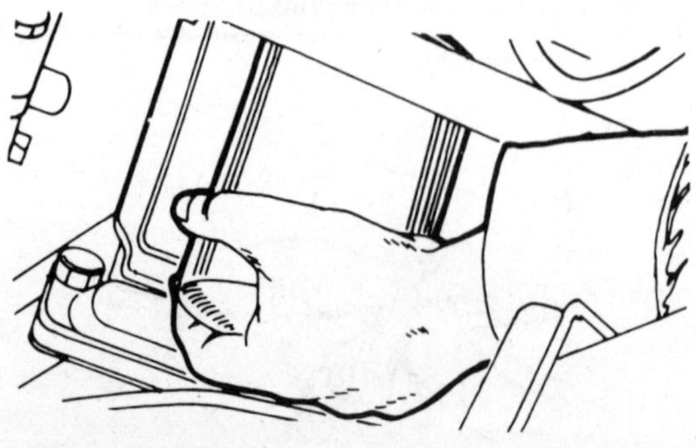

Install the new filter by hand only; DO NOT use a strap wrench to install!

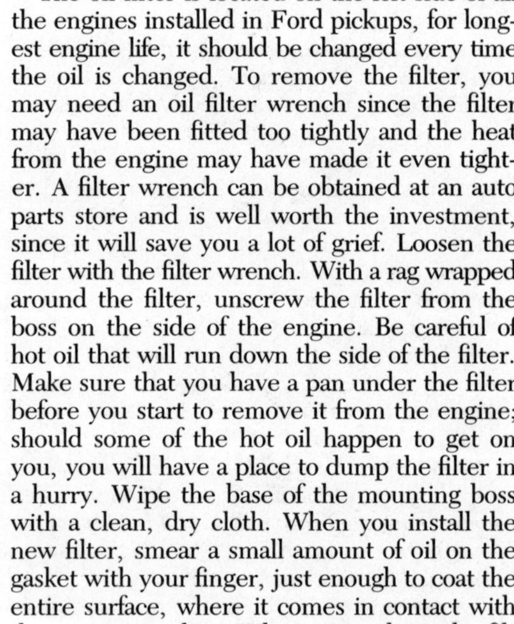

and not in the bottom of a pan of hot oil. Drain the oil into a suitable receptacle. *Be careful of the oil.* If it is at operating temperatures it is hot enough to burn you.

The oil filter is located on the left side of all the engines installed in Ford pickups, for longest engine life, it should be changed every time the oil is changed. To remove the filter, you may need an oil filter wrench since the filter may have been fitted too tightly and the heat from the engine may have made it even tighter. A filter wrench can be obtained at an auto parts store and is well worth the investment, since it will save you a lot of grief. Loosen the filter with the filter wrench. With a rag wrapped around the filter, unscrew the filter from the boss on the side of the engine. Be careful of hot oil that will run down the side of the filter. Make sure that you have a pan under the filter before you start to remove it from the engine; should some of the hot oil happen to get on you, you will have a place to dump the filter in a hurry. Wipe the base of the mounting boss with a clean, dry cloth. When you install the new filter, smear a small amount of oil on the gasket with your finger, just enough to coat the entire surface, where it comes in contact with the mounting plate. When you tighten the filter, rotate if only a half-turn after it comes in contact with the mounting boss.

Manual Transmission

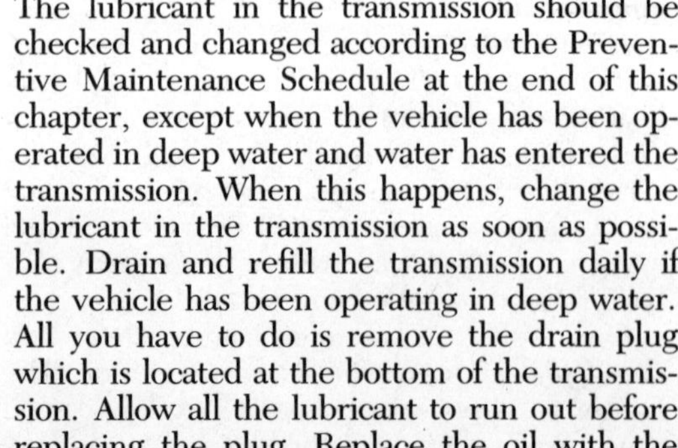

The lubricant in the transmission should be checked and changed according to the Preventive Maintenance Schedule at the end of this chapter, except when the vehicle has been operated in deep water and water has entered the transmission. When this happens, change the lubricant in the transmission as soon as possible. Drain and refill the transmission daily if the vehicle has been operating in deep water. All you have to do is remove the drain plug which is located at the bottom of the transmission. Allow all the lubricant to run out before replacing the plug. Replace the oil with the correct fluid. If you are experiencing hard shifting and the weather is very cold, use a lighter viscosity fluid in the transmission. If you don't have a pressure gun to install the oil, use a suction gun or kitchen-type baster.

Automatic Transmission

Aside from checking and adding fluid to the automatic transmission in order to keep the fluid level up to the proper level, there are no factory recommendations regarding the replacement of the automatic transmission fluid.

The extra load of operating the vehicle in deep sand, towing a heavy trailer, etc., causes the transmission to create more heat due to increased friction. This extra heat is transferred to the transmission fluid and, if the fluid is allowed to become too hot, it will change its chemical composition or become scorched. When this occurs, valve bodies become clogged and the transmission doesn't operate as efficiently as it should. Serious damage to the transmission can result.

You can tell if the transmission fluid is scorched by noting a distinctive "burned" smell and discoloration. Scorched transmission fluid is dark brown or black as opposed to its normal bright, clear red color. Since transmission fluid "cooks" in stages, it may develop forms of sludge or varnish. Pull the dip stick out and place the end on a tissue or paper towel. Particles of sludge can be seen more easily this way. If any of the above conditions do exist, the transmission fluid should be completely drained, the filtering screens cleaned, the transmission inspected for possible damage and new fluid installed.

To replace the fluid in the automatic transmission, follow the procedures following:

C4 AND C5 AUTOMATIC TRANSMISSION

1. Disconnect the fluid filler tube from the transmission oil pan to drain the fluid. Remove torque converter drain plug cover, remove the plug and allow the fluid to drain out. Replace the drain plug and cover.
2. When the fluid has stopped draining from the transmission, remove and thoroughly clean the pan and the screen. Discard the pan gasket.

CAUTION: *When removing the filter on C4 transmissions, be careful not to lose the*

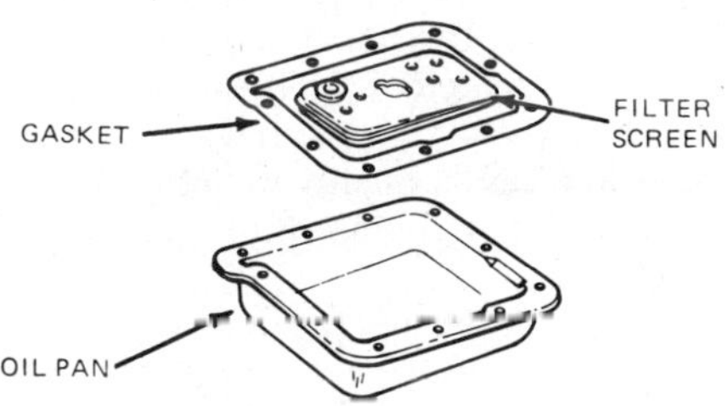

Automatic transmission filters are found above the transmission oil pan

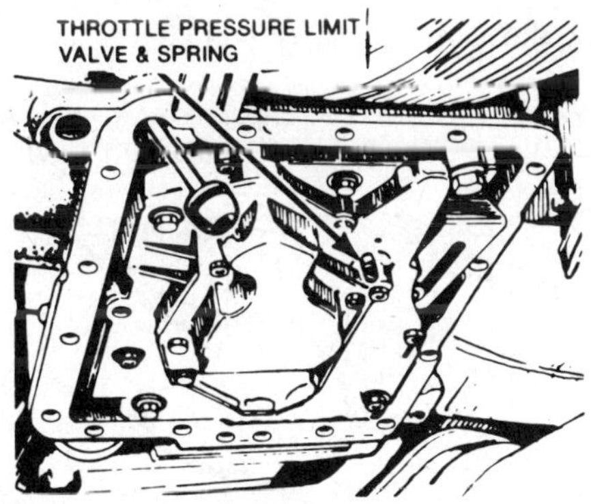

C4 throttle pressure limit valve and spring. They are held in place by the filter. The valve is installed with the large end toward the valve body; the spring fits over the valve stem

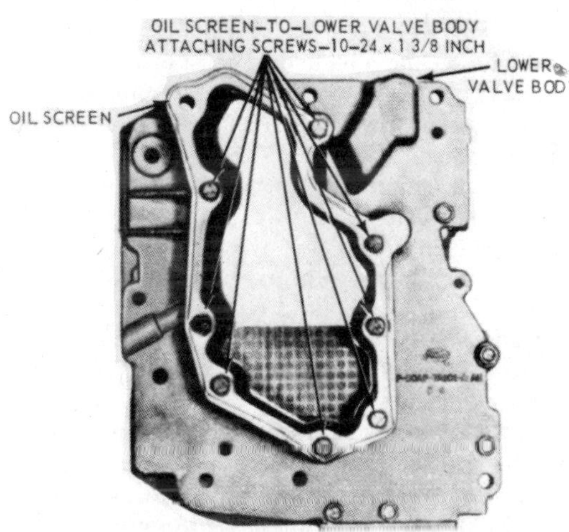

View of the automatic transmission fluid filter and attaching bolts, C4 model. Pan removed

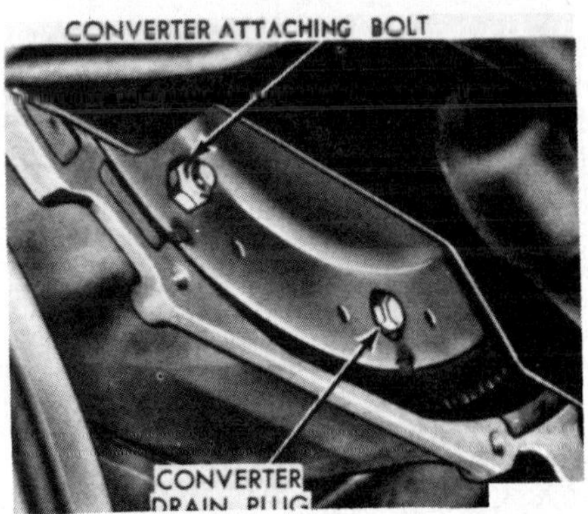

Torque converter drain plug on a C4 automatic transmission

throttle pressure limit valve and spring when separating the filter from the valve body.

3. Place a new gasket on the pan and install the pan on the transmission.

4. Connect the filler tube to the pan and tighten the fitting securely.

5. Add five quarts of fluid to the transmission through the filler tube. Add only three quarts if the converter wasn't drained.

6. Check the fluid level. With the transmission at room temperatures (70° F to 95° F) and the engine idling, the level should be between the middle and top holes on the dipstick. If the fluid level is below the middle hole, add enough fluid through the filler tube to raise the level to between the middle hole and the ADD mark. Please note that this check is only for when the transmission is at room temperatures. See the section on level checks for checking the transmission when it is at operating temperatures.

7. Replace the dipstick.

FMX; AUTOMATIC OVERDRIVE, C6 AUTOMATIC TRANSMISSION

1. Raise the vehicle on a hoist or jackstands.
2. Place a drain pan under the transmission.
3. Loosen the pan attaching bolts and drain the fluid from the transmission.
4. When the fluid has drained to the level of the pan flange, remove the rest of the pan bolts working from the rear and both sides of the pan to allow it to drop and drain slowly.
5. When all the fluid has drained from the transmission, remove the pan and thoroughly clean it and the screen. Discard the pan gasket.
6. Place a new gasket on the pan, and install the pan on the transmission.
7. Add three quarts of automatic transmission fluid to the transmission through the filler tube.
8. Check the fluid level.

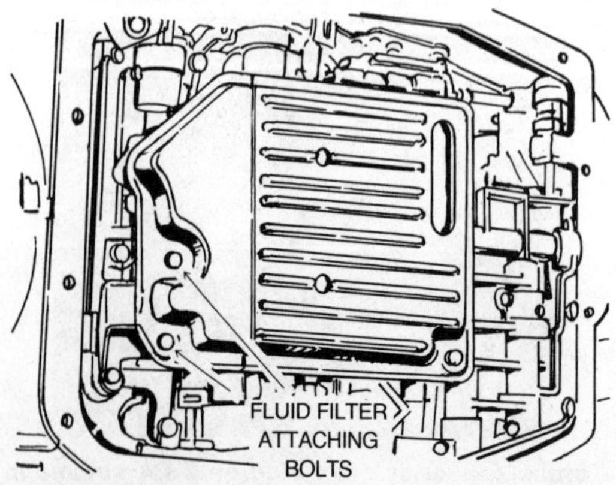

Fluid filter, automatic overdrive (AOD)

Front (4WD) and Rear Axle

Drain and refill the front and rear axle housings every 24,000 miles, or every day if the vehicle is operated in deep water. Remove the oil with a suction gun. Refill the axle housings with the proper oil. Be sure and clean the area around the drain plug before removing the plug. See the section on level checks.

Transfer Case

The transfer case is serviced at the same time and in the same manner as the transmission. Clean the area around the filler and drain plugs and remove the filler plug on the side of the transfer case. Remove the drain plug on the bottom of the transfer case and allow the lubricant to drain completely.

NOTE: *On the NP-203, loosen the front and rear lower cover bolts to drain the unit.*

Clean and install the drain plug. Add the proper lubricant. See the section on level checks.

Coolant

Completely draining and refilling the cooling system every two years at least will remove accumulated rust, seals and other deposits. This will increase the ability of the coolant to cool the engine.

1. Drain the existing antifreeze and coolant. Open the radiator and engine drain petcocks, or, if necessary, disconnect the bottom radiator hose, at the radiator outlet.
2. Close the petcock or re-connect the lower hose and fill the system with water.
3. Add a can of quality radiator flush.
4. Idle the engine until the upper radiator hose gets hot.
5. Drain the system again.
6. Repeat this process until the drained water is clear and free of scale.
7. Close all petcocks and connect all the hoses.
8. If equipped with a coolant recovery system, flush the reservoir with water and leave empty.
9. Determine the capacity of your cooling system. The capacity will be listed in the ca-

Open the radiator petcock to drain the cooling system. Spray first with penetrating oil

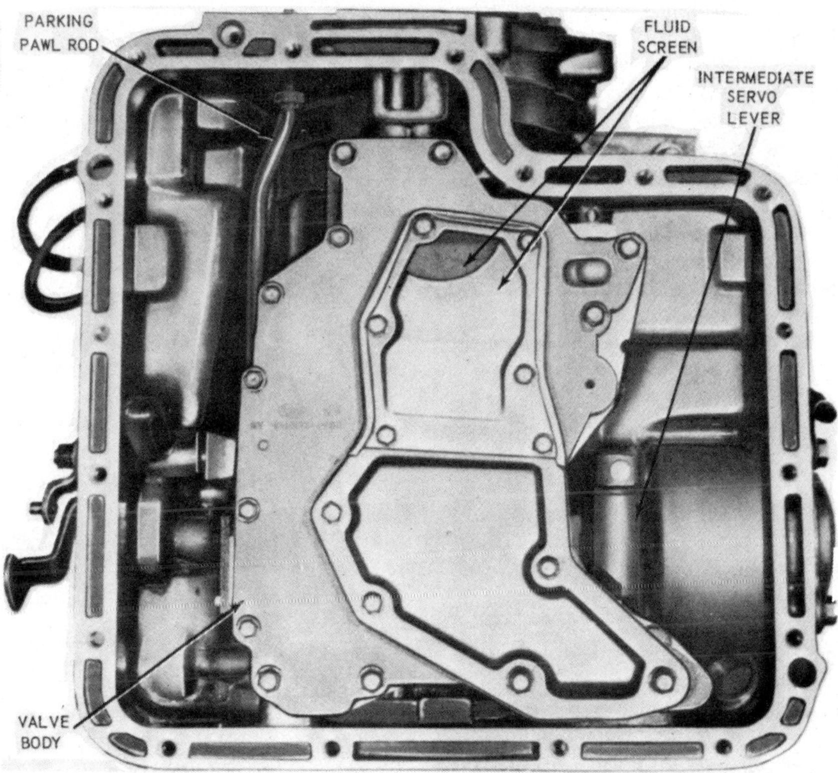

View of the C6 fluid filter and attaching bolts (pan removed)

pacities chart in this chapter. Add a 50/50 mix of quality antifreeze (ethylene glycol) and water to provide the desired protection.

10. Run the engine for 15 minutes with the radiator cap removed.

11. Stop the engine and check the coolant level. It should be 1″–2″ below the filler neck. With a coolant recovery system, the level should be at the overflow tube level in the radiator and at the "FULL" mark on the coolant reservoir.

12. Check the level of protection with a hydrometer, replace the cap and check for leaks.

Chassis Greasing

The lubrication chart indicates where the grease fittings are located. The vehicle should be greased according to the intervals in the Preventive Maintenance Schedule at the end of this chapter.

Wheel Bearings

The wheel bearings should be serviced (cleaned, inspected, repacked or replaced) according to the intervals in the Preventive Maintenance Schedule at the end of this chapter.

Before handling the bearings there are a few things that you should remember to do and try to avoid.

Do the following:

1. Remove all outside dirt from the housing before exposing the bearing.
2. Treat a used bearing as gently as you would a new one.
3. Work with clean tools in clean surroundings.
4. Use clean, dry canvas gloves, or at least clean, dry hands.
5. Clean solvents and flushing fluids are a must.
6. Use a clean paper when laying out the bearings to dry.
7. Protect disassembled bearings from rust and dirt. Cover them up.
8. Use clean rags to wipe bearings.
9. Keep the bearings in oil-proof paper when they are to be stored or are not in use.
10. Clean the inside of the housing before replacing the bearing.

Do NOT do the following:

1. Don't work in dirty surroundings.
2. Don't use dirty, chipped,or damaged tools.
3. Try not to work on wooden work benches or use wooden mallets.
4. Don't handle bearings with dirty or moist hands.

5. Do not use gasoline for cleaning; use a safe solvent.

6. Do not spin-dry bearings with compressed air. They will be damaged.

7. Do not spin unclean bearings.

8. Avoid using cotton waste or dirty cloths to wipe bearings.

9. Try not to scratch or nick bearing surfaces.

10. Do not allow the bearing to come in contact with dirt or rust at any time.

SERVICE

2WD Front

1. Jack the truck up until the wheel to be serviced is off the ground and can spin freely. It is easier to check all the bearings at the same time. If the equipment needed is available, raise the front end of the truck so that both front wheels are off the ground. Use jackstands or suitable blocks to support the vehicle. Make sure that the truck is completely stable before proceeding any further.

2. Remove the lug nuts and remove the wheel/tire assembly from the hub. On models with drum brakes it is possible to remove the hub assembly from the spindle with the wheel/tire assembly still attached, but the added weight makes handling of the entire assembly a little clumsy which could result in possible damage to the bearings or spindle.

On trucks with disc brakes, it is necessary to remove the caliper assembly from the rotor and caliper support. Do not disconnect the brake line from the caliper. Simply hang the caliper with a length of heavy wire above the hub. Be careful not to strain the flexible brake tube.

3. Remove the grease cap with a screwdriver or pliers.

4. Remove the cotter pin and discard it. *Cotter pins should never be reused.*

5. Remove the nut lock, adjusting nut, and washer from the spindle.

6. Wiggle the hub so that the outer wheel bearing comes loose and can be removed. Remove the outer bearing.

7. Remove the hub from the spindle and place it on a work surface, supported by two blocks of wood under the brake drum or hub.

NOTE: *On drum brake equipped models, if the hub will not come off easily, back off the brake shoe adjustment screw so that the shoes do not contact the brake drum.*

8. Place a block of wood or drift pin through the spindle hole and tap out the inner grease seal. Tap lightly so not to damage the bearing. When the seal falls out, so will the inner bearing. Discard the seal.

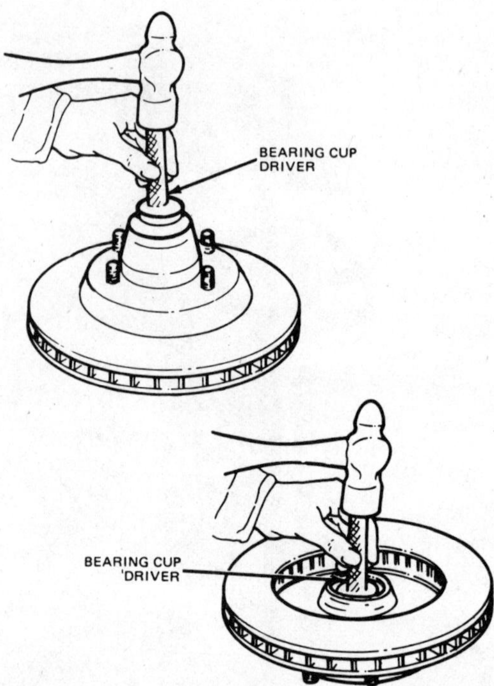

2WD front wheel bearing removal using bearing driver

Perform the above procedures to all the wheels that are going to be serviced.

9. Place all of the bearings, nuts, nut locks, washers and grease caps in a container of solvent. Use a light soft brush to thoroughly clean each part. Make sure that every bit of dirt and grease is rinsed off, then place each cleaned part on an absorbent cloth or paper and allow them to dry completely.

10. Clean the inside of the hub, including the bearing races, and the spindle. Remove all traces of old lubricant from these components.

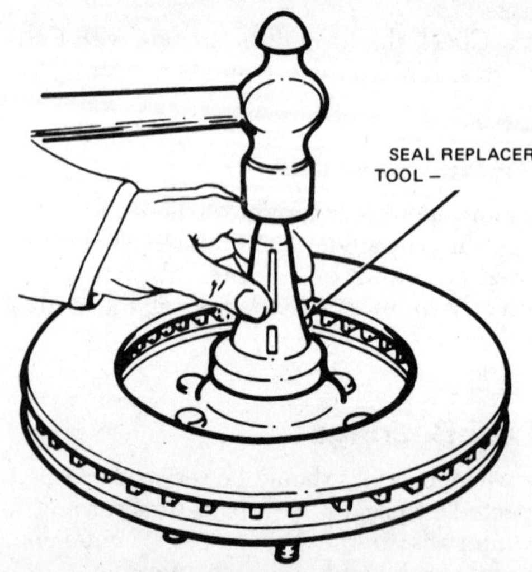

2WD front wheel bearing installation

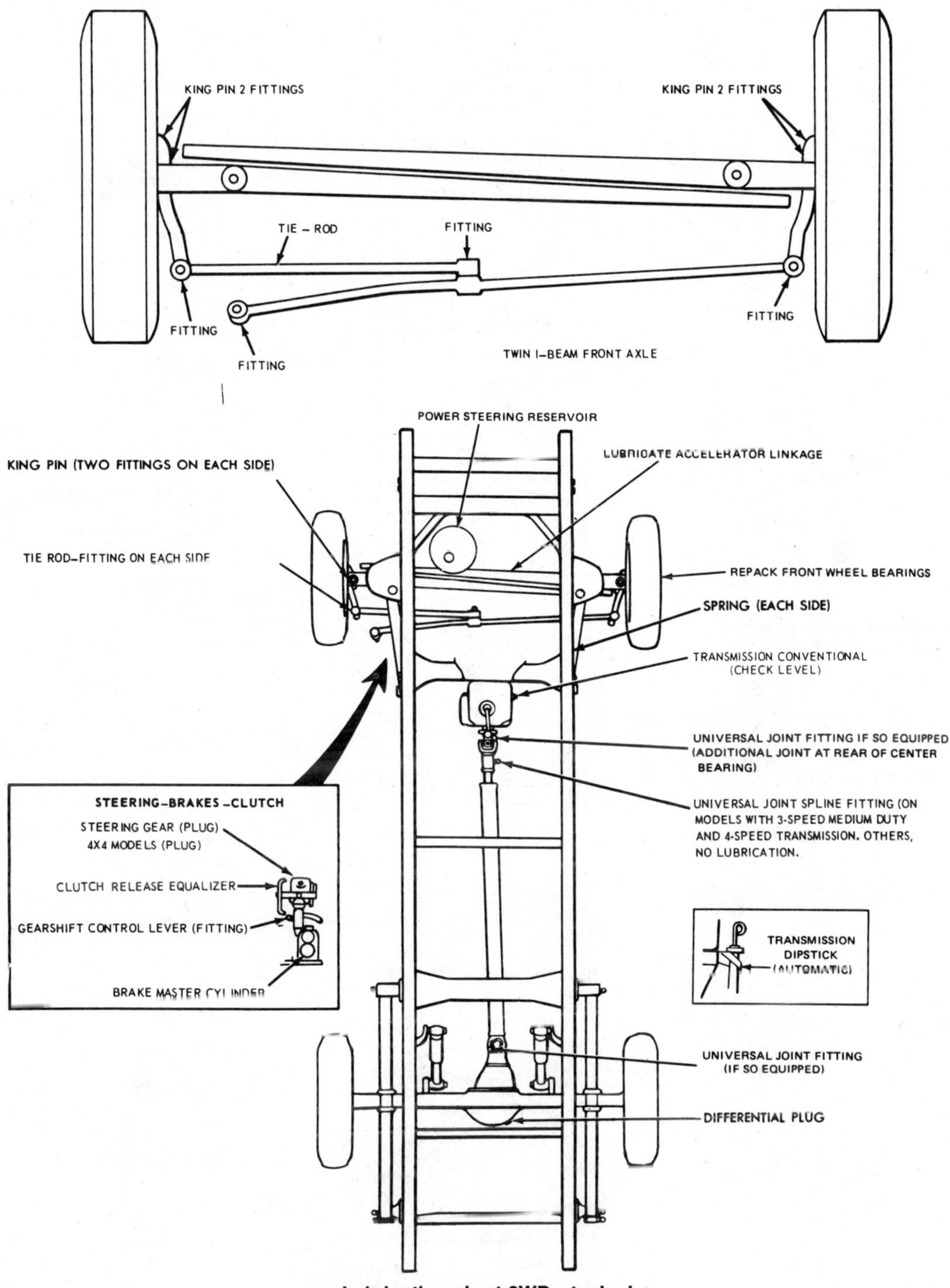

Lubrication chart 2WD—typical

11. Inspect the bearings for pitting, flat spots, rust, and rough areas. Check the races in the hub and the spindle for the same defects and rub them clean with a cloth that has been soaked in solvent. If the races show hair line cracks or worn shiny areas, they must be replaced. The races are installed in the hub with a press fit and are removed by driving them out with a suitable punch or drift. Place the new races squarely onto the hub and place a block of wood over them. Drive the race into place with a hammer, striking the block of wood. Never hit the race with any metal object.

Replacement seals, bearings, and other required parts can be bought at an auto parts store. The old parts should be taken along to be com-

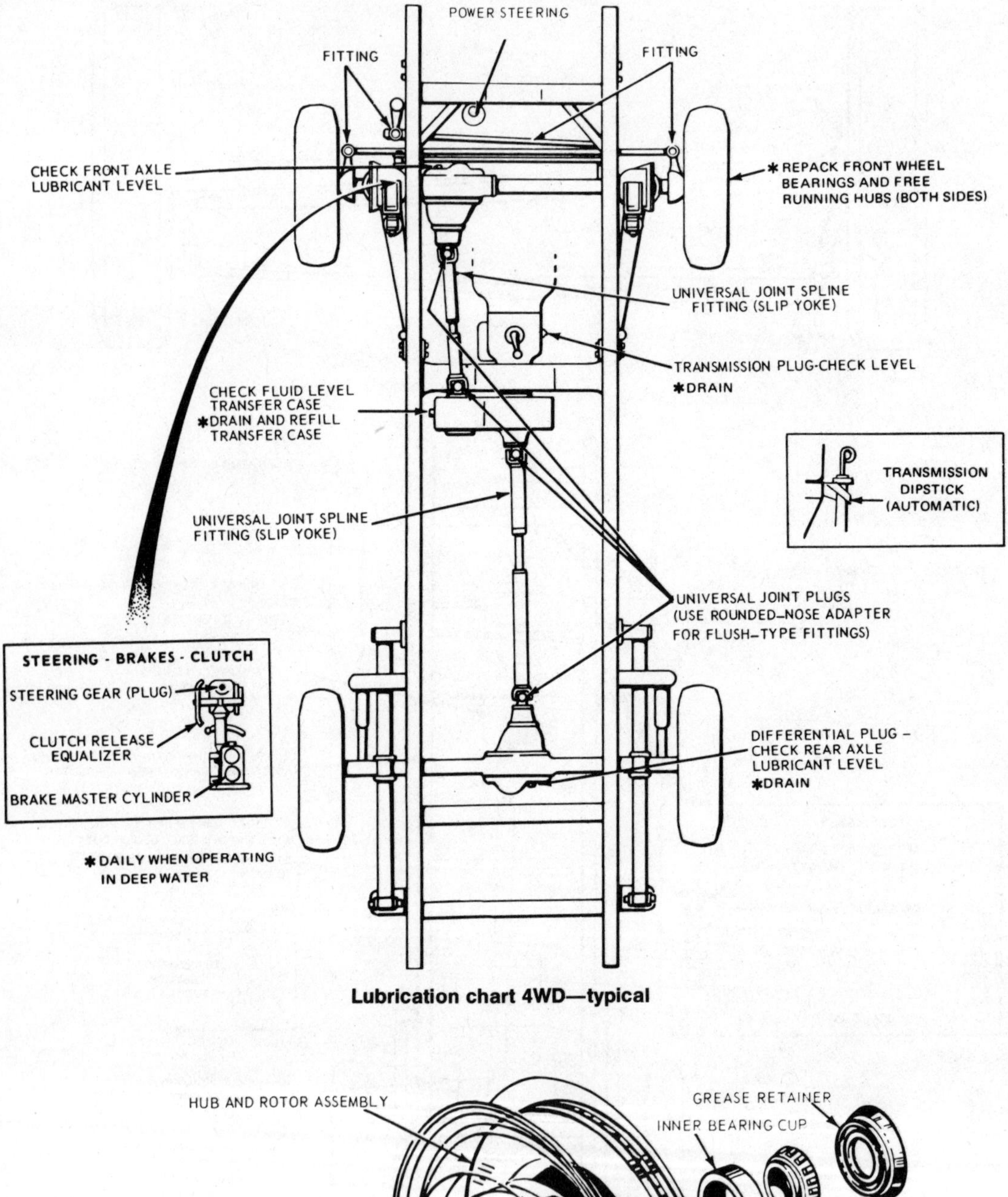

POWER STEERING
FITTING
FITTING
CHECK FRONT AXLE LUBRICANT LEVEL
✱ REPACK FRONT WHEEL BEARINGS AND FREE RUNNING HUBS (BOTH SIDES)
UNIVERSAL JOINT SPLINE FITTING (SLIP YOKE)
TRANSMISSION PLUG-CHECK LEVEL
✱DRAIN
CHECK FLUID LEVEL TRANSFER CASE
✱DRAIN AND REFILL TRANSFER CASE
TRANSMISSION DIPSTICK (AUTOMATIC)
UNIVERSAL JOINT SPLINE FITTING (SLIP YOKE)
UNIVERSAL JOINT PLUGS (USE ROUNDED–NOSE ADAPTER FOR FLUSH–TYPE FITTINGS)
STEERING - BRAKES - CLUTCH
STEERING GEAR (PLUG)
CLUTCH RELEASE EQUALIZER
BRAKE MASTER CYLINDER
DIFFERENTIAL PLUG – CHECK REAR AXLE LUBRICANT LEVEL
✱DRAIN
✱ DAILY WHEN OPERATING IN DEEP WATER

Lubrication chart 4WD—typical

HUB AND ROTOR ASSEMBLY
GREASE RETAINER
INNER BEARING CUP
OUTER BEARING CUP
OUTER BEARING CONE AND ROLLER
INNER BEARING CONE AND ROLLER
ADJUSTING NUT
GREASE CAP
WHEEL ASSEMBLY
WASHER
NUT LOCK
NUT
COTTER PIN
HUB BOLT

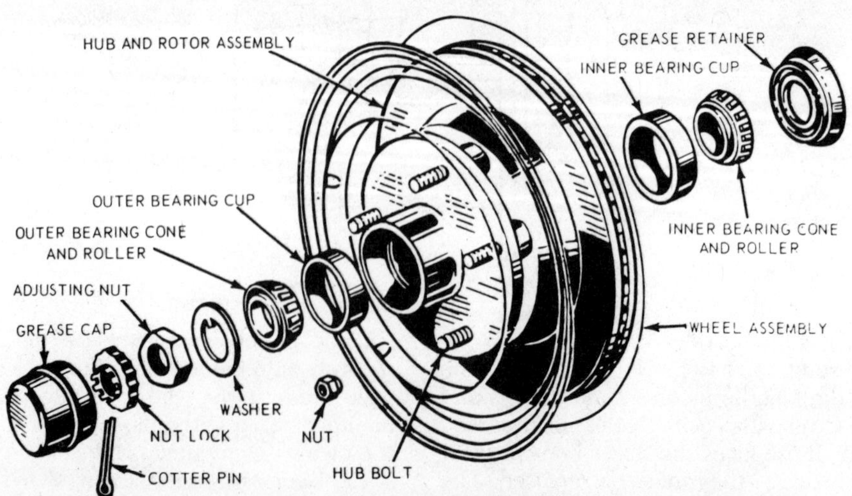

Front hub, bearing, and grease seal with disc brakes—2WD

pared with the replacement parts to ensure a perfect match.

12. Pack the wheel bearings with grease. There are special devices made for the specific purpose of greasing bearings, but if one is not available, pack the wheel bearings by hand. Put a large dab of grease in the palm of your hand and push the bearing through it with a sliding motion. The grease must be forced through the side of the bearing and in between each roller. Continue until the grease begins to ooze out the other side and through the gaps between the rollers; the bearing must be completely packed with grease.

NOTE: *Sodium based grease is not compatible with lithium based grease. Be careful not to mix the two types. The best way to prevent this is to completely clean all of the old grease from the hub and spindle before installing any new grease.*

13. Turn the hub assembly over so that the inner side faces up, making sure that the race and inner area are clean, and drop the inner wheel bearing into place. Using a hammer and a block of wood, tap the new grease seal in place. Never hit the seal with the hammer directly. Move the block of wood around the circumference until it is properly seated.

14. Slide the hub assembly onto the spindle and push it as far as it will go, making sure that it has completely covered the brake shoes. Keep the hub centered on the spindle to prevent damage to the grease seal and the spindle threads.

15. Place the outer wheel bearing in place over the spindle. Press it in until it is snug. Place the washer on the spindle after the bearing. Screw on the spindle nut and turn it down until a slight binding is felt.

16. With a torque wrench, tighten the nut to 17–25 ft. lbs. to seat the bearings. Install the nut lock over the nut so that the cotter pin hole in the spindle is aligned with a slot in the nut lock. Back off the adjusting nut and the nut lock two slots of the nut lock and install the cotter pin.

17. Bend the longer of the two ends opposite the looped end out and over the end of the spindle. Trim both ends of the cotter pin just enough so that the grease cap will fit, leaving the bent end shaped over the end of the spindle.

18. Install the grease cap, brake caliper if so equipped, and the wheel/tire assembly. The wheel should rotate freely with no noise or noticeable end-play.

19. Adjust the brakes on drum brake equipped trucks.

4WD Front Without Free-Running Hubs

NOTE: *Sodium based grease is not compatible with lithium based grease. Be careful not to mix the two types. The best way to prevent this is to completely clean all of the old grease from the hub assembly before installing any new grease.*

1. Raise the front of the vehicle and place jackstands under the vehicle. Remove the wheel.

2. Remove the front hub grease cap and driving hub snap-ring. On models equipped with free-running hubs, remove the retainer knob hub ring, actuator knob, snap-ring, outer clutch retaining ring, and actuating cam body.

3. Remove the splined driving hub and the pressure spring. This may require slight prying with a screwdriver.

4. Remove the wheel bearing locknut, lockring, and adjusting nut.

NOTE: *This may require the use of a front wheel bearing spanner #T59T-1197B for F-*

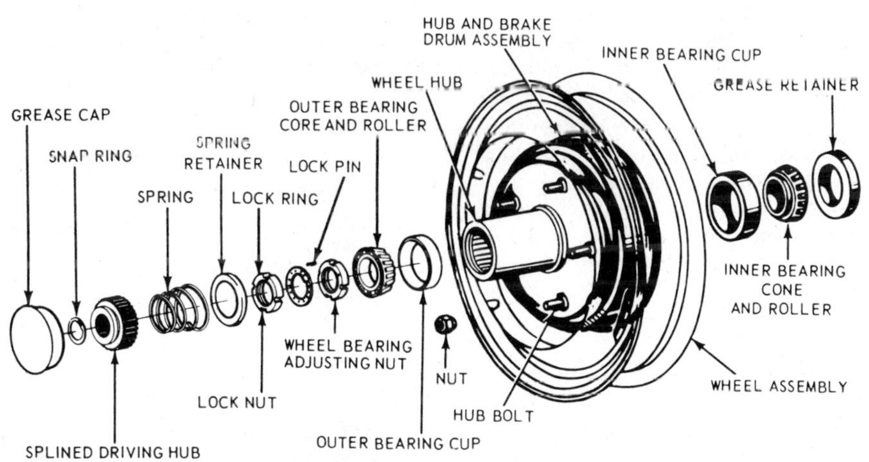

Front hub assembly without free-running hubs—4WD

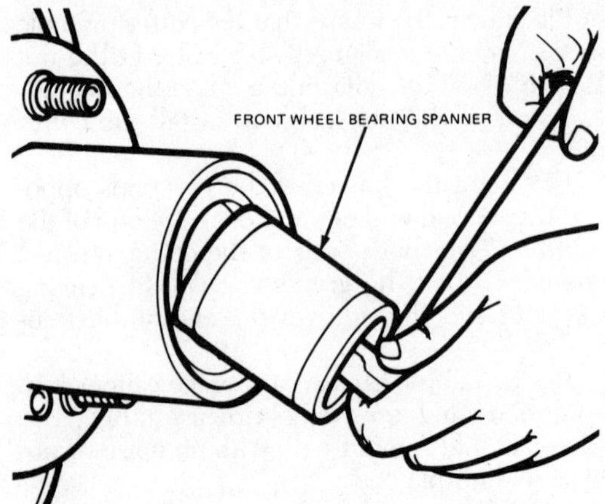

Lock nut, lock ring and adjusting nut removal using spanner

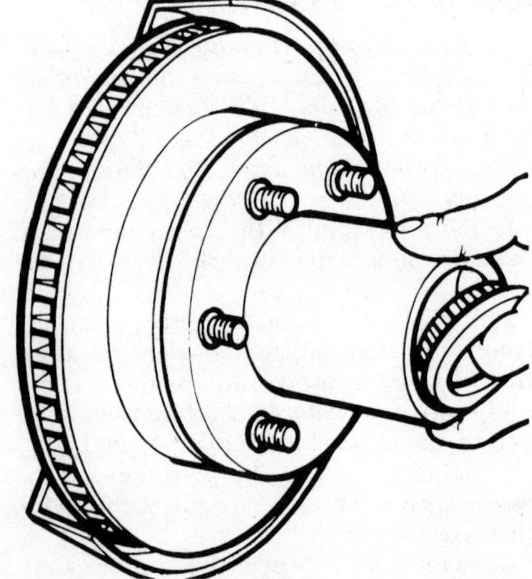
Outer bearing removal, 4×4

150, F-250, or #T78T-1197A for F-350 and heavy-duty F-250 models.

5. Drum Brakes: Remove the hub and drum assembly. This may require that the brake adjusting screw be backed off to move the brake shoes away from the brake drum. The outer wheel bearing and spring retainer will slide out as the hub is removed.

Disc Brakes: See the brake section, Chapter 9, for caliper removal. Suspend the caliper out of the way and remove the hub and rotor assembly.

6. Carefully drive out the inner bearing cone and grease seal from the hub.

7. Inspect the bearing cups (races) for cracks and pits. If the cups are excessively worn or there are pits or cracks visible, replace them along with the cones. The cups are removed from the hub by driving them out with a drift pin. They are installed in the same manner.

8. If it is determined that the cups are in satisfactory condition and are to remain in the hub, clean and inspect the cones (bearings). Refer to the bearing diagnosis chart. Replace the bearings if necessary. If it is necessary to replace either the cone or the cup, both parts should be replaced as a unit.

9. Thoroughly clean all components in a suitable solvent and blow them dry with compressed air or allow them to dry while resting on clean paper.

NOTE: *Do not spin the bearings with compressed air while drying them.*

10. Cover the spindle with a cloth and brush all loose dust and dirt from the brake assembly. Remove the cloth and thoroughly clean the inside of the hub and the spindle.

11. Pack the inside of the hub with wheel bearing grease. Add grease to the hub until the grease is flush with the inside diameter of the bearing cup.

12. Pack the bearing cone and roller assemblies with wheel bearing grease. A bearing packer is desirable for this operation. If a packer is not available place a large portion of grease into the palm of your hand and sliding the edge of the roller cage through the grease with your other hand, work as much grease in between the rollers as possible.

13. Position the inner bearing into the inner bearing cup and install the new grease seal.

14. Carefully position the hub assembly onto the spindle. Be careful not to damage the new seal. Install the drum or caliper.

15. Place the outer bearing into position on the spindle and into the bearing cup.

16. Install the bearing adjusting nut and tighten it to 50 ft. lbs. while rotating the hub back and forth to seat the bearings.

17. Back off the adjusting nut about 90°.

18. Assemble the lockring by turning the nut to the nearest notch where the dowel pin will enter.

19. Install the outer locknut and torque to 80–100 ft. lbs. The final end-play of the wheel on the spindle should be 0.001–0.010 in.

20. Install the pressure spring retainer, spring, the driving hub and driving hub snapring. This is for vehicles without free-running hubs.

21. Install the grease cap and adjust the brakes, if they were backed off to remove the hub assembly. Remove the jackstands and lower the vehicle.

4WD Front With Free-Running Hubs Thru 1979

NOTE: *For 1980–and later 4WD see Front Wheel Spindle Removal and Installation in Chapter 8.*

This procedure is much the same as for 4WD

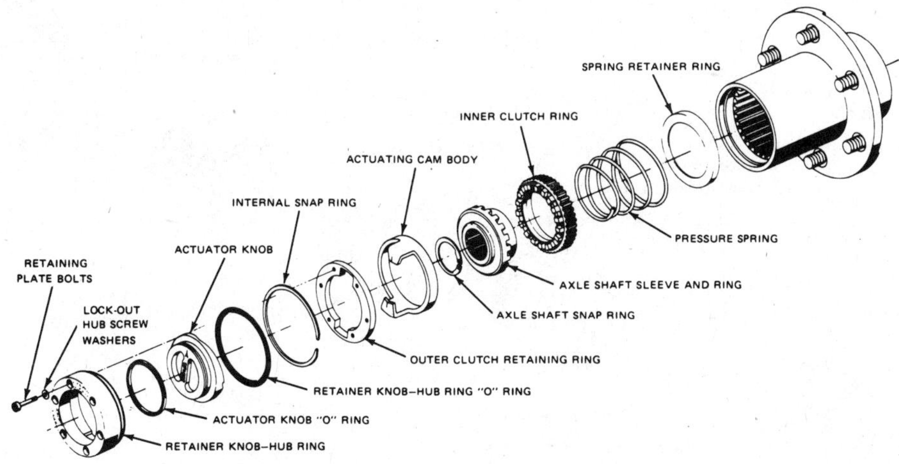

Free-running type front hub—light duty 4WD

Front Without Free-Running Hubs, once the hubs are removed. Use the following procedures for hub removal and installation.

NOTE: *These procedures are for the factory-installed hubs only. You will have to adapt the procedure for aftermarket hubs. The heavy duty hubs are found on some F-250 1350 models. The light duty hubs are used on all series.*

If the wheel bearings are not being packed at the same time as the hubs, make sure that you use the same type of grease as is packed around the wheel bearings. Sodium based and lithium based grease are not compatible with each other.

LIGHT DUTY

1. Remove the lock-out screw and washers.
2. Remove the hub ring and the knob.
3. Remove the internal snap-ring from the groove in the hub.
4. Remove the cam body ring and clutch retainer from the hub and disassemble the parts.
5. Remove the axle shaft snap-ring. It may be necessary to push in on the gear and pull out on the axle with a bolt to make the removal of the snap-ring easier.
6. Remove the drive gear and clutch gear. A slight rocking of the hub may make slide out easier.
7. Remove the coil spring and the spring retainer.
8. Clean all of the components in a suitable solvent and wipe out the hub with a clean cloth.
9. Grease the inside of the hub literally.
10. Install the spring retainer ring, with the under cut area facing in. Be sure it seats against the bearing.
11. Install the coil spring with the large end going in first.
12. Install the axle shaft sleeve and ring and the inner clutch ring with the teeth of both components meshed together in a locked position for easy assembly. It may be necessary to rock the hub to mesh the splines of the axle with those of the axle shaft sleeve and ring. Keep the two gears in the locked position.
13. Install the axle shaft snap-ring. Push in on the gear and pull out on the axle with a bolt to allow the snap-ring to go into the groove.
14. Install the actuating cam body ring into the outer clutch retaining ring and install them in the hub.
15. Install the internal snap-ring.
16. Apply a small amount of Lubriplate® grease to the ears of the cam.
17. Assemble the knob in the hub ring and assemble them to the axle with the knob in the locked position. Assemble the screws and washers alternately and evenly, making sure the retainer ring is not cocked in the hub.
18. Torque the six lock-out hub screws to 40 in lbs.

NOTE: *Do not drive the vehicle until you are sure that both of the lock-out hubs are either engaged or disengaged.*

HEAVY DUTY

1. Remove the free-running hub screws and washers.
2. Loosen the gear hub housing and slide it away from the hub and drum assembly.
3. Remove and discard the inner metal gasket, remove the gear hub housing, and remove and discard the outer gasket. Wipe the exposed parts clean with a clean rag.
4. Remove the snap-ring while holding pressure on the clutch gear.
5. The actuator knob should be in the lock position while performing this operation. Ease the clutch gear and pressure spring out of the assembly.

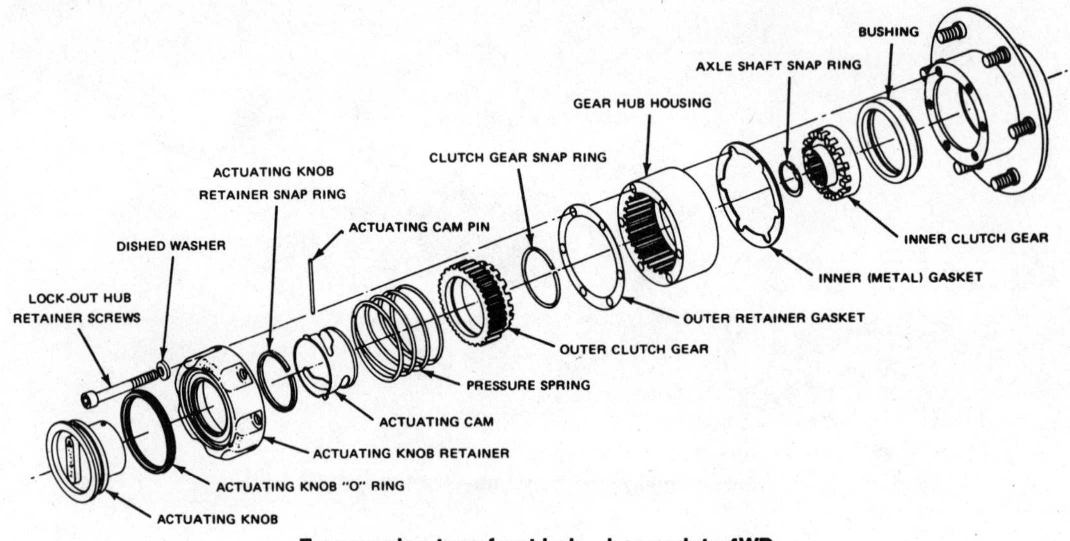

Free-running type front hub—heavy duty 4WD

6. Turn the actuator knob to the free position. Drive the cam lock pin out of the assembly with a drift.
7. Remove the actuating cam from the knob.
8. Remove the knob retainer snap-ring and remove the knob from the knob retainer.
9. Using a capscrew, pull out slightly on the axle shaft and remove the snap-ring which retains the bushing and inner clutch gear assembly.
10. Remove the inner clutch gear and the bushing behind it. Replace these two components as a set if excessive wear or damage is evident.
11. Inspect the splines of the axle shaft for nicks or burrs. Clean the threaded holes in the wheel hub.

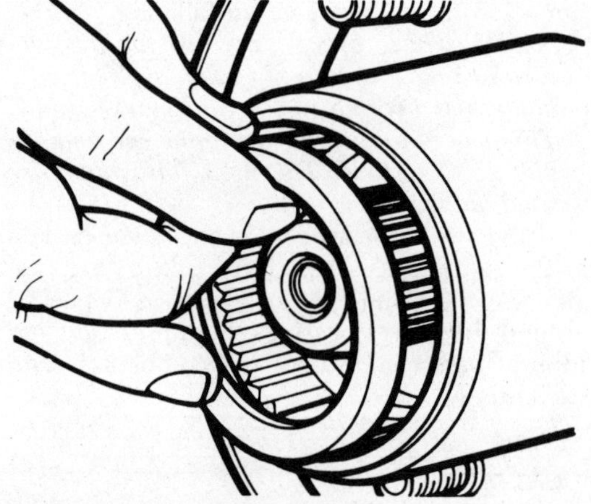

Spring retainer ring installation

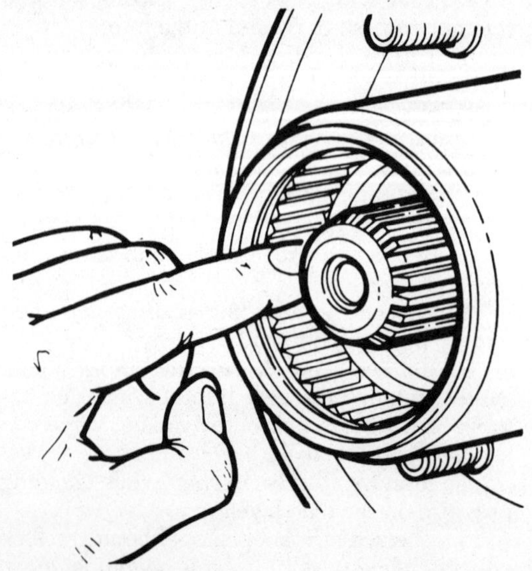

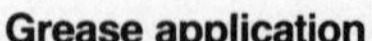
Grease application

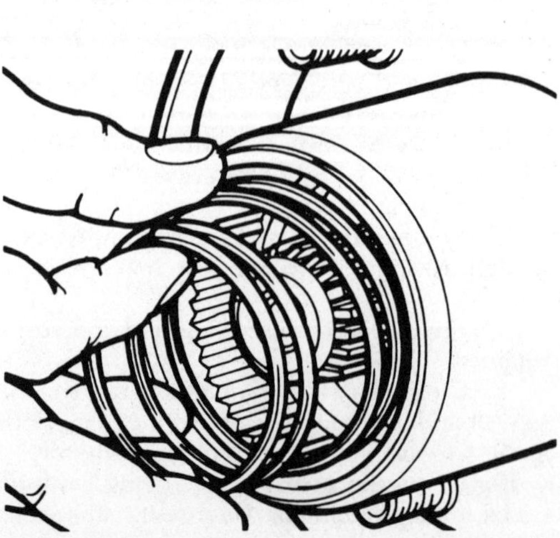

Coil spring installation

12. Apply Moly XL Hi-Speed grease to the back face and thrust face of the bushing and the splines of the inner clutch gear.

13. Assemble the inner clutch gear into the bushing.

14. Install the bushing and inner clutch gear onto the axle shaft mating the splines of the axle and the gear.

15. Install a new snap-ring to retain the bushing and gear. It may be necessary to pull out the axle with a capscrew to gain clearance for the snap-ring to be installed. Make sure that the snap-ring is fully seated.

16. Apply a small amount of O-ring lubricant on the actuator knob and assemble the O-ring to the actuator knob.

17. Install the actuating knob into the knob retainer with the arrow pointing to the free position.

18. Install the knob retainer snap-ring.

19. Install the actuating cam onto the knob, aligning the ears of the cam with the slots on the retainer. Position the parts on a small block of wood.

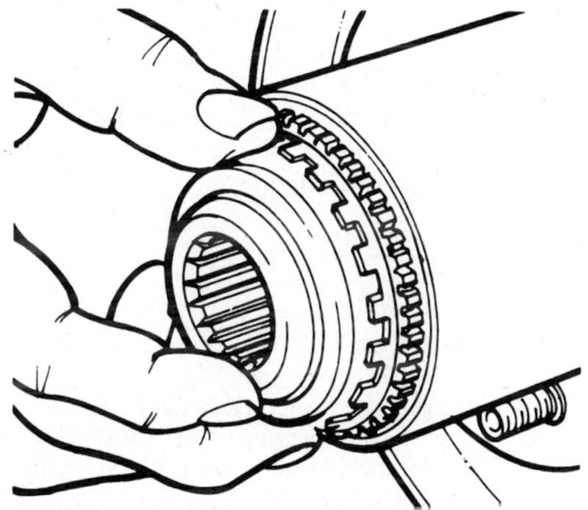

Axle shift sleeve and ring, and inner clutch ring installation

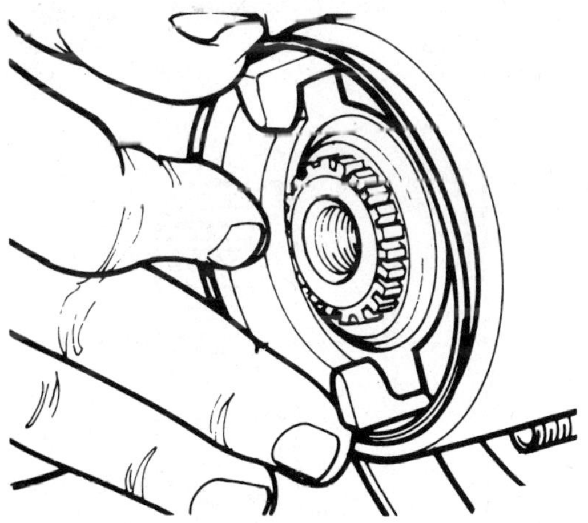

Installing the internal snap ring

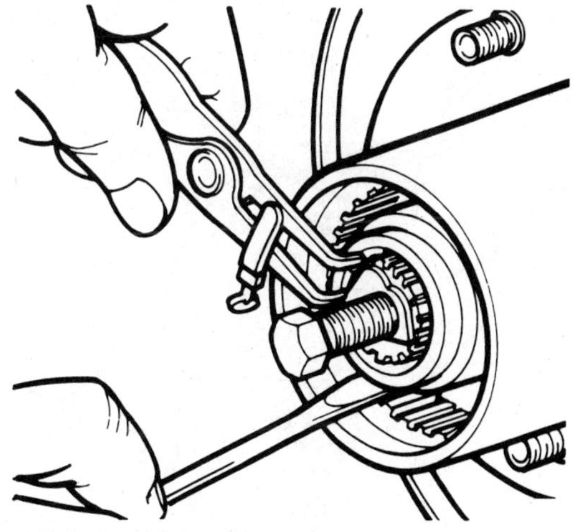

Installing the axle shaft snap ring

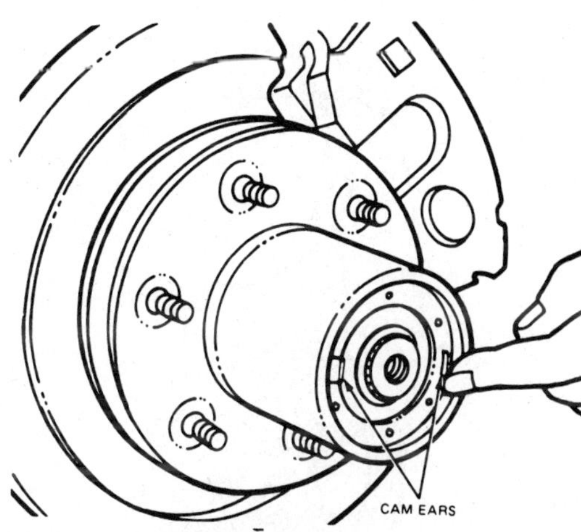

Applying a small amount of grease on the ears of the cam

20. Assemble the cam lock pin through the groove of the cam and the holes in the actuating knob. Be sure that the ends of the pin are flush with the outside diameter of the cam.

21. Turn the actuator knob to the lock position and apply a small amount of Moly XL Hi-Speed grease to both grooves of the cam.

22. Install the pressure spring and outer clutch gear. Compress the pressure spring by forcing the clutch gear down, then install the snap-ring. Be sure that the snap-ring is fully seated in the groove.

23. Turn the actuator knob to the free position. Assemble the six dished washers to the six retaining screws.

24. Install two screws with washers into the knob retainer to properly align the parts. Apply a small amount of Moly XL Hi-Speed grease to the outer spline and teeth of the outer clutch

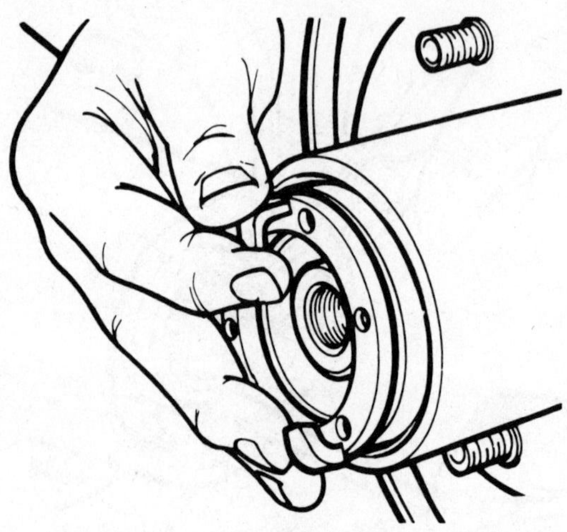

Installing the cam body ring into the clutch retaining ring

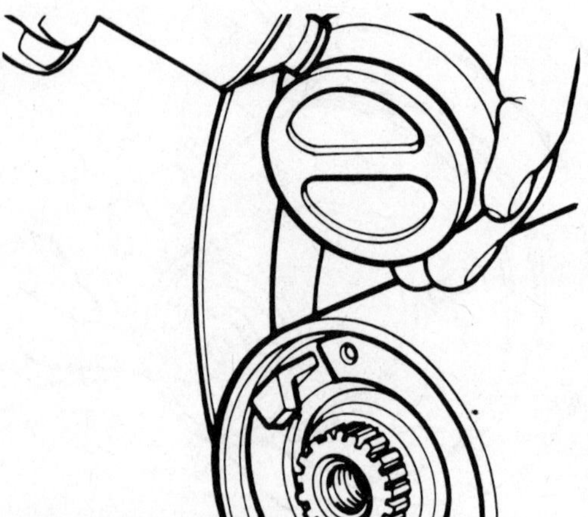

Lubricating the selector knob

gear. Remove any excess lubricant from the gasket surface of the retainer.

25. Install a new outer retainer gasket. Assemble the gear hub housing by aligning the splines of the housing with those on the outer clutch gear. Then install a new inner metal gasket on the hub housing.

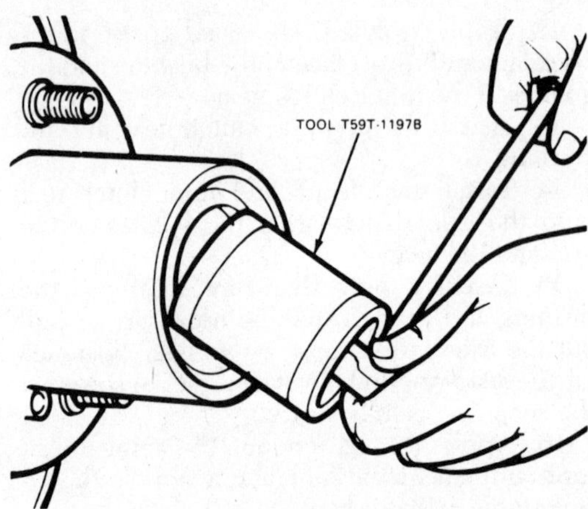

Lock nut, lock ring and adjusting nut removal

26. Position the free-running hub assembly to the axle and tighten the two installed retaining screws. Turn the actuator knob to the lock position.

27. Install the remaining four retainer screws with washers and tighten all screws in sequence to 30–35 ft. lbs.

NOTE: *The hubs may be hard to engage and disengage at first, but should loosen up after some use. Make sure that both the hubs are either engaged or disengaged before driving the truck.*

F-250 350 Rear

The wheel bearings on the F-250 350 full floating rear axle are packed with wheel bearing grease. Axle lubricant can also flow into the wheel hubs and bearings, however, wheel bearing grease is the primary lubricant. The wheel bearing grease provides lubrication until the axle lubricant reaches the bearings during normal operation.

1. Set the parking brake and loosen the axle shaft bolts.

2. Raise the rear wheels off the floor and place jackstands under the rear axle housing so that the axle is parallel with the floor.

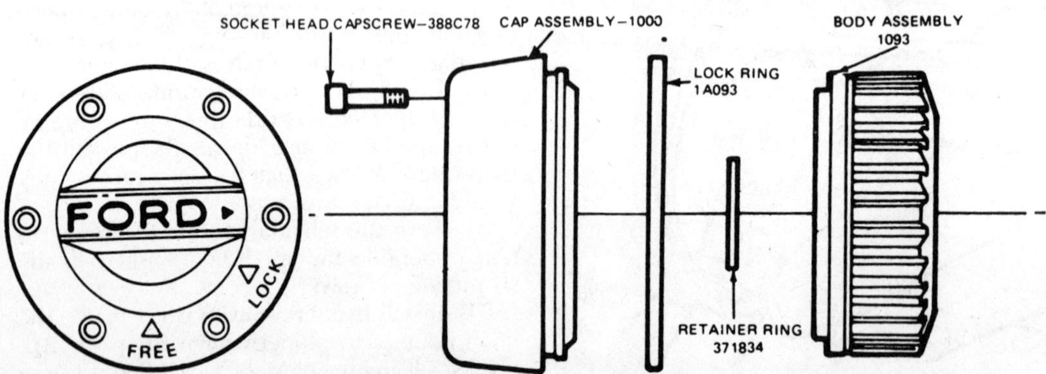

1980 and later manual locking hubs

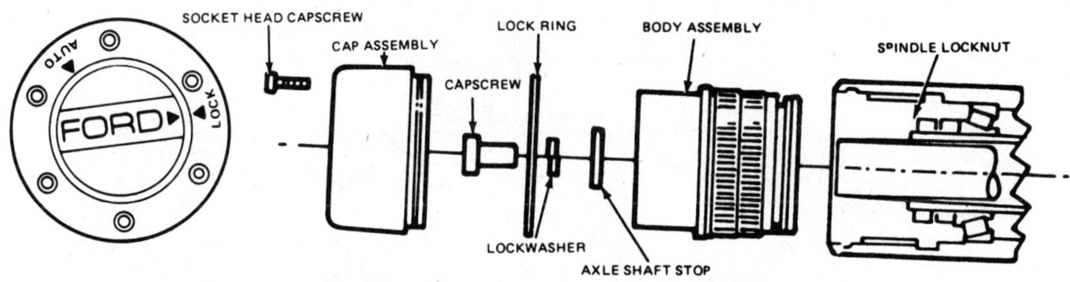

1980 and later automatic locking hubs

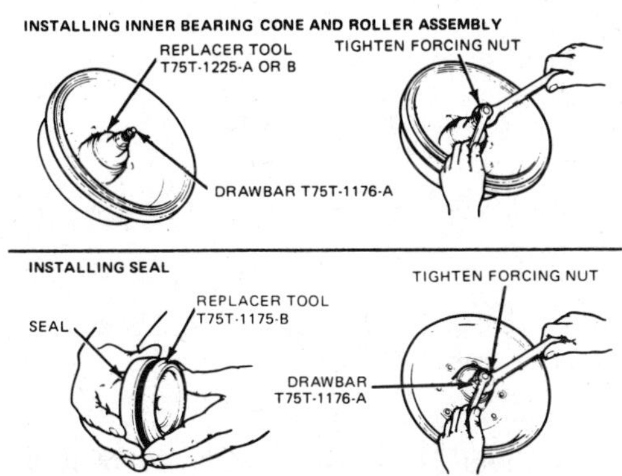

Rear wheel bearing and seal installation. Seal installation tools are very helpful here

3. Remove the axle shaft bolts.
4. Remove the axle shaft and gaskets.
5. With the axle shaft removed, remove the gasket from the axle shaft flange studs.
6. Bend the lockwasher tab away from the locknut, and then remove the locknut, lockwasher, and the adjusting nut.
7. Remove the outer bearing cone and pull the wheel straight off the axle.
8. With a piece of hardwood or a brass drift which will just clear the outer bearing cup, drive the inner bearing cone and inner seal out of the wheel hub.
9. Wash all the old grease or axle lubricant out of the wheel hub, using a suitable solvent.
10. Wash the bearing cups and rollers and inspect them for pitting, galling, and uneven wear patterns. Inspect the roller for end wear.
11. If the bearing cups are to be replaced, drive them out with a brass drift. Install the new cups with a block of wood and hammer or press them in.
12. If the bearing cups are properly seated, a 0.0015 in. feeler gauge will not fit between the cup and the wheel hub. The gauge should not fit beneath the cup. Check several places

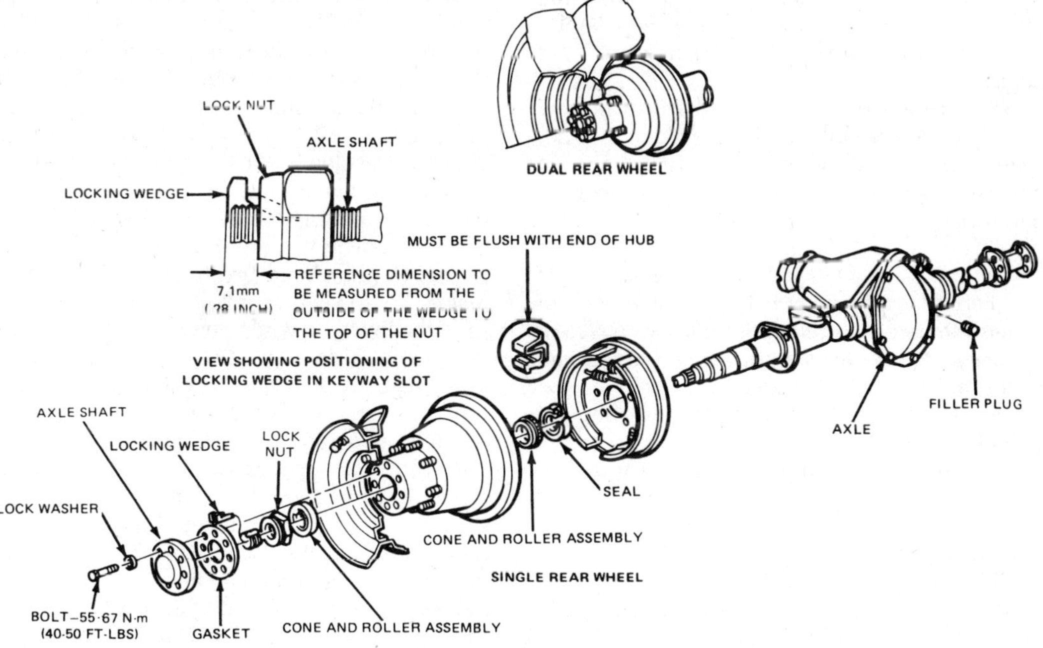

Rear wheel hub showing locking wedge positioning—F-350 (4 × 2) with dual rear wheels shown

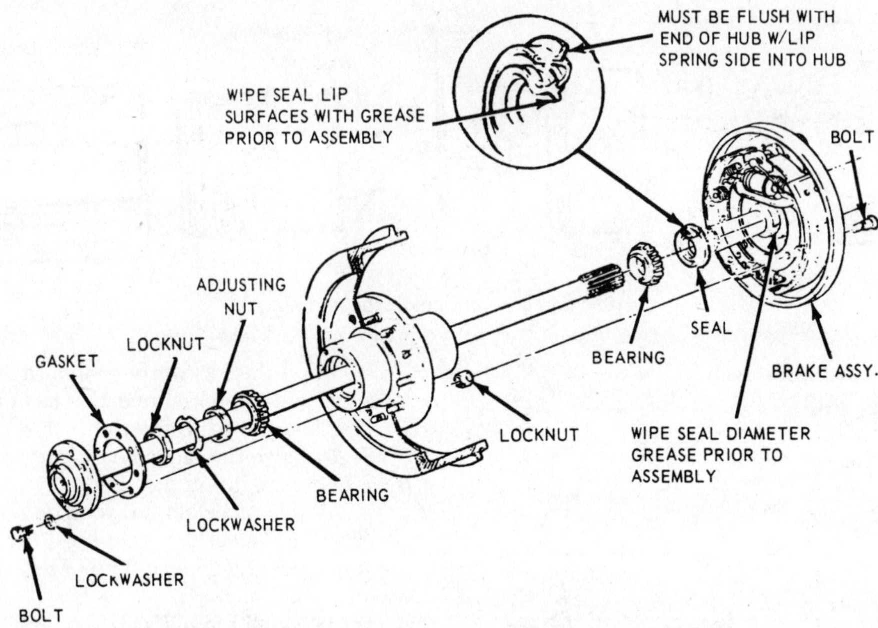

Single rear hub assembly with full-floating axles, F-250 only

to make sure the cups are squarely seated.

13. Pack each bearing cone and roller with a bearing packer or in the manner previously outlined for the front wheel bearings on 2WD trucks. Use a multi-purpose wheel bearing grease.

14. Place the inner bearing cone and roller assembly in the wheel hub. Install a new inner seal in the hub with a seal installation tool.

15. Install the wheel.

16. Install and tighten the bearing adjusting nut to 50–80 ft. lbs. while rotating the wheel.

17. Back off (loosen) the adjusting nut ⅜ of a turn.

18. Position the locking wedge in the keyway slot and carefully drive the wedge into position. The wedge must be bottomed against the shoulder of the adjusting nut when fully installed.

NOTE: *The locking wedge and the adjusting nut can be used over again, as long as the locking wedge cuts a new groove in the nylon retainer material within the ⅛ to ⅜ turn specified. The wedge must not be pressed into a previously cut groove.*

19. Apply axle lube to a new lockwasher and install it with the smooth side out.

20. Install the locknut and tighten it to 90–110 ft. lbs. The wheel must rotate freely after the locknut is tightened. The wheel end-play should be within 0.001–0.010 in.

21. Bend two lockwasher tabs inward over an adjusting nut flat and two lockwasher tabs outward over the locknut flat.

22. Install the axle shaft, gasket, lockbolts, and washers. Tighten the bolts to 40–50 ft. lbs.

23. Adjust the brakes, if necessary.

PUSHING AND TOWING

To push-start your vehicle, (manual transmission only), check to make sure that the bumpers of both vehicles are aligned so neither will be damaged. Be sure that all electrical system components are turned off (headlights, heater, blower, etc.). Turn on the ignition switch. Place the shift lever in Third or Fourth and push in the clutch pedal. At about 15 mph, signal the driver of the pushing vehicle to fall back, depress the accelerator pedal, and release the clutch pedal slowly. The engine should start.

When you are doing the pushing, make sure that the two bumpers match so you won't damage the vehicle you are to push. Another good idea is to put an old tire between the two vehicles. Try to keep your pick-up right up against the other vehicle while you are pushing. If the two vehicles do separate, stop and start over again instead of trying to catch up and ramming the other vehicle. Also try, as much as possible, to avoid riding or slipping the clutch.

If your pick-up has to be towed by a tow truck, it can be towed forward for any distance with the driveshaft connected as long as it is done fairly slowly. Otherwise disconnect the driveshaft at the rear axle and tie it up. On an F-250, the rear axle shafts can be removed and the hub covered to prevent lubricant loss. If your 4 WD pick-up has to be towed backward,

Preventive Maintenance Schedule

Model/Interval	Item	Service
	1965–72 Models	
Every 6 months or 6,000 miles	Centering yoke sockets and balls, 1967–72	MP grease—2 special fittings
	Crankcase	change oil and filter
	Differentials	check levels
	Steering linkage	MP grease—4 fittings
	Tires	rotate
	Transfer case	check level—50W
	U-joints and splines	MP grease—2 or 4 fittings
	Air cleaner elements, 1965–67	clean
	Air cleaner oil bath	30W
	Brake master cylinder	check level
	Cooling system	inspect hoses and fluid level
	Drive belts	inspect and adjust
	Oil filler cap	check and clean
	PCV filter, 1972	replace
	PCV system, 1965–71	test
	Power steering reservoir	check level—Type F trans. fluid
	Steering column U-joint	MP grease—1 fitting
	Steering gear-manual	check level—90W gear oil
	Automatic transmission	check level—Type F fluid only
Every 12 months or 12,000 miles	Hublock hobs	MP—repack
	Air cleaner element—1968 6-cyl, 1969–72 all	replace
	Cooling system—1965–69	inspect hoses
	Distributor	replace points, condenser and rotor
	Fuel mixture	check and adjust
	Fuel filter	replace
	Intake manifold—8 cylinder	torque
	PCV system, 1972	clean system—replace valve
	Spark delay valve—1972	replace
	Spark plugs	replace
	Thermactor air pump filter, 1965–67	replace
	Thermostatic air cleaner, 1972	inspect
	Throttle and choke linkage	inspect
	Valve clearance, 6 cylinder	adjust
Every 24 months or 24,000 miles	Brakes	inspect
	Front wheel bearings	MP grease—clean and repack
	Transfer case and front differential	Transfer case—SAE 50W; Axle—80/90W change lubricant
	Air cleaner element—1968, 8 cylinder	replace
	Cooling system	change coolant, flush system
	Distributor	replace cap
	EEC canister and purge hose, 1972	replace
	PCV filter, 1971	replace
	Speedometer and parking brake cables	MP grease
	Engine	check compression
Every 36 months or 36,000 miles	U-joints without fittings—1965–66, early 1967	repack with MP grease
	Air cleaner element, 1965–67	replace
	1973	
Every 4 months or 4,000 miles	Brakes	inspect
	Crankcase	change oil & filter
	Differential	check level
	Chassis fittings	lubricate
	Tires	rotate
	Transmission, automatic	adjust bands, check level
	Transmission, manual	check level
	Air cleaner, oil bath	clean and refill
	Brake master cylinder	check level
	Cooling system	inspect, change coolant

Preventive Maintenance Schedule (cont.)

Model/Interval	Item	Service
	1973 Models	
Every 4 months or 4,000 miles	Manifold heat riser	inspect
	PCV filter	replace
	Power steering reservoir	check level
	Spark plug, leader fuel	replace
	TRS or throttle solenoid fuse	check
Every 12 months or 12,000 miles	Air cleaner paper element	replace
	Breather cap	clean
	Distributor points, condenser, rotor	replace
	Drive belts	check and adjust
	EGR system	clean and inspect
	Fuel filter	replace
	Fuel vapor system	inspect
	Idle speed and mixture	check and adjust
	Ignition timing & dwell	check and adjust
	Intake manifold, 8 cylinder	torque
	Spark control system, F-100	inspect
	Spark delay valve	replace
	Spark plugs, unleading fuel	replace
	Thermostatic air cleaner	inspect
	Throttle and choke linkage	inspect
	Free running hubs	clean and repack
Every 24 months or 24,000	Differential, F-250	change lubricant
	Front wheel bearings	clean and repack
	Rear wheel bearings, F-250	clean and repack
	Transmission, manual	change lubricant
	Transfer case	change lubricant
	Distributor cap	replace
	Distributor shaft or wick	oil with 10W
	1974	
Every 4 months or 4,000 miles	Crankcase	change oil & filter
	Air cleaner oil bath	clean and refill
	Idle speed	adjust
	Manifold heat riser	inspect
Every 6 months or 6,000 miles	Brakes	inspect
	Differential	check level
	Chassis fittings	lubricate
	Transmission, automatic	adjust bands, check level
	Transmission, manual	check level
	Cooling system	change coolant
	Drive belts	check and adjust
	Fuel filter	replace
	Idle speed and mixture	adjust
	PCV filter	replace
	Power steering	check level
Every 6 months or 6,000 miles	Throttle and choke linkage	inspect
	Ignition timing	adjust
Every 12 months or 12 miles	Air cleaner paper element	replace
	Breather cap	clean
	Brake master cylinder	check level
	Distribution points, condenser, rotor	replace
	EGR system	clean and inspect
	Intake manifold, 8 cylinder	torque
	PCV valve	replace
	Spark plugs, leaded fuel	replace
	thermactor system	inspect
	Thermostatic air cleaner	inspect
	Free running hubs	clean and repack
Every 18 months or 18,000 miles	Distributor cap	replace
	Spark plugs, unleaded fuel	replace

Preventive Maintenance Schedule (cont.)

Model/Interval	Item	Service
	1974 Models	
Every 24 months or 24,000 miles	Front wheel bearings	clean and repack
	Rear wheel bearings, F-250	clean and repack
	Transfer case	change lubricant
	1975–76	
Every 5 months or 5,000 miles	Brakes	inspect
	Crankcase	change oil & filter
	Differential	check level
	Chassis fittings	lubricate
	Transmission, automatic	adjust bands, check level
	Transmission, manual	check level
	Air cleaner oil bath	clean and refill
	Power steering	check level
	Idle speed	adjust
	Throttle kickdown exc F-100	check
	Throttle solenoid-off speed	check
Every 6 months	Cooling system	inspect, change coolant
Every 15 months or 15,000 miles	Brake master cylinder	check level
	Parking brake linkage	oil with 10W
	Air cleaner element	replace
	Air cleaner temperature valve	check
	Choke system	inspect
	Distributor cap and rotor	inspect
	Distributor wick	oil with 10W
	Drive belts	check & adjust
	EGR system	clean and inspect
	Fuel filter	replace
	Ignition timing	adjust
	Intake manifold, 302 V8	torque
	Manifold heat riser	inspect
	PCV system	inspect
	Spark plugs	replace
	Spark plug wires	inspect
	Thermactor system	inspect
	Free running hubs	clean and repack
Every 20 months or 20,000 miles	Front wheel bearings	clean and repack
	Rear wheel bearings, Dana axle	clean and repack
Every 25 months or 25,000 miles	Differential, Dana	change lubricant
	Transmission, 4 speed	change lubricant
	Transfer case	change lubricant
Every 30 months or 30,000 miles	Air cleaner crankcase filter	replace
	EEC canister	inspect
	Fuel vapor system	inspect
	PCV valve	replace
	1977 and Later F-100 Only	
Every 6 months	Cooling system	change coolant
Every 7 months or 7,500 miles	Crankcase	change oil and filter
	Drive belts	check and adjust
	Idle speed and TSP-off speed	adjust
	Ignition timing	check and adjust
	Chassis fittings	lubricate
	Clutch linkage	inspect and oil
	Transmission, automatic	adjust bands, check level
Every 15 months or 15,000 miles	Exhaust system heat shields	inspect
Every 22 months or 22,500 miles	Spark plugs	replace
	Exhaust control valve, 300cid	inspect
	PCV valve	replace

Preventive Maintenance Schedule (cont.)

Model/Interval	Item	Service
	1977 and Later F-100 Only	
Every 22 months or 22,500 miles	Idle mixture	adjust
	Choke system	inspect
	Thermactor delay valve	inspect
Every 30 months or 30,000 miles	Air cleaner element	replace
	Air cleaner crankcase filter	replace
	Air cleaner temperature control valve	check
	Fuel vapor system	inspect
	Front wheel bearings	clean and repack
	Brakes	inspect
	Brake master cylinder	check level
	1977 and Later F-150, 250, 350 (Except Diesel)	
Every 6 months or 6,000 miles	Crankcase	change oil & filter
	Cooling system	change coolant
	Idle speed and TSP-off speed	adjust
	Ignition timing	adjust
	Decel throttle control system	check
	Chassis fittings	lubricate
	4 x 4 power cylinder	lubricate
	Clutch linkage	inspect and oil
	Exhaust system heat shields	inspect
	Transmission, automatic	adjust bands, check level
Every 15 months or 15,000 miles	Spark plugs	replace
	Exhaust control valve	check & lubricate
	Drive belts	check and adjust
	Air cleaner temperature control	check
	Choke system	check
	Thermactor system	check
	Chankcase breathe cap	clean
	EGR system	clean and inspect
	PCV system	clean and inspect
Every 30 months or 30,000 miles	PCV valve	replace
	Air cleaner element	replace
	Air cleaner crankcase filter	replace
	Fuel vapor system	inspect
	Brake master cylinder	check
	Brakes	inspect
	Free-running hubs	clean and repack
	Front wheel bearings	clean and repack
	Rear wheel bearings, Dana axles	clean and repack
	6.9L Diesel Models	
Every 6 months or 5,000 miles	Crankcase	change oil and filter
	Idle speed	check and adjust
	Throttle linkage	check operation
	Fuel/water separator	drain water
	U-joints	lubricate
	Front axle spindles	lubricate
Every 6 months or 15,000 miles	Fuel filter	replace
	Drive belts	check/adjust
	Steering linkage	lubricate
Every year	Coolant	check condition/replace
	Cooling hoses, clamps	check condition/replace

remove the front axle driving hubs, or disengage the lock-out hubs to prevent the front differential from rotating. If the drive hubs are removed, improvise a cover to keep out dust and dirt.

JACKING AND HOISTING

It is very important to be careful about running the engine, on vehicles equipped with limited slip differentials, while the vehicle is up on a jack. This is because if the drive train is engaged, power is transmitted to the wheel with the best traction and the vehicle will drive off the jack, resulting in possible damage or injury.

Jack a Ford pick-up from under the axles, radius arms, or spring hangers and the frame. Be sure and block the diagonally opposite wheel. Place jackstands under the vehicle at the points mentioned or directly under the frame when you are going to work under the vehicle.

Jump Starting a Dual-Battery Diesel

Ford pick-ups equipped with the 420 cu. in. (6.9L) V8 diesel utilize two 12 volt batteries, one on either side of the engine compartment. The batteries are connected in a parallel circuit (positive terminal to positive terminal, negative terminal to negative terminal). Hooking the batteries up in parallel circuit increases battery cranking power without increasing total battery voltage output—this remains at 12 volts. On the other hand, hooking two 12 volt batteries up in a series circuit (positive terminal to negative terminal, positive terminal to negative terminal) increases total battery output to 24 volts (12 volts plus 12 volts).

CAUTION: *NEVER hook the batteries up in a series circuit or the entire electrical system will go up in smoke, especially the starter.*

In the event that a diesel pickup needs to be jump started, use the following procedure.

1. Turn all lights off.
2. Turn "on" the heater blower motor to remove transient voltage.
3. Connect one jumper cable to the passenger side battery positive (+) terminal and the other cable clamp to the positive (+) terminal of the booster (good) battery.
4. Connect one end of the other jumper cable to the negative (−) terminal of the booster (good) battery and the other cable clamp to an engine bolthead, alternator bracket or other solid, metallic point on the diesel engine. DO NOT connect this clamp to the negative (−) terminal of the bad battery.

CAUTION: *Be very careful to keep the jumper cables away from moving parts (cooling fan, belts, etc.) on both engines.*

5. Start the engine of the donor car and run at moderate speed.
6. Start the engine of the diesel.
7. When the diesel starts, remove the cable from the engine block before disconnecting the positive terminal. The lights can now be turned "on".

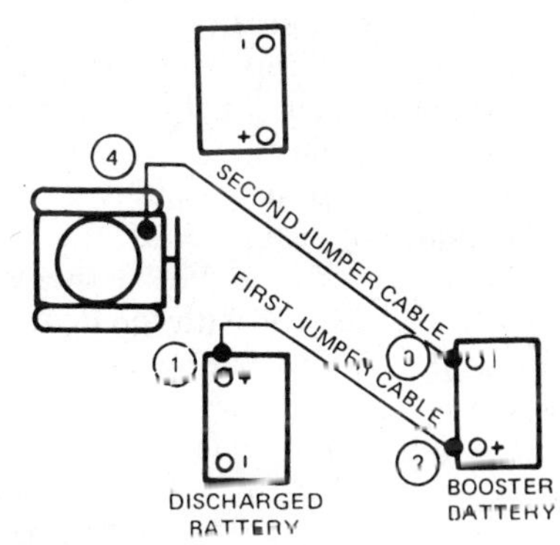

Diesel dual-battery jump starting diagram

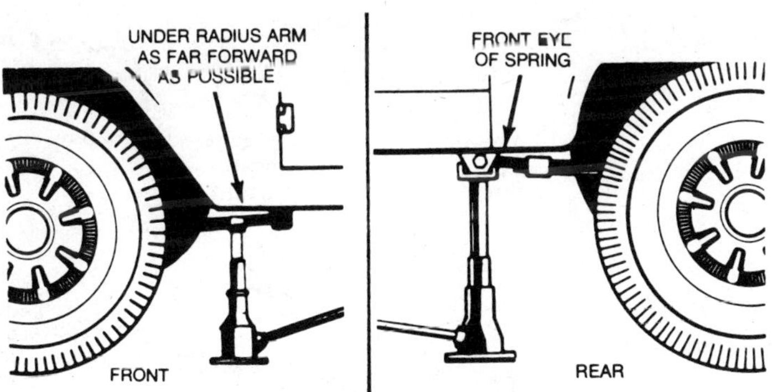

Proper jack placement

JUMP STARTING A DEAD BATTERY

The chemical reaction in a battery produces explosive hydrogen gas. This is the safe way to jump start a dead battery, reducing the chances of an accidental spark that could cause an explosion.

Jump Starting Precautions

1. Be sure both batteries are of the same voltage.
2. Be sure both batteries are of the same polarity (have the same grounded terminal).
3. Be sure the vehicles are not touching.
4. Be sure the vent cap holes are not obstructed.
5. Do not smoke or allow sparks around the battery.
6. In cold weather, check for frozen electrolyte in the battery.
7. Do not allow electrolyte on your skin or clothing.
8. Be sure the electrolyte is not frozen.

Jump Starting Procedure

1. Determine voltages of the two batteries; they must be the same.
2. Bring the starting vehicle close (they must not touch) so that the batteries can be reached easily.
3. Turn off all accessories and both engines. Put both cars in Neutral or Park and set the handbrake.
4. Cover the cell caps with a rag—do not cover terminals.
5. If the terminals on the run-down battery are heavily corroded, clean them.
6. Identify the positive and negative posts on both batteries and connect the cables in the order shown.
7. Start the engine of the starting vehicle and run it at fast idle. Try to start the car with the dead battery. Crank it for no more than 10 seconds at a time and let it cool off for 20 seconds in between tries.
8. If it doesn't start in 3 tries, there is something else wrong.
9. Disconnect the cables in the reverse order.
10. Replace the cell covers and dispose of the rags.

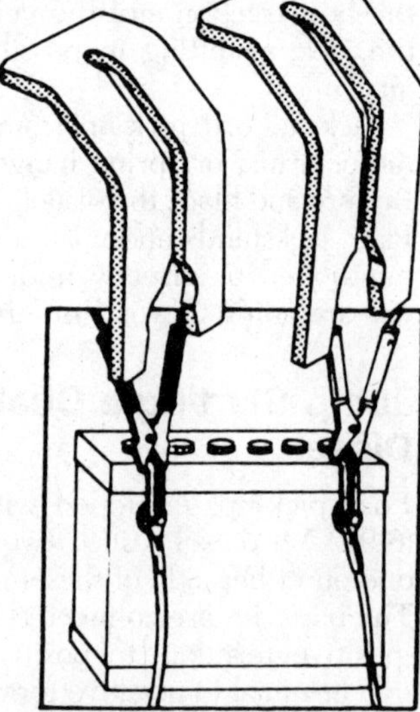

Side terminal batteries occasionally pose a problem when connecting jumper cables. There frequently isn't enough room to clamp the cables without touching sheet metal. Side terminal adaptors are available to alleviate this problem and should be removed after use.

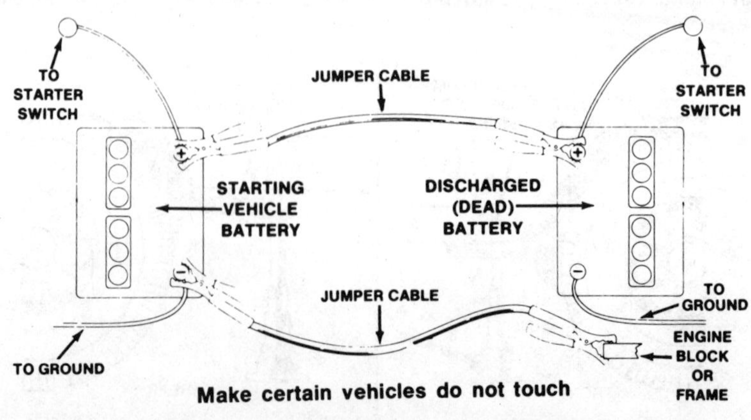

This hook-up for negative ground cars only

Tune-Up and Performance Maintenance 2

TUNE-UP PROCEDURES

Spark Plugs

A typical spark plug consists of a metal shell surrounding a ceramic insulator A metal electrode extends downward through the center of the insulator and protrudes a small distance. Located at the end of the plug and attached to the side of the outer metal shell is the side electrode. The side electrode bends in at a 90° angle so that its tip is even with, and parallel to, the tip of the center electrode. The distance between these two electrodes (measured in thousandths of an inch) is called the spark plug gap. The spark plug in no way produces a spark but merely provides a gap across which the current can arc. The coil produces anywhere from 20,000 to 40,000 volts which travels to the distributor where it is distributed through the spark plug wires to the spark plugs. The current passes along the center electrode and jumps the gap to the side electrode, and, in so doing, ignites the air/fuel mixture in the combustion chamber.

SPARK PLUG HEAT RANGE

Spark plug heat range is the ability of the plug to dissipate heat. The longer the insulator (or the farther it extends into the engine), the hotter the plug will operate; the shorter the insulator the cooler it will operate. A plug that absorbs little heat and remains too cool will quickly accumulate deposits of oil and carbon since it is not hot enough to burn them off. This leads to plug fouling and consequently to misfiring. A plug that absorbs too much heat will have no deposits, but, due to the excessive heat, the electrodes will burn away quickly and in some instances, preignition may result. Preignition takes place when plug tips get so hot that they glow sufficiently to ignite the fuel/air mixture before the actual spark occurs. This early ignition will usually cause a pinging during low speeds and heavy loads.

The general rule of thumb for choosing the correct heat range when picking a spark plug is: if most of your driving is long distance, high speed travel, use a colder plug; if most of your driving is stop and go, use a hotter plug. Original equipment plugs are compromise plugs, but most people never have occasion to change their plugs from the factory-recommended heat range.

REPLACING SPARK PLUGS

A set of spark plugs usually requires replacement after about 10,000 miles on cars with conventional ignition systems and after about 20,000 to 30,000 miles on trucks with electronic ignition, depending on your style of driving. In normal operation, plug gap increases about 0.001 in. for every 1,000–2,500 miles. As the gap increases, the plug's voltage requirement also increases. It requires a greater voltage to jump the wider gap and about two to three times as much voltage to fire a plug at high speeds than at idle.

When you're removing spark plugs, you should work on one at a time. Don't start by removing the plug wires all at once, because unless you number them, they may become mixed up. Take a minute before you begin and number the wires with tape. The best location for numbering is near where the wires come out of the cap.

1. Twist the spark plug boot and remove the boot and wire from the plug. Do not pull on the wire itself as this will ruin the wire.

2. If possible, use a brush or rag to clean the area around the spark plug. Make sure that all the dirt is removed so that none will enter the cylinder after the plug is removed.

3. Remove the spark plug using the proper size socket. A 13⁄16″ size socket may be used on all models from 1965–72. 1974 and later models

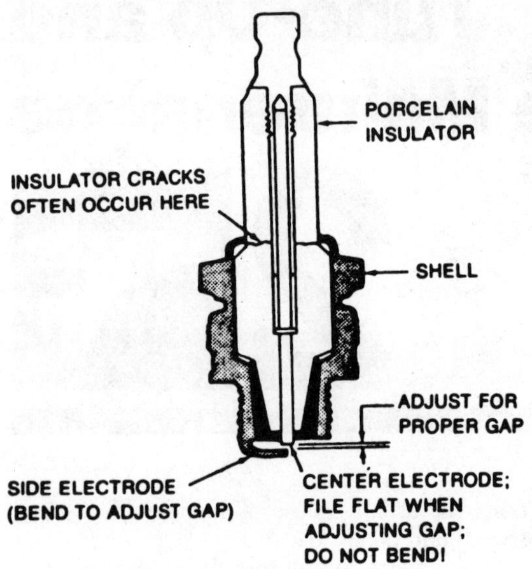

Cross section of a spark plug

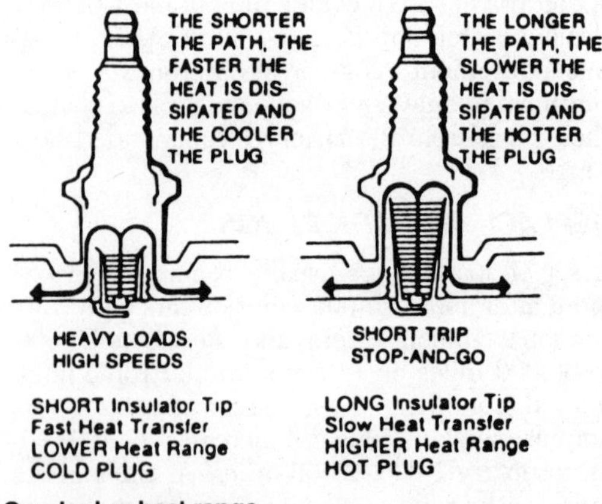

Spark plug heat range

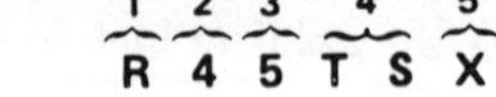

1 – R--INDICATES RESISTOR-TYPE PLUG.
2 – "4" INDICATES 14 mm THREADS.
3 – HEAT RANGE
4 – TS--TAPERED SEAT
S--EXTENDED TIP
5 – SPECIAL GAP

Spark plug type number chart, using the R45TSX as an example

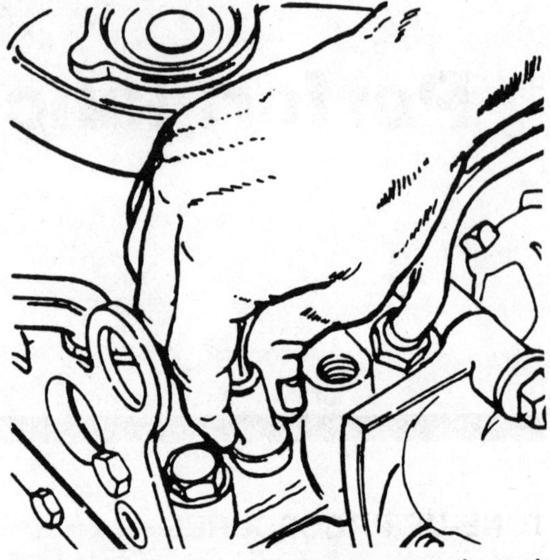

Twist and pull on the rubber boot to remove the spark plug wires; never pull on the wire itself

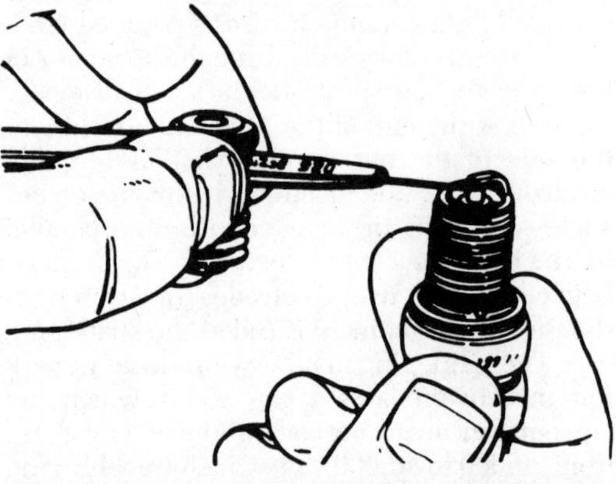

Always use a wire gauge to check the electrode gap; a flat feeler gauge may not give the proper reading

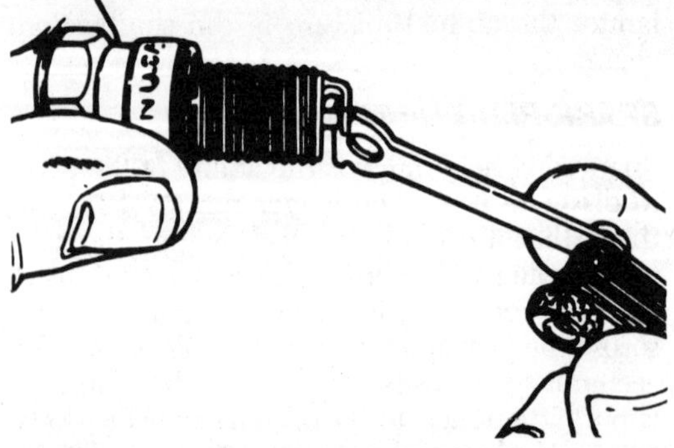

Adjust the electrode gap by bending the side electrode

use either a 5⁄8″ or 13⁄16″ size socket depending on the engine. Turn the socket counterclockwise to remove the plug. Be sure to hold the socket straight on the plug to avoid breaking the plug, or rounding off the hex on the plug.

4. Once the plug is out, check it against the plugs shown in the "Color" section of chapter four to determine engine condition. This is crucial since plug readings are vital signs of engine condition.

5. Use a round wire feeler gauge to check the plug gap. The correct size gauge should pass through the electrode gap with a slight drag. If

you're in doubt, try one size smaller and one larger. The smaller gauge should go through easily while the larger one shouldn't go through at all. If the gap is incorrect, use the electrode bending tool on the end of the gauge to adjust the gap. When adjusting the gap, always bend the side electrode. The center electrode is non-adjustable.

6. Squirt a drop of penetrating oil on the threads of the new plug and install it. Don't oil the threads too heavily. Turn the plug in clockwise by hand until it is snug.

7. When the plug is finger tight, tighten it with a wrench. If you don't have a torque wrench, tighten the plug as shown.

8. Install the plug boot firmly over the plug. Proceed to the next plug.

CHECKING AND REPLACING SPARK PLUG CABLES

Visually inspect the spark plug cables for burns, cuts, or breaks in the insulation. Check the spark plug boots and the nipples on the distributor cap and coil. Replace any damaged wiring. If no physical damage is obvious, the wires can be checked with an ohmmeter for excessive resistance. (See the tune-up and troubleshooting section.)

When installing a new set of spark plug cables, replace the cables one at a time so there will be no mixup. Start by replacing the longest cable first. Install the boot firmly over the spark plug. Route the wire exactly the same as the original. Insert the nipple firmly into the tower on the distributor cap. Repeat the process for each cable.

DISTRIBUTOR WIRING SEQUENCES AND FIRING ORDERS

To avoid confusion, replace spark plug wires one at a time.

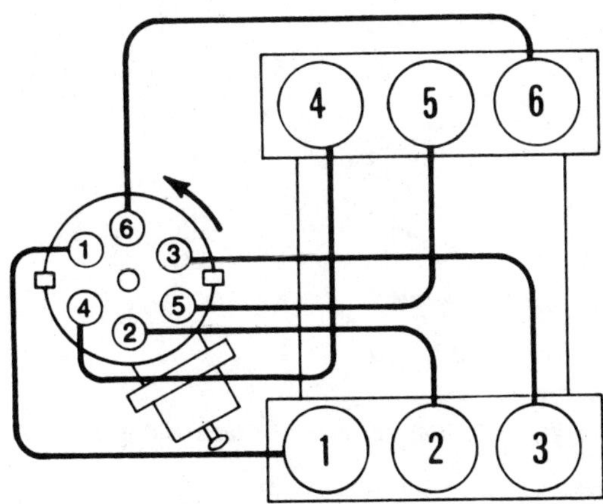

232 V6 wiring and distributor rotation
Firing order: 1-4-2-5-3-6
Rotation: counterclockwise

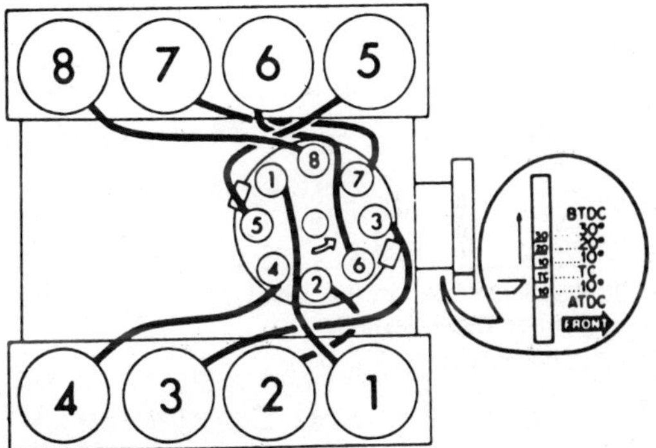

302, 352, 360, 390, 391, 460 V8 wiring and distributor rotation
Firing order: 1-5-4-2-6-3-7-8
Rotation: counterclockwise

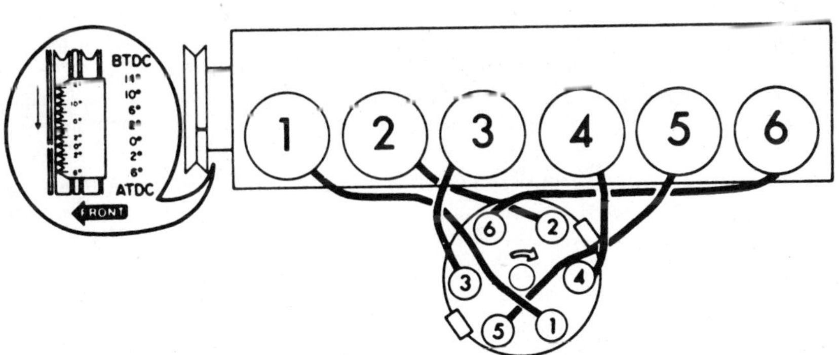

240, 300 inline six cylinder wiring and distributor rotation
Firing order: 1-5-3-6-2-4
Rotation: clockwise

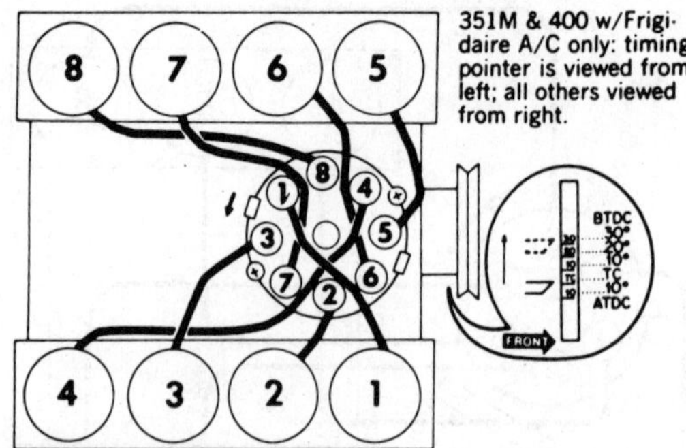

351W, 351M, 400 V8, 1978 and later wiring and distributor rotation
Firing order: 1-3-7-2-6-5-4
Rotation: counterclockwise

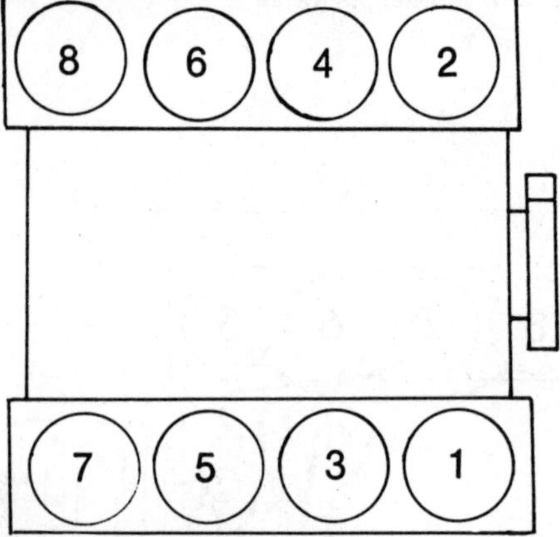

6.9L diesel cylinder arrangement
Firing order: 1-2-7-3-4-5-6-8

Breaker Points and Condenser

NOTE: *Some 1974 and all 1975 and later models are equipped with a breakerless, solidstate ignition system. The breakerless system eliminates the points and condenser completely.*

The points function as a circuit breaker for the primary circuit of the ignition system. The ignition coil must boost the 12 volts of electrical pressure supplied by the battery to as much as 25,000 volts in order to fire the spark plugs. To do this, the coil depends on the points and the condenser to make a clean break in the primary circuit.

The coil has both primary and secondary circuits. When the ignition is turned on, the battery supplies voltage through the coil and on to the points. The points are connected to ground, completing the primary circuit. As the current passes through the coil, a magnetic field is created in the iron center core of the coil. As the cam in the distributor turns, the points open and the primary circuit is interrupted. The magnetic field in the primary circuit of the coil collapses and cuts through the secondary circuit windings around the iron core. Because of the scientific phenomenon called "electromagnetic induction," the battery voltage is at this point increased to a level sufficient to fire the spark plugs.

When the points open, the electrical charge in the primary circuit jumps the gap created between the two open contacts of the points. If this electrical charge were not transferred elsewhere, the metal contacts of the points would melt and the gap between the points would start to change rapidly. If this gap is not maintained, the points will not break the primary circuit. If the primary circuit is not broken, the secondary circuit will not have enough voltage to fire the spark plugs.

The function of the condenser is to absorb excessive voltage from the points when they open and thus prevent the points from becoming pitted or burned.

The cycle must be completed by the ignition system every time a spark fires. In a V8 engine, all of the spark plugs fire once for every two revolutions of the crankshaft. That means that in one revolution, four spark plugs fire. So, when the engine is at an idle speed of 800 rpm, the points are opening and closing 3,200 times a minute.

There are two ways to check the breaker point gap: It can be done with a feeler gauge or a dwell meter. Either way you set the points, you are basically adjusting the amount of time that the points remain open. The time is measured in degrees of distributor rotation. When you measure the gap between the breaker points with a feeler gauge, you are setting the maximum amount the points will open when the rubbing block on the points is on a high point of the distributor cam. When you adjust the points with a dwell meter, you are adjusting the number of degrees that the points will remain closed before they start to open as a high point of the distributor cam approaches the rubbing block of the points.

When you replace a set of points, always replace the condenser at the same time. It's also wise to check the rotor for burns and cracks, and to replace it every other time you replace the points.

When you change the point gap or dwell, you will also have changed the ignition timing. So, if the point gap or dwell is changed, the ignition timing must be adjusted also. Changing the ignition timing, however, does not affect the dwell.

INSPECTION OF THE POINTS

1. Disconnect the high-tension wire from the top of the distributor and the coil.

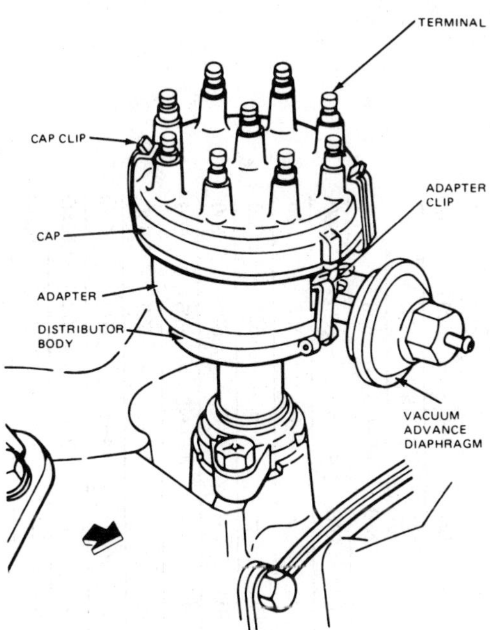

Typical distributor assembly

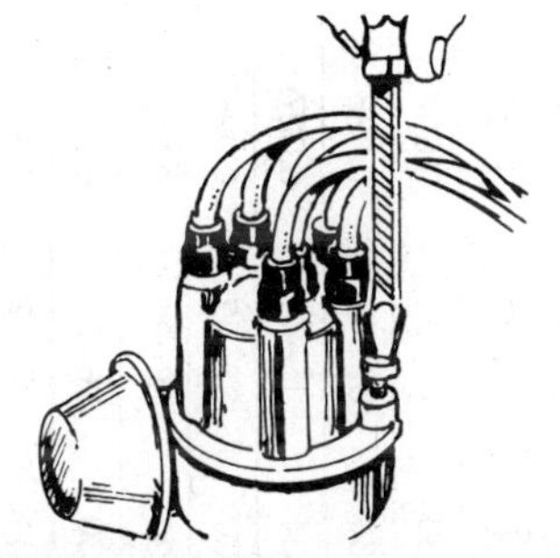

Remove the screws or metal clips to remove the distributor cap. Set the cap off to one side without removing any wires.

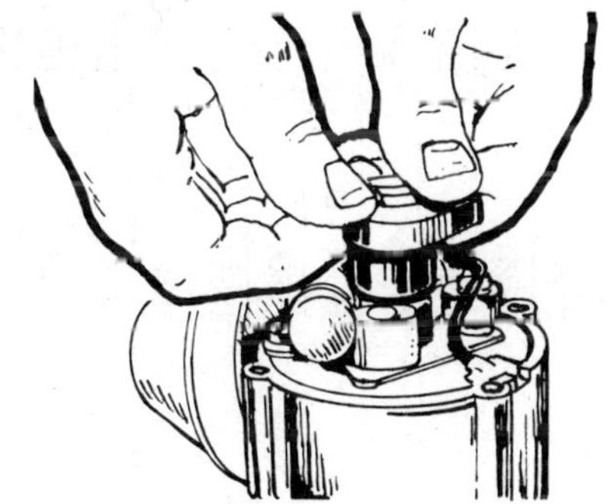

Remove the rotor by pulling straight up. It's a good idea to replace the rotor with each new set of points

2. Remove the distributor cap by prying off the spring clips on the side of the cap.

3. Remove the rotor from the distributor shaft by pulling it straight up. Examine the condition of the rotor. If it is cracked or the metal tip is excessively worn or burned, it should be replaced.

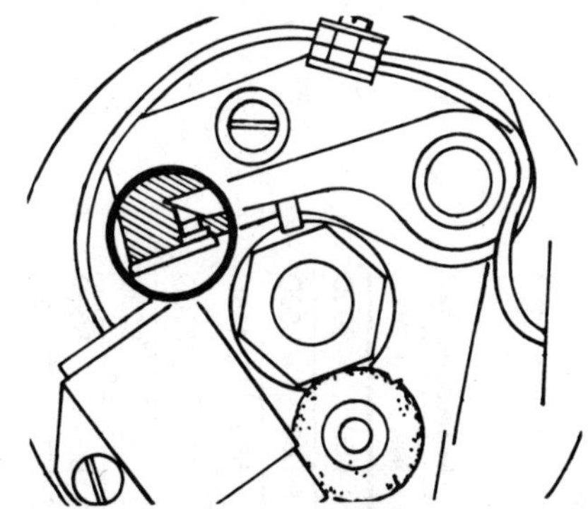

To check the point contact faces, move the breaker arm with a screwdriver blade. Also make sure the faces are properly aligned. Bend only the stationary contact if alignment is needed

4. Pry open the contacts of the points with a screwdriver and check the condition of the contacts. If they are excessively worn, burned or pitted, they should be replaced.

5. If the points are in good condition, adjust them, and replace the rotor and the distributor cap. If the points need to be replaced, follow the replacement procedure given below.

REPLACEMENT OF THE BREAKER POINTS AND CONDENSER

1. Remove the coil high-tension wire from top of the distributor cap. Remove the distributor cap from the distributor and place it out of the way. Remove the rotor from the distributor shaft.

2. Loosen the screw which holds the condenser lead to the body of the breaker points and remove the condenser lead from the points.

3. Remove the screw which holds and grounds the condenser to the distributor body. Remove the condenser from the distributor and discard it.

4. Remove the points assembly attaching screws and adjustment lockscrews. A screw-

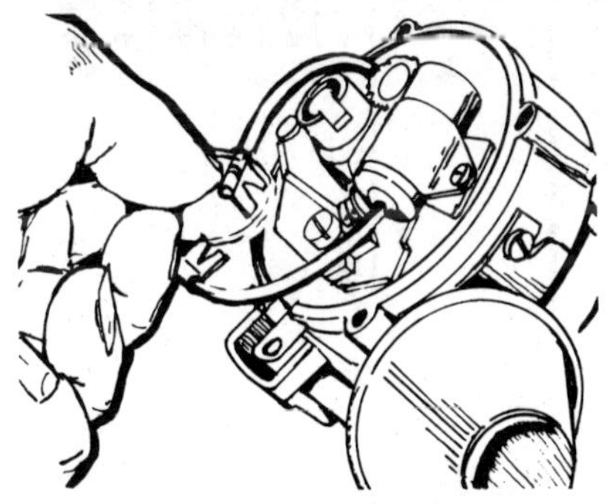

After removing the rotor, remove the wires from the points by first removing the screw

Tune-Up Specifications

When analyzing compression test results, look for uniformity among cylinders rather than specific pressures.

Year	Engine No. Cyl Displacement (cu in.)	Spark Plugs		Distributor		Ignition Timing (deg)		Intake Valve Opens (deg)	Fuel Pump Pressure (psi)	Idle Speed (rpm)▲	
		Orig Type	Gap (in.)	Point Dwell (deg)	Point Gap (in.)	Man	Auto			Man	Auto
1965	6-240	BTF-42	0.034	37–42	0.025	6	8	—	4–6	500	500D
	6-300	BTF-42	0.032	37–42	0.025	6	10	—	4–6	500	500D
	8-352	BF-42	0.034	26–31	0.017	6 ⑤	6 ⑤	—	5–6	550	475D
	8-361	BTF-31	0.030	26–31 ⑥	0.017 ⑦	12	12	—	4.5–6.5	525	500D
1966	6-240	BTF-31	0.032 ⑧	37–42	0.025	6	10	—	4–6	500	500D
	6-300	BTF-42	0.032 ⑧	37–42	0.025	6	10	—	4–6	500	500D
	8-352	BF-42	0.034	26–31	0.017	6 ⑤	6 ⑤	—	4.5–6.5	⑨	⑨
	8-361	BTF-31	0.030	26–31 ⑥	0.017 ⑦	10	10	—	4.5–6.5	525	500
	8-391	BTF-31	0.030	26–31 ⑥	0.017 ⑦	8	8	—	4.5–6.5	525	500
1967	6-240	BTF-42	0.034	37–42	0.025	6 ⑤	10 ⑤	12B	4–6	500	500D
	6-300	BTF-42	0.034	37–42	0.025	6 ⑤	10 ⑤	18B	4–6	500	500D
	8-352	BF-42	0.034	26–31	0.017	6 ⑤	6 ⑤	22B	4.5–6.5	⑨	⑨
	8-361	BTF-31	0.030	26–31	0.017	10	10	28B	4.5–6.5	525	500
	8-391	BTF-31	0.030	26–31	0.017	8	8	24B	4.5–6.5	525	500
1968	6-240	BTF-31	0.030	37–42	0.025	6	10	—	4–6	525	500
	6-300 LD	BTF-42	0.034	35–40	0.027	6	10	—	4–6	525	500
	6-300 HD	BTF-31	0.030	37–42	0.025	6	10	—	4–6	525	500
	8-361	BTF-31	0.030	26–31	0.017	10	10	—	4.5–6.5	525	500
	8-391	BTF-31	0.030	26–31	0.017	8	8	—	4.5–6.5	525	500
1969	6-240	BTF-42	0.034	37–42	0.025	6	6	—	4–6	600	525D
	6-300	BTF-42	0.034	35–40	0.027	6	6	—	4–6	600	525D
	8-302	BF-31	0.030	24–29	0.017	6	6	—	5–6	625	550D

	8-361	BF-32	0.030	26–31 ⑥	0.017 ⑦	6	6	—	4.5–6.5	550	500D
	8-391	BF-32	0.030	26–31 ⑥	0.017 ⑦	6	6	—	4.5–6.5	550	500D
1970	6-240 F-100	BTF-42B	0.035	35–40	0.027	6B	6B	12B	4–6	850/600	575
	6-240 F-250	BTF-42B	0.035	35–40	0.027	6B	6B	12B	4–6	600	550
	6-300 F-100	BTF-42B	0.035	35–40	0.027	6B	6B	12B	4–6	775/550	550
	6-300 F-250	BTF-42B	0.035	37–42	0.025	6B	6B	12B	4–6	600	550
	8-302	BTF-31B	0.030	24–29	0.021	6B	6B	16B	4–6	800/500	675
	8-360	BF-32B	0.035	24–29	0.017	6B	6B	13B	4–6	650	550
	8-390	BF-32B	0.035	24–29	0.021	6B	6B	13B	4–6	650	550
1971	6-240 F-100	BF-42B	0.035	35–40	0.027	6B	6B	12B	4–6	850/650	600
	6-240 F-250	BTF-31B	0.030	35–40	0.027	6B	6B	12B	4–6	600	550
	6-300 F-100	BTF-42B	0.035	35–40	0.027	6B	6B	12B	4–6	775/500	550
	6-300 F-250	BTF-31B	0.030	37–42	0.025	6B	6B	12B	4–6	600	550
	8-302	BTF-31B	0.030	24–29	0.021	6B	6B	16B	4–6	800/600	600
	8-360 F-100	BF-32B	0.035	24–29	0.017	6B	6B	13B	4–6	650	550
	8-360 F-250	BF-32B	0.035	26–31	0.017	6B	6B	13B	4–6	650	550
	8-390 F-100	BF-32B	0.035	24–29	0.021	6B	6B	13B	4–6	650	550
	8-390 F-250	BF-32B	0.035	26–31	0.017	6B	6B	13B	4–6	650	550
1972	6-240	BF-42B	0.035	35–39	0.027	6B	6B	12B	4–6	850/500	600
	6-300	BF-42B	0.035	35–39	0.027	6B	6B	12B	4–6	600	550
	8-302	BF-42B	0.035	26–30	0.017	6B	6B	16B	4–6	800/500	600
	8-360 F-100	BF-42B	0.035	26–30	0.017	8B	6B	13B	4–6	650	550
	8-360 F-250	BF-42B	0.035	26–30	0.017	6B	6B	13B	4–6	650	550
	8-390	BF-42B	0.035	26–30	0.017	6B	6B	13B	4–6	750/550	550
1973	6-240	BRF-42B	0.035	33–39	0.027	6B	6B	12B	4–6	850/600	650
	6-300	BRF-42B	0.035	33–39	0.027	10B	10B	12B	4–6	600	550
	8-302	BRF-42B	0.035	24–30	0.017	6B	6B	16B	4–6	1000	650
	8-360 F-100	BRF-42B	0.035	24–30	0.017	6B	3B	13B	4–6	850	700

Tune-Up Specifications (cont.)

When analyzing compression test results, look for uniformity among cylinders rather than specific pressures.

Year	Engine No. Cyl Displacement (cu in.)	Spark Plugs		Distributor		Ignition Timing (deg)		Intake Valve Opens (deg)	Fuel Pump Pressure (psi)	Idle Speed (rpm)▲	
		Orig Type	Gap (in.)	Point Dwell (deg)	Point Gap (in.)	Man	Auto			Man	Auto
1973	8-360 F-250	BRF-42B	0.035	24–30	0.017	6B	6B	13B	4–6	650	550
	8-390 F-100	BRF-42B	0.035	24–30	0.017	—	6B	13B	4–6	—	700
	8-390 F-250	BRF-42B	0.035	24–30	0.017	6B	6B	13B	4–6	650	550
1974	6-240	BRF-42B	0.034	33–39	0.027	6B	6B	12B	4–6	850/600	650
	6-300 F-100	BRF-31B	0.034	33–39 ①	0.027 ①	6B	—	12B	4–6	700	—
	6-300 F-250	BRF-31B	0.034	33–39 ①	0.027 ①	10B	10B	12B	4–6	600	550
	8-302	BRF-42B	②	24–30 ①	0.017 ①	②	②	16B	4–6	②	②
	8-360	BRF-42B	②	24–30 ①	0.017 ①	6B	3B ③	13B	4–6	②	②
	8-390	BRF-42B	②	24–30 ①	0.017 ①	②	②	13B	4–6	②	②
	8-460	ARF-52B	②	24–30 ①	0.017 ①	—	14B	—	4–6	—	650
1975–76	6-300	BRF-42B	0.044	Electronic		②	②	12B	4–6	②	②
	8-302	ARF-42B	0.044	Electronic		12B	6B	16B	4–6	850/550	650

	8-360	BRF-42B	②	Electronic	②	②	13B	4–6	②	②
	8-390	BRF-42B	②	Electronic	②	②	13B	4–6	②	②
	8-460	ARF-52B	②	Electronic	—	12B	—	4–6	—	650
1977	6-300	BSF-42B	0.044 ④	Electronic	②	②	12B	5–7	②	②
	8-302	ASF-42B	0.044	Electronic	②	②	16B	6–8	②	②
	8-351	ASF-42B	0.44	Electronic	②	②	—	6–8	②	②
	8-400	ASF-42B	0.044	Electronic	②	②	—	6–8	②	②
	8-460	ASF-42B	0.044	Electronic	②	②	—	5–7	②	②

① Breakerless ignition available in 1974
② See underhood specifications sticker
③ With underhood sticker #659: 6B
④ Engines built after 11/15/76: 0.054
⑤ With Exhaust Emission—TDC
⑥ Transistor ignition—22–24
⑦ Transistor ignition .020
⑧ Auto. Trans.—0.030
⑨ With exhaust emission:
Man. Trans.—.625
Auto. Trans.—550
Without exhaust emission
Man. Trans.—550
Auto. Trans.—475
▲ Where two figures are separated by a slash, the lower of the two is the rpm with the idle solenoid disconnected.

Tune-Up Specifications
1978–80

(For 1979 and 1980 Tune-Up Specifications consult the Vehicle Emissions Control Label, which is located on the engine of the vehicle. This decal will contain a calibration number which when used in conjunction with the chart below will yield the required tune-up information. If the information given in this chart disagrees with the information on the decal, use the information on the decal.)

Calibration	Spark Plug Gap	Ignition Timing	Fast Idle RPM High Cam	Fast Idle RPM Kick Down	Curb Idle rpm A/C ① Off/On	Curb Idle rpm Non A/C	Tsp Off rpm A/C	Tsp Off rpm Non A/C
9-87G-RO	.042–.046	8°BTDC	2700	—	—	600	—	—
9-97J-RO	.042–.046	8°BTDC	—	1600	650	—	—	—
9-97J-R11	.042–.046	8°BTDC	—	1600	650	—	—	—

① Only for A/C-TSP equipped, A/C compressor electromagnetic clutch deenergized.

Tune-Up Specifications
1981

(For 1981 Tune-Up Specifications consult the Vehicle Emissions Control Label, which is located on the engine of the vehicle. This decal will contain a calibration number which when used in conjunction with the chart below will yield the required tune-up information. If the information given in this chart disagrees with the information on the decal, use the information on the decal.)

Calibration Number	Engine	Spark Plug Gap	Ignition Timing °BTDC	Timing RPM	Fast Idle rpm High CAM	Fast Idle rpm Kick Down	Curb Idle rpm A/C On	Curb Idle rpm A/C off	Curb Idle rpm Non A/C
1-57G-R1	4.1L	.042–.046	4	800	2200	—	—	—	750
1-57G-R10	4.1L	.042–.046	4	800	2050	—	—	—	700
1-58-R0	4.1L	.042–.046	10	800	2000	—	—	—	575
1-51D-R0	4.9L	.042–.046	6	800	—	1400	700	600	600
1-51D-R10	4.9L	.042–.046	6	800	—	1250	650	550	550
1-51D-R12	4.9L	.042–.046	6	800	—	1250	650	550	550
1-51E-R0	4.9L	.042–.046	6	800	—	1400	700	600	600
1-51F-R0	4.9L	.042–.046	6	800	—	1250	650	550	550
1-51G-R0	4.9L	.042–.046	6	800	—	1250	650	550	550
1-51H-R0	4.9L	.042–.046	6	800	—	1250	650	550	550
1-51K-R0	4.9L	.042–.046	6	800	—	1250	650	550	550
1-51L-R0	4.9L	.042–.046	6	800	—	1250	650	550	550
1-51E-R10	4.9L	.042–.046	6	800	—	1400	700	600	600
1-51F-R10	4.9L	.042–.046	6	800	—	1250	650	550	550
1-51G-R10	4.9L	.042–.046	6	800	—	1250	650	550	550
1-51H-R10	4.9L	.042–.046	6	800	—	1250	650	550	550
1-51K-R10	4.9L	.042–.046	6	800	—	1250	650	550	550
1-51L-R10	4.9L	.042–.046	6	800	—	1250	650	550	550
1-51S-R0	4.9L	.042–.046	6	800	—	1400	700	600	600
1-51S-R10	4.9L	.042–.046	6	800	—	1250	650	550	550
1-51T-R0	4.9L	.042–.046	6	800	—	120	650	550	550

Tune-Up Specifications (cont.)
1981

(For 1981 Tune-Up Specifications consult the Vehicle Emissions Control Label, which is located on the engine of the vehicle. This decal will contain a calibration number which when used in conjunction with the chart below will yield the required tune-up information. If the information given in this chart disagrees with the information on the decal, use the information on the decal.)

Calibration Number	Engine	Spark Plug Gap	Ignition Timing °BTDC	Timing RPM	Fast Idle rpm		Curb Idle rpm		
					High CAM	Kick Down	A/C On	A/C off	Non A/C
1-52G-R0	4.9L	.042–.046	10	800	—	1400	—	—	550
1-52H-R0	4.9L	.042–.046	10	800	—	1250	—	—	500
1-52K-R0	4.9L	.042–.046	10	800	—	1250	—	—	500
1-52L-R0	4.9L	.042–.046	10	800	—	1250	—	—	500
1-52G-R10	4.9L	.042–.046	10	800	—	1400	—	—	550
1-52H-R10	4.9L	.042–.046	10	800	—	1250	—	—	500
1-52K-R10	4.9L	.042–.046	10	800	—	1250	—	—	500
1-52L-R10	4.9L	.042–.046	10	800	—	1250	—	—	500
1-52S-R0	4.9L	.042–.046	10	800	—	1400	—	—	550
1-52T-R0	4.9L	.042–.046	10	800	—	1250	—	—	550
5-77-R1	4.9L	.042–.046	10	800	—	1500	—	—	600(A)
5-78-R1	4.9L	.042–.046	10	800	—	1500	—	—	700(M)
9-77J-R12	4.9L	.042–.046	12	800	1600	—	—	—	700
9-77S-R10	4.9L	.042–.046	10	800	1600	—	—	—	700
9-78J-R0	4.9L	.042–.046	12	800	—	1500	—	—	550
9-78J-R11	4.9L	.042–.046	12	800	1600	—	—	—	550
1-53D-R0	5.0L	.042–.046	8	800	2200	—	—	—	700
1-53F-R0	5.0L	.042–.046	8	800	2050	—	—	—	650
1-53G-R0	5.0L	.042–.046	8	800	2050	—	—	—	650
1-53H-R0	5.0L	.042–.046	8	800	2050	—	—	—	650
1-53K-R0	5.0L	.042–.046	8	800	2050	—	—	—	650
1-53D-R10	5.0L	.042–.046	8	800	2200	—	—	—	700
1-53G-R10	5.0L	.042–.046	8	800	2050	—	—	—	650
1-53K-R10	5.0L	.042–.046	8	800	2050	—	—	—	650
1-53D-R12	5.0L	.042–.046	8	800	2050	—	—	—	650
1-53F-R11	5.0L	.042–.046	8	800	2050	—	—	—	650
1-53G-R12	5.0L	.042–.046	8	800	2050	—	—	—	650
1-53H-R11	5.0L	.042–.046	8	800	2050	—	—	—	650
1-53K-R13	5.0L	.042–.046	8	800	2050	—	—	—	650
1-54D-R1	5.0L	.042–.046	8	800	2000	—	—	—	575
1-54K-R0	5.0L	.042–.046	8	800	1850	—	—	—	525
1-54F-R0	5.0L	.042–.046	8	800	2000	—	—	—	575
1-54G-R0	5.0L	.042–.046	8	800	2000	—	—	—	575
1-54H-R0	5.0L	.042–.046	8	800	2000	—	—	—	575
1-54L-R2	5.0L	.042–.046	8	800	2000	—	—	—	575

Tune-Up Specifications (cont.)
1981

(For 1981 Tune-Up Specifications consult the Vehicle Emissions Control Label, which is located on the engine of the vehicle. This decal will contain a calibration number which when used in conjunction with the chart below will yield the required tune-up information. If the information given in this chart disagrees with the information on the decal, use the information on the decal.)

Calibration Number	Engine	Spark Plug Gap	Ignition Timing °BTDC	Timing RPM	Fast Idle rpm		Curb Idle rpm		
					High CAM	Kick Down	A/C On	A/C off	Non A/C
1-54L-R10	5.0L	.042–.046	8	800	1850	—	—	—	525
1-54P-R0	5.0L	.042–.046	—	—	1350	—	—	—	—
1-54R-R0	5.0L	.042–.046	—	—	1350	—	—	—	—
1-54P-R10	5.0L	.042–.046	—	—	1350	—	—	—	—
1-54R-R10	5.0L	.042–.046	—	—	1200	—	—	—	—
7-79-R1	5.0L	.042–.046	6	800	—	1250	—	—	750
7-80-R0	5.0L	.042–.046	6	800	—	1500	—	—	650
1-59A-R0	5.8L	.042–.046	10	800	2000	—	650	—	650
1-59B-R0	5.8L	.042–.046	10	800	2000	—	650	—	650
1-59G-R0	5.8L	.042–.046	10	800	2000	—	650	—	650
1-59H-R0	5.8L	.042–.046	10	800	2000	—	650	—	650
1-59K-R0	5.8L	.042–.046	10	800	2000	—	650	—	650
1-59A-R10	5.8L	.042–.046	10	800	2000	—	650	—	650
1-59B-R10	5.8L	.042–.046	10	800	1850	—	600	—	600
1-59G-R10	5.8L	.042–.046	10	800	1850	—	600	—	600
1-59H-R10	5.8L	.042–.046	10	800	1850	—	600	—	600
1-59K-R10	5.8L	.042–.046	10	800	1850	—	600	—	600
1-60A-R0	5.8L	.042–.046	6	800	2200	—	—	—	—
1-60B-R0	5.8L	.042–.046	6	800	2200	—	—	—	—
1-60H-R1	5.8L	.042–.046	6	800	2000	—	625	550	550
1-60J-R0	5.8L	.042–.046	6	800	2000	—	625	550	550
1-60K-R0	5.8L	.042–.046	6	800	2000	—	625	550	550
1-60A-R10	5.8L	.042–.046	6	800	2000	—	625	550	550
1-60B-R10	5.8L	.042–.046	6	800	1850	—	575	500	500
1-60H-R10	5.8L	.042–.046	6	800	1850	—	575	500	500
1-60J-R10	5.8L	.042–.046	6	800	1850	—	575	500	500
1-60K-R10	5.8L	.042–.046	6	800	1850	—	575	500	500
1-63T-R0	5.8L	.042–.046	—	—	1700	—	—	—	—
1-64A-R0	5.8L	.042–.046	8	800	2000	—	625	550	550
1-64G-R1	5.8L	.042–.046	10	600	2000	—	625	550	550
1-64H-R2	5.8L	.042–.046	10	600	2000	—	625	550	550
1-64R-R1	5.8L	.042–.046	—	—	1650	—	—	—	—
1-64S-R0	5.8L	.042–.046	—	—	1500	—	—	—	—
1-64T-R0	5.8L	.042–.046	—	—	1500	—	—	—	—
7-76J-R11	5.8L	.042–.046	6	800	1700	—	—	—	600

Tune-Up Specifications (cont.)
1981

(For 1981 Tune-Up Specifications consult the Vehicle Emissions Control Label, which is located on the engine of the vehicle. This decal will contain a calibration number which when used in conjunction with the chart below will yield the required tune-up information. If the information given in this chart disagrees with the information on the decal, use the information on the decal.)

Calibration Number	Engine	Spark Plug Gap	Ignition Timing °BTDC	Timing RPM	Fast Idle rpm High CAM	Fast Idle rpm Kick Down	Curb Idle rpm A/C On	Curb Idle rpm A/C off	Curb Idle rpm Non A/C
9-71J-R10	5.8L	.042–.046	10	800	1750	—	—	—	600
9-71J-R11	5.8L	.042–.046	10	800	1750	—	—	—	600
9-72J-R11	5.8L	.042–.046	10	800	2000	—	—	—	600
9-72J-R12	5.8L	.042–.046	10	800	2000	—	—	—	600
9-83G-R12	6.1L	.042–.046	6	800	2200	—	—	—	600
9-83H-R11	6.1L	.042–.046	6	800	2500	—	—	—	600
9-83H-R14	6.1L	.042–.046	2	800	2500	—	—	—	600
9-73J-R11	6.6L	.042–.046	6	800	1750	—	—	—	600
9-73J-R12	6.6L	.042–.046	6	800	1750	—	—	—	600
9-74J-R11	6.6L	.042–.046	3	800	2000	—	—	—	600
9-74J-R12	6.6L	.042–.046	6	800	2000	—	—	—	600
9-87G-R11	7.0L	.042–.046	6	800	2700	—	—	—	600
9-97J-R0	7.5L	.042–.046	8	800	1600	—	—	—	650
7-93J-R0	7.8L	.038–.042	10	800	2500	—	—	—	600
7-95J-R0	8.8L	.038–.042	10	800	2500	—	—	—	600

Tune-Up Specifications
1982

(For 1982 Tune-Up Specifications consult the Vehicle Emissions Control Label, which is located on the engine of the vehicle. This decal will contain a calibration number which when used in conjunction with the chart below will yield the required tune-up information. If the information given in this chart disagrees with the information on the decal, use the information on the decal.)

Calibration	Engine	Spark Plug Gap	Ignition Timing	Fast Idle rpm	Curb Idle rpm
2-54R-R0	5.0L	.042–.046	—	1350	—
2-54X-R1	5.0L	.042–.046	12° BTDC	2100	650
1-63T-R0	5.8L	.042–.046	—	1700	—
1-63T-R10B	5.0L	.042–.046	—	1700	—
1-64H-R2	5.8L	.042–.046	10° BTDC	2000	625
1-64R-R1	5.8L	.042–.046	—	1650	—
1-64S-R0	5.8L	.042–.046	—	1650	—
1-64T-R0	5.8L	.042–.046	—	1650	—
1-64T-R10	5.8L	.042–.046	—	1650	—
2-63Y-R10B	5.8L	.042–.046	—	1700	—
2-64X-R0	5.8L	.042–.046	14° BTDC	2000	625
2-64Y-R10B	5.8L	.042–.046	—	1650	—

Tune-Up Specifications (cont.)
1982

(For 1982 Tune-Up Specifications consult the Vehicle Emissions Control Label, which is located on the engine of the vehicle. This decal will contain a calibration number which when used in conjunction with the chart below will yield the required tune-up information. If the information given in this chart disagrees with the information on the decal, use the information on the decal.)

Calibration	Engine	Spark Plug Gap	Ignition Timing	Fast Idle rpm	Curb Idle rpm
9-77J-R12	4.9L	.042–.046	12° BTDC	1600	—
9-77G-R10	4.9L	.042–.046	10° BTDC	1600	—
9-78J-R0	4.9L	.042–.046	12° BTDC	1600	—
9-78J-R11	4.9L	.042–.046	12° BTDC	1600	—
2-75J-R17	5.8L	.042–.046	5° BTDC	1500	700 ④
2-76J-R17	5.8L	.042–.046	5° BTDC	1500	—
7-75J-R14	5.8L	.042–.046	6° BTDC	1500	700 ④
7-76J-R11	5.8L	.042–.046	6° BTDC	1700	—
7-76J-R13	5.8L	.042–.046	12° BTDC	1600	500
7-76J-R14	5.8L	.042–.046	6° BTDC	1700	—
7-76J-R15	5.8L	.042–.046	6° BTDC	1700	—
9-83G-R12	6.1L	.042–.046	6° BTDC	2200	600
9-83H-R11	6.1L	.042–.046	6° BTDC	2500	600
9-83H-R14	6.1L	.042–.046	2° BTDC	2500	600
9-73J-R11	6.6L	.042–.046	6° BTDC	1750	600 ④
9-73J-R12	6.6L	.042–.046	6° BTDC	1750	600 ④
9-73J-R13	6.6L	.042–.046	6° BTDC	1750	600 ④
9-73J-R14	6.6L	.042–.046	6° BTDC	1750	600 ④
9-74J-R11	6.6L	.042–.046	6° BTDC	2000	—
9-74J-R12	6.6L	.042–.046	6° BTDC	2000	—
9-74J-R13	6.6L	.042–.046	3° BTDC	2000	—
9-74J-R14	6.6L	.042–.046	6° BTDC	2000	—
9-87G-R11	7.0L	.042–.046	6° BTDC	—	600
9-97J-R12	7.5L	.042–.046	8° BTDC	—	650

① A/C on—50 RPM Less if NON A/C
② A/C on—600 NON A/C
③ 100 RPM Less for NON A/C or A/C off
④ NON A/C.

Tune-Up Specifications
1983

(For 1983 Tune-Up Specifications consult the Vehicle Emissions Control Label, which is located on the engine of the vehicle. This decal will contain a calibration number which when used in conjunction with the chart below will yield the required tune-up information. If the information given in this chart disagrees with the information on the decal, use the information on the decal.)

Calibration	Engine	Spark Plug Gap	Ignition Timing	Fast Idle rpm	Curb Idle rpm
3-41D-R01	2.0L	.032–.036	6° BTDC	2000	800
3-41D-R10	2.0L	.032–.036	6° BTDC	2000	800
3-41P-R02	2.0L	.032–.036	6° BTDC	2000	800

Tune-Up Specifications (cont.)
1983

(For 1983 Tune-Up Specifications consult the Vehicle Emissions Control Label, which is located on the engine of the vehicle. This decal will contain a calibration number which when used in conjunction with the chart below will yield the required tune-up information. If the information given in this chart disagrees with the information on the decal, use the information on the decal.)

Calibration	Engine	Spark Plug Gap	Ignition Timing	Fast Idle rpm	Curb Idle rpm
3-41P-R11	2.0L	.032–.036	6° BTDC	2000	800
3-41P-R12	2.0L	.032–.036	6° BTDC	2000	800
3-49S-R01	2.3L	.032–.036	6° BTDC	2000	850 ①
3-49S-R10	2.3L	.032–.036	6° BTDC	2000	850 ①
3-49S-R11	2.3L	.032–.036	6° BTDC	2000	850 ①
3-49X-R01	2.3L	.032–.036	10° BTDC	2000	850
3-49X-R11	2.3L	.032–.036	10° BTDC	2000	850
3-50S-R01	2.3L	.032–.036	8° BTDC	2000	750
3-50S-R01	2.3L	.032–.036	8° BTDC	2000	800
3-50X-R10	2.3L	.032–.036	8° BTDC	2000	800
3-50X-R11	2.3L	.032–.036	10° BTDC	2000	800
3-49G-R20	2.3L	.042–.046	6° BTDC	2000	850 ①
3-49H-R17	2.3L	.042–.046	6° BTDC	2000	850 ①
3-49S-R16	2.3L	.042–.046	6° BTDC	2000	850 ①
3-49T-R20	2.3L	.042–.046	6° BTDC	2000	850 ①
3-49T-R20	2.3L	.042–.046	6° BTDC	2000	850 ①
3-49Y-R19	2.3L	.042–.046	10° BTDC	2000	850 ①
3-50S-R18	2.3L	.042–.046	6° BTDC	2000	800
3-50Y-R18	2.3L	.042–.046	10° BTDC	2000	800
4-61F-R00	2.8L	.042–.046	10° BTDC	3000	850–900 ②
4-62D-R00	2.8L	.042–.046	10° BTDC	3000	850–900 ②
4-62S-R01	2.8L	.042–.046	10° BTDC	3000	850–900 ②
4-62S-R10	2.8L	.042–.046	10° BTDC	3000	800–900 ③
3-55D-R00	3.8L	.042–.046	2° BTDC	1300	550
3-56D-R00	3.8L	.042–.046	10° BTDC	2200	550
3-51D-R00	4.9L	.042–.046	6° BTDC	1600	700 ④
3-51E-R01	4.9L	.042–.046	6° BTDC	1600	700 ④
2-63Y-R12	5.8L	.042–.046	—	1700	750
2-64X-R00	5.8L	.042–.046	14° BTDC	2000	625 ⑩
2-64Y-R11	5.8L	.042–.046	—	1650	600
2-64Y-R12	5.8L	.042–.046	—	1650	600
5-77-R01	4.9L	.042–.046	10° BTDC	1500	600 ⑪
5-78-R01	4.9L	.042–.046	10° BTDC	1500	600 ⑪
9-77J-R12	4.9L	.042–.046	12° BTDC	1600	700
9-77S-R10	4.9L	.042–.046	10° BTDC	1600	700
9-78J-R00	4.9L	.042–.046	12° BTDC	1600	550

Tune-Up Specifications (cont.)
1983

(For 1983 Tune-Up Specifications consult the Vehicle Emissions Control Label, which is located on the engine of the vehicle. This decal will contain a calibration number which when used in conjunction with the chart below will yield the required tune-up information. If the information given in this chart disagrees with the information on the decal, use the information on the decal.)

Calibration	Engine	Spark Plug Gap	Ignition Timing	Fast Idle rpm	Curb Idle rpm
9-78J-R11	4.9L	.042–.046	12° BTDC	1600	550
7-79-R01	5.0L	.042–.046	6° BTDC	1250	750
7-80-R00	5.0L	.042–.046	6° BTDC	1600	650
2-75A-R10	5.8L	.042–.046	8° BTDC	1500	650
2-75J-R20	5.8L	.042–.046	8° BTDC	1500	650
2-76A-R10	5.8L	.042–.046	8° BTDC	1500	650
2-76J-R20	5.8L	.042–.046	8° BTDC	1500	650
9-83G-R12	6.1L	.042–.046	6° BTDC	2200	600
9-83G-R14	6.1L	.042–.046	6° BTDC	1600	600
9-83H-R11	6.1L	.042–.046	6° BTDC	2500	600
9-83H-R14	6.1L	.042–.046	2° BTDC	2500	600
9-87G-R11	7.0L	.042–.046	6° BTDC	2700	600
9-97J-R13	7.5L	.042–.046	8° BTDC	1600	600
9-98S-R00	7.5L	.042–.046	6° BTDC	1500	600

① 800—w/o Power Steering
② 750–800—Auto. Trans
③ 700–800—Auto. Trans
④ 600—Non A/c or A/c off
⑤ 550—Non A/c or A/c off
⑥ 800—A/c on
⑦ 600—Non A/c or A/c off
⑧ 675—A/c on
⑨ 900—Throttle solenoid on, 600 throttle solenoid off
⑩ 550—A/c off and Non A/c
⑪ 700—Manual Trans.

Tune-Up Specifications
1984

(For 1984 Tune-Up Specifications consult the Vehicle Emissions Control Label, which is located on the engine of the vehicle. This decal will contain a calibration number which when used in conjunction with the chart below will yield the required tune-up information. If the information given in this chart disagrees with the information on the decal, use the information on the decal.)

Calibration	Engine	Spark Plug Gap	Ignition Timing	Fast Idle rpm	Curb Idle rpm
3-41P-R15	2.0L	.032–.036	8° BTDC	2000	800
3-41S-R18	2.0L	.032–.036	9° BTDC	2000	800
3-49G-R20	2.3L	.042–.046	6° BTDC	2000	850 ①
3-49G-R20	2.3L	.042–.046	6° BTDC	2200	850 ①
3-49G-R17	2.3L	.042–.046	6° BTDC	2000	850 ①
3-49S-R16	2.3L	.042–.046	6° BTDC	2000	850 ①
3-49T-R20	2.3L	.042–.046	6° BTDC	2000	850 ①
3-49Y-R20	2.3L	.042–.046	10° BTDC	2000	850 ①
3-50H-R18	2.3L	.042–.046	6° BTDC	2000	800
3-50S-R18	2.3L	.042–.046	6° BTDC	2000	800

Tune-Up Specifications (cont.)

1984

(For 1984 Tune-Up Specifications consult the Vehicle Emissions Control Label, which is located on the engine of the vehicle. This decal will contain a calibration number which when used in conjunction with the chart below will yield the required tune-up information. If the information given in this chart disagrees with the information on the decal, use the information on the decal.)

Calibration	Engine	Spark Plug Gap	Ignition Timing	Fast Idle rpm	Curb Idle rpm
3-50Y-R18	2.3L	.042–.046	10° BTDC	2000	800
4-61F-R00	2.8L	.042–.046	10° BTDC	3000	800–900 ②
4-61F-R10	2.8L	.042–.046	10° BTDC	3000	800–900 ②
4-61G-R00	2.8L	.042–.046	10° BTDC	3000	700–800
4-61K-R01	2.8L	.042–.046	10° BTDC	3000	850–950 ②
4-61S-R00	2.8L	.042–.046	10° BTDC	3000	800–900 ②
4-62D-R00	2.8L	.042–.046	10° BTDC	3000	800–900 ②
4-62D-R10	2.8L	.042–.046	10° BTDC	3000	800–900 ②
4-62S-R01	2.8L	.042–.046	10° BTDC	3000	800–900 ②
4-62S-R10	2.8L	.042–.046	10° BTDC	3000	800–900 ②
4-51D-R01	4.9L	.042–.046	10° BTDC	1600	600–700 ③
4-51E-R00	4.9L	.042–.046	10° BTDC	1600	600–700 ③
4-51K-R00	4.9L	.042–.046	10° BTDC	1600	600–700 ③
4-51L-R00	4.9L	.042–.046	10° BTDC	1600	600–700 ③
4-51R-R00	4.9L	.042–.046	10° BTDC	1600	600–700 ③
4-51S-R00	4.9L	.042–.046	10° BTDC	1600	600–700 ③
4-51S-R01	4.9L	.042–.046	10° BTDC	1600	600–700 ③
4-51S-R02	4.9L	.042–.046	10° BTDC	1600	600–700 ③
4-51T-R00	4.9L	.042–.046	10° BTDC	1600	600–700 ③
4-51Z-R00	4.9L	.042–.046	10° BTDC	1600	600–700 ③
4-51L-R00	4.9L	.042–.046	10° BTDC	1600	600–700 ③
4-52R-R00	4.9L	.042–.046	10° BTDC	1600	600–700 ③
4-52S-R00	4.9L	.042–.046	10° BTDC	1600	600–700 ③
4-52T-R00	4.9L	.042–.046	10° BTDC	1600	600–700 ③
4-52W-R00	4.9L	.042–.046	10° BTDC	1600	600–700 ③
4-53F-R00	5.0L	.042–.046	8° BTDC	2100	800 ④
4-53F-R10	5.0L	.042–.046	8° BTDC	2100	800 ④
4-53G-R00	5.0L	.042–.046	8° BTDC	2100	800 ④
4-53G-R10	5.0L	.042–.046	8° BTDC	2100	800 ④
4-53K-R00	5.0L	.042–.046	8° BTDC	2100	800 ④
4-53K-R10	5.0L	.042–.046	8° BTDC	2100	800 ④
4-53Z-R00	5.0L	.042–.046	8° BTDC	2100	800 ④
4-53Z-R10	5.0L	.042–.046	8° BTDC	2100	800 ④
4-54E-R00	5.0L	.042–.046	8° BTDC	2100	800 ④
4-53E-R10	5.0L	.042–.046	8° BTDC	2100	800 ④
4-54J-R00	5.0L	.042–.046	8° BTDC	2100	800 ④

Tune-Up Specifications (cont.)
1984

(For 1984 Tune-Up Specifications consult the Vehicle Emissions Control Label, which is located on the engine of the vehicle. This decal will contain a calibration number which when used in conjunction with the chart below will yield the required tune-up information. If the information given in this chart disagrees with the information on the decal, use the information on the decal.)

Calibration	Engine	Spark Plug Gap	Ignition Timing	Fast Idle rpm	Curb Idle rpm
4-54J-R10	5.0L	.042–.046	8° BTDC	2100	800 ④
4-54L-R00	5.0L	.042–.046	8° BTDC	2100	800 ④
4-54L-R10	5.0L	.042–.046	8° BTDC	2100	800 ④
4-54R-R00	5.0L	.042–.046	10° BTDC	2000	575
4-54R-R10	5.0L	.042–.046	10° BTDC	2000	575
4-54T-R00	5.0L	.042–.046	10° BTDC	2000	575
4-54T-R10	5.0L	.042–.046	10° BTDC	2000	575
4-54W-R00	5.0L	.042–.046	12° BTDC	2100	675 ⑤
4-54W-R10	5.0L	.042–.046	12° BTDC	2100	675 ⑤
4-63H-R00	5.8L	.042–.046	10° BTDC	2000	750
4-64H-R00	5.8L	.042–.046	10° BTDC	2000	600
4-64H-R00	5.8L	.042–.046	10° BTDC	2000	600
4-64T-R00	5.8L	.042–.046	10° BTDC	2000	600
4-64T-R00	5.8L	.042–.046	10° BTDC	2000	600
4-64Y-R00	5.8L	.042–.046	10° BTDC	2000	600
5-77-R01	4.9L	.042–.046	10° BTDC	1500	600 ⑥
5-78-R01	4.9L	.042–.046	10° BTDC	1500	600 ⑥
9-77J-R12	4.9L	.042–.046	12° BTDC	1600	700 ⑦
9-78J-R00	4.9L	.042–.046	12° BTDC	1600	550
9-78J-R11	4.9L	.042–.046	12° BTDC	1600	550
7-79-R01	5.0L	.042–.046	6° BTDC	1500	750 ⑧
7-80-R00	5.0L	.042–.046	6° BTDC	1500	750 ⑧
2-75A-R10	5.8L	.042–.046	8° BTDC	1500	800 ⑧
2-75J-R20	5.8L	.042–.046	8° BTDC	1500	700 ⑧
2-76A-R10	5.8L	.042–.046	8° BTDC	1500	800 ⑧
2-76J-R20	5.8L	.042–.046	8° BTDC	1500	700 ⑧
9-83G-R12	6.1L	.042–.046	6° BTDC	2200	600
9-83G-R14	6.1L	.042–.046	6° BTDC	1600	600
9-83H-R11	6.1L	.042–.046	6° BTDC	2500	600
9-87G-R11	7.0L	.042–.046	6° BTDC	2700	600
9-97J-R10	7.5L	.042–.046	8° BTDC	1600	800 ⑨
3-98S-R10	7.5L	.042–.046	8° BTDC	1600	800 ⑨
4-98S-R00	7.5L	.042–.046	8° BTDC	1600	800 ⑨
4-37A-R00	2.0L	—	—	1450	725–775
4-37B-R00	2.0L	—	—	1450	725–775
3-47D-R00	2.2L	—	—	1450	780–830

Tune-Up Specifications (cont.)
1984

(For 1984 Tune-Up Specifications consult the Vehicle Emissions Control Label, which is located on the engine of the vehicle. This decal will contain a calibration number which when used in conjunction with the chart below will yield the required tune-up information. If the information given in this chart disagrees with the information on the decal, use the information on the decal.)

Calibration	Engine	Spark Plug Gap	Ignition Timing	Fast Idle rpm	Curb Idle rpm
4-68J-R00	6.9L	—	—	—	650–700
4-68X-R00	6.9L	—	—	—	650–700

① 800 without P/S
② 700–800 RPM—Auto. Trans. in DRIVE
③ 550–650 RPM—Auto. Trans. in DRIVE
④ 700—Non a/c or A/C off
⑤ 700—Non a/c or A/C off
⑥ 700—Manual Trans.
⑦ 600—TSP off
⑧ 650—"D" auto trans; 525—TSP off
⑨ 650—DRIVE

Tune-Up Specifications
1985–86

(For 1985–86 Tune-Up Specifications consult the Vehicle Emissions Control Label, which is located on the engine of the vehicle. This decal will contain a calibration number which when used in conjunction with the chart below will yield the required tune-up information. If the information given in this chart disagrees with the information on the decal, use the information on the decal.)

Calibration	Engine	Spark Plug Gap	Ignition Timing	Fast Idle rpm	Curb Idle rpm
5-41D-R00	2.0L	.042–.046	6° BTDC	1700	775–825
5-41D-R10	2.0L	.042–.046	6° BTDC	1700	775–825
5-49F-R01	2.3L	.042–.046	10° BTDC	—	575–725
5-49S-R01	2.3L	.042–.046	10° BTDC	—	575–725
5-50H-R02	2.3L	.042–.046	10° BTDC	—	625–725
5-50S-R02	2.3L	.042–.046	10° BTDC	—	625–775
5-61F-R01	2.8L	.042–.046	10° BTDC	3000	800–900 ①
5-61S-R01	2.8L	.042–.046	14° BTDC	3200	800–900 ①
5-62E-R01	2.8L	.042–.046	10° BTDC	3000	800–900 ①
5-62R-R01	2.8L	.042–.046	10° BTDC	3000	800–900 ①
4-51R-R00	4.9L	.042–.046	10° BTDC	1600	600–700 ②
4-51S-R02	4.9L	.042–.046	10° BTDC	1600	600–700 ③
4-51T-R00	4.9L	.042–.046	10° BTDC	1600	600–700 ②
4-52G-R00	4.9L	.042–.046	10° BTDC	1600	600–700 ②
4-52G-R10	4.9L	.042–.046	10° BTDC	1600	600–700 ②
4-52L-R00	4.9L	.042–.046	10° BTDC	1600	600–700 ②
4-52L-R10	4.9L	.042–.046	10° BTDC	1600	600–700 ②
4-52R-R00	4.9L	.042–.046	10° BTDC	1600	600–700 ②
4-52S-R00	4.9L	.042–.046	10° BTDC	1600	600–700 ②
4-52S-R10	4.9L	.042–.046	10° BTDC	1600	600–700 ②
4-52T-R00	4.9L	.042–.046	10° BTDC	1600	600–700 ②
5-51D-R00	4.9L	.042–.046	10° BTDC	1600	600–700 ②

Tune-Up Specifications (cont.)
1985–86

(For 1985–86 Tune-Up Specifications consult the Vehicle Emissions Control Label, which is located on the engine of the vehicle. This decal will contain a calibration number which when used in conjunction with the chart below will yield the required tune-up information. If the information given in this chart disagrees with the information on the decal, use the information on the decal.)

Calibration	Engine	Spark Plug Gap	Ignition Timing	Fast Idle rpm	Curb Idle rpm
5-51E-R00	4.9L	.042–.046	10° BTDC	1600	600–700 ②
5-51F-R00	4.9L	.042–.046	10° BTDC	1600	600–700 ②
5-51H-R00	4.9L	.042–.046	10° BTDC	1600	600–700 ②
5-51K-R00	4.9L	.042–.046	10° BTDC	1600	600–700 ②
5-51L-R00	4.9L	.042–.046	10° BTDC	1600	600–700 ②
5-51V-R00	4.9L	.042–.046	10° BTDC	1600	600–700 ②
5-51Z-R00	4.9L	.042–.046	10° BTDC	1600	600–700 ②
5-52E-R00	4.9L	.042–.046	10° BTDC	1600	600–700 ②
5-52K-R00	4.9L	.042–.046	10° BTDC	1600	600–700 ②
5-52W-R00	4.9L	.042–.046	10° BTDC	1600	600–700 ②
5-52Y-R00	4.9L	.042–.046	10° BTDC	1600	600–700 ②
4-54R-R12	5.0L	.042–.046	10° BTDC	2000	575D
4-54R-R13	5.0L	.042–.046	10° BTDC	2000	575D
4-54R-R14	5.0L	.042–.046	10° BTDC	2000	575D
5-53D-R00	5.0L	.042–.046	10° BTDC	—	—
5-53D-R01	5.0L	.042–.046	8° BTDC	—	—
5-53F-R00	5.0L	.042–.046	10° BTDC	—	—
5-53F-R01	5.0L	.042–.046	8° BTDC	—	—
5-53H-R00	5.0L	.042–.046	10° BTDC	—	—
5-53H-R01	5.0L	.042–.046	8° BTDC	—	—
5-54Q-R00	5.0L	.042–.046	10° BTDC	—	—
5-54Q-R01	5.0L	.042–.046	10° BTDC	—	—
5-54S-R00	5.0L	.042–.046	10° BTDC	—	—
5-54S-R01	5.0L	.042–.046	10° BTDC	—	—
5-54W-R00	5.0L	.042–.046	10° BTDC	—	—
5-54X-R00	5.0L	.042–.046	10° BTDC	—	—
4-64G-R00	5.8L(F)	.042–.046	10° BTDC	1900	650D
4-64G-R02	5.8L(F)	.042–.046	10° BTDC	1900	650D
4-64G-R02	5.8L(E)	.042–.046	10° BTDC	1900	650D
4-64T-R00	5.8L(F)	.042–.046	10° BTDC	2000	600D
4-64T-R00	5.8L(E)	.042–.046	10° BTDC	2000	600D
4-64Z-R10	5.8L(F)	.042–.046	14° BTDC	1900	650D
4-64Z-R10	5.8L(E)	.042–.046	14° BTDC	1900	650D
5-63H-R00	5.8L	.042–.046	10° BTDC	2000	700
5-63Y-R00	5.8L	.042–.046	10° BTDC	2000	700

① 700–800 in Drive A/T
② 550–650 in Drive A/T

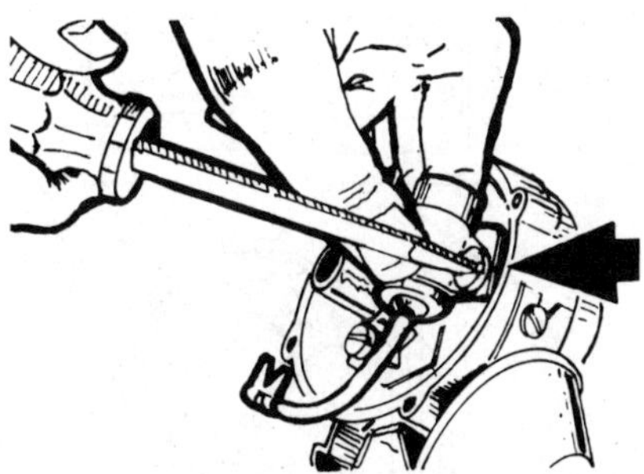

Use a magnetic screwdriver to remove the condenser hold-down screw. Be careful not to drop the screw into the distributor

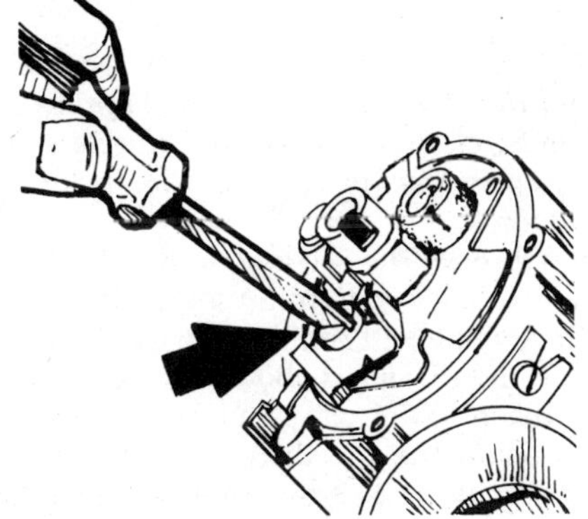

Remove the points hold-down screw with a magnetic screwdriver

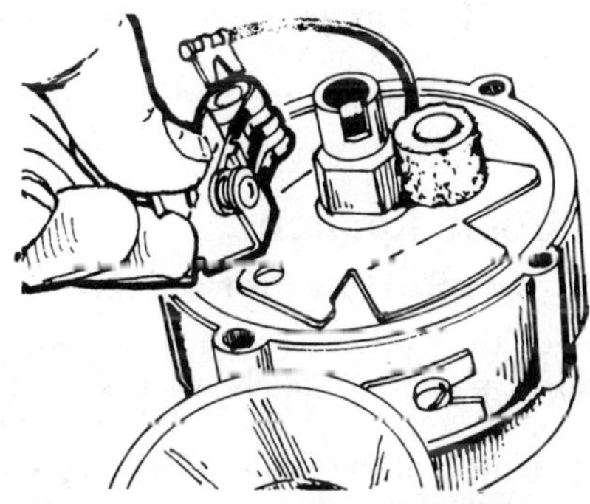

Wipe off the cam lobes before installing new points. Dab a small amount of fresh grease on the plastic rubbing block on the points. Place the points set on the distributor plate so the locating pin fits in its hole in the plate. Using the magnetic screwdriver, install the points screw, condenser, and hook up the wires

driver with a holding mechanism will come in handy here so that you don't drop a screw into the distributor and have to remove the entire distributor to retrieve it.

5. Remove the points by lifting them straight up and off the locating dowel on the plate. Wipe off the cam and apply new cam lubricant. Discard the old set of points.

6. Slip the new set of points onto the locating dowel and install the screws that hold the

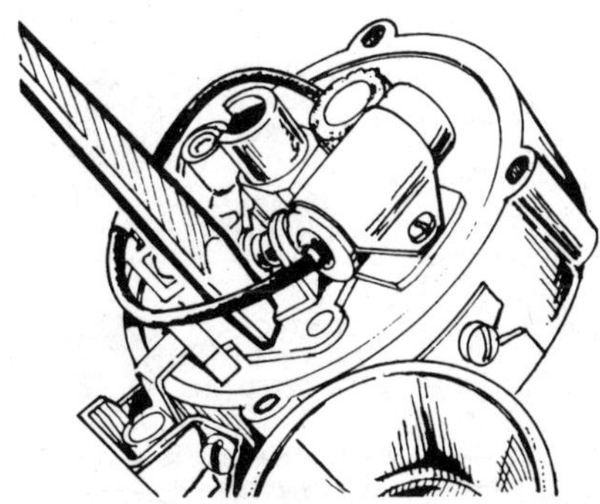

Turn the engine over by hand so the points rubbing block is up on the peak of one of the distributor cam lobes. Open the gap by inserting a screwdriver in the adjusting slot and twisting

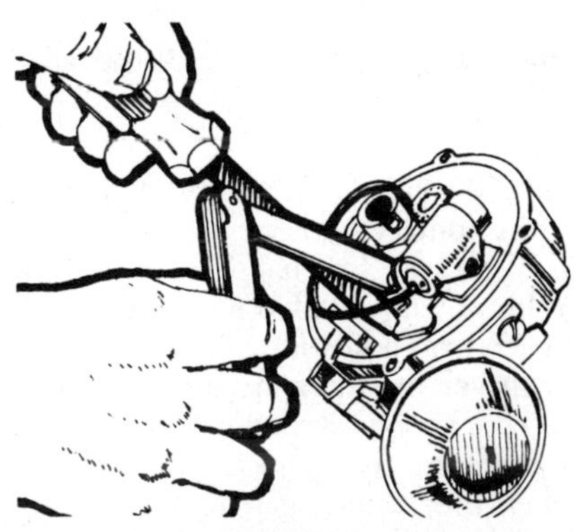

Insert the correct size feeler gauge between the open contacts. When the gauge slides through with just a slight drag, tighten the points screw

assembly onto the plate. Do not tighten them all the way.

7. Attach the new condenser to the plate with the ground screw.

8. Attach the condenser lead to the points at the proper place.

9. Apply a small amount of cam lubricant to the shaft where the rubbing block of the points touches.

ADJUSTMENT OF THE BREAKER POINTS WITH A FEELER GAUGE

1. If the contact points of the assembly are not parallel, bend the stationary contact so that they make contact across the entire surface of the contacts. Bend only the stationary bracket part of the point assembly; not the moveable contact.

2. Turn the engine until the rubbing block of the points is on one of the high points of the distributor cam. You can do this by either turning the ignition switch to the start position and releasing it quickly ("bumping" the engine) or by using a wrench on the bolt which holds the crankshaft pulley to the crankshaft.

3. Place the correct size feeler gauge be-

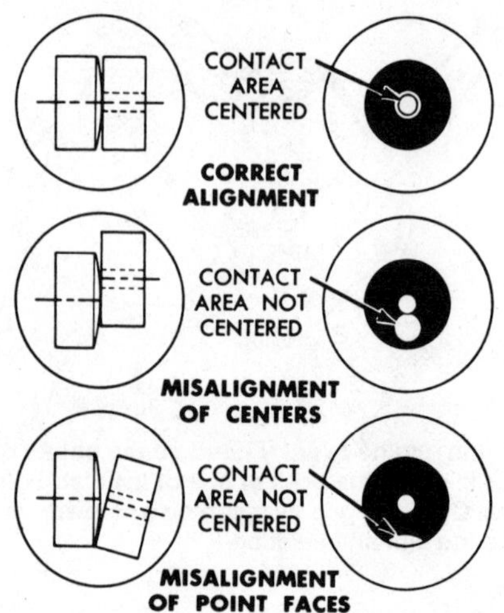

Alignment of the breaker points. Proper alignment is critical

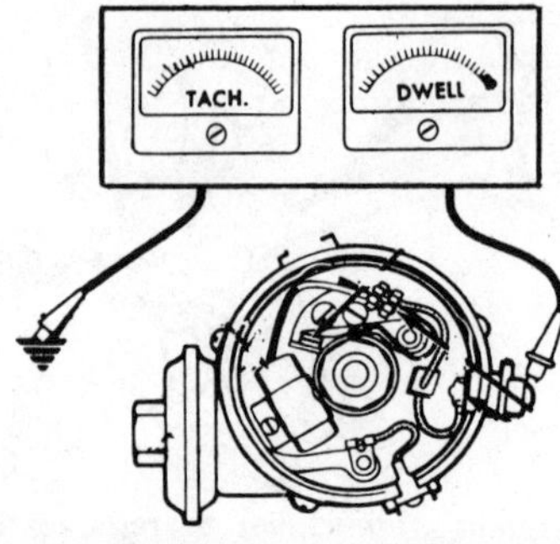

Typical dwell meter connections: one lead connects to ground, the other to the coil terminal on the distributor

tween the contacts. Make sure that it is parallel with the contact surfaces.

4. With your free hand, insert a screwdriver into the notch provided for adjustment or into the eccentric adjusting screw, then twist the screwdriver to either increase or decrease the gap to the proper setting.

5. Tighten the adjustment lockscrew and recheck the contact gap to make sure that it didn't change when the lockscrew was tightened.

6. Replace the rotor and distributor cap, and the high-tension wire that connects the top of the distributor and the coil. Make sure that the rotor is firmly seated all the way onto the distributor shaft and that the tab of the rotor is aligned with the notch in the shaft. Align the tab in the base of the distributor cap with the notch in the distributor body. Make sure that the cap if firmly seated on the distributor and that the retainer clips are in place. Make sure that the end of the high-tension wire is firmly placed in the top of the distributor and the coil.

ADJUSTMENT OF THE BREAKER POINTS WITH A DWELL METER

1. Adjust the points with a feeler gauge as described earlier.

2. Connect the dwell meter to the ignition circuit according to the manufacturer's instructions. One lead of the meter is connected to a ground and the other lead is to be connected to the coil terminal on the distributor. An adapter is usually provided for this purpose.

3. If the dwell meter has a set line on it, adjust the meter to zero the indicator.

4. Start the engine.

NOTE: *Be careful when working on any vehicle while the engine is running. Make sure that the transmission is in Neutral or Park and that the parking brake is applied. Keep hands, clothing, tools, and the wires of the test instruments clear of the rotating fan blades.*

5. Observe the reading on the dwell meter. If the reading is within the specified range, turn off the engine and remove the dwell meter.

6. If the reading is above the specified range, the breaker point gap is too small. If the reading is below the specified range, the gap is too large. In either case, the engine must be stopped and the gap adjusted in the manner previously covered. After making the adjustment, start the engine and check the reading on the dwell meter. When the correct reading is obtained, disconnect the dwell meter.

7. Check the adjustment of the ignition timing.

Electronic Ignition

BASIC OPERATING PRINCIPLES

In mid 1974, Ford Motor Company introduced in selected models its new Solid-State Ignition System. In 1975, it became standard equipment in all pick-up models. This system was designed primarily to provide a hotter spark necessary to fire the leaner fuel/air mixtures required by today's emission control standards.

The Ford Solid-State Ignition is a pulse-triggered, transistor controlled breakerless ignition system. With the ignition switch "on," the primary circuit is on and the ignition coil is energized. When the armature spokes approach the magnetic pick-up coil assembly, they induce a voltage which tells the amplifier to turn the coil primary current off. A timing circuit in the amplifier module will turn the current on again after the coil field has collapsed. When the current is on, it flows from the battery through the ignition switch, the primary windings of the ignition coil, and through the amplifier module circuits to ground. When the current is off, the magnetic field built up in the ignition coil is allowed to collapse, inducing a high voltage into the second windings of the coil. High voltage is produced each time the field is thus built up and collapsed.

Although the systems are basically the same, Ford refers to their solid-state ignition in several different ways. 1974–76 systems are referred to simply as Breakerless systems. In 1977, Ford named their ignition system Dura-Spark I and Dura-Spark II. In 1982 Ford dropped the Dura-Spark I and introduced the Dura-Spark III (while continuing the Dura-Spark II). This system is based on Electronic Engine Control (EEC). The EEC system controls spark advance in response to various engine sensors. This includes a crankshaft position sensor which replaces the stator and armature assembly in the distributor. Dura-Spark II is the version used in all states except California. Dura-Spark I and III are the systems used in California V8's only. Basically, the only difference between the two is that the coil charging currents are higher in the California vehicles. This is necessary to fire the leaner fuel/air mixtures required by California's stricter emission laws. The difference in coils alters some of the test values.

Ford has used several different types of wiring harness on their solid-state ignition systems, due to internal circuitry changes in the electronic module. Wire continuity and color have not been changed, but the arrangement of the terminals in the connectors is different for each year. Schematics of the different years are included here, but keep in mind that the writing in all diagrams has been simplified and as a result, the routing of your wiring may not match the wiring in the diagram. However, the wire colors and terminal connections are the same.

Wire color-coding is critical to servicing the Ford Solid-State Ignition. Battery current reaches the electronic module through either the *white* or *red* wire, depending on whether the engine is cranking or running. When the engine is cranking, battery current is flowing through the *white* wire. When the engine is running, battery current flows through the *red* wire. All distributor signals flow through the *orange* and *purple* wires. The *green* wire carries primary current from the coil to the module. The *black* wire is a ground between the distributor and the module. Up until 1975, a *blue* wire provides transient voltage protection. In 1976, the *blue* wire was dropped when a zener diode was added to the module. The *orange* and *purple* wires which run from the stator to the module must *always* be connected to the same color wire at the module. If these connections are crossed, polarity will be reversed and the system will be thrown out of phase. Some replacement wiring harnesses were sold with the wiring crossed, which complicates the problem considerably. As previously noted, the *black* wire is the ground wire. The screw which grounds the black wire also, of course, grounds the entire primary circuit. If this screw is loose, dirty, or corroded, a seemingly incomprehensible ignition problem will develop. Several other cautions should be noted here. Keep in mind that on vehicles equipped with catalytic converters, any test that requires removal of a spark plug wire while the engine is running should be kept to a thirty second maximum. Any longer than this may damage the converter. In the event you are testing spark plug wires, do not pierce them. Test the wires at their terminals only.

TROUBLESHOOTING THE FORD SOLID-STATE IGNITION SYSTEM

NOTE: *Ford has substantially altered their 1978 and later electronic ignition test procedure. Due to the sensitive nature of the system and the complexity of the test procedures, it is recommended that you refer to your dealer if you suspect a problem in your 1978 and later electronic ignition system. The system can, of course, be tested by substituting known good components (module, stator, etc.).*

Basic troubleshooting for the Dura Spark and TFI systems can be found at the beginning of chapter 3.

This system, which at first appears to be extremely complicated, is actually quite simple to diagnose and repair. Diagnosis does, however, require the use of a voltmeter and an ohmmeter. You will also need several jumper wires with both blade ends and alligator clips.

The symptoms of a defective component within the solid state system are exactly the same as those you would encounter in a conventional system. Some of these systems are:

- Hard or no starting
- Rough idle
- Poor fuel economy
- Engine misses while under load or while accelerating

If you suspect a problem in your ignition system, first perform a spark intensity test to pinpoint the problem. Using insulated pliers, hold the end of one of the spark plug leads about ½ in. away from the engine block or other good ground, and crank the engine. If you have a nice, fat spark, then your problem is not in the ignition system. If you have no spark or a very weak spark, then proceed to the following tests.

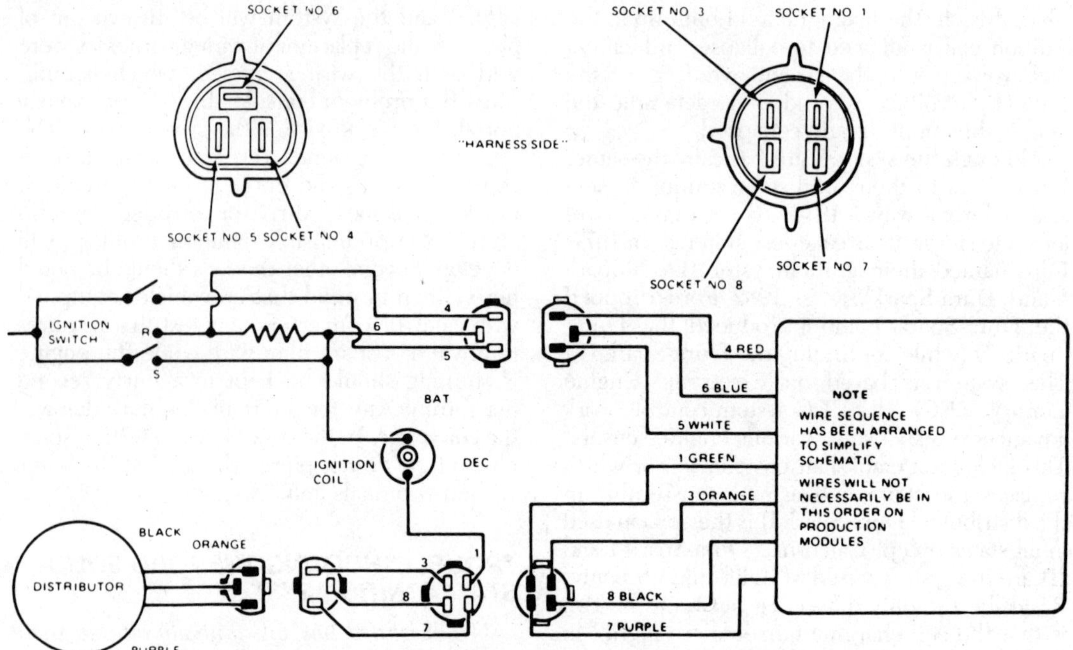

1975 ignition wiring schematic

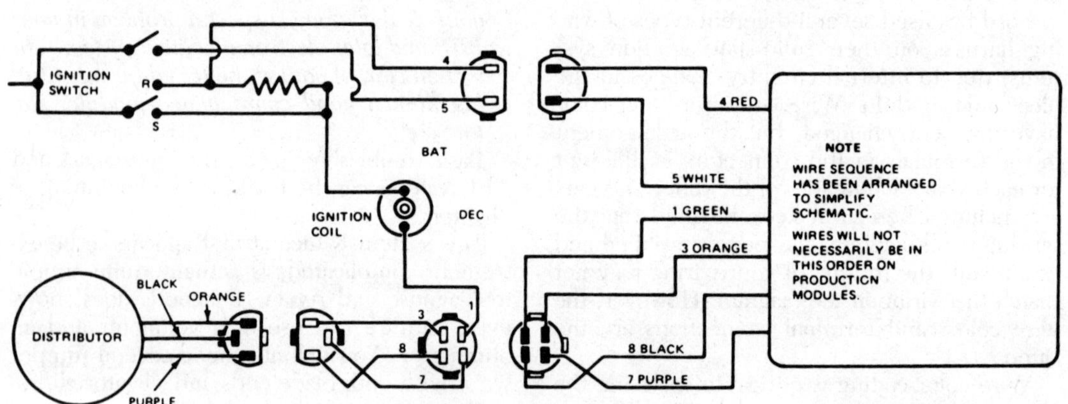

1976 ignition wiring schematic

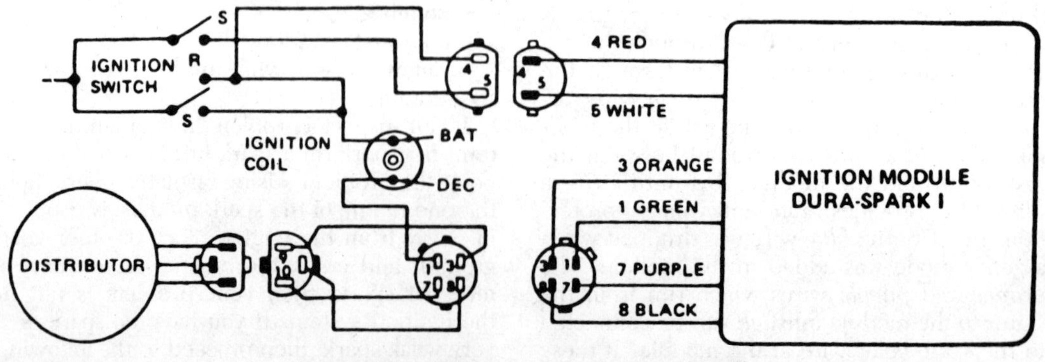

1977–79 Dura Spark I ignition wiring schematic

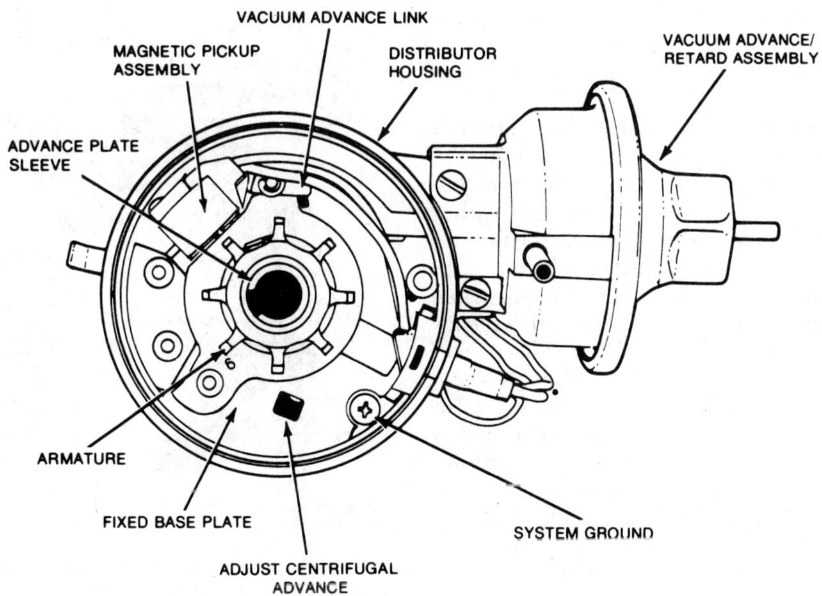

V8-type electronic distributor components

Stator Test

To test the stator (also known as the magnetic pickup assembly), you will need an ohmmeter. Run the engine until it reaches operating temperature, then turn the ignition switch to the "off" position. Disconnect the wire harness from the distributor. Connect the ohmmeter between the orange and purple wires. Resistance should be between 400 and 800 ohms. Next, connect the ohmmeter between the black wire and a good ground on the engine. Operate the vacuum advance either by hand or with an external vacuum source. Resistance should be zero ohms. Finally, connect the ohmmeter between the orange wire and ground, and then the purple wire and ground. Resistance should be over 70,000 ohms in both cases. If any of your ohmmeter readings differ from the above specifications, then the stator is defective and must be replaced as a unit.

If the stator is good, then either the electronic module or the wiring connections must be checked next. Because of its complicated electronic nature, the module itself cannot be checked, except by substitution. If you have access to a module which you know to be good, then perform a substitution test at this time. If this cures the problem, then the original module is faulty and must be replaced. If it does not cure the problem or if you cannot locate a known-good module, then disconnect the two

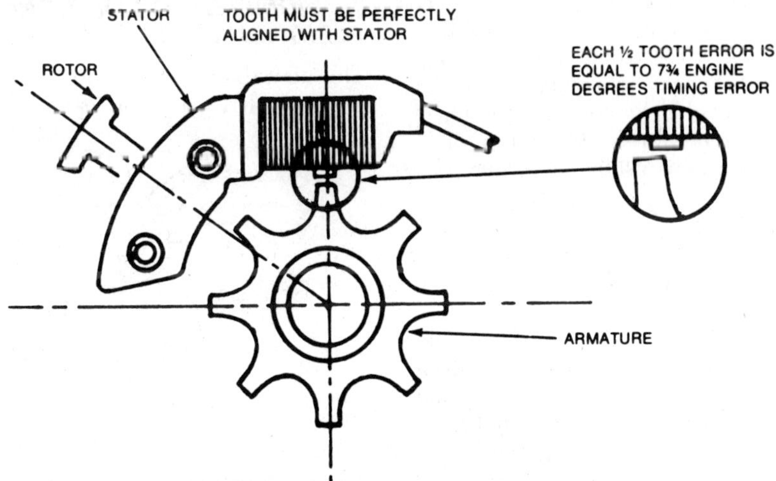

V8 electronic distributor, static timing position

wiring harnesses from the module, and, using a voltmeter, check the following circuits.

NOTE: *Make no tests at the module side of the connectors.*

1. Starting circuit—Connect the voltmeter leads to ground and to the corresponding female socket of the white male lead from the module (you will need a jumper wire with a blade end). Crank the engine over. The voltage should be between 8 and 12 volts.

2. Running circuit—Turn the ignition switch to the "on" position. Connect the voltmeter leads to ground and the corresponding female socket of the red male lead from the module. Voltage should be battery voltage plus or minus 0.1 volts.

3. Coil circuit—Leave the ignition switch "on." Connect the voltmeter leads to ground and to the corresponding female socket of the green male lead from the module. Voltage should be battery voltage plus or minus 0.1 volts.

If any of the preceding readings are incorrect, inspect and repair any loose, broken, frayed or dirty connections. If this doesn't solve the problem, perform a battery source test.

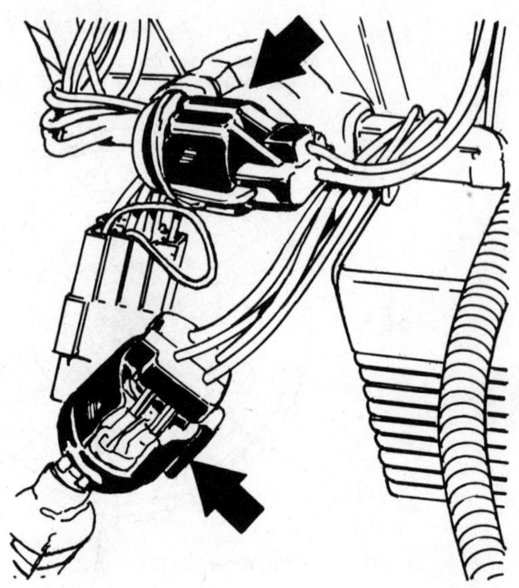

When you're working on the electronic ignition, unplug the module connectors here. Leave the module side alone or you'll short out the module (shown on right)

Battery Source Test

To make this test, *do not* disconnect the coil.

Connect the voltmeter leads to the BAT terminal at the coil and a good ground. Connect a jumper wire from the DEC terminal at the coil to a good ground. Make sure all lights and accessories are off. Turn the ignition to the "on" position. Check the voltage. If the voltage is below 4.9 volts (11 volts for Dura-Spark I), then check the primary wiring for broken strands, cracked or frayed wires, or loose or dirty terminals. Repair or replace any defects. If, however, the voltage is above 7.9 volts (14 volts for Dura-Spark I), then you have a problem in the resistance wiring and it must be replaced.

It should be noted here that if you do have a problem in your electronic ignition system, most of the time it will be a case of loose, dirty or frayed wires. The electronic module, being completely solid-state, is not ordinarily subject to failure. It is possible for the unit to fail, of course, but as a general rule, the source of an ignition system probably will be somewhere else in the circuit.

MODULE TEST

If the electronic module is suspected of being defective, proceed as follows:

1. Without removing the existing module from the vehicle, unplug the connectors from the electronic module. Connect a known good module. The substitute module does not have to be fastened to the vehicle to operate properly.

2. Attempt to start the engine. If the engine starts and accelerates properly, proceed to step three. If the engine will still not start, the fault is in the wiring or other vehicle systems. Inspect and repair as necessary.

3. Reconnect the original module. Again attempt to start and run the engine. If the engine once again will not start, remove the original module and replace with a new one. If, however, the engine will now start and run on the original module, the module is not defective.

4. With the engine operating, check all connections in the primary wiring of the ignition system for such faults as poor wire crimp to terminal or improper engagement. The faulty connection will be observed when the engine misfires or stops. Correct as necessary.

TACHOMETER-TO-COIL CONNECTION—ELECTRONIC IGNITION

The new solid state ignition coil connector allows a tachometer test lead with an alligator-

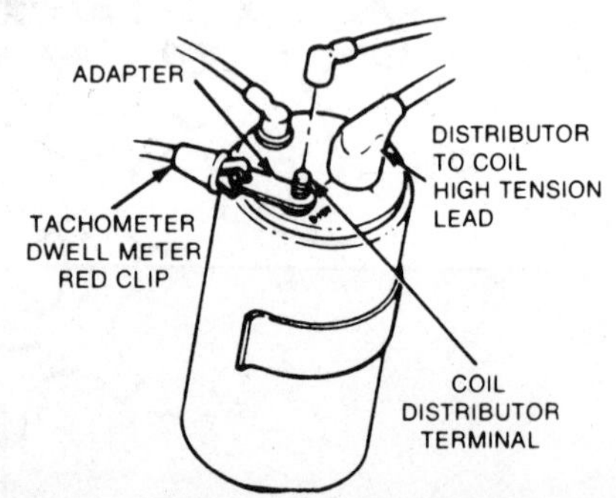

Dwell/tach installation showing adaptor on coil, 1974 and earlier models

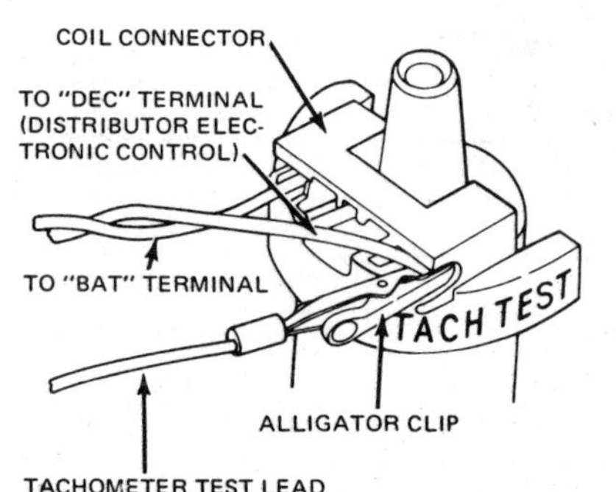

Attaching a tachometer lead to the coil connector, 1975 and later

type clip to be connected to the DEC (Distributor Electronic Control) terminal without removing the connector.

When engine rpm must be checked, install the tachometer alligator clip into the "TACH TEST" cavity as shown. If the coil connector must be removed, grasp the wires and pull horizontally until it disconnects from the terminals.

Ignition Wires

TESTING

CAUTION: *Do not, under any circumstances, puncture an ignition wire with any type of probing device.*

1975 Test Sequence

	Test Voltage Between	Should Be	If Not, Conduct
Key On	Socket #4 and Engine Ground	Battery Voltage ± 0.1 Volt	Module Bias Test
	Socket #1 and Engine Ground	Battery Voltage ± 0.1 Volt	Battery Source Test
Cranking	Socket #5 and Engine Ground	8 to 12 volts	Cranking Test
	Jumper #1 to #8 Read #6	more than 6 volts	Starting Circuit Test
	Pin #7 and Pin #8	½ volt minimum AC or any DC volt wiggle	Distributor Hardware Test
Key Off	Socket #7 and #3 Socket #8 and Engine Ground Socket #7 and Engine Ground Socket #3 and Engine Ground	400 to 800 ohms 0 ohms more than 70,000 ohms	Magnetic Pick-up (Stator) Test
	Socket #4 and Coil Tower Socket #1 and Pin #6	7,000 to 13,000 ohms 1.0 to 2.0 ohms	Coil Test
	Socket #1 and Engine Ground	more than 4.0 ohms	Short Test
	Socket #4 and Pin #6	1.0 to 2.0 ohms	Resistance Wire Test

1976 Test Sequence

	Test Voltage Between	Should Be	If Not, Conduct
Key On	Socket #4 and Engine Ground	Battery Voltage ± 0.1 Volt	Battery Source Test
	Socket #1 and Engine Ground	Battery Voltage ± 0.1 Volt	Battery Source Test
Cranking	Socket #5 and Engine Ground	8 to 12 volts	Check Supply Circuit (starting) through Ignition Switch
	Jumper #1 to #8 Read #6	more than 6 volts	Starting Circuit Test
	Pin #3 and Pin #8	½ volt minimum AC or any DC volt wiggle	Distributor Hardware Test
Key Off	Socket #8 and #3 Socket #7 and Engine Ground Socket #8 and Engine Ground Socket #3 and Engine Ground	400 to 800 ohms 0 ohms more than 70,000 ohms more than 70,000 ohms	Magnetic Pick-up (Stator) Test
	Socket #4 and Coil Tower	7,000 to 13,000 ohms	Coil Test
	Socket #1 and Engine Ground	more than 4.0 ohms	Short Test

1977–80 Test Sequence

	Test Voltage Between	Should Be	If Not, Conduct
Key On	Socket #4 and Engine Ground	Battery Voltage ± 0.1 Volt	Module Bias Test
	Socket #1 and Engine Ground	Battery Voltage ± Volt	Battery Source Test
Cranking	Socket #5 and Engine Ground	8 to 12 volts	Cranking Test
	Jumper #1 to #8—Read Coil "Bat" Term & Engine Ground	more than 6 volts	Standing Circuit Test
	Sockets #7 and #3	½ volt minimum wiggle	Distributor Hardware Test
Key Off	Socket #7 and #3 Socket #8 and Engine Ground Socket #7 and Engine Ground Socket #3 and Engine Ground	400 to 800 ohms 0 ohms more than 70,000 ohms more than 70,000 ohms	Magnetic Pick-up (Stator) Test
	Socket #4 and Coil Tower	7,000 to 13,000 ohms	Coil Test
	Socket #1 and Coil "Bat" Term	1.0 to 2.0 ohms Breakerless & Dura-Spark II	
		0.5 to 1.5 ohms Dura-Spark I	
	Socket #1 and Engine Ground	more than 4.0 ohms	Short Test
	Socket #4 and Coil "Bat" Term (Except Dura-Spark I)	1.0 to 2.0 ohms Breakerless	Resistance Wire Test
		0.7 to 1.7 ohms Dura-Spark II	

1. Remove the distributor cap from the distributor.
2. Check to make sure the spark plug wires are firmly seated in the cap.
3. Disconnect the spark plug end of the suspect wire(s).
4. Using a volt/ohmmeter, measure the resistance from the wire terminal inside the cap to the spark plug terminal (inside the spark plug boot). If resistance is less than 5,000 ohms per inch, the plug wire resistance is OK; if resistance exceeds 5,000 ohms per inch replace the wire(s).

Checking ignition wire resistance

Distributor Cap and Rotor

On late models equipped with electronic ignition the distributor rotor has been coated with a silicone compound, which is used to reduce radio interference caused by the high-voltage ignition system. Due to centrifugal force and time, this compound is thrown off the rotor onto the distributor cap terminals. As this substance ages, it takes on the appearance of dirt or a contaminant on the cap and rotor terminals. This condition is normal and causes no performance loss; *do not replace the cap and rotor for this condition only.*

NOTE: *When replacing the rotor, apply sil-*

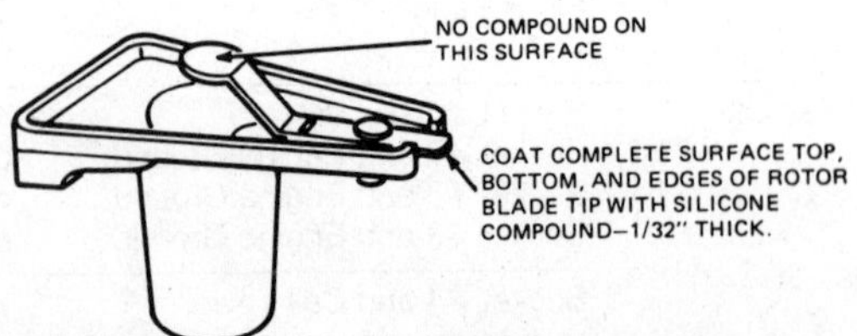

Silicone-compound application to distributor rotor

icone dielectric compound (Ford part D7AZ-19A331 or equivalent) approximately 1/32 in. thick, to all sides and edges of the brass terminal outside the plastic body. See the accompanying illustration for specific details.

Ignition Timing

Ignition timing is the measurement, in degrees of crankshaft rotation, of the point at which the spark plugs fire in each of the cylinders. It is measured in degrees before or after Top Dead Center (TDC) of the compression stroke. Ignition timing is controlled by turning the distributor body in the engine.

Ideally, the air/fuel mixture in the cylinder will be ignited by the spark plug just as the piston passes TDC of the compression stroke. If this happens, the piston will be beginning the power stroke just as the compressed and ignited air/fuel mixture starts to expand. The expansion of the air/fuel mixture then forces the piston down on the power stroke and turns the crankshaft.

Because it takes a fraction of a second for the spark plug to ignite the mixture in the cylinder, the spark plug must fire a little before the piston reaches TDC. Otherwise, the mixture will not be completely ignited as the piston passes TDC and the full power of the explosion will not be used by the engine.

The timing measurement is given in degrees of crankshaft rotation before the piston reaches TDC (BTDC, or Before Top Dead Center). If the setting for the ignition timing is 5° BTDC, each spark plug must fire 5° before each piston reaches TDC. This only holds true, however, when the engine is at idle speed.

As the engine speed increases, the pistons go faster. The spark plugs have to ignite the fuel even sooner if it is to be completely ignited when the piston reaches TDC. To do this, the distributor has a means to advance the timing of the spark as the engine speed increases. This is accomplished by centrifugal weights within the distributor and a vacuum diaphragm mounted on the side of the distributor. It is necessary to disconnect the vacuum lines from the diaphragm when the ignition timing is being set.

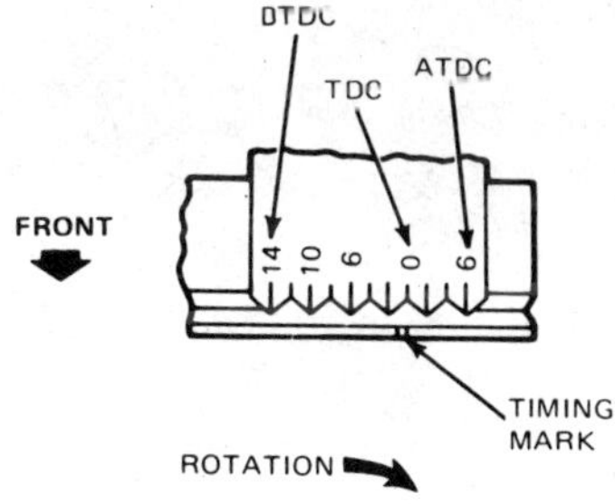

Typical inline-six and 232 V6 timing marks; degree scale on timing pointer, marks on pulley rim

If the ignition is set too far advanced (BTDC), the ignition and expansion of the fuel in the cylinder will occur too soon and tend to force the piston down while it is still traveling up. This causes engine ping. If the ignition spark is set too far retarded after TDC (ATDC), the piston will have already passed TDC and started on its way down when the fuel is ignited. This will cause the piston to be forced down for only a portion of its travel. This will result in poor engine performance and lack of power.

The timing is best checked with a timing light. This device is connected in series with the No. 1 spark plug. The current that fires the spark plug also causes the timing light to flash.

There is a notch on the crankshaft pulley on all 6 cyl. engines. A scale of degrees of crankshaft rotation is attached to the engine block in such a position that the notch will pass close by the scale. On the V8 engines, the scale is located on the crankshaft pulley and a pointer is attached to the engine block so that the scale will pass close by. When the engine is running, the timing light is aimed at the mark on the crankshaft pulley and the scale.

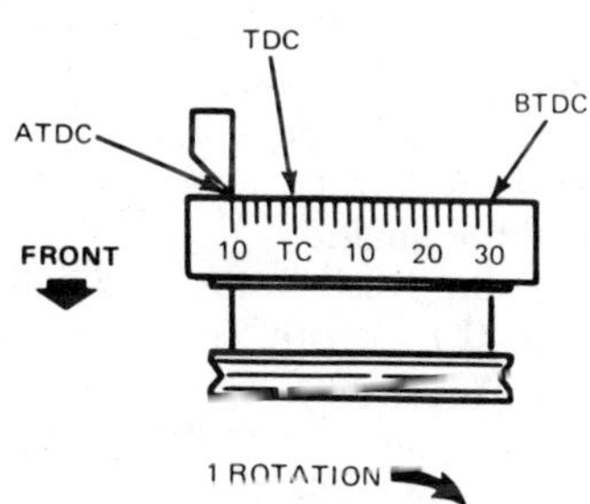

Typical V8 timing marks; some engines have both scale and marks on pulley, pointer separate

IGNITION TIMING ADJUSTMENT

1. Locate the timing marks on the crankshaft pulley and the front of the engine.
2. Clean the timing marks so that you can see them.
3. Mark the timing marks with a piece of chalk or with paint. Color the mark on the scale that will indicate the correct timing when it is aligned with the mark on the pulley or the pointer. It is also helpful to mark the notch in the pulley or the tip of the pointer with a small dab of color.
4. Attach a tachometer to the engine.
5. Attach a timing light according to the

Stay out of direct sunlight when timing the engine, as the sunlight will overpower the timing light flashes

manufacturer's instructions. If the timing light has three wires, one is attached to the No. 1 spark plug with an adapter. The other wires are connected to the battery. The red wire goes to the positive side of the battery and the black wire is connected to the negative terminal of the battery.

6. Disconnect the vacuum line to the distributor at the distributor and plug the vacuum line. A golf tee does a fine job.

7. Check to make sure that all of the wires clear the fan and then start the engine.

8. Adjust the idle to the correct setting.

9. Aim the timing light at the timing marks. If the marks that you put on the flywheel or pulley and the engine are aligned when the light flashes, the timing is correct. Turn off the engine and remove the tachometer and the timing light. If the marks are not in alignment, proceed with the following steps.

10. Turn off the engine.

11. Loosen the distributor lockbolt just enough so that the distributor can be turned with a little effort.

12. Start the engine. Keep the wires of the timing light clear of the fan.

13. With the timing light aimed at the pulley and the marks on the engine, turn the distributor in the direction of rotor rotation to retard the spark, and in the opposite direction of rotor rotation to advance the spark. Align the marks on the pulley and the engine with the flashes of the timing light.

14. When the marks are aligned, tighten the distributor lockbolt and recheck the timing with the timing light to make sure that the distributor did not move when you tightened the lockbolt.

15. Turn off the engine and remove the timing light.

Carburetor

This Section contains only tune-up adjustment procedures for carburetors. Descriptions, adjustments and overhaul procedures for carburetors can be found in the "Fuel System" Section (Chapter 4) of this book.

When the engine in your pick-up is running, the air/fuel mixture from the carburetor is being drawn into the engine by a partial vacuum created by the downward movement of the pistons on the intake stroke. The amount of air/fuel mixture that enters the engine is controlled by the throttle plate(s) in the bottom of the carburetor. When the engine is not running, the throttle plates are closed, completely blocking off the air/fuel passage(s) at the bottom of the carburetor. The throttle plates are connected by the throttle linkage to the accelerator pedal in the passenger compartment. When you depress the pedal, you open the throttle plates in the carburetor to admit more air/fuel mixture to the engine.

When the engine is idling, it is necessary to have the throttle plates open slightly. To prevent having to hold your foot on the pedal, an idle speed adjusting screw is located on the carburetor linkage.

The idle adjusting screw contacts a lever

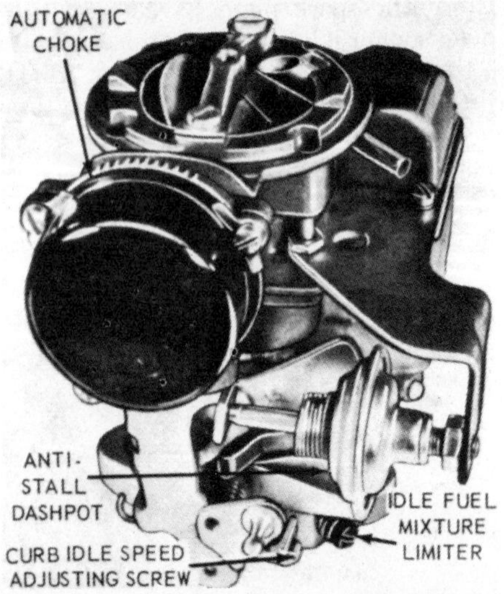

Carter model YF 1-bbl carburetor with a dashpot—used on 6-cylinder engines

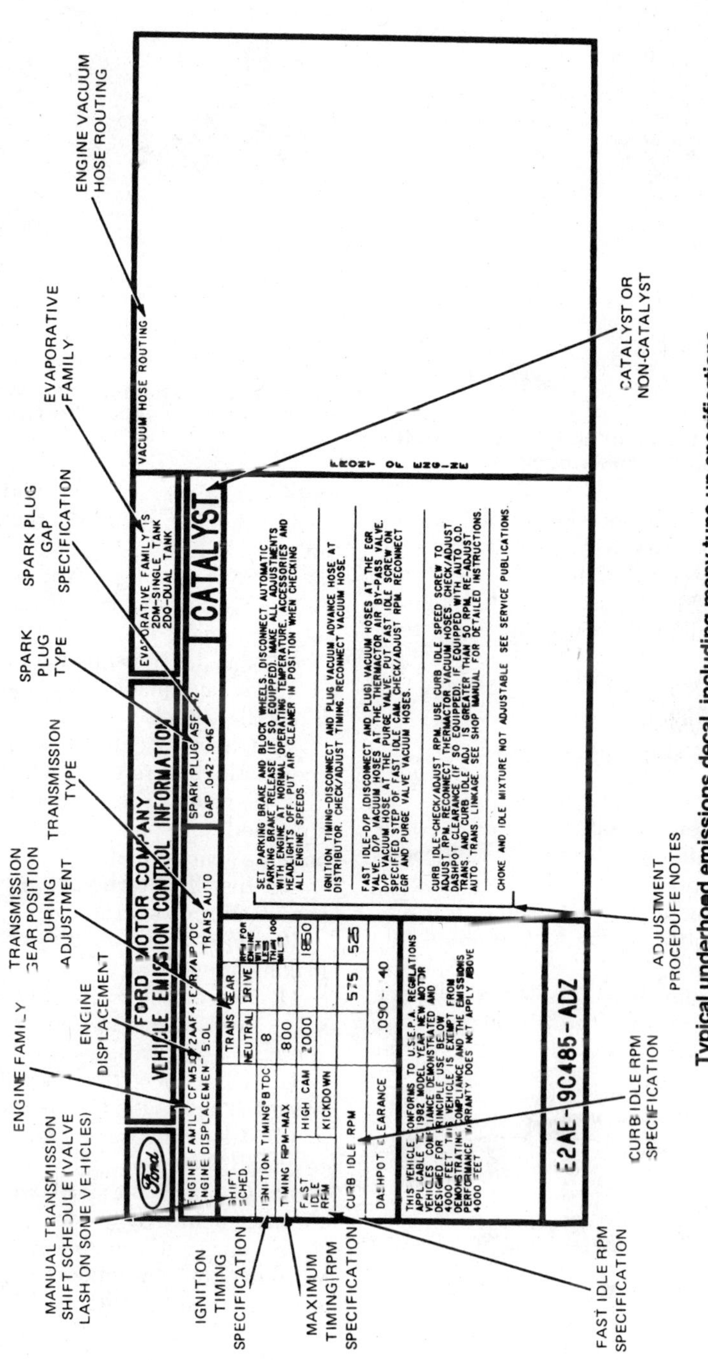

Typical underhood emissions decal, including many tune-up specifications

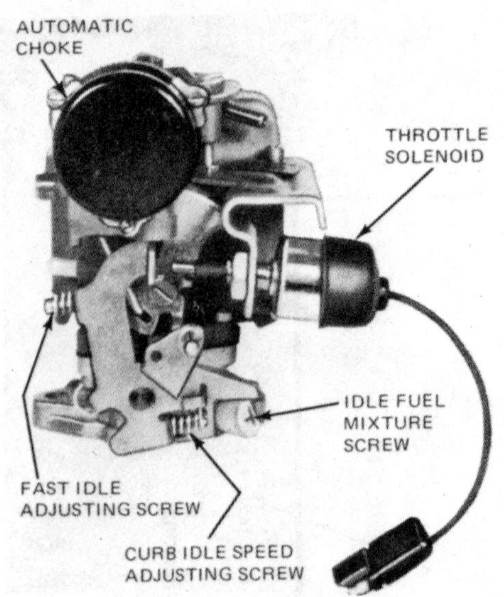

Carter model YF 1-bbl carburetor with a throttle solenoid—used on 6-cylinder engines

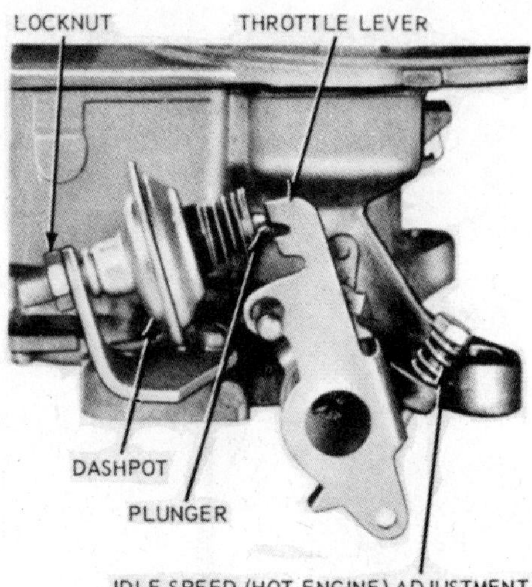

Idle speed adjustment on an Autolite model 2100 2-bbl carburetor with a dashpot

(throttle lever) on the outside of the carburetor. When the screw is turned, it opens or closes the throttle plates of the carburetor, raising or lowering the idle speed of the engine. This screw is called the curb idle adjusting screw.

GASOLINE ENGINES

Idle Speed and Mixture Adjustment

1965–73

1. With the engine off, turn the idle fuel mixture screw and limiter cap to the full counterclockwise position.
2. Turn the idle speed adjusting screw(s) out until the throttle plate(s) seats in the throttle bore(s).
3. Make certain that the solenoid plunger is not interfering with the throttle lever.
4. Turn the idle speed adjusting screw in until it just contacts the stop on the throttle shaft and lever assembly, then turn the screw inward 1½ turns.
5. Start the engine and warm it up.
6. Check, and if necessary, adjust the ignition timing.
7. Put the transmission in neutral (manual) or drive (automatic). Set the parking brake. Block the wheels.
8. Check that the choke plate is in the full open position; turn the headlights on high beam (this activates the solenoid on models so equipped, and puts a maximum electrical load on nonsolenoid models.
9. Install a tachometer according to the manufacturer's instructions.
10. If possible leave the air cleaner on while making adjustments.
11. Loosen the solenoid locknut and turn the solenoid in or out to obtain the specified idle speed.
12. Disconnect the solenoid lead wire and place the automatic transmission in neutral.
13. Adjust the carburetor throttle stop screw to obtain 500 rpm.
14. Connect the lead wire and open the throttle slightly by hand.
15. Turn the mixture adjusting screw(s) inward to obtain the smoothest possible idle with the air cleaner installed.

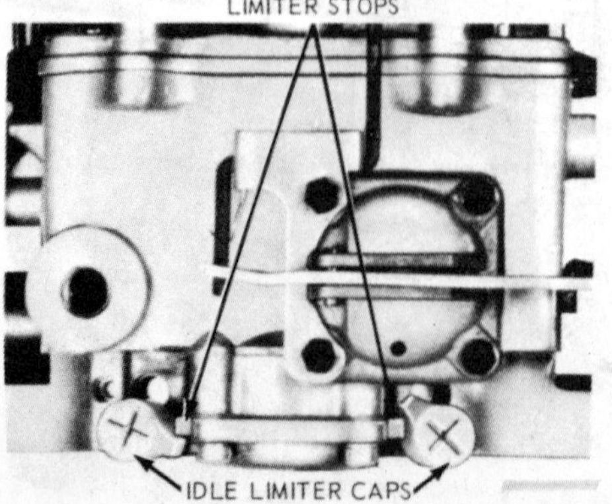

Idle fuel mixture adjusting screw with limiter cap on 2-bbl carburetor

Idle Speed Adjustment

1974–76

1. Remove the air cleaner and plug the vacuum lines.
2. Set the parking brake and block the wheels.

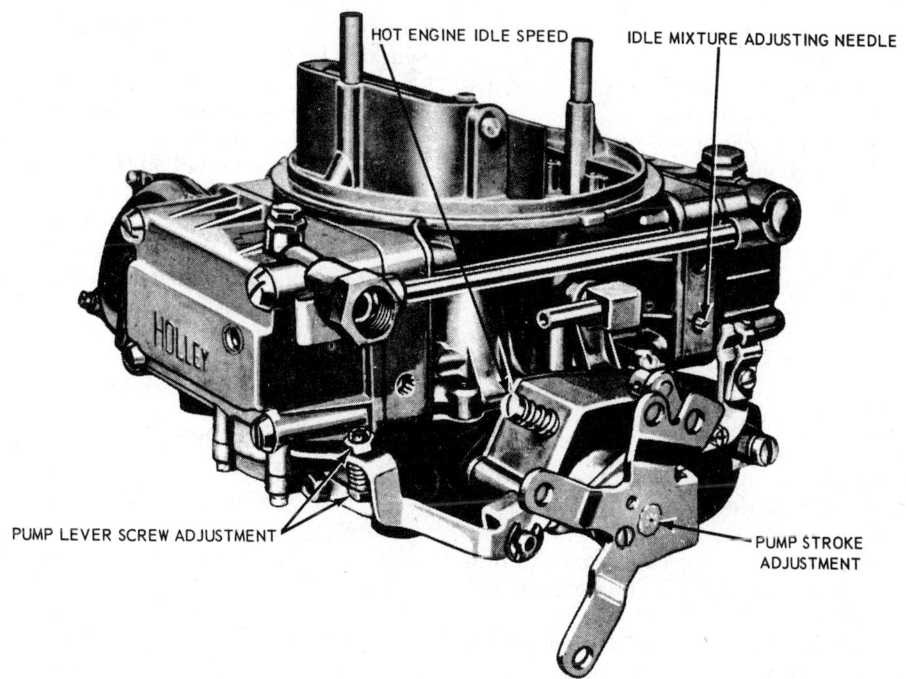

Holley 2300 carburetor

3. Connect a tachometer according to the manufacturer's instructions.

4. Run the engine to normalize underhood temperatures.

5. Check, and if necessary, reset the ignition timing.

6. Make certain that the choke plate is fully open.

7. Place the manual transmission in neutral; the automatic in Drive. Block the wheels. Turn on the headlights to "high beam" (see no. 8 above).

8. Turn the solenoid adjusting screw in or out to obtain the specified idle speed. The idle speed is the higher of the two rpm figures on the underhood specifications sticker.

9. Disconnect the solenoid lead wire. Place the automatic transmission in neutral.

10. Turn the solenoid-off adjusting screw to obtain the solenoid off rpm. This is the lower of the two rpm figures on the underhood specifications sticker.

11. Connect the solenoid lead wire and open the throttle slightly to allow the solenoid plunger to extend.

12. Stop the engine, replace the air cleaner and connect the vacuum lines. Check the idle speed. Readjust if necessary with the air cleaner installed.

1977–84

1. Remove the air cleaner and disconnect and plug the vacuum lines.

2. Block the wheels, apply the parking brake, turn off all accessories, start the engine and run it to normalize underhood temperatures.

3. Check that the choke plate is fully open and connect a tachometer according to the manufacturer's instructions.

4. Check the throttle stop positioner (TSP)-off speed as follows:

   a. collapse the plunger by forcing the throttle lever against it.

   b. place the transmission in neutral and check the engine speed. If necessary, adjust to specified TSP-Off speed with the throttle adjusting screw. See the underhood sticker.

5.. Place the manual transmission in neutral; the automatic in Drive and make certain the TSP plunger is extended.

6. Turn the TSP until the specified idle speed is obtained.

7. Install the air cleaner and connect the vacuum lines. Check the idle speed. Adjust, if necessary, with the air cleaner on.

Idle Mixture Adjustment

1974 AND LATER

NOTE: *For this procedure, Ford recommends a propane enrichment procedure. This requires special equipment not available to the general public. In lieu of this equipment the following procedure may be followed to obtain a satisfactory idle mixture.*

1. Block the wheels, set the parking brake

and run the engine to bring it to normal operating temperature.

2. Disconnect the hose between the emission canister and the air cleaner.

3. On engines equipped with the Thermactor air injection system, the routing of the vacuum lines connected to the dump valve will have to be temporarily changed. Mark them for reconnection before switching them.

4. For valves with one or two vacuum lines at the side, disconnect and plug the lines.

5. For valves with one vacuum line at the top, check the line to see if it is connected to the intake manifold or an intake manifold source such as the carburetor or distributor vacuum line. If not, remove and plug the line at the dump valve and connect a temporary length of vacuum hose from the dump valve fitting to a source of intake manifold vacuum.

6. Remove the limiter caps from the mixture screws by CAREFULLY cutting them with a sharp knife.

7. Place the transmission in neutral and run the engine at 2500 rpm for 15 seconds.

8. Place the automatic transmssion in Drive; the manual in neutral.

9. Adjust the idle speed to the higher of the two figures given on the underhood sticker.

10. Turn the idle mixture screws to obtain the highest possible rpm, leaving the screws in the leanest position that will maintain this rpm.

11. Repeat steps 7 thru 10 until further adjustment of the mixture screws does not increase the rpm.

12. Turn the screws in until the lower of the two idle speed figures is reached. Turn the screws in ¼ turn increments each to insure a balance.

13. Turn the engine off and remove the tachometer. Reinstall all equipment.

NOTE: *Rough idle, that cannot be corrected by normal service procedures on 1977 and later models, may be caused by leakage between the EGR valve body and diaphragm. To determine if this is the cause:*

1. Tighten the EGR bolts to 15 ft. lb. Connect a vacuum gauge to the intake manifold.

2. Lift to exert a sideways pressure on the diaphragm housing. If the idle changes or the reading on the vacuum gauge varies, replace the EGR valve.

6.9L V8 DIESEL

Curb Idle Adjustment

1. Place the transmission in neutral or park.

2. Bring the engine up to normal operating temperature.

3. Idle speed is measured with manual transmission in neutral and automatic transmission in Drive with the wheels blocked and parking brake ON.

4. Check the curb idle speed, using a magnetic pickup tachometer suitable for diesel engines. The part number for the Ford tachometer is Rotunda® 99-0001. Adjust the idle speed to 600–700 rpm.

NOTE: *Always check the underhood emissions control information sticker for the latest idle and adjustment specifications.*

5. Place the transmission in neutral or park and momentarily speed up the engine. Allow the rpm to drop to idle and recheck the idle speed. Readjust if necessary.

Fast Idle Adjustment

1. Place the transmission in neutral or park.

2. Start the engine and bring up to normal operating temperature.

3. Disconnect the wire from the fast idle solenoid.

4. Apply battery voltage to activate the solenoid plunger.

5. Speed up the engine momentarily to set the plunger.

6. The fast idle should be between 850–900 rpm. Adjust the fast idle by turning the solenoid plunger in or out.

7. Speed up the engine momentarily and recheck the fast idle. Readjust if necessary.

8. Remove the battery voltage from the solenoid and reconnect the solenoid wire.

Valve Lash

Valve adjustment determines how far the valves enter the cylinder and how long they stay open and closed.

If the valve clearance is too large, part of the lift of the camshaft will be used in removing the excessive clearance. Consequently, the valve will not be opening as far as it should. This condition has two effects: the valve train components will emit a tapping sound as they take up the excessive clearance and the engine will perform poorly because the valves don't open fully and allow the proper amount of gases to flow into and out of the engine.

If the valve clearance is too small, the intake valve and the exhaust valves will open too far and they will not fully seat on the cylinder head when they close. When a valve seats itself on the cylinder head, it does two things: it seals the combustion chamber so that none of the gases in the cylinder escape and it cools itself by transferring some of the heat it absorbs from the combustion in the cylinder to the cylinder head and to the engine's cooling system. If the valve clearance is too small, the engine will run poorly because of the gases escaping from the combustion chamber. The valves will also become overheated and will warp, since they cannot transfer heat unless they are touching the valve seat in the cylinder head.

NOTE: *While all valve adjustments must be made as accurately as possible, it is better to have the valve adjustment slightly loose than slightly tight as a burned valve may result from overly tight adjustments.*

ADJUSTMENT

240 and 300 6 Cyl.

1. Crank the engine until the TDC mark on the crankshaft damper is aligned with timing pointer on the cylinder front cover.
2. Scribe a mark on the damper at this point.
3. Scribe two more marks on the damper,

Chilton's Three "C's" Diesel Engine Diagnosis Procedure

Condition	Cause	Correction
Rough Idle	Improper adjustment	Adjust idle
	Accelerator control cable binding	Repair or lubricate
	Air or water in the fuel system	Clear air or water from fuel system
	Injection nozzle clogged	Check and clean injector nozzles
	Improper valve clearance	Check valve adjustment
	Injection pump malfunction	Check injection pump
Poor Performance	Air cleaner clogged	Check element
	Accelerator control cable binding	Check control cable for free movement
	Restricted fuel flow (water or air)	Check lines and filter
	Incorrect injection timing	Check injection timing
	Injection pump malfunction	Replace injection pump
Excessive Exhaust Smoke	Restricted air cleaner	Check element
	Air or water in fuel filter	Remove air or water from fuel system
	Improper grade fuel	Check fuel in tank
	Incorrect injection timing	Check injection timing
	Injection pump malfunction	Replace injection pump
	Injection nozzle stuck open	Check injector nozzles
Excessive Fuel Consumption	Restricted air cleaner	Check element
	Leak in fuel lines	Check for leaks
	Incorrect idle speed	Check idle
	Restricted exhaust system	Check exhaust
	Improper grade of fuel	Check fuel in tank
	Injection pump malfunction	Check injection pump operation
Loud Knocking in Engine	Defective fuel injector	Replace fuel injector

Note: If the problem persists after performing these preliminary checks, disassembly and inspection of internal engine components may be necessary for further diagnosis.

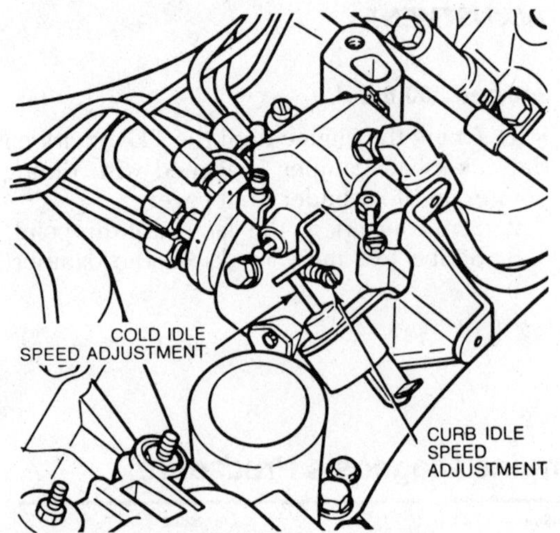

6.9L diesel injection pump showing idle speed adjustment. Pump mounted on top (front) of intake manifold

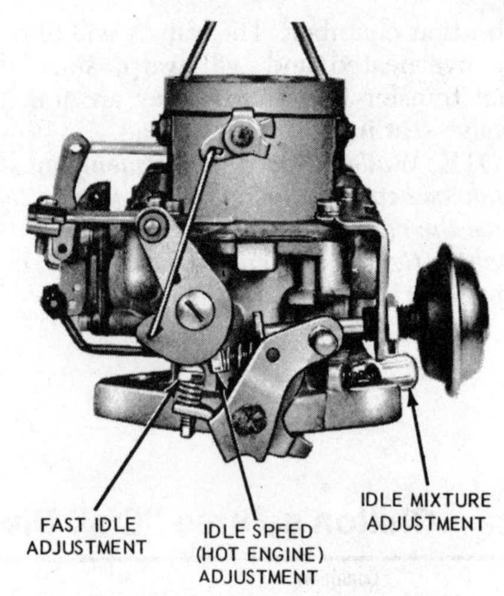

Autolite 1101A 1-bbl carburetor

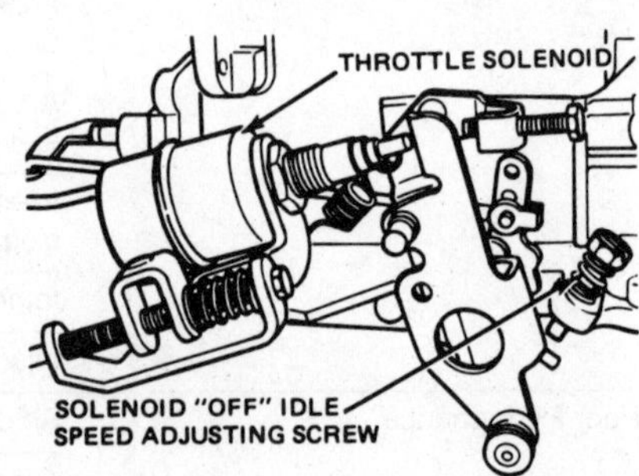

Autolite 2150 with solenoid throttle positioner

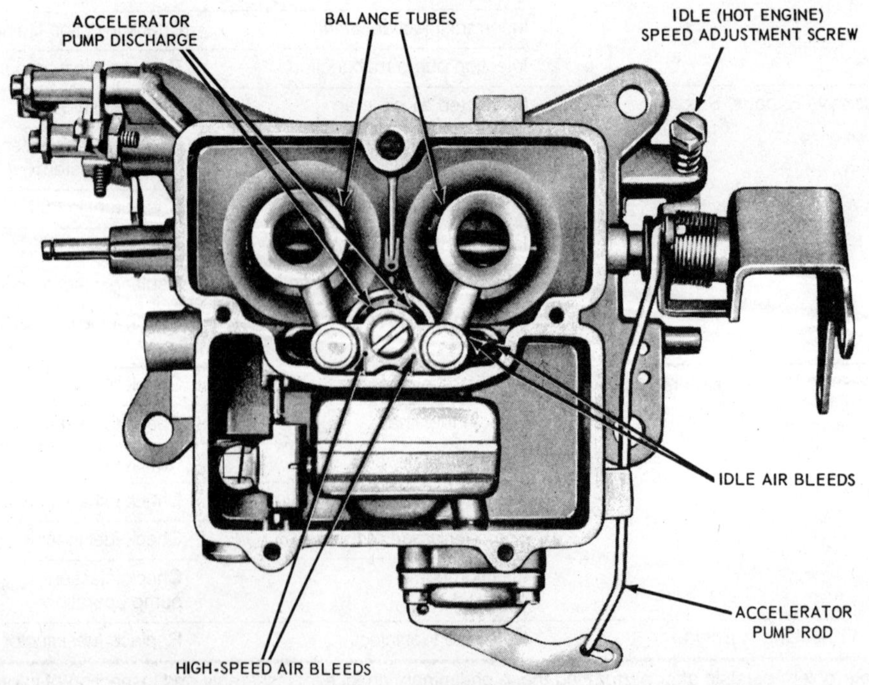

Autolite 2100A 2-bbl used on the 1965 352 cu in. engine (top view)

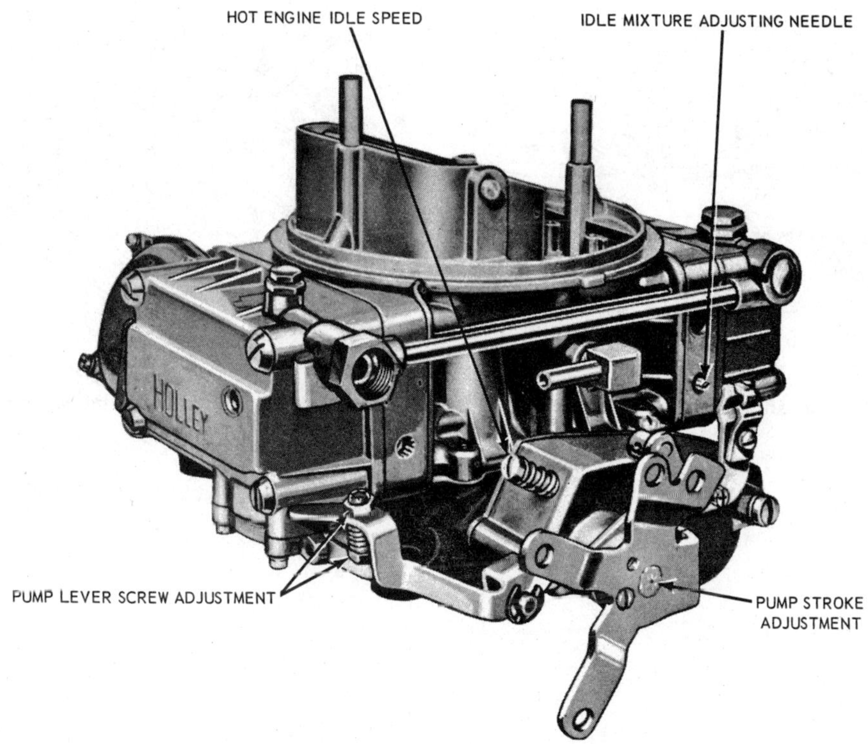

Holley 4350 4-bbl carburetor

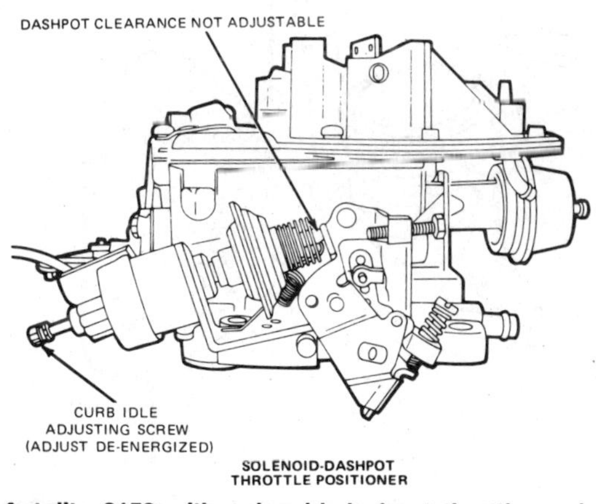

Autolite 2150 with solenoid dashpot throttle positioner

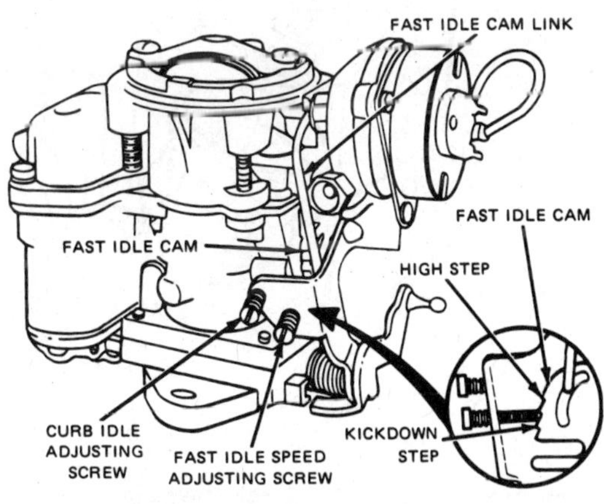

Carter YFA 1-bbl carburetor

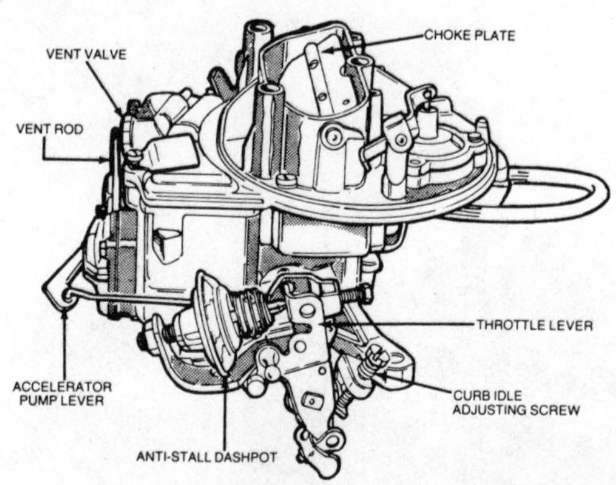

Autolite 2100 2-bbl showing curb idle screw

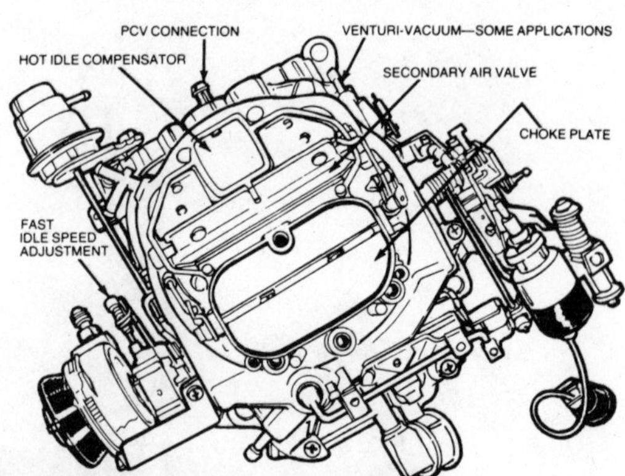

Autolite model 4300 4-bbl. Some models do not have throttle solenoid

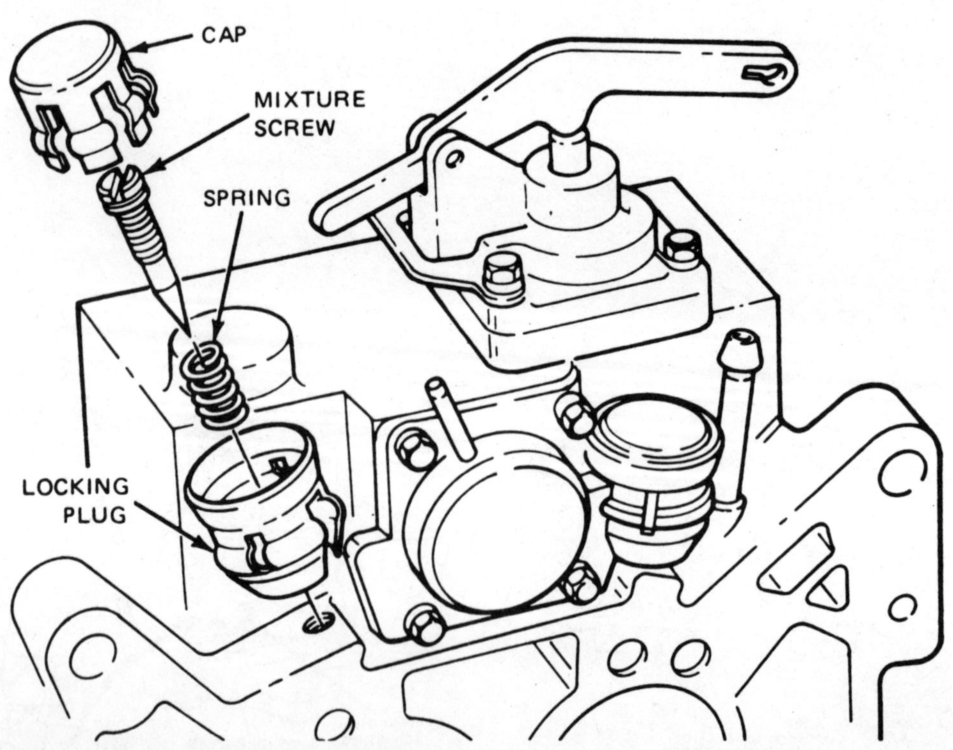

Some 1980 and later 2150 2-bbls have 2-piece metal plugs and caps in place of the plastic limiter caps on the idle mixture adjusting screws. They should be carefully removed before attempting any adjustments

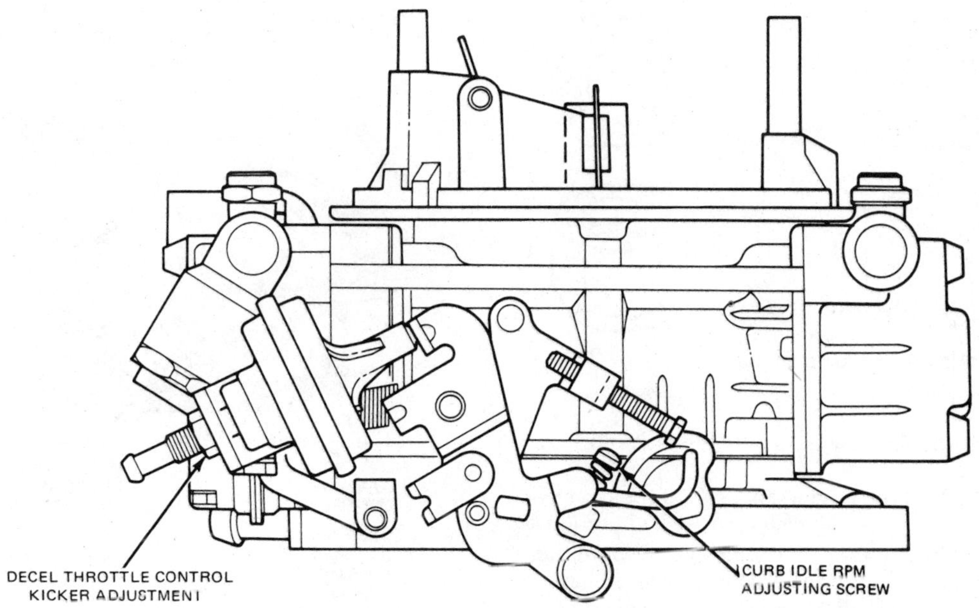

Curb idle screw locations, 4180C 4-bbl on 460 V8s

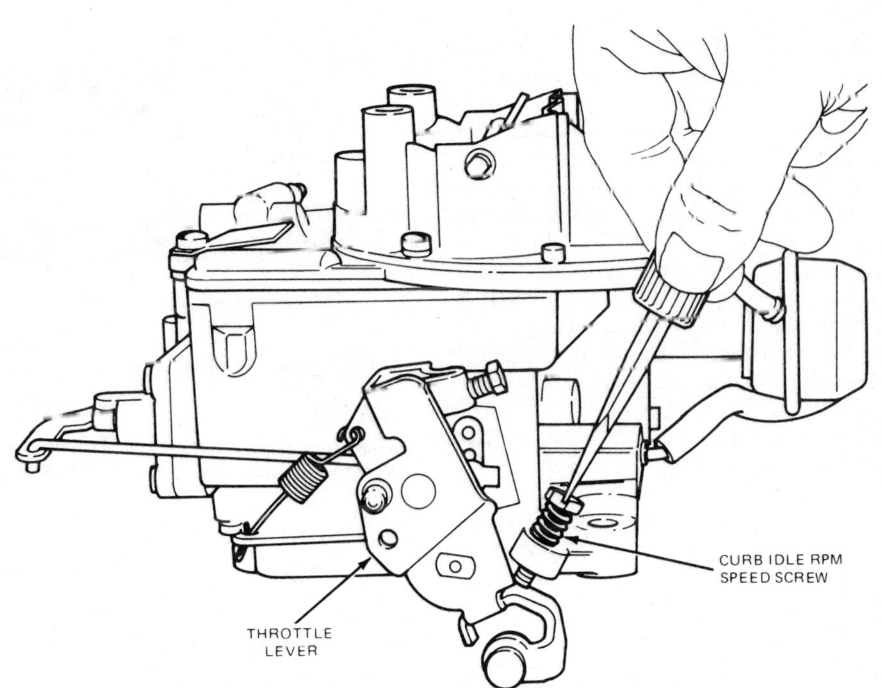

2150 2-bbl curb idle adjustment, 302 and 351 Canadian V8s

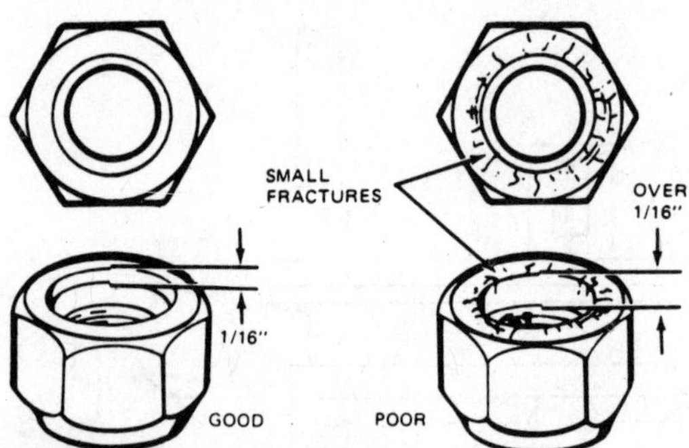

Checking the rocker stud nut

each equally spaced from the first mark (see illustration).

4. With the engine on TDC of the compression stroke, (mark A aligned with the pointer) back off the rocker arm adjusting nut until there is end-play in the pushrod. Tighten the adjusting nut until all clearance is removed, then tighten the adjusting nut one additional turn. To determine when all clearance is removed from the rocker arm, turn the pushrod with the fingers. When the pushrod can no longer be turned, all clearance has been removed.

5. Repeat this procedure for each valve, turning the crankshaft ⅓ turn to the next mark each time and following the engine firing order of 1-5-3-6-2-4.

302 Cu In. V8

Some early models of the 302 cu in. V8 are equipped with adjustable rockers whereas the later models are equipped with positive stop type rocker mounting studs. Positive stop equipped rockers are adjusted by turning the adjusting nut down until it stops. You can identify a positive stop mounting stud by determining whether or not the shank portion of the stud that is exposed just above the cylinder head is the same diameter as the threaded portion at the top of the stud, to which the rocker arm retaining nut attaches. If the shank portion is larger than the threaded area, it is a positive stop mounting stud. Use the procedure given below for adjusting the valve lash on positive stop type mounting stud equipped vehicles.

There are two different procedures for adjusting the valves on the V8 engines. One is a preferred procedure and one is an alternate procedure. The preferred procedure is recommended, but the alternate procedure may be used.

NOTE: *These procedures are not tune-up procedures, but rebuild procedures to be performed only after valve train reassembly.*

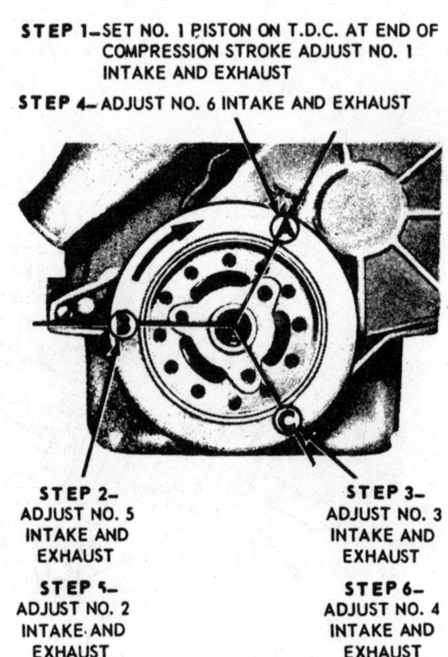

Position of crankshaft for valve adjustment, 240 and 300 inline sixes

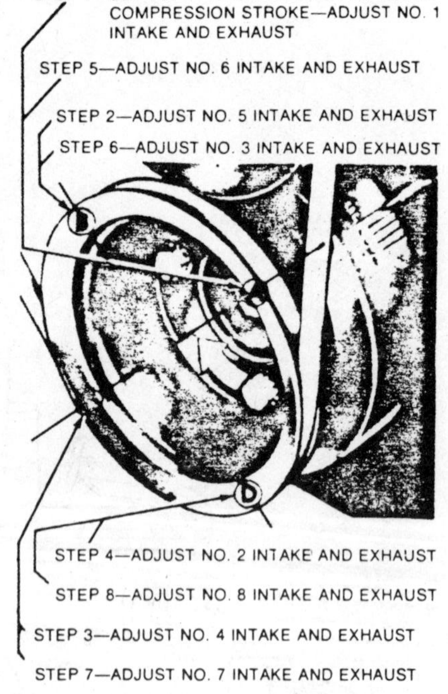

Position of crankshaft for valve adjustment—1969 302 V8 without positive-stop rocker arm stud

PREFERRED PROCEDURE THROUGH 1969

1. Position the piston(s) on TDC of the compression stroke, using the timing mark on the crankshaft pulley as a reference for starting with the No. 1 cylinder. You can tell if a piston is coming up on its compression stroke by removing the spark plug of the cylinder you are

working on and placing your thumb over the hole while the engine is cranked over. Air will try to force its way past your thumb when the piston comes upon the compression stroke. Make sure that the hightension coil wire leading to the distributor is removed before cranking the engine. Remove the valve covers.

2. Starting with No. 1 cylinder, and the piston in the position as mentioned above, apply pressure to slowly bleed down the valve lifter until the plunger is completely bottomed.

3. While holding the valve lifter in the fully collapsed position, check the available clearance between the rocker arm and the valve stem tip. Use a feeler gauge.

4. If the clearance is not within the specified amount, rotate the rocker arm stud nut clockwise to decrease the clearance and counterclockwise to increase the clearance. Normally, one turn of the rocker arm stud nut will vary the clearance by 0.066 in. Check the breakaway torque of each stud nut with a torque wrench, turning it counterclockwise. It should be anywhere from 4.5 to 15 ft. lbs. Replace the nut and/or the stud as necessary.

5. When both valves for the No. 1 cylinder have been adjusted, proceed on to the other valves, following the firing order sequence 1–5–4–2–6–3–7–8.

6. Replace the valve covers and gaskets.

ALTERNATE PROCEDURE THROUGH 1969

Follow Step 1 of the preferred procedure given above, but instead of collapsing the lifter as in Step 2, loosen the rocker retaining nut until there is endplay present in the pushrod; then tighten the nut to remove all pushrod-to-rocker arm clearance. When the pushrod-to-rocker arm clearance has been eliminated, tighten the stud nut an additional ¾ turn to place the lifter plunger in the desired operating range.

Repeat this procedure for all of the cylinders, using the firing order sequence as a guide. It takes ¼ turn of the crankshaft to bring the next piston in the firing order sequence up to TDC at the end of its compression stroke. Collapsed Tappet Gap Clearance:

- Allowable: .071–.193
- Desired: .096–.165

POSITIVE STOP TYPE MOUNTING STUD FROM 1970

351, 400, 460 and 1970 and Later 302V8.

1. Crank the engine until the No. 1 cylinder is at TDC of the compression stroke and the timing pointer is aligned with the mark on the crankshaft damper.

2. Scribe a mark on the damper at this point.

3. Scribe two additional marks on the damper (see illustration).

4. With the timing pointer aligned with mark 1 on the damper, tighten the following valves to the specified torque:

- *302 and 460:* Nos. 1, 7 and 8 Intake; Nos. 1, 5 and 4 Exhaust
- *351 and 400:* Nos. 1, 4 and 8 Intake; Nos. 1, 3 and 7 Exhaust

5. Rotate the crankshaft 180° to point 2 and tighten the following valves:

- *302 and 460:* Nos. 5 and 4 Intake; Nos. 2 and 6 Exhaust
- *351 and 400:* Nos. 3 and 7 Intake; Nos. 2 and 6 Exhaust

6. Rotate the crankshaft 270° to point 3 and tighten the following valves:

- *302 and 460:* Nos. 2, 3 and 6 Intake; Nos. 7, 3 and 8 Exhaust
- *351 and 400:* Nos. 2, 5 and 6 Intake; Nos. 4, 5 and 8 Exhaust

7. Rocker arm tightening specifications are: 302 and 351W—tighten nut until it contacts the rocker shoulder, then torque to 18–20 ft. lbs.; 400—tighten bolt to 18–25 ft. lbs.; 460—tighten nut until it contacts rocker shoulder, then torque to 18–22 ft. lbs.

With No. 1 at TDC at end of compression stroke make a chalk mark at points 2 and 3 approximately 90 degrees apart.

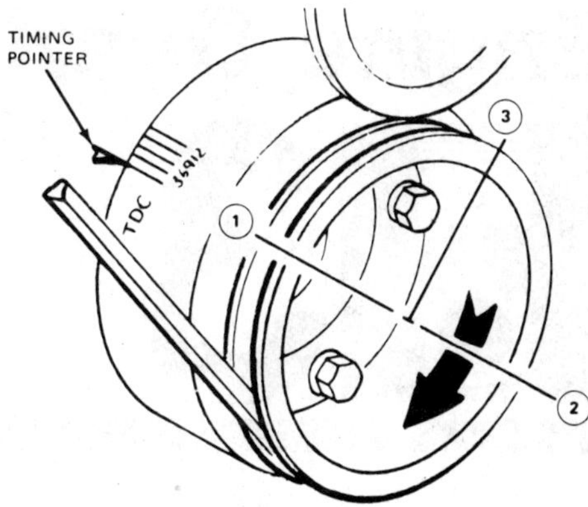

POSITION 1 – No. 1 at TDC at end of compression stroke.
POSITION 2 – Rotate the crankshaft 180 degrees (one half revolution) clockwise from POSITION 1.
POSITION 3 – Rotate the crankshaft 270 degrees (three quarter revolution clockwise from POSITION 2

Position of the crankshaft for checking and adjusting valve clearance, 351, 400, 460 and 1970 and later 302 V8s.

Engine and Engine Overhaul

3

ENGINE ELECTRICAL

Dura Spark Electronic Ignition Systems

Four different electronic ignition systems are used on Ford Motor Company vehicles, depending on year, engine and model. The four systems are:

1. Dura Spark I
2. Dura Spark II
3. Dura Spark III
4. TFI-IV (Thick Film Integrated)

Dura Spark I and Dura Spark II systems are nearly identical in operation, and virtually identical in appearance. The Dura Spark I uses a special control module which senses current flow through the ignition coil and adjust the dwell, or coil "on" time for maximum spark intensity. If the Dura Spark I module senses that the ignition is ON, but the distributor shaft is not turning, the current to the coil is turned OFF by the module. The Dura Spark II system does not have this feature, the coil is energized for the full amount of time that the ignition switch is ON. Keep this in mind when servicing the Dura Spark II system, as the ignition system could inadvertently "fire" while performing ignition system services (such as distributor cap removal) while the ignition is ON.

Dura Spark III is based on the previous systems, but the input signal is controlled by the EEC system, rather than as a function of engine timing and distributor armature position. The distributor, rotor cap, and control module are unique to this system; the spark plugs and plug wires are the same as those used with the Dura Spark II system. Although the Dura Spark II and III control modules are similar in appearance, they cannot be interchanged between systems.

The TFI-IV ignition system features a universal ditributor using no centrifugal or vacuum advance. The distributor has a die cast base which incorporates an integrally mounted TFI (Thick Film Integrated) ignition module, a "Hall Effect" vane switch stator assembly and provision for fixed octane adjustment. The TFI system uses an E-Core ignition coil in lieu of the Dura Spark coil. No distributor calibration is required and initial timing is not a normal adjustment, since advance etc. is controlled by the EEC-IV system.

GENERAL TESTING

Ignition Coil Test

The ignition coil must be diagnosed separately from the rest of the ignition system.

1. Primary resistance is measured between the two primary (low voltage) coil terminals, with the coil connector disconnected and the ignition switch off. Primary resistance must be 0.71–0.77 ohms for Dura Spark I. For Dura Spark II, it must be 1.13–1.23 ohms. For TFI systems, the primary resistance should be 0.3–1.0 ohms.
2. On Dura Spark ignitions, the secondary resistance is measured between the BATT and high voltage (secondary) terminals of the ignition coil with the ignition off, and the wiring from the coil disconnected. Secondary resistance must be 7350–8250 ohms on Dura Spark I systems. Dura Spark II figure is 7700–9300 ohms. For TFI systems, the primary resistance should be 8000–11500 ohms.
3. If resistance tests are okay, but the coil is still suspected, test the coil on a coil tester by following the test equipment manufacturer's instructions for a standard coil. If the reading differs from the original test, check for a defective harness.

Resistance Wire Test

Replace the resistance wire if it doesn't show a resistance of 1.05–1.15 for Dura Spark II. The resistance wire isn't used on Dura Spark I or TFI Systems.

Spark Plug Wire Resistance

Resistance on these wires must not exceed 5000 ohms per inch. To properly measure this, remove the wires from the plugs, and remove the distributor cap. Measure the resistance through the distributor cap at that end. Do not pierce any ignition wire for any reason. Measure only from the two ends.

NOTE: *Silicone grease must be reapplied to the spark plug wires whenever they are removed. When removing the wires from the spark plugs, a special tool should be used. Do not pull on the wires. Grasp and twist the boot to remove the wire. Whenever the high tension wires are removed from the plugs, coil, or distributor, silicone grease must be applied to the boot before reconnection. Use a clean small screwdriver blade to coat the entire interior surface with Ford silicone grease D7AZ–19A331–A, Dow Corning #111, or General Electric G–627.*

Adjustments

The air gap between the armature and magnetic pick-up coil in the distributor is not adjustable, nor are there any adjustments for the amplifier module. Inoperative components are simply replaced. Any attempt to connect components outside the vehicle may result in component failure.

TROUBLESHOOTING DURA SPARK I

The following Dura Spark II troubleshooting procedures may be used on Dura Spark I systems with a few variations. The Dura Spark I module has internal connections which shut off the primary circuit in the run mode when the engine stalls. To perform the above troublehooting procedures, it is necessary to by-pass these connections. However, with these connections by-passed, the current flow in the primary becomes so great that it will damage both the ignition coil and module unless a ballast resistor is installed in series with the primary circuit at the BAT terminal of the ignition coil. Such a resistor is available from Ford (Motorcraft part number DY–36). A 1.3 ohm, 100 watt wire-wound power resistor can also be used. To install the resistor, proceed as follows:

1. Release the BAT terminal lead from the coil by inserting a paper clip through the hole in the rear of the horseshoe coil connector and manipulating it against the locking tab in the connector until the lead comes free.
2. Insert a paper clip in the BAT terminal of the connector on the coil. Using jumper leads, connect the ballast resistor as shown.
3. Using a straight pin, pierce both the red and white leads of the module to short these two together. This will by-pass the internal connections of the module which turn off the ignition circuit when the engine is not running.

CAUTION: *Pierce the wires only AFTER the ballast resistor is in place or the ignition coil and module will be damaged.*

4. With the ballast resistor and by-pass in place, proceed with the Dura Spark II troubleshooting procedures. The resistor will become very hot during testing.

TROUBLESHOOTING DURA SPARK II

The following procedures can be used to determine whether the ignition system is working or not. If these procedures fail to correct the problem, a full troubleshooting procedure should be performed.

Preliminary Checks

1. Check the battery's state of charge and connections.
2. Inspect all wires and connections for breaks, cuts, abrasions, or burn spots. Repair as necessary.
3. Unplug all connectors one at a time and inspect for corroded or burned contacts. Repair and plug connectors back together. DO NOT remove the dielectric compound in the connectors.
4. Check for loose or damaged spark plug or coil wires. A wire resistance check is given at the end of this section. If the boots or nipples are removed on 8mm ignition wires, reline the inside of each with new silicone dielectric compound (Motorcraft WA 10).

Special Tools

To perform the following tests, two special tools are needed; an ignition test jumper and a modified spark plug. The test jumper must be used when performing the following tests. The modified spark plug is basically a spark plug with the side electrode removed. Ford makes a special tool called a Spark Tester for this purpose, which besides not having a side electrode is equipped with a spring clip so that it can be grounded to engine metal. It is recommended that the Spark Tester be used as there is less chance of being shocked.

Run Mode Spark Test

NOTE: *The wire colors given here are the main colors of the wires, not the dots or hashmarks.*

STEP 1

1. Remove the distributor cap and rotor from the distributor.

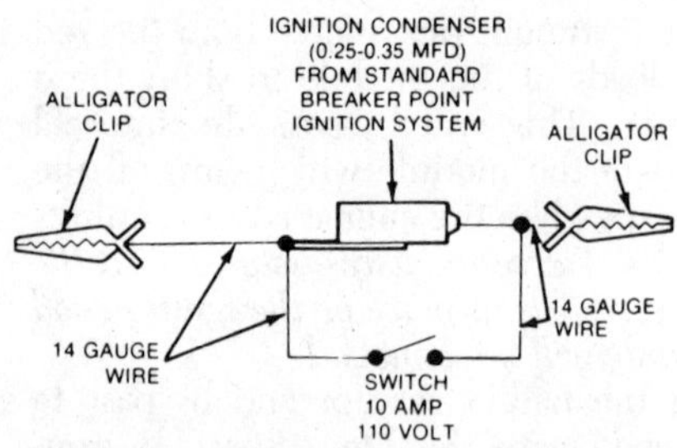

Test jumper switch used for troubleshooting the Dura Spark II ignition system;

2. With the ignition OFF, turn the engine over by hand until one of the teeth on the distributor armature aligns with the magnet in the pick-up coil.

3. Remove the coil wire from the distributor cap. Install the modified spark plug (see Special Tools, above) in the coil wire terminal and using heavy gloves and insulated pliers, hold the spark plug shell against the engine block.

4. Turn the ignition to RUN (not START) and tap the distributor body with a screwdriver handle. There should be a spark at the modified spark plug or at the coil wire terminal.

5. If a good spark is evident, the primary circuit is OK: perform Start Mode Spark Test. If there is no spark, proceed to Step 2.

STEP 2

1. Unplug the module connector(s) which contain(s) the green and black module leads.

2. In the harness side of the connector(s), connect the special test jumper (see Special Tools, above) between the leads which connect to the green and black leads of the module pig tails. Use paper clips on connector socket holes to make contact. Do not allow clips to ground.

3. Turn the ignition switch to RUN (not START) and close the test jumper switch. Leave closed for about 1 second, then open. Repeat several times. There should be a spark each time the switch is opened. On Dura Spark I systems, close the test switch for 10 seconds on the first cycle. After that, 1 second is adequate.

4. If there is no spark, the problem is probably in the primary circuit through the ignition switch, the coil, the green lead or the black lead, or the ground connection in the distributor: perform Step 3. If there is a spark, the primary circuit wiring and coil are probably OK. The problem is probably in the distributor pick-up, the module red wire, or the module: perform Step 6.

STEP 3

1. Disconnect the test jumper lead from the black lead and connect it to a good ground. Turn the test jumper switch on and off several times as in Step 2.

2. If there is no spark, the problem is probably in the green lead, the coil, or the coil feed circuit: perform Step 5.

3. If there is spark, the problem is probably in the black lead or the distributor ground connection: perform Step 4.

STEP 4

Connect an ohmmeter between the black lead and ground. With the meter on its lowest scale, there should be no measurable resistance in the circuit. If there is resistance, check the distributor ground connection and the black lead from the module. Repair as necessary, remove the ohmmeter, plug in all connections and repeat Step 1. If there is no resistance, the primary ground wiring is OK: perform Step 6.

STEP 5

Disconnect the test jumper from the green lead and ground and connect it between the TACH-TEST terminal of the coil and a good ground on the engine. With the ignition switch in the RUN position, turn the jumper switch on. Hold it on for about 1 second then turn it off as in Step 2. Repeat several times. There should be a spark each time the switch is turned off. If there is no spark, the problem is probably in the primary circuit running through the ignition switch to the coil BAT terminal, or in the coil itself. Check coil resistance (test given later in this section), and check the coil for internal shorts or opens. Check the coil feed circuit for opens, shorts or high resistance. Repair as necessary, reconnect all connectors and repeat Step 1. If there is spark, the coil and its feed circuit are OK. The problem could be in the green lead between the coil and the module. Check for open or short, repair as necessary, reconnect all connectors and repeat Step 1.

STEP 6

To perform this step, a voltmeter which is not combined with a dwell meter is needed. The slight needle oscillations may not be detectable on the combined voltmeter/dwell meter unit.

1. Connect a voltmeter between the orange and purple leads on the harness side of the module connectors.

CAUTION: *On the catalytic converter equipped cars, disconnect the air supply line between the Thermactor by-pass valve and the manifold before cranking the engine with the ignition off. This will prevent damage to the catalytic converter. After Testing, run the engine for at least 3 minutes before reconnecting the by-pass valve, to clear excess fuel from the exhaust system.*

2. Set the voltmeter on its lowest scale and crank the engine. The meter needle should oscillate slightly. If the meter does not oscillate, check the circuit through the magnetic pick-up in the distributor for open, shorts, shorts to ground and resistance. Resistance between the orange and purple leads should be 400–1000 ohms, and between each lead and ground should be more than 70,000 ohms. Repair as necessary, reconnect all connectors and repeat Step 1. If the meter oscillates, the problem is probably in the power feed to the module (red wire) or in the module itself: proceed to Step 7.

STEP 7

1. Remove all meters and jumpers and plug in all connectors.

2. Turn the ignition switch to the RUN position and measure voltage between the battery positive terminal and engine ground. It should be 12 volts.

3. Measure voltage between the red lead of the module and engine ground. To make this measurement, it will be necessary to pierce the red wire with a straight pin and connect the voltmeter to the straight pin and to ground. DO NOT ALLOW THE STRAIGHT PIN TO GROUND ITSELF.

4. The two readings should be within one volt of each other. If not within one volt, the problem is in the power feed to the red lead. Check for shorts, open, or high resistance and correct as necessary. After repairs, repeat Step 1. If the readings are within one volt, the problem is probably in the module. Replace with a good module and repeat Step 1. If this corrects the problem, reconnect the old module and repeat Step 1. If problem returns, permanently install the new module.

Start Mode Spark Test

NOTE: *The wire colors given here are the main colors of the wires, not the dots or hashmarks.*

1. Remove the coil wire from the distributor cap. Install the modified spark plug mentioned under "Special Tools" in the coil wire and ground it to engine metal either by its sporing clip (Spark Tester) or by holding the spark plug shell against the engine block with insulated pliers.

NOTE: *See "CAUTION" under Step 6 of "Run Mode Spark Test," above.*

2. Have an assistant crank the engine using the ignition switch and check for spark. If there is good spark, the problem is probably in the distributor cap, rotor, ignition cables or spark plugs. If there is no spark, proceed to Step 3.

3. Measure the battery voltage. Next, measure the voltage at the white wire of the module while cranking the engine. To make this measurement, it will be necessary to pierce the white wire with a straight pin and connect the voltmeter to the straight pin and to ground. DO NOT ALLOW THE STRAIGHT PIN TO GROUND ITSELF. The battery voltage and the voltage at the white wire should be within 1 volt of each other. If the readings are not within 1 volt of each other, check and repair the feed through the ignition switch to the white wire. Recheck for spark (Step 1). If the readings are within 1 volt of each other, or if there is still no spark after power feed to white wire is repaired, proceed to Step 4.

4. Measure the coil BAT terminal voltage while cranking the engine. The reading should be within 1 volt of battery voltage. If the readings are not within 1 volt of each other, check and repair the feed through the ignition switch to the coil. If the readings are within 1 volt of each other, the problem is probably in the ignition module. Substitute another module and repeat test for spark (Step 1).

TROUBLESHOOTING DURA SPARK III

PRELIMINARY CHECKOUT

NOTE: *When making these tests, make sure to follow wiring back to the module for color coding purposes. All instrument checks for wiring integrity should be accompanied by visual inspection and by wiggling of connectors to check for either bad insulation or loose connections.*

Begin troubleshooting by inspecting all vacuum hoses and both high tension and wiring harness wiring for proper routing and secure connections. Check also for damaged insulation and burned connectors.

Make sure the battery is fully charged and turn off all accessories before starting tests. The procedure requires the following equipment:

1. A precise volt/ohmmeter, preferably with digital readout.

2. A commercially available spark tester that can replace a spark plug in the circuit and provide visible evidence of a hot spark.

3. A diagnostic test adapter designed for the Dura Spark III system. This must plug into the three wire connector going to the ignition module an apply voltage to the right module circuit for testing it direclty from the battery.

4. A 12 volt test light and a supply of straight pins for testing for voltage and resistance in the wiring.

TEST 1

1. Disconnect the three wire ignition module connector. Inspect the connector for damage, dirt, or corrosion. If none are present,

proceed with Step 2. Otherwise, make repairs as necessary.

2. Install the test adapter between the two halves of the connector. Pull the coil high tension lead out of the distributor, install and ground the spark tester. Turn the ignition switch to the "RUN" position.

3. Touch the lead to the test adapter to the battery positive terminal while observing the spark tester. There should be a spark as the lead touches the terminal. Test repeatedly. If spark occurs consistently, go to Test 2. Otherwise, see Test 4.

TEST 2

1. Remove the diagnostic test adapter from the ignition module circuit, and reconnect the connector. Leave the spark tester in place, and observe it while cranking the engine. If there is no spark, go on to test three. If there is spark, follow the rest of the steps in this test.

2. Inspect the distributor cap, rotor, and adapter for cracks or carbon tracking and replace parts as necessary. Make sure there is silicone compound to protect the tip of the rotor.

3. If the inspections above do not reveal and cure the problem, check the distributor rotor alignment and correct as necessary.

TEST 3

1. If the starter relay has an "I" terminal, disconnect the cable from the starter relay to the starter motor. If it has no "I" terminal, disconnect the wire to the "S" terminal of the relay.

2. Insert a straight pin through the center of the white wire leading to the ignition module. Make sure it does not contact any ground.

3. Measure the voltage existing between the positive and negative battery terminals.

4. Connect the VOM negative lead to a good engine ground. Use a pin to get a connection to the white wire going to the ignition module (without grounding the pin). Connect the positive lead to the VOM to the pin. Finally, turn the ignition switch to the START position and read the voltage while wiggling the wiring.

5. Connect the positive lead of the VOM to the "Batt" terminal of the ignition coil and with the ignition switch in the START position, repeat the test.

6. If either reading was less than 90 percent of battery voltage, refer to a wiring diagram and repair wiring and connectors in the faulty circuit. Otherwise, replace the ignition switch.

7. Remove the straight pin and reconnect the wiring to the starter relay. If the required repairs do not resolve the problem, or if both circuits passed the test, proceed to Test 4.

TEST 4

1. Connect a test lamp between the TACH terminal of the ignition coil and a ground on the engine. Connect the diagnostic test adapter into the ignition system as in the first test. Turn the ignition switch to the "RUN" position.

2. Touch the test lead for the adapter to the battery positive terminal repeatedly while observing the test light.

3. Remove the diagnostic connector and test light and reconnect the three prong connector. If the light flashes consistently, go to Test 5; if not, go to Test 6.

TEST 5

1. Disconnect the coil high tension wire and connector. Inspect the wire and connector for a burned appearance and replace parts as necessary. Inspect the coil for cracks or carbon tracking in the high tension connector, and replace it if necessary.

2. Test the high tension lead with an ohmmeter by removing it and connecting the meter to either end. Resistance should be 5,000 ohms per inch or less. If resistance is too high, replace the wire.

3. Measure the coil secondary circuit resistance by connecting the ohmmeter between the coil BATT terminal and the high voltage connector. Resistance must be between 7,700 ohms and 10,500 ohms. If resistance is either above or below this range, replace the coil.

4. Replace or reconnect parts as necessary.

TEST 6

1. If the starter relay has an "I" terminal, disconnect the cable from the relay to the starter motor. If there is no "I" terminal on the relay, disconnect the wire to the 'S' terminal of the relay. Insert straight pins into the centers of the red and white module wires. DO NOT GROUND. Measure the exact voltage by connecting the voltmeter between the positive and negative battery terminals.

2. Connect the voltmeter negative lead between the base of the distributor and the pin passing through the red lead. Turn the ignition switch to the "RUN" position. Measure the voltage while wiggling the wiring.

3. Connect the voltmeter positive lead over to the pin running through the white wire. Turn the ignition switch to the START position and read the voltage while wiggling the wiring.

4. Repeat the step above, but with the positive lead attached to the BATT terminal on the ignition coil to test the ballast resistor bypass. Turn the ignition switch off, remove the straight pins, and reconnect the starter wiring.

5. If the voltage was more than 90 percent

of battery voltage in every case, go on to the next test. If voltage was lower than 90 percent of battery voltage, inspect the wiring harness for faulty circuits and repair as necessary. Replace the ignition switch, or replace the radio interference capacitor on the coil as necessary until the system can pass the test.

TEST 7

1. Attach the negative lead of the voltmeter to an engine ground, and the positive lead to the BATT terminal on the coil.

2. With the ignition switch in the RUN position, measure the voltage.

3. Turn the ignition switch off and remove the voltmeter leads. If the voltage is 6 to 8 volts, proceed to Test 8; if it is less than 6 volts or greater than 8 volts, proceed to Test 9.

TEST 8

1. Disconnect the ignition module three wire connector and the connector at the coil from the wire from the ignition module. Repair or replace bad connectors as necessary.

2. Connect an ohmmeter between an engine ground ([MIN]) and the TACH terminal of the coil. Reconnect module and coil connectors. If resistance is greater than one ohm, replace the module. If it is one ohm or less, just inspect the wiring harness between the module and coil to make sure there are no wiring problems.

TEST 9

1. Disconnect the ignition coil primary connectors. Measure coil primary resistance by connecting an ohmmeter between the BATT and TACH terminals. Disconnect the ohmmeter and reconnect connectors.

2. If resistance is between .8 and 1.6 ohms, proceed to Test 10. If resistance is less than or greater than specification, replace the coil.

TEST 10

1. Insert a straight pin into the green wire at the module without grounding it.

2. Attach the negative lead of the voltmeter to an engine ground. Then, turn the ignition switch on and measure the voltage, first at the straight pin in the green wire and then at the TACH terminal of the ignition coil. If the difference in voltage is more than .5 volts, inspect and repair the green module-to-coil wire as necessary. If it is less than .5 volts, but more than 1.5, proceed to Test 12. If it is 1.5 volts or less, proceed to the test of the ballast resistor (Test 11).

3. Turn the ignition off and remove the leads and straight pin.

TEST 11

1. Disconnect the two wire connector to the ignition module. Repair any defects in the connectors. Disconnect the coil primary connector.

2. Use an ohmmeter to measure resistance of the circuit between the BATT terminal of the ignition coil connector and the wiring harness connector mating with the red wire from the module. In both cases, measure on the wiring harness side not at the coil or at the wire leading to the module.

3. If the resistance is .8–1.6 ohms, replace the ignition module. If it is less than .8 or greater than 1.6 ohms, replace the ballast resistor.

4. Remove the ohmmeter and reconnect connectors as necessary.

TEST 12

1. Insert a straight pin into the black wire at the ignition module without grounding it.

2. Connect a voltmeter between the pin and an engine ground, with the positive lead at the pin. Turn the ignition switch to RUN position.

3. If the voltage read is less than .5 volt, replace the ignition module. If it is greater than .5 volts, proceed to the final test for further diagnosis of problems in the ground circuit.

4. Turn the ignition switch off, remove the voltmeter connectors and remove the straight pin.

TEST 13

1. Disconnect the three-wire connector to the module. Connect an ohmmeter between an engine ground and the harness side terminal mating with the black wire from the module. Read the resistance while wiggling the harness.

2. If resistance is less than one ohm, look for a problem in the wiring harness connectors and the module black wire. The problem is either intermittent or not in the ignition system. If resistance is greater than one ohm, inspect the harness and connectors between the module and ground connection. Repair wiring as necessary, disconnect the ohmmeter, and reconnect the connector.

Rotor Alignment Dura Spark III

1. Remove the distributor cap, noting the approximate location of the high tension wire going to No. 1 cylinder. Rotate the engine until No. 1 cylinder firing position is being approached by the rotor and the engine nears 0 degrees TDC. Remove the rotor and position a distributor alignment tool so that when the alignment slots reach an aligned position, the tool will slip into place.

2. Turn the engine very slowly until the tool just slips into the alignment slots, and then stop rotating the engine. Read the position of the timing mark on the vibration damper. If it is between 4 degrees Before Top Center and 4 degrees After Top Center, the rotor alignment meets specification. In this case, remove the tool, and reposition the rotor and cap. If the timing mark is outside these limits, proceed with the steps that follow.

3. Remove the alignment tool. Rotate the engine until the timing marks align at 0 degrees, TDC.

4. Loosen the two sleeve assembly adjustment screws. Then, rotate the sleeve assembly until the alignment tool can be inserted. With the tool in position, tighten the adjusting screws. Then, remove the tool, and install the rotor and cap.

TROUBLESHOOTING THE TFI–IV SYSTEM

NOTE: *After performing any test which requires piercing a wire with a straight pin, remove the straight pin and seal the holes in the wire with silicone sealer.*

Ignition Coil Secondary Voltage

1. Disconnect the secondary (high voltage) coil wire from the distributor cap and install a spark tester (see Special Tools, located with the Dura Spark Troubleshooting) between the coil wire and ground.

2. Crank the engine. A good, strong spark should be noted at the spark tester. If spark is noted, but the engine will not start, check the spark plugs, spark plug wiring, and fuel system. If there is no spark at the tester: Check the ignition coil secondary wire resistance; it should be no more than 5000 ohms per inch. Inspect the ignition coil for damage and/or carbon tracking. With the distributor cap removed, verify that the distributor shaft turns with the engine; if it does not, repair the engine as required. If the fault was not found proceed to the next test.

Ignition Coil Primary Circuit Switching

1. Insert a small straight pin in the wire which runs from the coil negative (−) terminal to the TFI module, about one inch from the module.

CAUTION: *The pin must not touch ground.*

2. Connect a 12VDC test lamp between the straight pin and an engine ground.

3. Crank the engine, noting the operation of the test lamp. If the test lamp flashes, proceed to the next test. If the test lamp lights but does not flash, proceed to the Wiring Harness test. If the test lamp does not light at all, proceed to the Primary Circuit Continuity test.

Ignition Coil Resistance

Refer to the General Testing for an explanation of the resistance tests. Replace the ignition coil if the resistance is out of the specification range.

Wiring Harness

1. Disconnect the wiring harness connector from the TFI module; the connector tabs must be PUSHED to disengage the connector. Inspect the connector for damage, dirt, and corrosion.

2. Attach the negative lead of a voltmeter to the base of the distributor. Attach the other voltmeter lead to a small straight pin. With the ignition switch in the RUN position, insert the straight pin into the No. 1 terminal of the TFI module connector. Note the voltage reading. With the ignition switch in the RUN position, move the straight pin to the No. 2 connector terminal. Again, note the voltage reading. Move the straight pin to the No. 3 connector terminal, then turn the ignition switch to the START position. Note the voltage reading then turn the ignition OFF.

3. The voltage readings should all be at least 90% of the available battery voltage. If the readings are okay, proceed to the Stator Assembly and Module test. If any reading is less than 90% of the battery voltage, inspect the wiring, connectors, and/or ignition switch for defects. If the voltage is low only at the No. 1 terminal, proceed to the ignition coil primary voltage test.

Stator Assembly and Module

1. Remove the distributor from the engine.

2. Remove the TFI module from the distributor.

3. Inspect the distributor terminals, ground screw, and stator wiring for damage. Repair as necessary.

4. Measure the resistance of the stator assembly, using an ohmmeter. If the ohmmeter reading is 800–975 ohms, the stator is okay, but the TFI module must be replaced. If the ohmmeter reading is less than 800 ohms or more than 975 ohms; the TFI module is okay, but the stator module must be replaced.

5. Repair as necessary and reinstall the TFI module and the distributor.

TFI Module

1. Remove the distributor cap from the distributor, and set it aside (spark plug wires intact).

2. Disconnect the TFI harness connector.

3. Remove the distributor.

4. Remove the two TFI module retaining screws.

5. To disengage the modules terminals from the distributor base connector, pull the right side of the module down the distributor mounting flange and then back up. Carefully pull the module toward the flange and away from the distributor.

CAUTION: *Step 5 must be followed EXACTLY; failure to do so will result in damage to the distributor module connector pins.*

6. Coat the TFI module baseplate with a thin layer of silicone grease (FD7AZ–19A331–A or its equivalent).

7. Place the TFI module on the distributor base mounting flange. Position the module assembly toward the distributor bowl and carefully engage the distributor connector pins. Install and torque the two TFI module retaining screws to 9–16 inch lbs.

8. Install the distributor assembly.

9. Install the distributor cap and check the engine timing.

Primary Circuit Continuity

This test is performed in the same manner as the previous Wiring Harness test, but only the No. 1 terminal conductor is tested (ignition switch in RUN position). If the voltage is less than 90% of the available battery voltage, proceed to the coil primary voltage test.

Ignition Coil Primary Voltage

1. Attach the negative lead of a voltmeter to the distributor base.

2. Turn the ignition switch ON and connect the positive voltmeter lead to the negative (−) ignition coil terminal. Note the voltage reading and turn the ignition OFF. If the voltmeter reading is less than 90% of the available battery voltage, inspect the wiring between the ignition module and the negative (−) coil terminal, then proceed to the last test, which follows.

Ignition Coil Supply Voltage

1. Attach the negative lead of a voltmeter to the distributor base.

2. Turn the ignition switch ON and connect the positive voltmeter lead to the positive (+) ignition coil terminal. Note the voltage reading then turn the ignition OFF. If the voltage reading is at least 90% of the battery voltage, yet the engine will still not run; first, check the ignition coil connector and terminals for corrosion, dirt, and/or damage; second, replace the ignition switch if the connectors and terminal are okay.

3. Connect any remaining wiring.

Distributor

REMOVAL

1. Remove the air cleaner assembly, taking note of the hose locations.

2. On models equipped with a conventional ignition system, disconnect the primary wire at the coil. On models equipped with breakerless ignition, disconnect the distributor wiring connector from the vehicle wiring harness.

3. Noting the position of the vacuum line(s) on the distributor diaphragm, disconnect the lines at the diaphragm. Unsnap the two distributor cap retaining clamps and remove the cap. Position the cap and ignition wires to one side.

NOTE: *If it is necessary to disconnect ignition wires from the cap to get enough room to remove the distributor, make sure to label every wire and the cap for easy and accurate reinstallation.*

4. Using chalk or paint, carefully mark the position of the distributor rotor in relation to the distributor housing and mark the position of the distributor housing in relation to the engine block. When this is done, you should have a line on the distributor housing directly in line with the tip of the rotor and another line on the engine block directly in line with the mark on the distributor housing. This is very important because the distributor must be reinstalled in the exact same location from which it was removed, if correct ignition timing is to be maintained.

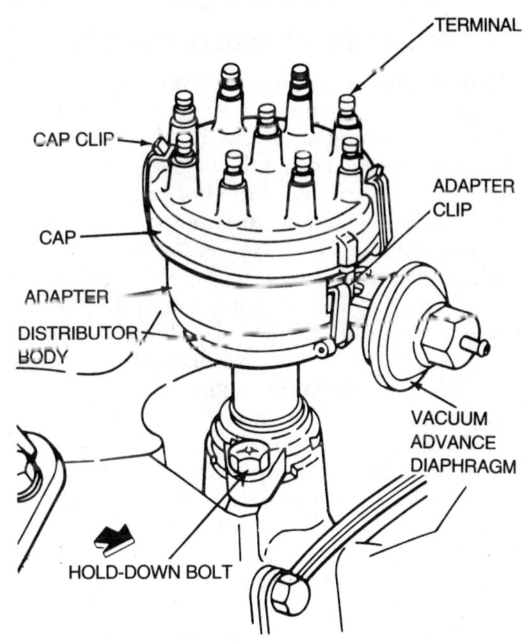

Distributor assembly. Arrow points to front

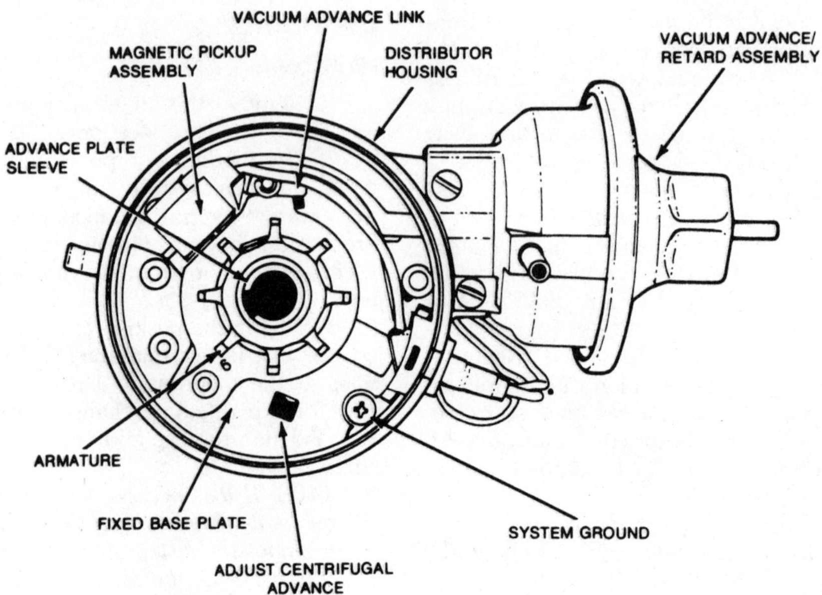

V8 breakerless (electronic) distributor, cap and rotor removed

5. Remove the distributor hold-down bolt and clamp. Remove the distributor from the engine. Make sure that the oil pump (intermediate) driveshaft does not come out with the distributor. If it does, remove it from the distributor shaft, coat its lower end with heavy grease, and reinsert it, making sure that it fully engages the oil pump drive.

NOTE: *Do not disturb the engine while the distributor is removed. If you turn the engine over with the distributor removed, you will have to retime the engine.*

INSTALLATION—ENGINE DISTURBED

If the engine was cranked (disturbed) with the distributor removed, it will now be necessary to retime the engine. If the distributor has been installed incorrectly and the engine will not start, remove the distributor from the engine and start over again. Hold the distributor close to the engine and install the cap on the distributor in its normal position. Locate the No. 1 spark plug tower on No. 1 spark plug and crank the engine over until the No. 1 cylinder is on its compression stroke. To accomplish this, place a wrench on the lower engine pulley and turn the engine slowly in a clockwise or counterclockwise (V8) direction until the TDC mark on the crankshaft damper aligns with the timing pointer. If you place your finger in the No. 1 spark plug hole, you will feel air escaping as the piston rises in the combustion chamber. On conventional ignition systems, the rotor must be at the No. 1 firing position to install the distributor. On breakerless ignition systems, one of the armature segments must be aligned with the stator as shown in the accompanying illustration to install the distributor. Make sure that the oil pump intermediate shaft properly engages the distributor shaft. It may be necessary to crank the engine with the starter, after the distributor drive gear is partially engaged, in order to engage the oil pump intermediate shaft. Install, but do not tighten the retaining clamp and bolt. Rotate the distributor to advance the timing to a point where the armature tooth is aligned properly (breakerless ignition), or to a point where the points are just starting to open (conventional ignition). Tighten the clampbolt.

INSTALLATION—ENGINE NOT DISTURBED

If the engine was not cranked (disturbed) when the distributor was removed, position the distributor in the block with the rotor aligned with the mark previously scribed on the distributor body and the marks on the distributor body and cylinder block in alignment. Install the distributor hold-down bolt and clamp fingertight.

1. Install the distributor cap and wires.
2. On models equipped with conventional ignition, connect the primary wire at the coil. On models equipped with breakerless ignition, connect the distributor wiring connector to the wiring harness.
3. Install the Thermactor air pump mounting bolt, if removed, and adjust the air pump drive belt tension, if necessary, as outlined in Chapter 1.
4. Install the air cleaner, if removed.
5. Check the ignition timing as outlined in Chapter 2.

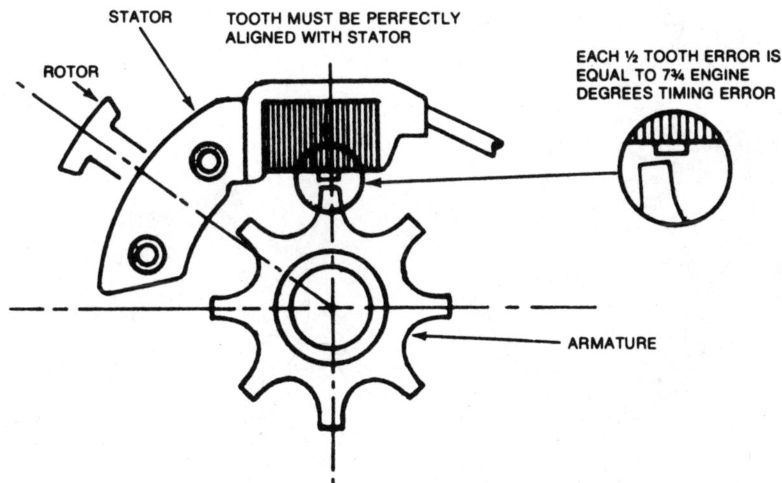

V8 breakerless distributor, static timing position. V6 similar

Alternator

The alternator charging system is a negative (−) ground system which consists of an alternator, a regulator, a charge indicator, a storage battery and wiring connecting the components.

The alternator is belt-driven from the engine. Energy is supplied from the alternator/regulator system to the rotating field through two brushes to two slip-rings. The slip-rings are mounted on the rotor shaft and are connected to the field coil. This energy supplied to the rotating field from the battery is called excitation current and is used to initially energize the field to begin the generation of electricity. Once the alternator starts to generate electricity, the excitation current comes from its own output rather than the battery.

The alternator produces power in the form of alternating current. The alternating current is rectified by 6 diodes into direct current. The direct current is used to charge the battery and power the rest of the electrical system.

ALTERNATOR PRECAUTIONS

To prevent damage to the alternator and regulator, the following precautions should be taken when working with the electrical system.

1. Never reverse the battery connections.
2. Booster batteries for starting must be connected properly—positive-to-positive and negative-to-negative.
3. Disconnect the battery cables before using a fast charger; the charger has a tendency to force current through the diodes in the opposite direction for which they were designed. This burns out the diodes.
4. Never use a fast charger as a booster for starting the vehicle.
5. Never disconnect the voltage regulator while the engine is running.

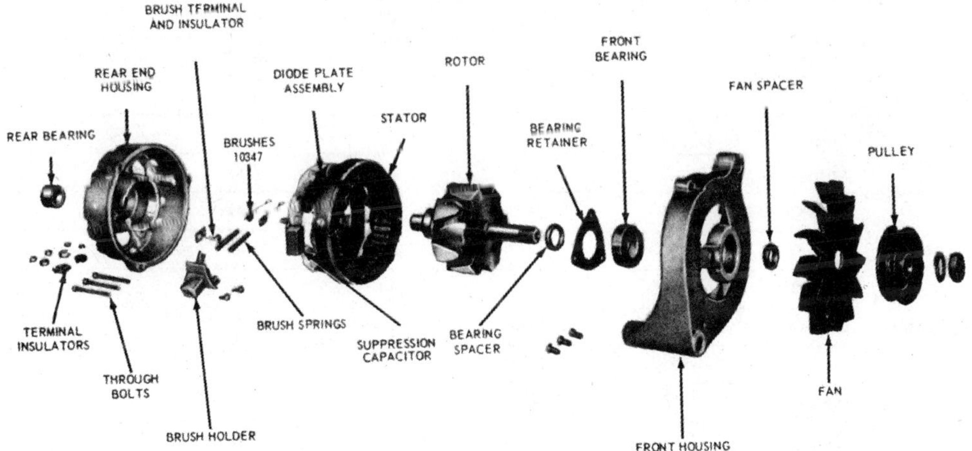

Exploded view of typical alternator

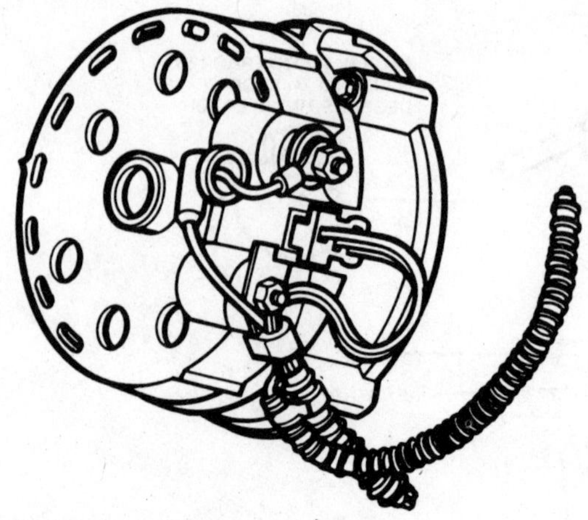

Side terminal alternator

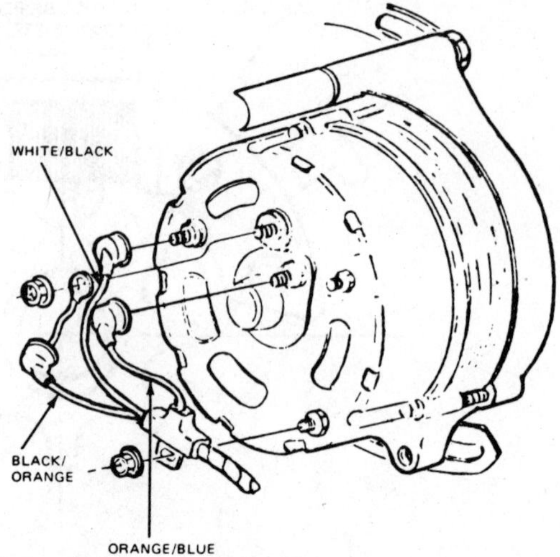

Rear terminal alternator

6. Avoid long soldering times when replacing diodes or transistors. Prolonged heat is damaging to AC generators.

7. Do not use test lamps of more than 12 volts (V) for checking diode continuity.

8. Do not short across or ground any of the terminals on the AC generator.

9. The polarity of the battery, generator, and regulator must be matched and considered before making any electrical connections within the system.

10. Never operate the alternator on an open circuit. Make sure that all connections within the circuit are clean and tight.

11. Disconnect the battery terminals when performing any service on the electrical system. This will eliminate the possibility of accidental reversal of polarity.

12. Disconnect the battery ground cable if arc welding is to be done on any part of the car.

REMOVAL AND INSTALLATION

While internal alternator repairs are possible, they require specialized tools and training. Therefore, it is advisable to replace a defective alternator, or have it repaired by a qualified shop.

Alternator Specifications

Year	Color Code	Output Amps	Output Watts	Field Current Amps	Cut-in rpm	Brush Length Inches New	Brush Length Inches Limit
1966–74	Purple	38	570	2.5	400	½	5/16
	Orange	42	630	2.9	400	½	5/16
1975	Purple	38	570	2.5	400	½	5/16
	Orange	42	630	2.9	400	½	5/16
	Red	55	825	2.9	400	½	5/16
	Green	61	915	2.9	400	½	5/16
1976–81	Orange	40	600	2.9	400	½	5/16
	Green	60	900	2.9	400	½	5/16
	Green*	60	900	4.0	400	½	3/16
1982 and Later	Orange	40	600	4.3	900	½	5/16
	Green	60	900	4.3	1025	½	5/16
	Black	70	1050	4.0	780	½	¼
	Red	100	1500	—	930	½	¼

*Blue ink on pulley face

1. Open the hood and disconnect the battery ground cable.
2. Remove the adjusting arm bolt.
3. Remove the alternator through-bolt. Remove the drive belt from the alternator pulley and lower the alternator.
4. Label all of the leads to the alternator so that you can install them correctly and disconnect the leads from the alternator.
5. Remove the alternator from the vehicle.
6. To install, reverse the above procedure.

Belt Tension Adjustment

The fan belt drives the alternator and water pump. If the belt is too loose, it will slip and the alternator will not be able to produce its rated current. Also, the water pump will not operate efficiently and the engine could overheat.

Check the tension of the belt by pushing your thumb down on the longest span of the belt, midway between the pulleys. Belt deflection should be approximately ½ in.

To adjust belt tension, proceed as follows:

1. Loosen the alternator mounting bolt and the adjusting arm bolts.
2. Apply pressure on the alternator front housing only, moving the alternator away from the engine to tighten the belt. Do not apply pressure to the rear of the cast aluminum housing of an alternator; damage to the housing could result.
3. Tighten the alternator mounting bolt and the adjusting arm bolts when the correct tension is reached.

Regulator

The alternator regulator has been designed to control the charging system's rate of charge and to compensate for seasonal temperature changes. The electro-mechanical regulator on 1968 and later vehicles is calibrated at the factory and is not adjustable. The regulator on 1965 through 1967 models is adjustable.

REMOVAL AND INSTALLATION

1. Disconnect the positive terminal of the battery.
2. Disconnect all of the electrical leads at the regulator. Label them as removed, so you can replace them in the correct order on the replacement unit.
3. Remove all of the hold-down screws, then remove the unit from the vehicle.
4. Install the new voltage regulator using the hold-down screws from the old one, or new ones if they are provided with the replacement regulator. Tighten the hold-down screws.
5. Connect all the leads to the new regulator.

ADJUSTMENT (1965–1967 MODELS ONLY)

To make any adjustments to the voltage regulator, the unit has to be removed from the vehicle. See the removal and installation procedure for instructions.

FIELD RELAY ADJUSTMENT

Air Gap

Place a 0.010 to 0.018 in. feeler gauge on top of the coil core closest to the contact points. Hold the armature down on the gauge. Do not push down on the contact spring arm. Bend the contact post arm until the bottom contact just touches the upper contact. Remove the feeler gauge.

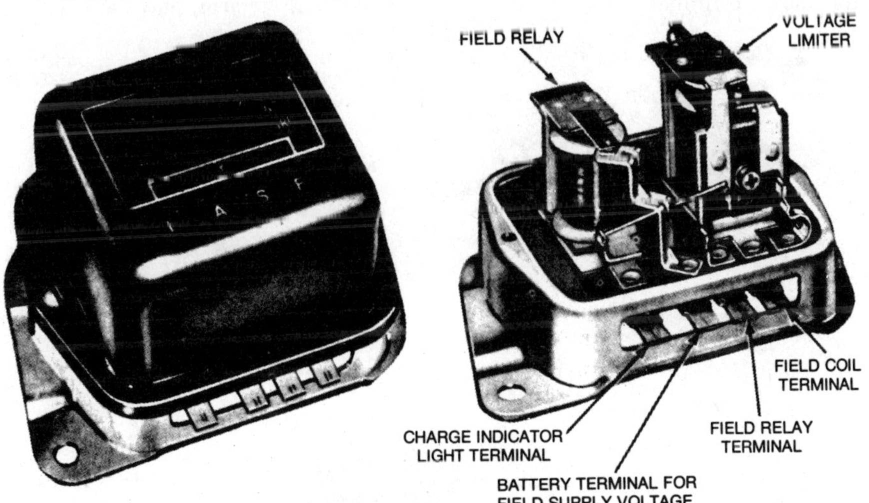

1965–69 regulator with cover installed and removed

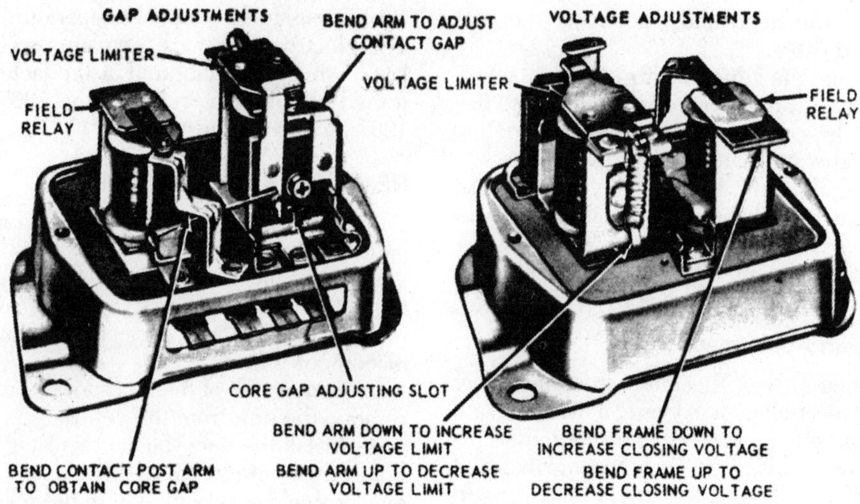

1965–67 regulator adjustments

VOLTAGE LIMITER ADJUSTMENT

The voltage limiter is adjusted by bending the voltage limiter spring arm. To increase the voltage setting, bend the adjusting arm downward. To decrease the voltage setting, bend the adjusting arm upward. Final adjustment of the regulator must be made with the regulator at normal operating temperatures. The voltage limiter should be set to between 13.6 and 15.1 volts read with a voltmeter installed between the battery/alternator terminal of the starter relay and the positive terminal of the battery.

Starter Motor

REMOVAL

Positive Engagement Type

1. Disconnect the positive battery terminal.
2. Raise the vehicle and disconnect the starter cable at the starter terminal.
3. Remove all of the starter attaching bolts that attach the starter to the bellhousing.
4. Remove the starter from the engine.
5. Install the starter in the reverse order of removal.

Solenoid Actuated Type—1976–77 With 460 Eng.

1. Disconnect the battery ground cable.
2. Raise the vehicle and disconnect the cables and wires at the starter solenoid.
3. Turn the front wheels to the right and remove the two bolts attaching the steering idler arm to the frame.
4. Remove the starter mounting bolts and remove the starter.
5. Install in the reverse order of removal.

STARTER DRIVE REPLACEMENT

1. Remove the cover of the starter drive's plunger lever arm, and the brush cover band.

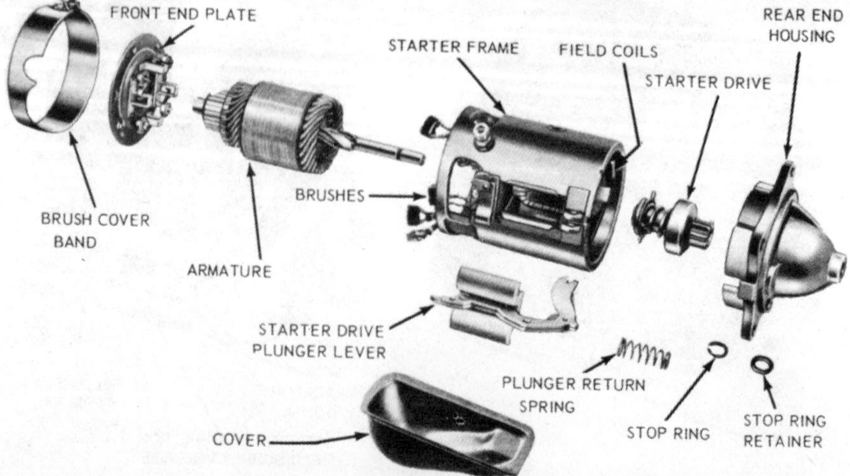

Positive engagement starter

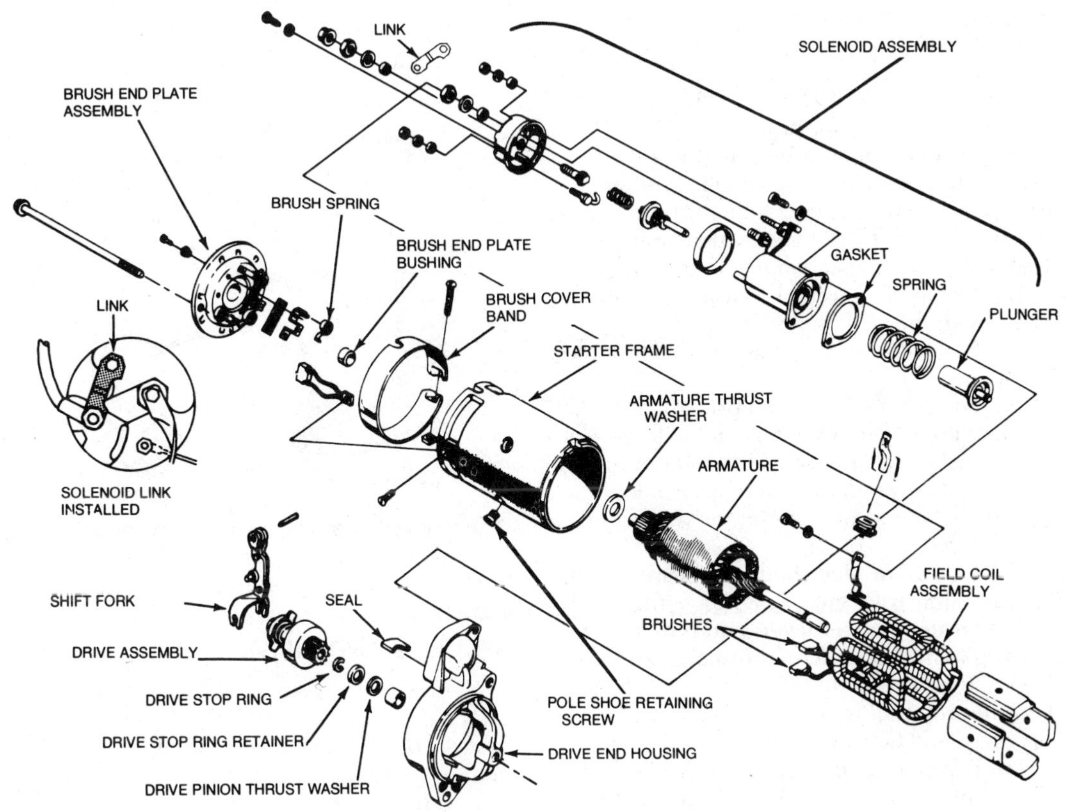

Solenoid actuated type starter

Remove the through-bolts, starter drive gear housing, and the return spring of the driver gear's actuating lever.

2. Remove the pivot pin which retains the starter gear plunger lever and remove the lever.

3. Remove the stop-ring retainer. Remove and discard the stop-ring which holds the drive gear to the armature shaft and then remove the drive gear assembly.

To install the drive gear assembly:

4. Lightly Lubriplate® the armature shaft splines and install the starter drive gear assembly on the shaft. Install a new stop-ring and stop-ring retainer.

5. Position the starter drive gear plunger lever to the frame and starter drive assembly.

6. Install the pivot pin.

7. Position the drive plunger lever return spring and the drive gear housing to the frame, then install and tighten the throughbolts. Be sure that the stopring retainer is properly seated in the drive housing.

8. Position the starter drive plunger lever cover and the brush cover band on the starter. Tighten the brush cover band retaining screw.

BRUSH REPLACEMENT

Replace the starter brushes when they are worn to ¼ in. Always install a complete set of new brushes.

1. Remove the starter from the truck.

2. Loosen and remove the brush cover band, gasket, and starter drive plunger lever cover. Remove the commutator brushes from their holders.

3. Remove the two through-bolts from the starter frame.

4. Remove the drive end housing and the plunger lever return spring.

5. Remove the starter drive plunger lever pivot pin and lever, and remove the armature.

6. Remove the brush end plate.

7. Remove the ground brush attaching screws from the frame and remove the brushes.

8. Cut the insulated brush leads from the field coils as close to the field connection as possible.

9. Clean and inspect the starter motor. Use a brush or air to clean the field coils, armature, commutator, armature shaft, brush end plate, and drive end housing. Wash all of the other parts in solvent and dry them.

Inspect the armature windings for broken or burned insulation and unsoldered connections.

10. Replace the brush end plate if the insulator between the field brush holder and the end plate is cracked or broken.

11. Position the new insulated field brushes lead on the field coil connection. Position and crimp the clip provided with the brushes to hold the brush lead to the connection. Solder the lead, clip, and connection together.

12. Install the ground brush leads to the frame with the attaching screws.

13. Clean the commutator with 00 or 000 sandpaper.

14. Position the brush end plate to the starter frame, with the end plate boss in the frame slot.

15. Install the armature in the starter frame.

16. Install the starter drive gear plunger lever to the frame and starter drive assembly, and install the pivot pin.

17. Fill drive end housing bearing bore about ¼ full with grease. Position the return spring on the plunger lever, and the drive end housing to the starter frame. Install the through-bolts and tighten them to 55–75 in. lbs. Be sure that the stop ring retainer is seated properly in the drive end housing.

18. Install the commutator brushes in the brush holders. Center the brush springs on the brushes.

19. Position the plunger lever cover and the brush cover band, with its gasket on the starter. Tighten the band attaching screw.

20. Connect the starter to the battery to check its operation. If it works, install it in the engine.

STARTER RELAY REPLACEMENT

The starter relay is mounted on the inside of the right wheel well. To replace it, disconnect the positive battery cable from the battery, disconnect all of the electrical leads from the relay and remove the relay from the fender well. Replace in the reverse order of removal.

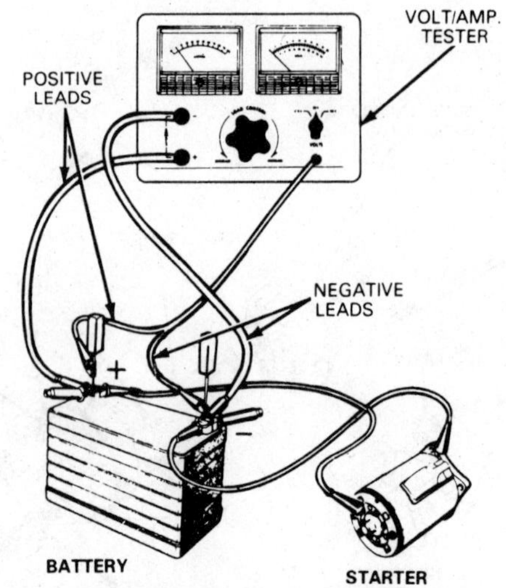

Starter no-load test with starter on test bench

Battery

REMOVAL AND INSTALLATION

1. Loosen the nuts which secure the cable ends to the battery terminals. Lift the battery cables from the terminals with a twisting motion.

2. If there is a battery cable puller available, make use of it.

3. Remove the hold-down nuts from the battery hold-down bracket and remove the bracket and the battery. Lift the battery straight up and out of the vehicle, being sure to keep the battery level to avoid spilling the battery acid.

4. Before installing the battery in the vehicle, make sure that the battery terminals are clean and free from corrosion. Use a battery terminal cleaner on the terminals and on the inside of the battery cable ends. If a cleaner is not available, use coarse grade sandpaper to remove the corrosion. A mixture of baking soda and water poured over the terminals and cable ends will help remove and neutralize any acid

Battery and Starter Specifications

Year	Engine No. Cyl Displacement (cu in.)	Battery: Ampere Hour Capacity	Battery: Volts	Battery: Terminal Grounded	Starters: Lock Test: Amps	Starters: Lock Test: Volts	Starters: Lock Test: Torque (ft. lbs.)	Starters: No-Load Test: Amps	Starters: No-Load Test: Volts	Starters: No-Load Test: rpm	Brush Spring Tension (oz)
1965–86	All	45–83 ⑥	12 ④	Neg	460 ①	—	9 ②	70 ⑤	12	—	40 ③

① With 4.5 in. diameter starter—670 amps
② With 4.5 in. diameter starter—15.5 ft. lbs.
③ 1978–84 with 4.5 in. diameter starter—80
④ F-250/350 w/6.9L Diesel have two 12 volt batteries
⑤ 4.5 in. diameter starter—80 amps
⑥ Varies according to engine

buildup. Before installing the cables onto the terminals, cut a piece of felt cloth, or something similar into a circle about 3 in. across. Cut a hole in the middle about the size of the battery terminals at their base. Push the cloth pieces over the terminals so that they lay flat on the top of the battery. Soak the pieces of cloth with oil. This will keep oxidation to a minimum.

5. Place the battery in the vehicle. Install the cables onto the terminals. Tighten the nuts on the cable ends.

NOTE: *See Chapter 1 for battery maintenance illustrations.*

6. Smear a light coating of grease on the cable ends and tops of the terminals. This will further prevent the buildup of oxidation on the terminals and the cable ends.

7. Install and tighten the nuts of the battery hold-down bracket.

ENGINE MECHANICAL

Engine Removal and Installation

Inline Six Cylinder

1. Drain the cooling system and the crankcase. Remove the hood and the air cleaner. Disconnect the positive battery cable.

2. Disconnect the heater hose from the water pump and coolant outlet housing. Disconnect the flexible fuel line from the fuel pump.

3. Remove the radiator.

4. Remove the fan, water pump pulley, and fan belt.

5. Disconnect the accelerator cable at the carburetor. Remove the throttle return spring. On trucks equipped with power brakes, disconnect the brake booster vacuum hose at the

General Engine Specifications

Engine No. Cyl Displacement (cu in.)	Carburetor	Bore x Stroke	Compression Ratio	Oil Pressure @ 2000 rpm
6-232	2 bbl	3.81 x 3.39	8.65:1	40–60
6-240	1 bbl	4.00 x 3.18	①	40–60
6-300	1 bbl	4.00 x 3.98	②	40–60
8-255	2 bbl	3.68 x 3.00	8.2:1	40–60
8-302	2 bbl	4.00 x 3.00	③	40–60
8-351M	2 bbl	4.00 x 3.50	8.0:1	50–75
8-352	2 bbl	4.00 x 3.50	8.9:1	35–55
8-360	2 bbl	4.05 x 3.50	④	35–60
8-361	2 bbl	4.05 x 3.50	⑥	45–70
8-390	2 bbl	4.05 x 3.78	⑤	35–50
8-391	2 bbl	4.05 x 3.79	⑦	45–70
8-400	2 bbl	4.00 x 4.00	8.0:1	50–75
8-460	4 bbl	4.36 x 3.85	8.0:1	40–65
8-420	Diesel	4.00 x 4.18	20.7:1	40–60

① 1965: 8.75:1
1966–70: 9.2:1
1971: 8.8:1
1972–73: 8.5:1
② 1965: 8.4:1
1966–67: 8.0:1
1968–71: 8.8:1
1972–73: 8.4:1
③ 1969–71: 8.6:1
1972–73: 8.2:1
④ 1965: 7.6:1
1966–67: 7.4:1
1968–69: 7.2:1
1970–71: 8.4:1
1972: 8.0:1
⑤ 1966: 7.4:1
1967: 7.4:1
1968–69: 7.2:1
1970–71: 8.6:1
1972: 8.2:1
⑥ 1965: 7.6:1
1966–69: 7.4:1
⑦ 1965: 7.6:1
1966–67: 7.4:1
1968–69: 7.2:1

intake manifold. On trucks with automatic transmissions, disconnect the transmission kickdown rod at the bellcrank assembly.

6. Disconnect the exhaust pipe from the exhaust manifold.

7. Disconnect the body ground strap and the battery ground cable from the engine.

8. Disconnect the engine wiring harness at the ignition coil, the coolant temperature sending unit, and the oil pressure sending unit. Position the wiring harness out of the way.

9. Remove the alternator mounting bolts and position the alternator out of the way.

10. On a truck equipped with power steering, remove the power steering pump from the mounting brackets and move it to one side, leaving the lines attached.

11. Raise the truck on a hoist and remove the starter and automatic transmission filler tube bracket, if so equipped. Also, remove the rear engine plate upper right bolt.

12. On manual transmission equipped trucks, remove the flywheel housing lower attaching bolts and disconnect the clutch return spring.

13. On automatic transmission equipped trucks, remove the converter housing access cover assembly and remove the flywheel-to-converter attaching nuts. Secure the converter in the housing. Remove the transmission oil cooler lines from the retaining clip at the engine. Remove the lower converter housing-to-engine attaching bolts.

14. Remove the nut from each of the two front engine mounts.

15. Lower the vehicle and position a jack under the transmission and support it. Remove the remaining bellhousing-to-engine attaching bolts.

16. Attach the engine lifting device and raise the engine slightly and carefully pull it from the transmission. Lift the engine out of the vehicle.

To install the engine:

17. Place a new gasket on the muffler inlet pipe.

18. Carefully lower the engine into the truck. Make sure that the dowels in the engine block engage the holes in the bellhousing.

19. On manual transmission equipped trucks, start the transmission input shaft into the clutch disc. It may be necessary to adjust the position of the engine or transmission in order for the input shaft to enter the clutch disc. If necessary, turn the crankshaft until the input shaft splines mesh with the clutch disc splines.

20. On automatic transmission equipped trucks, start the converter pilot into the crankshaft. Unsecure the converter in the housing.

21. Install the bellhousing upper attaching bolts. Remove the jack supporting the transmission.

22. Lower the engine until it rests on the engine mounts. Remove the lifting device.

23. Install the engine mount nuts and tighten them to 45–55 ft. lbs.

24. Install the automatic transmission coil cooler lines bracket, if so equipped.

25. Install the remaining bellhousing attaching bolts.

26. Connect the clutch return spring, if so equipped.

27. Install the starter and connect the starter cable. Attach the automatic transmission fluid filler tube bracket, if so equipped.

28. On trucks with automatic transmissions, install the transmission oil cooler lines in the bracket at the cylinder block.

29. Connect the exhaust pipe to the exhaust manifold. Tighten the nuts to 25–35 ft. lbs.

30. Connect the engine ground strap and negative battery cable.

31. On a truck with an automatic transmission, connect the kick-down rod to the bellcrank assembly on the intake manifold.

32. Connect the accelerator linkage to the carburetor and install the return spring.

33. On a truck with power brakes, connect the brake booster vacuum line to the intake manifold.

34. Connect the coil primary wire, oil pressure and coolant temperature sending unit wires, fuel line, heater hoses, and the battery positive cable.

35. Install the alternator to its mounting bracket. Install the power steering pump to its bracket, if so equipped.

36. Install the water pump pulley, spacer, fan, and fan belt. Adjust the belt tension.

37. Install the radiator and connect the upper and lower radiator hoses to the radiator and engine. Connect the automatic transmission oil cooler lines, if so equipped.

38. Install and adjust the hood.

39. Fill the cooling system. Fill the crankcase.

40. Start the engine and check for leaks. Bleed the cooling system. Adjust the clutch pedal free-play or the automatic transmission control linkage. Install the air cleaner.

V6 and Gasoline V8 Except 460

1. Drain the cooling system and crankcase. Remove the hood.

2. Disconnect the battery and alternator cables from the cylinder block.

3. Remove the air cleaner and intake duct assembly, plus the crankcase ventilation hose.

4. Disconnect the upper and lower radia-

tor hoses, and, if so equipped, the automatic transmission oil cooler lines.

5. Remove the fan shroud and lay it over the fan. Remove the radiator and fan, shroud, fan, spacer, pulley, and belt.

6. Disconnect the alternator leads and the alternator adjusting bolts. Allow the alternator to swing down out of the way.

7. Disconnect the oil pressure sending unit lead from the sending unit.

8. Disconnect the fuel tank-to-pump fuel line at the fuel pump and plug the line.

9. Disconnect the accelerator linkage at the carburetor. Disconnect the automatic transmission kick-down rod and remove the return spring, if so equipped.

10. Disconnect the heater hoses from the water pump and intake manifold. Disconnect the temperature sending unit wire from the sending unit.

11. Remove the upper bellhousing-to-engine attaching bolts.

12. Disconnect the primary wire from the coil. Remove the wiring harness from the left rocker arm cover and position the wires out of the way. Disconnect the ground strap from the cylinder block.

13. Raise the front of the truck and disconnect the starter cable from the starter. Remove the starter.

14. Disconnect the exhaust pipe from the exhaust manifolds.

15. Disconnect the engine mounts from the brackets on the frame.

16. On trucks with automatic transmissions, remove the converter inspection plate and remove the torque converter-to-flywheel attaching bolts.

17. Remove the remaining bellhousing-to-engine attaching bolts.

18. Lower the vehicle and support the transmission with a jack.

19. Install an engine lifting device.

NOTE: *On the V6, the intake manifold is aluminum. If a lifting device is attached to the manifold, all manifold bolts must be installed and torqued.*

20. Raise the engine slightly and carefully pull it out from the transmission. Lift the engine out of the engine compartment.

21. Install the engine in the reverse order of removal. Make sure that the dowels in the engine block engage the holes in the bellhousing through the rear cover plate. If the engine hangs up after the transmission input shaft enters the clutch disc (manual transmission only), turn the crankshaft with the transmission in gear until the input shaft splines mesh with the clutch disc splines.

Tighten the exhaust pipe-to-exhaust manifold nuts to 25–35 ft. lbs., and all others as follows:

- ¼ in. 20—6–9 ft. lbs.
- 5⁄16 in. 18—12–18 ft. lbs.
- ⅜ in. 16—22–32 ft. lbs.
- 7⁄16 in. 14—45–57 ft. lbs.
- ½ in. 13—55–80 ft. lbs.
- 9⁄16 in.—85–120 ft. lbs.

460 V8

1. Remove the hood.

2. Drain the cooling system, the radiator, and the cylinder block.

3. Disconnect the negative battery cable and remove the air cleaner assembly.

4. Disconnect the upper and lower radiator hoses and the transmission oil cooler lines from the radiator.

5. Remove the fan shroud from the radiator and remove the fan from the water pump. Remove the fan and shroud from the engine compartment.

6. Remove the upper support and remove the radiator.

7. If the truck is equipped with air conditioning, remove the compressor from the engine and position it out of the way. If the compressor must be removed completely, loosen the air conditioning service valves (disconnect) carefully to discharge the air conditioning system. Remove the compressor.

8. Remove the power steering pump from the engine, if so equipped, and position it to one side. Do not disconnect the fluid lines.

9. Disconnect the fuel pump inlet line from the pump and plug the line.

10. Remove the alternator drive belts and disconnect the alternator from the engine, positioning it aside.

11. Disconnect the ground cable from the right front corner of the engine.

12. Disconnect the heater hoses.

13. Remove the transmission fluid filler tube attaching bolt from the right-side valve cover and position the tube out of the way.

14. Disconnect all vacuum lines at the rear of the intake manifold.

15. Disconnect the speed control cable at the carburetor, if so equipped. Disconnect the accelerator rod and the transmission kickdown rod and secure them out of the way.

16. Disconnect the engine wiring harness at the connector on the fire wall.

17. Raise the vehicle and disconnect the exhaust pipes at the exhaust manifolds.

18. Disconnect the starter cable and remove the starter. Bring the starter forward and rotate the solenoid outward to remove the assembly.

19. Remove the access cover from the con-

Valve Specifications

Year	Engine Displacement Cu In. (cc)	Seat Angle (deg)	Face Angle (deg)	Spring Test Pressure (lbs. @ in.)	Spring Installed Height (in.)	Stem to Guide Clearance (in.)		Stem Diameter (in.)	
						Intake	Exhaust	Intake	Exhaust
1982–83	6-232	45	44	202 @ 1.28	1.70	.0010–.0025	.0015–.0032	.3422	.3415
1965–66	6-240	45	44	①	1,700	.00185	.00185	.34195	.34195
1967–72	6-240	45	44	197 @ 1.300	1.700	.00185	.00185	.34195	.34195
1973–74	6-240	45	44	②	③	.00185	.00185	.34195	.34195
1975–86	6-300	45	44	②	③	.00185	.00185	.34195	.34195
1982	8-255	45	46	⑧	⑨	.0010–.0027	.0010–.0027	.3420	.3415
1969–71	8-302	45	44	180 @ 1.230	1.660	.00185	.00185	.34195	.34195
1972	8-302	45	44	180 @ 1.230	1.660	.00185	.00235	.34195	.34145
1973–78	8-302	45	44	200 @ 1.310	1.690	.00185	.00235	.34195	.34145
1979–86	8-302	45	44	④	⑤	.00185	.00235	.34195	.34145
1975–86	8-351W	45	44	⑩	1.80	.0010–.0027	.0015–.0032	.3420	.3415⑪
1977–80	8-351M	45	44	226 @ 1.390	1.812	.00185	.00235	.34195	.34145
1965–67	8-352	45	44	189 @ 1.420	1 13/16–1 27/32	.00170	.00270	.37150	.3705

1970–71	8-360	45	44	90 @ 1.82	1 13/16–1 27/32	.0010–.0027	.0020–.0034	.3711–.3718	.3711–.3718
1972	8-360	45	44	90 @ 1.82	1 13/16–1 27/32	.0010–.0027	.0010–.0027	.3711–.3718	.3706–.3713
1973–76	8-360	45	44	⑥	1 13/16 ⑦–1 27/32	.0010–.0027	.0015–.0032	.3711–.3718	.3706–.3713
1965–69	8-361	45	44	80 @ 1.67	1 41/64–1 11/16	.0010–.0027	.0020–.0037	.3711–.3718	.4338–.4348
1970–71	8-390	45	44	90 @ 1.82	1 13/16–1 27/32	.0010–.0027	.0020–.0034	.3711–3718	.3711–3718
1972	8-390	45	44	90 @ 1.82	1 13/16–1 27/32	.0010–.0027	.0010–.0027	.3711–.3718	.3706–.3713
1973–76	8-390	45	44	⑥	1 13/16 ⑦–1 27/32	.0010–.0027	.0015–.0032	.3711–.3718	.3706–.3713
1965–67	8-391	45	44	80 @ 1.67	1 15/64–1 1/4	.0010–.0024	.0020–.0037	.3711–.3718	.4338–.4348
1966–69	8-391	45	44	80 @ 1.67	1 41/64–1 11/16	.0010–.0024	.0020–.0037	.3711–.3718	.4338–.4348
1977–80	8-400	45	44	80 @ 1.82	1 13/16–1 27/32	.0010–.0027	.0015–.0032	.3416–.3423	.3411–.3418
1983–86	8-420 ⑫	⑬	⑬	60 @ 1.798	N.A.	.0012–.0029	.0012–.0029	.37165–.37235	.37165–.37235
1974–86	8-460	45	44	80 @ 1.81	1 51/64–1 53/64	.0010–.0027	.0010–.0027	.3416–.3423	.3416–.3423

N.A.: Not available at time of publication
① Intake: 190 @ 1.325
Exhaust: 197 @ 1.300
② Intake: 190 @ 1.300
Exhaust: 192 @ 1.180
1985–86: 180 @ 1.240
③ Intake: 1.700
Exhaust: 1.690
④ Intake: 202 @ 1.360
Exhaust: 200 @ 1.200
⑤ Intake: 1.780
Exhaust: 1.600
⑥ F-100 exhaust only—1.83 @ 1.24 in.;
F-100 intake only—90 @ 1.82;
F-250 intake and exhaust 220 @ 1.38
⑦ F-100 exhaust only—1 23/32–1 11/61 in.
⑧ Intake: 204 @ 1.36
Exhaust: 200 @ 1.20
⑨ Intake: 1.78
Exhaust: 1.60
⑩ Intake: 200 @ 1.36
Exhaust: 200 @ 1.20
⑪ 1982: .3420
⑫ V8 Diesel
⑬ Intake angle: 30°
Exhaust angle: 37.5°

Piston and Ring Specifications

All measurements given in inches

			Ring Side Clearance			Ring Gap		
Year	Engine	Piston to Bore Clearance	Top Compres-sion	Bottom Compres-sion	Oil Control	Top Compres-sion	Bottom Compres-sion	Oil Control
1982–83	6-232	.0014–.0022	.0020–.0040	.0020–.0040	Snug	.0100–.0200	.0100–.0200	.015–.055
1965–71	6-240	.0014–.0022	.0019–.0036	.0020–.0040	Snug	.0100–.0200	.0100–.0200	.015–.055
1972–74	6-240	.0014–.0022	.0024–.0041	.0025–.0045	Snug	.0100–.0200	.0100–.0200	.015–.055
1975–76	6-300	.0014–.0022	.0024–.0041	.0025–.0045	Snug	.0100–.0200	.0100–.0200	.015–.055
1977	6-300	.0014–.0022	.0019–.0036	.0020–.0040	Snug	.0100–.0200	.0100–.0200	.010–.035
1978	6-300	.0002–.0004	.0019–.0036	.0020–.0040	Snug	.0100–.0200	.0100–.0200	.015–.055
1979–86	6-300	.0014–① .0022	.0019–.0036	.0020–.0040	Snug	.0100–.0200	.0100–.0200	.010–.035
1982	8-255	.0014–.0024	.0020–.0040	.0020–.0040	Snug	.0100–.0200	.0100–.0200	.015–.055
1969–72	8-302	.0018–.0026	.0019–.0036	.0020–.0040	Snug	.0100–.0200	.0100–.0200	.015–.069
1973–74	8-302	.0018–.0026	.0020–.0040	.0020–.0040	Snug	.0100–.0200	.0100–.0200	.015–.069
1975–76	8-302	.0018–.0026	.0020–.0040	.0020–.0040	Snug	.0100–.0200	.0100–.0200	.015–.055
1977	8-302	.0018–.0026	.0020–.0040	.0020–.0040	Snug	.0100–.0200	.0100–.0200	.010–.035
1978	8-302	.0018–.0026	.0020–.0040	.0020–.0040	Snug	.0100–.0200	.0100–.0200	.015–.055
1979–86	8-302	.0018–.0026	.0020–.0040	.0020–.0040	Snug	.0100–.0200	.0100–.0200	.015–.035
1977–86	8-351W	.0022–.0030	.0019–.0036	.0020–.0040	Snug	.0010–.0020	.0010–.0020	.015–.035
1977–80	8-351M	.0014–.0022	.0019–.0036	.002–.004	Snug	.010–.020	.010–.020	.010–.035
1965–67	8-352	.0015–.0023	.0024–.0041	.0020–.0040	Snug	.010–.020	.010–.020	.015–.066
1970–76	8-360	.0015–.0023	.0020–.0040	.0020–.0040	Snug	.010–.020	.010–.020	.015–.035
1965	8-361	.0023–.0029	.0024–.0041	.0020–.0040	Snug	.015–.036	.015–.036	.015–.055
1966–67	8-361	.0017–.0025	.0024–.0041	.0030–.0050	Snug	.015–.036	.015–.036	.015–.055
1968	8-361	.0025–.0033	.0024–.0041	.0024–.0041	.0190–.0360	.015–.036	.015–.036	.015–.038
1969	8-361	.0025–.0033	.0029–.0046	.0029–.0046	.0036–.0039	.015–.034	.015–.036	.015–.036
1970–76	8-390	.0015–.0023	.0020–.0040	.0020–.0040	Snug	.010–.020	.010–.020	.015–.035

Piston and Ring Specifications (cont.)

All measurements given in inches

Year	Engine	Piston to Bore Clearance	Ring Side Clearance			Ring Gap		
			Top Compression	Bottom Compression	Oil Control	Top Compression	Bottom Compression	Oil Control
1965	8-391	.0023–.0029	.0024–.0041	.0020–.0040	Snug	.015–.036	.015–.036	.015–.055
1966–67	8-391	.0017–.0025	.0024–.0041	.0030–.0050	Snug	.015–.036	.015–.036	.015–.055
1968	8-391	.0025–.0033	.0024–.0041	.0024–.0041	.0190–.0360	.015–.036	.015–.036	.015–.038
1969	8-391	.0025–.0033	.0029–.0046	.0029–.0046	.0036–.0039	.015–.034	.015–.034	.015–.036
1977–80	8-400	.0014–.0022	.0019–.0036	.002–.004	Snug	.010–.020	.010–.020	.010–.035
1983–84	8-420	.0055–.0075	.002–.004	.002–.004	.001–.003	.014–.024	.010–.070	.060–.024
1974–76	8-460	.0022–.0030	.002–.004	.002–.004	Snug	.010–.020	.010–.020	.015–.055
1977	8-460	.0014–.0022	.0025–.0045	.0025–.0045	Snug	.010–.020	.010–.020	.010–.030
1978	8-460	.0022–.0030	.0025–.0045	.0025–.0045	Snug	.010–.020	.010–.020	.010–.030
1974–86	8-460	.0022–.0030	.0019–.0036	.002–.004	Snug	.010–.020	.010–.020	.010–.035

① 1985–86: .0010–.0018

Crankshaft and Connecting Rod Specifications

Year	Engine No. Cyl Displacement (cu in.)	Crankshaft				Connecting Rod		
		Main Bearing Journal Diameter	Main Bearing Oil Clearance	Shaft End-Play	Thrust on No.	Journal Diameter	Oil Clearance	Side Clearance
1982–83	6-232	2.5188–2.5192	.0009–.0027	.004–.008	3	2.3105 2.3109	.0009–.0027	.004–.011
1965	6-240	①	.0006–.0024	.004–.008	5	②	.0006–.0022	.006–.013
1966–69	6-240	2.3982–2.3990	.0005–.0015	.004–.008	5	2.1228–2.1236	.0008–.0015	.006–.013
1970–74	6-240	2.3982–2.3990	.0010–.0015 ③	.004–008	5	2.1228–2.1236	.0010–.0015 ④	.006–013
1982	8-255	2.2488–2.2492	.0005–.0024 ⑩	.004–.008	3	2.1230–2.1234	.0008–.0025	.010–.020
1965	6-300	2.3982–2.3990	.0006–.0026	.004–.008	5	2.1228–2.1236	.0006–.0022	.006–.013
1966–72	6-300	2.3982–2.3990	.0009–.0028	.004–.008	5	2.1228–2.1236	.0009–.0027	.006–.013
1973	6-300	2.3982–2.3990	.0009–.0015	.004–.008	5	2.1228–2.1236	⑤	.006–.013
1974	6-300	2.3982–2.3990	.0009–.0015	.004–.008	5	2.1228–2.1236	⑥	.006–.013

Crankshaft and Connecting Rod Specifications (cont.)

Year	Engine No. Cyl Displacement (cu in.)	Crankshaft				Connecting Rod		
		Main Bearing Journal Diameter	Main Bearing Oil Clearance	Shaft End-Play	Thrust on No.	Journal Diameter	Oil Clearance	Side Clearance
1975–86	6-300	2.3982–2.3990	.0008–.0015	.004–.008	5	2.1228–2.1236	.0008–.0015	.006–.013
1969	8-302	2.2482–2.2490	.0010–.0015	.004–.008	3	2.1228–2.1236	.0008–.0015	.010–.020
1970–72	8-302	2.2482–2.2490	.0010–.0015	.004–.008	3	2.1228–2.1236	.0010–.0015	.010–.020
1973–86	8-302	2.2482–2.2490	.0005–.0015 ⑦	.004–.008	3	2.1228–2.1236	.0008–.0015	.010–.020
1977–80	8-351M	2.994–3.0002	.0008–.0015	.004–.008	3	2.3103–2.3111	.0008–.0015	.010–.020
1975–86	8-351W	2.994–3.0002	.0005–.0015 ⑦	.004–.008	3	2.3103–2.3111	.0008–.0015	.010–.020
1965	8-352	2.7484–2.7492	.0005–.0028 ⑧	.004–.010	3	2.4380–2.4388	.0007–.0028	.010–.020
1966–67	8-352	2.7484–2.7492	.0005–.0015	.004–.010	3	2.4380–2.4388	.0007–.0028	.010–.020
1970–74	8-360	2.7484–2.7492	.0005–.0024	.004–.010	3	2.4380–2.4388	.0008–.0026	.010–.020
1975–76	8-360	2.7484–2.7492	.0005–.0015	.004–.010	3	2.4380–2.4388	.0008–.0015	.008–.025
1965–69	8-361	2.7479–2.7487	.0010–.0015	.004–.010	3	2.4377–2.4385	.0010–.0029	.010–.020
1970–72	8-390	2.7484–2.7492	.0010–.0015	.004–.010	3	2.4380–2.4385	.0010–.0015	.010–.020
1973	8-390	2.7484–2.7492	.0005–.0015	.004–.010	3	2.4380–2.4385	.0008–.0025	.008–.025
1974	8-390	2.7484–2.7492	.001–.0015	.004–.010	3	2.4380–2.4385	.0008–.0015	.008–.025
1975–76	8-390	2.7484–2.7492	.0005–.0015	.004–.010	3	2.4380–2.4385	.0008–.0015	.010–.020
1966–69	8-391	2.7479–2.7487	.0010–.0020	.004–.010	3	2.4377–2.4385	.0011–.0020	.010–.020
1977–81	8-400	2.9994–3.0002	.0008–.0015	.004–.008	3	2.3103–2.3111	.0008–.0015	.010–.020
1974–86	8-460	2.9994–3.0002	.0012–.0015 ⑨	.004–.008	3	2.4992–2.5000	.0008–.0015	.010–.020
1983–86	8-420 ⑪	3.1228–3.1236	.0018–.0036	.0020–.0090	3	2.4980–2.4990	.0011–.0026	.008–.020

① Coded red: 2.3986–2.3990
Coded blue: 2.3982–2.3986
② Coded red: 2.1232–2.3990
Coded blue: 2.1228–2.1232
③ 1973–74—.0005–.0015
④ 1973–74—.008–.0015
⑤ (L.D.) Light duty .0008–.0015
(H.D.) Heavy duty .0009–.0027
⑥ (L.D.) Light duty .0008–.0015
(H.D.) Heavy duty .0009–.0015
⑦ #1: .0001–.0015
⑧ #1: .0007–.0031
⑨ #1: .0004–.0015
⑩ #1: .0004–.0020
⑪ Diesel V8

Torque Specifications

All readings in ft. lbs.

Year	Engine No. Cyl Displacement (cu in.)	Cylinder Head Bolts	Rod Bearing Bolts	Main Bearing Bolts	Crankshaft Pulley Bolt	Flywheel to Crankshaft Bolts	Manifold	
							Intake	Exhaust
1982–83	6-232	65–81	30–36	62–81	85–100	75–85	18	15–22
1965–66	6-240	70–75	40–45	60–70	130–145	75–85	20–35	20–25
1967–74	6-240	70–75	40–45	60–70	130–145	75–85	23–28	23–28
1975–76	6-300	70–75	40–45	60–70	130–150	75–85	23–28	23–28
1977–86	6-300	70–75	40–45	60–70	130–150	75–85	22–32	28–33
1982	8-255	65–72	19–24	60–70	70–90	75–85	18–20	18–24
1969	8-302	65–72	19–24	60–70	70–90	75–85	20–22	15–20
1970	8-302	65–72	19–24	60–70	70–90	75–85	23–25	12–16
1971–74	8-302	65–72	19–24	60–70	100–130	75–85	23–25	12–16
1975–86	8-302	65–72	19–24	60–70	70–90	75–85	23–25	18–24
1977–86	8-351W	95–105 ⑦	40–45	35–45	70–90	75–85	①	18–24
1978–80	8-351M	95–105	40–45	95–105	70–90	75–85	①	18–24
1965–67	8-352	80–90	40–45	95–105	70–90	75–85	32–35	12–18
1970–71	8-360	80–90	40–45	95–105	150–175	75–85	32–35	18–24
1972	8-360	80–90	40–45	95–105	70–90	75–85	32–35	18–24
1973–74	8-360	80–90	40–45	95–105	70–90	75–85	40–45	18–24
1975–76	8-360	80–90	40–45	95–105	130–150	75–85	40–45	12–18
1965	8-361	80–90	40–45	95–105	70–90	75–85	32–35	12–18
1966–69	8-361	80–90	40–45	95–105	150–175	75–85	32–35	18–24
1970–74	8-390	80–90	40–45	95–105	70–90	75–85	32–35	12–18
1975–76	8-390	80–90	40–45	95–105	130–150	75–85	40–45	18–24
1966–69	8-391	80–90	40–45	95–105	150–175	75–85	32–35	18–24
1977	8-400	95–105	40–45	35–45	70–90	75–85	①	18–24
1978–80	8-400	95–105	40–45	95–105	70–90	75–85	①	18–24
1983–86	8-420 ②	③	④	⑤	90	47	⑥	30
1974–86	8-460	130–140	40–45	95–105	70–90	75–85	25–30	28–33

① 3/8″ 22–32
5/16″ 17–25
② V8 Diesel
③ Torque in sequence shown in Chapter 3: Torque bolts to 40 ft. lbs.; then to 65 ft. lbs.; then to 75 ft. lbs.; then retorque all bolts at 75 ft. lbs.
④ Torque to 38 ft. lbs., then to 46–51 ft. lbs.
⑤ Torque to 75 ft. lbs., then to 95 ft. lbs.
⑥ 3/8″—22–33 ft. lbs.
1/4″—12–18 ft. lbs.
5/16″—14 ft. lbs.
⑦ 1985–86: 105–112 ft. lbs.

Camshaft Specifications

(All measurements in inches)

Engine	Journal Diameter 1	2	3	4	5	Bearing Clearance	Lobe Lift Intake	Exhaust	Camshaft End Play
240, 300	2.0170–2.0180	2.0170–2.0180	2.0170–2.0180	2.1070–2.0180	—	.001–.003	.2490	.2490	.001–.007
302	2.0805–2.0815	2.0655–2.0665	2.0505–2.0515	2.0355–2.0365	2.0205–2.0215	.001–.003	.2303 ①	.2375 ②	.001–.003
351W	2.0805–2.0815	2.0655–2.0665	2.0505–2.0515	2.0355–2.0365	2.0205–2.0215	.001–.003	.2600	.2600	.001–.007
400	2.1248–2.1328	2.0655–2.0665	2.0505–2.0515	2.0355–2.0365	2.0505–2.0215	.001–.003	.2474 ③	.2500	.001–.006
420 (diesel)	2.0990–2.1000	2.0990–2.1000	2.0990–2.1000	2.0990–2.1000	2.0990–2.1000	.001–.005	.2535	.2530	.001–.009
460	2.1238–2.1248	2.1238–2.1248	2.1238–2.1248	2.1238–2.1248	2.1238–2.1248	.001–.003	.2530	.2780	.001–.006

① 1977 & 1980–86: .2375
② 1977 & 1980–86: .2470
③ 1979: .2500

verter housing and remove the fly-wheel-to-converter attaching nuts. Remove the lower converter housing-to-engine attaching bolts.

20. Remove the engine mount through bolts attaching the rubber insulators to the frame brackets.

21. Lower the vehicle and place a jack under the transmission to support it.

22. Remove the converter housing-to-engine block attaching bolts (left-side).

23. Disconnect the coil wire and remove the coil and bracket assembly from the intake manifold.

24. Attach the engine lifting device and carefully lift the engine from the engine compartment.

25. Install the engine in the reverse order of removal.

Tighten the alternator pivot bolt to 45–57 ft. lbs. and all the rest of the nuts and bolts as is outlined in Step 21 of the preceding "V8 except 460 Removal and Installation" procedure.

6.9L Diesel Engine

1. Take off the hood and engine cover, drain the coolant, remove the air cleaner and intake duct assembly and cover the air intake opening with a clean rag to keep out dirt. Remove the upper grille support bracket and upper air conditioning condenser mounting brackets.

2. On vehicles equipped with air conditioning, the system MUST be discharged to remove the condenser.

NOTE: *DO NOT attempt to do this yourself, unless you are trained in A/C repair. Have a professional disconnect it.*

3. Remove the radiator fan shroud halves. Remove the fan and clutch assembly as described under water pump removal in this chapter.

4. Detach the radiator hoses and the transmission cooler lines, if so equipped. Remove the radiator assembly.

5. Remove the power steering pump and position it out of the way. Disconnect the fuel supply line heater and alternator wires at the alternator.

6. Disconnect the oil pressure sending unit wire at the sending unit, remove the sender from the dash panel and lay it on the engine.

7. Disconnect the accelerator cable and the speed control cable, if so equipped, from the injection pump. Remove the cable bracket with cables attached, from the intake manifold and position it out of the way.

8. Disconnect the transmission kickdown rod from the injection pump, if so equipped.

9. Disconnect the main wiring harness connector from the right side of the engine and the ground strap from the rear of the engine. Remove the fuel return hose from the left rear of the engine.

10. Remove the two upper transmission-to-engine attaching bolts. Disconnect the heater hoses, water temperature sender wire, over-

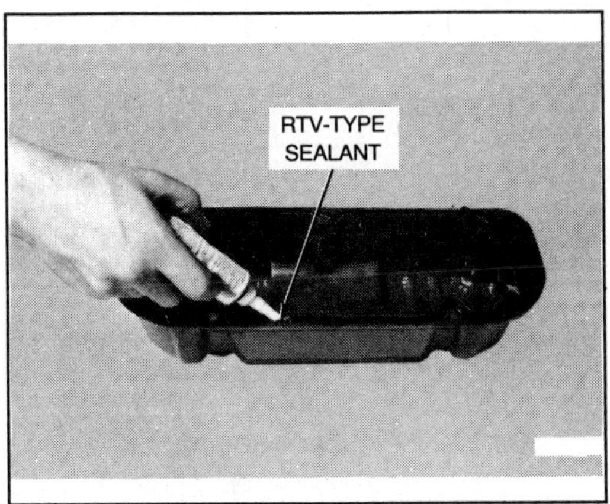

Use a silicone sealant when reinstalling the valve covers

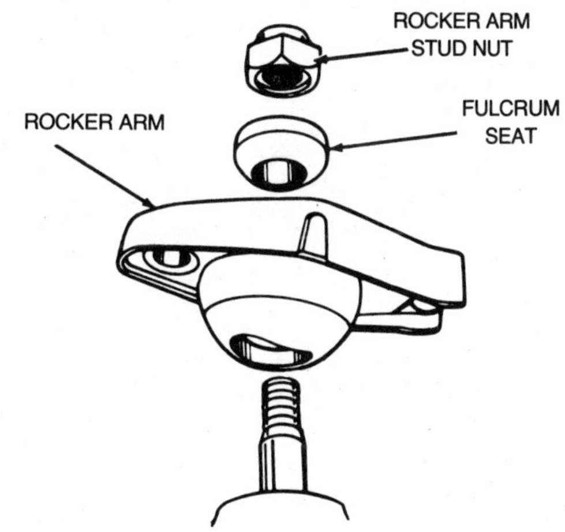

240 and 300 inline six rocker arm assembly

heat light switch wire and position the wires out of the way.

11. Raise the truck and support on jack stands. Disconnect the battery ground cables from the front of the engine and the starter cables from the starter.

12. Remove the fuel inlet line and plug the fuel line at the fuel pump. Detach the exhaust pipe at the exhaust manifold. Disconnect the engine insulators from the no. 1 crossmember.

13. Remove the flywheel inspection plate and the four converter-to-flywheel attaching nuts, if equipped with automatic transmission.

14. Remove the jackstands and lower the truck. While supporting the transmission, remove the four lower transmission attaching bolts. Attach an engine lifting sling and remove the engine from the truck.

15. To install the engine, align the converter to the flex plate and the engine dowels to the transmission. Reverse all the previous steps for the remainder of the installation.

Rocker Studs

REMOVAL AND INSTALLATION

6-240, 6-300, 8-255, 302

Rocker arm studs which are broken or have damaged threads may be replaced with standard studs. Studs which are loose in the cylinder head must be replaced with oversize studs which are available for service. The amount of oversize and diameter of the studs are as follows:

- 0.006 in. oversize—0.3774–0.7781 in.
- 0.010 in. oversize—0.3814–0.3821 in.
- 0.015 in. oversize—0.3864–0.3871 in.

A tool kit for replacing the rocker studs is available and contains a stud remover and two oversize reamers: one for 0.006 in. and one for 0.015 in. oversize studs. For 0.010 in. oversize

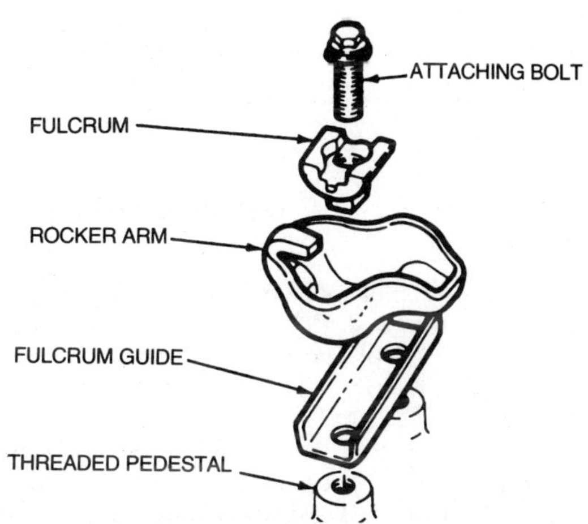

302, 351W valve rocker assembly, 1980 only

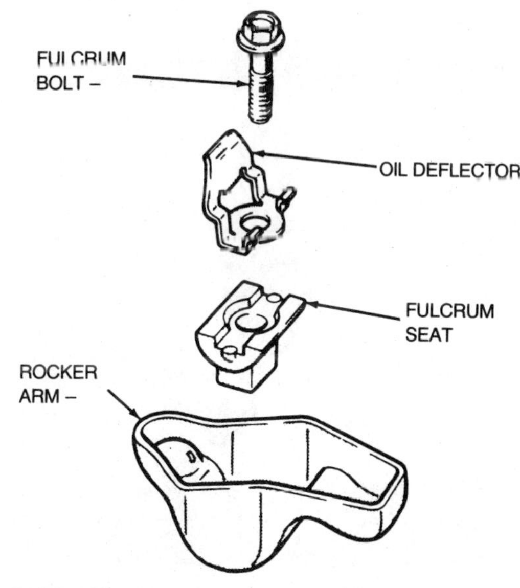

351M, 400, 460 rocker arm assembly

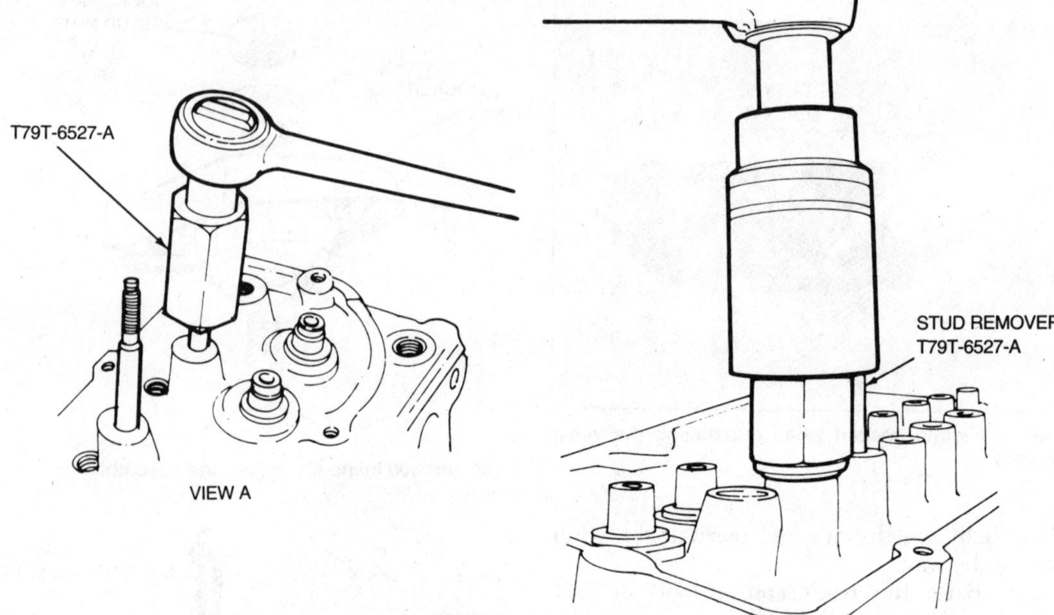

Removing the rocker arm stud on the 240 and 300 inline sixes

studs, use reamer tool T66P-6A527-B. to press the replacement studs into the cylinder head, use the stud replacer tool T69P-6049-D. Use the smaller reamer tool first when boring the hole for oversize studs.

1. Remove the valve rocker cover(s) by moving all hoses aside and unbolting the cover(s). Position the sleeve of the rocker arm stud remover over the stud with the bearing end down. When working on a 302 V8, cut the threaded part of the stud off with a hacksaw. Thread the puller into the sleeve and over the stud until it is fully bottomed. Hold the sleeve with a wrench and rotate the puller clockwise to remove the stud.

An alternate method of removing the rocker studs without the special tool is to put spacers over the stud until just enough threads are left showing at the top so a nut can be screwed onto the top of the rocker arm stud and get a full bite. Turn the nut clockwise until the stud is removed, adding spacers under the nut as necessary.

NOTE: *If the rocker stud was broken off flush*

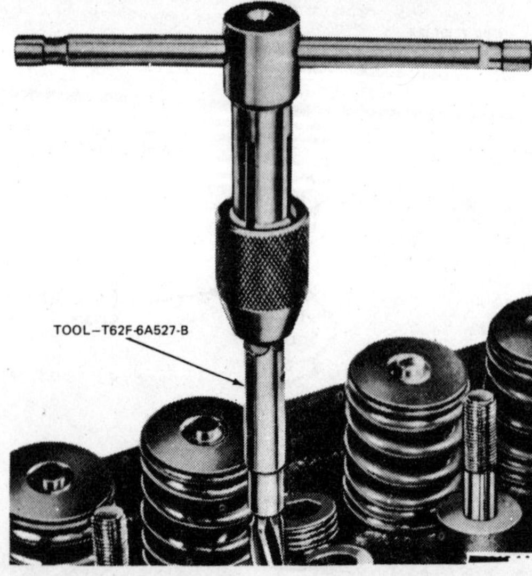

Reaming the rocker arm stud holes

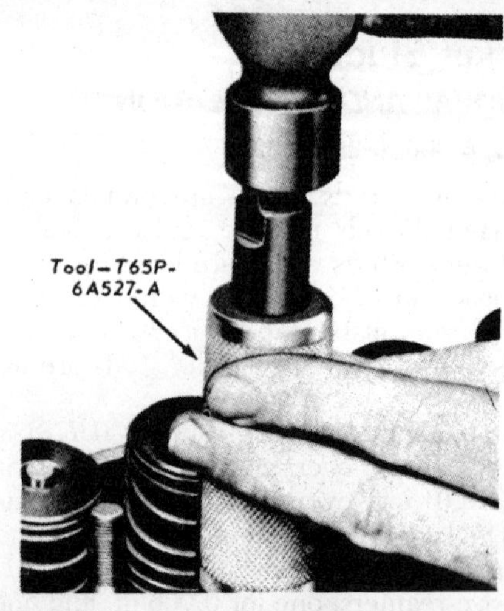

Installing a new rocker arm stud

with the stud boss, use an easy-out tool to remove the broken off part of the stud from the cylinder head.

2. If a loose rocker arm stud is being replaced, ream the stud bore for the selected oversize stud.

NOTE: *Keep all metal particles away from the valves.*

3. Coat the end of the new stud with Lubriplate®. Align the stud and installer with the stud bore and tap the sliding driver until it bottoms. When the installer contacts the stud boss, the stud is installed to its correct height.

Valve Rocker Arm Shaft Assembly

REMOVAL AND INSTALLATION

352, 360, 361, 390, and 391 Cu. In. Engine

1. Remove air cleaner, disconnect spark plug leads and remove leads from bracket on the valve rocker cover.
2. Remove crankcase ventilation hose from rocker cover, then remove rocker cover. On left rocker cover the wiring harness must be removed.
3. On right side, start at No. 4 cylinder (rearmost) and loosen the support bolts in sequence, two turns at a time. Remove the shaft assembly and baffle plate after all the bolts have been loosened. The same procedure is followed on the left bank, except that the bolt-loosening sequence starts with the No. 5 cylinder (foremost).

CAUTION: *The above bolt-loosening procedure must be followed to avoid damage to the rocker arm shaft.*

4. To install, apply Lubriplate® to the pad end of the rocker arms, to the tip of the valve stems and to both ends of the pushrods.
5. Rotate engine to 45 degrees *past* No. 1 cylinder TDC.
6. With the pushrods in place, position rocker arm shaft assembly and baffle plate on the cylinder head such that *oil holes are on the bottom and identification notch is down and toward the front on the right bank and toward the rear on the left bank.* Tighten support bolts finger tight.
7. On the right bank, start at No. 4 cylinder and tighten the support bolts two turns at a time in sequence (4-3-2-1) until the supports are fully in contact with the cylinder head. Then tighten the support bolts to 40–45 ft. lbs. torque. The same procedure is followed on the left valve rocker arm shaft support bolts, starting with the No. 5 cylinder. This procedure allows time for the hydraulic lifter leakdown and thus prevents damage to pushrods, valves and rocker arms.
8. Check valve clearances and adjust if necessary.
9. Install rocker cover, using new gaskets and sealer.
10. Tighten cover retaining bolts to 10–12 ft. lbs., wait two minutes, then tighten to the same torque again.
11. Install crankcase ventilation regulator valve and hose(s), connect spark plug wires and crankcase vent hose, and install air cleaner.

Rocker Arms

REMOVAL AND INSTALLATION

6.9L Diesel V8

1. Disconnect the ground cables from both batteries.
2. Remove the valve cover attaching screws and remove both valve covers.
3. Remove the valve rocker arm post mounting bolts. Remove the rocker arms and

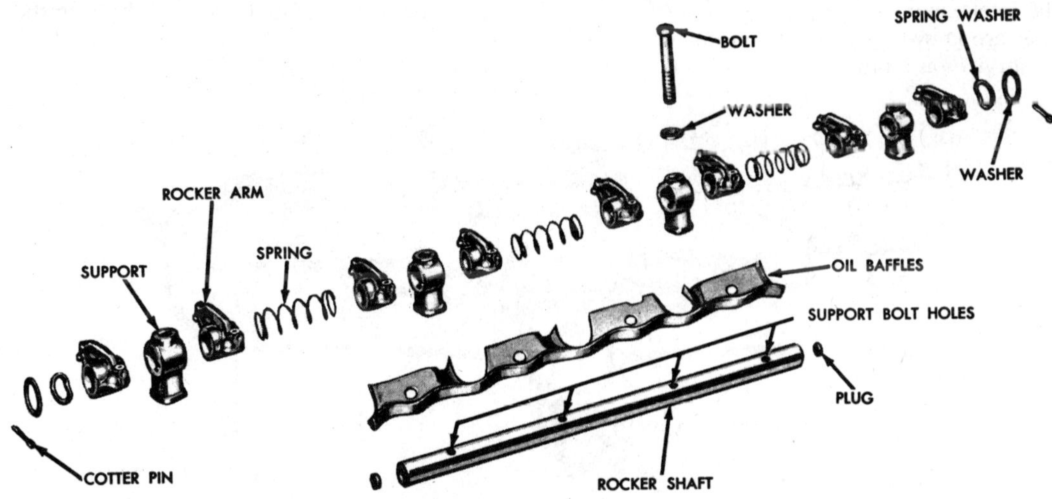

Rocker shaft assembly—352, 360, 361, 390 and 391 V8s

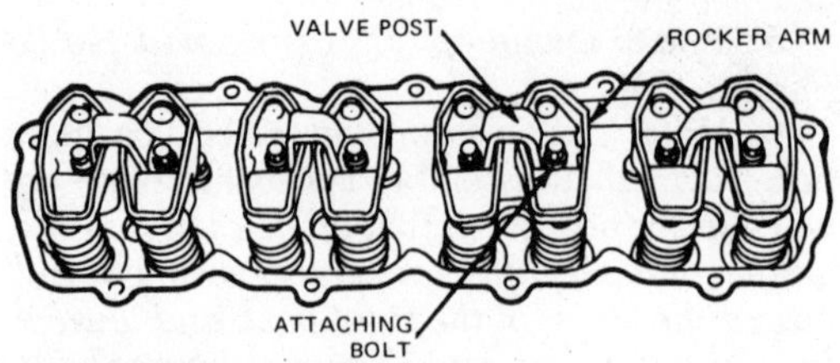

Diesel V8 rocker arm assembly

posts in order and mark them with tape so they can be installed in their original positions.

4. If the cylinder heads are to be removed, then the pushrods can now be removed. Make a holder for the pushrods out of a piece of wood or cardboard, and remove the pushrods in order. *It is very important that the pushrods be re-installed in their original order.* The pushrods can remain in position if no further disassembly is required.

5. If the pushrods were removed, install them in their original locations. Make sure they are fully seated in the tappet seats.

NOTE: *The copper colored end of the pushrod goes toward the rocker arm.*

6. Apply a polyethylene grease to the valve stem tips. Install the rocker arms and posts in their original positions.

7. Turn the engine over by hand until the valve timing mark is at the 11:00 position, as viewed from the front of the engine. Install all of the rocker arm post attaching bolts and torque to 27 ft. lbs.

8. Install new valve cover gaskets and install the valve covers. Install the battery cables, start the engine and check for leaks.

Intake Manifold

REMOVAL AND INSTALLATION

6-300

The intake and exhaust manifolds on these engines are known as combination manifolds and are services as a unit.

1. Remove the air cleaner. Disconnect the choke cable at the carburetor. Disconnect the accelerator cable or rod at the carburetor. Remove the accelerator retracting spring.

2. On a vehicle with automatic transmission, remove the kick-down rod-retracting spring. Remove the accelerator rod bellcrank assembly.

3. Disconnect the fuel inlet line and the distributor vacuum line from the carburetor.

4. Disconnect the muffler inlet pipe from the exhaust manifold.

5. Disconnect the power brake vacuum line, if so equipped.

6. Remove the bolts and nuts attaching the manifolds to the cylinder head. Lift the manifold assemblies from the engine. Remove and discard the gaskets.

7. To separate the manifolds, remove the nuts joining the intake and exhaust manifolds.

8. Clean the mating surfaces of the cylinder head and the manifolds.

9. If the intake and exhaust manifolds have been separated, coat the mating surfaces lightly with graphite grease and place the exhaust manifold over the studs on the intake manifold. Install the lockwashers and nuts. Tighten them finger tight.

10. Install a new intake manifold gasket.

11. Coat the mating surfaces lightly with graphite grease. Place the manifold assemblies in position against the cylinder head. Make sure that the gaskets have not become dislodged. Install the attaching washers, bolts and nuts. Tighten the attaching nuts and bolts in the proper sequence to 26 ft. lbs. If the intake and exhaust manifolds were separated, tighten the nuts joining them.

12. Position a new gasket on the muffler inlet pipe and connect the inlet pipe to the exhaust manifold.

13. Connect the crankcase vent hose to the intake manifold inlet tube and position the hose clamp.

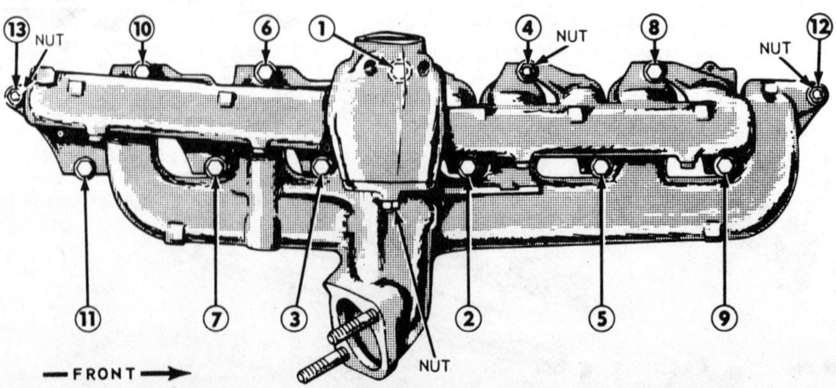

240 and 300 six cylinder intake and exhaust manifold torque sequence

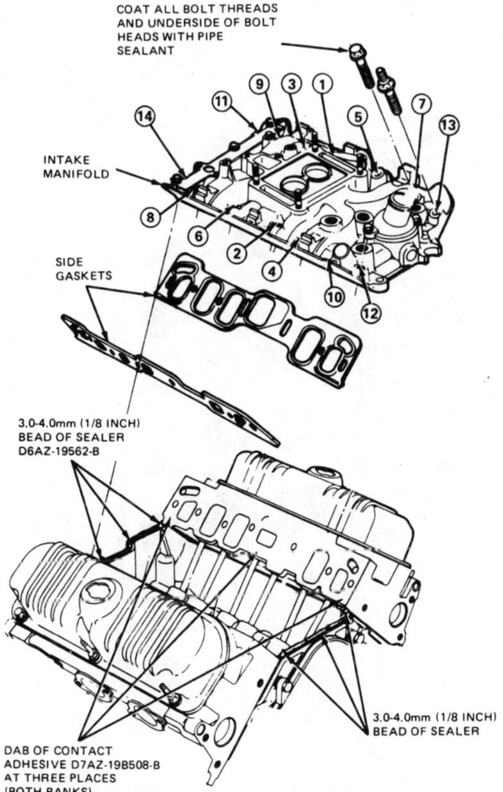

V6 intake manifold removal and installation. Part numbers are Ford—equivalent sealers and adhesives may be used

14. Connect the fuel inlet line and the distributor vacuum line to the carburetor.
15. Connect the accelerator cable to the carburetor and install the retracting spring. Connect the choke cable to the carburetor.
16. On a vehicle with an automatic transmission, install the bellcrank assembly and the kick-down rod retracting spring. Adjust the transmission control linkage.
17. Install the air cleaner.

Gasoline V8 and V6 Except 460 & EFI Models

1. Drain the cooling system, remove the air cleaner and the intake duct assembly.
2. Disconnect the accelerator rod from the carburetor and remove the accelerator retracting spring. Disconnect the automatic transmission kick-down rod at the carburetor, if so equipped.
3. Disconnect the high-tension lead and all other wires from the ignition coil.
4. Disconnect the spark plug wires from the spark plugs by grasping the rubber boots and twisting and pulling at the same time. Remove the wires from the brackets on the rocker covers. Remove the distributor cap and spark plug wire assembly.
5. Remove the carburetor fuel inlet line and the distributor vacuum line from the carburetor.
6. Remove the distributor lockbolt and remove the distributor and vacuum line. See "Distributor Removal and Installation."

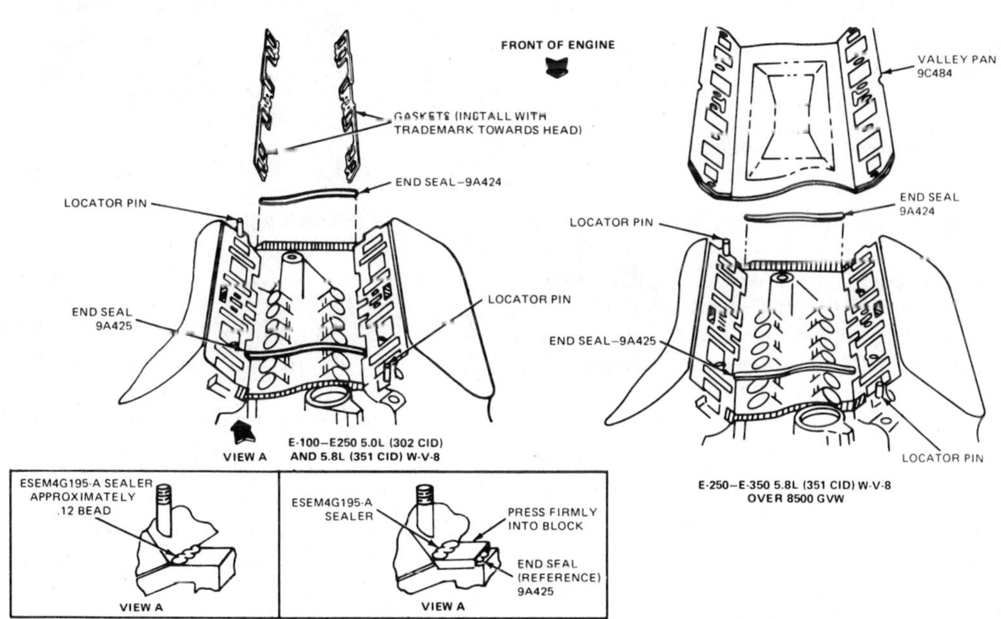

302 and 351W V8 intake manifold sealing and gaskets, late model shown

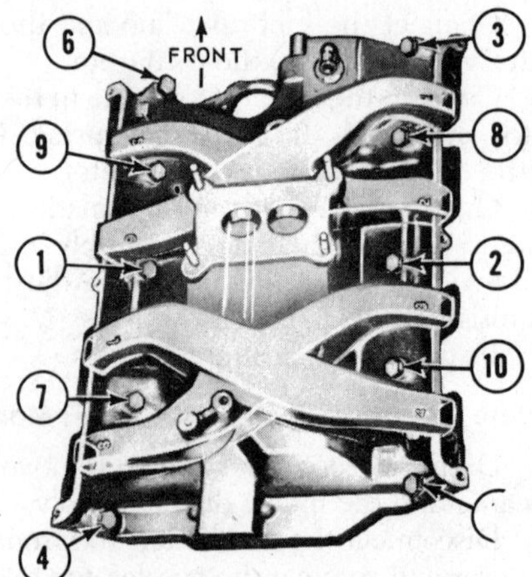

Intake manifold bolt tightening sequence for the 352, 360, 361, 390, and 391 V8s

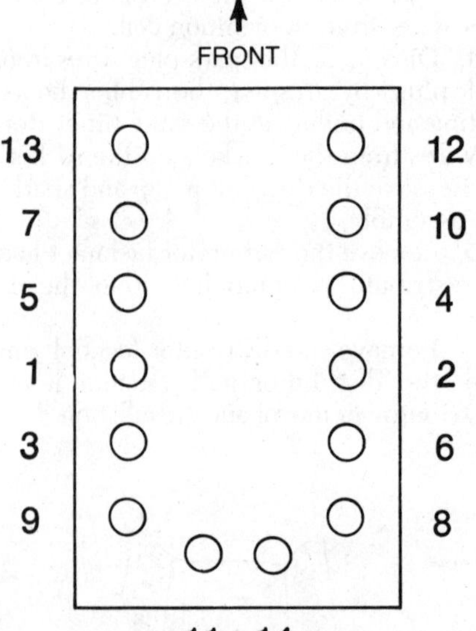

V6 intake manifold torque sequence

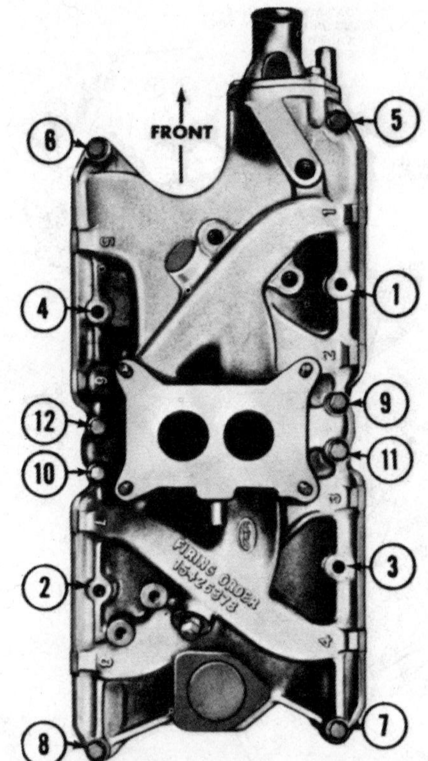

Intake manifold bolt tightening sequence for the 302 V8

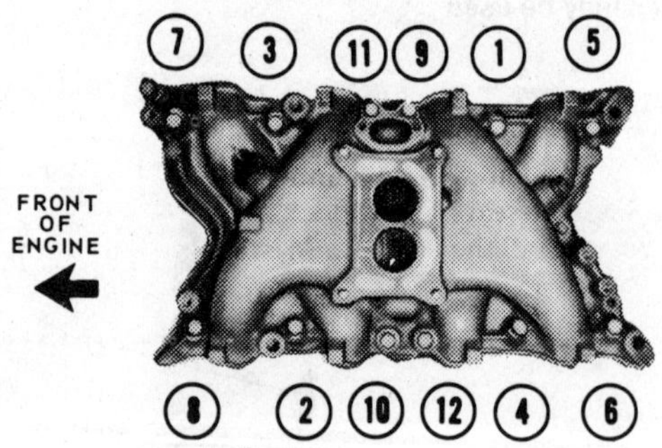

Intake manifold bolt tightening sequence for 351, 351M, and 400 V8s

7. Disconnect the upper radiator hose from the coolant outlet housing and the temperature sending unit wire at the sending unit. Remove the heater hose from the intake manifold.

8. Loosen the clamp on the water pump bypass hose at the coolant outlet housing and slide the hose off the outlet housing.

9. Disconnect the PCV hose at the rocker cover.

10. If the engine is equipped with the Thermactor exhaust emission control system, remove the air pump to cylinder head air hose at the air pump and position it out of the way. Also remove the air hose at the backfire suppressor valve. Remove the air hose bracket from the valve rocker arm cover and position the air hose out of the way.

11. On the 352, 360, 361, 390, 391 V8s, remove the rocker arm shafts and pushrods. *The pushrods must be reinstalled in their original positions.*

12. Remove the intake manifold and carburetor as an assembly. It may be necessary to pry the intake manifold from the cylinder head. Remove all traces of the intake manifold-to-cylinder head gaskets and the two end seals from both the manifold and the other mating surfaces of the engine.

Installation is as follows:

1. Clean the mating surfaces of the intake manifold, cylinder heads and block with laquer

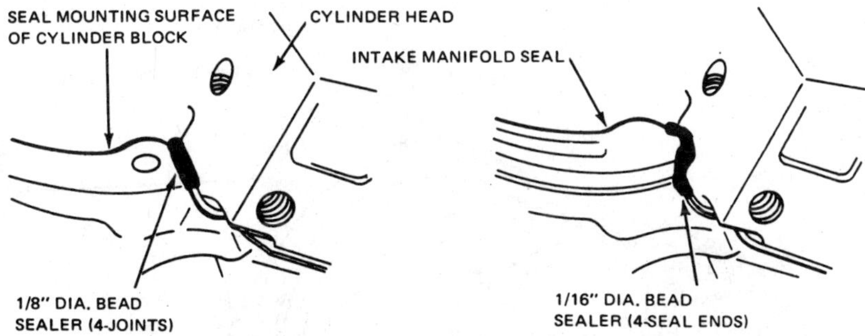

Sealer application area for intake manifold installation on all V8s except 460

thinner or similar solvent. Apply a 1/8 in. bead of silicone-rubber RTV sealant at the points shown in the accompanying diagram.

CAUTION: *Do not apply sealer to the waffle portions of the seals as the sealer will rupture the end seal material.*

2. Position new seals on the block and press the seal locating extensions into the holes in the mating surfaces.

3. Apply a 1/16 in. bead of sealer to the outer end of each manifold seal for the full length of the seal (4 places). As before, do not apply sealer to the waffle portion of the end seals.

NOTE: *This sealer sets in about 15 minutes, depending on brand, so work quickly but carefully. DO NOT DROP ANY SEALER INTO THE MANIFOLD CAVITY. IT WILL FORM AND SET AND PLUG THE OIL GALLERY.*

4. Position the manifold gasket onto the block and heads with the alignment notches under the dowels in the heads. Be sure gasket holes align with head holes.

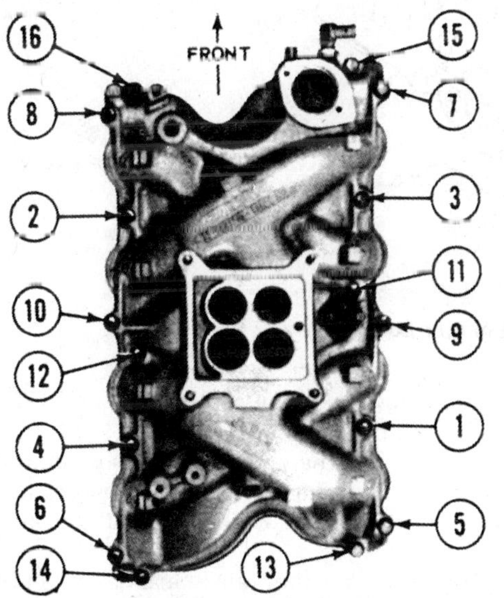

Intake manifold bolt tightening sequence for the 460 V8

5. Install the manifold and related equipment in reverse order of removal.

Fuel Injected

NOTE: *Discharge fuel system pressure before starting any work that involves disconnecting fuel system lines. See "Fuel Supply Manifold" removal and installation procedures (Gasoline Fuel System section).*

1. To remove the upper manifold: Remove the air cleaner. Disconnect the electrical connectors at the air bypass valve, throttle position sensor and EGR position sensor.

2. Disconnect the throttle linkage at the throttle ball and the AOD transmission linkage from the throttle body. Remove the bolts that secure the bracket to the intake and position the bracket and cables out of the way.

3. Disconnect the upper manifold vacuum fitting connections by removing all the vacuum lines at the vacuum tree (label lines for position identification). Remove the vacuum lines to the EGR valve and fuel pressure regulator.

4. Disconnect the PCV system by disconnecting the hose from the fitting at the rear of the upper manifold.

5. Remove the two canister purge lines from the fittings at the throttle body.

6. Disconnect the EGR tube from the EGR valve by loosening the flange nut.

7. Remove the bolt from the upper intake support bracket to upper manifold. Remove the upper manifold retaining bolts and remove the upper intake manifold and throttle body as an assembly.

8. Clean and inspect all mounting surfaces of the upper and lower intake manifolds.

9. Position a new mounting gasket on the lower intake manifold and install the upper manifold in the reverse order of removal. Mounting bolts are torqued to 12–18 ft. lbs.

10. To remove the lower intake manifold: Upper manifold and throttle body must be removed first.

11. Drain the cooling system. Remove the distributor assembly, cap and wires.

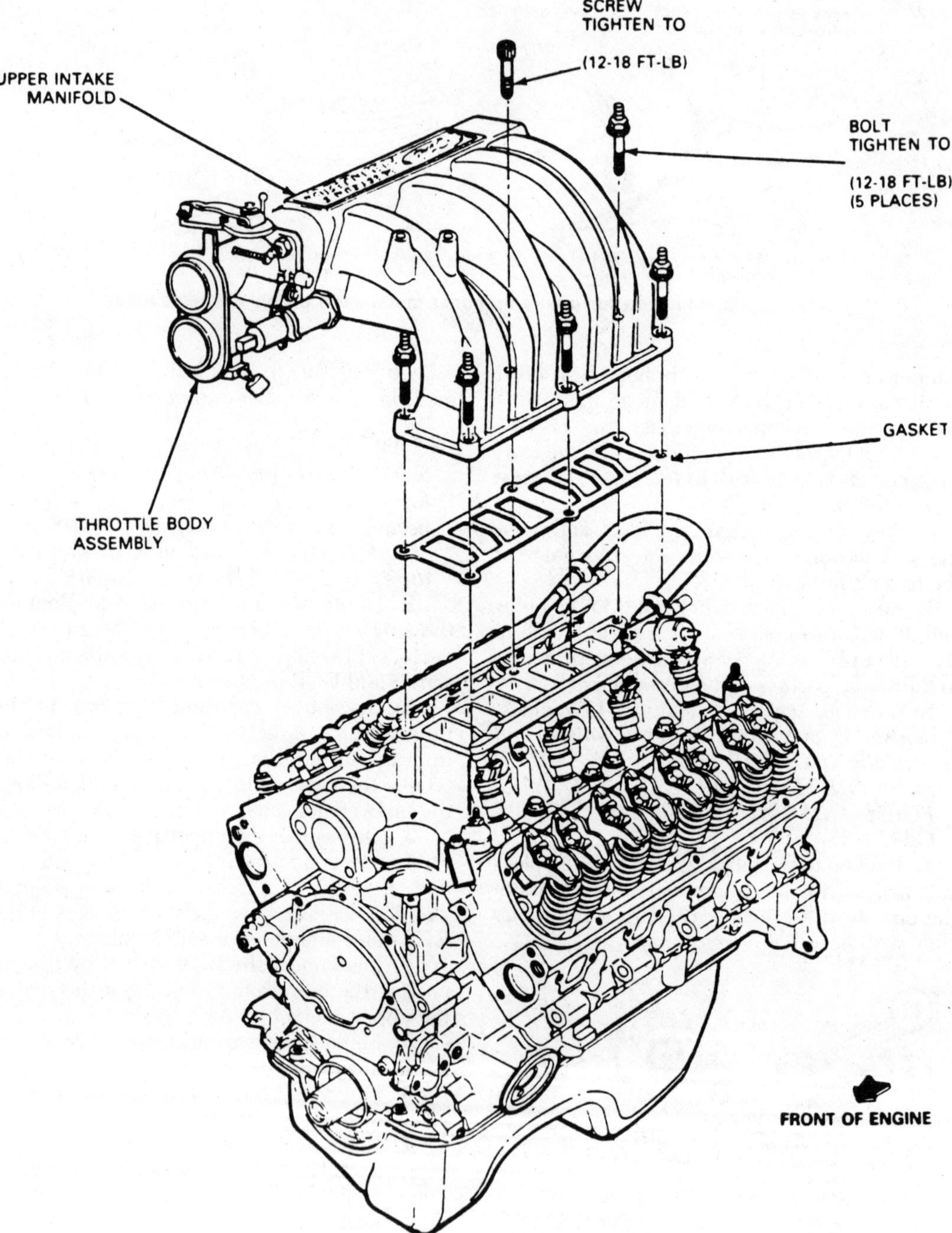

Upper intake manifold and throttle body—EFI

12. Disconnect the electrical connectors at the engine coolant temperature sensor and sending unit, at the air charge temperature sensor and at the knock sensor.

13. Disconnect the injector wiring harness from the main harness asssembly. Remove the ground wire from the intake manifold stud. The ground wire must be installed at the same position it was removed from.

14. Disconnect the fuel supply and return lines from the fuel rails.

15. Remove the upper radiator hose from the thermostat housing. Remove the bypass hose. Remove the heater outlet hose at the intake manifold.

16. Remove the air cleaner mounting bracket. Remove the intake manifold mounting bolts and studs. Pay attention to the loca-

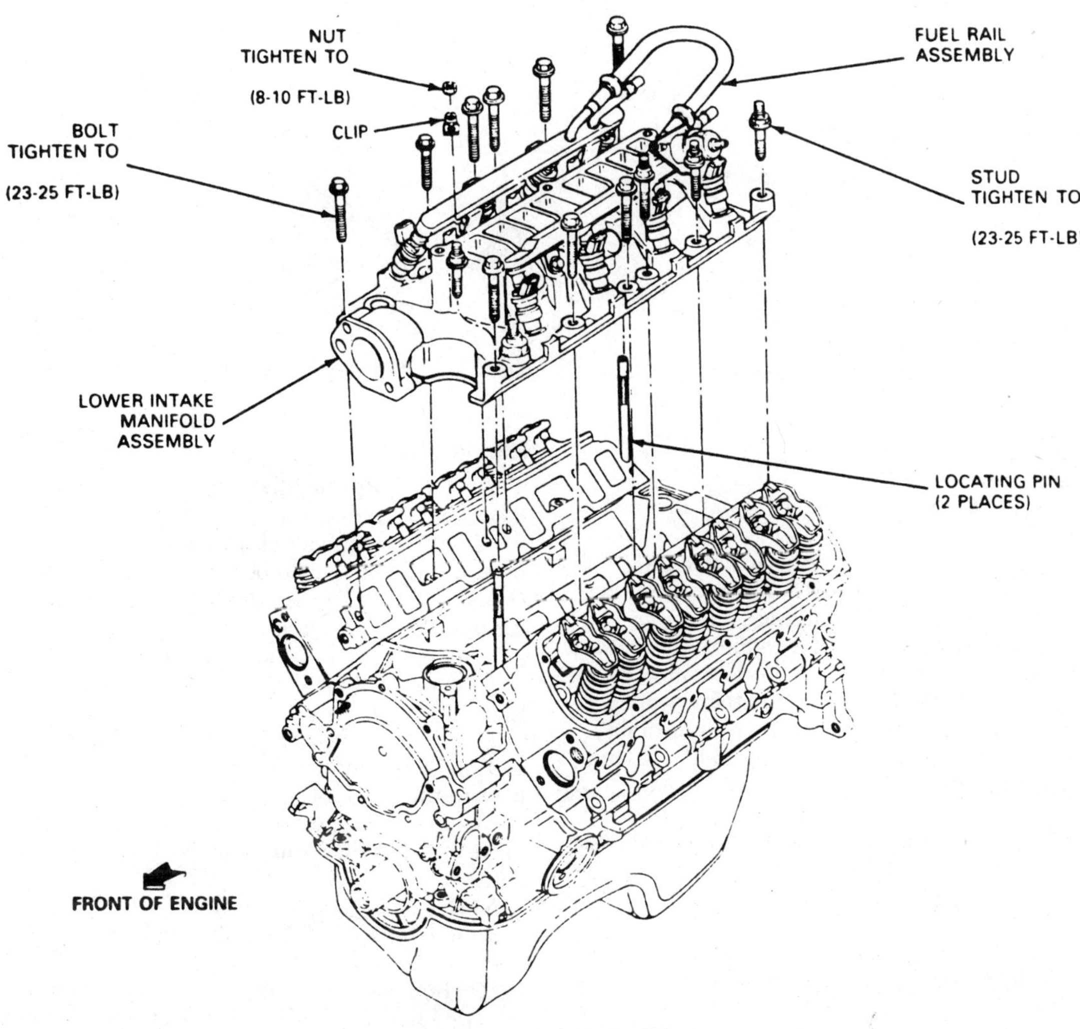

Lower intake manifold—EFI

tion of the bolts and studs for reinstallation. Remove the lower intake manifold assembly.

17. Clean and inspect the mounting surfaces of the heads and manifold.

18. Apply a ¹⁄₁₆ inch bead of RTV sealer to the ends of the manifold seal (the junction point of the seals and gaskets). Install the end seals and intake gaskets on the cylinder heads. The gaskets must interlock with the seal tabs.

19. Install locator bolts at opposite ends of each head and carefully lower the intake manifold into position. Install and tighten the mounting bolts and studs to 23–25 ft. lbs. Install the remaining components in the reverse order of removal.

460 V8

1. Drain the cooling system and remove the air cleaner assembly.

2. Disconnect the upper radiator hose at the engine.

3. Disconnect the heater hoses at the intake manifold and the water pump. Position them out of the way. Loosen the water pump by-pass hose clamp at the intake manifold.

4. Disconnect the PCV valve and hose at right valve cover. Disconnect all of the vacuum lines at the rear of the intake manifold and tag them for proper reinstallation.

5. Disconnect the wires at the spark plugs, and remove the wires from the brackets on the valve covers. Disconnect the high-tension wire from the coil and remove the distributor cap and wires as an assembly.

6. Disconnect all of the distributor vacuum lines at the carburetor and vacuum control valve and tag them for proper installation. Remove the distributor and vacuum lines as an assembly.

7. Disconnect the accelerator linkage at the carburetor. Remove the speed control linkage bracket, if so equipped, from the manifold and carburetor.

8. Remove the bolts holding the accelera-

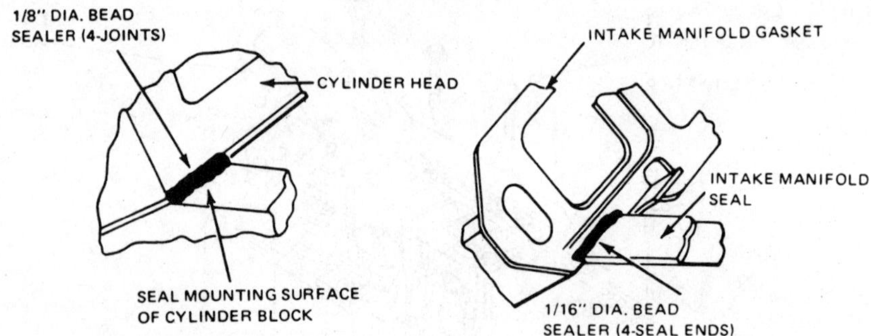

Sealer application areas for intake manifold installation of on 460 V8

tor linkage bellcrank and position the linkage and return springs out of the way.

9. Disconnect the fuel line at the carburetor.

10. Disconnect the wiring harness at the coil battery terminal, engine temperature sending unit, oil pressure sending unit, and other connections as necessary. Disconnect the wiring harness from the clips at the left valve cover and position the harness out of the way.

11. Remove the coil and bracket assembly.

12. Remove the intake manifold attaching bolts and lift the manifold and carburetor from the engine as an assembly. It may be necessary to pry the manifold away from the cylinder heads. Do not damage the gasket sealing surfaces.

Installation is as follows:

1. Clean the mating surfaces of the intake manifold, cylinder heads and block with laquer, thinner or similar solvent. Apply a ⅛ in. bead of silicone-rubber RTV sealant at the points shown in the accompanying diagram.

CAUTION: *Do not apply sealer to the waffle portions of the seals as the sealer will rupture the end seal material.*

2. Position new seals on the block and press the seal locating extensions into the holes in the mating surfaces.

3. Apply a $\frac{1}{16}$ in. bead of sealer to the outer end of each manifold seal for the full length of the seal (4 places). As before, do not apply sealer to the waffle portion of the end seals.

NOTE: *This sealer sets in about 15 minutes, depending on brand, so work quickly but carefully. DO NOT DROP ANY SEALER INTO THE MANIFOLD CAVITY. IT WILL FORM AND SET AND PLUG THE OIL GALLERY.*

4. Position the manifold gasket onto the block and heads with the alignment notches under the dowels in the heads. Be sure gasket holes align with head holes.

5. Install the manifold and related equipment in reverse order of removal.

6.9L V8 Diesel

1. Open the hood and remove both battery ground cables.

2. Remove the air cleaner and install clean rags into the air intake of the intake manifold. *It is important that no dirt or foreign objects get into the diesel intake.*

3. Remove the injection pump as described in Chapter 4 under Diesel Fuel Systems.

4. Remove the fuel return hose from no. 7 and no. 8 rear nozzles and remove the return hose to the fuel tank.

5. Label the positions of the wires and remove the engine wiring harness from the engine.

NOTE: *The engine harness ground cable must be removed from the back of the left cylinder head.*

6. Remove the bolts attaching the intake manifold to the cylinder heads and remove the manifold.

7. Remove the CDR tube grommet from the valley pan.

8. Remove the bolts attaching the valley pan strap to the front of the engine block, and remove the strap.

9. Remove the valley pan drain plug and remove the valley pan.

10. Apply a ⅛ in. bead of RTV sealer to each

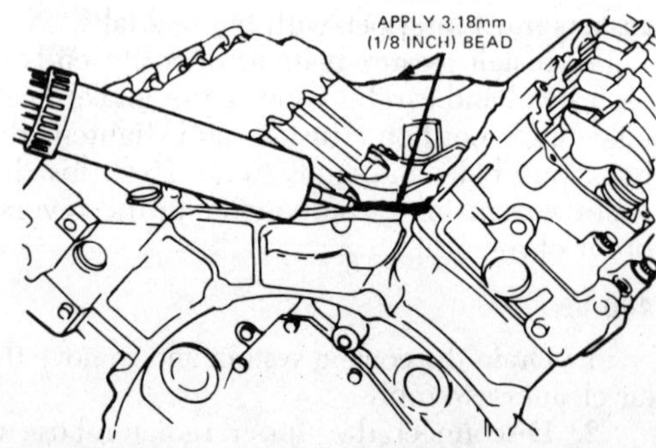

Apply sealer to the diesel cylinder block-to-intake manifold mating surfaces on each end

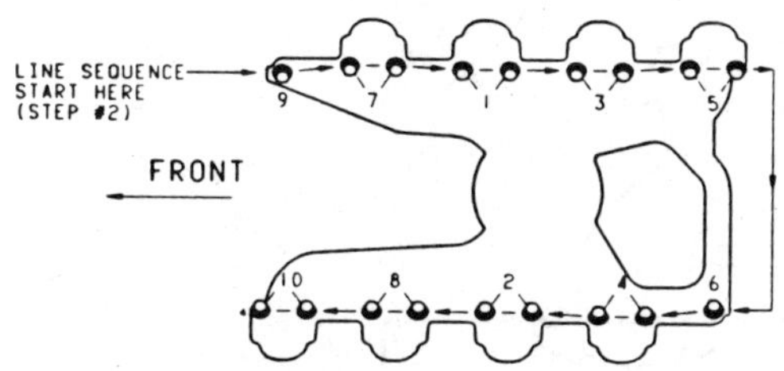

STEP 1. TORQUE BOLTS TO 33 N·m (24 lbf-ft), IN NUMBERED SEQUENCE SHOWN ABOVE.
STEP 2. TORQUE BOLTS TO 33 N·m (24 lbf-ft), IN LINE SEQUENCE SHOWN ABOVE.

6.9L diesel intake manifold torque sequence

end of the cylinder block as shown in the accompanying illustration.

NOTE: *The RTV sealer should be applied immediately prior to the valley pan installation.*

12. Install the valley pan drain plug, CDR tube and new grommet into the valley pan.
13. Install a new O-ring and new back-up ring on the CDR valve.
14. Install the valley pan strap on the front of the valley pan.
15. Install the intake manifold and torque the bolts to 24 ft. lbs. using the sequence shown in the illustration.
16. Reconnect the engine wiring harness and the engine ground wire located to the rear of the left cylinder head.
17. Install the injection pump using the procedure shown in Chapter 4 under Diesel Fuel Systems.
18. Install the no. 7 and no. 8 fuel return hoses and the fuel tank return hose.
19. Remove the rag from the intake manifold and replace the air cleaner. Reconnect the battery ground cables to both batteries.
20. Run the engine and check for oil and fuel leaks.

NOTE: *If necessary, purge the nozzle high pressure lines of air by loosening the connector one half to one turn and cranking the engine until solid stream of fuel, devoid of any bubbles, flows from the connection.*

CAUTION: *Keep eyes and hands away from the nozzle spray. Fuel spraying from the nozzle under high pressure can penetrate the skin.*

21. Check and adjust the injection pump timing, as described in Chapter 4 under Diesel Fuel Systems.

Exhaust Manifold

REMOVAL AND INSTALLATION

6-300

The intake and exhaust manifold on these engines are known as combination manifolds and are serviced as a unit. See "Intake Manifold Removal and Installation."

V6 and Gasoline V8

1. Remove the air cleaner if the manifold being removed has the carburetor heat stove attached to it. On 351 and 400 remove the oil filter.
2. Remove the dipstick tube assembly on the 360 and 390 V8s. On the 302 V8, just remove the bracket. On 351 and 400 V8 vehicles with a column mounted automatic transmission lever, disconnect the selector lever cross-shaft for clearance.
3. Disconnect the power steering pump bracket from the cylinder block and move it out of the way on 360, 361 and 390, 391 V8s.
4. Disconnect the exhaust pipe or catalytic converter from the exhaust manifold. Remove and discard the donut gasket.
5. When the left manifold is being removed on the 352 engine remove the exhaust heat control valve and gasket.
6. Remove the exhaust manifold attaching screws and remove the manifold from the cylinder head.
7. Install the exhaust manifold in the reverse order of removal. Apply a light coat of graphite grease to the mating surface of the manifold. Install and tighten the attaching bolts, starting from the center and working to both ends alternately. Tighten to the proper specifications.

6.9L V8 Diesel

1. Disconnect the ground cables from both batteries.
2. Jack up the truck and safely support it with jackstands.
3. Disconnect the muffler inlet pipe from the exhaust manifolds.
4. Lower the truck to remove the right manifold. When removing the left manifold, jack the truck up. Bend the tabs on the manifold attaching bolts, then remove the bolts and manifolds.
5. Before installing, clean all mounting surfaces on the cylinder heads and the manifolds. Apply an antiseize compound on the manifold bolt threads and install the left manifold, using a new gasket and new locking tabs.
6. Torque the bolts to specifications and bend the tabs over the flats on the bolt heads to prevent the bolts from loosening.
7. Jack up the truck to install the right manifold. Install the right manifold following procedures 5 and 6 above.
8. Connect the inlet pipes to the manifold and tighten. Lower the truck, connect the bat-

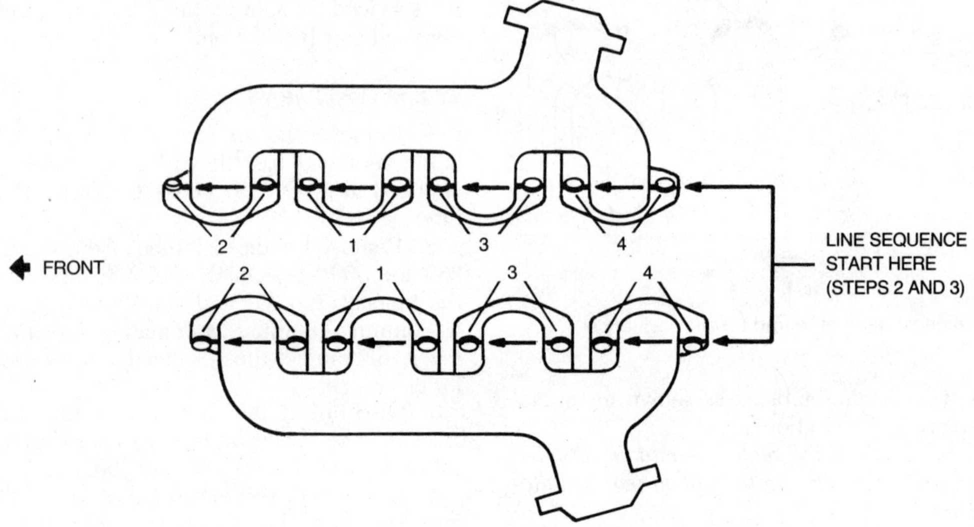

6.9L diesel V8 exhaust manifold torque sequence

teries and run the engine to check for exhaust leaks.

Cylinder Head

REMOVAL AND INSTALLATION

6-300

1. Drain the cooling system. Remove the air cleaner. Remove the oil filler tube. Disconnect the battery cable at the cylinder head.
2. Disconnect the muffler inlet pipe at the exhaust manifold. Pull the muffler inlet pipe down. Remove the gasket.
3. Disconnect the accelerator rod or cable retracting spring. Disconnect the choke control cable if applicable and the accelerator rod at the carburetor.
4. Disconnect the transmission kickdown rod. Disconnect the accelerator linkage at the bellcrank assembly.
5. Disconnect the fuel inlet line at the fuel filter hose, and the distributor vacuum line at the carburetor. Disconnect other vacuum lines as necessary for accessibility and identify them for proper connection.
6. Remove the radiator upper hose at the coolant outlet housing.
7. Disconnect the distributor vacuum line at the distributor. Disconnect the carburetor fuel inlet line at the fuel pump. Remove the lines as an assembly.
8. Disconnect the spark plug wires at the spark plugs and the temperature sending unit wire at the sending unit.
9. Grasp the PCV vent hose near the PCV valve and pull the valve out of the grommet in the valve rocker arm cover. Disconnect the PCV vent hose at the hose fitting in the intake manifold spacer and remove the vent hose and PCV valve.
10. Disconnect the carburetor air vent tube and remove the valve rocker arm cover.
11. Remove the valve rocker arm shaft assembly. Remove the pushrods in sequence so that they can be identified and reinstalled in their original positions.
12. Remove the cylinder head bolts and remove the cylinder head. *Do not pry between*

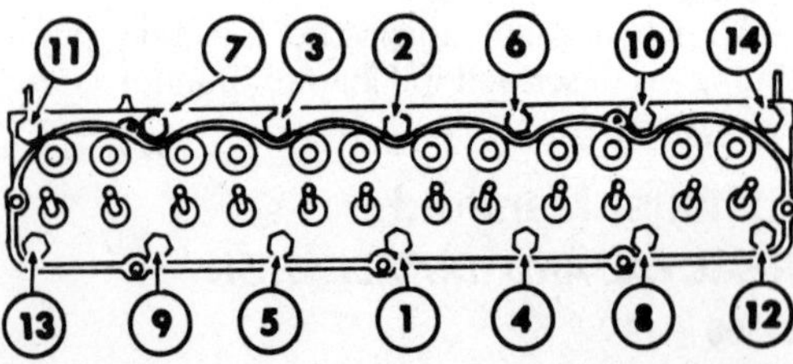

Cylinder head torque sequence for 240 and 300 inline sixes

ENGINE OVERHAUL

Most engine overhaul procedures are fairly standard. In addition to specific parts replacement procedures and complete specifications for your individual engine, this chapter also is a guide to accepted rebuilding procedures. Examples of standard rebuilding practice are shown and should be used along with specific details concerning your particular engine.

Competent and accurate machine shop services will ensure maximum performance, reliability and engine life. Procedures marked with the symbol shown above should be performed by a competent machine shop, and are provided so that you will be familiar with the procedures necessary to a successful overhaul.

In most instances it is more profitable for the do-it-yourself mechanic to remove, clean and inspect the component, buy the necessary parts and deliver these to a shop for actual machine work.

On the other hand, much of the rebuilding work (crankshaft, block, bearings, pistons, rods, and other components) is well within the scope of the do-it-yourself mechanic.

Tools

The tools required for an engine overhaul or parts replacement will depend on the depth of your involvement. With a few exceptions, they will be the tools found in a mechanic's tool kit (see Chapter 1). More in-depth work will require any or all of the following:

- a dial indicator (reading in thousandths) mounted on a universal base
- micrometers and telescope gauges
- jaw and screw-type pullers
- scraper
- valve spring compressor
- ring groove cleaner
- piston ring expander and compressor
- ridge reamer
- cylinder hone or glaze breaker
- Plastigage®
- engine stand

Use of most of these tools is illustrated in this chapter. Many can be rented for a one-time use from a local parts jobber or tool supply house specializing in automotive work.

Occasionally, the use of special tools is called for. See the information on Special Tools and the Safety Notice in the front of this book before substituting another tool.

Inspection Techniques

Procedures and specifications are given in this chapter for inspecting, cleaning and assessing the wear limits of most major components. Other procedures such as Magnaflux and Zyglo can be used to locate material flaws and stress cracks. Magnaflux is a magnetic process applicable only to ferrous materials. The Zyglo process coats the material with a flourescent dye penetrant and can be used on any material. Check for suspected surface cracks can be more readily made using spot check dye. The dye is sprayed onto the suspected area, wiped off and the area sprayed with a developer. Cracks will show up brightly.

Overhaul Tips

Aluminum has become extremely popular for use in engines, due to its low weight. Observe the following precautions when handling aluminum parts:

- Never hot tank aluminum parts (the caustic hot-tank solution will eat the aluminum)
- Remove all aluminum parts (identification tag, etc.) from engine parts prior to hot-tanking.
- Always coat threads lightly with engine oil or anti-seize compounds before installation, to prevent seizure.
- Never over-torque bolts or spark plugs, especially in aluminum threads.

Stripped threads in any component can be repaired using any of several commercial repair kits (Heli-Coil, Microdot, Keenserts, etc.)

When assembling the engine, any parts that will be in frictional contact must be prelubed to provide lubrication at initial start-up. Any product specifically formulated for this purpose can be used, but engine oil is not recommended as a pre-lube.

When semi-permanent (locked, but removable) installation of bolts or nuts is desired, threads should be cleaned and coated with Loctite® or other similar, commercial non-hardening sealant.

Repairing Damaged Threads

Several methods of repairing damaged threads are available. Heli-Coil® (shown here), Keenserts® and Microdot® are among the most widely used. All involve basically the same principle—drilling out stripped threads, tapping the hole and installing a prewound insert—making welding, plugging and oversize fasteners unnecessary.

Two types of thread repair inserts are usually supplied—a standard type for most Inch Coarse, Inch Fine, Metric Coarse and Metric Fine thread sizes and a spark plug type to fit most spark plug port sizes. Consult the individual manufacturer's catalog to determine exact applications. Typical thread repair kits will contain a selection of prewound threaded inserts, a tap (corresponding to the outside diameter threads of the insert) and an installation tool. Spark plug inserts usually differ because they require a tap equipped with pilot threads and a combined reamer/tap section. Most manufacturers also supply blister-packed thread repair inserts separately in addition to a master kit containing a variety of taps and inserts plus installation tools.

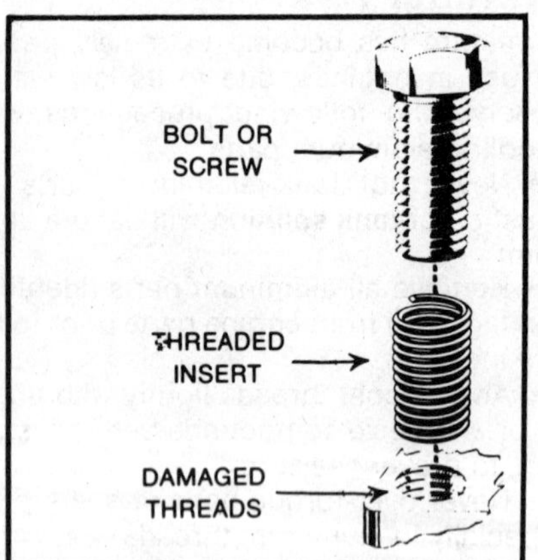

Damaged bolt holes can be repaired with thread repair inserts

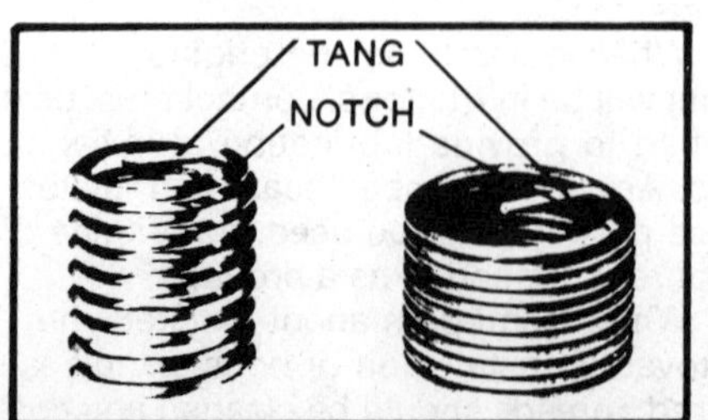

Standard thread repair insert (left) and spark plug thread insert (right)

Before effecting a repair to a threaded hole, remove any snapped, broken or damaged bolts or studs. Penetrating oil can be used to free frozen threads; the offending item can be removed with locking pliers or with a screw or stud extractor. After the hole is clear, the thread can be repaired, as follows:

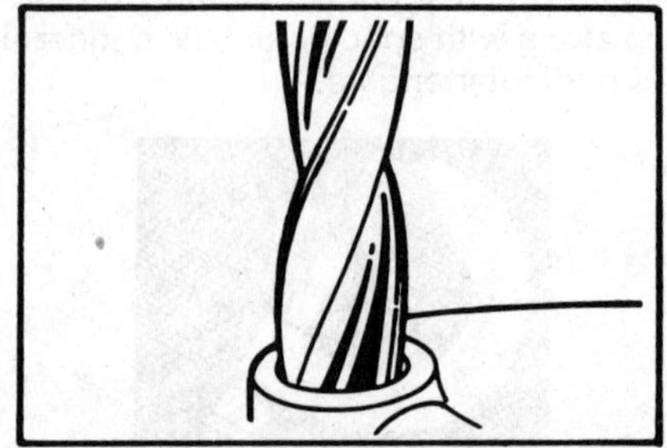

Drill out the damaged threads with specified drill. Drill completely through the hole or to the bottom of a blind hole

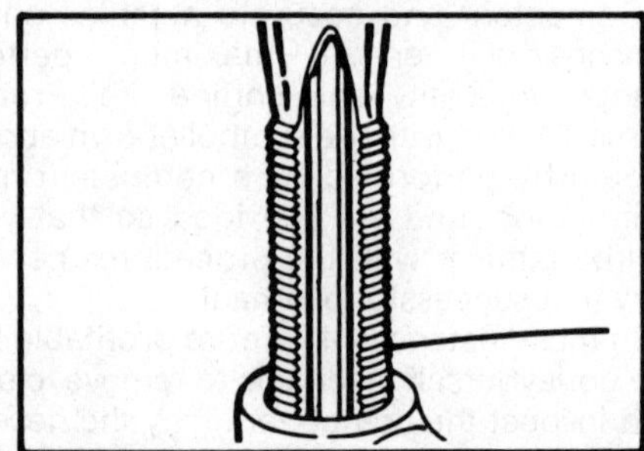

With the tap supplied, tap the hole to receive the thread insert. Keep the tap well oiled and back it out frequently to avoid clogging the threads

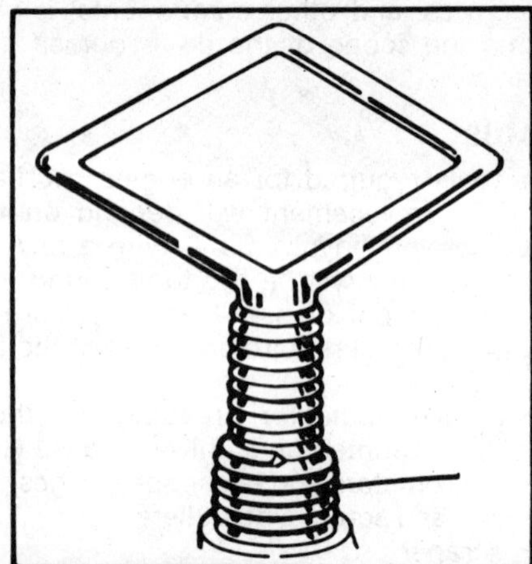

Screw the threaded insert onto the installation tool until the tang engages the slot. Screw the insert into the tapped hole until it is ¼–½ turn below the top surface, After installation break off the tang with a hammer and punch

Standard Torque Specifications and Fastener Markings

In the absence of specific torques, the following chart can be used as a guide to the maximum safe torque of a particular size/grade of fastener.

- There is no torque difference for fine or coarse threads.
- Torque values are based on clean, dry threads. Reduce the value by 10% if threads are oiled prior to assembly.
- The torque required for aluminum components or fasteners is considerably less.

U.S. Bolts

SAE Grade Number	1 or 2			5			6 or 7		
Number of lines always 2 less than the grade number.									
Bolt Size	Maximum Torque			Maximum Torque			Maximum Torque		
(Inches)—(Thread)	Ft./Lbs.	Kgm	Nm	Ft./Lbs.	Kgm	Nm	Ft./Lbs.	Kgm	Nm
¼—20	5	0.7	6.8	8	1.1	10.8	10	1.4	13.5
—28	6	0.8	8.1	10	1.4	13.6			
5/16—18	11	1.5	14.9	17	2.3	23.0	19	2.6	25.8
—24	13	1.8	17.6	19	2.6	25.7			
⅜—16	18	2.5	24.4	31	4.3	42.0	34	4.7	46.0
—24	20	2.75	27.1	35	4.8	47.5			
7/16—14	28	3.8	37.0	49	6.8	66.4	55	7.6	74.5
—20	30	4.2	40.7	55	7.6	74.5			
½—13	39	5.4	52.8	75	10.4	101.7	85	11.75	115.2
—20	41	5.7	55.6	85	11.7	115.2			
9/16—12	51	7.0	69.2	110	15.2	149.1	120	16.6	162.7
—18	55	7.6	74.5	120	16.6	162.7			
⅝—11	83	11.5	112.5	150	20.7	203.3	167	23.0	226.5
—18	95	13.1	128.8	170	23.5	230.5			
¾—10	105	14.5	142.3	270	37.3	366.0	280	38.7	379.6
—16	115	15.9	155.9	295	40.8	400.0			
⅞— 9	160	22.1	216.9	395	54.6	535.5	440	60.9	596.5
—14	175	24.2	237.2	435	60.1	589.7			
1— 8	236	32.5	318.6	590	81.6	799.9	660	91.3	894.8
—14	250	34.6	338.9	660	91.3	849.8			

Metric Bolts

Relative Strength Marking	4.6, 4.8			8.8		
Bolt Markings						
Bolt Size	Maximum Torque			Maximum Torque		
Thread Size x Pitch (mm)	Ft./Lbs.	Kgm	Nm	Ft./Lbs.	Kgm	Nm
6 x 1.0	2–3	.2–.4	3–4	3–6	.4–.8	5–8
8 x 1.25	6–8	.8–1	8–12	9–14	1.2–1.9	13–19
10 x 1.25	12–17	1.5–2.3	16–23	20–29	2.7–4.0	27–39
12 x 1.25	21–32	2.9–4.4	29–43	35–53	4.8–7.3	47–72
14 x 1.5	35–52	4.8–7.1	48–70	57–85	7.8–11.7	77–110
16 x 1.5	51–77	7.0–10.6	67–100	90–120	12.4–16.5	130–160
18 x 1.5	74–110	10.2–15.1	100–150	130–170	17.9–23.4	180–230
20 x 1.5	110–140	15.1–19.3	150–190	190–240	26.2–46.9	160–320
22 x 1.5	150–190	22.0–26.2	200–260	250–320	34.5–44.1	340–430
24 x 1.5	190–240	26.2–46.9	260–320	310–410	42.7–56.5	420–550

CHECKING ENGINE COMPRESSION

A noticeable lack of engine power, excessive oil consumption and/or poor fuel mileage measured over an extended period are all indicators of internal engine wear. Worn piston rings, scored or worn cylinder bores, blown head gaskets, sticking or burnt valves and worn valve seats are all possible culprits here. A check of each cylinder's compression will help you locate the problems.

As mentioned in the "Tools and Equipment" section of Chapter 1, a screw-in type compression gauge is more accurate than the type you simply hold against the spark plug hole, although it takes slightly longer to use. It's worth it to obtain a more accurate reading. Follow the procedures below for gasoline and diesel-engined cars.

Gasoline Engines

1. Warm up the engine to normal operating temperature.
2. Remove all spark plugs.

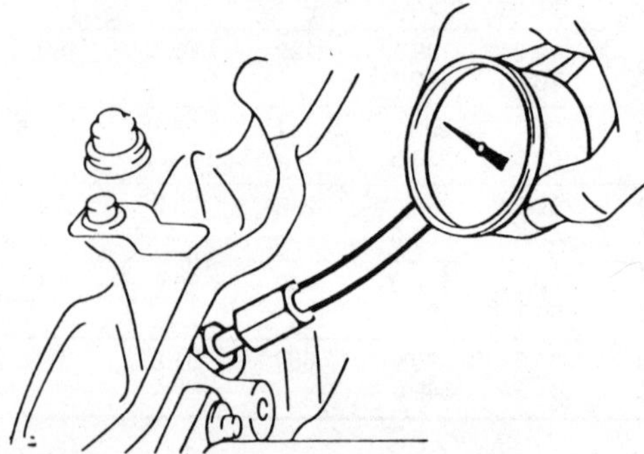

The screw-in type compression gauge is more accurate

3. Disconnect the high-tension lead from the ignition coil.
4. On carbureted cars, fully open the throttle either by operating the carburetor throttle linkage by hand or by having an assistant "floor" the accelerator pedal. On fuel-injected cars, disconnect the cold start valve and all injector connections.
5. Screw the compression gauge into the No. 1 spark plug hole until the fitting is snug.

NOTE: *Be careful not to crossthread the plug hole. On aluminum cylinder heads use extra care, as the threads in these heads are easily ruined.*

6. Ask an assistant to depress the accelerator pedal fully on both carbureted and fuel-injected cars. Then, while you read the compression gauge, ask the assistant to crank the engine two or three times in short bursts using the ignition switch.
7. Read the compression gauge at the end of each series of cranks, and record the highest of these readings. Repeat this procedure for each of the engine's cylinders. Compare the highest reading of each cylinder to the compression pressure specifications in the "Tune-Up Specifications" chart in Chapter 2. The specs in this chart are maximum values.

A cylinder's compression pressure is usually acceptable if it is not less than 80% of maximum. The difference between each cylinder should be no more than 12–14 pounds.

8. If a cylinder is unusually low, pour a tablespoon of clean engine oil into the cylinder through the spark plug hole and repeat the compression test. If the compression comes up after adding the oil, it appears that that cylinder's piston rings or bore are damaged or worn. If the pressure remains low, the valves may not be seating properly (a valve job is needed), or the head gasket may be blown near that cylinder. If compression in any two adjacent cylinders is low, and if the addition of oil doesn't help the compression, there is leakage past the head gasket. Oil and coolant water in the combustion chamber can result from this problem. There may be evidence of water droplets on the engine dipstick when a head gasket has blown.

Diesel Engines

Checking cylinder compression on diesel engines is basically the same procedure as on gasoline engines except for the following:

1. A special compression gauge adaptor suitable for diesel engines (because these engines have much greater compression pressures) must be used.
2. Remove the injector tubes and remove the injectors from each cylinder.

NOTE: *Don't forget to remove the washer underneath each injector; otherwise, it may get lost when the engine is cranked.*

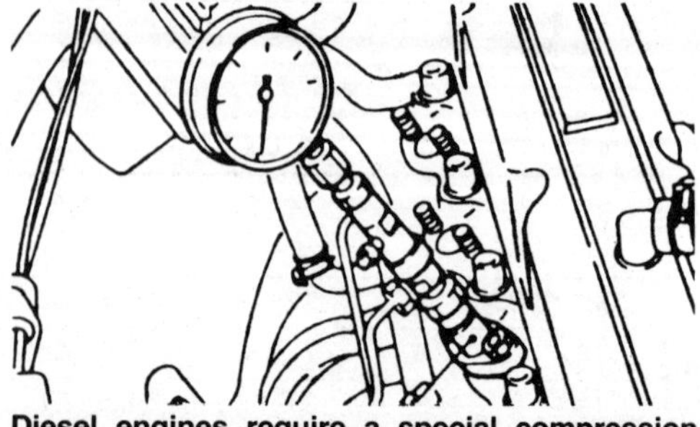

Diesel engines require a special compression gauge adaptor

3. When fitting the compression gauge adaptor to the cylinder head, make sure the bleeder of the gauge (if equipped) is closed.
4. When reinstalling the injector assemblies, install new washers underneath each injector.

the cylinder head and the block as the gasket surfaces may be damaged.

To install the cylinder head:

1. Clean the head and block gasket surfaces. If the cylinder head was removed for a gasket change, check the flatness of the cylinder head and block.
2. Apply sealer to both sides of the new cylinder head gasket. Position the gasket on the cylinder block.
3. Install a new gasket on the flange of the muffler inlet pipe.
4. Lift the cylinder head above the cylinder block and lower it into position using two head bolts installed through the head as guides.
5. Coat the threads of the No. 1 and 6 bolts for the right-side of the cylinder head with a small amount of water-resistant sealer. Oil the threads of the remaining bolts. Install, but do not tighten, two bolts at the opposite ends of the head to hold the head and gasket in position.
6. The cylinder head bolts are tightened in 3 progressive steps. Torque them (in the proper sequence) to 55 ft. lbs., then 65 ft. lbs., and finally to 75 ft. lbs.
7. Apply Lubriplate® to both ends of the pushrods and install them in their original positions.
8. Install the valve rocker arm shaft assembly.
9. Adjust the valves, as necessary.
10. Install the muffler inlet pipe lockwashers and attaching nuts.
11. Connect the radiator upper hose at the coolant outlet housing.
12. Position the distributor vacuum line and the carburetor fuel inlet line on the engine. Connect the fuel line at the fuel filter hose and install a new clamp. Install the distributor vacuum line at the carburetor. Connect the accelerator linkage at the bellcrank assembly. Connect the transmission kickdown rod.
13. Connect the accelerator rod retracting spring. Connect the choke control cable (if applicable) and the accelerator rod at the carburetor.
14. Connect the distributor vacuum line at the distributor. Connect the carburetor fuel inlet line at the fuel pump. Connect all the vacuum lines using their previous identification for proper connection.
15. Connect the temperature sending unit wire at the sending unit. Connect the spark plug wires. Connect the battery cable at the cylinder head.
16. Fill the cooling system.
17. Install the valve rocker cover. Connect the carburetor air vent tube.
18. Connect the PCV vent hose at the carburetor spacer fitting. Insert the PCV valve with the vent hose attached, into the valve rocker arm cover grommet. Install the air cleaner, start the engine and check for leaks.

V6

1. Drain the cooling system.
2. Disconnect the cable from the battery negative terminal.
3. Remove the air cleaner assembly including air intake duct and heat tube.
4. Loosen the accessory drive belt idler. Remove the drive belt.
5. If the left cylinder head is being removed:
   a. If equipped with power steering, remove the pump mounting brackets' attaching bolts, leaving the hoses connected, place the pump/bracket assembly aside in a position to prevent the fluid from leaking out.
   b. If equipped with air conditioning, remove the mounting brackets' attaching bolts, leaving the hoses connected, position the compressor aside.
6. If the right cylinder head is being removed:
   a. Disconnect the thermactor diverter valve and hose assembly at the by-pass valve and downstream air tube.
   b. Remove the assembly.
   c. Remove the accessory drive idler.
   d. Remove the alternator.
   e. Remove the thermactor pump pulley. Remove the thermactor pump.
   f. Remove the alternator bracket.
   g. Remove the PCV valve.
7. Remove the intake manifold.
8. Remove the valve rocker arm cover attaching screws. Loosen the silicone rubber gasketing material by inserting a putty knife under the cover flange. Work the cover loose and re-

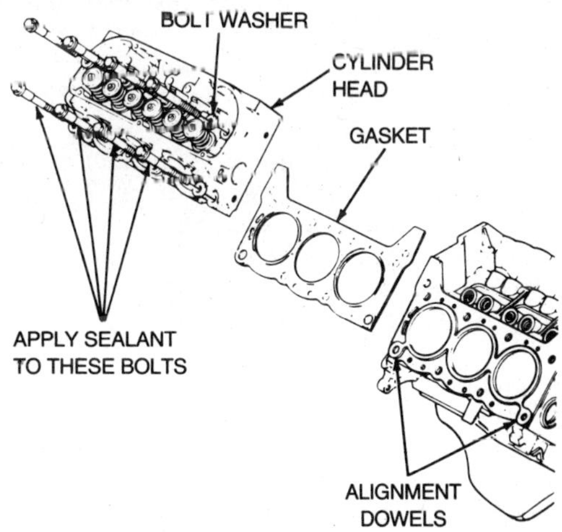

232 V6 cylinder head installation

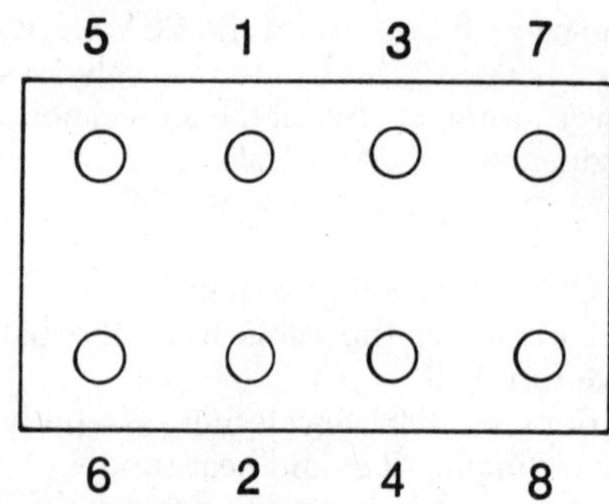

232 V6 cylinder head torque sequence

move. *The plastic rocker arm covers will break if excessive prying is applied.*

9. Remove the exhaust manifold(s).

10. Loosen the rocker arm fulcrum attaching bolts enough to allow the rocker arm to be lifted off the pushrod and rotated to one side.

11. Remove the pushrods. The position of each rod should be installed in the original position during assembly.

12. Remove the cylinder head attaching bolts. Remove the cylinder head(s).

13. Remove and discard the old cylinder head gasket(s). Discard the cylinder head bolts.

14. Lightly oil all bolt and stud bolt threads before installation except those specifying special sealant.

15. Clean the cylinder head, intake manifold, valve rocker arm cover and cylinder head gasket surfaces. If the cylinder head was removed for a cylinder head gasket replacement, check the flatness of the cylinder head and block gasket surfaces.

16. Position new head gasket(s) on the cylinder block using the dowels for alignment.

17. Position the cylinder heads to the block.

18. Apply a thin coating of pipe sealant or equivalent to the threads of the short cylinder head bolts (nearest to the exhaust manifold). Do not apply sealant to the long bolts. Lightly oil the cylinder head bolt flat washers. Install the flat washers and cylinder head bolts (Eight each side).

CAUTION: *Always use new cylinder head bolts to assure a leak tight assembly. Torque retention with used bolts can vary, which may result in coolant or compression leakage at the cylinder head mating surface area.*

19. Tighten the attaching bolts in sequence. Back-off the attaching bolts 2–3 turns. Repeat tightening sequence.

NOTE: *When the cylinder head attaching bolts have been tightened using the above sequential procedure, it is not necessary to retighten the bolts after extended engine operation. However, the bolts can be checked for tightness if desired.*

20. Dip each pushrod end in heavy engine oil. Install the push rods in their original position. For each valve rotate the crankshaft until the tappet rests on the heel (base circle) of the camshaft lobe.

21. Position the rocker arms over the push rods, install the fulcrums, and tighten the fulcrum attaching bolts to 61–132 in. lbs.

CAUTION: *Fulcrums must be fully seated in cylinder head and pushrods must be seated in rocker arm sockets prior to final tightening.*

22. Lubricate all rocker arm assemblies with heavy engine oil. Final tighten the fulcrum bolts to 19–25 ft. lbs. For final tightening, the camshaft may be in any position.

NOTE: *If the original valve train components are being installed, a valve clearance check is not required. If a component has been replaced, perform a valve clearance check.*

23. Install the exhaust manifold(s).

24. Apply a 1/8–3/16 inch bead of RTV silicone sealant to the rocker arm cover flange. Make sure the sealer fills the channel in the cover flange. The rocker arm cover must be installed within 15 minutes after the silicone sealer application. After this time, the sealer may start to set-up, and its sealing effectiveness may be reduced.

25. Position the cover on the cylinder head and install the attaching bolts. Note the location of the wiring harness routing clips and spark plug wire routing clip stud bolts. Tighten the attaching bolts to 36–60 in. lbs. torque.

26. Install the intake manifold.

27. Install the spark plugs, if necessary.

28. Connect the secondary wires to the spark plugs.

29. Install the oil fill cap. If equipped with air conditioning, install the compressor mounting and support brackets.

Loosen the rockers and rotate out of the way to remove the pushrods. Keep them in order; note pushrod holder made out of cardboard in background

30. On the right cylinder head:
a. Install the PCV valve.
b. Install the alternator bracket. Tighten attaching nuts to 30–40 ft. lbs.
c. Install the thermactor pump and pump pulley.
d. Install the alternator.
e. Install the accessory drive idler.
f. Install the thermactor diverter valve and hose assembly. Tighten the clamps securely.
31. Install the accessory drive belt and tighten to specified tension.
32. Connect the cable to the battery negative terminal.
33. Fill the cooling system with the specified coolant.

CAUTION: *This engine has an aluminum cylinder head and requires a special unique corrosion inhibited coolant formulation to avoid radiator damage.*

34. Start the engine and check for coolant, fuel, and oil leaks.
35. Check and, if necessary, adjust the curb idle speed.
36. Install the air cleaner assembly including the air intake duct and heat tube.

Gasoline V8 Except 460

1. Remove the intake manifold, carburetor or EFI.
2. Remove the rocker arm cover(s).
3. If the right cylinder head is to be removed, loosen the alternator adjusting arm bolt and remove the alternator mounting bracket bolt and spacer. Swing the alternator down and out of the way. Remove the air cleaner inlet duct from the right cylinder head assembly. Remove the ignition coil on 360, 361 and 390, 391 V8s. On 351 and 400 remove the ground strap at the rear of the head.

If the left cylinder head is being removed, remove the bolts fastening the accelerator shaft assembly at the front of the cylinder head. On vehicles equipped with air conditioning, the system must be discharged and the compressor removed. The procedure is best left to an air conditioning specialist. Persons not familiar with A/C systems can be easily injured when working on the systems.

4. Disconnect the exhaust manifold(s) from the muffler inlet pipe(s).
5. Loosen the rocker arm stud nuts so that the rocker arms can be rotated to the side. Remove the pushrods and identify them so that they can be reinstalled in their original positions.
6. Remove the cylinder head bolts and lift the cylinder head from the block.

To install the cylinder head(s):

1. Clean the cylinder head, intake manifold, and the valve cover and head gasket surfaces.

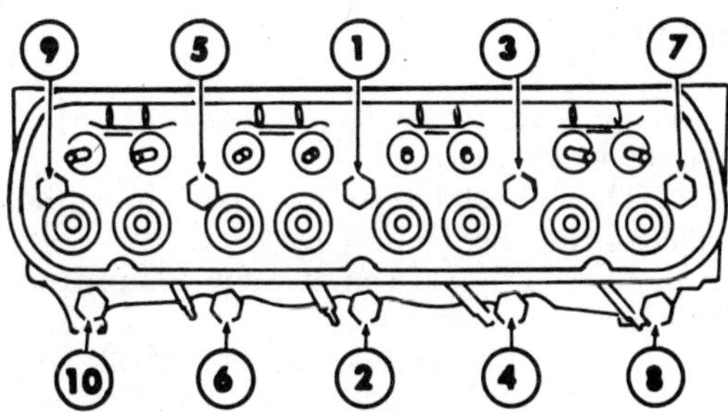

Cylinder head bolt torque sequence, all gasoline V8s

2. A specially treated composition head gasket is used. *Do not apply sealer to a composition gasket.* Position the new gasket over the locating dowels on the cylinder block. Then, position the cylinder head on the block and install the attaching bolts.
3. The cylinder head bolts are tightened in 3 progressive steps. Tighten all the bolts in the proper sequence to 50 ft. lbs., 60 ft. lbs., and finally to 70 ft. lbs. of torque on the 302 V8. On all V8's except the 302, 351M and 400 tighten to 70 ft. lbs., 80 ft. lbs., and finally to 90 ft. lbs. On 351M and 400 V8s, tighten to 70, 80 then 95–105 ft. lbs.
4. Clean the pushrods. Blow out the oil passage in the rods with compressed air. Check the pushrods for straightness by rolling them on a piece of glass. Never try to straighten a pushrod; always replace it.
5. Apply Lubriplate® to the ends of the pushrods and install them in their original positions.
6. Apply Lubriplate® to the rocker arms and their fulcrum seats and install the rocker arms. Adjust the valves.
7. Position a new gasket(s) on the muffler inlet pipe(s) as necessary. Connect the exhaust manifold(s) at the muffler inlet pipe(s).
8. If the right cylinder head was removed, install the alternator, ignition coil and air cleaner duct on the right cylinder head. Adjust the drive belt.

If the left cylinder head was removed, install the accelerator shaft assembly at the front of the cylinder head.

9. Clean the valve rocker arm cover and the cylinder head gasket surfaces. Place the new gaskets in the covers, making sure that the tabs of the gasket engage the notches provided in the cover. Install the compressor, evaluate, charge and leak test the system. Let an air conditioning specialist do this.
10. Install the intake manifold and related parts.

460 V8

1. Remove the intake manifold and carburetor as an assembly.
2. Disconnect the exhaust pipe from the exhaust manifold.
3. Loosen the air conditioning compressor drive belt, if so equipped.
4. Loosen the alternator attaching bolts and remove the bolt attaching the alternator bracket to the right cylinder head.
5. Disconnect the air conditioning compressor from the engine and move it aside, out of the way. *Do not discharge the air conditioning system.*
6. Remove the bolts securing the power steering reservoir bracket to the left cylinder head. Position the reservoir and bracket out of the way.
7. Remove the valve rocker arm covers. Remove the rocker arm bolts, rocker arms, oil deflectors, fulcrums and pushrods in sequence so that they can be reinstalled in their original positions.
8. Remove the cylinder head bolts and lift the head and exhaust manifold off the engine. If necessary, pry at the forward corners of the cylinder head against the casting bosses provided on the cylinder block. *Do not damage the gasket mating surfaces of the cylinder head and block by prying against them.*
9. Remove all gasket material from the cylinder head and block. Clean all gasket material from the mating surfaces of the intake manifold. If the exhaust manifold was removed, clean the mating surfaces of the cylinder head and exhaust manifold. Apply a thin coat of graphite grease to the cylinder head exhaust port areas and install the exhaust manifold.
10. Position two long cylinder head bolts in the two rear lower bolt holes of the left cylinder head. Place a long cylinder head bolt in the rear lower bolt hole of the right cylinder head. Use rubber bands to keep the bolts in position until the cylinder heads are installed on the cylinder block.
11. Position new cylinder head gaskets on the cylinder block dowels. *Do not apply sealer to the gaskets, heads, or block.*
12. Place the cylinder heads on the block, guiding the exhaust manifold studs into the exhaust pipe connections. Install the remaining cylinder head bolts. The longer bolts go in the lower row of holes.
13. Tighten all the cylinder head attaching bolts in the proper sequence in three stages: 75 ft. lbs., 105 ft. lbs., and finally, to 135 ft. lbs. When this procedure is used, it is not necessary to retorque the heads after extended use.
14. Make sure that the oil holes in the pushrods are open and install the pushrods in their original positions. Place a dab of Lubriplate® to the ends of the pushrods before installing them.
15. Lubricate and install the valve rockers. Make sure that the pushrods remain seated in their lifters.
16. Connect the exhaust pipes to the exhaust manifolds.
17. Install the intake manifold and carburetor assembly. Tighten the intake manifold attaching bolts in the proper sequence to 25–30 ft. lbs.
18. Install the air conditioning compressor to the engine.
19. Install the power steering reservoir to the engine.
20. Apply oil-resistant sealer to one side of the new valve cover gaskets and lay the cemented side in place in the valve covers. Install the covers.
21. Install the alternator to the right cylinder head and adjust the alternator drive belt tension.
22. Adjust the air conditioning compressor drive belt tension.
23. Fill the radiator with coolant.
24. Start the engine and check for leaks.

6.9L V8 Diesel

1. Open the hood and disconnect the negative cables from both batteries.
2. Drain the cooling system and remove the radiator fan shroud halves.

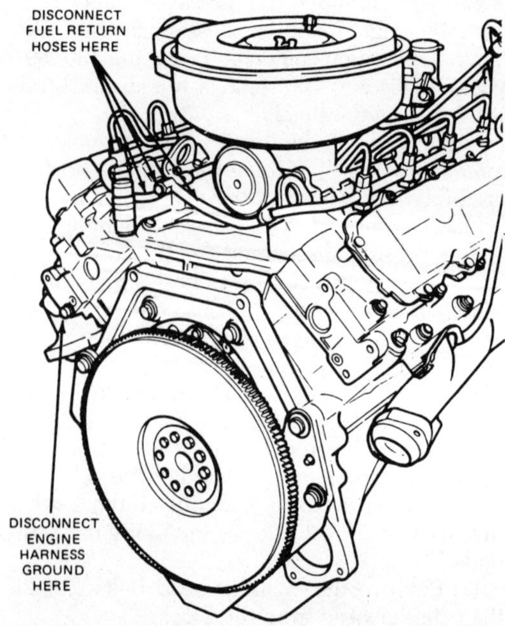

6.9L V8 Diesel fuel hose and engine ground harness connections

3. Remove the radiator fan and clutch assembly using special tool T83T-6312-A and B. This tool is available through the Owatonna Tool Co. whose address is listed in the front of this book, or through Ford Dealers. It is also available through many tool rental shops.

NOTE: *The fan clutch uses a left-hand thread and must be removed by turning the nut clockwise.*

4. Label and disconnect the wiring from the alternator.

5. Remove the adjusting bolts and pivot bolts from the alternator and the vacuum pump and remove both units.

6. Remove the fuel filter lines and cap to prevent fuel leakage.

7. Remove the alternator, vacuum pump, and fuel filter brackets with the fuel filter attached.

8. Remove the heater hose from the cylinder head.

9. Remove the fuel injection pump as described in Chapter 4 under Diesel Fuel Systems.

10. Remove the intake manifold and valley cover.

11. Jack up the truck and safely support it with jackstands.

12. Disconnect the exhaust pipes from the exhaust manifolds.

13. Remove the clamp holding the engine oil dipstick tube in place and the bolt attaching the transmission oil dipstick to the cylinder head.

14. Lower the truck.

15. Remove the engine oil dipstick tube.

16. Remove the valve covers, rocker arms and pushrods. Keep the pushrods in order so they can be returned to their original positions.

17. Remove the nozzles and glow plugs as described in Chapter 4 under Diesel Fuel Systems.

18. Remove the cylinder head bolts and attach lifting eyes, using special tool T70P-6000 or equivalent, to each end of the cylinder heads.

19. Carefully lift the cylinder heads out of the engine compartment and remove the head gaskets.

NOTE: *The cylinder head prechambers may fall out of the heads upon removal.*

To install:

20. Position the cylinder head gasket on the engine block and carefully lower the cylinder head in place.

NOTE: *Use care in installing the cylinder heads to prevent the prechambers from falling out into the cylinder bores.*

21. Install the cylinder head bolt and torque in 4 steps using the sequence shown in the illustration.

NOTE: *Lubricate the threads and the mating surfaces of the bolt heads and washers with engine oil.*

22. Dip the pushrod ends in clean engine oil and install the pushrods with the copper colored ends toward the rocker arms, making sure the pushrods are fully seated in the tappet pushrod seats.

23. Install the rocker arms and posts in their original positions. Apply a Lubriplate® grease to the valve stem tips. Turn the engine over by hand until the timing mark is at the 11 o'clock position as viewed from the front. Install the

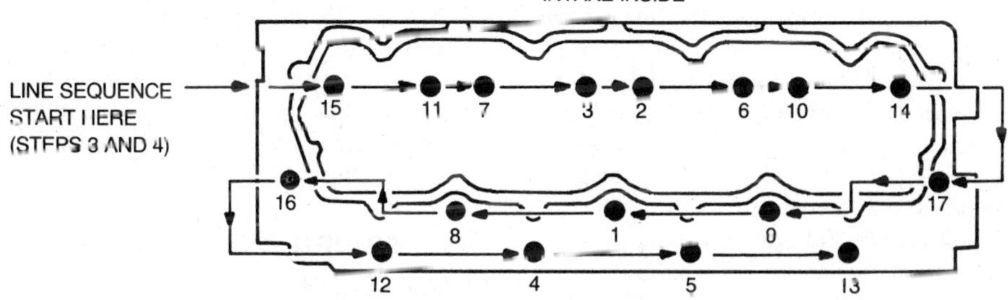

CYLINDER HEAD BOLTS

STEP 1. TORQUE BOLTS TO 40 FT. LBS. IN NUMBERED SEQUENCE SHOWN ABOVE.

STEP 2. TORQUE BOLTS TO 65 FT. LBS. IN NUMBERED SEQUENCE SHOWN ABOVE.

STEP 3. TORQUE BOLTS TO 75 FT. LBS. IN LINE SEQUENCE SHOWN ABOVE.

STEP 4. REPEAT STEP 3.

420 V8 Diesel—cylinder head bolt tightening sequence

rocker arm posts, bolts, and torque to 27 ft. lbs. Install the valve covers.

24. Install the valley pan and the intake manifold.

25. Install the fuel injection pump as described in Chapter 4 under Diesel Fuel Systems.

26. Connect the heater hose to the cylinder head.

27. Install the fuel filter, alternator, vacuum pump, and their drive belts.

28. Install the engine oil and transmission dip sticks.

29. Connect the exhaust pipe to the exhaust manifolds.

30. Reconnect the alternator wiring harness and replace the air cleaner. Connect both battery ground cables.

31. Refill and bleed the cooling system.

32. Run the engine and check for fuel, coolant and exhaust leaks.

NOTE: *If necessary, purge the high pressure fuel lines of air by loosening the connector one half to one turn and cranking the engine until a solid stream of fuel, free from any bubbles, flows from the connection.*

33. Check the injection pump timing. Refer to chapter 4 for these procedures.

34. Install the radiator fan and clutch assembly using special tools T83T-6312A and B or equivalent.

NOTE: *The fan clutch uses a left-hand thread. Tighten by turning the nut counterclockwise. Install the radiator fan shroud halves.*

CLEANING AND INSPECTION

1. With the valves installed to protect the valve seats, remove deposits from the combustion chambers and valve heads with a scraper and a wire brush. Be careful not to damage the cylinder head gasket surface. After the valves are removed, clean the valve guide bores with a valve guide cleaning tool. Using cleaning solvent to remove dirt, grease and other deposits, clean all bolts holes; be sure the oil passage is clean (V-8 engines).

2. Remove all deposits from the valves with a fine wire brush or buffing wheel.

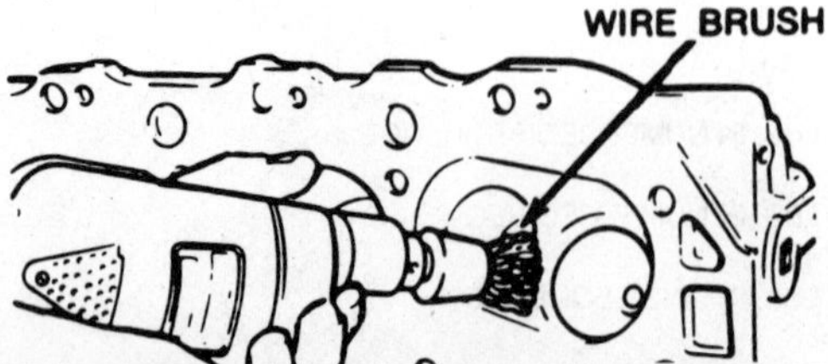

Remove combustion chamber carbon from the cylinder head with a wire brush and electric drill. Make sure all carbon is removed and not just burnished

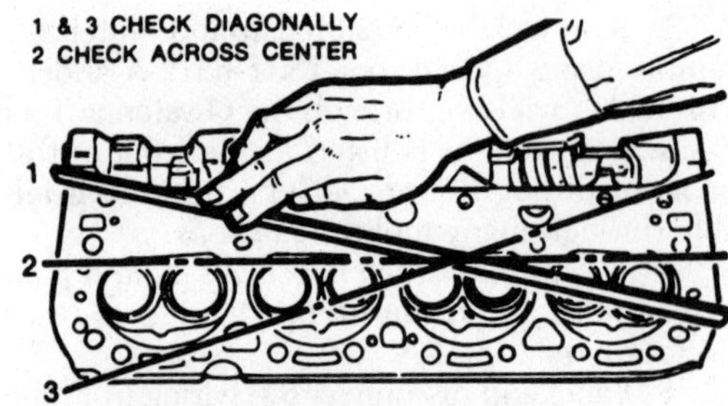

Checking the cylinder head for warpage

3. Inspect the cylinder heads for cracks or excessively burned areas in the exhaust outlet ports.

4. Check the cylinder head for cracks and inspect the gasket surface for burrs and nicks. Replace the head if it is cracked.

5. On cylinder heads that incorporate valve seat inserts, check the inserts for excessive wear, cracks or looseness.

RESURFACING

Cylinder Head Flatness

When a cylinder head is removed, check the flatness of the cylinder head gasket surface.

1. Place a straight-edge across the gasket surface of the cylinder head. Using feeler gauges, determine the clearance at the center of the straight-edge.

2. If warpage exceeds .003″ in a 6″ span, or .006″ over the total length, the cylinder head must be resurfaced.

3. If necessary to refinish the cylinder head gasket surface, do not plane or grind off more than .254 mm (0.010 inch) from the original gasket surface.

NOTE: *When milling the cylinder heads of V-8 engines, the intake manifold mounting position is altered, and must be corrected by milling the manifold flange a proportionate amount. Consult an experienced machinist about this.*

Valves and Springs

VALVE LASH

Valve adjustment determines how far the valves enter the cylinder and how long they stay open and closed.

If the valve clearance is too large, part of the lift of the camshaft will be used in removing the excessive clearance. Consequently, the valve will not be opening as far as it should. This condition has two effects: the valve train components will emit a tapping sound as they take up the excessive clearance and the engine will perform poorly because the valves don't open fully and allow the proper amount of gases to flow into and out of the engine.

If the valve clearance is too small, the intake valve and the exhaust valves will open too far and they will not fully seat on the cylinder head when they close. When a valve seats itself on the cylinder head, it does two things: it seals the combustion chamber so that none of the gases in the cylinder escape and it cools itself by transferring some of the heat it absorbs from the combustion in the cylinder to the cylinder head and to the engine's cooling system. If the valve clearance is too small, the engine will run poorly because of the gases escaping from the combustion chamber. The valves will also become overheated and will warp, since they cannot transfer heat unless they are touching the valve seat in the cylinder head.

NOTE: *While all valve adjustments must be made as accurately as possible, it is better to have the valve adjustment slightly loose than slightly tight as a burned valve may result from overly tight adjustments.*

ENGINES WITH HYDRAULIC LIFTERS

All of the engines covered in this guide are equipped with hydraulic valve lifters, which due to their design, constantly take up the lash in the valve train. Because of this, these engines require no periodic adjustment to their valves. However, in the event of cylinder head removal or any operation which requires disturbing the rocker arms, the rocker arms will have to be adjusted.

240 and 300 cu. in. Inline Six

1. Crank the engine until the TDC mark on the crankshaft damper is aligned with timing pointer on the cylinder front cover.
2. Scribe a mark on the damper at this point.
3. Scribe two more marks on the damper, each equally spaced from the first mark (see illustration).
4. Scribe two more marks on the damper, each equally spaced from the first mark (see illustration).
4. With the engine on TDC of the compression stroke, (mark A aligned with the pointer) back off the rocker arm adjusting nut until there is end-play in the pushrod. Tighten the adjusting nut until all clearance is removed, then tighten the adjusting nut one additional turn. To determine when all clearance is removed from the rocker arm, turn the pushrod with the fingers. When the pushrod can no longer be turned, all clearance has been removed.
5. Repeat this procedure for each valve, turning the crankshaft ⅓ turn to the next mark each time and following the engine firing order of 1-5-3-6-2-4.

302 Cu In. V8

Some early models of the 302 cu in. V8 are equipped with adjustable rockers whereas the later models are equipped with positive stop type rocker mounting studs. Positive stop equipped rockers are adjusted by turning the adjusting nut down until it stops. You can identify a positive stop mounting stud by determining whether or not the shank portion of the stud that is exposed just above the cylinder head is the same diameter as the threaded portion at the top of the stud, to which the rocker arm retaining nut attaches. If the shank portion is larger than the threaded area, it is a positive

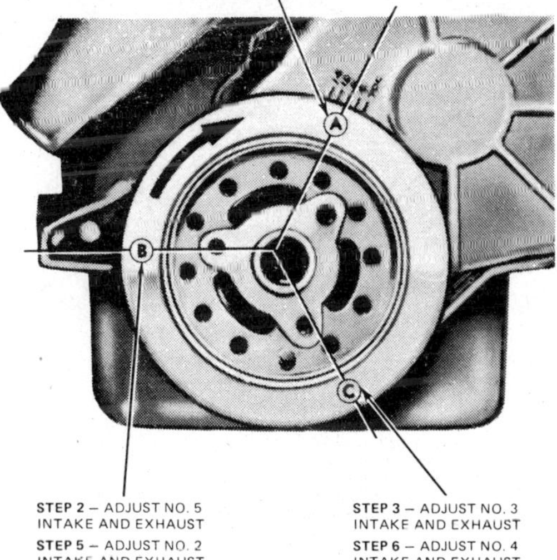

240 and 300 inline six crankshaft positioning for valve clearance adjustment

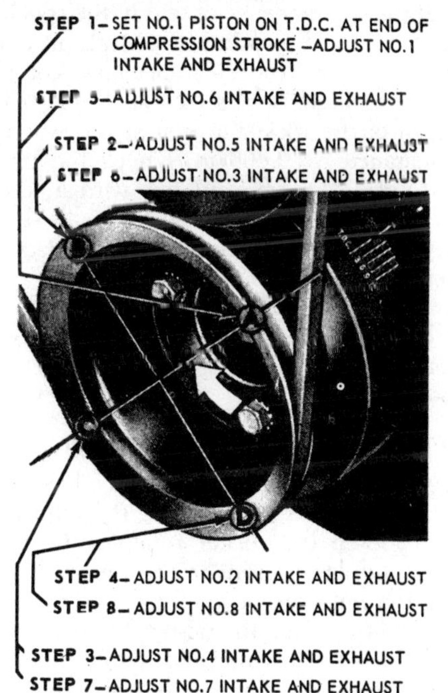

Position of crankshaft for valve adjustment—1969 302 V8 without positive stop rocker arm stud

stop mounting stud. Use the procedure given below for adjusting the valve lash on positive stop type mounting stud equipped vehicles.

There are two different procedures for adjusting the valves on the V8 engines. One is a preferred procedure and one is an alternate procedure. The preferred procedure is recommended, but the alternate procedure may be used.

NOTE: *These procedures are not tune-up procedures, but rebuild procedures to be performed only after valve train reassembly.*

PREFERRED PROCEDURE THROUGH 1969

1. Position the piston(s) on TDC of the compression stroke, using the timing mark on the crankshaft pulley as a reference for starting with the No. 1 cylinder. You can tell if a piston is coming up on its compression stroke by removing the spark plug of the cylinder you are working on and placing your thumb over the hole while the engine is cranked over. Air will try to force its way past your thumb when the piston comes upon the compression stroke. Make sure that the high tension coil wire leading to the distributor is removed before cranking the engine. Remove the valve covers.
2. Starting with No. 1 cylinder, and the piston in the position as mentioned above, apply pressure to slowly bleed down the valve lifter until the plunger is completely bottomed.
3. While holding the valve lifter in the fully collapsed position, check the available clearance between the rocker arm and the valve stem tip. Use a feeler gauge.
4. If the clearance is not within the specified amount, rotate the rocker arm stud nut clockwise to decrease the clearance and counterclockwise to increase the clearance. Normally, one turn of the rocker arm stud nut will vary the clearance by 0.066 in. Check the breakaway torque of each stud nut with a torque wrench, turning it counterclockwise. It should be anywhere from 4.5 to 15 ft. lbs. Replace the nut and/or the stud as necessary.
5. When both valves for the No. 1 cylinder have been adjusted, proceed on to the other valves, following the firing order sequence 1-5-4-2-6-3-7-8.

ALTERNATE PROCEDURE THROUGH 1969

Follow Step 1 of the preferred procedure given above, but instead of collapsing the lifter as in Step 2, loosen the rocker retaining nut until there is endplay present in the pushrod; then tighten the nut to remove all pushrod-to-rocker arm clearance. When the pushrod-to-rocker arm clearance has been eliminated, tighten the stud nut an additional ¾ turn to place the lifter plunger in the desired operating range.

Repeat this procedure for all of the cylinders, using the firing order sequence as a guide. It takes ¼ turn of the crankshaft to bring the next piston in the firing order sequence up to TDC at the end of its compression stroke. Collapsed Tappet Gap Clearance:

Allowable: .071–.193
Desired: .096–.165

POSITIVE STOP TYPE MOUNTING STUD FROM 1970

351, 400, 460 and Later 302 V8

1. Crank the engine until the No. 1 cylinder is at TDC of the compression stroke and the timing pointer is aligned with the mark on the crankshaft damper.
2. Scribe a mark on the damper at this point.
3. Scribe two additional marks on the damper (see illustration).
4. With the timing pointer aligned with the mark on the damper, tighten the following valves to the specified torque:
   - *302 and 460:* No. 1, 7 and 8 Intake; No. 1, 5 and 4 Exhaust
   - *351 and 400:* No. 1, 4 and 8 Intake; No. 1, 3 and 7 Exhaust
5. Rotate the crankshaft 180° to position 2 and tighten the following valves:
   - *302 and 460:* No. 5 and 4 Intake; No. 2 and 6 Exhaust
   - *351 and 400:* No. 3 and 7 Intake; No. 2 and 6 Exhaust
6. Rotate the crankshaft 270° to position 3 and tighten the following valves:

With No. 1 at TDC at end of compression stroke make a chalk mark at points 2 and 3 approximately 90 degrees apart.

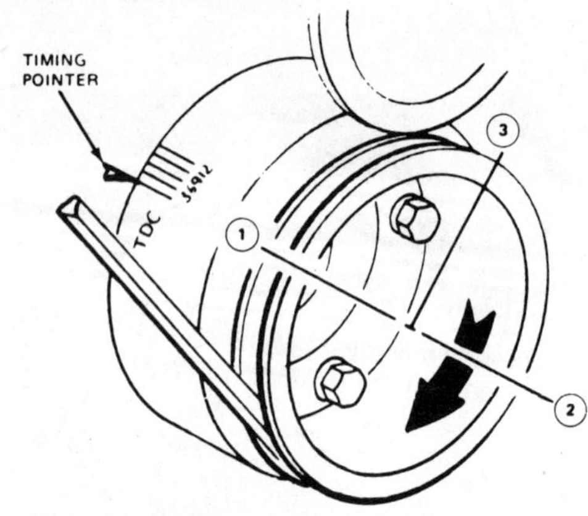

POSITION 1 – No. 1 at TDC at end of compression stroke.
POSITION 2 – Rotate the crankshaft 180 degrees (one half revolution) clockwise from POSITION 1.
POSITION 3 – Rotate the crankshaft 270 degrees (three quarter revolution clockwise from POSITION 2.

Crankshaft positions for positive stop-type valve adjustment, 1970 and later 302

- *302 and 460:* No. 2, 3 and 6 Intake; No. 7, 3 and 8 Exhaust
- *351 and 400:* No. 2, 5 and 6 Intake; No. 4, 5 and 8 Exhaust

7. Rocker arm tightening specifications are: 302 and 351 W—tighten nut until it contacts the rocker shoulder, then torque to 18–20 ft. lbs.; 400—tighten bolt to 18–25 ft. lbs.; 460—tighten nut until it contacts rocker shoulder, then torque to 18–22 ft. lbs.

Valve Spring, Retainer and Valve Seal

REMOVAL AND INSTALLATION

Broken valve springs or damaged valve stem seals and retainers may be replaced without removing the cylinder head, provided damage to the valve or valve seat has not occurred.

NOTE: *The following procedure requires the use of special tools: air compressor, air line adapter tool to fit the spark plug hole, and a valve spring compressor tool designed to be used with the cylinder head on the engine. If the head has been removed from the engine the procedure will only require the use of a valve spring compressor tool designed to be used with the head off.*

1. Remove the valve rocker arm cover.
2. Remove the applicable spark plug or glow plugs on diesels and bring the piston to top of the bore to prevent accidental loss of the valve into the cylinder.
3. Remove the valve rocker arm fulcrum bolts, fulcrum seats, rocker arms and push rods from the applicable cylinder.
4. Install an air line with an adapter in the spark plug hole and apply air pressure to hold the valve(s) in the closed position. Failure to hold the valve(s) closed is an indication of valve seat damage and requires removal of the cylinder head.

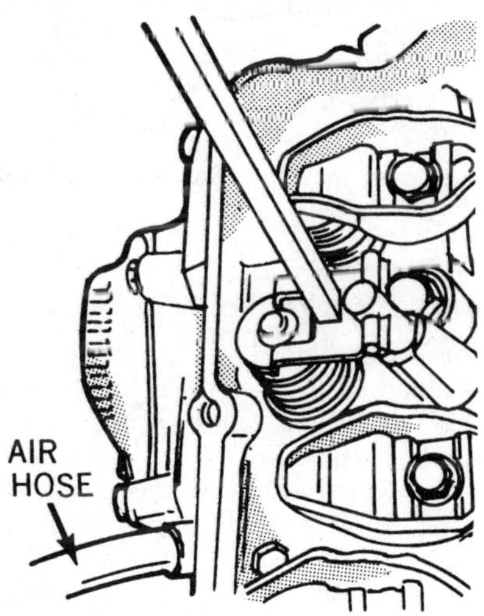

Compressing gasoline engine valve spring. Note spring compressor position and air hose. Cylinder at TDC

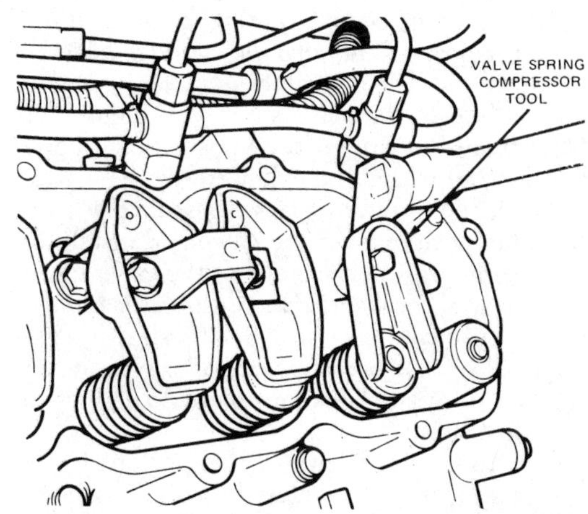

Compressing valve spring on the 6.9L diesel using special tool

5. Install the fulcrum bolt or the stud nut and position the compressor tool. Compress the valve spring and remove the retainer locks, spring retainer and valve spring.
6. Remove and discard the valve stem seal.
7. If air pressure has forced the piston to the bottom of the cylinder, any removal of air pressure will allow the valve(s) to fall into the cylinder. A rubber band wrapped around the end of the valve stem will prevent this condition and will still allow enough travel to check the valve for binds.
8. Inspect the valve stem for damage. Rotate the valve and check the valve stem tip for eccentric movement during rotation. Move the valve up and down through normal travel in the valve guide and check the stem for binds.

Removing or installing valve stem oil seals using air line

NOTE: *If the valve has been damaged, it will be necessary to remove the cylinder head.*

9. If the valve condition proves satisfactory, lubricate the valve stem with engine oil. Hold the valve in the closed position and apply air pressure within the cylinder.

10. Install a new valve stem seal. Place the spring in position over the valve and install the valve spring retainer. Compress the valve spring and install the valve spring compressor tool.

11. Lubricate the push rod ends with Lubriplate® or equivalent and install the push rod. Apply Lubriplate® or equivalent to the tip of the valve stem.

12. Apply Lubriplate® or equivalent to the rocker arm, fulcrum seat and stud nut or bolt.

13. Turn off the air and remove the air line and adapter. Install the spark plug and connect the spark plug wire.

14. Clean and install the rocker arm cover.

INSPECTION

VALVES

Minor pits, grooves, ect., may be removed. Discard valves that are severely damaged, or if the face runout cannot be corrected by refinishing or if the stem clearance exceeds specifications. Discard any worn or damaged valve train parts.

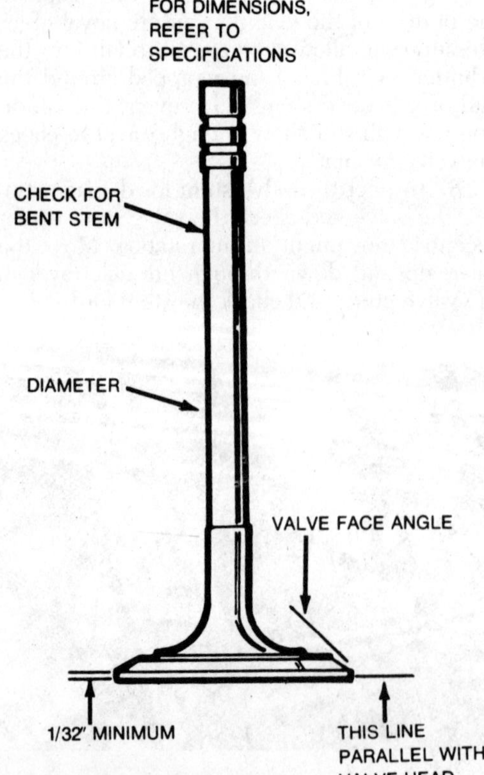

Critical valve dimensions

REFACING VALVES

NOTE: *The valve seat refacing operation should be coordinated with the valve refacing operations so that the finished angles of the valve seat and valve face will be to specifications and provide a compression-tight fit. Valve refacing and all related machine work should be handled by a qualified machinist.*

If the valve face runout is excessive and/or to remove pits and grooves, reface the valves to a true 44 degree angle. Remove only enough stock to correct the runout or to clean up the grooves and pits.

If the edge of the head is less than 0.794mm (1/32 inch) thick after grinding, replace the valve because the valve will run too hot for the engine. The interference fit of the valve and seat should not be lapped out.

Remove all grooves or score marks from the end of the valve stem, and chamfer it as necessary. Do not remove more than 0.254mm (0.010 inch) from the end of the valve stem.

If the valve and/or valve seat has been refaced, it will be necessary to check the clearance between the rocker arm pad and the valve stem tip with the valve train assembly installed in the engine.

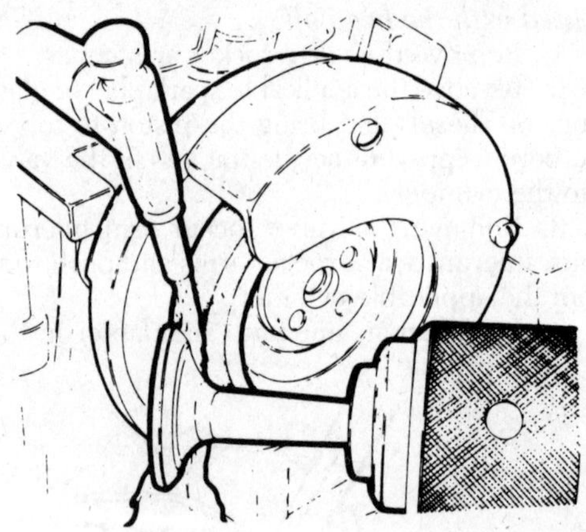

A well-equipped machine shop can handle valve refacing jobs

CHECKING VALVE SPRINGS

Check the valve spring for proper pressure at the specified spring lengths using valve spring pressure tool. Weak valve springs cause poor performance; therefore, if the pressure of any spring is lower than the service limit, replace the spring. Springs should be ±5 lbs of all other springs.

Check each valve spring for squareness. Stand the spring on a flat surface next to a square. Measure the height of the spring, and rotate the spring slowly and observe the space be-

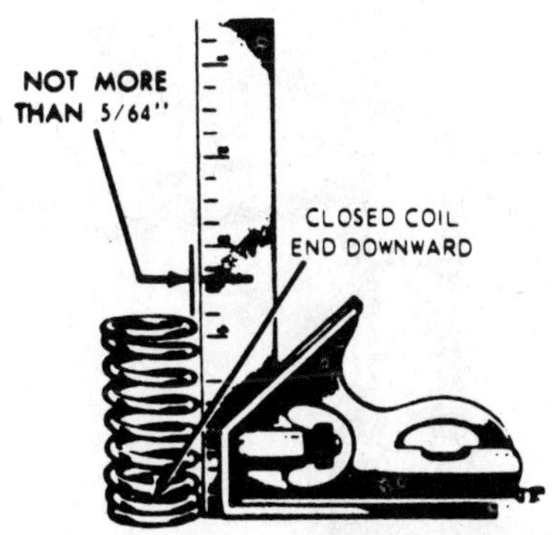

Check the valve spring free length and squareness

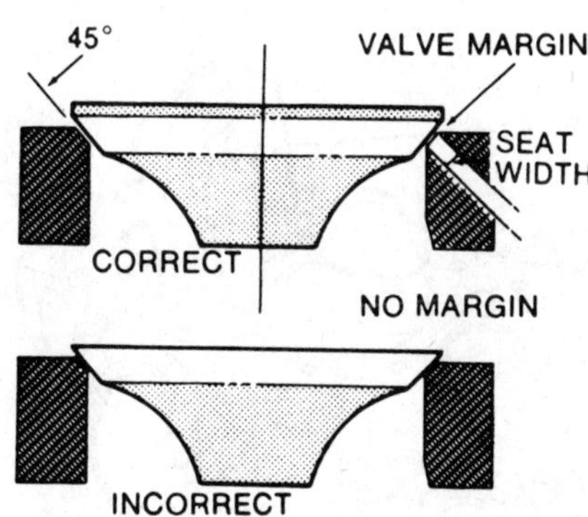

Valve seat width and centering after proper reaming

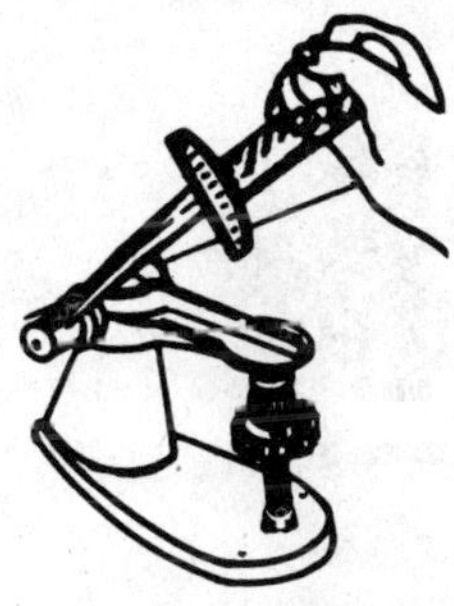

Have the valve spring test pressure checked at a machine shop. Make sure the readings are within specifications

tween the top coil of the spring and the square. If the spring is out of square more than 5⁄64 inch or the height varies (by comparison) by more than 1⁄16 inch, replace the spring.

CUTTING THE SEATS

NOTE: *The valve refacing operation should be coordinated with the refacing of the valve seats so that the finished angles of the valve seat and valve face will be to specifications and provide a compression tight fit.*

Grind the valve seats of all engines to a true 45 degree angle. Remove only enough stock to clean up pits and grooves or to correct the valve seat runout.

The finished valve seat should contact the approximate center of the valve face. It is good

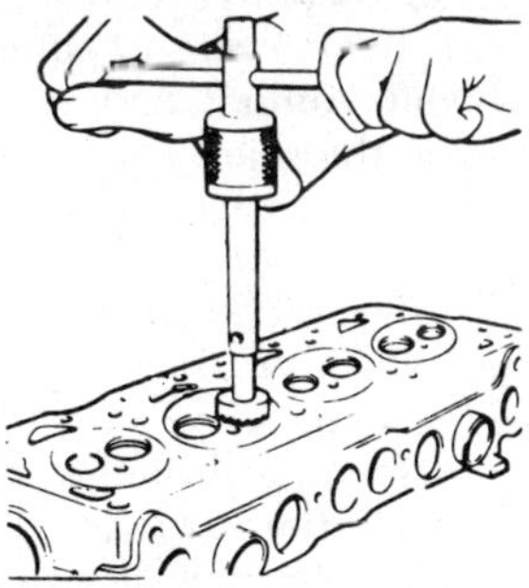

Reaming valve seat with a hand reamer

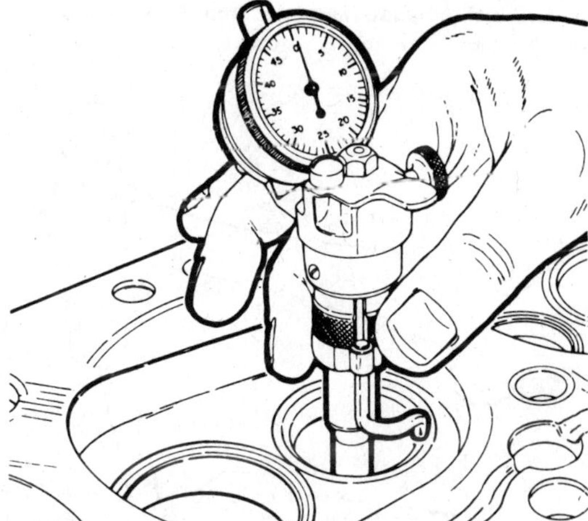

Checking valve seat concentricity with a dial gauge

practice to determine where the valve seat contacts the valve face, (seat concentricity). To do this, coat the seat with Prussian blue and set the valve in place. Rotate the valve with light pressure. If the blue is transferred to the top edge of the valve face, lower the valve seat. If the blue is transferred to the bottom edge of the valve face, raise the valve seat.

You can also check for seat concentricity using a dial gauge. Install the dial gauge pilot into the valve guide, and the rest of the arm on the valve seat. Zero the gauge, and rotate the arm around the seat. Run-out should not exceed .002 in.

Valve Seats

REMOVAL AND INSTALLATION

420 (6.9L) V8 Diesel

NOTE: *The 6.9L diesel is the only engine covered in this guide which has removable valve seats.*

1. Using Ford Rotunda tool 14-0309 the exhaust valve seats may be removed. Position the remover collet into the insert and rotate the

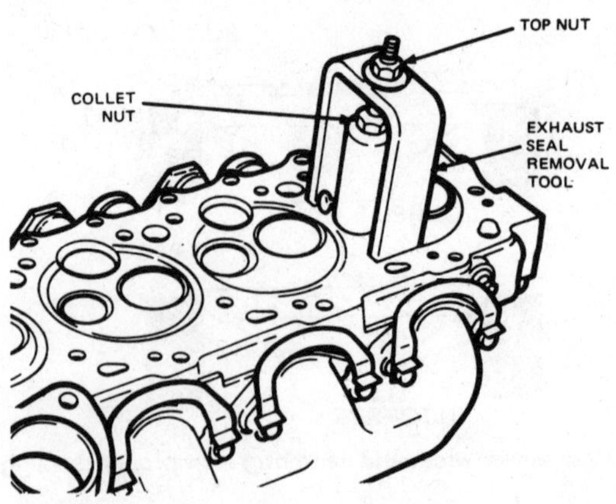

6.9L diesel exhaust valve seat insert removal using special tool

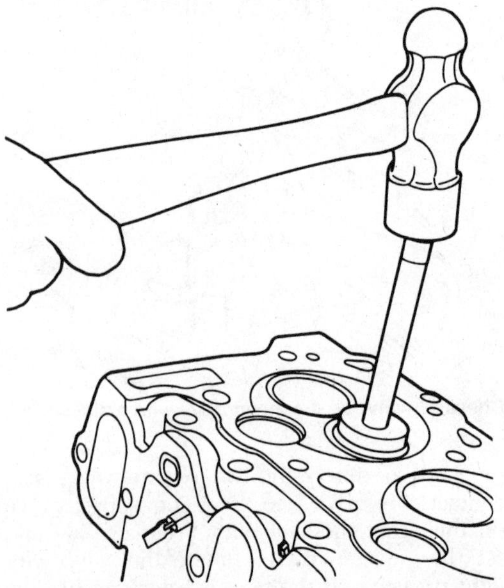

Installing diesel exhaust valve seats using special tool

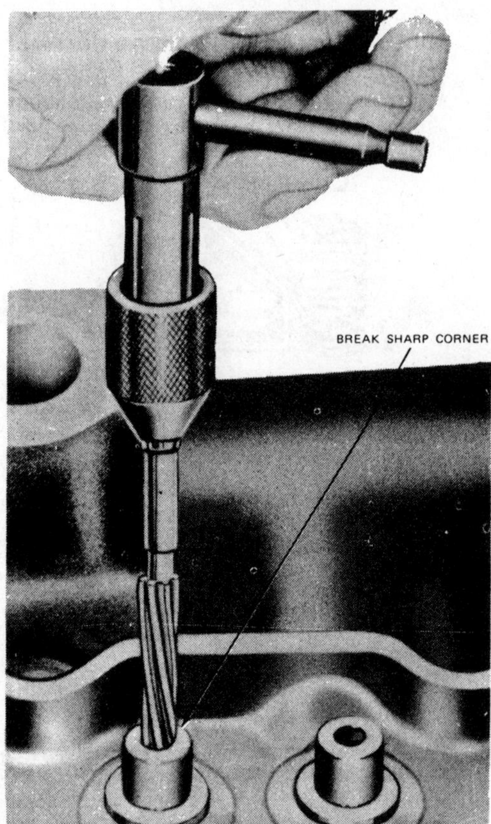

Reaming valve guides

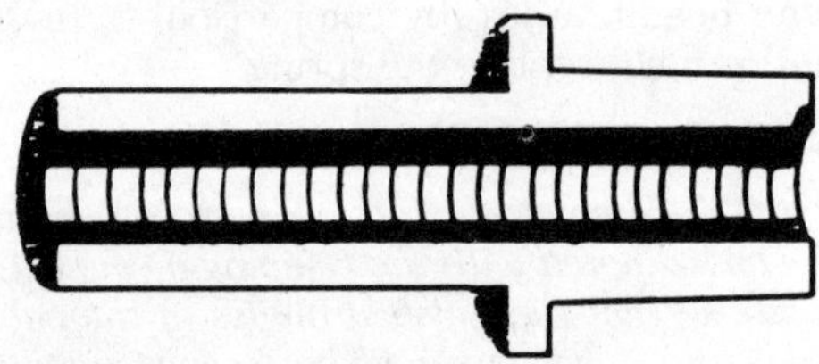

Cross-section of a knurled valve guide

collet nut clockwise to expand the collet jaws under the lip of the seat insert.

2. Rotate the top nut clockwise to remove the insert.

NOTE: *If an oversize seat insert is required, the cylinder head should be sent out to a qualified machine shop.*

3. To install a new exhaust valve seat, drive the seat in place using Rotunda tool 14-0309 and a hammer.

Valve seat inserts are supplied for service in standard size, .015 in. oversize and .030 in. oversize.

Valve Guides

REAMING VALVE GUIDES

If it becomes necessary to ream a valve guide to install a valve with an oversize stem, a reaming kit is available which contains an oversize reamers and pilot tools.

When replacing a standard size valve with an oversize valve always use the reamer in sequence (smallest oversize first, then next smallest, etc.) so as not to overload the reamers. Always re-face the valve seat after the valve guide has been reamed, and use a suitable scraper to break the sharp corner at the top of the valve guide.

KNURLING

Valve guides which are not excessively worn or distorted may, in some cases, be knurled rather than reamed. Knurling is a process in which metal inside the valve guide bore is displaced and raised (forming a very fine cross-hatch pattern), thereby reducing clearance.

Knurling also provides for excellent oil control. The possibility of knurling rather than reaming the guides should be discussed with a machinist.

STEM-TO-GUIDE CLEARANCE

Valve stem-to-guide clearance should be checked upon assembling the cylinder head, and is especially necessary if the valve guides have been reamed or knurled, or if oversize valves have been installed. Excessive oil consumption often is a result of too much clearance between the valve guide and valve stem.

Clean the valve stem with laquer thinner or a similar solvent to remove all gum and varnish. Clean the valve guides using solvent and an expanding wire-type valve guide cleaner (a rifle cleaning brush works well here).

2. Mount a dial indicator so that the stem is at 90° to the valve stem and as close to the valve guide as possible.

3. Move the valve off its seat, and measure the valve guide-to stem clearance by rocking the stem back and forth to actuate the dial indicator. Measure the valve stems using a micrometer and compare to specifications, to determine whether stem or guide wear is responsible for excessive clearance.

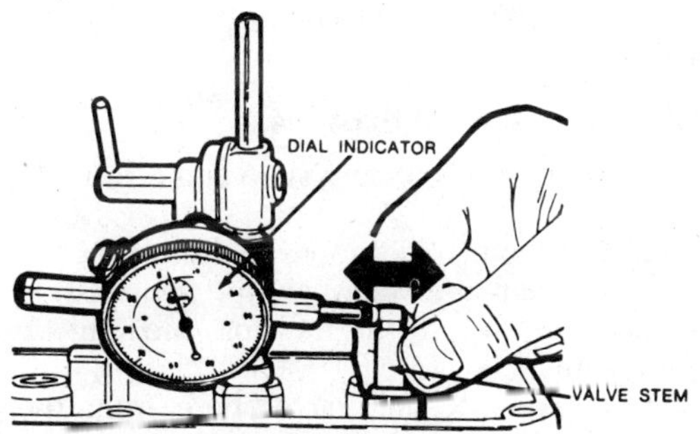

Measuring valve stem-to-guide clearance. Make sure the indicator is mounted at 90° to the valve stem and as close to the guide as possible

VALVE LAPPING

The valves must be lapped into their seats after resurfacing, to ensure proper sealing. Even if the valves have not been refaced, they should be lapped into the head before reassembly.

Set the cylinder head on the workbench, combustion chamber side up. Rest the head on wooden blocks on either end, so there are two or three inches between the tops of the valve guides and the bench.

1. Lightly lube the valve stem with clean engine oil. Coat the valve seat completely with valve grinding compound. Use just enough compound so that the full width and circumference of the seat are covered.

Lapping the valves by hand. When done, the finish on both valve faces and seats should be smooth and evenly shiny

2. Install the valve in its proper location in the head. Attach the suction cup end of the valve lapping tool to the valve head. It usually helps to put a small amount of saliva into the suction cup to aid it sticking to the valve.

3. Rotate the tool between the palms, changing position and lifting the tool often to prevent grooving. Lap the valve in until a smooth, evenly-polished seat and valve face are evident.

4. Remove the valve from the head. Wipe away all traces of grinding compound from the valve face and seat. Wipe out the port with a solvent-soaked rag, and swab out the valve guide with a piece of solvent-soaked rag to make sure there are no traces of compound grit inside the guide. *This cleaning is very important, as the engine will ingest any grit remaining when started.*

5. Proceed through the remaining valves, one at a time. Make sure the valve faces, seats, cylinder ports and valve guides are clean before reassembling the valve train.

Timing Gear or Chain Front Cover and Oil Seal

REMOVAL AND INSTALLATION

240 and 300 Inline Sixes

1. Drain the cooling system and disconnect the radiator upper hose at the coolant outlet elbow and remove the two upper radiator retaining bolts.

2. Raise the vehicle and drain the crankcase.

3. Remove the splash shield and the automatic transmission oil cooling lines, if so equipped, then remove the radiator.

4. Loosen and remove the fan belt, fan and pulley.

Use a puller (which can be rented) to remove the crankshaft vibration damper on all engines

5. Use a gear puller to remove the crankshaft pulley damper.

6. Remove the cylinder front cover retaining bolts and gently pry the cover away from the block. Remove the gasket.

7. Drive out the old seal with a pin punch from the rear of the cover. Clean out the recess in the cover.

8. Coat the new seal with grease and drive it into the cover until it is fully seated. Check the seal to make sure that the spring around the seal is in the proper position.

9. Clean the cylinder front cover and the gasket surface of the cylinder block. Apply an oil-resistant sealer to the new front cover gasket and install the gasket onto the cover.

10. Position the front cover assembly over the end of the crankshaft and against the cylinder block. Start, but do not tighten, the cover and pan attaching screws. Slide a front cover alignment tool (Ford part no. T68P-6019-A or equivalent) over the crank stub and into the seal bore of the cover. Tighten all front cover and oil pan attaching screws to 12–18 ft. lbs.—front cover; 10–15 ft. lbs.—oil pan, *tightening the oil pan screws first.*

NOTE: *Trim away the exposed portion of the old oil pan gasket flush with the front of the engine block. Cut and position the required portion of a new gasket to the oil pan and apply sealer to both sides.*

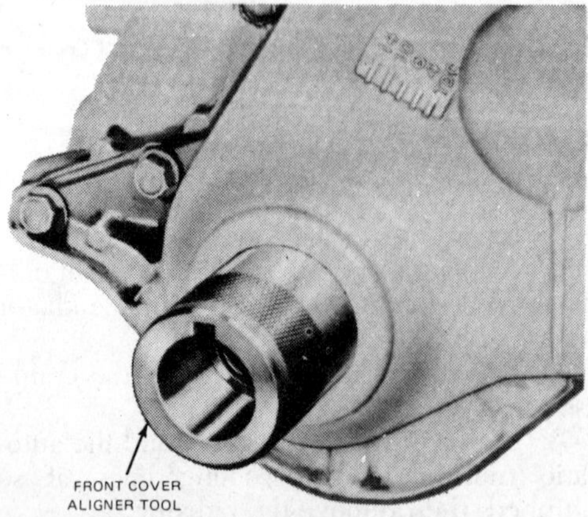

Aligning the front timing cover on the inline six cylinder crankshaft

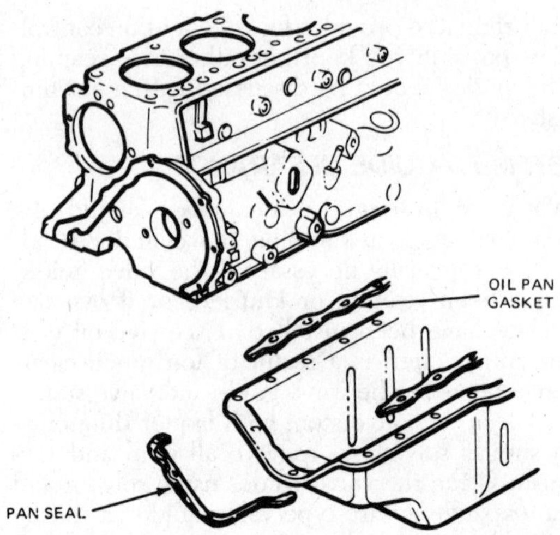

Front pan/cover seal, inline six cylinder engines

11. Lubricate the hub of the crankshaft damper pulley with Lubriplate® to prevent damage to the seal during installation or on initial starting of the engine.

12. Install and assemble the remaining components in the reverse order of removal, starting from Step 4. Start the engine and check for leaks.

V6 and Gasoline V8 Except 460

1. Drain the cooling system and the crankcase.

2. Disconnect the upper and lower radiator hoses from the water pump, transmission oil cooler lines from the radiator, and remove the radiator.

3. Disconnect the heater hose from the

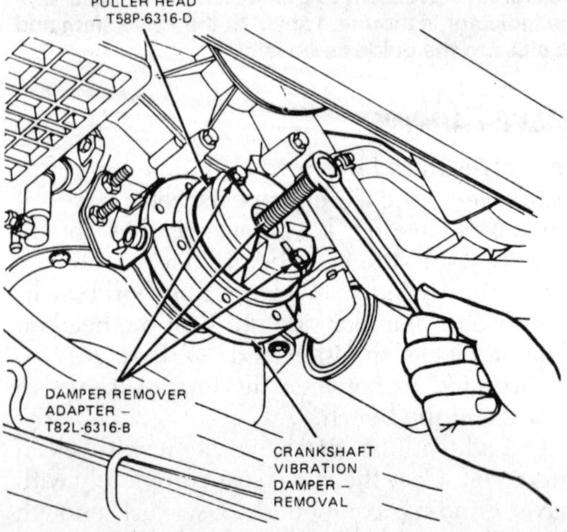

Access to the damper is often better from underneath. 232 V6 shown

water pump. Slide the water pump by-pass hose clamp toward the water pump.

4. Loosen the alternator pivot bolt and the bolt which secures the alternator adjusting arm to the water pump. Position the alternator out of the way.

5. Remove the power steering pump and air conditioning compressor from their mounting brackets, if so equipped.

6. Remove the bolts holding the fan shroud to the radiator, if so equipped. Remove the fan, spacer, pulley and drive belts.

7. Remove the crankshaft pulley from the crankshaft damper. Remove the damper attaching bolt and washer and remove the damper with a puller. On the 352, 360, 361, 390, 391 V8, remove the crankshaft sleeve with a puller.

8. Disconnect the fuel pump outlet line at the fuel pump. Disconnect the vacuum inlet and outlet lines from the fuel pump. Remove the fuel pump attaching bolts and lay the pump to one side with the fuel inlet line still attached.

9. Remove the oil level dipstick and the bolt holding the dipstick tube to the exhaust manifold on the 302 V8.

10. Remove the oil pan-to-cylinder front cover attaching bolts. Use a sharp, thin cutting blade to cut the oil pan gasket flush with the cylinder block. Remove the front cover and water pump as an assembly.

11. Discard the front cover gasket.

12. Place the front seal removing tool (Ford part no. T70P-6B070-A or equivalent) onto the front cover plate and over the front of the seal as shown in the illustration. Tighten the two through bolts to force the seal puller under the seal flange, then alternately tighten the four puller bolts *a half turn at a time* to pull the oil seal from the cover.

13. Coat a new front cover oil seal with Lubriplate® or equivalent and place it onto the front oil seal alignment and installation tool (Ford part no. T70P-6B070-A or equivalent) as shown in the illustration. Place the tool and the seal onto the end of the crankshaft and push it to-

302, 351W, 351M and 400 V8 front crankshaft seal installation

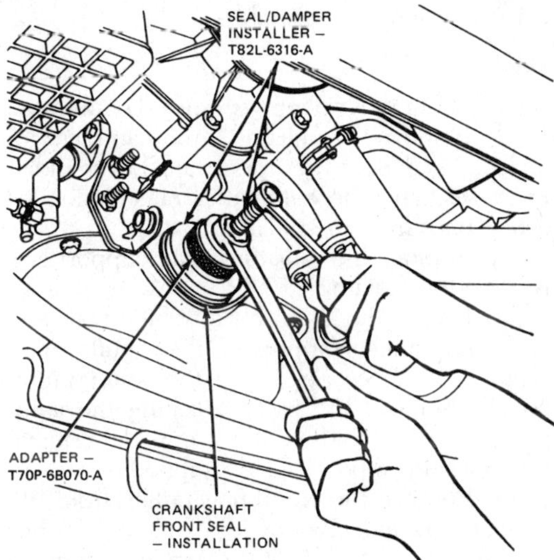

V6 front oil seal installation, shown from underneath truck

Vibration damper installation, 351M and 400 V8s

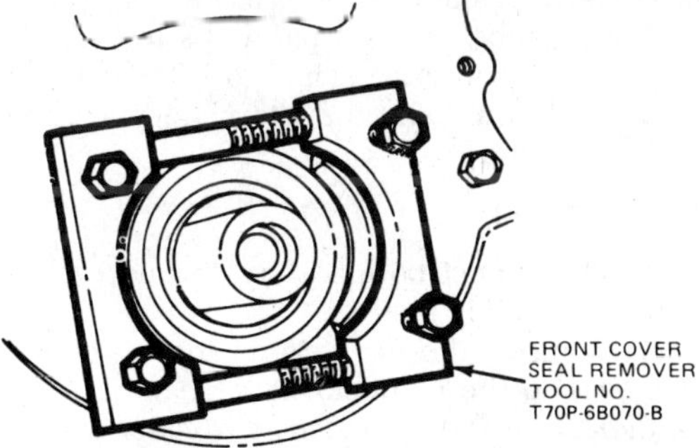

Removing the front crankshaft seal on 302 and 351W V8s

ward the engine until the seal starts into the front cover.

14. Place the installation screw, washer and nut onto the end of the crankshaft, then thread the screw into the crankshaft. Tighten the nut against the washer and tool to force the seal into the front cover plate. Remove the tool.

15. Apply Lubriplate® or equivalent to the oil seal rubbing surface of the vibration damper inner hub to prevent damage to the seal. Coat the front of the crankshaft with engine oil for damper installation.

16. To install the damper, line up the damper keyway with the key on the crankshaft, then install the damper onto the crankshaft. Install the cap screw and washer, and tighten the screw to 80 ft. lbs. Install the crankshaft pulley.

17. Assemble the rest of the engine in the reverse order of disassembly.

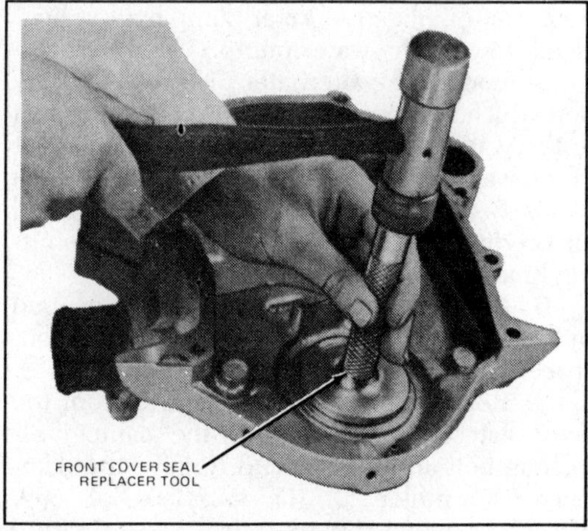

Installing oil seal into 460 V8 front cover. Tool makes it easier to drive in seal evenly

460 V8

1. Drain the cooling system and crankcase.
2. Remove the radiator shroud and fan.
3. Disconnect the upper and lower radiator hoses, and the automatic transmission oil cooler lines from the radiator.
4. Remove the radiator upper support and remove the radiator.
5. Loosen the alternator attaching bolts and air conditioning compresser idler pulley and remove the drive belts with the water pump pulley. Remove the bolts attaching the compressor support to the water pump and remove the bracket (support), if so equipped.
6. Remove the crankshaft pulley from the vibration damper. Remove the bolt and washer attaching the crankshaft damper and remove the damper with a puller. Remove the woodruff key from the cranksahft.
7. Loosen the by-pass hose at the water pump, and disconnect the heater return tube at the water pump.
8. Disconnect and plug the fuel inlet and outlet lines at the fuel pump, and remove the fuel pump.
9. Remove the bolts attaching the front cover to the cylinder block. Cut the oil pan seal flush with the cylinder block face with a thin knife blade prior to separating the cover from the cylinder block. Remove the cover and water pump as an assembly. Discard the front cover gasket and oil pan seal.
10. Transfer the water pump if a new cover is going to be installed. Clean all of the gasket sealing surfaces on both the front cover and the cylinder block.
11. Coat the gasket surface of the oil pan with sealer. Cut and position the required sections of a new seal on the oil pan. Apply sealer to the corners.
12. Drive out the old front cover oil seal with a pin punch. Clean out the seal recess in the cover. Coat a new seal with Lubriplate® or equivalent grease. Install the seal, making sure the seal spring remains in the proper position. A front cover seal tool, Ford part no. T72J-1177 or equivalent, makes installation easier.
12. Coat the gasket surfaces of the cylinder block and cover with sealer and position the new gasket on the block.
13. Position the front cover on the cylinder block. Use care not to damage the seal and gasket or mislocate them.
14. Coat the front cover attaching screws with sealer and install them.

NOTE: *It may be necessary to force the front cover downward to compress the oil pan seal in order to install the front cover attaching bolts. Use a screwdriver or drift to engage the cover screw holes through the cover and pry downward.*

15. Assemble and install the remaining components in the reverse order of removal. Tighten the front cover bolts to 15–20 ft. lbs., the water pump attaching scews to 12–15 ft. lbs., the crankshaft damper to 70–90 ft. lbs., the crankshaft pulley to 35–50 ft. lbs., fuel pump to 19–27 ft. lbs., the oil pan bolts to 9–11 ft. lbs. for the 5/16 in. screws and to 7–9 ft. lbs. for the 1/4 in. screws, and the alternator pivot bolt to 45–57 ft. lbs.

6.9L V8 Diesel

1. Disconnect both battery ground cables. Drain the cooling system.
2. Remove the air cleaner and cover the air intake on the manifold with clean rags. *Do not allow any foreign material to enter the intake.*
3. Remove the radiator fan shroud halves.

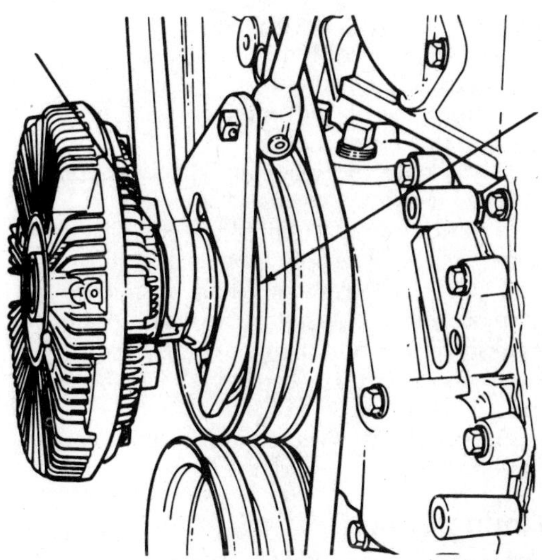
Removing the 6.9L diesel fan clutch using puller (arrows)

4. Remove the fan and fan clutch assembly. You will need a puller or Ford tool no. T83T-6312-A for this.

NOTE: *The nut is a left-hand thread; remove by turning the nut clockwise.*

5. Remove the injection pump as described in Chapter 4 under Diesel Fuel Systems.

6. Remove the water pump.

7. Jack up the truck and safely support it with jackstands.

8. Remove the crankshaft pulley and vibration damper as described in this chapter.

9. Remove the engine ground cables at the front of the engine.

10. Remove the five bolts attaching the engine front cover to the engine block and oil pan.

11. Lower the truck.

12. Remove the front cover.

NOTE: *The front cover oil seal on the diesel must be driven out with an arbor press and*

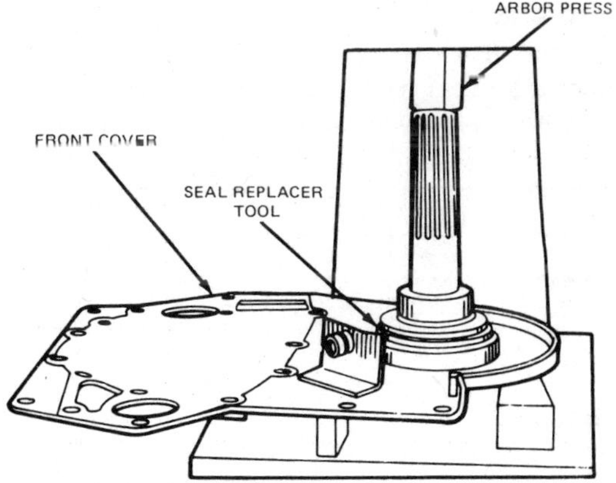

6.9L diesel front oil seal removal and installation using arbor press

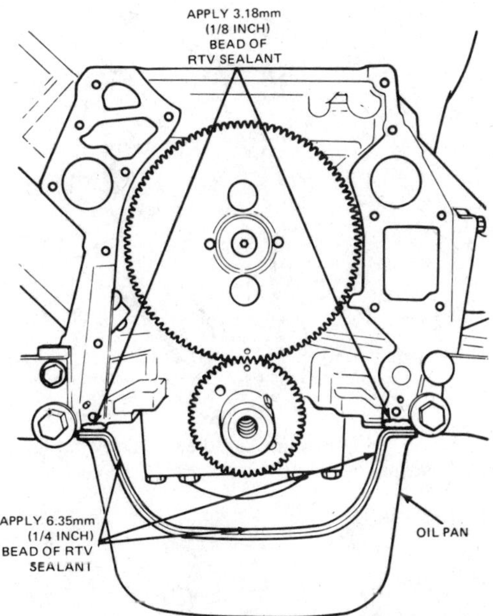

RTV sealer application, 6.9L diesel. Make sure you install the front cover within 15 minutes or the sealant will "set up", reducing its effectiveness

a 3¼ in. spacer. Take the cover to a qualified machinist or engine specialist for this procedure. See also steps 14 and 15.

13. Remove all old gasket material from the front cover, engine block, oil pan sealing surfaces and water pump surfaces.

14. Coat the new front oil seal with Lubriplate® or equivalent grease.

15. The new seal must be installed using a seal installation tool, Ford part no. T83T-6700-A and an arbor press. A qualified machinist or engine specialist can handle seal installation as well as removal. When the seal "bottoms out" on the front cover surface, it is installed at the proper depth.

16. Install alignment dowels into the engine block to align the front cover and gaskets. These can be made out of round stock. Apply a gasket sealer to the engine block sealing surfaces, then install the gaskets on the block.

17. Apply a ⅛ in. bead of RTV sealer on the front of the engine block as shown in the illustration. Apply a ¼ in. bead of RTV sealer on the oil pan as shown.

18. Install the front cover immediately after applying RTV sealer. The sealer will begin to cure and lose its effectiveness unless the cover is installed quickly.

19. Install the water pump gasket on the engine front cover. Apply RTV sealer to the four water pump bolts illustrated. Install the water pump and hand tighten all bolts.

CAUTION: *The two top water pump bolts must be no more than 1¼ in. (31.75 mm)*

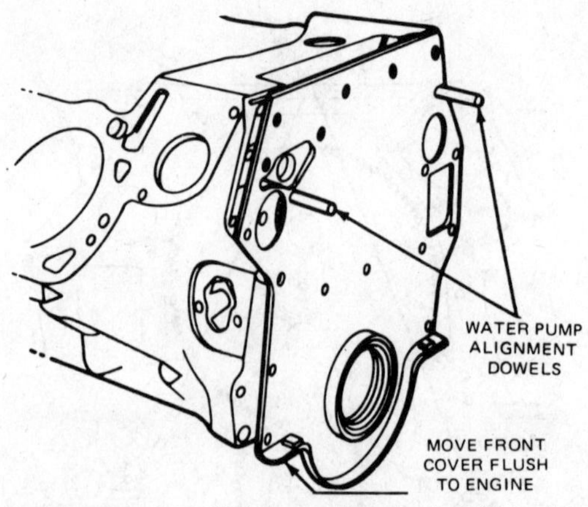

Front cover installation on diesel, showing alignment dowels.

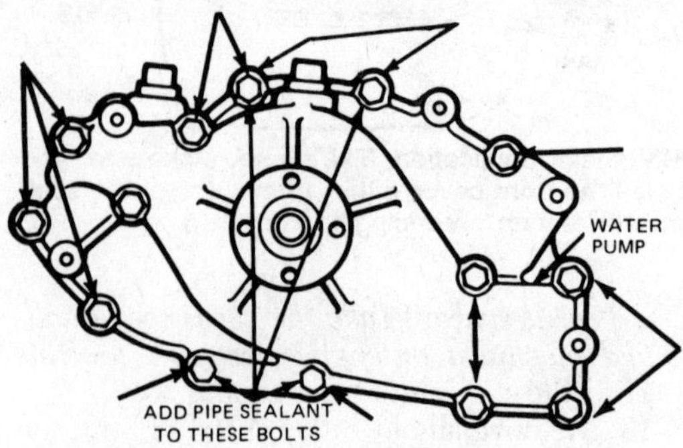

Water pump-to-front cover installation, 6.9L diesel. The two top pump bolts must be no more than 1¼ in. long.

long—bolts any longer will interfere with (hit) the engine drive gears.

20. Torque the water pump bolts to 19 ft. lbs. Torque the front cover bolts to specifications according to bolt size (see Torque Specifications chart).

21. Install the injection pump adaptor and injection pump as described in Chapter 4 under Diesel Fuel System.

22. Install the heater hose fitting in the pump using pipe sealant, and connect the heater hose to the water pump.

23. Jack up the truck and safely support it with jackstands.

24. Lubricate the front of the crankshaft with clean engine oil. Apply RTV sealant to the engine side of the retaining bolt washer to prevent oil seepage past the keyway. Install the crankshaft vibration damper using Ford special tools T83T-6316B. Torque the damper-to-crankshaft bolt to 90 ft. lbs.

25. Install the remaining engine components in the reverse order of removal.

Timing Chain

REMOVAL AND INSTALLATION

V6 and V8

1. Remove the front cover.
2. Rotate the crankshaft counterclockwise to take up the slack on the leftside of the chain.
3. Establish a reference point on the cylinder block and measure from this point to the chain.
4. Rotate the crankshaft in the opposite direction to take up the slack on the rightside of the chain.
5. Force the left-side of the chain out with your fingers and measure the distance between the reference point and the chain. The timing chain deflection is the difference between the two measurements. If the deflection exceeds ½ in., replace the timing chain and sprockets.

To replace the timing chain and sprockets:

6. Turn the crankshaft until the timing marks on the sprockets are aligned vertically.
7. Remove the camshaft sprocket retaining screw and remove the fuel pump eccentric and washers.

Torque Limits—6.9L V-8 Diesel Engine

NOTE: Unless otherwise specified, use standard torque chart. Torque values are with threads and washer faces coated with engine oil. Torque values are listed without tolerance. Variations to torque will occur due to torque wrench calibration. Variation should be within 10% of nominal values.

Standard Torque

¼ x 20 UNC	5/16-18 UNC	3/8-16 UNC	7/16-14 UNC	½ x 13 UNC
9.5 N·m (7 ft-lb)	19 N·m (14 ft-lb)	32 N·m (24 ft-lb)	51 N·m (38 ft-lb)	81 N·m (60 ft-lb)

Pipe Threads

1/8 x 27	¼ x 18	3/8 x 18	½ x 14
7–11 N·m (5–8 ft-lb)	17–24 N·m (12–18 ft-lb)	30–44 N·m (22–33 ft-lb)	34–47 N·m (25–35 ft-lb)

V6 and V8 timing chain showing valve timing marks

Oil slinger and fuel pump eccentric installation, V8s

8. Alternately slide both of the sprockets and timing chain off the crankshaft and camshaft until free of the engine.

9. Position the timing chain on the sprockets so that the timing marks on the sprockets are aligned vertically. Alternately slide the sprockets and chain onto the crankshaft and camshaft sprockets.

10. Install the fuel pump eccentric washers and attaching bolt on the camshaft sprocket. Tighten to 40–45 ft. lbs.

11. Install the front cover.

Timing Gears

REMOVAL AND INSTALLATION

6-300

1. Drain the cooling system and remove the front cover.

2. Crank the engine until the timing marks on the camshaft and crankshaft gears are aligned.

3. Use a gear puller to remove both of the timing gears.

4. Before installing the timing gears, be sure that the key and spacer are properly installed. Align the gear key way with the key and install the gear on the camshaft. Be sure that the timing marks line up on the camshaft and the crankshaft gears and install the crankshaft gear.

5. Install the front cover, and assemble the

Alignment of the crankshaft oil seal and camshaft timing marks on the 240 and 300 inline sixes

240 and 300 inline six camshaft timing gear installation. Crankshaft gear requires one puller each for removal and installation

240 and 300 inline six cylinder timing mark alignment

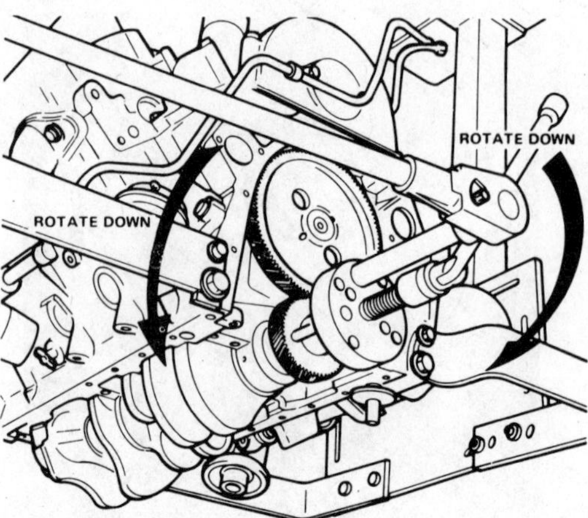

6.9L diesel crankshaft drive gear removal; engine shown out of truck

rest of the engine in the reverse order of disassembly. Fill the cooling system.

6.9L (420) V8 Diesel

1. Follow the procedures for timing gear cover removal and installation, and remove the front cover.

2. To remove the crankshaft gear, install gear puller (Ford part) no. T83T-6316-A or equivalent, and using a breaker bar to prevent the crankshaft from rotating, remove the crankshaft gear. To install the crankshaft gear use tool (Ford part) no. T83T-6316-B or equivalent while aligning the timing marks as shown in the illustration, and press the gear into place.

3. The camshaft gear may be removed by taking out the Allen screw and installing a gear puller, Ford part no. T83T-6316-A or equivalent and removing the gear. The gear may be replaced by using tool (Ford part) no. T83T-6316-B or equivalent. Torque the Allen screw to 12–18 ft. lbs.

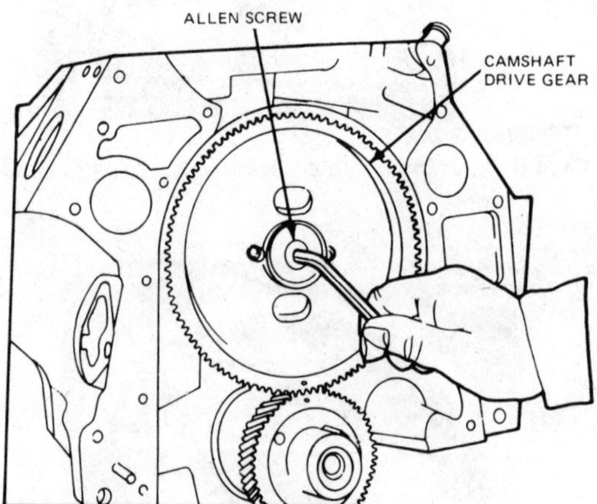

V8 diesel camshaft timing gear installation

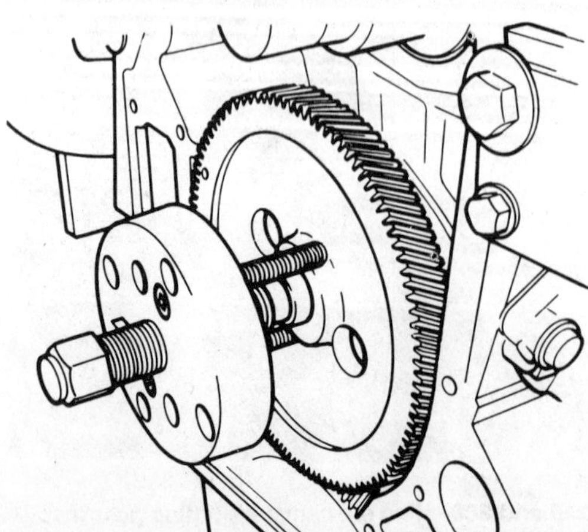

Removing the 6.9L diesel camshaft timing gear

Camshaft

REMOVAL AND INSTALLATION

240 and 300 Six-Cylinder

1. Remove the grille, radiator, and timing cover.

2. Remove the distributor, fuel pump, oil pan and oil pump.

3. Align the timing marks. Unbolt the camshaft thrust plate, working through the holes in the camshaft gear.

4. Loosen the rocker arms, remove the pushrods, take off the side cover and remove the valve lifters with a magnet.

5. Remove the camshaft very carefully to prevent nicking the bearings.

6. Oil the camshaft bearing journals and use Lubriplate® or something similar on the lobes. Install the camshaft, gear, and thrust plate, aligning the gear marks. Tighten down the thrust plate. Make sure that the camshaft end-play is not excessive.

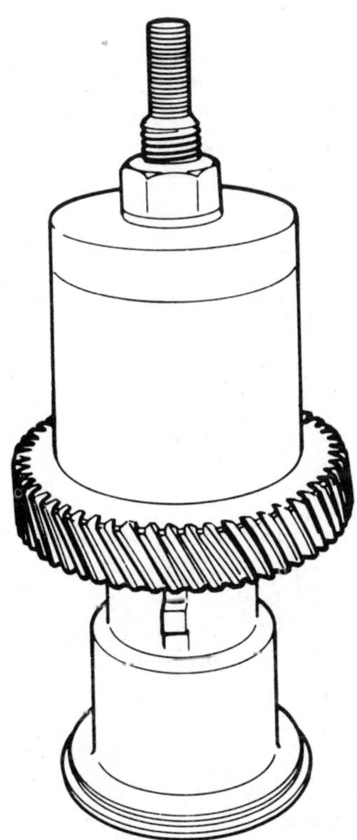

Special installation tool installed on diesel crankshaft drive gear

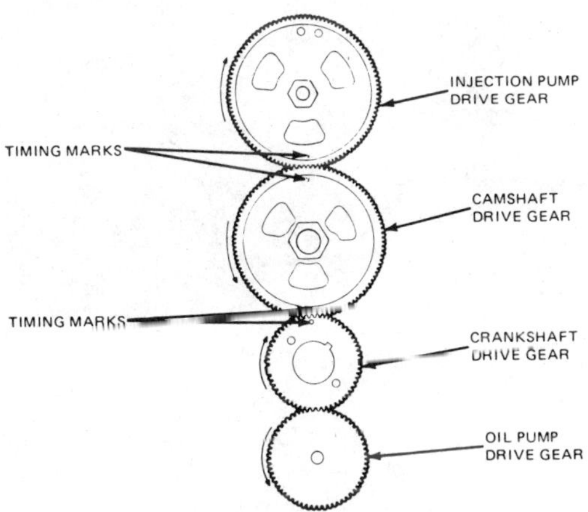

Aligning timing marks, 6.9L V8 diesel

7. The last item to be replaced is the distributor. The rotor should be at the firing position for no. 1 cylinder, with the timing gear marks aligned.

V6 and V8 Including Diesel

NOTE: *Ford recommends removing the engine of 6.9L diesel models for camshaft removal.*

1. Remove the intake manifold and valley pan, if so equipped.

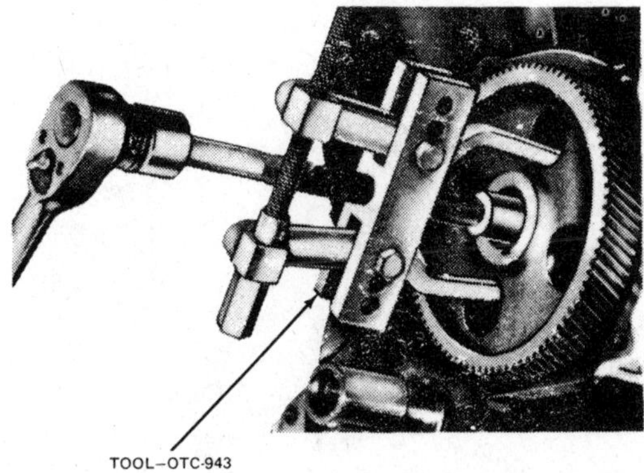

240 and 300 inline six cylinder camshaft gear removal

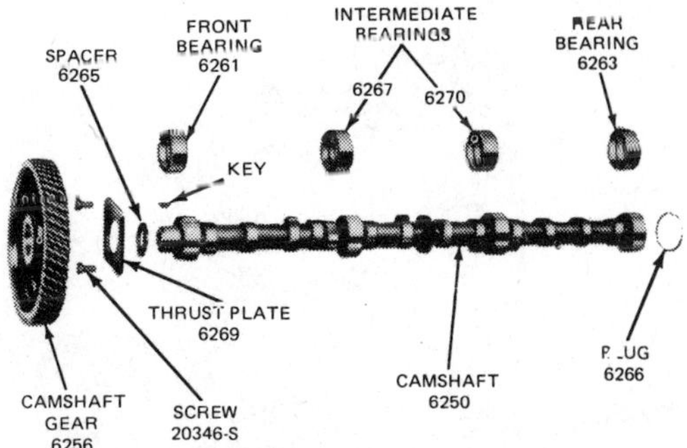

240 and 300 six cylinder camshaft assembly

2. Remove the rocker covers, and either remove the rocker arm shafts or loosen the rockers on their pivots and remove the pushrods. The pushrods must be reinstalled in their original positions.

3. Remove the valve lifters in sequence with a magnet. *They must be replaced in their original positions.*

4. Remove the timing gear cover and timing chain (timing gear on V8 diesel) and sprockets.

5. In addition to the radiator and air conditioning condenser, if so equipped, it may be necessary to remove the front grille assembly and the hood lock assembly to gain the necessary clearance to slide the camshaft out the front of the engine.

6. On the V6, remove the camshaft thrust button and spring. Remove the camshaft thrust plate attaching screws and carefully slide the camshaft out of its bearing bores. Use extra caution not to scratch the bearing journals with the camshaft lobes.

NOTE: *A camshaft removal tool, Ford part no. T65L-6250-A and adaptor 14-0314 are needed to remove the diesel camshaft.*

7. Install the camshaft in the reverse order of removal. Coat the camshaft with engine oil liberally before installing it. Slide the camshaft into the engine very carefully so as not to scratch

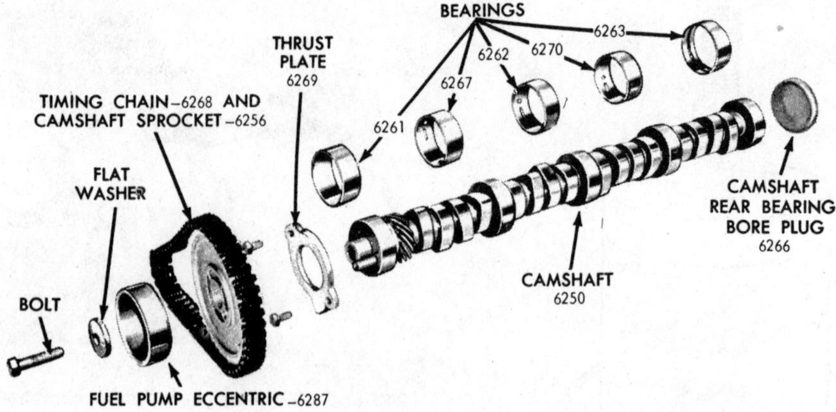

V8 camshaft and related parts

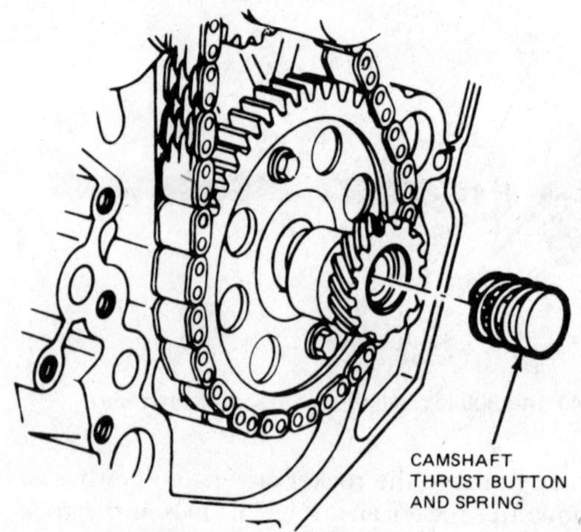

Note proper position of V6 camshaft thrust button and spring when reinstalling

the bearing bores with the camshaft lobes. Install the camshaft thrust plate and tighten the attaching screws to 9–12 ft. lbs. Measure the camshaft end-play. If the end-play is more than 0.009 in., replace the thrust plate. Assemble the remaining components in the reverse order of removal.

CHECKING CAMSHAFT

Camshaft Lobe Lift

Check the lift of each lobe in consecutive order and make a note of the reading.

1. Remove the fresh air inlet tube and the air cleaner. Remove the heater hose and crankcase ventilation hoses. Remove valve rocker arm cover(s).
2. Remove the rocker arm stud nut or fulcrum bolts, fulcrum seat and rocker arm.
3. Make sure the push rod is in the valve tappet socket. Install a dial indicator D78P-4201-B (or equivalent) so that the actuating point of the indicator is in the push rod socket (or the

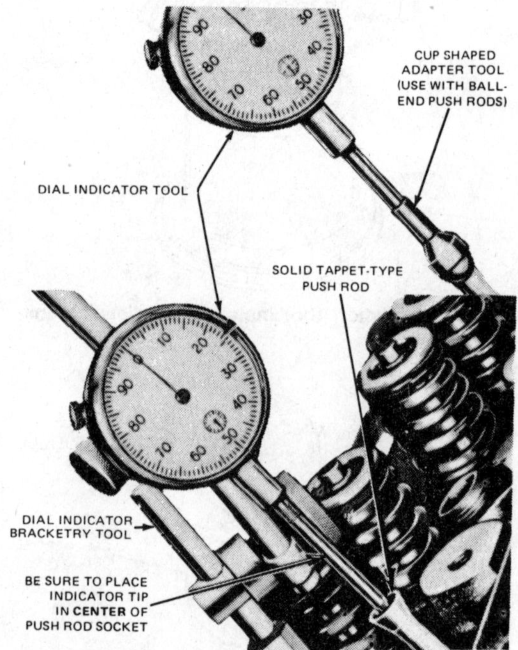

Checking camshaft lobe lift

indicator ball socket adapter Tool 6565-AB is on the end of the push rod) and in the same plane as the push rod movement.

4. Disconnect the I terminal and the S terminal at the stater relay. Install an auxiliary stater switch between the battery and S terminals of the stater relay. Crank the engine with the ignition switch off. Turn the crankshaft over until the tappet is on the base circle of the camshaft lobe. At this position, the push rod will be in its lowest position.
5. Zero the dial indicator. Continue to rotate the crankshaft slowly until the push rod is in the fully raised position.
6. Compare the total lift recorded on the dial indicator with the specification shown on the "Camshaft Specification" chart.

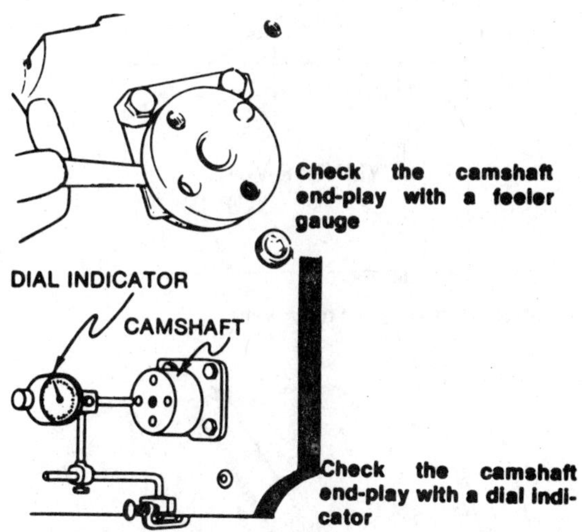

Checking camshaft end play

To check the accuracy of the original indicator reading, continue to rotate the crankshaft until the indicator reads zero. If the lift on any lobe is below specified wear limits listed, the camshaft and the valve tappet operating on the worn lobe(s) must be replaced.

7. Remove the dial indicator and auxiliary stater switch.

8. Install the rocker arm, fulcrum seat and stud nut or fulcrum bolts. Check the valve clearance. Adjust if required (refer to procedure in this chapter).

9. Install the valve rocker arm cover(s) and the air cleaner.

Camshaft End Play

NOTE: *On all gasoline V-8 engines, prying against the aluminum-nylon camshaft sprocket, with the valve train load on the camshaft, can break or damage the sprocket. Therefore, the rocker arm adjusting nuts must be backed off, or the rocker arm and shaft assembly must be loosened sufficiently to free the camshaft. After checking the camshaft end play, check the valve clearance. Adjust if required (refer to procedure in this chapter).*

1. Push the camshaft toward the rear of the engine. Install a dial indicator (Tools D78P-4201-F, -G or equivalent so that the indicator point is on the camshaft sprocket attaching screw.

2. Zero the dial indicator. Position a prybar between the camshaft gear and the block. Pull the camshaft forward and release it. Compare the dial indicator reading with the specifications.

3. If the end play is excessive, check the spacer for correct installation before it is removed. If the spacer is correctly installed, replace the thrust plate.

4. Remove the dial indicator.

CAMSHAFT BEARING REPLACEMENT

1. Remove the engine following the procedures in this chapter and install it on a work stand.

2. Remove the camshaft, flywheel and crankshaft, following the appropriate procedures. Push the pistons to the top of the cylinders.

3. Remove the camshaft rear bearing bore plug. Remove the camshaft bearings with Tool T65L-6250-A or equivalent.

4. Select the proper size expanding collet and back-up nut and assemble on the mandrel. With the expanding collet collapsed, install the collet assembly in the camshaft bearing and tighten the back-up nut on the expanding mandrel until the collet fits the camshaft bearing.

5. Assemble the puller screw and extension (if necessary) and install on the expanding mandrel. Wrap a cloth around the threads of the puller screw to protect the front bearing or journal. Tighten the pulling nut against the

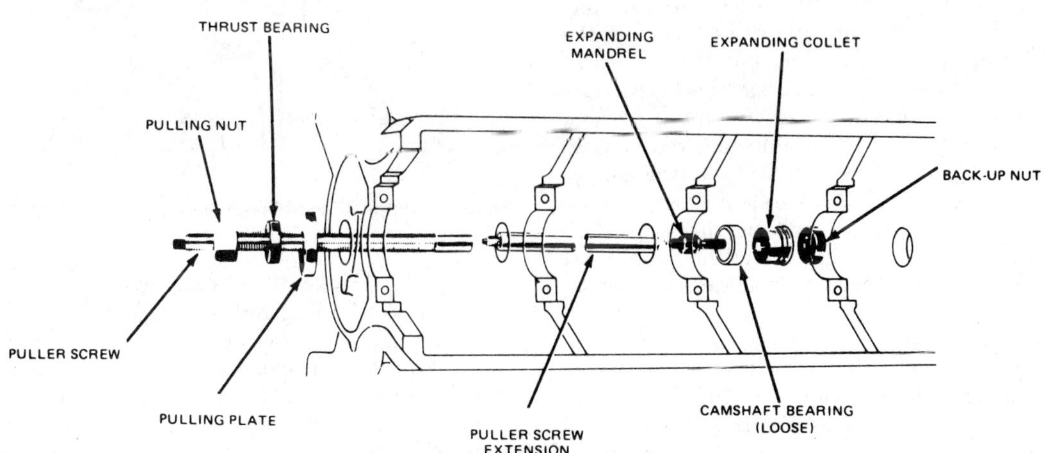

Camshaft bearing replacement

thrust bearing and pulling plate to remove the camshaft bearing. Be sure to hold a wrench on the end of the puller screw to prevent it from turning.

6. To remove the front bearing, install the puller from the rear of the cylinder block.

7. Position the new bearings at the bearing bores, and press them in place with tool T65L-6250-A or equivalent. *Be sure to center the pulling plate and puller screw to avoid damage to the bearing. Failure to use the correct expanding collet can cause severe bearing damage.* Align the oil holes in the bearings with the oil holes in the cylinder block before pressing bearings into place.

NOTE: *Be sure the front bearing is installed .51–.89 mm (0.020–0.035 in.) for the inline six cylinder engines, 0.127–0.508 mm (0.005–0.020 in.) for the gasoline V8, .040–.060 for the diesel V8, below the front face of the cylinder block.*

8. Install the camshaft rear bearing bore plug.

9. Install the camshaft, crankshaft, flywheel and related parts, following the appropriate procedures.

10. Install the engine in the truck, following the procedures described earlier in this chapter.

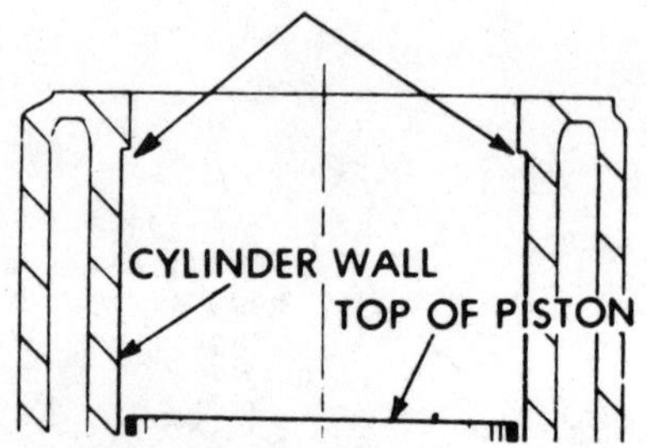

Ridge caused by cylinder wear

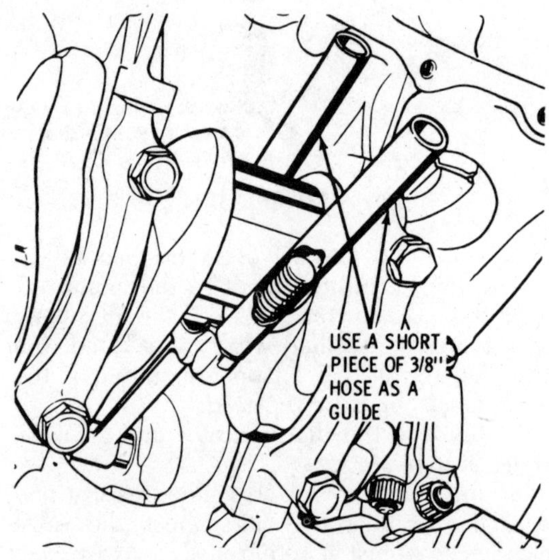

Make connecting rod bolt guides out of rubber tubing; these also protect the cylinder walls and crank journal from scratches

Pistons and Connecting Rods

REMOVAL AND INSTALLATION

6-Cylinder

1. Drain the cooling system and the crankcase.

2. Remove the cylinder head.

3. Remove the oil pan, the oil pump inlet tube and the oil pump.

4. Turn the crankshaft until the piston to be removed is at the bottom of its travel and place a cloth on the piston head to collect filings. Using a ridge reaming tool, remove any ridge of carbon or any other desposit from the upper cylinder walls where piston travel ends. *Do not cut into the piston ring travel area more than 1/32 in. while removing the ridge.*

5. Mark all of the connecting rod caps so that they can be reinstalled in the original positions from which they are removed and remove the connecting rod bearing cap. Also identify the piston assemblies as they, too, must be reinstalled in the same cylinder from which removed.

6. With the bearing caps removed, the connecting rod bearing bolts are potentially damaging to the cylinder walls during removal. To guard against cylinder wall damage, install four or five inch lengths of 3/8 in. rubber tubing onto the connecting rod bolts. These will also protect the crankshaft journal from scratches when the connecting rod is installed, and will serve as a guide for the rod.

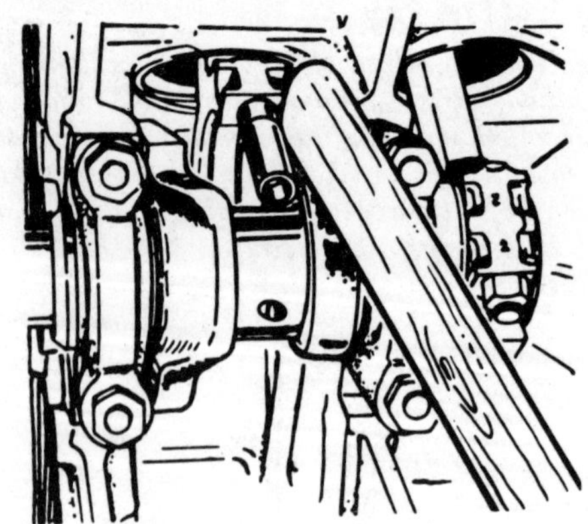

Push the piston assembly out with a hammer handle

7. Squirt some clean engine oil into each cylinder before removing the pistons. Using a wooden hammer handle, push the connecting rod and piston assembly out the top of the cylinder (pushing from the bottom of the rod). Be

careful to avoid damaging both the crank journal and the cylinder wall when removing the rod and piston assembly.

8. Before installing the piston/connecting rod assembly, be sure to clean all gasket mating surfaces, oil the pistons, piston rings and the cylinder walls with light engine oil.

9. Be sure to install the pistons in the cylinders from which they were removed. The connecting rod and bearing caps are numbered from 1 to 6 beginning at the front of the engine. The numbers on the connecting rod and bearing cap must be on the same side when installed in the cylinder bore. If a connecting rod is ever transposed from one engine or cylinder to another, new bearings should be fitted and the connecting rod should be numbered to correspond with the new cylinder number. The notch on the piston head goes toward the front of the engine.

10. Make sure the ring gaps are properly spaced around the circumference of the piston. Make sure rubber hose lengths are fitted to the rod bolts. Fit a piston ring compressor around the piston and slide the piston and connecting rod assembly down into the cylinder bore, pushing it in with the wooden hammer handle. Push the piston down until it is only slightly below the top of the cylinder bore. Guide the connecting rods onto the crankshaft bearing journals carefully, using the rubber hose lengths, to avoid damaging the crankshaft.

11. Check the bearing clearance of all the rod bearings, fitting them to the crankshaft bearing journals.

12. After the bearings have been fitted, apply a light coating of engine oil to the journals and bearings.

13. Turn the crankshaft until the appropriate bearing journal is at the bottom of its stroke, then push the piston assembly all the way down until the connecting rod bearing seats on the crankshaft journal. Be careful not to allow the bearing cap screws to strike the crankshaft bearing journals and damage them.

14. After the piston and connecting rod as-

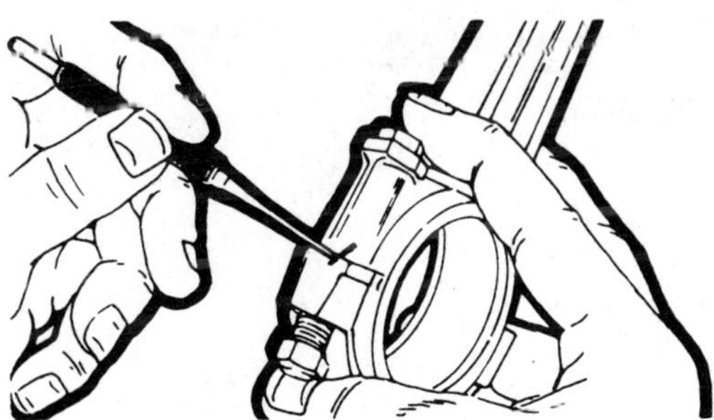

Match the connecting rods to their caps with a scribe mark for reassembly

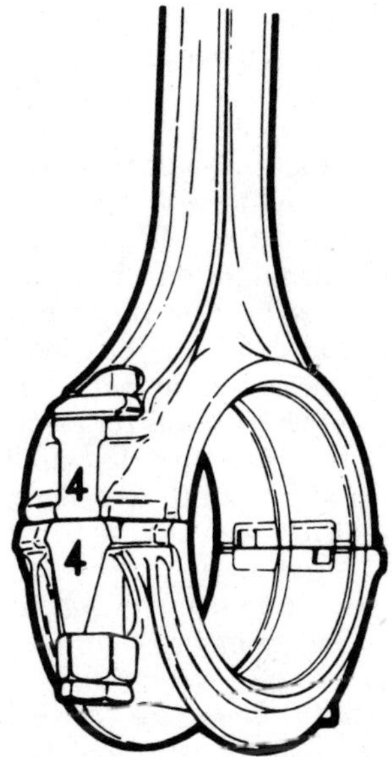

Number each rod and cap with its cylinder number for correct assembly

semblies have been installed, check the connecting rod side clearance on each crankshaft journal.

15. Prime and install the oil pump and the oil pump intake tube, then install the oil pan.

16. Reassemble the rest of the engine in the reverse order of disassembly.

V8 Engines Including Diesel

1. Drain the cooling system and the crankcase. Remove the intake manifold, cylinder heads, oil pan and the oil pump.

2. Turn the crankshaft until the piston to be removed is at the bottom of its travel, then place a cloth on the piston head to collect filings. Remove any ridge of deposits at the end of the piston travel from the upper cylinder bore, using a ridge reaming tool. Do not cut into the piston ring travel area more than $\frac{1}{32}$ in. when removing the ridge.

3. Make sure that all of the connecting rod bearing caps can be identified, so they will be reinstalled in their original positions.

4. Turn the crankshaft until the connecting rod that is to be removed is at the bottom of its stroke and remove the connecting rod nuts and bearing cap.

5. With the bearing caps removed, the connecting rod bearing bolts are potentially damaging to the cylinder walls during removal. To guard against cylinder wall damage, install four or five inch lengths of $\frac{3}{8}$ in. rubber tubing onto the connecting rod bolts. These will also protect the crankshaft journal from scratches when the connecting rod is installed, and will serve as a guide for the rod.

6. Squirt some clean engine oil into each cylinder before removing the piston assemblies. Using a wooden hammer handle, push the connecting rod and piston assembly out the top of the cylinder (pushing from the bottom of the rod). Be careful to avoid damaging both the crank journal and the cylinder wall when removing the rod and piston assembly.

6. Remove the bearing inserts from the connecting rod and cap if the bearings are to be replaced, and place the cap onto the piston/rod assembly from which it was removed.

7. Install the piston/rod assemblies in the same manner as that for the 6 cylinder engines. See the procedure given for 6 cylinder engines.

NOTE: *The connecting rod and bearing caps are numbered from 1 to 4 in the right bank and from 5 to 8 in the left bank, beginning at the front of the engine. The numbers on the rod and cap must be on the same side when they are installed in the cylinder bore. Also, the largest chamfer at the bearing end of the rod should be positioned toward the crank pin thrust face of the crankshaft and the notch in the head of the piston faces toward the front of the engine.*

8. Assemble the engine in the reverse order of disassembly.

Piston Ring and Wrist Pin

REMOVAL

All of the Ford gasoline engines covered in this guide utilize pressed-in wrist pins, which can only be removed by an arbor press. The 6.9L diesel pistons are removed in the same way, only the pistons are heated before the wrist pins are pressed out. On both gasoline and diesel engines, the piston/connecting rod assemblies should be taken to an engine specialist or qualified machinist for piston removal and installation.

A piston ring expander is necessary for removing piston rings without damaging them; any other method (screwdriver blades, pliers, etc.) usually results in the rings being bent,

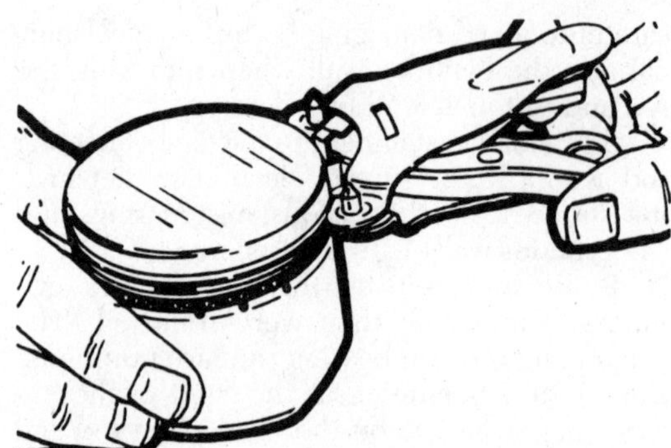

Remove and install the rings with a ring expander

scratched or distorted, or the piston itself being damaged. When the rings are removed, clean the ring grooves using an appropriate ring groove cleaning tool, using care not to cut too deeply. Thoroughly clean all carbon and varnish from the piston with solvent.

CAUTION: *Do not use a wire brush or caustic solvent (acids, etc.) on pistons.*

Inspect the pistons for scuffing, scoring, cracks, pitting, or excessive ring groove wear. If these are evident, the piston must be replaced.

The piston should also be checked in relation to the cylinder diameter. Using a telescoping gauge and micrometer, or a dial gauge, measure the cylinder bore diameter perpendicular (90%) to the piston pin, 2½ in. below the cylinder block deck (surface where the block mates with the heads). Then, with the micrometer, measure the piston, perpendicular to its wrist pin on the skirt. The difference between the two measurements is the piston clearance. If the clearance is within specifications or slightly below (after the cylinders have been bored or honed), finish honing is all that is necessary. If the clearance is excessive, try to obtain a slightly larger piston to bring clearance to within specifications. If this is not possible, obtain the first oversize piston and hone (or if necessary, bore) the cylinder to size. Generally, if the cylinder bore is tapered .005 in. or more or is out-of-round .003 in. or more, it is advisable to rebore

Use needle-nose or snap-ring pliers to remove the piston pin clips

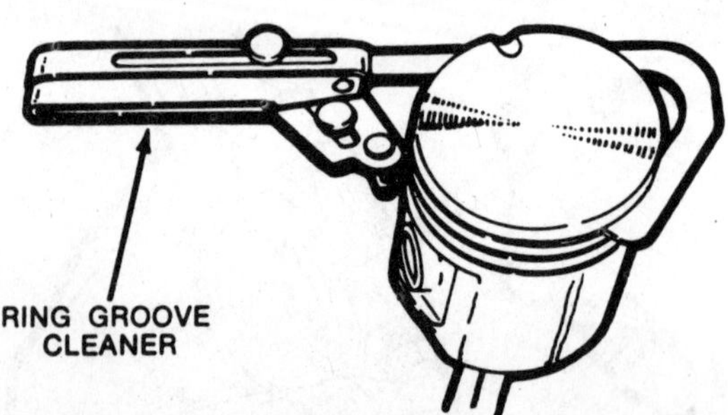

Clean the ring grooves with this tool or the edge of an old ring

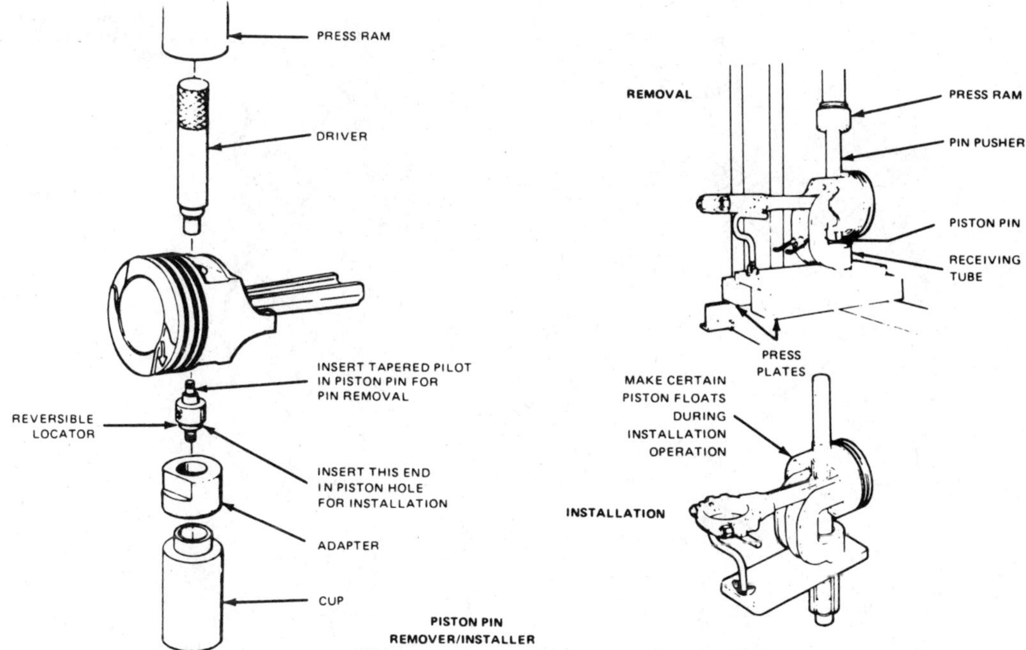

Have the wrist pins pressed in and out with an arbor press. This applies to all engines covered in this guide

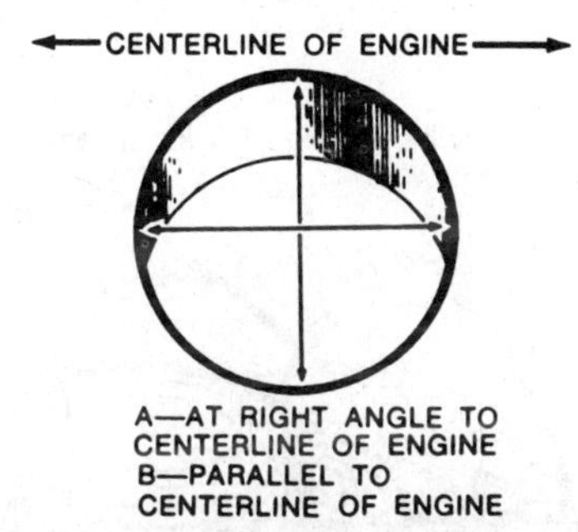

Cylinder bore measuring points. Take top measurement ½ in. below top of block deck, bottom measurement ½ in. above top of piston when piston is at B.D.C.

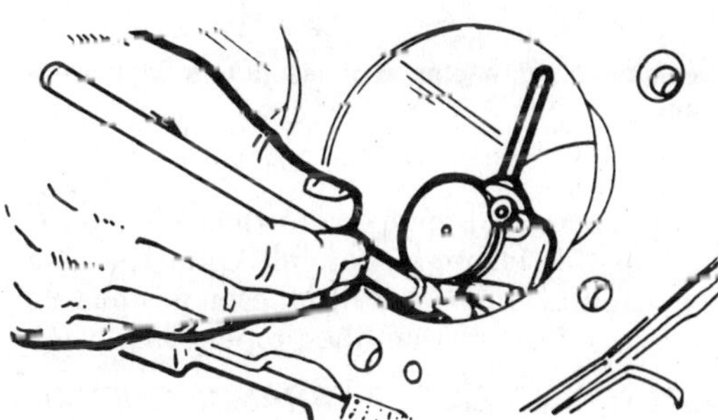

Measuring cylinder bore with a dial gauge

for the smallest possible oversize piston and rings.

After measuring, mark pistons with a felttip pen for reference and for assembly.

NOTE: *Cylinder honing and/or boring should be performed by a reputable, professional mechanic with the proper equipment. In some cases, "clean-up" honing can be done with the cylinder block in the car, but most excessive honing and all cylinder boring must be done with the block stripped and removed from the car.*

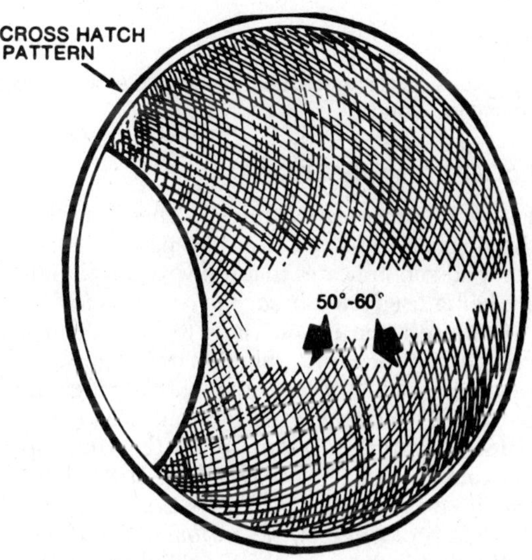

Proper cylinder bore cross-hatching after honing

NOTE: *Before honing the 6.9L diesel cylinders, the piston oil cooling jets must be removed. This procedure should be handled by a diesel specialist, as special tools are needed. Jets cannot be reused; new jets should be fitted.*

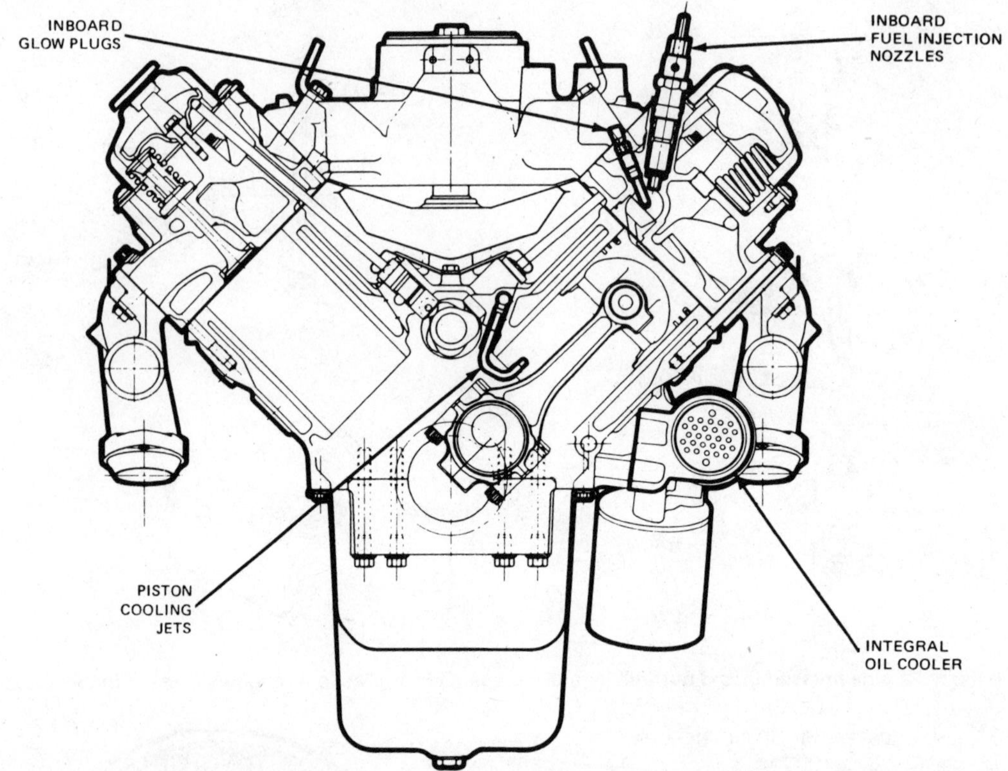

6.9L diesel V8 cross-section showing piston oil cooling jets which must be removed prior to any cylinder honing or boring

PISTON RING END GAP

Piston ring end gap should be checked while the rings are removed from the pistons. Incorrect end gap indicates that the wrong size rings are being used; *ring breakage could occur*.

Compress the piston rings to be used in a cylinder, one at a time, into that cylinder. Squirt clean oil into the cylinder, so that the rings and the top 2 inches of cylinder wall are coated. Using an inverted piston, press the rings approximately 1 in. below the deck of the block (on diesels, measure ring gap clearance with the ring positioned at the *bottom* of ring travel in the bore). Measure the ring end gap with a feeler gauge, and compare to the "Ring Gap" chart in this chapter. Carefully pull the ring out of the cylinder and file the ends squarely with a fine file to obtain the proper clearance.

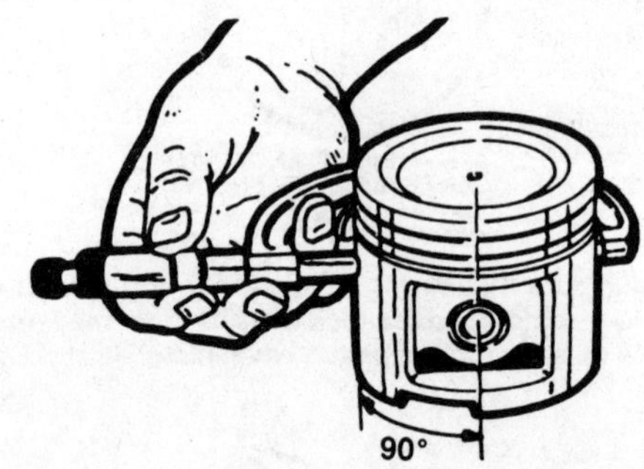

Check piston diameter at these points with a micrometer

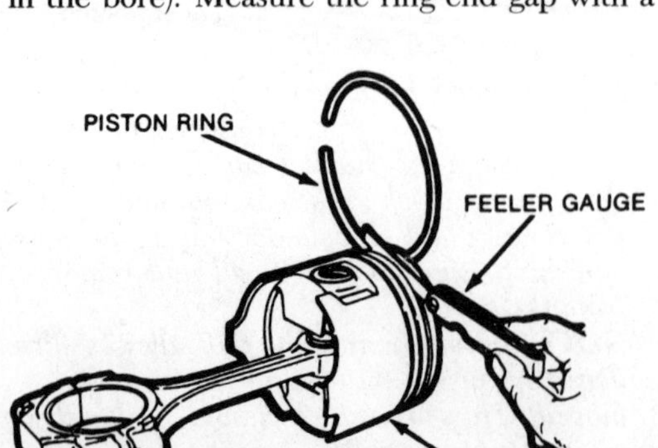

Checking ring side clearance

PISTON RING SIDE CLEARANCE CHECK AND INSTALLATION

Check the pistons to see that the ring grooves and oil return holes have been properly cleaned. Slide a piston ring into its groove, and check the side clearance with a feeler gauge. On gasoline engines, make sure you insert the gauge between the ring and its lower land (lower edge of the groove), because any wear that occurs

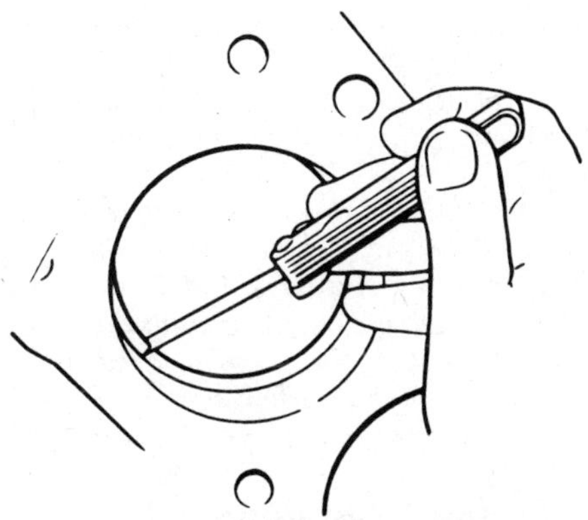

Check piston ring end gap with a feeler gauge, with the ring positioned in the cylinder one inch below the deck of the block

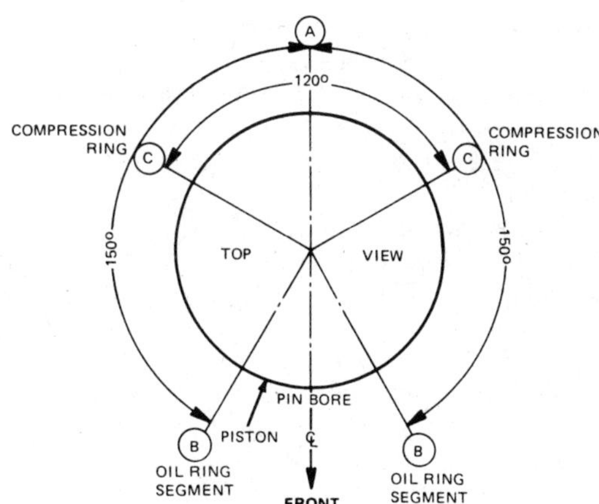

6.9L diesel piston ring spacing

forms a step at the inner portion of the lower land. On diesels, insert the gauge between the ring and the *upper* land. If the piston grooves have worn to the extent that relatively high steps exist on the lower land, the piston grooves have worn to the extent that relatively high steps exist on the lower land, the piston should be replaced, because these will interfere with the operation of the new rings and ring clearances will be excessive. Piston rings are not furnished in oversize widths to compensate for ring groove wear.

Install the rings on the piston, *lowest ring first,* using a piston ring expander. There is a high risk of breaking or distorting the rings, or scratching the piston, if the rings are installed by hand or other means.

Position the rings on the piston as illustrated; *spacing of the various piston ring gaps is crucial to proper oil retention and even cylinder wear.* When installing new rings, refer to the installation diagram furnished with the new parts.

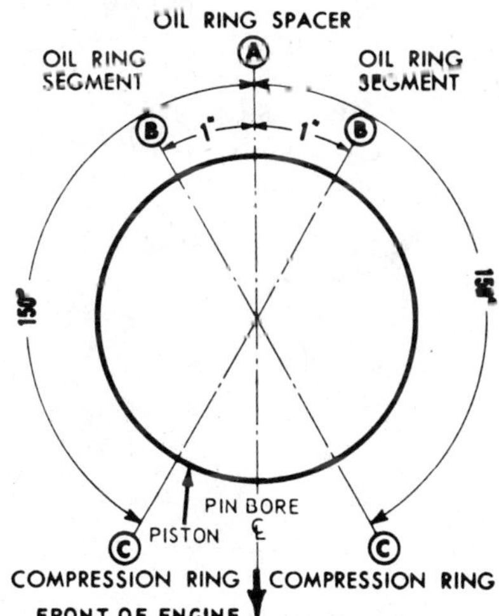

Proper spacing of the piston ring gaps around the circumference of the piston—gasoline engines

Connecting Rod Bearings

INSPECTION

Connecting rod bearings for the engines covered in this guide consist of two halves or shells which are interchangeable in the rod and cap. When the shells are placed in position, the ends extend slightly beyond the rod and cap surfaces so that when the rod bolts are torqued the shells will be clamped tightly in place to insure positive seating and to prevent turning. A tang holds the shells in place.

NOTE: *The ends of the bearing shells must never be filed flush with the mating surface of the rod and cap.*

If a rod bearing becomes noisy or is worn so that its clearance on the crank journal is sloppy, a new bearing of the correct undersize must be selected and installed since there is a provision for adjustment.

CAUTION: *Under no circumstances should the rod end or cap be filed to adjust the bearing clearance, nor should shims of any kind be used.*

Inspect the rod bearings while the rod assemblies are out of the engine. If the shells are scored or show flaking, they should be replaced. If they are in good shape, check for proper clearance on the crank journal (see below). Any scoring or ridges on the crank journal means the crankshaft must be reground and fitted with undersized bearings, or replaced.

CHECKING BEARING CLEARANCE AND REPLACING BEARINGS

NOTE: *Make sure connecting rods and their caps are kept together, and that the caps are installed in the proper direction.*

Replacement bearings are available in standard size, and in undersizes for reground crankshafts. Connecting rod-to-crankshaft bearing clearance is checked using Plastigage® at either the top or bottom of each crank journal. The Plastigage® has a range of .001 in. to .003 in.

1. Remove the rod cap with the bearing shell. Completely clean the bearing shell and the crank journal, and blow any oil from the oil hole in the crankshaft.

NOTE: *The journal surfaces and bearing shells must be completely free of oil, because Plastigage® is soluble in oil.*

2. Place a strip of Plastigage® lengthwise along the bottom center of the lower bearing shell, then install the cap with shell and torque the bolt or nuts to specification. DO NOT TURN the crankshaft with the Plastigage® installed in the bearing.

3. Remove the bearing cap with the shell. The flattened Plastigage® will be found sticking to either the bearing shell or crank journal. *Do not remove it yet.*

4. Use the printed scale on the Plastigage® envelope to measure the flattened material at its widest point. The number within the scale which most closely corresponds to the width of the Plastigage® indicates bearing clearance in thousandths of an inch.

5. Check the specifications chart in this chapter for the desired clearance. It is advisable to install a new bearing if clearance exceeds .003 in.; however, if the bearing is in good condition and is not being checked because of bearing noise, bearing replacement is not necessary.

6. If you are installing new bearings, try a standard size, then each undersize in order until one is found that is within the specified limits when checked for clearance with Plastigage®. Each undersize shell has its size stamped on it.

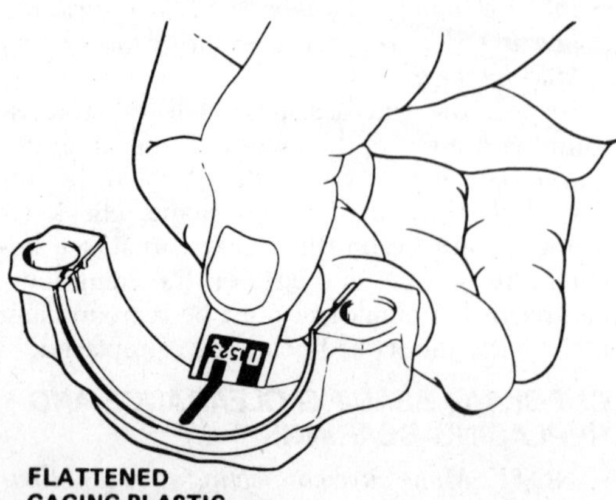

Checking rod bearing clearance with Plastigage® or equivalent

7. When the proper size shell is found, clean off the Plastigage® material from the shell, oil the bearing thoroughly, reinstall the cap with its shell and torque the rod bolt nuts to specification.

NOTE: *With the proper bearing selected and the nuts torqued, it should be possible to move the connecting rod back and forth freely on the crank journal as allowed by the specified connecting rod end clearance. If the rod cannot be moved, either the rod bearing is too far undersize or the rod is misaligned.*

Piston and Connecting Rod

ASSEMBLY AND INSTALLATION

Install the connecting rod to the piston making sure piston installation notches and any marks on the rod are in proper relation to one another. Lubricate the wrist pin with clean engine oil and install the pin into the rod and piston assembly by using an arbor press as required. Install wrist pin snap-rings if equipped, and rotate them in their grooves to make sure they are seated. To install the piston and rod assemblies:

1. Make sure connecting rod big-end bearings (including end cap) are of the correct size and properly installed.

2. Fit rubber hoses over the connecting rod bolts to protect the crankshaft journals, as in the "Piston Removal" procedure. Coat the rod bearings with clean oil.

3. Using the proper ring compressor, insert the piston assembly into the cylinder so that the notch in the top of the piston faces the front of the engine (this assumes that the dimple(s) or other markings on the connecting rods are in correct relation to the piston notch(s)).

4. From beneath the engine, coat each crank journal with clean oil. Pull the connecting rod, with the bearing shell in place, into position against the crank journal.

5. Remove the rubber hoses. Install the bearing cap and cap nuts and torque to specification.

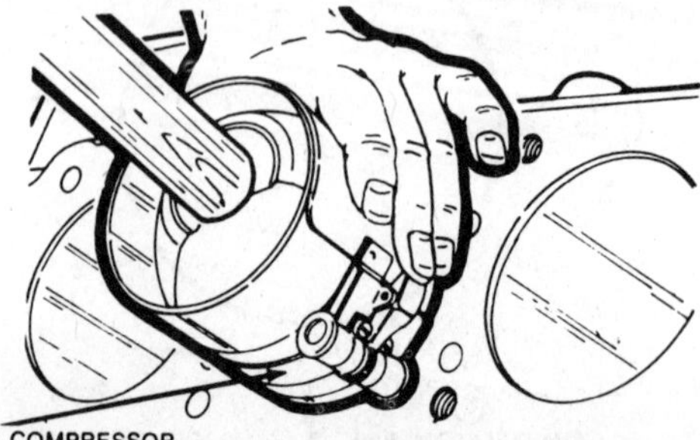

Tap the piston assembly into the cylinder with a wooden hammer handle. Notches on piston crown face the front of the engine

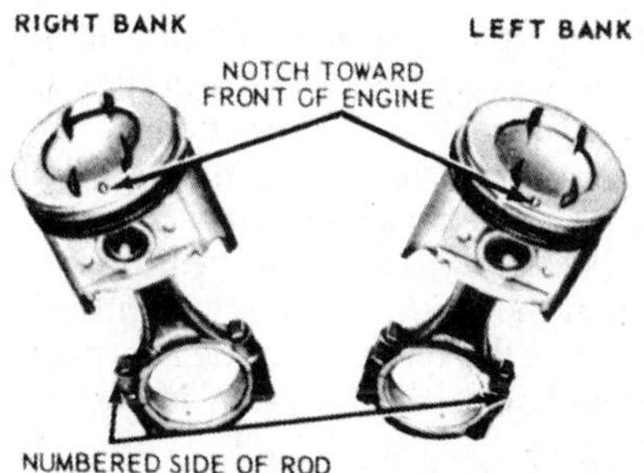

V6-232, V8-302, 351 and 400 piston and rod assemblies showing piston installation notches

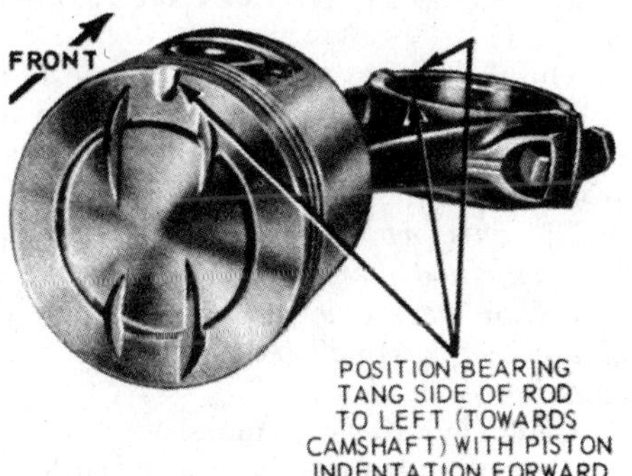

Inline six-cylinder rod and piston assembly

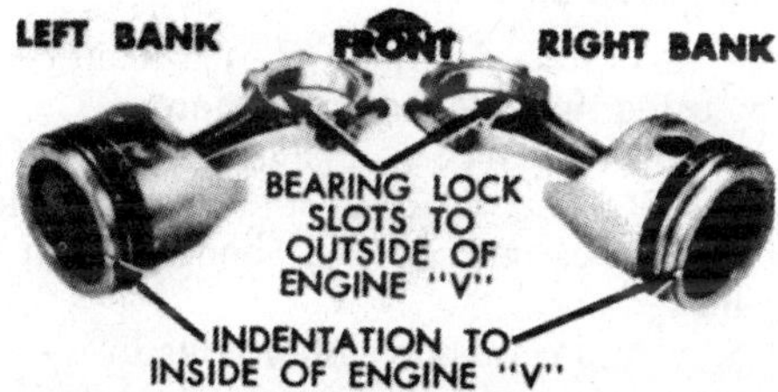

Connecting rod and piston installation—360, 361 and 391 V8s

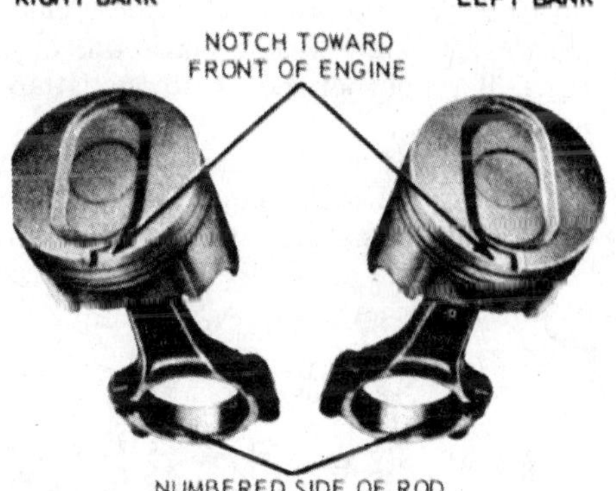

460 V8 piston and rod installation

NOTE: *When more than one rod and piston assembly is being installed, the connecting rod cap attaching nuts should only be tightened enough to keep each rod in position until all have been installed. This will ease the installation of the remaining piston assemblies.*

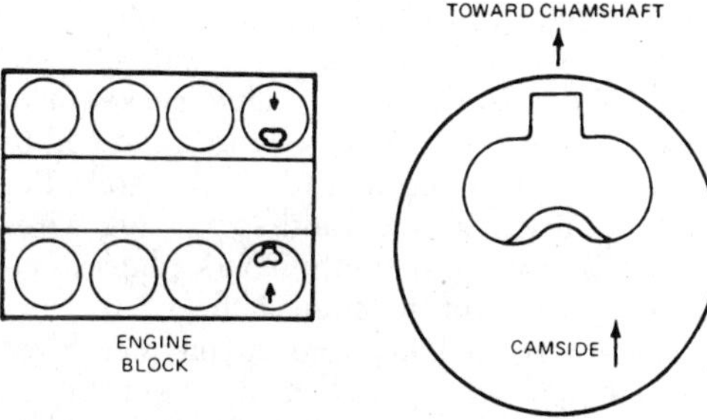

6.9L diesel piston positioning

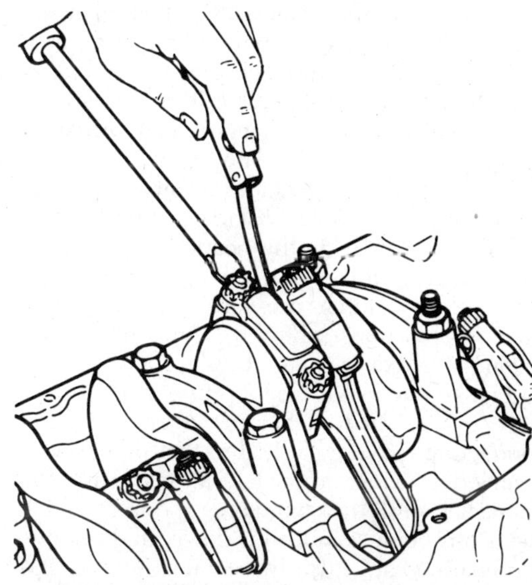

Checking connecting rod side clearance with a feeler gauge. Use a small pry bar to spread the connecting rods

6. Check the clearance between the sides of the connecting rods and the crankshaft using a feeler gauge. Spread the rods slightly with a screwdriver to insert the gauge. If clearance is below the minimum tolerance, the rod may be machined to provide adequate clearance. If clearance is excessive, substitute an unworn rod, and recheck. If clearance is still outside specifications, the crankshaft must be welded and reground, or replaced.
7. Replace the oil pump if removed and the oil pan.
8. Install the cylinder head(s) and intake manifold.

Crankshaft and Main Bearings

REMOVAL AND INSTALLATION

Engine Removed

1. With the engine removed from the vehicle and placed in a work stand, disconnect

the spark plug wires from the spark plugs and remove the wires and bracket assembly from the attaching stud on the valve rocker arm cover(s) if so equipped. Disconnect the coil to distributor high-tension lead at the coil. Remove the distributor cap and spark plug wires as an assembly. Remove the spark plugs to allow easy rotation of the crankshaft.

2. Remove the fuel pump and oil filter. Slide the water pump by-pass hose clamp (if so equipped) toward the water pump. Remove the alternator and mounting brackets.

3. Remove the crankshaft pulley from the crankshaft vibration damper. Remove the capscrew and washer from the end of the crankshaft. Install a universal puller, Tool T58P-6316-D or equivalent on the crankshaft vibration damper and remove the damper.

4. Remove the cylinder front cover and crankshaft gear, refer to "Cylinder Front Cover and Timing Chain" in this chapter.

5. Invert the engine on the work stand. Remove the clutch pressure plate and disc (manual-shift trans.). Remove the flywheel and engine rear cover plate. Remove the oil pan and gasket. Remove the oil pump.

6. Make sure all bearing caps (main and connecting rod) are marked so that they can be installed in their original locations. Turn the crankshaft until the connecting rod from which the cap is being removed is down, and remove the bearing cap. Push the connecting rod and piston assembly up into the cylinder. Repeat this procedure until all the connecting rod bearing caps are removed.

7. Remove the main bearing caps.

8. Carefully lift the crankshaft out of the block so that the thrust bearing surfaces are not damaged. Handle the crankshaft with care to avoid possible fracture to the finished surfaces.

9. Remove the rear journal seal from the block and rear main bearing cap.

10. Remove the main bearing inserts from the block and bearing caps.

11. Remove the connecting rod bearing inserts from the connecting rods and caps.

12. If the crankshaft main bearing journals have been refinished to a definite undersize, install the correct undersize bearings. *Be sure the bearing inserts and bearing bores are clean. Foreign material under the inserts will distort the bearing and cause a failure.*

13. Place the upper main bearing inserts in position in the bores with the tang fitting in the slot. Be sure the oil holes in the bearing inserts are aligned with the oil holes in the cylinder block.

14. Install the lower main bearing inserts in the bearing caps.

15. Clean the rear journal oil seal groove and the mating surfaces of the block and rear main bearing cap.

16. Dip the lip-type seal halves in clean engine oil. Install the seals in the bearing cap and block with the undercut side of the seal toward the front of the engine.

NOTE: *This procedure applies only to engines with two piece rear main bearing oil seals. Those having one piece seals (inline six-cylinder engines) will be installed after the crankshaft is in place.*

17. Carefully lower the crankshaft into place. Be careful not to damage the bearing surfaces.

CHECKING MAIN BEARING CLEARANCES

18. Check the clearance of each main bearing by using the following procedure:

a. Place a piece of Plastigage® or its equivalent, on bearing surface across full width of bearing cap and about ¼ inch off center.

b. Install cap and tighten bolts to specificiations. *Do not turn crankshaft while Plastigage® is in place.*

c. Remove the cap. Using Plastigage® scale, check width of Plastigage® at widest point to get the minimum clearance. Check at narrowest point to get maximum clearance. Difference between readings is taper of journal.

d. If clearance exceeds specified limits, try a 0.001 or 0.002 inch undersize bearing in combination with the standard bearing.

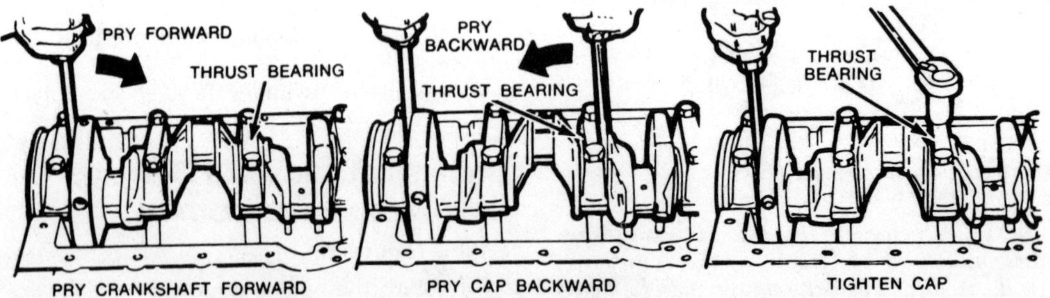

Crankshaft thrust bearing alignment

Bearing clearance must be within specified limits. If standard and 0.002 inch undersize bearing does not bring clearance within desired limits, refinish crankshaft journal, then install undersize bearings.

NOTE: *Refer to "Rear Main Oil Seal removal and installation", for special instructions in applying RTV sealer to rear main bearing cap.*

19. Apply engine oil to the journals and bearings.

20. Install all the bearing caps except the thrust bearing cap (no. 3 bearing on all except the 6-240, 300 which use the no. 5 as the thrust bearing). Be sure the main bearing caps are installed in their original locations. Tighten the bearing cap bolts to specifications.

21. Install the thrust bearing cap with the bolts finger tight.

22. Pry the crankshaft forward against the thrust surface of the upper half of the bearing.

23. Hold the crankshaft forward and pry the thrust bearing cap to the rear. This will align the thrust surfaces of both halves of the bearing.

24. Retain the forward pressure on the crankshaft. Tighten the cap bolts to specifications.

25. Check the crankshaft end play using the following procedures:

a. Force the crankshaft toward the rear of the engine.

b. Install a dial indicator (tools D78P-4201-F, -G or equivalent) so that the contact point rests against the crankshaft flange and the indicator axis is parallel to the crankshaft axis.

c. Zero the dial indicator. Push the crankshaft forward and note the reading on the dial.

d. If the end play exceeds the wear limit listed in the "Crankshaft and Connecting Rod Specifications" chart, replace the thrust bearing. If the end play is less than the minimum limit, inspect the thrust bearing faces for scratches, burrs, nicks, or dirt. If the thrust faces are not damaged or dirty, then they probably were not aligned properly. Lubricate and install the new thrust bearing and align the faces following procedures 21 thru 24.

26. On 6-240 and 6-300 engines with one piece rear main bearing oil seal, coat a new crankshaft rear oil seal with oil and install using Tool T65P-6701-A or equivalent. Inspect the seal to be sure it was not damaged during installation.

27. Install new bearing inserts in the connecting rods and caps. Check the clearance of each bearing, following the procedure (18.a thru d).

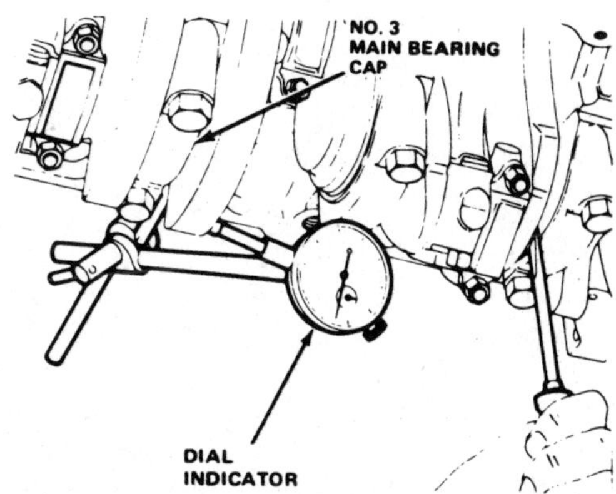

Checking crankshaft end-play with a dial indicator

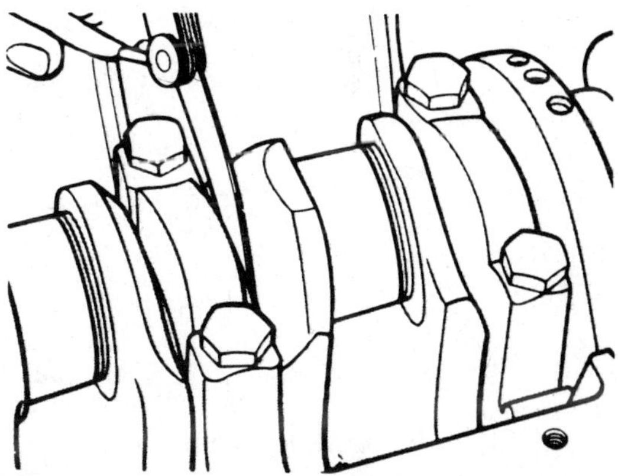
Crankshaft end play can also be checked with a feeler gauge

28. After the connecting rod bearings have been fitted, apply a light coat of engine oil to the journals and bearings.

29. Turn the crankshaft throw to the bottom of its stroke. Push the piston all the way down until the rod bearing seats on the crankshaft journal.

30. Install the connecting rod cap. Tighten the nuts to specifications.

31. After the piston and connecting rod assemblies have been installed, check the side clearance with a feeler gauge between the connecting rods on each connecting rod crankshaft journal. Refer to "Crankshaft and Connecting Rod Specifications" chart in this chapter.

32. Install the timing chain and sprockets or gears, cylinder front cover and crankshaft pulley and adapter, following steps under "Cylinder Front Cover and Timing Chain Installation" in this chapter.

Engine In Car

1. With the oil pan, oil pump and spark plugs removed, remove the cap from the main bearing needing replacement and remove the bearing from the cap.

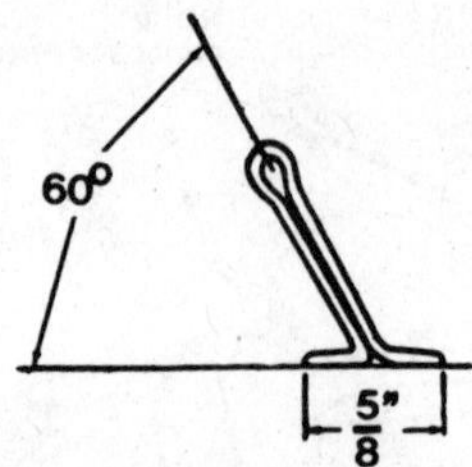

Make a bearing roll-out pin from a cotter pin

2. Make a bearing roll-out pin, using a bent cotter pin as shown in the illustration. Install the end of the pin in the oil hole in the crankshaft journal.

3. Rotate the crankshaft clockwise as viewed from the front of the engine. This will roll the upper bearing out of the block.

4. Lube the new upper bearing with clean engine oil and insert the plain (unnotched) end between the crankshaft and the indented or notched side of the block. Roll the bearing into place, making sure that the oil holes are aligned. Remove the roll pin from the oil hole.

5. Lube the new lower bearing and install it in the main bearing cap. Install the main bearing cap onto the block, making sure it is positioned in proper direction with the matchmarks in alignment.

6. Torque the main bearing cap to specification.

NOTE: *See "Crankshaft Installation" for thrust bearing alignment.*

CRANKSHAFT CLEANING AND INSPECTION

NOTE: *Handle the crankshaft carefully to avoid damage to the finish surfaces.*

1. Clean the crankshaft with solvent, and blow out all oil passages with compressed air. On the 6-240 and 6-300 engine, clean the oil seal contact surface at the rear of the crankshaft with solvent to remove any corrosion, sludge or varnish deposits.

2. Use crocus cloth to remove any sharp edges, burrs or other imperfections which might damage the oil seal during installation or cause premature seal wear.

NOTE: *Do not use crocus cloth to polish the seal surfaces. A finely polished surface may produce poor sealing or cause premature seal wear.*

3. Inspect the main and connecting rod journals for cracks, scratches, grooves or scores.

4. Measure the diameter of each journal at least four places to determine out-of-round, taper or undersize condition.

5. On an engine with a manual transmission, check the fit of the clutch pilot bearing in the bore of the crankshaft. A needle roller bearing and adapter assembly is used as a clutch pilot bearing. It is inserted directly into the engine crank shaft. The bearing and adapter assembly cannot be serviced separately. A new bearing must be installed whenever a bearing is removed.

6. Inspect the pilot bearing, when used, for roughness, evidence of overheating or loss of lubricant. Replace if any of these conditions are found.

7. On the 6-240 and 6-300 engine, inspect the rear oil seal surface of the crankshaft for deep grooves, nicks, burrs, porosity, or scratches which could damage the oil seal lip during installation. Remove all nicks and burrs with crocus cloth.

Main Bearings

1. Clean the bearing inserts and caps thoroughly in solvent, and dry them with compressed air.

NOTE: *Do not scrape varnish or gum deposits from the bearing shells.*

2. Inspect each bearing carefully. Bearings that have a scored, chipped, or worn surface should be replaced.

3. The copper-lead bearing base may be visible through the bearing overlay in small localized areas. This may not mean that the bearing is excessively worn. It is not necessary to replace the bearing if the bearing clearance is within recommended specifications.

4. Check the clearance of bearings that appear to be satisfactory with Plastigage® or its equivalent. Fit the new bearings following the procedure "Crankshaft and Main Bearings removal and installation" in this chapter.

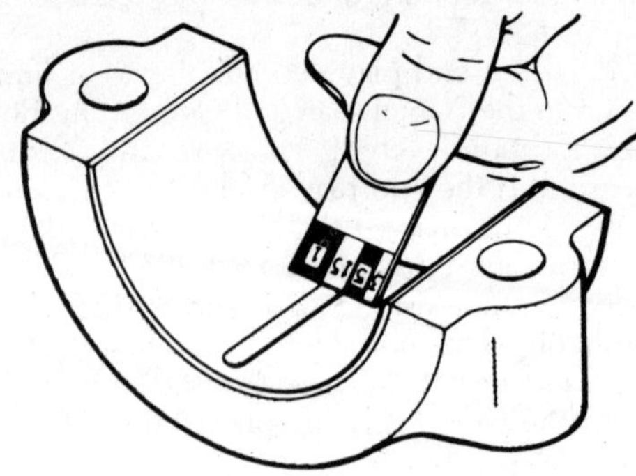

Checking main bearing clearance with Plastigage®

REGRINDING JOURNALS

NOTE: *Crankshaft regrinding should be handled by a qualified machinist.*

1. Dress minor scores with an oil stone. If the journals are severely marred or exceed the service limit, they should be reground to size for the next undersize bearing.

2. Regrind the journals to give the proper clearance with the next undersize bearing. If the journal will not clean up to maximum undersize bearing available, replace the crankshaft.

3. Always reproduce the same journal shoulder radius that existed originally. Too small a radius will result in fatigue failure of the crankshaft. Too large a radius will result in bearing failure due to radius ride of the bearing.

4. After regrinding the journals, chamfer the oil holes, then polish the journals with a #320 grit polishing cloth and engine oil. Crocus cloth may also be used as a polishing agent.

Oil Pan

REMOVAL AND INSTALLATION

240 and 300 Inline Six Cylinder

1. Drain the crankcase and also drain the cooling system.

2. Remove the radiator.

3. Raise the vehicle on a hoist.

4. Remove the engine front support insulator to support bracket nuts and washers on both supports. Raise the front of the engine with a transmission jack and wood block and place 1-inch thick wood blocks between the front support insulators and support brackets. Lower the engine and remove the transmission jack.

5. Remove the oil pan attaching bolts and lower the pan to the crossmember. Remove the 2 oil pump inlet tube and screw assembly bolts and drop the assembly in the pan. Remove the oil pan. Remove the oil pump inlet tube attaching bolts. Remove the inlet tube and screen assembly from the oil pump and leave it in the bottom of the oil pan. Remove the oil pan gaskets. Remove the inlet tube and screen from the oil pan.

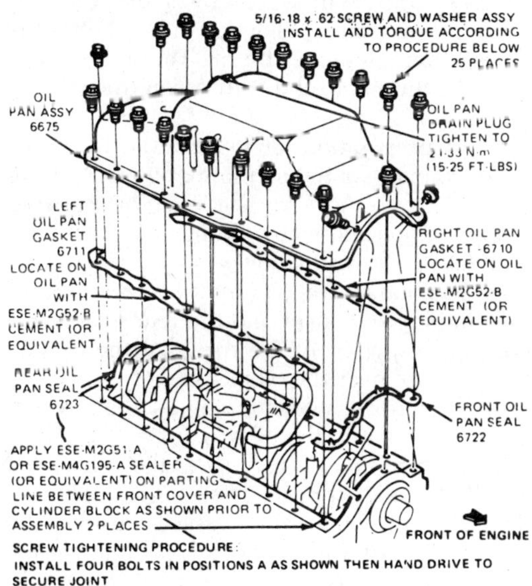

240 and 300 inline six oil pan removal

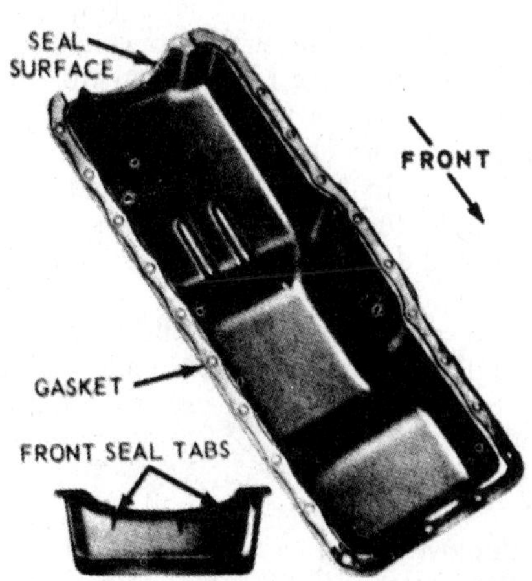

Inline six cylinder pan gasket and oil seal installation

6. Clean the gasket surfaces of the oil pump, oil pan and cylinder block. Remove the rear main bearing cap to oil pan seal and cylinder front cover to oil pan seal. Clean the seal grooves.

7. Apply oil-resistant sealer in the cavities between the bearing cap and cylinder block. Install a new seal in the rear main bearing cap and apply a bead of oil-resistant sealer to the tapered ends of the seal.

8. Install new side gaskets on the oil pan with oil-resistant sealer. Position a new oil pan to cylinder front cover seal on the oil pan.

9. Clean the inlet tube and screen assembly and place it in the oil pan.

10. Position the oil pan under the engine. Install the inlet tube and screen assembly on the oil pump with a new gasket. Tighten the screws to 5–7 ft. lb. Position the oil pan against the cylinder block and install the attaching bolts. Tighten the bolts in sequence to 10–12 ft. lb.

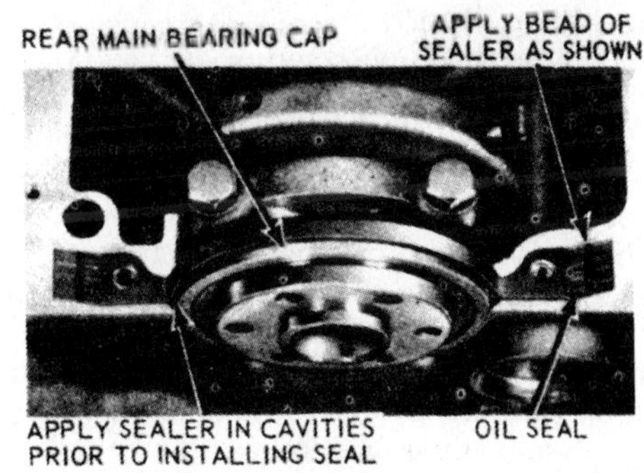

Oil pan rear seal installation on inline six cylinder engines

11. Raise the engine with a transmission jack and remove the wood blocks from the engine front supports. Lower the engine until the front support insulators are positioned on the support brackets. Install the washers and nuts on the insulator studs and tighten the nuts.
12. Install the starter and connect the starter cable.
13. Lower the vehicle. Install the radiator.
14. Fill the crankcase and cooling systm.
15. Start the engine and check for coolant and oil leaks.

8-302 1966–79

1. Remove the air cleaner and the air cleaner duct. Remove the oil dipstick and dipstick tube.
2. Drain the crankcase and remove the oil pan retaining bolts. Remove the oil pan, seals and gasket.
3. Remove the oil pump pick-up tube and screen assembly.
4. Clean the oil pump pick-up tube and screen assembly and the oil pan and cylinder block mating surfaces before reassembling the engine.
5. Position the new oil pan gasket and end seals to the cylinder block then install the oil pump pick-up tube and screen assembly with the retaining bolts and nut.
6. Position the oil pan onto the block and then install the retaining bolts.
7. Install the oil dipstick tube and the dipstick. Install the air cleaner duct and the air cleaner.

8-302, 351W 1980–and later

1. Remove the oil dipstick (on pan entry models only).
2. Remove the bolts attaching the fan shroud to the radiator and position the shroud over the fan.
3. Remove the nuts and lockwashers attaching the engine support insulators to the chassis bracket.
4. If equipped with an automatic transmission, disconnect the oil cooler line at the left side of the radiator.
5. Raise the engine and place wood blocks under the engine supports.
6. Drain the crankcase.
7. Remove the oil pan attaching bolts and lower the oil pan onto the crossmember.
8. Remove the two bolts attaching the oil pump pickup tube to the oil pump. Remove nut attaching oil pump pickup tube to the number 3 main bearing cap stud. Lower the pick-up tube and screen into the oil pan.
9. Remove the oil pan from the vehicle.
10. Clean oil pan, inlet tube and gasket surfaces. Inspect the gasket sealing surface for damages and distortion due to overtightening of the bolts. Repair and straighten as required.
11. Position a new oil pan gasket and seals to the cylinder block.
12. Position the oil pick-up tube and screen to the oil pump, and install the lower attaching bolt and gasket loosely. Install nut attaching to number 3 main bearing cap stud.
13. Place the oil pan on the crossmember. Install the upper pick-up tube bolt. Tighten the pick-up tube bolts.
14. Position the oil pan to the cylinder block and install the attaching bolts. Tighten to 10–12 ft. lb.

V6-232 and Other V8s

1. Raise and support the truck on jackstands. Remove the oil dipstick.
2. Remove the bolts attaching the fan shroud and position it over the fan.
3. Remove the engine support insulators-to-chassis bracket attaching nuts and washers. Disconnect the exhaust pipe at the manifolds.
4. If the vehicle is equipped with an automatic transmission, disconnect the oil cooler line at the left-side of the radiator.
5. Raise the engine with a jack placed under the crankshaft damper and a block of wood to act as a cushion. Place wood blocks under the engine supports.
6. Drain the crankcase. Remove the oil filter on the 460 V8.
7. Remove the oil pan attaching screws and lower the oil pan onto the crossmember. Remove the two bolts attaching the oil pump pick-up tube to the oil pump. Lower the assembly from the oil pump. Leave it in the bottom of the oil pan. Remove the oil pan and gaskets. Remove the inlet tube and screen from the oil pan.
8. In preparation for installation, clean the gasket surfaces of the oil pump, oil pan and cylinder block. Remove the rear main bearing cap-to-oil pan seal and engine front cover-to-oil pan seal. Clean the seal grooves.
9. Position the oil pan front and rear seal on the engine front cover and the rear main bearing cap, respectively. Be sure that the tabs on the seals are over the oil pan gasket.
10. Clean the inlet tube and screen assembly and place it in the oil pan.
11. Position the oil pan under the engine and install the inlet tube and screen assembly on the oil pump with a new gasket. Position the oil pan against the cylinder block and install the retaining bolts.
12. Assemble the rest of the engine in the reverse order of disassembly, starting with Step 7. Fill the crankcase with oil.

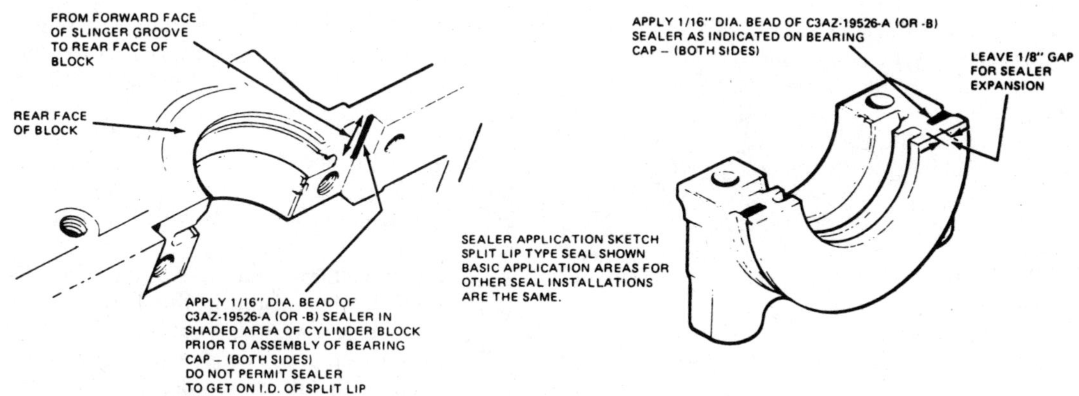

Apply RTV sealant to the main bearing cap and block on all 1974 and later gasoline engines except the 240 and 300 sixes

Rear Main Oil Seal

REPLACEMENT—TWO PIECE SEAL

All Engines 1965–73

1. Drain the crankcase and remove the oil pan, and, if necessary, the oil pump.
2. Remove the lower half of the rear main bearing cap and, after removing the old seal from the cap, drive out the pin in the bottom of the seal groove with a punch.
3. Loosen all the main bearing caps and allow the crankshaft to lower slightly.

NOTE: *Do not allow the crankshaft to drop more than 1/32 in.*

4. With a 6 in. length of 3/16 in. brazing rod, drive up on either exposed end of the top half of the oil seal. When the opposite end of the seal starts to protrude, grasp it with a pair of pliers and gently pull, while the driven end is being tapped.
5. After removing both halves of the old original rope seal and the retaining pin from the lower half of the bearing cap, carefully clean the seal grooves in the cap and block with solvent.
6. Soak the new rubber replacement seals in clean engine oil.
7. Install the upper half of the seal in the block with the undercut side of the seal toward the front of the engine. Slide the seal around the crankshaft journal until 3/8 in. protrudes beyond the base of the block.

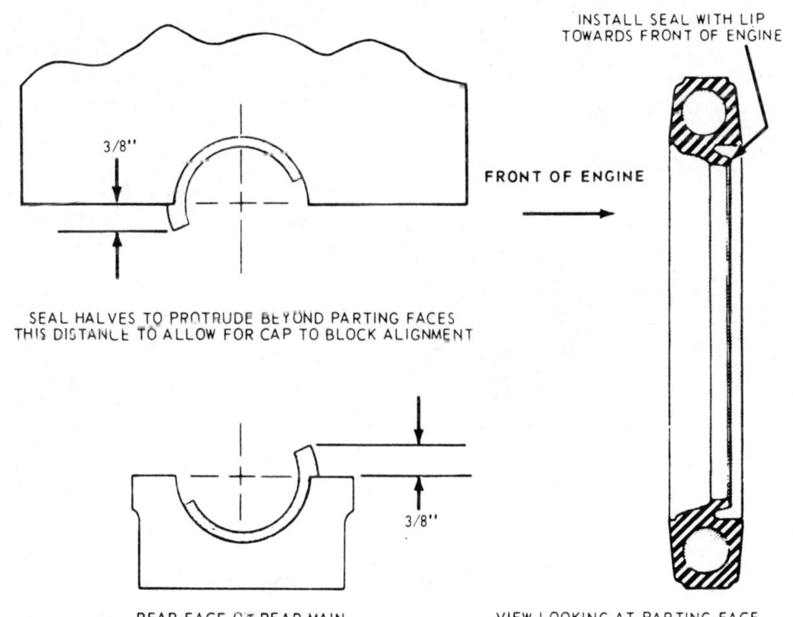

Crankshaft rear main seal installation on all V6 and V8 engines including 6.9L diesel

8. Repeat the above procedure for the lower seal, allowing an equal amount of the seal to protrude beyond the opposite end of the bearing cap.

9. Install the rear bearing cap and torque all the main bearings to the proper specification. Apply sealer only to the rear of the seals.

10. Dip the bearing cap side seals in oil, then immediately install them. Do not use any sealer on the side seals. Tap the seals into place and do not clip the protruding ends.

11. Install the oil pump and oil pan. Fill the crankcase with oil, start the engine and check for leaks.

All Engines 1974–and later Except Inline Sixes

1. Remove the oil pan and the oil pump (if required).

2. Loosen all the main bearing cap bolts, thereby lowering the crankshaft slightly but not to exceed /32 inch.

3. Remove the rear main bearing cap, and remove the oil seal from the bearing cap and cylinder block. On the block half of the seal use a seal removal tool, or install a small metal screw in one end of the seal, and pull on the screw to remove the seal. Exercise caution to prevent scratching or damaging the crankshaft seal surfaces.

4. Remove the oil seal retaining pin from the bearing cap if so equipped. The pin is not used with the split-lip seal.

5. Carefully clean the seal groove in the cap and block with a brush and solvent such as lacquer thinner, spot remover, or equivalent, orf trichlorethylene. Also, clean the area where sealer is later to be applied. Dry the area thoroughly, so that no solvent touches the seal.

6. Dip the split lip-type seal halves in clean engine oil.

7. Carefully install the upper seal (cylinder block) into its groove with undercut side of seal toward the FRONT of the engine, by rotating it on the seal journal of the crankshaft until approximately 3/8 inch protrudes below the parting surface.

Be sure no rubber has been shaved from the outside diameter of the seal by the bottom edge of the groove. Do not allow oil to get on the sealer area.

8. Tighten the remaining bearing cap bolts to the specifications listed in the Torque chart at the beginning of this chapter.

9. Install the lower seal in the rear main bearing cap with undercut side of seal toward the FRONT of the engine, allow the seal to protrude approximately 3/8 inch abovve the parting surface to mate with the upper seal when the cap is installed.

10. Apply an even 1/16 inch bead of RTF silicone rubber sealer, to the areas shown, following the procedure given in the illustration.

NOTE: *This sealer sets-up in 15 minutes.*

Install the rear main bearing cap. Tighten the cap bolts to specifications.

11. Install the oil pump and oil pan. Fill the crankcase with the proper amount and type of oil.

12. Operate the engine and check for oil leaks.

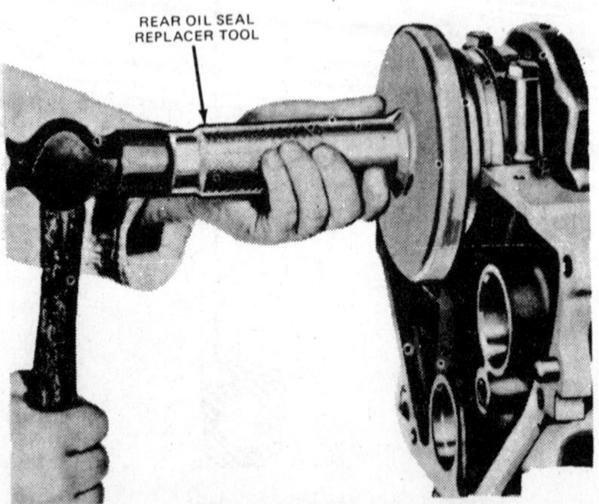

240 and 300 inline six rear oil seal installation using special tool

240 and 300 Inline Sixes

If the crankshaft rear oil seal replacement is the only operation being performed, it can be done in the vehicle as detailed in the following procedure. If the oil seal is being replaced in conjunction with a rear main bearing replacement, the engine must be removed from the vehicle and installed on a work stand.

1. Remove the starter.

2. Remove the transmission from the vehicle, following the procedures in Chapter 6.

3. On a manual-shift transmission, remove the pressure plate and cover assembly and the clutch disc following the procedure in Chapter 6.

4. Remove the flywheel attaching bolts and remove the flywheel and engine rear cover plate.

5. Use an awl to punch two holes in the crankshaft rear oil seal. Punch the holes on opposite sides of the crankshaft and just above the bearing cap to cylinder block split line. Install a sheet metal screw in each hole. Use two large screwdrivers or small pry bars and pry against both screws at the same time to remove the crankshaft rear oil seal. It may be necessary to place small blocks of wood against the cylinder block to provide a fulcrum point for the pry bars. *Use caution throughout this procedure to*

avoid scratching or otherwise damaging the crankshaft oil seal surface.

6. Clean the oil seal recess in the cylinder block and main bearing cap.

7. Clean, inspect and polish the rear oil seal rubbing surface on the crankshaft. Coat a new oil seal and the crankshaft with a light film of engine oil. Start the seal in the recess with the seal lip facing forward and install it with a seal driver. Keep the tool straight with the centerline of the crankshaft and install the seal until the tool contacts the cylinder block surface. Remove the tool and inspect the seal to be sure it was not damaged during installation.

8. Install the engine rear cover plate. Position the flywheel on the crankshaft flange. Coat the threads of the flywheel attaching bolts with oil-resistant sealer and install the bolts. Tighten the bolts in sequence across from each other to the specifications listed in the Torque chart at the beginning of this Chapter.

9. On a manual-shift transmission, install the clutch disc and the pressure plate assembly following the procedure in Chapter 6.

10. Install the transmission, following the procedure in Chapter 6.

6.9L Diesel V8

1. Remove the transmission, clutch and flywheel assemblies.

2. Remove the engine rear cover.

3. Using an arbor press and a 4⅛ in. diameter spacer, press out the rear oil seal from the cover.

4. To install, clean the rear cover and engine block surfaces. Remove all traces of old RTV sealant from the oil pan and rear cover sealing surface by cleaning with a suitable solvent and drying thoroughly.

5. Coat the new rear oil seal with Lubriplate® or equivalent. Using an arbor press and spacer, install the new seal into the cover.

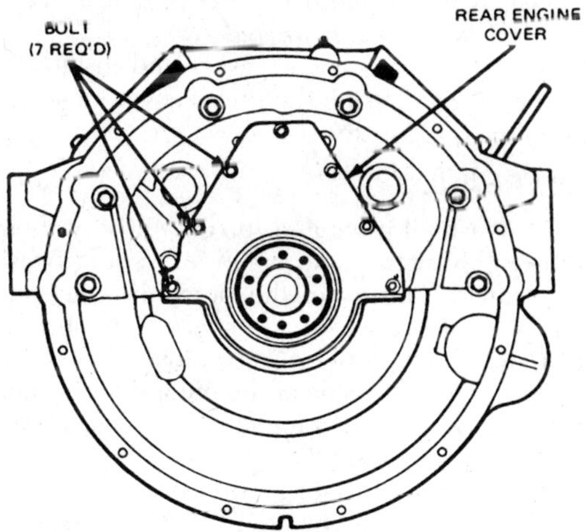

6.9L diesel rear cover removal

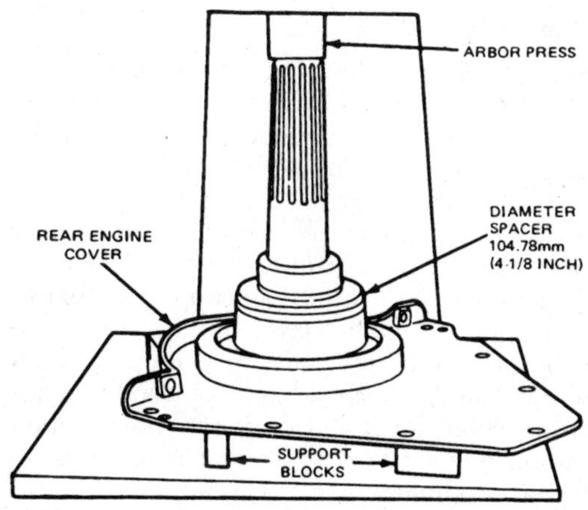

The 6.9L diesel rear oil seal must be pressed in and out

NOTE: *The seal must be installed from the engine block side of the rear cover, flush with the seal bore inner surface.*

6. Install a seal pilot, Ford part no. T83T-6701B or equivalent onto the crankshaft.

7. Apply gasket sealant to the engine block gasket surfaces, and install the rear cover gasket to the engine.

8. Apply a ¼ in. bead of RTV sealant onto the oil pan sealing surface, *immediately* after rear cover installation.

9. Push the rear cover into position on the engine and install the cover bolts. Torque to specification.

10. Position the flywheel on the crankshaft flange. Coat the threads of the flywheel attaching bolts with sealant and install the bolts and flexplate, if equipped. Torque the bolts to specification, alternating across from each bolt.

11. Install the clutch and transmission. Run the engine and check for oil leaks.

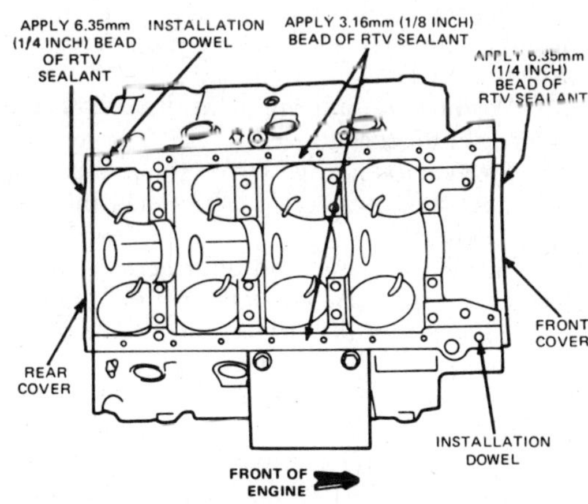

Oil pan sealer application, 6.9L diesel

One Piece Seal

1. Remove the transmission, clutch assembly or converter and flywheel.
2. (See Step 7 for diesel engines). Lower the oil pan if necessary for working room.
3. On engines except 2.2L and 6.9L diesels, use an awl to punch two small holes on opposite sides of the seal just above the split between the main bearing cap and engine block. Install a sheet metal screw in each hole. Use two small pry bars and pry evenly on both screws using two small blocks of wood as a fulcrum point for the pry bars. Use caution throughout to avoid scratching or damage to the oil seal mounting surfaces.
4. When the seal has been removed, clean the mounting recess.
5. Coat the seal and block mounting surfaces with oil. Apply white lube to the contact surface of the seal and crankshaft. Start the seal into the mounting recess and install with seal mounting tool Ford number T82L–6701–A or equivalent.
6. Install the remaining components in the reverse.
7. On the 2.2L and 6.9L diesel engines; the oil seal is one piece but mounted on a retaining plate. Remove the mounting plate from the rear of the engine and replace the seal. Reinstall in reverse order of removal.

Oil Pump

REMOVAL AND INSTALLATION

Except V6

1. Remove the oil pan.
2. Remove the oil pump inlet tube and screen assembly.
3. Remove the oil pump attaching bolts and remove the oil pump gasket and intermediate driveshaft.
4. Before installing the oil pump, prime it by filling the inlet and outlet port with engine oil and rotating the shaft of the pump to distribute it.
5. Position the intermediate driveshaft into the distributor socket.
6. Position the new gasket on the pump body and insert the intermediate driveshaft into the pump body.
7. Install the pump and intermediate driveshaft as an assembly. *Do not force the pump if it does not seat readily.* The driveshaft may be misaligned with the distributor shaft. To align it, rotate the intermediate driveshaft into a new position.
8. Install the oil pump attaching bolts and torque them to 12–15 ft. lbs. on the inline sixes and to 20–25 ft. lbs. on the V8s.

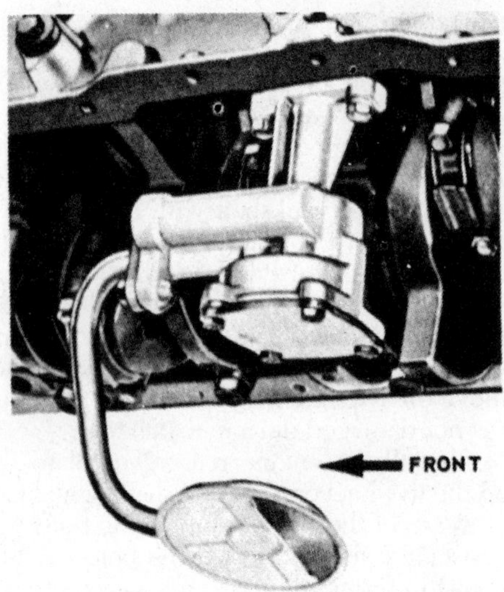

Typical six cylinder oil pump; V8 pumps similar

V6

Unlike the inline sixes and V8s, the 232 V6 oil pump is mounted on the engine front timing cover.

1. Remove the oil filter. The oil pump is the assembly to which the filter screws.
2. Remove the oil pump cover attaching bolts, and remove the cover.
3. Lift the pump gears out of the pocket in the front cover, and remove the cover gasket and discard.
4. To install, make sure the gear pocket is lightly packed with petroleum jelly, or liberally coat all the gear surfaces with an oil conditioner or heavy engine oil. *Do not use chassis lubricants.*
5. Install the gears in the cover pocket, making sure the petroleum jelly fills all voids between the gears and the pocket.

   CAUTION: *Failure to coat the oil pump gears may result in failure of the pump to prime when the engine is started.*
6. Position the cover gasket and install the pump cover. Torque the pump cover attaching bolts to 18–22 ft. lbs.

OVERHAUL

1. Wash all parts in a solvent and dry them thoroughly with compressed air. Use a brush to clean the inside of the pump housing and the pressure relief valve chamber. Be sure all dirt and metal particles are removed.
2. Check the inside of the pump housing and the outer race and rotor for damage or excessive wear or scoring.
3. Check the mating surface of the pump cover for wear. If the cover mating surface is worn, scored or grooved, replace the pump.

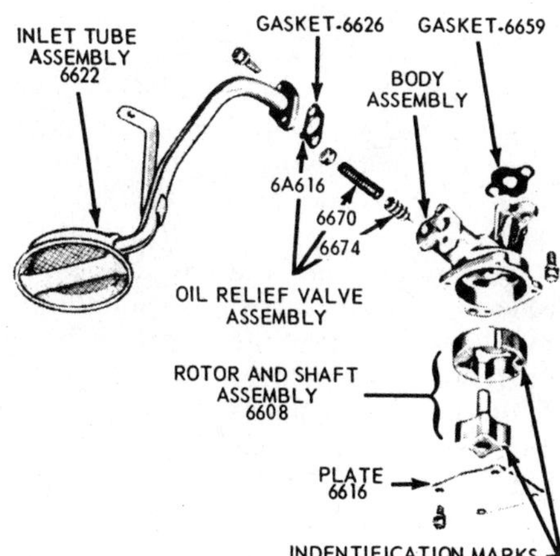

Exploded view of the typical V8 oil pump

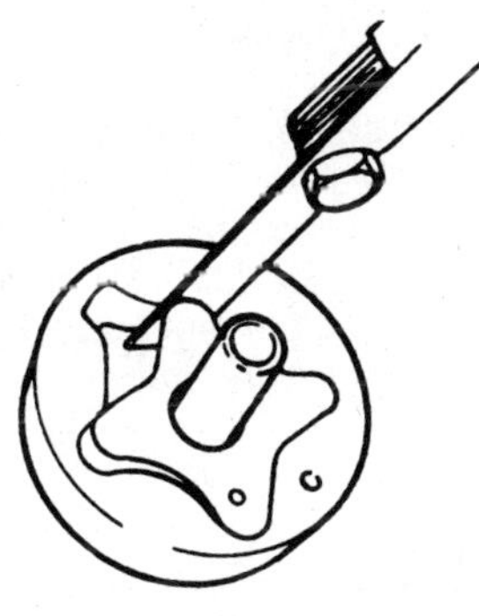

Checking inner rotor tip clearance

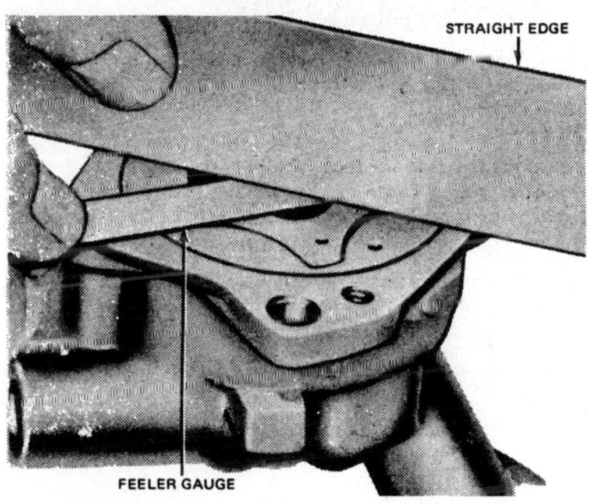

Checking rotor end play

4. Measure the inner rotor tip clearance.

5. With the rotor assembly installed in the housing, place a straight edge over the rotor assembly and the housing. Measure the clearance (rotor end play) between the straight edge and the rotor and the outer race.

6. Check the drive shaft to housing bearing clearance by measuring the OD of the shaft and the ID of the housing bearing.

7. Components of the oil pump are not serviced. If any part of the oil pump requires replacement, replace the complete pump assembly.

8. Inspect the relief valve spring to see if it is collapsed or worn.

9. Check the relief valve piston for scores and free operation in the bore.

Oil Cooler

REMOVAL AND INSTALLATION

6.9L Diesel

The diesel oil cooler should be disassembled if the cooler O-rings begin to leak.

1. Gently rap the front and oil cooler headers to loosen the O-rings. Carefully twist the oil cooler apart.

2. Using a suitable solvent, thoroughly clean the oil cooler and the front and filter headers.

3. Always use new O-rings when reassembling. Lubricate the new rings and all O-ring mating surfaces with clean engine oil. Install the two narrow O-rings into their respective grooves inside the front and filter headers.

4. Place the large O-ring over the oil cooler shell.

5. Press the assembly together, making sure the locating clips align in the slots.

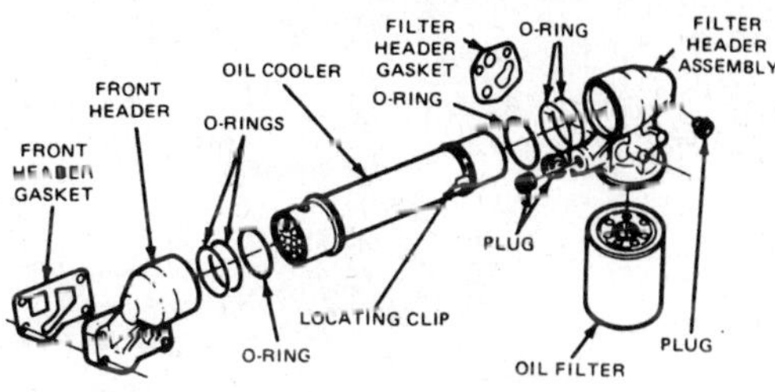

6.9L diesel oil cooler and filter assembly

Flywheel and Ring Gear

REMOVAL AND INSTALLATION

1. Remove the transmission, following the procedures in chapter 6 "Clutch and Transmission".

2. On a manual-shift transmission, remove the clutch pressure plate and cover assembly and clutch disc, following the procedures in Chapter 6 "Clutch and Transmission".

3. Remove the flywheel attaching bolts and remove the flywheel.

4. Position the flywheel on the crankshaft flange. Coat the threads of the flywheel attach-

ing bolts with Loctite® or equivalent and install the bolts. Tighten the bolts in sequence across from each other to 75–85 ft. lbs. on all except the diesel. Torque the diesel bolts in sequence across from each other to 38 ft. lbs.

5. On a manual shift transmission, install the clutch disc and pressure plate and cover assembly following the procedures in Chapter 6 "Clutch and Transmission".

6. Install the transmission following the procedure in Chapter 6 "Clutch and Transmission".

RING GEAR REPLACEMENT

NOTE: *This procedure is for manual-shift transmission only. On automatic transmission if the ring gear has worn, chipped or cracked teeth, replace the flywheel assembly.*

1. Heat the ring gear with a blow torch on the engine side of the gear, and knock it off the flywheel. *Do not hit the flywheel when removing the ring gear.*

2. Heat the new ring gear evenly until the gear expands enough to slip onto the flywheel. Make sure the gear is properly seated against the shoulder. Do not heat any part of the gear more than 500 degrees F. If this limit is exceeded, the hardness will be removed from the ring gear teeth.

ENGINE COOLING

The satisfactory performance of any engine is controlled to a great extent by the proper operation of the cooling system. The engine block is fully waterjacketed to prevent distortion of the cylinder walls. Directed cooling and water holes in the cylinder head causes water to flow past the valve seats, which are one of the hottest parts of any engine, to carry heat away from the valves and seats.

The minimum temperature of the coolant is controlled by the thermostat, mounted in the coolant outlet passage of the engine. When the coolant temperature is below the temperature rating of the thermostat, the thermostat remains closed and the coolant is directed through the radiator by-pass hose to the water pump and back into the engine. When the coolant temperature reaches the temperature rating of the thermostat, the thermostat opens and allows coolant to flow past it and into the top of the radiator. The radiator dissipates the excess engine heat

The cooling system is pressurized and operating pressure is regulated by the rating of the radiator cap which contains a relief valve. The reason for a pressurized cooling system is to allow for higher engine operating temperatures with a higher coolant boiling point.

Radiator

REMOVAL AND INSTALLATION

1. Drain the cooling system.

2. Disconnect the transmission cooling lines from the bottom of the radiator, if so equipped.

3. Remove the retaining bolts at each of the 4 corners of the shroud, if so equipped, and

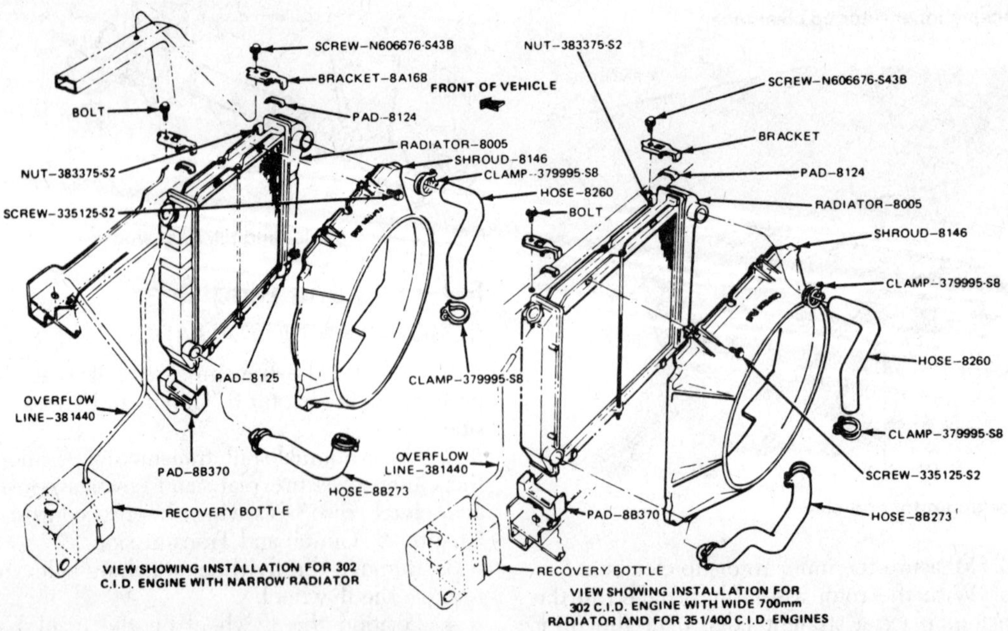

Radiator assembly, late models

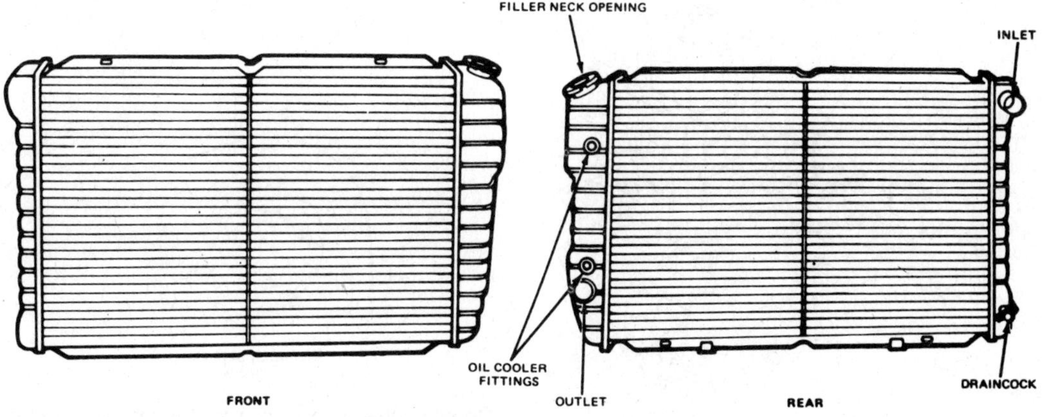

Typical crossflow radiator. Diesel models use vertical-flow radiator

position the shroud over the fan, clear of the radiator.

4. Disconnect the upper and lower hoses from the radiator.

5. Remove the radiator retaining bolts or the upper supports and lift the radiator from the vehicle.

6. Install the radiator in the reverse order of removal. Fill the cooling system and check for leaks.

Water Pump

REMOVAL AND INSTALLATION

Inline 6 Cylinder Engines

1. Drain the cooling system.
2. Disconnect the lower radiator hose from the water pump.
3. Remove the drive belt, fan, fan spacer, fan shroud, if so equipped, and water pump pulley. On the 6-240 and 6-300, remove the alternator pivot arm from the pump.
4. Disconnect the heater hose at the water pump.
5. Remove the water pump.
6. Before installing the old water pump, clean the gasket mounting surfaces on the pump and on the cylinder block. If a new water pump is being installed, remove the heater hose fitting from the old pump and install it on the new one. Coat the new gaskets with sealer on both sides and install the water pump in the reverse order of removal.

V8 and V6 Engines

NOTE: *See Timing Cover procedures for diesel water pump removal and installation and pump bolt installation illustration.*

1. Drain the cooling system.
2. Remove the bolts securing the fan shroud to the radiator, if so equipped, and position the shroud over the fan.
3. Disconnect the lower radiator hose, heater hose and by-pass hose at the water pump. Remove the drive belts, fan, fan spacer and pulley. Remove the fan shroud, if so equipped.

NOTE: *On the 1978–79 351M and 400 V8's it is necessary to remove the air conditioning compressor from the pump. Do not disconnect any refrigerant lines! Simply support the compressor out of the way!*

4. Loosen the alternator pivot bolt and the bolt attaching the alternator adjusting arm to the water pump. Remove the power steering pump bracket from the water pump and position it out of the way.
5. Remove the bolts securing the water pump to the timing chain cover and remove the water pump.
6. Install the water pump in the reverse order of removal, using a new gasket.

Thermostat

REMOVAL AND INSTALLATION

1. Drain the cooling system below the level of the coolant outlet housing. Use the petcock valve at the bottom of the radiator to drain the system. It is not necessary to remove any of the hoses.
2. Remove the coolant outlet housing retaining bolts and slide the housing with the hose attached to one side.
3. Turn the thermostat counterclockwise to unlock it from the outlet.
4. Remove the gasket from the engine block and clean both mating surfaces.
5. To install the thermostat, coat a new gasket with water resistant sealer and position it on the outlet of the engine. The gasket must be in place before the thermostat is installed.
6. Install the thermostat with the bridge (opposite end from the spring) inside the elbow connection and turn it clockwise to lock it in

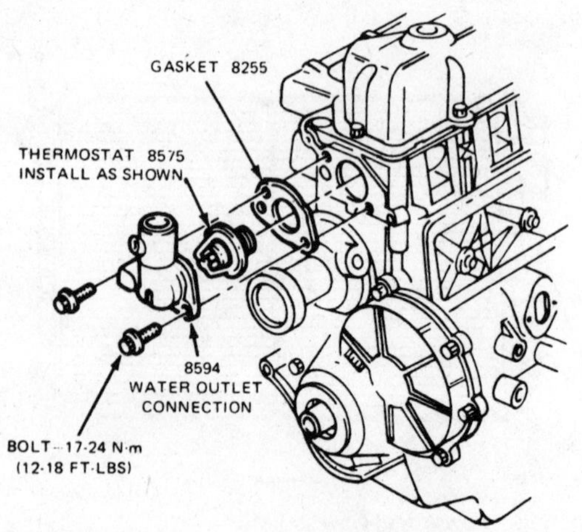

Inline six cylinder thermostat installation. V8 thermostat mounted vertically on front of engine, diesel is on side of front of intake manifold

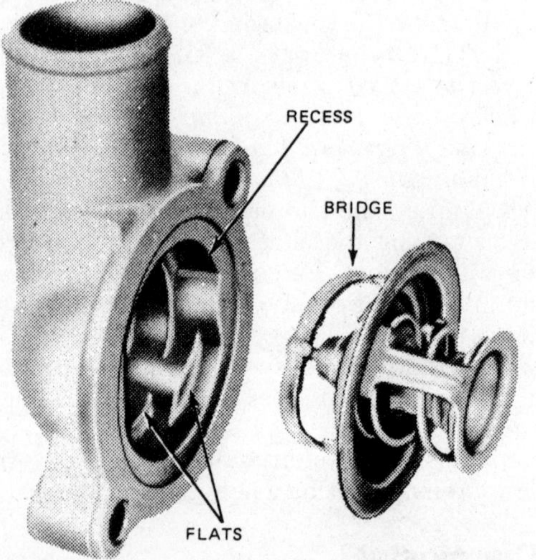

Thermostat spring always faces "down" in all engines

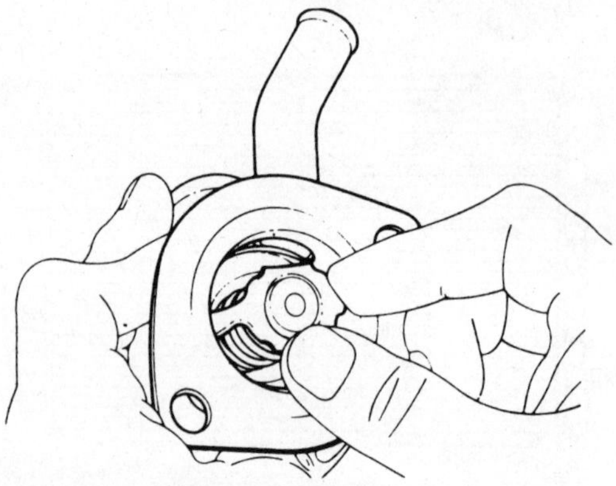

On all gasoline engines, turn the thermostat clockwise to lock it into position on the flats in the outlet elbow

position, with the bridge against the flats cast into the elbow connection.

7. Position the elbow connection onto the mounting surface of the outlet, so that the thermostat flange is resting on the gasket and install the retaining bolts.

8. Fill the radiator and operate the engine until it reaches operating temperature. Check the coolant level and adjust as necessary.

NOTE: *It is a good practice to check the operation of a new thermostat before it is installed in an engine. Place the thermostat in a pan of boiling water. If it does not open more than ¼ in., do not install it in the engine.*

Emission Controls and Fuel System

4

There are three types of automobile pollutants that concern automotive engineers: crankcase fumes, exhaust gases—oxides of nitrogen (NO_x) and carbon monoxide (CO) and gasoline vapors from evaporation. The devices and systems used to limit these pollutants are commonly called emission control equipment.

The emission control devices required on a Ford truck are determined by the weight classification. Light duty models use the same emission controls as passenger cars; these are generally those with a GVW (Gross Vehicle Weight) of 6000 pounds or less. Heavy duty models operate under less stringent rules and use a few less devices; these are generally those with a GVW over 6000 lbs.

CRANKCASE EMISSION CONTROLS

The crankcase emission control equipment consists of a positive crankcase ventilation (PCV) valve, a closed or open oil filler cap and the hoses that connect this equipment.

When the engine is running, a small portion of the gases which are formed in the combustion chamber leak by the piston rings and enter the crankcase. Since these gases are under pressure they tend to escape from the crankcase and enter into the atmosphere. If these gases were allowed to remain in the crankcase for any length of time, they would contaminate the engine oil and cause sludge to build up. If the gases are allowed to escape into the atmosphere, they would pollute the air, as they contain unburned hydrocarbons. The crankcase emission control equipment recycles these gases back into the engine combustion chamber, where they are burned.

Crankcase gases are recycled in the following manner. While the engine is running, clean filtered air is drawn into the crankcase either directly through the oil filler cap or through

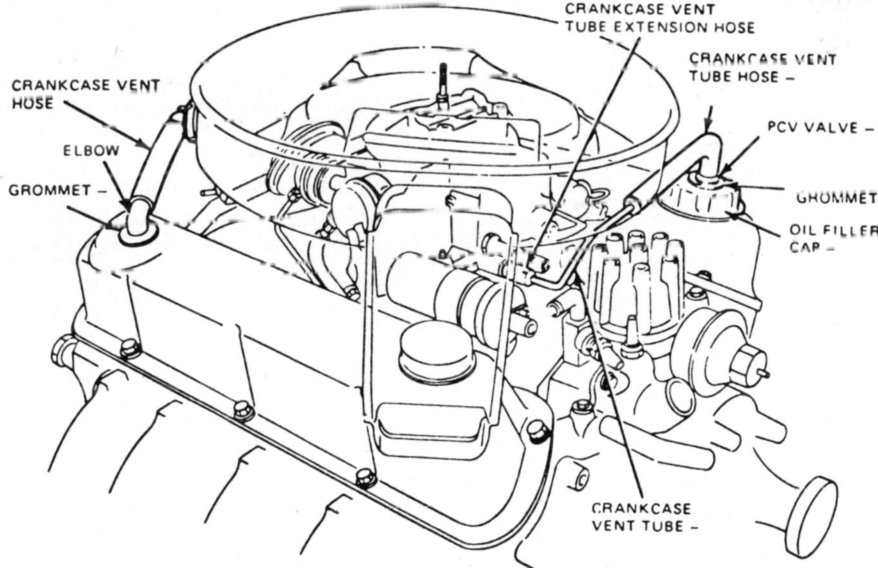

Positive Crankcase Ventilation system—V8 engines

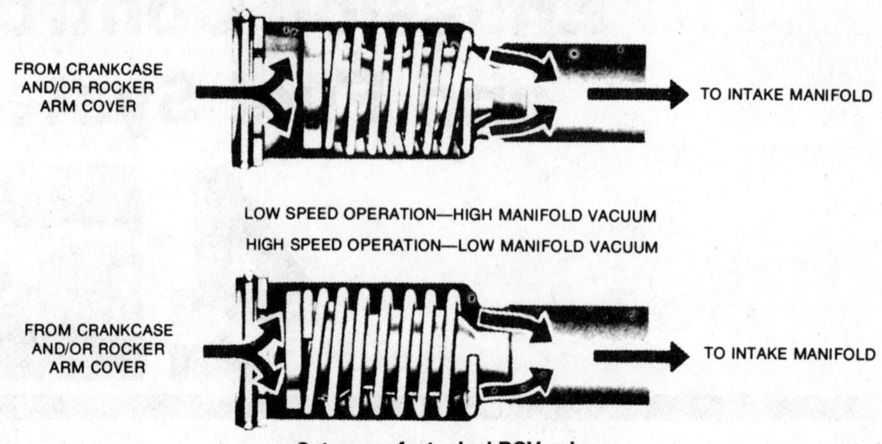

Cutaway of a typical PCV valve

the carburetor air filter and then through a hose leading to the oil filler cap. As the air passes through the crankcase it picks up the combustion gases and carries them out of the crankcase, up through the PCV valve and into the intake manifold. After they enter the intake manifold they are drawn into the combustion chamber and are burned.

The most critical component of the system is the PCV valve. This vacuum-controlled valve regulates the amount of gases which are recycled into the combustion chamber. At low engine speeds the valve is partially closed, limiting the flow of gases into the intake manifold. As engine speed increases, the valve opens to admit greater quantities of the gases into the intake manifold. If the valve should become blocked or plugged, the gases will be prevented from escaping the crankcase by the normal route. Since these gases are under pressure, they will find their own way out of the crankcase. This alternate route is usually a weak oil seal or gasket in the engine. As the gas escapes by the gasket, it also creates an oil leak. Besides causing oil leaks, a clogged PCV valve also allows these gases to remain in the crankcase for an extended period of time, promoting the formation of sludge in the engine.

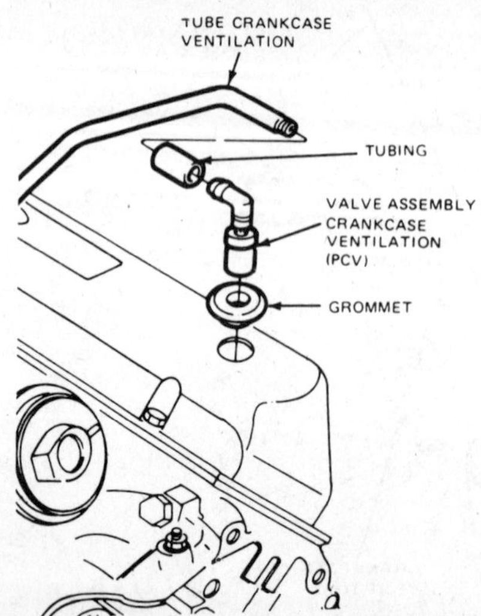

PCV valve mounting in valve cover, V8 shown. V6 and inline six similar

The above explanation and the troubleshooting procedure which follows applies to all of the engines installed in Ford trucks, since all are equipped with PCV systems.

TROUBLESHOOTING

With the engine running, pull the PCV valve and hose from the valve rocker cover rubber grommet.

A hissing noise should be heard as air passes through the valve and a strong vacuum should be felt when you place a finger over the valve inlet if the valve is working properly. While you have your finger over the PCV valve inlet, check for vacuum leaks in the hose and at the connections.

When the PCV valve is removed from the engine, a metallic clicking noise should be heard when it is shaken. This indicates that the metal check ball inside the valve is still free and is not gummed up.

REPLACEMENT

1. Pull the PCV valve and hose from the rubber grommet in the rocker cover.
2. Remove the PCV valve from the hose. Inspect the inside of the PCV valve. If it is dirty, disconnect it from the intake manifold and clean it in a suitable, safe solvent.

To install, proceed as follows:

1. If the PCV valve hose was removed, connect it to the intake manifold.

2. Connect the PCV valve to its hose.
3. Install the PCV valve into the rubber grommet in the valve rocker cover.

EVAPORATIVE EMISSION CONTROLS

Beginning in 1970, F-100 pick-ups produced for sale in California were equipped with evaporative emission controls on the fuel system. For 1971, the system was modified somewhat and used on all F-100 pick-ups as standard equipment.

After 1974, F-250 pick-ups sold in California were equipped with the evaporative emission system.

Changes in atmospheric temperature cause fuel tanks to "breathe"; that is, the air within the tank expands and contracts with outside temperature changes. As the temperature rises, air escapes through the tank vent tube or the vent in the tank cap. The air which escapes contains gasoline vapors. In a similar manner, the gasoline which fills the carburetor float bowl expands when the engine is stopped. Engine heat causes this expansion. The vapors escape through the carburetor and air cleaner.

The Evaporative Emission Control System provides a sealed fuel system with the capability to store and condense fuel vapors. The system has three parts: a fill control vent system; a vapor vent and storage system; and a pressure and vacuum relief system (special fill cap).

The fill control vent system is a modification to the fuel tank. It uses a dome air space within the tank which is 10–12% of the tank's volume. The air space is sufficient to provide for the thermal expansion of the fuel. The space also serves as part of the in-tank vapor vent system.

The in-tank vent system consists of the dome air space previously described and a vapor separator assembly. The separator assembly is mounted to the top of the fuel tank and is secured by a cam-lock-ring, similar to the one which secures the fuel sending unit. Foam material fills the vapor separator assembly. The foam material separates raw fuel and vapors, thus retarding the entrance of fuel into the vapor line.

From 1971 and later the vapor separator is an orifice valve located in the dome of the tank. The restricted size of the orifice (0.050 in.) tends to allow only vapor to pass out of the tank. The orifice valve is connected to the vent line which runs forward to the carbon-filled canister in the engine compartment.

The sealed filler cap has a pressure-vacuum relief valve. Under normal operating conditions, the filler cap operates as a check valve, allowing air to enter the tank to replace the fuel consumed. At the same time, it prevents vapors from escaping through the cap. In case of excessive pressure within the tank, the filler cap valve opens to relieve the pressure.

Because the filler cap is sealed, fuel vapors have only one place through which they may escape—the vapor separator assembly at the top of the fuel tank. The vapors pass through the foam material and continue through a single vapor line which leads to a canister in the engine compartment. The canister is filled with activated charcoal.

Another vapor line runs from the top of the carburetor float chamber to the charcoal canister.

As the fuel vapors (hydrocarbons), enter the charcoal canister, they are absorbed by the charcoal. The air is dispelled through the open bottom of the charcoal canister, leaving the hydrocarbons trapped within the charcoal. When the engine is started, vacuum causes fresh air to be drawn into the canister from its open bottom. The fresh air passes through the charcoal picking up the hydrocarbons which are trapped there and feeding them into the carburetor for burning with the fuel mixture.

EXHAUST EMISSION CONTROLS

There are many devices used on the engines installed in Ford pick-ups to control emission of exhaust gases into the atmosphere.

All of the engines may use the air injection reactor system, the Ford terminology for which is the "Thermactor" exhaust emission control system. This system is used on all engines, from 1970 to the present.

The exhaust emission control air injection system consists of a belt-driven air pump, which directs compressed air through connecting hoses to an air manifold and through air nozzles in the exhaust ports adjacent to each exhaust valve. The air, with its normal oxygen content, reacts with the hot, but incompletely burned exhaust gases and permits further combustion in the exhaust port or manifold.

Another emission control system common to all of the engines since 1974 is the Exhaust Gas Recirculation (EGR) system. This system is designed to reduce the amount of oxides of nitrogen (NO_x) emitted into the atmosphere by reintroducing small amounts of exhaust gas into the combustion cycle. The amount of recycled exhaust gas depends chiefly on engine vacuum and temperature.

New for 1975 models is the catalytic converter. The converter is a muffler-type device installed in the vehicle's exhaust system containing a chemical catalyst. When exhaust gases pass over and through the catalyst, further chemical reaction occurs and the pollutants are broken down into harmless elements.

The above paragraphs are just a brief summary of the main exhaust emission control systems. Individual components of the various systems, their functions, construction, and repair are discussed further in the following sections.

Air Pump

The air injection pump is a positive-displacement vane type which is permanently lubricated and requires little periodic maintenance. The only serviceable parts on the air pump are the exhaust tube and relief valve. The relief valve decreases the airflow when the pump pressure reaches a preset level. This occurs at high engine rpm. The relief valve also serves to prevent damage to the pump and to limit maximum exhaust manifold temperatures.

Inlet air for the Thermactor system is cleaned by a centrifugal filter fan mounted on the air pump driveshaft, thus an element-type air cleaner (filter) is not required.

The air supply from the air pump is controlled by the air by-pass valve. Normally, the air by-pass valve is closed and the air is directed to the check valve(s) and air manifold(s) for distribution to the cylinder head exhaust ports. During engine deceleration, the air by-pass valve opens and air delivery to the cylinder head exhaust ports is momentarily diverted to the atmosphere.

A check valve is used in the inlet air side of the air manifold(s) to prevent exhaust gases from flowing back into the air pump and air by-pass valve during the air by-pass cycle or during air pump and/or drive belt failure.

Air Delivery Manifold

The air delivery manifold distributes the air from the pump to each of the air delivery tubes in a uniform manner. This applies only to the 6 cylinder engines, as the air delivery manifold is integral with the cylinder head on the V8 engines.

Air By-Pass Valve

The air by-pass valve prevents engine backfire by briefly interrupting the air being injected into the exhaust manifold during periods of deceleration or rapid throttle closure. The valve opens when a sudden increase in manifold vacuum overcomes the diaphragm spring tension. With the valve in the open position, the airflow is vented to the atmosphere. In addition to preventing backfiring in the exhaust manifold as previously mentioned, the valve also prevents possible damage to the engine by not allowing the overly rich fuel mixture from being burned in the exhaust manifold. A rich mixture in the exhaust manifold is the result of deceleration or rapid throttle closure and to promote its further combustion by injecting air would cause backfiring.

Carburetor

The carburetors used on engines equipped with emission controls have specific flow characteristics that differ from the carburetors used on vehicles not equipped with emission control devices. All carburetors have limiter caps installed on the idle fuel mixture adjustment screws. These limiter caps prevent an overly rich mixture adjustment from being made. The correct adjustment can usually be reached within the range of the limiter caps. These carburetors are identified by number. The same type carburetor should be used when replacement is necessary.

Thermostatically Controlled Air Cleaner System (TAC)

This system consists of a heat shroud which is integral with the right-side exhaust manifold, a hot air hose and a special air cleaner assembly equipped with a thermal sensor and vacuum motor and air valve assembly.

The temperature of the carburetor intake air is thermostatically controlled by means of a valve plate and a vacuum override built into a duct assembly attached to the air cleaner. The exhaust manifold shroud tube is attached to the shroud over the exhaust manifold for the source of heated air.

The thermal sensor is attached to the air valve actuating lever, along with the vacuum motor lever, both of which control the position of the air valve to supply either heated air from the exhaust manifold or cooler air from the engine compartment.

During the warm-up period, when the under-the-hood temperatures are low, the thermal sensor doesn't exert enough tension on the air valve actuating lever to close (heat off) the air valve. Thus, the carburetor receives heated air from around the exhaust manifold.

As the temperature of the air entering the air cleaner approaches approximately 100° F, the thermal sensor begins to push on the air valve actuating lever and overcome the spring tension which holds the air valve in the open

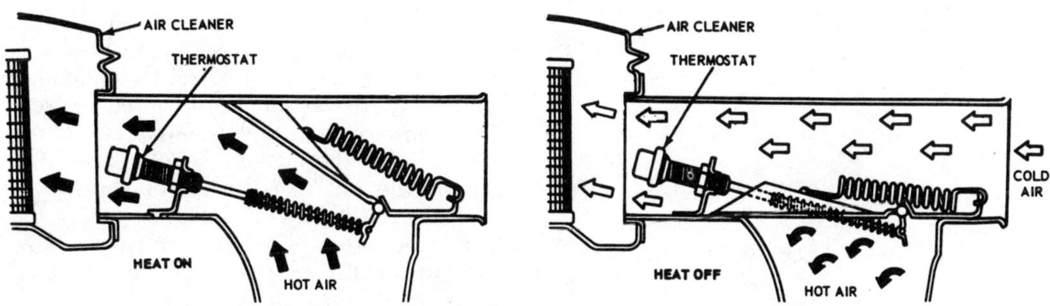

Operation of the thermostatically-controlled air cleaner

(heat on) position. The air valve begins to move to the closed (heat off) position, allowing only under-the-hood air to enter the air cleaner.

The air valve in the air cleaner will also open, regardless of the air temperature, during heavy acceleration to obtain maximum airflow through the air cleaner. The extreme decrease in intake manifold vacuum during heavy acceleration permits the vacuum motor to override the thermostatic control. This opens the system to both heated air and air from the engine compartment.

The purpose of TAC is to get hot air into the carburetor as soon as possible because the engine will emit less pollutants on a lean mixture.

Dual Diaphragm Distributor

The dual diaphragm distributor has two diaphragms which operate independently. The outer (primary) diaphragm makes use of carburetor vacuum to advance the ignition timing. The inner (secondary) diaphragm uses intake manifold vacuum to provide additional retardation of ignition timing during closed-throttle deceleration and idle, resulting in the reduction of hydrocarbon emissions.

Ported Vacuum Switch Valve (PVS)

The PVS valve is a temperature sensing valve usually found on the distributor vacuum advance line, and is installed in the coolant outlet elbow. During prolonged periods of idle, or any other situation which causes engine operating temperatures to be higher than normal, the valve, which under normal conditions simply connects the vacuum advance diaphragm to its vacuum source within the carburetor, closes the normal source vacuum port and engages an alternate source vacuum port. This alternate

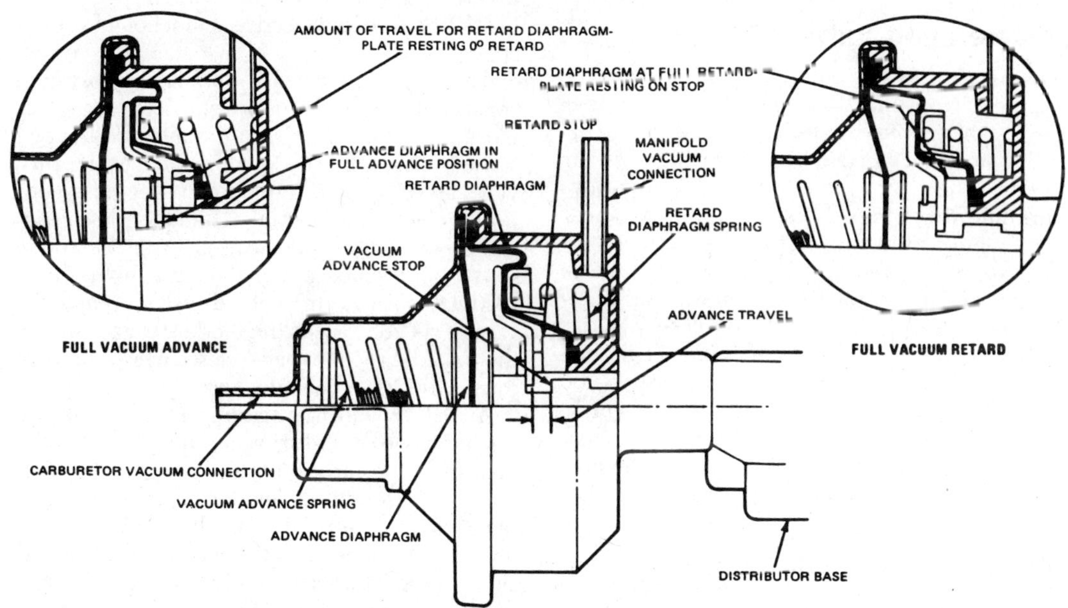

Dual diaphragm vacuum advance and retard mechanism for the distributor

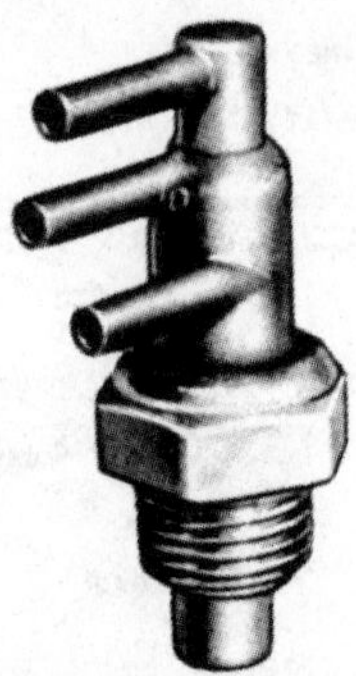

A ported vacuum switch

source is from the intake manifold which, under idle conditions, maintains a high vacuum. This increase in vacuum supply to the distributor diaphragm advances the timing, increasing the idle speed. The increase in idle speed causes a directly proportional increase in the operation of the cooling system. When the engine has cooled sufficiently, the vacuum supply is returned to its normal source, the carburetor.

These switches are used in several places in the emission systems. They can have anywhere from two to four ports and can be used to turn vacuum on and off, or to switch between two vacuum sources for a third delivery point.

When cold, a typical three-port PVS provides a path through the center and top holes. When hot, the top port is closed off and the center and bottom ports are open. The vacuum sources would be connected to the top and bottom ports.

Deceleration Valve

Some engines were equipped with a distributor vacuum advance control valve (deceleration valve) which is used with dual diaphragm distributors to further aid in controlling ignition timing. The deceleration valve is in the vacuum line which runs from the outer (advance) diaphragm to the carburetor, the normal vacuum supply for the distributor. During deceleration, the intake manifold vacuum rises causing the deceleration valve to close off the carburetor vacuum source and connect the intake manifold vacuum source to the distributor advance diaphragm. The increase in vacuum provides maximum ignition timing advance, thus providing more complete fuel combustion and decreasing exhaust system backfiring.

Exhaust Gas Recirculation System (EGR)

There are two types of EGR valves; one vacuum operated, and the other (only found on EEC systems) electrically operated. In the first system, a vacuum-operated EGR flow valve is attached to the carburetor spacer (except on the 302 V8). A passage in the carburetor spacer mates with a hole in the mounting face of the EGR valve or the intake manifold. The EGR valve on the 302 V8 is located on the rear of the intake manifold. On all engines except the 302 V8, the system allows exhaust gases to flow from the exhaust crossover, through the control valve and through the spacer into the intake manifold below the carburetor. For those engines where exhaust gases cannot be picked up from the exhaust crossover (6 cylinder) as described above, the gases are picked up from the choke stove located on the exhaust manifold or directly from the exhaust manifold. The exhaust gases are routed to the carburetor spacer through steel tubing.

The vacuum signal which operates the EGR valve originates at the EGR vacuum port in the carburetor. This signal is controlled by at least one, and sometimes, two series of valves.

A water temperature sensing valve (the EGR PVS) which is closed until the water temperature reaches either 60° F or 125° F, depending on application, is always used.

The position of the EGR vacuum port in the carburetor and calibration of the EGR valve can be varied to give the required modulation of EGR during acceleration and low speed cruise conditions. However, a more complicated system using a second series valve is sometimes needed to provide control of EGR for accepting engine operation at high speed cruise conditions. The second valve: the high speed modulator valve, is controlled as a function of vehicle speed.

The high speed EGR modulator subsystem consists of a speed sensor, an electronic module and a solenoid vacuum valve. The speed sensor, driven by the speedometer cable, provides an AC signal in relation to engine speed, to the electronic module. The electronic module processes the information from the speed sensor and sends a signal to the high speed modulator (vacuum solenoid) valve. When the vehicle speed exceeds the module trigger speed, the solenoid vacuum valve closes which, in turn, causes the EGR valve to close.

An EGR venturi vacuum amplifier takes a relatively weak venturi vacuum signal from the venturi of the carburetor and uses this vacuum to control the strong intake manifold vacuum signal to operate the EGR valve. This makes it possible to achieve an accurate, repeatable, and almost exact proportion between the airflow in the carburetor and the EGR flow. The amplifier includes a vacuum reservoir and a check valve to maintain an adequate supply of vacuum despite changes in manifold vacuum. The relief valve also "dumps" the EGR vacuum signal whenever the venturi vacuum is equal to, or greater than, the intake manifold vacuum. This allows the EGR valve to close at or near wide open throttle (acceleration), when maximum performance from the engine is required.

Another system working in conjunction with the EGR system is the EGR/CSC system. This system regulates both the distributor spark advance and operation of the EGR valve according to the temperature of the engine coolant. The system consists of: a 95°F EGR PVS valve, a spark delay valve, and a vacuum check valve.

When the engine coolant is below 82°F, the EGR PVS valve admits carburetor EGR port vacuum directly to the distributor advance diaphragm through a one-way check valve. At the same time, the EGR PVS valve shuts off carburetor EGR vacuum to the EGR valve and transmission diaphragm.

When the engine coolant temperature is above 95°F, the EGR PVS valve is actuated and directs carburetor EGR vacuum to the EGR valve and transmission instead of the distributor.

The spark delay valve (SDV) delays carburetor spark advance vacuum to the distributor advance diaphragm by restricting the vacuum through the SDV valve for a predetermined time. During normal acceleration, little or no vacuum is admitted to the distributor advance diaphragm until acceleration is completed, because of the time delay of the SDV valve, and the re-routing of the EGR port vacuum, if the engine coolant temperature is 95°F or higher. The check valve blocks vacuum from the SDV valve to the EGR PVS valve so that carburetor spark vacuum will not be dissipated when the EGR PVS valve is actuated above 95°F.

The 235°F PVS valve is not part of the EGR/CSC system, but is connected to the distributor vacuum advance to prevent engine overheating while idling. At idle speeds, no vacuum is generated at the carburetor spark port or the EGR port and the ignition timing is fully retarded. When the engine coolant reaches 235°F, the valve is actuated to admit intake manifold vacuum to the distributor advance diaphragm which advances the ignition timing. The result is the engine speed increases and the increase in coolant circulation and fan speed cools the engine.

Engines equipped with the Electronic Engine Control (EEC) system utilize an electronically-controlled EGR valve. In this system, exhaust gas flow is controlled according to the demands of the EEC computer. An electronic sensor attached to the EGR valve signals the computer.

Cold Temperature Activated Vacuum System

The cold temperature activated vacuum (CTAV) system was first used in 1974 on 460 V8 engines in F-100 trucks built for sale in California.

The CTAV system more accurately matches spark advance to the engine requirements under cold ambient temperature conditions. The system can select from two vacuum sources for spark advance depending on the ambient tem-

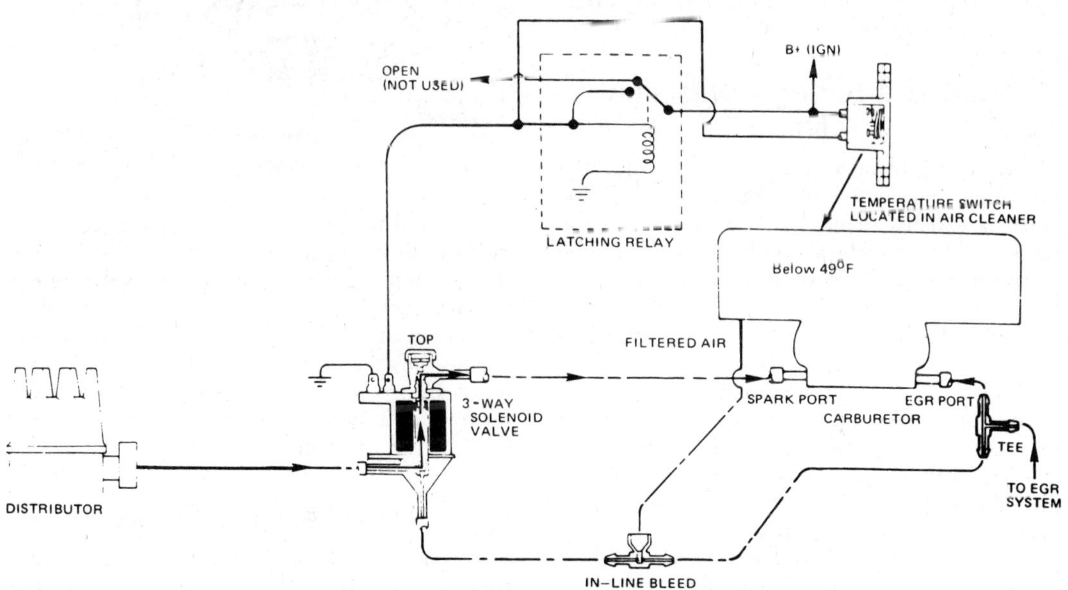

Operation of the CTAV system below 49° F

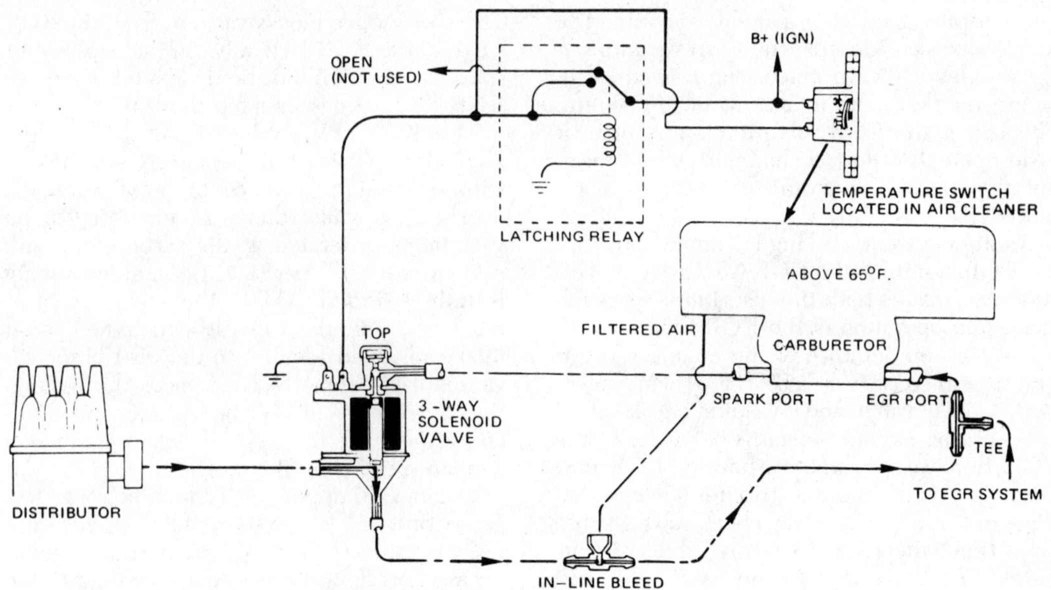

Operation of the CTAV system above 65° F

perature: below 49°F—carburetor spark port vacuum; above 65°F—EGR vacuum. In between these two temperature ranges the system will select either source of vacuum, depending on the cycle it is in.

The CTAV system consists of an ambient temperature switch, a three-way vacuum switch, inline vacuum bleed, and a latching relay.

The vacuum from both the spark port of the carburetor and the EGR port is supplied to the three-way solenoid valve. The ambient temperature switch provides the signal that determines which of the sources will be selected. The latching relay provides for only one cycle each time the ignition switch is turned on.

Vacuum and Spring Controlled Heat Control Valve

The heat control valve, commonly known as the heat riser, is mounted between the exhaust pipe and the exhaust manifold. The purpose of the device is to provide a quick warm-up of the carburetor and the rest of the induction system.

Fuel will condense on the cold surfaces of the induction system, which causes air/fuel ratios to fluctuate. These variations can cause uneven acceleration and increased emissions. The exhaust control valve, which is thermostatically-controlled, is closed when the engine is cold and routes hot exhaust gases through a passage under the carburetor and over to the opposite exhaust manifold which has no heat control valve and thus no restriction to block the flow of exhaust gases. This quickly warms

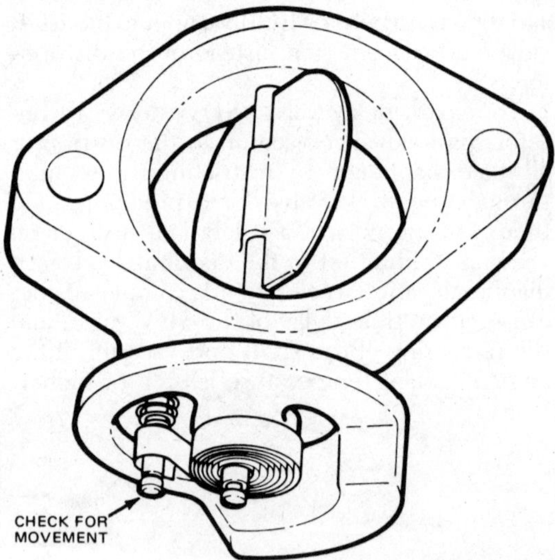

A spring-operated exhaust heat control valve

the air/fuel mixture delivery passages and provides improved mixture control and driveability. As the engine warms up, the valve opens and reduces the flow of exhaust gases through the warm-up passage.

The valve is either operated by a bi-metal temperature sensitive spring or a vacuum motor operated by intake manifold vacuum routed through a PVS switch.

Electrically-Assisted Choke

Some pick-ups use an electrically heated choke thermostatic spring housing as an aid to fast choke release and better emission characteristics during engine warm-up. The heater operates from a lead off the alternator only when the engine is actually running.

The heater element operates only when ambient temperatures are above 60°F (when long periods of choke operation are not necessary for engine driveability). When temperatures are below 60°F, the choke thermostatic spring is heated in the normal manner; via a tube running from an exhaust manifold heat stove.

EMISSION CONTROL SERVICE

Gasoline Engines

NOTE: *Complete and detailed procedures for the servicing of the crankcase ventilation system are found in the "Maintenance" Section of Chapter 1.*

Thermactor System

AIR BY-PASS VALVE REPLACEMENT

1. Disconnect the air and vacuum hoses at the air by-pass valve body.
2. Position the air by-pass valve and connect the respective hoses.

CHECK VALVE REPLACEMENT

1. Disconnect the air supply hose at the valve. Use a 1¼ in. crowfoot wrench. The valve has a standard, right-hand pipe thread.
2. Clean the threads on the air manifold adapter (air supply tube on the V8 engines) with a wire brush. Do not blow compressed air through the check valve in either direction.
3. Install the check valve and tighten.
4. Connect the air supply hose.

AIR MANIFOLD REPLACEMENT

Six-Cylinder Engines

1. Disconnect the air supply hose at the check valve, position the hose out of the way and remove the valve.
2. Loosen all of the air manifold-to-cylinder head tube coupling nuts (compression fittings). Inspect the air manifold for damaged threads and fittings and for leaking connections. Repair or replace as required. Clean the manifold and associated parts with kerosene. Do not dry the parts with compressed air.
3. Position the air manifold on the cylinder head. Be sure that all of the tube coupling nuts are aligned with the cylinder head.
4. Screw each coupling nut into the cylinder head, one or two threads. Tighten the tube coupling nuts.
5. Install the check valve and tighten it.
6. Connect the air supply hose to the check valve.

AIR SUPPLY TUBE REPLACEMENT

V8 Engines Only

1. Disconnect the air supply hose at the check valve and position the hose out of the way.
2. Remove the check valve.
3. Remove the air supply tube volt and seal washer.
4. Carefully remove the air supply tube and seal washer from the cylinder head. Inspect the air supply tube for evidence of leaking threads or seal surfaces. Examine the attaching bolt head, seal washers, and supply tube surface for leaks. Inspect the attaching bolt and cylinder head threads for damage. Clean the air supply tube, seal washers, and bolt with kerosene. Do not dry the parts with compressed air.
5. Install the seal washer and air supply tube on the cylinder head. Be sure that it is positioned in the same manner as before removal.
6. Install the seal washer and mounting bolt. Tighten the bolt.
7. Install the check valve and tighten it.
8. Connect the air supply hose to the check valve.

AIR NOZZLE REPLACEMENT

Six-Cylinder Engines Only

Normally, air nozzles should be replaced during cylinder head reconditioning. A nozzle may be replaced, however, without removing the cylinder head, by removing the air manifold and using a hooked tool.

Clean the nozzle with kerosene and a stiff brush. Inspect the air nozzles for eroded tips.

AIR PUMP AND FILTER FAN REPLACEMENT

1. Loosen the air pump attaching bolts.
2. Remove the drive pulley attaching bolts and pull the pulley off the air pump shaft.
3. Pry the outer disc loose, then remove the centrifugal filter fan. Care must be used to prevent foreign matter from entering the air intake hole, especially if the fan breaks during removal. Do not attempt to remove the metal drive hub.
4. Install the new filter fan by drawing it into position with the pulley bolts.

AIR PUMP REPLACEMENT

1. Disconnect the air outlet hose at the air pump.
2. Loosen the pump belt tension adjuster.
3. Disengage the drive belt.
4. Remove the mounting bolt and air pump.

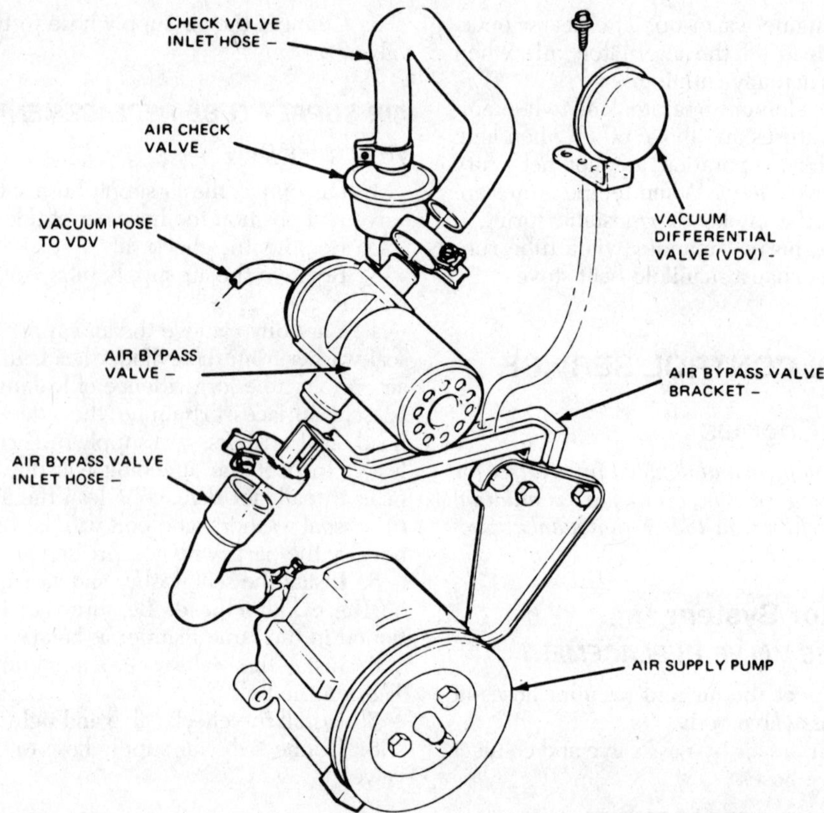

Thermactor air pump system components. Locations vary slightly among engines

5. Position the air pump on the mounting bracket and install the mounting bolt.
6. Place the drive belt in the pulley and attach the adjusting arm to the air pump.
7. Adjust the drive belt tension and tighten the adjusting arm and mounting bolts.
8. Connect the air outlet hose to the air pump.

RELIEF VALVE REPLACEMENT

Do not disassemble the air pump on the car to replace the relief valve; remove the pump from the engine.

1. Remove the relief valve with the aid of a slide hammer.
2. Position the relief valve on the pump housing and hold it in position with a block of wood.
3. Use a hammer to lightly tap the wood block until the relief valve is seated.

RELIEF VALVE PRESSURE-SETTING PLUG REPLACEMENT

1. Compress the locking tabs inward (together) and remove the plastic pressure-setting plug.
2. Before installing the new plug, be sure that the plug is the correct one. The plugs are color-coded.
3. Insert the plug in the relief valve hole and push in until it snaps into place.

DISTRIBUTOR TEMPERATURE-SENSING VACUUM CONTROL VALVE TEST

1. Check the routing and connection of all the vacuum hoses.
2. Bring the engine up to the normal operating temperature. The engine must not be overheated.
3. Note the engine rpm, with the transmission in Neutral, and the throttle at curb idle.
4. Disconnect the vacuum hose from the intake manifold at the temperature-sensing valve. Plug or clamp the hose.
5. Note the idle rpm with the hose disconnected. If there is no change in rpm, the valve is good. If there is a drop of 100 or more rpm, the valve should be replaced. Replace the vacuum line.
6. Check to make sure that the all-season coolant mixture meets specifications and that the correct radiator cap is in place and functioning.
7. Block the radiator airflow to induce a higher-than-normal temperature condition.
8. Continue to operate the engine until the temperature or heat indicator shows above normal.

If the engine speed, by this time, has increased 100 or more rpm, the temperature-sensing valve is satisfactory. If not, it should be replaced.

DISTRIBUTOR DECELERATION VACUUM CONTROL VALVE TEST

1. Connect a tachometer to the engine and bring the engine to the normal operating temperature.

2. Check the idle speed and set it to specifications with the headlights on high beam, as necessary.

3. Turn off the headlights and note the idle rpm.

4. Remove the plastic cover from the valve. Slowly turn the adjusting screw counterclockwise without pressing in. After 5, and no more than 6 turns, the idle speed should suddenly increase to about 1000 rpm. If the speed does not increase after six turns, push inward on the valve spring retainer and release. Speed should now increase.

5. Slowly turn the adjusting screw clockwise until the idle speed drops to the speed noted in step 3. Make one more turn clockwise.

6. Increase the engine speed to 2000 rpm, hold for 5 seconds, and release the throttle. The engine speed should return to idle speed within 4 seconds. If idle is not resumed in 4 seconds, back off the dashpot adjustment and repeat the check. If the idle is not resumed in 3 seconds with the dashpot backed off, turn the deceleration valve adjustment screw an additional quarter turn clockwise and repeat the check. Repeat the quarter turn adjustment and idle return checks until the engine returns to idle within the required time.

7. If it takes more than one complete turn from Step 5 to meet the idle return time specification, replace the valve.

DUAL DIAPHRAGM VACUUM ADVANCE AND VACUUM RETARD FUNCTIONAL CHECK

1. To check vacuum advance, disconnect the vacuum lines from both the advance (outer) and retard (inner) diaphragms. Plug the line removed from the retard diaphragm.

Connect a tachometer and timing light to the engine. Increase the idle speed by setting the screw on the first step of the fast idle cam. Note the ignition timing setting, using a timing light.

Connect the carburetor vacuum line to the advance diaphragm. If the timing advances immediately, the advance unit is functioning properly. Adjust the idle speed to 550–600 rpm.

2. Check the vacuum retardation as follows: using a timing light, note the ignition timing. Remove the plug from the manifold vacuum line and connect the line to the inner diaphragm. Timing should retard immediately.

3. If vacuum retardation is not to specifications, replace the dual diaphragm advance unit. If the advance (vacuum) does not function properly, calibrate the unit on a distributor test stand. If the advance part of the unit cannot be calibrated, or if either diaphragm is leaking, replace the dual diaphragm vacuum advance unit.

EVAPORATIVE EMISSION CONTROL SYSTEM CHECK

Other than a visual check to determine that none of the vapor lines are broken, there is no test for this equipment.

ELECTRONIC SPARK CONTROL SYSTEM OPERATION TEST

1. Raise the rear of the vehicle until the rear wheels are clear of the ground by at least 4 in. Support the rear of the vehicle with jackstands.

CAUTION: *The rear of the vehicle must be firmly supported during this test. If one of the rear wheels should come in contact with the ground while it is turning, the vehicle will move forward very rapidly and unexpectedly. As an extra precaution, chock the front wheels and do not stand in front of the vehicle while the wheels are turning.*

2. Disconnect the vacuum hose from the distributor vacuum advance chamber. This is the outer hose on cars with dual diaphragm vacuum advance units.

3. Connect the hose to a vacuum gauge.

4. Pour hot water on the temperature-sensing switch to make sure that it is above 65°F.

5. Start the engine and apply the foot brake. Depress the clutch and shift the transmission into High gear. Rlease the hand brake and slowly engage the clutch.

6. Have an assistant observe the vacuum gauge while you raise the speed of the engine until the speedometer reads 35 mph, at which time the vacuum gauge should show a reading.

7. If the vacuum gauge shows a reading below 35 mph, a component in the electronic spark control system is defective. If the vacuum gauge does not show a reading, even above 35 mph, there is either a defective component in the electronic spark control system, or there is a broken or clogged vacuum passage between the carburetor and the distributor.

HEATED AIR INTAKE TEST

1. With the engine completely cold, look inside the cold air duct and make sure that the valve plate is fully in the up position (closing the cold air duct).

2. Start the engine and bring it to operating temperature.

3. Stop the engine and look inside the cold air duct again. The valve plate should be down, allowing an opening from the cold air duct into the air cleaner.

4. If the unit appears to be malfunctioning, remove it and examine it to make sure that the springs are not broken or disconnected, and replace the thermostat if all other parts appear intact and properly connected.

TRANSMISSION-REGULATED SPARK

Transmission Valve Test

1. Attach a test light to the wire which connects the transmission valve to the distributor modulator valve.

2. Jack up and support the vehicle, so that the rear wheels are free to turn.

3. Start the engine and engage the transmission in Low gear. Observe the test light, which should be lighted at this time.

4. On standard transmissions, engage High gear and check to see that the light goes out.

5. On automatic transmissions, place the vehicle in Drive and allow it to upshift. Upon the shift into High gear, the test light should go out.

6. If the test lamp fails to function properly, replace the transmission valve.

EGR System

EGR VALVE OPERATION TEST

1. Disconnect the EGR valve vacuum supply line and plug the source side of the line.

2. Start the engine and allow it to reach operating temperature.

3. Supply vacuum to the EGR valve vacuum supply line. The stem of the EGR valve should visibly move. As more vacuum is applied to the valve, it should open fully and the engine idle should roughen, rpm drop, and/or the engine stop completely.

4. If the idle quality doesn't change, there is no EGR taking place. Remove the EGR valve and either replace it or try to clean it. After cleaning, repeat the above test. If the valve still does not perform satisfactorily, replace it.

5. If the valve opens when vacuum is applied and disrupts the engine idle, but the engine doesn't return to a smooth idle when no vacuum is applied to the valve, then the valve may not be closing and sealing properly. Remove the valve and/or clean or replace it. Recheck the operation of the valve if it is cleaned or replaced.

EGR CARBURETOR PORT CHECK

1. Disconnect the vacuum line from the EGR carburetor vacuum port.

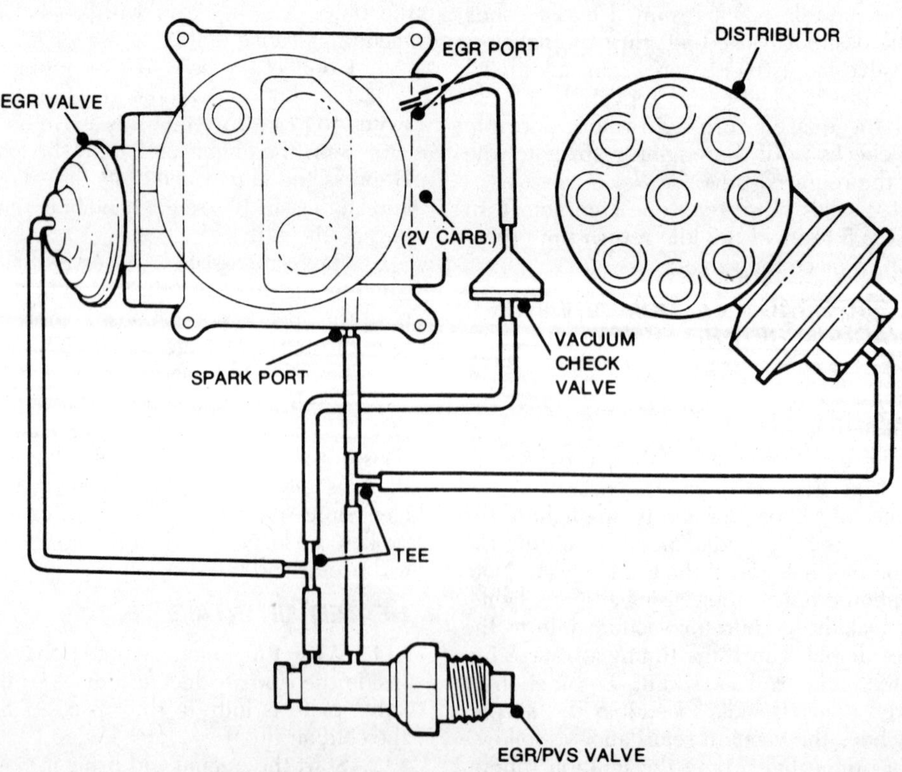

EGR valves are located adjacent to the carburetor

2. Open and release the throttle very quickly at least to the ½ open position. Be careful not to overrev the engine. Have a finger placed over the port at the same time the throttle is blipped.

3. Vacuum should be present when the throttle is opened. If no vacuum can be detected, the port is blocked and should be cleaned.

PVS OPERATION CHECK

On PVS units with two or three outlets, vacuum should pass through the PVS when the engine is started and allowed to reach normal operating temperature.

On PVS units with four outlets, vacuum should be routed between the two outlets marked "D" and "M" when the engine is started and allowed to reach normal operating temperature.

EGR VALVE CLEANING

1. Remove the EGR valve from the engine.

2. Use a small hand drill to clean the orifice hole in the EGR valve body if it is blocked or

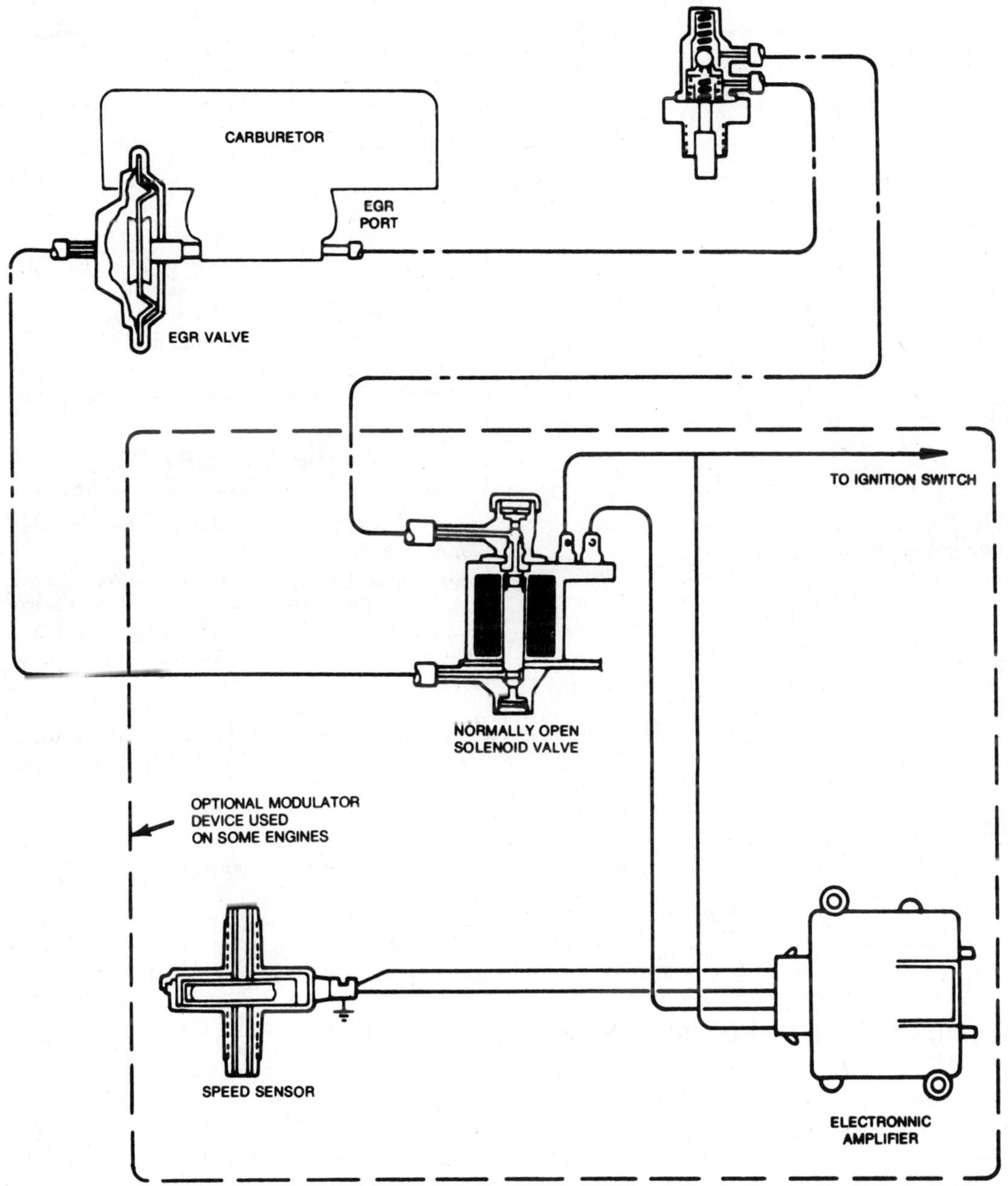

EGR system schematic

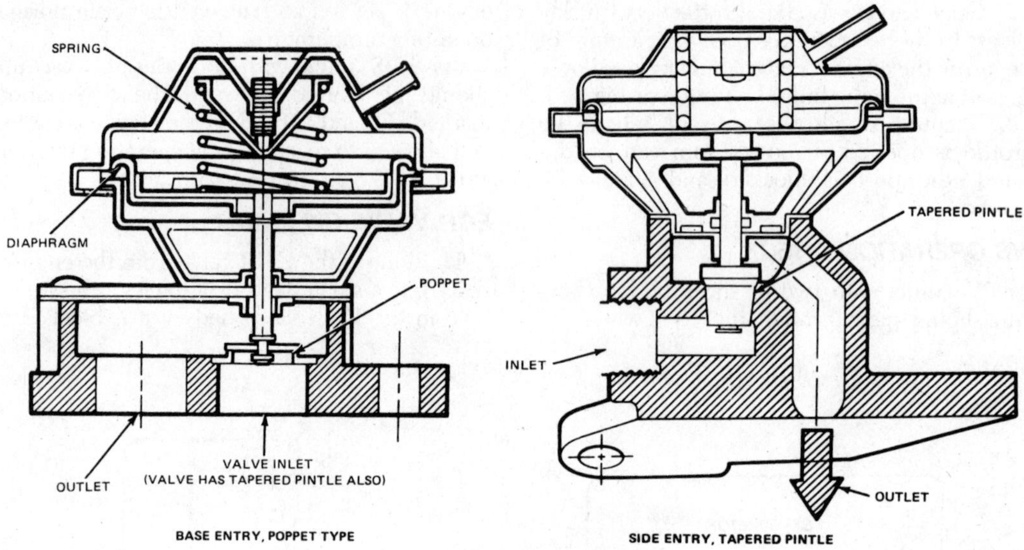

Vacuum-type EGR valve cutaways

restricted by deposits. Use EXTREME care not to enlarge the hole or damage the surface.

3. Separate the diaphragm section from the main mounting body.

4. Clean the valve plate, stem, and the mounting plate with a small rotary type wire brush powered by an electric drill. Take care not to damage any parts.

5. Remove deposits between the stem and the valve disc with a steel blade or shim stock. The poppet must be free to wobble and move axially before reassembly.

6. Clean the cavity and passages in the main body section with the rotary type wire brush.

7. Remove all debris with compressed air.

8. Reassemble the diaphragm to the main body using a new gasket between them. Tighten the attaching screws to 28 in. lbs.

9. Clean the orifice plate and the counterbore in the valve body and reinstall the orifice by using a small amount of cement to retain the plate in place while assembling the valve to the engine. Apply cement only to the outer edges of the orifice plate to avoid restricting the orifice.

NOTE: *Some EGR valves are riveted together and cannot be taken apart for cleaning. These must be discarded if they cannot be cleaned enough to perform satisfactorily.*

EXHAUST HEAT CONTROL VALVE (HEAT RISER) CHECK

Check and make sure that the valve is free to operate and not frozen or restricted from moving by rust. When the engine is first started (cold) the valve should remain closed. As the engine heats up, the valve should gradually open until the engine reaches normal operating temperatures when the valve should be completely open. Check the PVS, if the valve is vacuum-operated, in the manner previously described. Make sure that the vacuum line is in good condition and is not restricted in any way.

COLD TEMPERATURE ACTUATED VACUUM SYSTEM (CTAV) DIAGNOSES

1. Connect a tachometer to the engine. Connect a vacuum gauge to the vacuum line leading to the distributor vacuum advance diaphragm. Make sure that the temperature sensing switch is above 65°F. Disconnect the electrical lead from the 3-way solenoid vacuum valve.

2. Start the engine and rev it to 1,500 rpm. There should be about 15 in. Hg of vacuum present at the distributor advance diaphragm. If no vacuum reading is observed, check the vacuum source back to the carburetor spark port.

3. Connect the electrical lead to the 3-way solenoid vacuum valve. No or low vacuum should be present at the distributor. If the vacuum is substantial, check the vacuum valve ground and electrical source back to the ignition switch.

4. Rev the engine at 3,000 rpm. The vacuum present at the distributor should be about 9 in. Hg. If no vacuum is present, check the vacuum source back to the carburetor.

5. If Steps 2 through 4 are positive, the vacuum system is normal and the engine can be shut off.

6. Attach a grounded test light to the 3-

way solenoid vacuum valve. Disconnect the electrical connector at the temperature switch located in the air cleaner. Turn the ignition to On.

7. If the test light glows, replace the latching relay.

8. If the test light does not glow, reconnect the electrical connector at the temperature switch in the carburetor air cleaner. The light should come on.

9. If the test light does not glow, check the temperature switch and electrical source back to the ignition switch.

10. If the test light came on in Step 8, disconnect the connector at the temperature sensing switch in the air cleaner. The light should remain on. If the light goes out, replace the latching relay.

11. Connect the test light to the temperature switch terminal and cool the switch to below 49°F. The light should go out when the switch is cooled. If the light remains on, replace the temperature switch.

GASOLINE ENGINE FUEL SYSTEM

Fuel Pump

The mechanical fuel pump is camshaft eccentric-actuated and located on the lower left center of the engine block on six-cylinder engines and the left-side of the front cover on V8 engines.

REMOVAL

1. Disconnect the fuel inlet and outlet lines at the fuel pump. Discard the fuel inlet retainig clamp

2. Remove the pump retaining bolts then

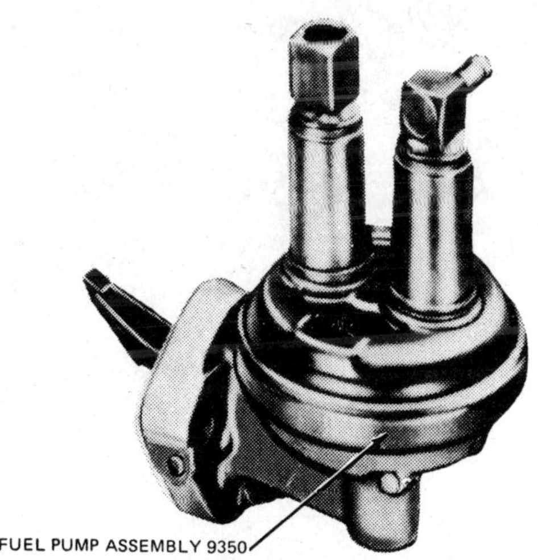

Inline-six type mechanical fuel pump

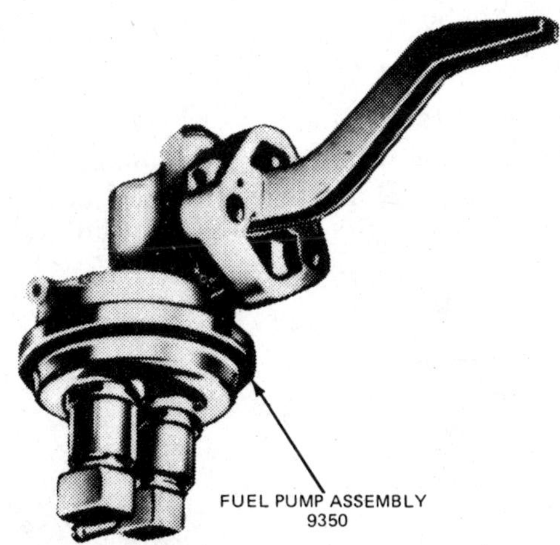

Gasoline V8 type fuel pump

remove the pump assembly and gasket from the engine. Discard the gasket.

INSTALLATION

1. If a new pump is to be installed, remove the fuel line connector fitting from the old pump and install it in the new pump.

2. Remove all gasket material from the mounting pad and pump flange. Apply oil resistant sealer to both sides of a new gasket.

3. Position the new gasket on the pump flange and hold the pump in position against the mounting pad. Make sure that the rocker arm is riding on the camshaft eccentric.

4. Press the pump tight against the pad, install the retaining bolts and alternately torque them to 12–15 ft. lbs. on 6 cylinder engines and 20–24 ft. lbs. on the 302; 14–20 on 351 and 400; 19–27 on 352, 360, 361, 390, 391 engines. Connect the fuel lines. Use a new clamp on the fuel inlet lines.

5. Operate the engine and check for leaks.

TESTING

Incorrect fuel pump pressure and low volume (flow rate) are the two most likely fuel pump troubles that will affect engine performance. Low pressure will cause a lean mixture and fuel starvation at high speeds and excessive pressure will cause high fuel consumption and carburetor flooding.

To determine that the fuel pump is in satisfactory operating condition, tests for both fuel pump pressure and volume should be performed.

The tests are performed with the fuel pump installed on the engine and the engine at normal operating temperature and at idle speed.

Before the test, make sure that the replaceable fuel filter has been changed at the proper mileage interval. If in doubt, install a new filter.

Pressure Test

1. Remove the air cleaner assembly. Disconnect the fuel inlet line of the fuel filter at the carburetor. Use care to prevent fire, due to fuel spillage. Place an absorbent cloth under the connection before removing the line to catch any fuel that might flow out of the line.

2. Connect a pressure gauge, a restrictor and a flexible hose between the fuel filter and the carburetor.

3. Position the flexible hose and the restric-

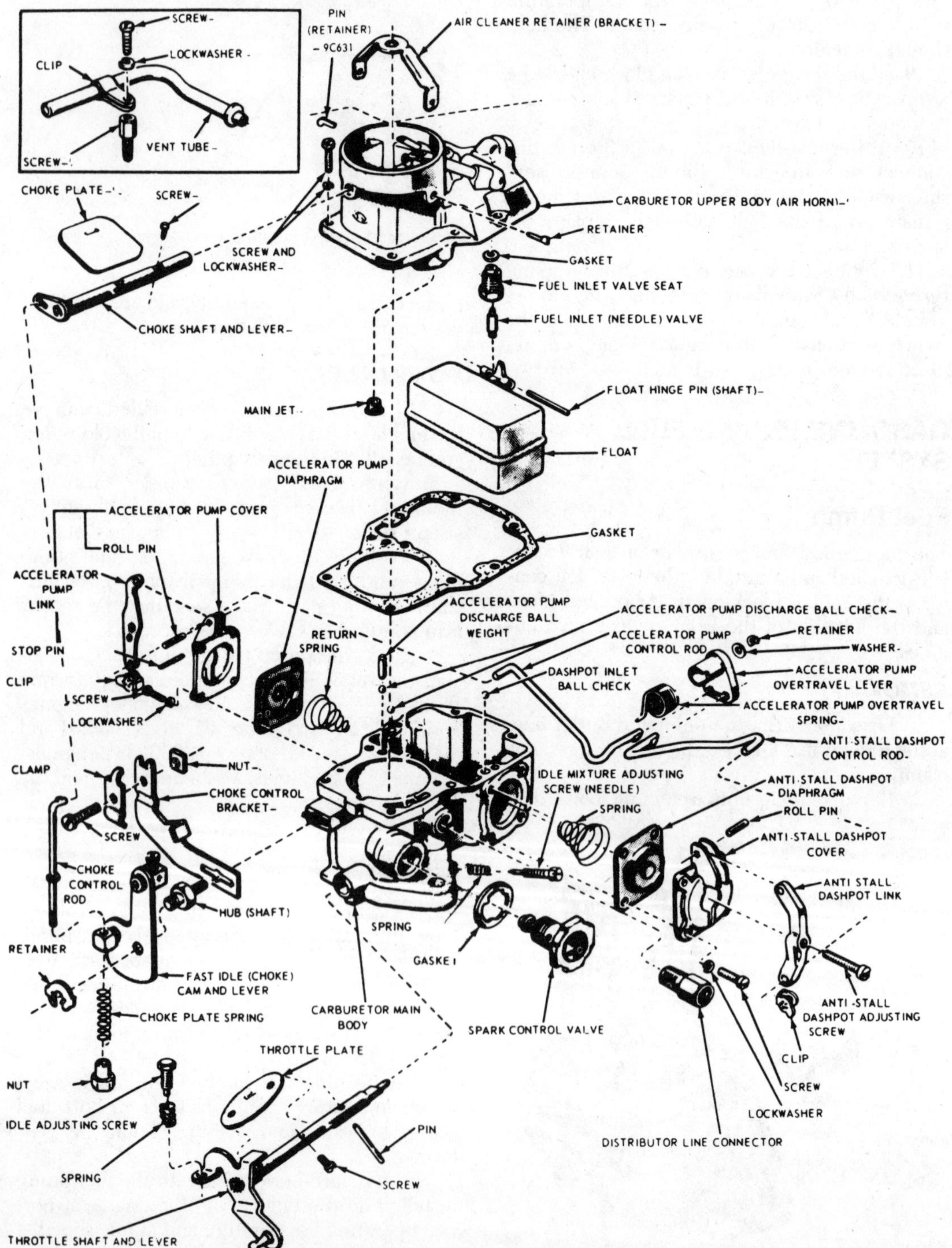

Exploded view of the Ford 1100 1-bbl carburetor

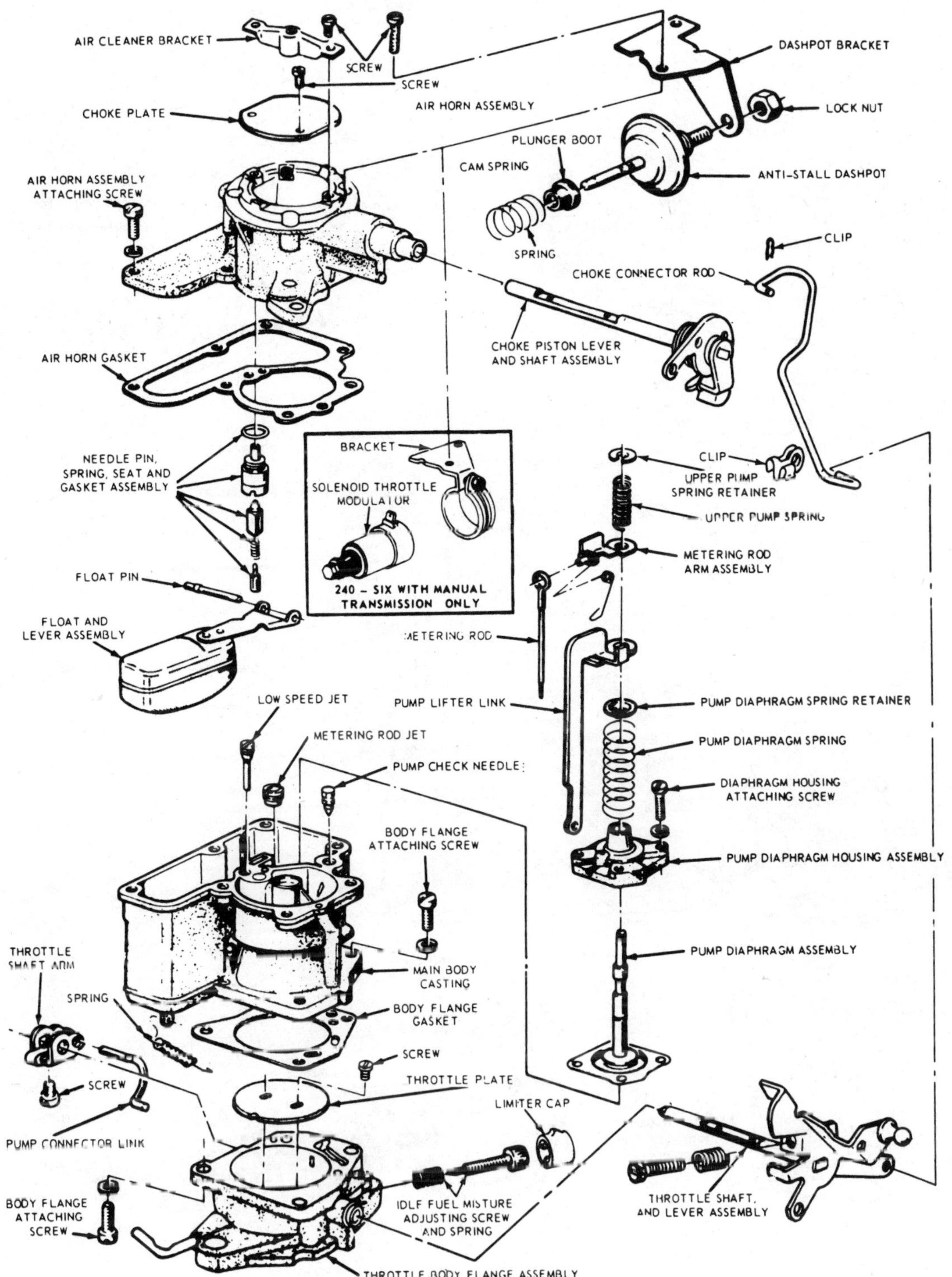

An exploded view of the Carter YF 1-bbl carburetor

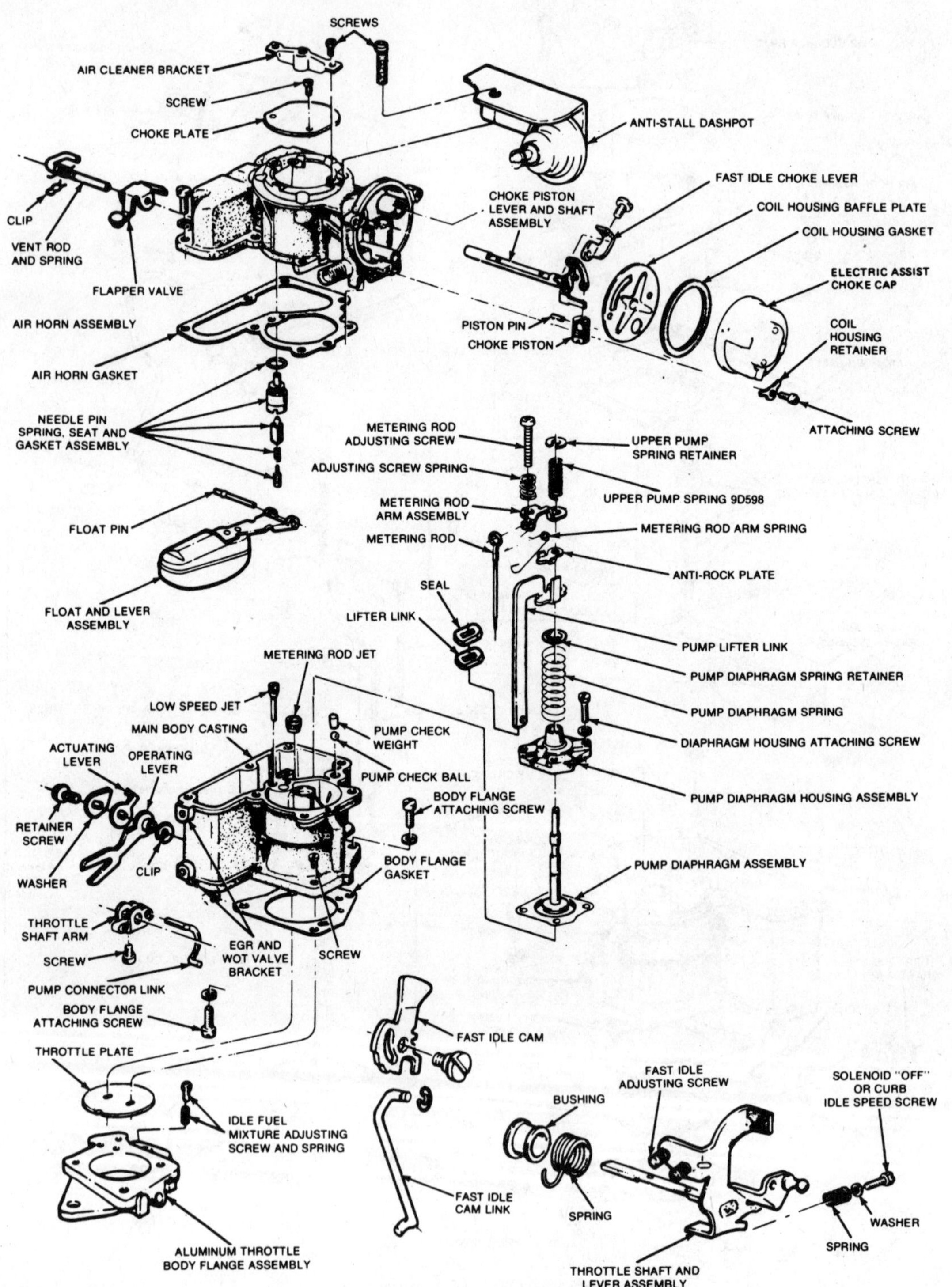

Carter YFA (non-feedback), exploded view

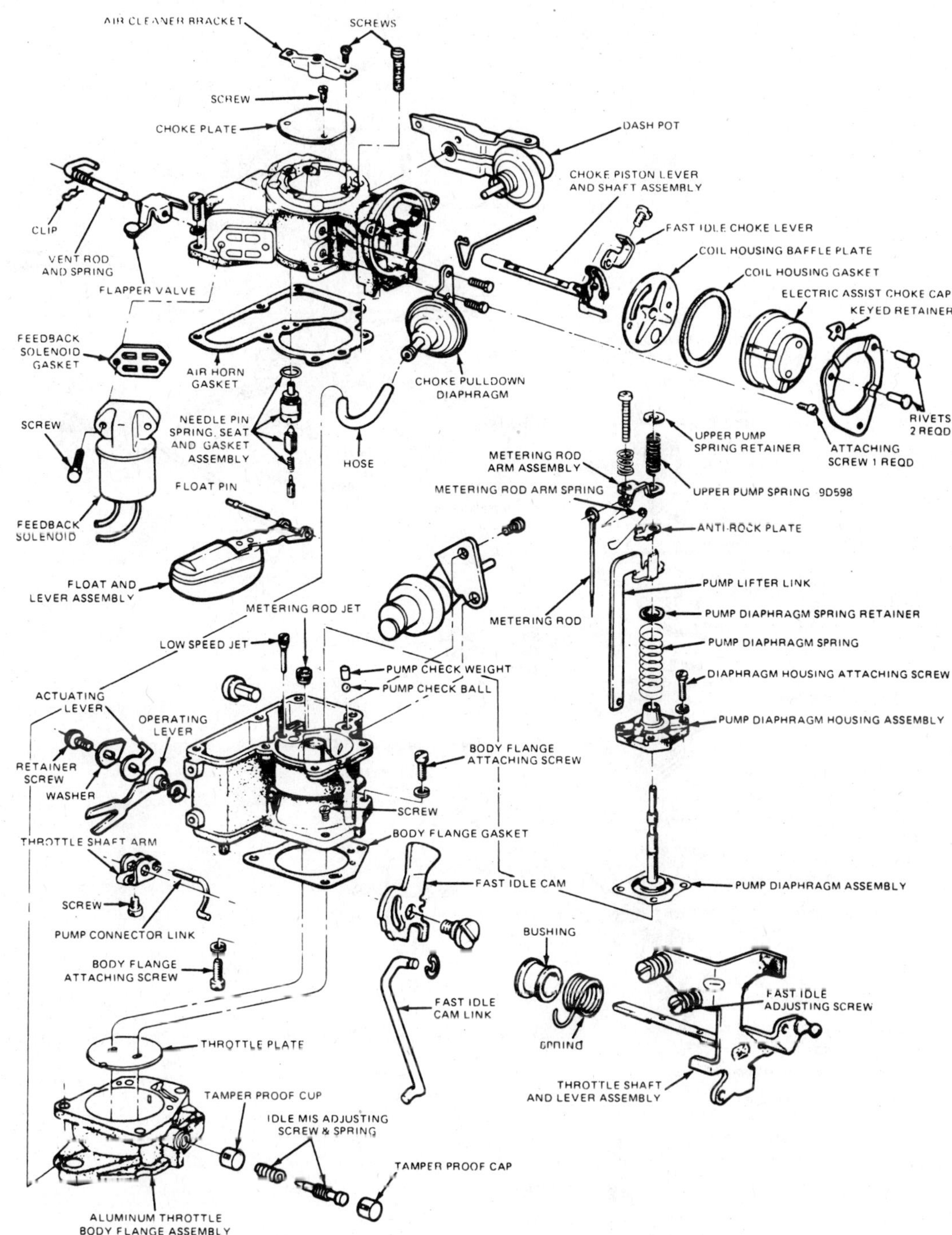

Exploded view of the Carter YFA feedback carburetor

tor so that the fuel can be discharged into a suitable, graduated container.

4. Before taking a pressure reading, operate the engine at the specified idle rpm and vent the system into the container by opening the hose restrictor momentarily.

5. Close the hose restrictor, allow the pressure to stabilize and note the reading. The pressure should be 5 psi.

If the pump pressure is not within 4–6 psi and the fuel lines and filter are in satisfactory condition, the pump is defective and should be replaced.

If the pump pressure is within the proper range, perform the test for fuel volume.

Volume Test

1. Operate the engine at the specified idle rpm.

2. Open the hose restrictor and catch the

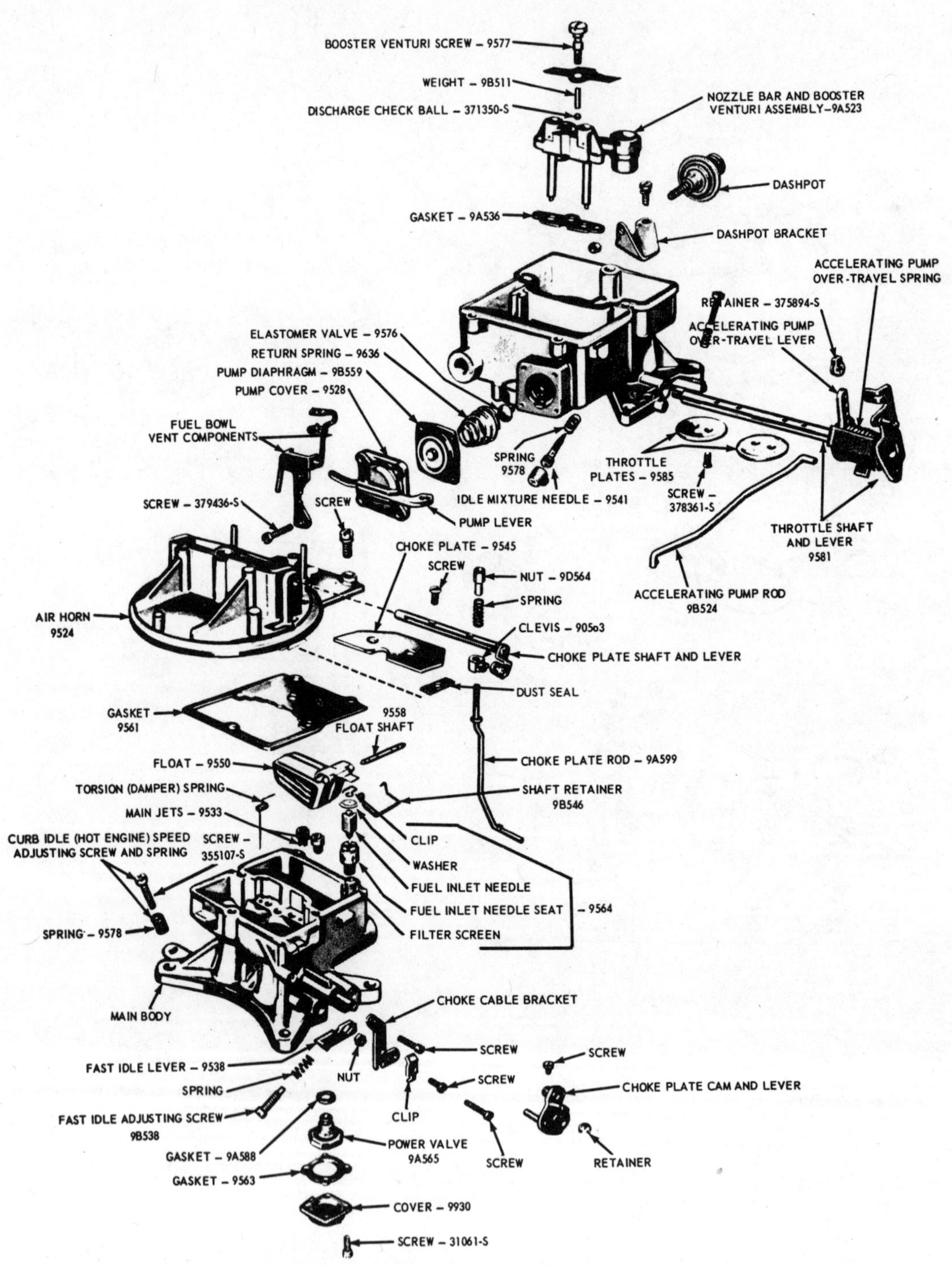

Autolite 2100 2-bbl carburetor

fuel in the container while observing the time it takes to pump 1 pint. It should take 30 seconds for 1 pint to be expelled on all vehicles made prior to the 1974 model year. On 1974 vehicles, 1 pint should be expelled in 15 seconds. On 1975 and later models, 1 pint should be pumped in 20 seconds. If the pump does not pump to specifications, check for proper fuel tank venting or a restriction in the fuel line leading from the fuel tank to the carburetor before replacing the fuel pump.

Electric Fuel Pump

Two electric pumps are used on injected models; a low pressure boost pump mounted in the gas tank and a high pressure pump mounted on the vehicle frame. Models equipped with the

7.5L engine use a single low pressure pump mounted in the gas tank.

On injected models the low pressure pump is used to provide pressurized fuel to the inlet of the high pressure pump and helps prevent noise and heating problems. The externally mounted high pressure pump is capable of supplying 15.9 gallons of fuel an hour. System pressure is controlled by a pressure regulator mounted on the engine.

On internal fuel tank mounted pumps tank removal is required. Frame mounted models can be accessed from under the vehicle. Prior to servicing release system pressure (see Fuel Supply Manifold details). Disconnect the negative battery cable prior to pump removal.

REMOVAL AND INSTALLATION

In-Tank Pump

1. Disconnect the negative battery cable.
2. Depressurize the system and drain as much gas from the tank by pumping out through the filler neck.
3. Raise the back of the vehicle and safely support on jackstands.
4. Disconnect the fuel supply, return and vent lines at the right and left side of the frame.
5. Disconnect the wiring harness to the fuel pump.
6. Support the gas tank, loosen and remove the mounting straps. Remove the gas tank.
7. Disconnect the lines and harness at the pump flange.
8. Clean the outside of the mounting flange and retaining ring. Turn the fuel pump lock ring counterclockwise and remove.
9. Remove the fuel pump.
10. Clean the mounting surfaces. Put a light coat of grease on the mounting surfaces and on the new sealing ring. Install the new fuel pump.
11. Installation is in the reverse order of removal. Fill the tank with at least 10 gals. of gas. Turn the ignition key ON for three seconds. Repeat 6 or 7 times until the fuel system is pressurized. Check for any fitting leaks. Start the engine and check for leaks.

External Pump

1. Disconnect the negative battery cable.
2. Depressurize the fuel system.
3. Raise and support the rear of the vehicle on jackstands.
4. Disconnect the inlet and outlet fuel lines.
5. Remove the pump from the mounting bracket.
6. Install in reverse order, make sure the pump is indexed correctly in the mounting bracket insulator.
7. Disconnect the fuel inlet line of the fuel filter at the carburetor. Use care to prevent fire, due to fuel spillage. Place an absorbent cloth under the connection before removing the line to catch any fuel that might flow out of the line.
8. Connect a pressure gauge, a restrictor and flexible hose between the fuel filter and the carburetor.
9. Position the flexible hose and the restrictor so that the fuel can be discharged into a suitable, graduated container.
10. Before taking a pressure reading, operate the engine at the specified idle rpm and vent the system into the container by opening the hose restrictor momentarily.
11. Close the hose restrictor, allow the pressure to stabilize and note the reading. The prssure should be 5 psi. If the pump pressure is not within 4–6 psi and the fuel lines and filter are in satisfactory condition, the pump is defective and should be replaced. If the pump pressure is within the proper range, perform the test for fuel volume.

Volume Test

1. Operate the engine at the specified idle rpm.
2. Open the hose restrictor and catch the fuel in the container while observing the time it takes to pump 1 pint. 1 pint should be pumped in 20 seconds. If the pump does not pump to specifications, check for proper fuel tank venting or a restriction in the fuel line leading from the fuel tank to the carburetor before replacing the fuel pump.

"Quick-Connect" Line Fittings

REMOVAL AND INSTALLATION

NOTE: *"Quick-Connect" (push) type fittings must be disconnected using proper procedures or the fitting may be damaged. Two types of retainers are used on the push connect fittings. Line sizes of 3/8 in. and 5/16 in. use a "hairpin" clip retainer. 1/4 line connectors use a "duck bill" clip retainer.*

Hairpin Clip

1. Clean all dirt and/or grease from the fitting. Spread the two clip legs about an 1/8 inch each to disengage from the fitting and pull the clip outward from the fitting. Use finger pressure only, do not use any tools.
2. Grasp the fitting and hose assembly and pull away from the steel line. Twist the fitting and hose assembly slightly while pulling, if necessary, when a sticking condition exists.
3. Inspect the hairpin clip for damage, replace the clip if necessary. Reinstall the clip in position on the fitting.
4. Inspect the fitting and inside of the con-

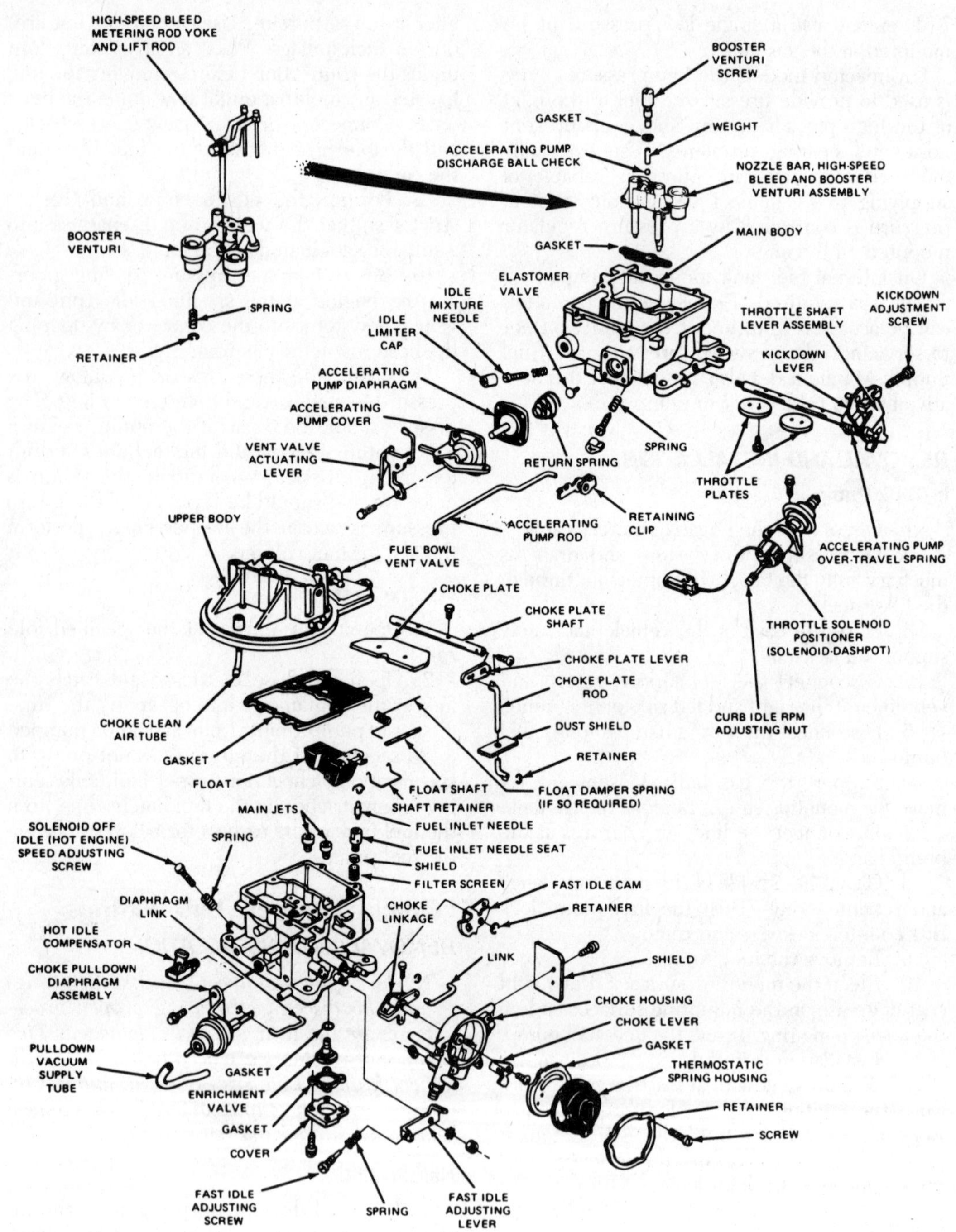

Exploded view of the Autolite 2150 carburetor

nector to insure freedom of dirt or obstruction. Install fitting into the connector and push together. A click will be heard when the hairpin snaps into proper connection. Pull on the line to insure full engagement.

Duck Bill Clip

1. A special tool is available from Ford for removing the retaining clips (Ford Tool No. T82L–9500–AH). If the tool is not on hand see Step 2. Align the slot on the push connector disconnect tool with either tab on the retaining clip. Pull the line from the connector.

2. If the special clip tool is not available, use a pair of narrow 6 in. channel lock pliers with a jaw width of 0.2 in. or less. Align the jaws of the pliers with the openings of the fitting case and compress the part of the retaining clip that

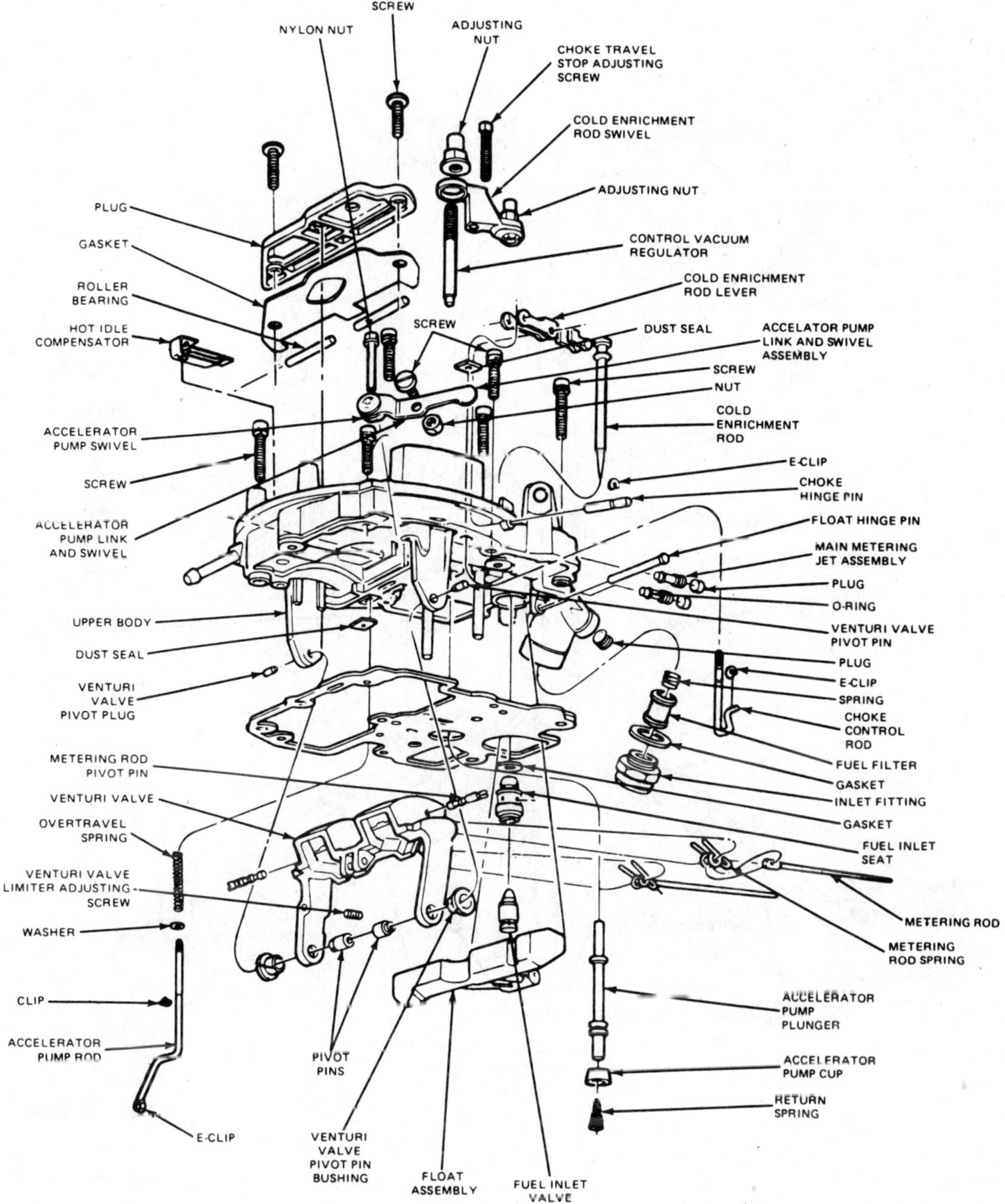

Motorcraft 7200VV (variable venturi) 2-bbl carburetor upper body

engages the case. Compressing the retaining clip will release the fitting which may be pulled from the connector. Both sides of the clip must be compressed at the same time to disengage.

3. Inspect the retaining clip, fitting end and connector. Replace the clip if any damage is apparent.

4. Push the line into the steel connector until a click is heard, indicating the clip is in place. Pull on the line to check engagement.

Carburetors

REMOVAL AND INSTALLATION

1. Remove the air cleaner.

2. Remove the throttle cable or rod from the throttle lever. Disconnect the distributor vacuum line, EGR vacuum line, if so equipped, the inline fuel filter and the choke heat tube at the carburetor.

3. Disconnect the choke clean air tube from

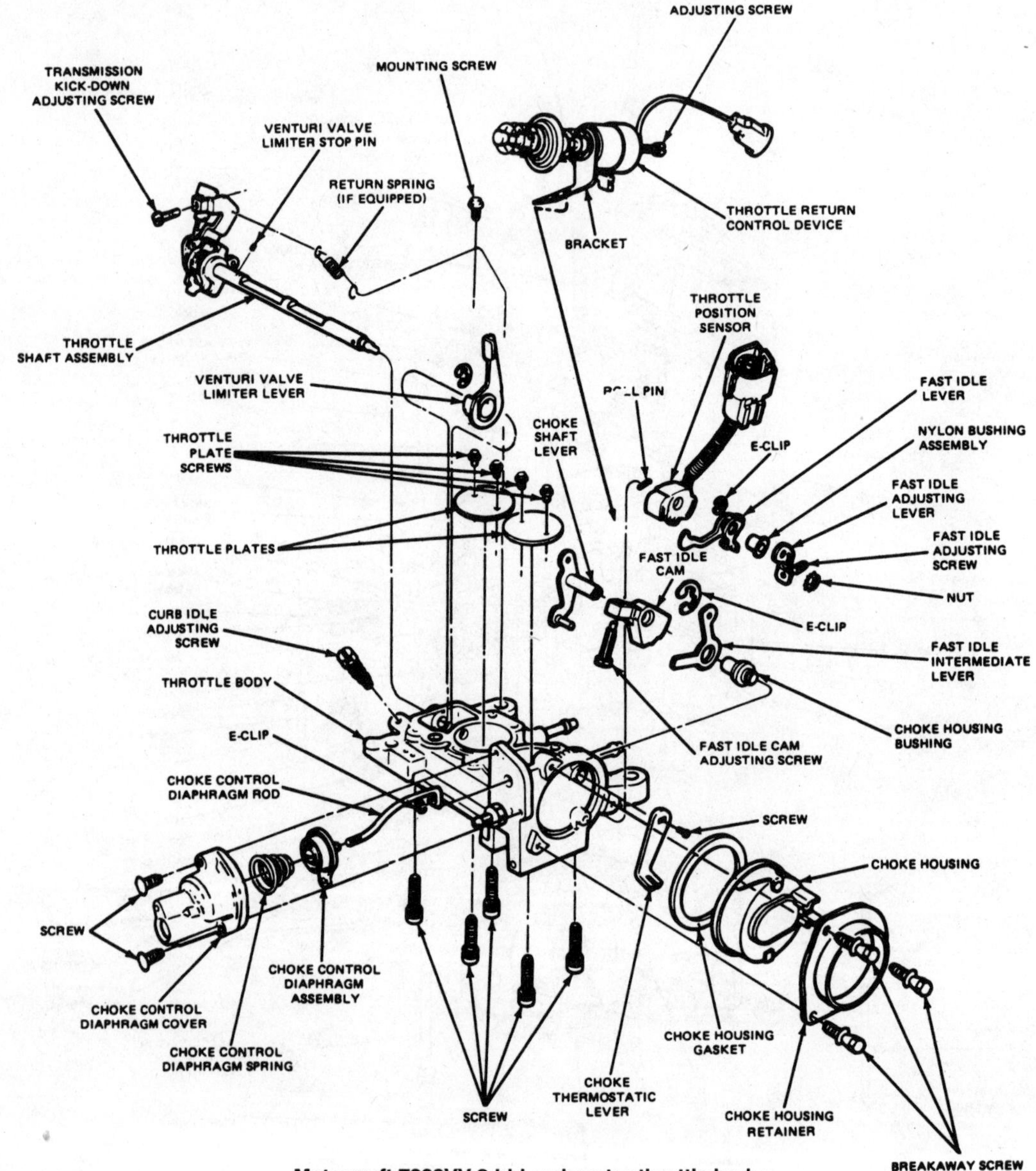

Motorcraft 7200VV 2-bbl carburetor throttle body

the air horn. Disconnect the choke actuating cable, if so equipped.

4. Remove the carburetor retaining nuts then remove the carburetor. Remove the carburetor mounting gasket, spacer (if so equipped), and the lower gasket from the intake manifold.

5. Before installing the carburetor, clean the gasket mounting surfaces of the spacer and carburetor. Place the spacer between two new gaskets and position the spacer and gaskets on the intake manifold. Position the carburetor body flange, snug the nuts, then alternately tighten each nut in a criss-cross pattern.

6. Connect the inline fuel filter, throttle cable, choke heat tube, distributor vacuum line, EGR vacuum line, and choke cable.

7. Connect the choke clean air line to the air horn.

8. Adjust the engine idle speed, the idle fuel mixture and anti-stall dashpot (if so equipped). Install the air cleaner.

FLOAT AND FUEL LEVEL ADJUSTMENT

Carter Model YR 1-bbl
Carter Model YFA 1-bbl
Carter Model YFA Feedback 1-bbl
Autolite Model 1101 1-bbl

1. Remove the carburetor air horn and gasket from the carburetor.

2. Invert the air horn assembly, and check the clearance from the top of the float to the

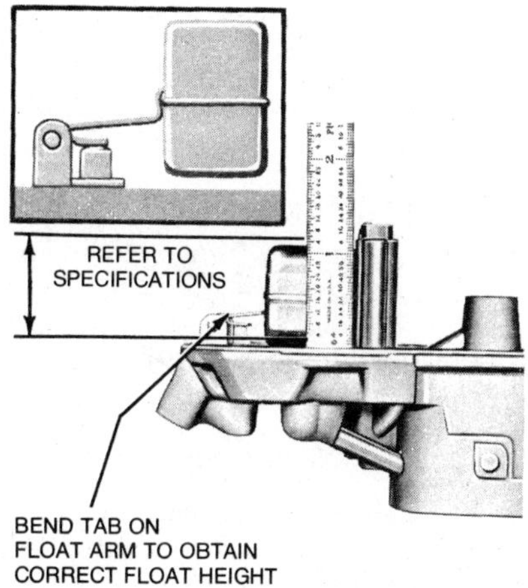

Adjusting the float level—Autolite 1101A

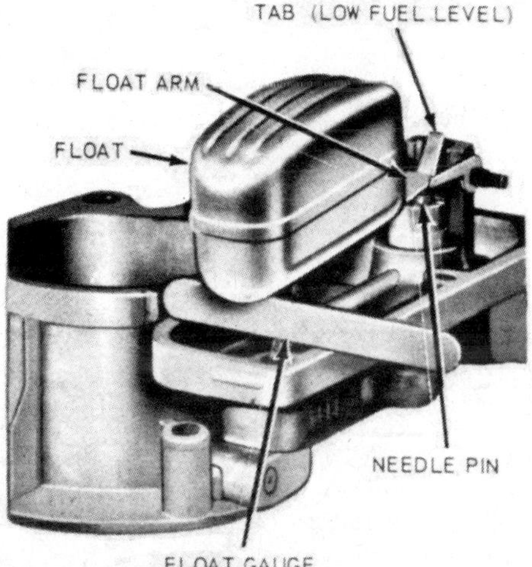

Adjusting the float level—Carter YF, YFA and YFA feedback 1-bbls.

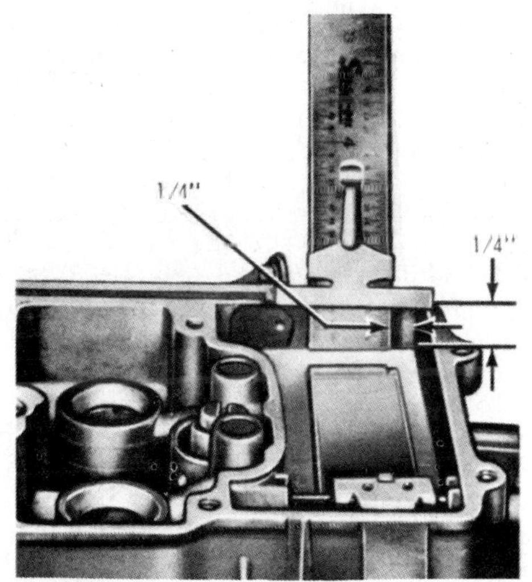

Float level adjustment (wet)—Autolite 2100, 2100A, and 2150 2-bbl

bottom of the air horn with a float level gauge. Hold the air horn at eye level when gauging the float level. The float arm (lever) should be resting on the needle pin. Do not load the needle when adjusting the float. Bend the float arm as necessary to adjust the float level (clearance). Do not bend the tab at the end of the float arm, because it prevents the float from striking the bottom of the fuel bowl when empty.

3. Turn the air horn over and hold it upright and let the float hang free. Measure the maximum clearance from the top of the float to the bottom of the air horn with the float gauge. Hold the air horn at eye level when gauging the dimension. The float drop should be 1¼ in. To adjust the float drop, bend the tab at the end of the float arm to obtain the specified setting.

4. Install the carburetor air horn with a new gasket.

Autolite Model 2100, 2100A and 2150 2-bbl (Wet Adjustment)

1. Run the engine until it reaches normal operating temperature. Place the vehicle on a level surface and stop the engine.

2. Remove the carburetor air cleaner assembly.

3. Remove the air horn attaching screws and the carburetor identification tag. Temporarily, leave the air horn and gasket in position on the carburetor main body and start the engine. Let the engine idle for a few minutes, then rotate the air horn out of the way and remove the air horn gasket to provide access to the float assembly.

4. While the engine is idling, use a standard depth scale to measure the vertical distance from the top machined surface to the carburetor main body to the level of the fuel in the fuel bowl. The measurement must be made at least ¼ in. away from any vertical surface to assure an accurate reading, because thesurface of the fuel is concave—being higher at the edges than in the center. Care must be exercised to measure the fuel level at the point of contact with the float.

5. If any adjustment is required, stop the engine to minimize the hazard of fire due to spilled gasoline. To adjust the fuel level, bend the float tab contacting the fuel inlet valve upward in relation to the original position to raise the fuel level, and downward to lower it. Each time the float is adjusted, the engine must be started and permitted to idle for a few minutes to stabilize the fuel level. Check the fuel level after each adjustment, until the specified level is obtained.

6. Assemble the carburetor in the reverse order of disassembly, using a new gasket be-

tween the air horn and the main carburetor body.

Motorcraft Model 7200 VV Feedback 2-bbl

1. Remove the upper body assembly and the gasket.
2. Fabricate a gauge to the specified dimensions.
3. With the upper body inverted, place the fuel level gauge on the case surface of the upper body and measure the vertical distance from the cast surface of the upper body and the bottom of the float.
4. To adjust, bend the float operating lever away from the fuel inlet needle to decrease the setting and toward the needle to increase the setting.
5. Check and/or adjust the float drop using the following procedures.
   a. Fabricate a gauge to the specified dimension.
   b. With the upper body assembly held in the uprght position, place the gauge against the cast surface of the upper body and measure the vertical distance between the cast surface of the upper body and the bottom of the float.
   c. To adjust, bend the stop tab on the float lever away from the hinge pin to increase the setting and toward the hinge pin to decrease the setting.
5. Reinstall the upper body assembly and new gasket.

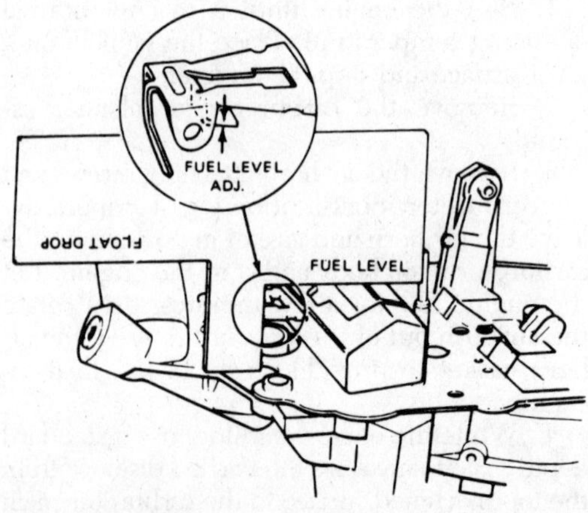

Float level adjustment for the Motorcraft 7200VV 2-bbl carburetor

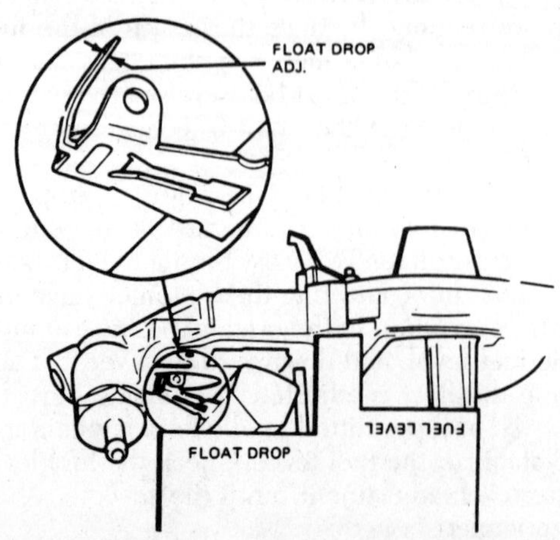

Float drop adjustment for the Motorcraft 7200VV 2-bbl carburetor

Autolite Model 4300 and 4350 4-bbl

1. Remove and invert the carburetor air horn.
2. Measure the distance from the top of the float to the air horn gasket surface. Align the float pontoons if necessary by twisting them.
3. If necessary bend the primary needle tab downward to raise the float and upward to lower the float.

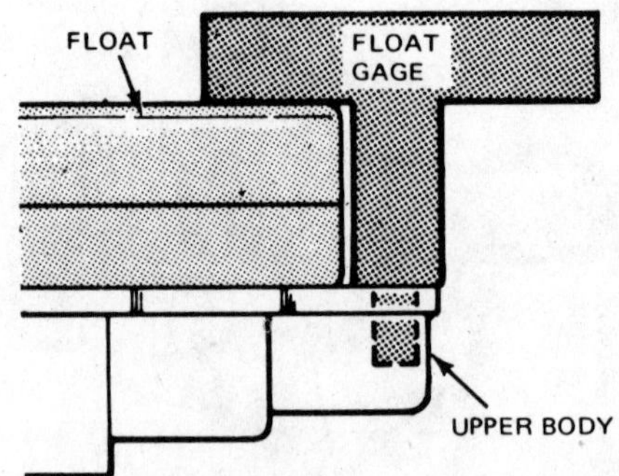

Float level adjustment on an Autolite 4300 and 4350 4-bbl carburetor

Holly Model 2300 2-bbl
Holley Model 4150 4-bbl
Holley Model 4160 4-bbl
Holley Model 4180 4-bbl

To perform a preliminary dry float adjustment on both the primary and secondary fuel bowl float assemblies, remove the fuel bowls and invert them allowing the float to rest on the fuel inlet valve and seat assembly. The fuel inlet valve and seat can be rotated until the float is parallel with the fuel bowl floor (actually the top of the fuel bowl chamber inverted). Note that this is an initial dry float setting which must be rechecked with the carburetor assembled and on the engine to obtain the proper wet fuel level.

This carburetor has an external adjustable needle and seat assembly which allows the fuel level to be checked and adjusted without removing the carburetor from the engine.

1. Run the engine with the vehicle resting on a level surface until the engine temperature has normalized.

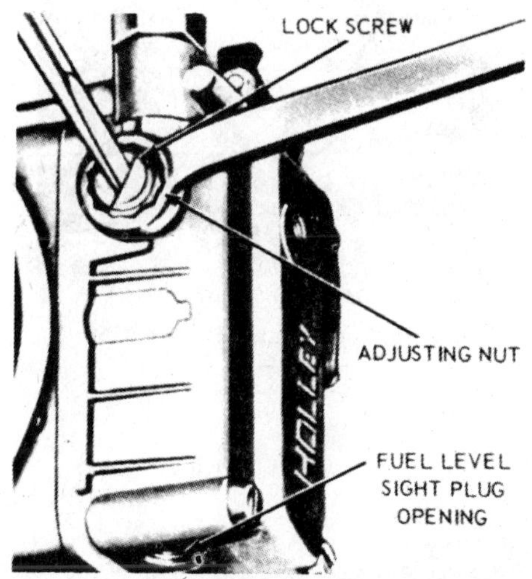

Float level adjustment (wet)—Holley 2300 2-bbl, Holley 4150, 4160, 4180C 4-bbl

2. Remove the air cleaner assembly.
3. Place a suitable container or an absorbent cloth below the fuel level sight plug in the fuel bowl.
4. Stop the engine and remove the sight plug and gasket. The fuel level in the bowl should be at the lower edge of the sight plug hole, plus or minus 1/16 in.
5. To adjust the fuel level, install the sight plug and gasket, loosen one on the lower fuel bowl retaining screws and drain the fuel from the bowl only if the level is too high. Loosen the lockscrew on top of the fuel bowl just enough to allow the adjusting nut to be turned. Turn the adjusting nut about ½ of a turn in to lower the fuel level and out to raise the fuel level. By turning the adjusting nut 1/6 of a turn, the fuel level will change 3/64 in. at the sight plug.
6. Start the engine and allow the fuel level to stabilize. Check the fuel level as outlined in Step 4.
7. Install the air cleaner assembly if no further adjustments are necessary.

FAST IDLE ADJUSTMENT

Ford Model 1100, 1101 1-bbl

The fast idle is controlled by the idle adjusting screw bearing against the bottom of the choke cam and lever during idle or closed-throttle conditions. The choke cam and lever opens the throttle slightly, through contact of the idle adjusting screw with the cam, as the manual choke position is selected. Higher engine idle speeds are automatically provided through contact of the idle adjusting screw with the cam. The curb idle must be adjusted correctly for the fast idle to be proper during application of the choke.

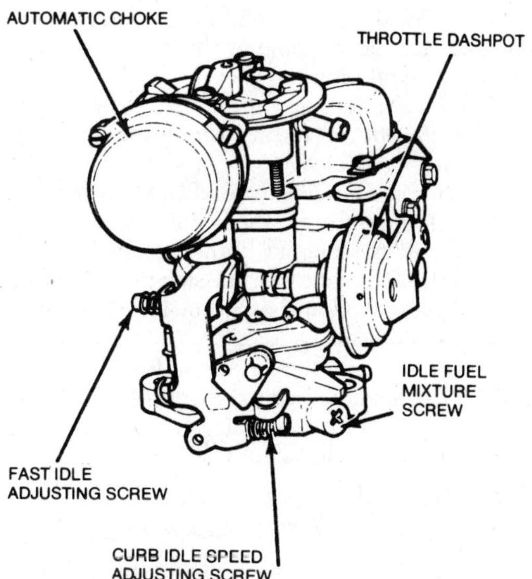

Carter YF series speed adjustments; Canadian leaded fuel models similar

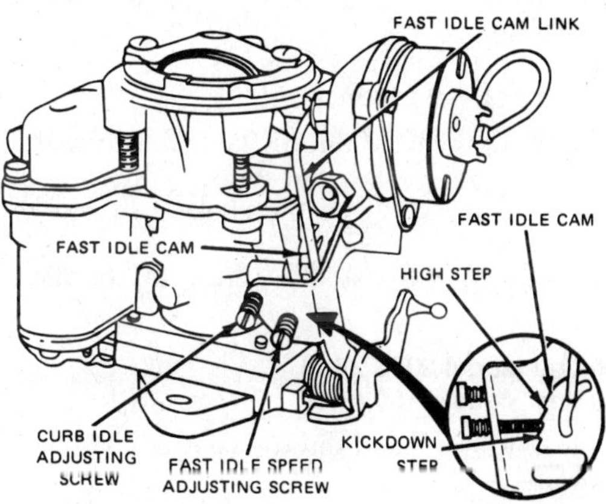

Fast idle adjusting screw—Carter YFA (U.S. models)

Holly Model 4180 4-bbl
Carter Model YFA 1-bbl

1. Remove the spark delay valve, if so equipped, from the distributor vacuum advance line, and route the vacuum line directly to the advance side of the distributor.
2. Trace the EGR signal vacuum line from the EGR valve to the carburetor and if there is a EGR/PVS valve or temperature vacuum switch located in the vacuum line routing, disconnect the EGR vacuum line at the EGR valve and plug the line.
3. If not equipped with an EGR/PVS valve or temperature vacuum switch do not detach the EGR vacuum line.
4. Trace the purge valve vacuum line from the purge valve located on the canister, to the first point where the vacuum line can be de-

tached from the underhood hose routing. Disconnect the vacuum line at that point, cap the open port, and plug the vacuum line.

CAUTION: *To prevent damage to the purge valve do not disconnect the vacuum line at the purge valve.*

5. With the engine running at normal operating temperature, the choke plate fully opened and the manual transmission in Neutral and the automatic transmission in Park, place the fast idle level on the 2nd or kickdown step of the fast idle cam.

6. Adjust the fast idle screw to within 100 rpm of the specified speed given on the Vehicle Emission Control Decal.

7. Reconnect all vacuum lines.

Carter Model YF-1 bbl

CANADIAN 300 INLINE SIXES (LEADED FUEL)

1. Place the transmission in Neutral or Park.
2. Run the engine up to normal operating temperature.
3. Place the fast idle screw on the specified step of the fast idle cam. Adjust the fast idle to specifications.

Autolite Model 2100A 2-bbl

1. Push the hand throttle knob fully inward.
2. Position the fast idle adjustment screw on the index mark "V" on the choke cam and lever.
3. Adjust the fast idle screw to specifications.

Holley Model 2300 2-bbl
Holley Model 4150 4-bbl

1. Push the hand throttle control knob fully inward.
2. Attach a tachometer to the engine.
3. Disconnect the choke cable housing from the choke cable bracket clamp.
4. Pull the choke cable housing rearward until the choke plate operating lever is against the stop on the choke cable bracket. Hold the plate open all the way to keep the engine running.
5. To adjust the fast idle turn the fast idle screw with a 3/16 in. wrench.

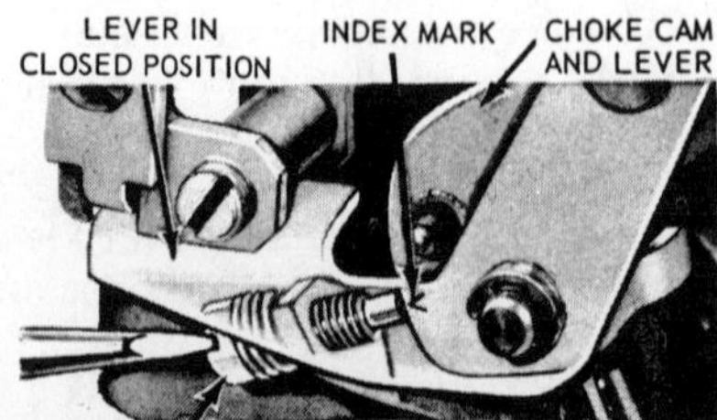

Fast idle adjusting screw—Autolite 2100A

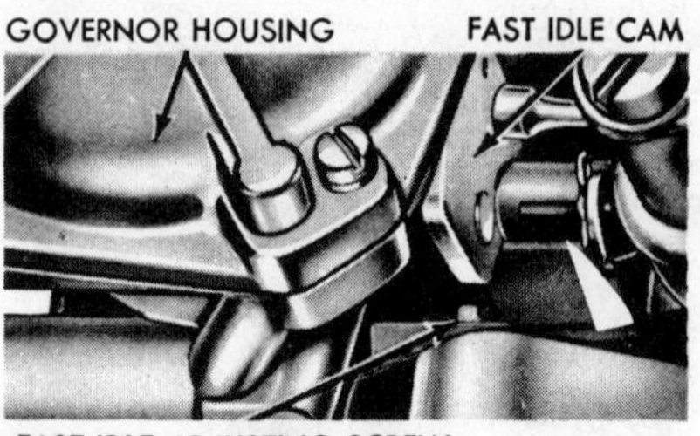

Fast idle adjusting screw—Holley 4150

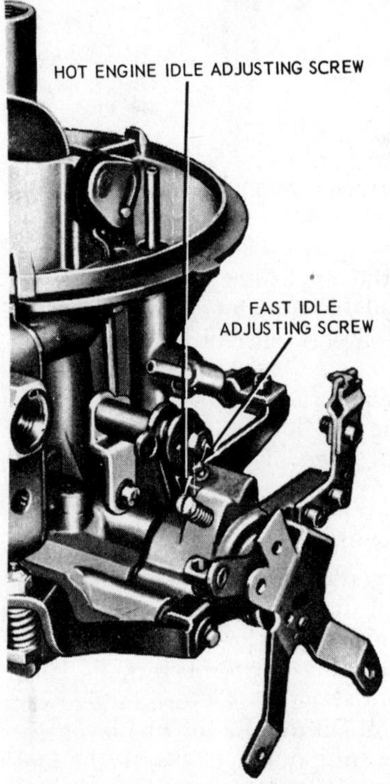

Fast idle adjusting screw—Holley 2300

NOTE: *On the 4 BBL carburetor a 3/16 in. wrench with a 90° head will be necessary.*

6. Turn off the engine and remove the tachometer.
7. Push the choke lever, cable and housing forward to the full choke position and clamp the choke cable housing to the choke cable bracket.
8. Install the air cleaner.

Carter Model YF 1-bbl

1. Position the fast idle screw on the kickdown step of the fast idle cam against the shoulder of the high step.
2. Adjust by bending the choke plate connecting rod to obtain the proper clearance between the lower edge of the choke plate and the carburetor air horn. Use the proper drill bit inserted between the lower edge of the choke plate and the carburetor air horn.

3. With the engine at operating temperature, air cleaner removed and a tachometer attached according to the manufacturer's instructions, manually rotate the fast idle cam to the top step while holding the choke plate fully open. Turn the fast idle adjusting screw inward or outward as required to obtain the proper rpm.

4. When setting the fast idle speed, all vacuum distributor and EGR controls must be disconnected and plugged to insure proper speeds during cold operation.

Autolite Model 2100 2-bbl

1970–72

1. Loosen the choke thermostatic spring housing retaining screws and position the housing 90° in the rich direction.
2. Position the fast idle speed screw at the kick-down step of the fast idle cam. This kick-down step is identified by a small "V" stamped in the side of the casting.
3. Be sure that the fast idle cam is in the kick-down position while checking or adjusting the fast idle cam clearance. Check the clearance between the lower edge of the choke plate and the wall of the air horn by inserting a drill of the specified diameter between them. Adjustment may be accomplished by turning the fast idle cam adjusting screw clockwise to increase or counterclockwise to decrease the clearance.
4. Set the choke thermostatic spring housing to specifications, and adjust the antistall dashpot, idle speed, and fuel mixture.

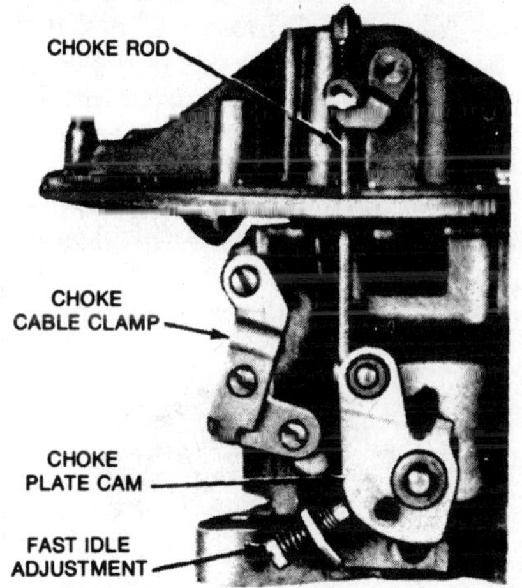

Fast idle speed adjustment for the Autolite 2100, 2150 2-bbl carburetor

Autolite Model 2100 and 2150 2-bbl

1973–80

1. Loosen the choke thermostatic spring housing retaining screws and rotate the housing 90° in the right direction.
2. Position the fast idle speed screw or lever on the high step of the cam.
3. Depress the choke pull-down diaphragm against the diaphragm stop screw thereby placing the choke in the pull-down position.
4. While holding the choke pull-down diaphragm depressed, slightly open the throttle and allow the fast idle cam to fall.
5. Close the throttle and check the position of the fast idle cam or lever. When the fast idle cam is adjusted correctly, the screw should contact the "V" mark on the cam. Adjustment is accomplished by rotating the fast idle cam adjusting screw as needed.

Autolite Model 2150A and 2150 Feedback

1. Set the parking brake and block the wheels.
2. Place the transmission in Neutral or Park.
3. Run the engine up to normal operating temperature.
4. Disconnect the electric connector on the EVAP purge solenoid (feedback models). Disconnect and purge the vacuum signal hose at the EVAP purge valve on non-feedback 2150s.
5. Disconnect and plug the vacuum signal hose at the EGR valve.
6. Place the fast idle adjustment mechanism on the top step of the fast idle cam. Check and adjust the fast idle rpm to specifications.
7. Remove the plug from the EGR hose and reconnect. Remove the plugs from the other plugged hoses and reconnect them to their original locations.

Autolite Model 2150 2-bbl

Canadian 302 and 351 Leaded Fuel Engines

1. Set the parking brake and put the transmission in Park or Neutral.
2. Run the engine up to normal operating temperature.
3. Place the fast idle cam on the second step of the fast idle cam.
4. Check and/or adjust the fast idle rpm to specifications.

Motorcraft Model 7200 VV 2-bbl

1. Place the transmission in park or neutral.
2. Bring the engine to normal operating temperature.
3. Disconnect the purge hose on the canister side of the evaporator purge solenoid. Check to see that purge vacuum is present (solenoid has opened—will require 3 to 5 minute wait after starting the engine) followed by a short time at part throttle. Reconnect the purge hose.
4. Disconnect and plug the vacuum hose at the EGR and purge valves.
5. Place the fast idle lever on the second step

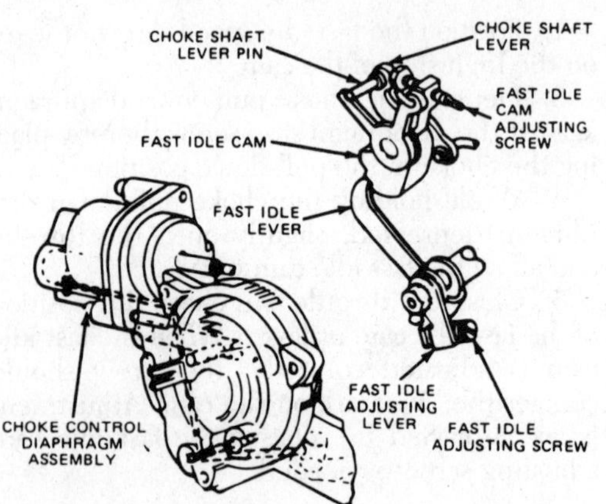

Fast idle adjustment for the Motorcraft 7200VV 2-bbl carburetor

of the fast idle cam. (third step on California models)

6. Adjust the fast idle rpm to specifications.

7. Reconnect the EGR and purge vacuum hoses.

Holley Model 4180C 4-bbl

1. Set the parking brake, put the transmission in Park or Neutral and run the engine up to operating temperature.

2. Turn off the air conditioning and heater controls.

3. Disconnect and plug the vacuum hoses at the air control valve and EGR valve and purge control valves.

4. Place the transmission in the position specified on the underhood decal.

5. If necessary, check and adjust the curb idle rpm.

6. Place the transmission in Neutral or Park and rev the engine. Place the transmission in the specified position according to the underhood decal and recheck the curb idle rpm. Readjust if necessary.

7. Connect an external vacuum source which provides a minimum of 10 inches of vac-

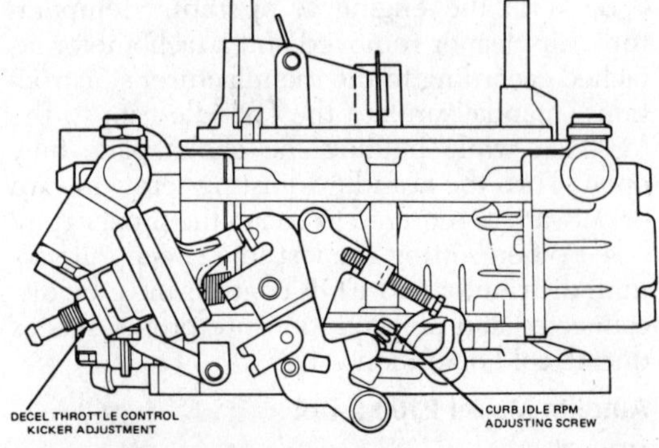

Holley 4180C 4-bbl curb idle and VOTM kicker adjustments locations

uum to the VOTM (Vacuum Operated Throttle Modulator) kicker.

8. Place the transmission in the specified position.

9. Adjust the VOTM (throttle kicker) locknut if necessary to obtain the proper idle rpm.

10. Reconnect all vacuum hoses.

Autolite Model 4300 and 4350 4-bbl

1. Loosen the choke thermostatic spring housing retaining screws and position the housing 90° in the rich direction.

2. Position the fast idle speed screw at the kick-down step of the fast idle cam. This kick-down step is identified by a small "V" stamped in the side of the casting.

3. Be sure that the fast idle cam is in the kick-down position while checking or adjusting the fast idle cam clearance. Check the clearance between the lower edge of the choke plate and the wall of the air horn by inserting a drill of the specified diameter between them. Adjustment may be accomplished by turning the fast idle cam adjusting screw clockwise to increase or counterclockwise to decrease the clearance.

4. Set the choke thermostatic spring hous-

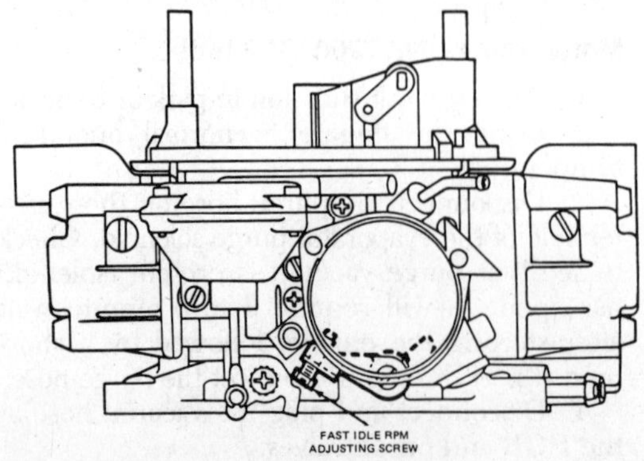

Holley 4180C 4-bbl fast idle adjustment

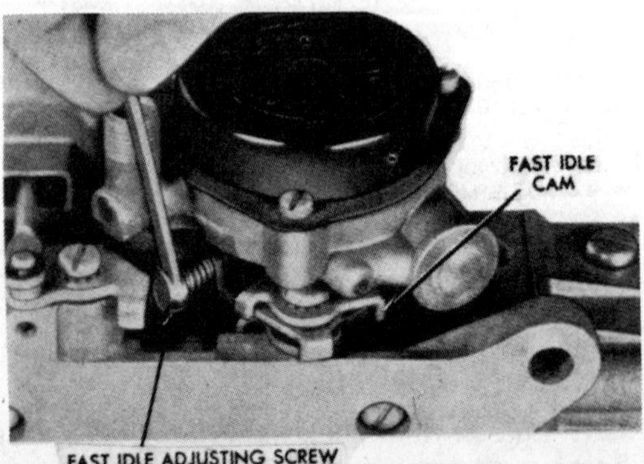

Fast idle adjustment on the Holley 4160 4-bbl

ing to specifications, and adjust the antistall dashpot, idle speed, and fuel mixture.

Holley Model 4160 4-bbl

1. Make sure that the engine idle speed and mixture are adjusted correctly. The fast idle speed is adjusted with the engine at normal operating temperature.
2. With the choke in the wide open position, turn the fast idle adjusting screw in until it just touches the fast idle cam, then back it off ⅛ to ¼ of a turn.

CHOKE PLATE PULL-DOWN CLEARANCE ADJUSTMENT

Carter Model YF 1-bbl
Carter Model YFA 1-bbl

1. Remove the carburetor air cleaner, and remove the choke thermostatic spring housing.
2. Bend a section of 0.026 in. diameter wire at a 90° angle approximately ⅛ in. from one end.
3. Insert the bent end of the wire gauge between the choke piston slot and the right-hand slot in the choke housing. Rotate the choke piston lever counterclockwise until the gauge is snug in the piston slot.
4. Exert light pressure upon the choke piston lever to hold the gauge in position. Check the specified clearance with a drill of the correct diameter between the lower edge of the choke plate and the carburetor bore.
5. Choke plate pull-down clearance may be adjusted by bending the choke piston lever as required to obtain the desired clearance. It is recommended that the choke piston lever be removed prior to bending, in order to prevent distorting the piston link.
6. Install the choke thermostatic spring housing and gasket, and set the housing to the proper specification.

Choke plate pull-down adjustment on the Carter YF 1-bbl

Autolite Model 1101A 1-bbl (Manual Choke 1965)

1. Place the choke linkage in the full choke position.
2. Gradually bend the choke lever tang until a gauge or drill of the specified size will pass through between the choke plate and body.

Autolite Model 2100A 2-bbl (Manual Choke-1965)

1. Pull the choke cam and lever to the full choke position.
2. Insert the specified size drill or gauge between the downward side of the choke plate and the air horn wall.
3. Adjust the choke operating (pull down) rod adjusting nut to just contact the plastic swivel.

Autolite Model 2100 2-bbl

1. Remove the air cleaner.
2. With the engine at its normal operating temperature, loosen the choke thermostatic spring housing retaining screws, and set the housing 90° in the rich direction.
3. Disconnect and remove the choke heat tube from the choke housing.
4. Turn the fast idle adjusting screw outward one full turn.
5. Start the engine. Use a drill of the specified diameter to check the clearance between the lower edge of the choke plate and the air horn wall.
6. To adjust the clearance, turn the diaphragm stopscrew (located on the underside of the choke diaphragm housing). Turning clockwise will decrease the clearance; counterclockwise will increase it.
7. Connect the choke heat tube, and set the choke thermostatic spring housing to the proper specification. Adjust the fast idle speed to specifications.

Autolite Model 2150 2-bbl

1. Remove the air cleaner assembly.
2. Set the throttle on the top step of the fast idle cam.
3. Noting the position of the choke housing cap, loosen the retaining screws and rotate the cap 90 degrees in the rich (closing) direction.
4. Activate the pull-down motor by manually forcing the pull-down control diaphragm link in the direction of applied vacuum or by applying vacuum to the external vacuum tube.

5. Using a drill gauge of the specified diameter, measure the clearance between the choke plate and the center of the air horn wall nearest the fuel bowl.

6. To adjust, reset the diaphram stop on the end of the choke pull-down diaphragm.

7. After adjusting, reset the choke housing cap to the specified notch. Check and reset fast idle speed, if necessary. Install the air cleaner.

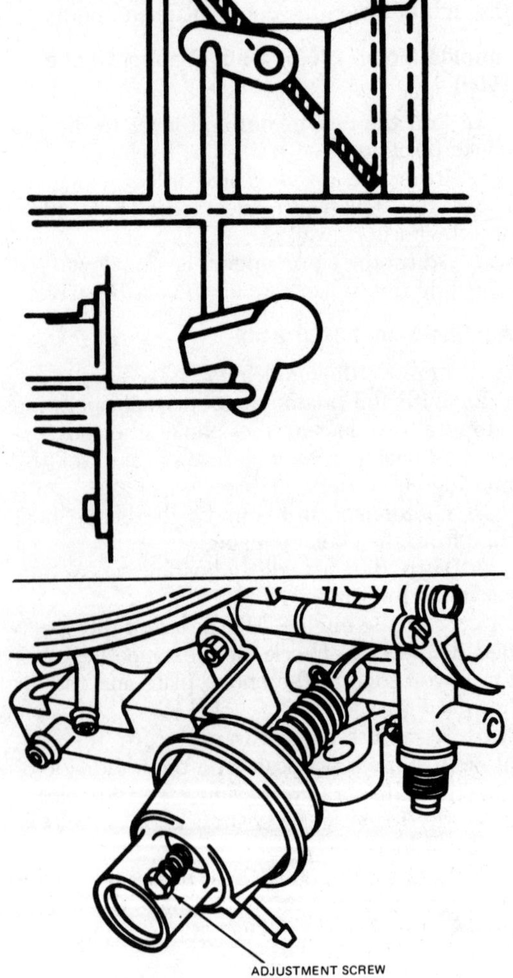

Autolite 2150 2-bbl choke plate pulldown adjustment

Autolite Model 4300 and 4350 4-bbl

1. Remove the air cleaner assembly.

2. Remove the choke cover and thermostatic coil assembly. Block the throttle valve half open so that the fast idle screw does not contact the fast idle cam.

3. Bend a 0.036 in. wire gauge at a 90° angle about ⅛ in. from the end. Insert the bent end between the lower edge of the choke piston slot and the upper edge of the right-hand slot in the choke housing.

4. Move the piston lever counterclockwise until the gauge fits snugly in the slot. Hold the gauge in place by exerting light pressure on the lever.

5. Insert a drill or gauge of the specified thickness (see "Carburetor Specifications" chart) between the lower edge of the choke plate and the air horn wall.

6. To adjust, loosen the hex head screw (left-hand thread) on the choke plate shaft and pry the link away from the tapered shaft. Using a drill gauge 0.010 in. thinner than the specified clearance (to allow for tolerances in the linkage), insert the gauge between the lower edge of the choke plate and the air horn wall. Hold the choke plate against the gauge and maintain a light pressure in a counterclockwise direction on the choke lever. Then, with the choke piston snug against the 0.036 in. wire gauge and the choke plate against the 0.010 in. smaller drill gauge, tighten the hex head screw (left-hand thread) on the choke plate shaft. After tightening the hex head screw, make a final check using a drill gauge of the specified clearance between the choke plate and air horn.

7. After adjustment, install the choke cover and adjust as outlined under "Automatic Choke Housing Adjustment." Install the air cleaner.

Holley Model 4180 4-bbl (Hot Air System)

1. Remove the choke thermostat housing, gasket and retainer.

2. Insert a piece of wire into the choke piston bore to move the piston down against the stop screw.

3. Measure the gap between the lower edge of the choke plate and the air horn wall.

4. Turn the adjustment screw to specifications.

5. Reinstall the choke thermostat housing, gasket and retainer.

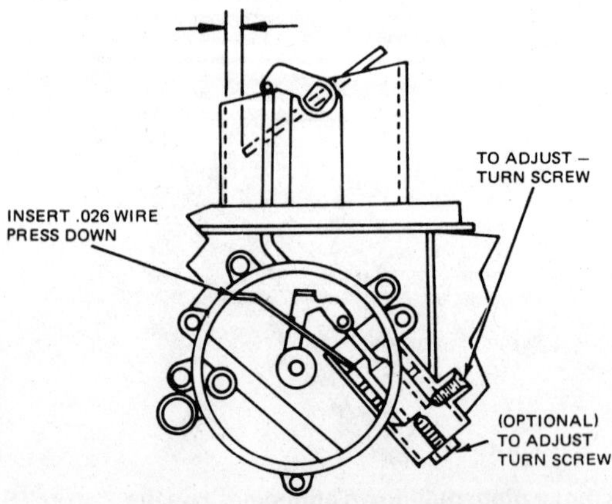

Holley 4180 4-bbl choke pulldown adjustment

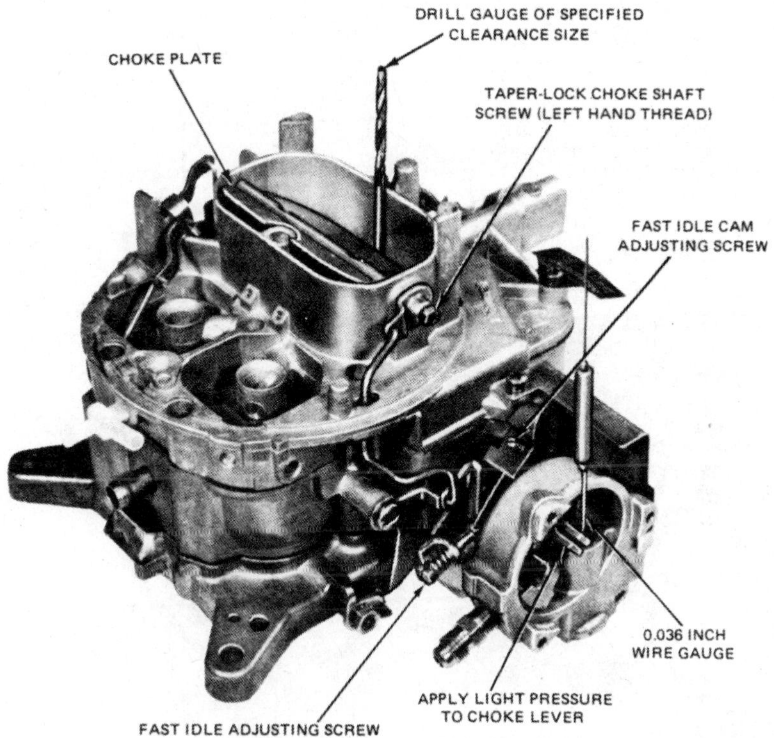

Fast idle and choke plate pull-down adjustment on the Autolite 4300 4-bbl carburetor. The 4350 4-bbl is similar

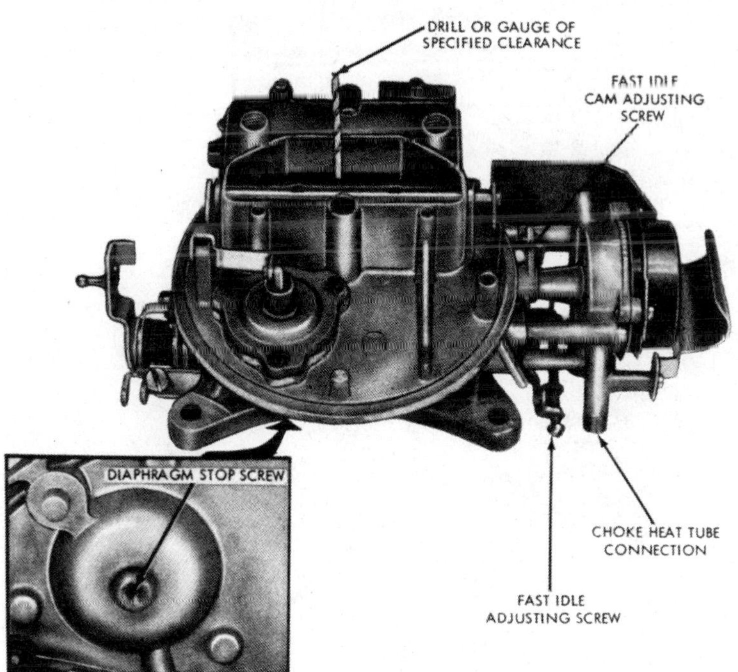

Choke plate pull-down adjustment—Autolite 2100 2-bbl

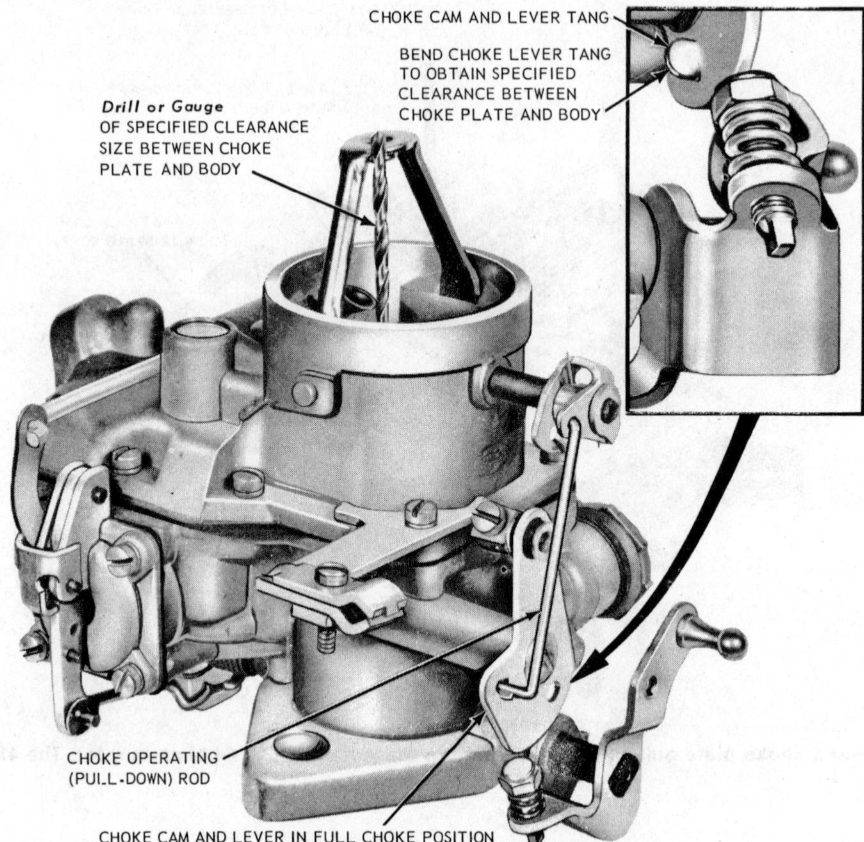

Choke plate pull-down adjustment—Autolite 1101A

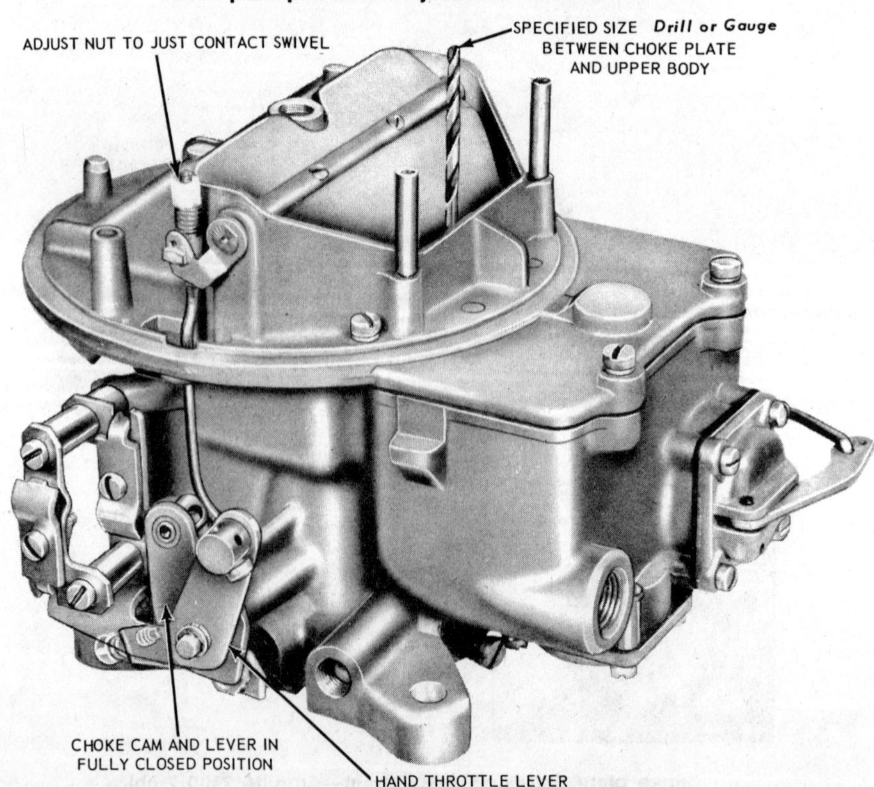

Choke plate pull-down adjustment—Autolite 2100A

AUTOMATIC CHOKE HOUSING ADJUSTMENT

All Carburetors

By rotating the spring housing of the automatic choke, the reaction of the choke to engine temperature can be controlled. To adjust, remove the air cleaner assembly, loosen the thermostatic spring housing retaining screws and set the spring housing to the specified index mark. The marks are shown in the accompanying illustration. After adjusting the setting, tighten the retaining screw and replace the air cleaner assembly to the carburetor.

Automatic choke housing adjustment

DECHOKE CLEARANCE ADJUSTMENT

Carter Model 1-bbl

1. Remove the carburetor air cleaner.
2. Hold the throttle plate to the full open position while closing the choke plate as far as possible without forcing it. Use a drill of the proper diameter (see "Carburetor Specifications" chart) to check the clearance between the choke plate and air horn.
3. Adjust as necessary by bending the pawl on the fast idle speed lever. Bend forward to increase clearance and backward to decrease clearance.

Autolite Model 4300 and 4350 4-bbl

1. Remove the air cleaner assembly.
2. Remove the automatic choke spring housing from the carburetor.
3. With the throttle plate wide open and the choke plate closed as far as possible without forcing it, insert a drill gauge of the specified diameter between the choke plate and air horn.
4. To adjust, bend the arm on the choke trip lever. Bend downward to increase clearance and

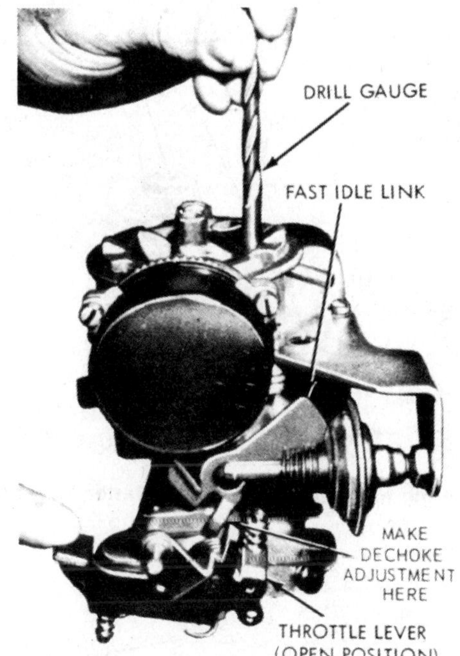

Dechoke clearance adjustment on the Carter YF 1-bbl

upward to decrease clearance. After adjusting, recheck the clearance.

5. Install the automatic choke housing, taking care to engage the thermostatic spring with the tang on the choke lever and shaft assembly.
6. Adjust the automatic choke setting. Install the air cleaner. Adjust the idle speed and dashpot, if so equipped.

METERING ROD ADJUSTMENT

Carter Model YF 1-bbl

With the carburetor air horn and gasket removed from the carburetor, unscrew the idle speed adjusting screw until the throttle plate is tightly closed in the throttle bore. Press downward on the end of the diaphragm shaft until the metering rod arm contacts the lifter link at the diaphragm stem. With the metering rod in the preceding position, turn the rod adjustment screw (see the accompanying illustration) until the metering rod just bottoms in the body casting. Turn the metering rod adjusting screw one additional turn in the clockwise direction. Install the carburetor air horn along with a new gasket.

ACCELERATOR PUMP CLEARANCE SETTING

Autolite Model 1101A 1-bbl

1. Insert a roll pin in the lower hole (HI) position of the lever stop hole.

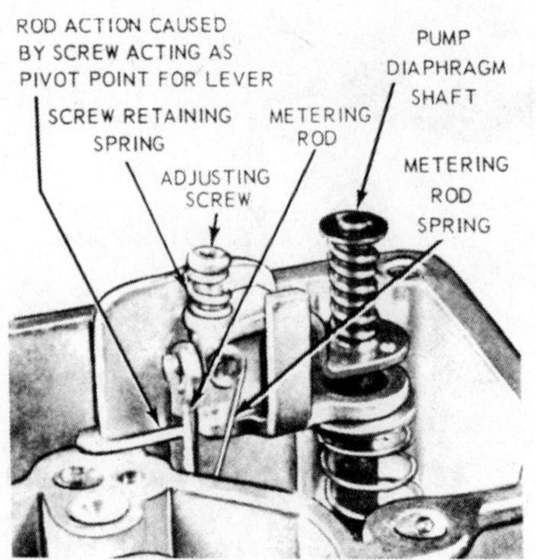

Metering rod adjustment on the Carter YF 1-bbl

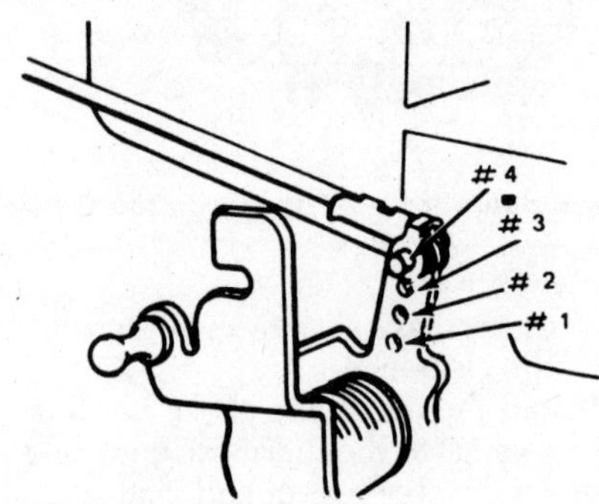

Accelerator pump stroke adjustment on the Autolite 2150 2-bbl

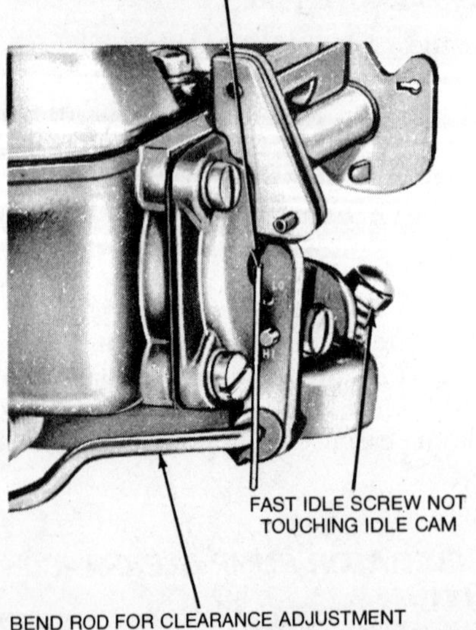

Accelerator pump clearance setting—Autolite 1101A

2. Position the throttle and choke linkage so that the throttle plate will seat in the throttle bore.
3. Hold the throttle plates in the closed position.
4. Position a gauge or drill of the specified thickness given in the Carburetor Specifications Chart between the roll pin and the cover surface.
5. Bend the accelerating pump actuating rod to adjust.

Holley Model 2300 2-bbl

1. With a feeler gauge measure the distance between the accelerating pump operating lever adjustment screw head and the pump arm when the pump arm is depressed manually and the throttle plates are in the wide open position.
2. To adjust loosen the adjusting screw locknut and turn the adjusting screw in to increase the clearance and out to decrease the clearance. One-half turn is equal to approximately 0.015 inch.
3. Hold the adjusting screw in position and tighten the locknut.

ACCELERATOR PUMP STROKE ADJUSTMENT

Autolite Model 1101A 1-bbl

Accelerator requirements in various climates are controlled by the amount of fuel discharged by the accelerating pump. The pump stroke is changed by the location of the roll pin in the lever stop hole. See the Carburetor Specifications Chart.

Holley Model 2300 2-bbl

To satisfy acceleration requirements in various climates, the accelerating pump discharge can be adjusted.

1. The bottom hole (No. 2) in the accelerating pump cam and the throttle lever provides the maximum pump discharge for extreme cold weather and the top hole (No. 1) provides the minimum pump discharge for warm weather operation.
2. To adjust remove the retaining screw, place in the proper hole and make sure the plastic accleerating pump cam, located behind the throttle lever is properly aligned (indexed) with the numbered hole in the throttle lever before replacing the retaining screw.
3. Whenever adjustments are made to the accelerator pump the fuel bowl vent clearance must be checked and adjusted.

Accelerator pump stroke adjustment on the Autolite 2100 2-bbl

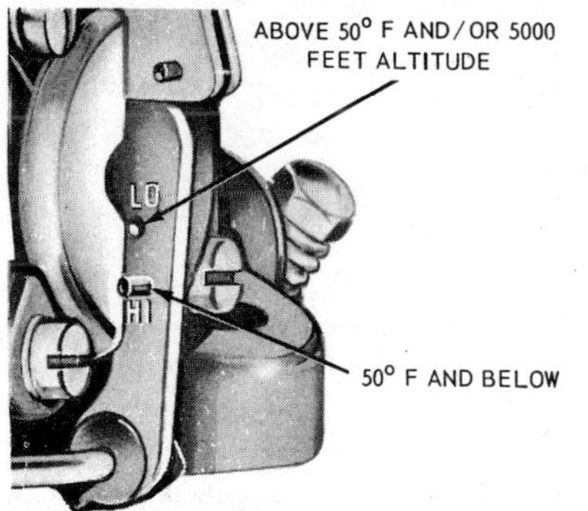

Accelerator pump stroke adjustment—Autolite 1101A

FUEL BOWL VENT CLEARANCE ADJUSTMENT

Holley Model 2300 2-bbl

1. With the air cleaner removed and the engine at operating temperature check the clearance between the bottom of the rubber vent valve and the top of the fuel bowl at the vent opening.
2. To adjust loosen the lock nut on the vent rod adjusting screw and raise or lower the screw, as necessary, to obtain the specified clearance. (0.070–.090)
3. After adjustment has been made hold the screw in place and tighten the locknut with a wrench.

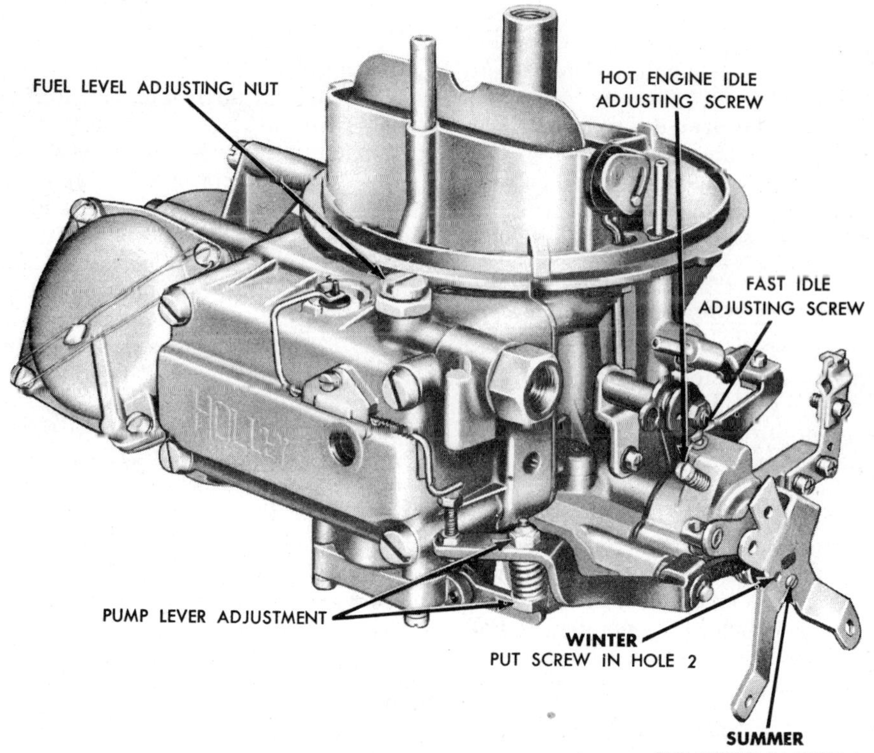

Accelerator pump clearance and stroke adjustment—Holley 2300

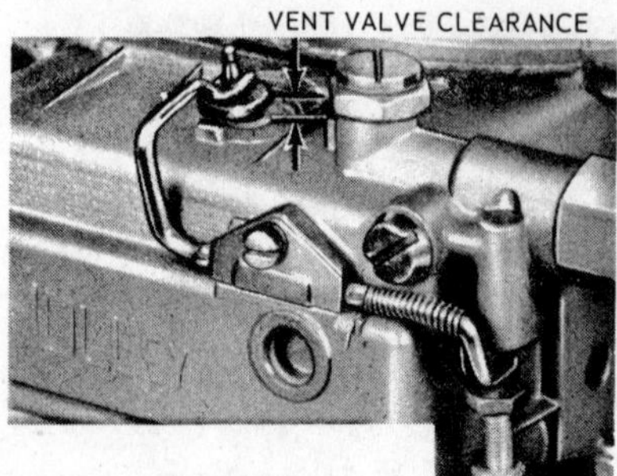

Fuel bowl vent clearance adjustment—Holley 2300

Autolite Model 2100, 2100A and 2150 2-bbl

In order to keep the exhaust emission level of the engine within the specified limits, the accelerating pump stroke has been preset at the factory. The additional holes are provided for differing engine-transmission-body applications only. The primary throttle shaft lever (overtravel lever) has four holes and the accelerating pump link two holes to control the pump stroke. The accelerating pump operating rod should be in the overtravel lever hole number listed in the "Carburetor Specifications" chart, and in the inboard hole (hole closest to the pump plunger) in the accelerating pump link. If the pump stroke has been changed from the specified settings, use the following procedure to correct the stroke.

1. Release the operating rod from the retaining clip by pressing the tab end of the clip toward the rod while pressing the rod away from the clip until it disengages.
2. Position the clip over the specified hole (see "Carburetor Specifications" chart) in the overtravel lever. Press the ends of the clip together and insert the operating rod through the clip and the overtravel lever. Release the clip to engage the rod.

Autolite Model 4300 4-bbl

The pump stroke is preset at the factory to limit exhaust emissions. The additional holes in the operating arm are provided for different engine applications. The stroke should not be changed from the specified hole (see "Carburetor Specifications" chart).

The only adjustments possible are the pump stroke and pump stem height. To change the pump stroke, merely remove the pivot pin and reposition it in the specified hole. To adjust the pump stem height, bend the operating rod at the angles, taking care not to cause binds in the system.

Autolite Model 4350 4-bbl

The accelerator pump adjustment is preset at the factory for reduced exhaust emissions. Adjustment is provided only for different engine installations. The adjustment is internal, with three piston-to-shaft pin positions in the pump piston.

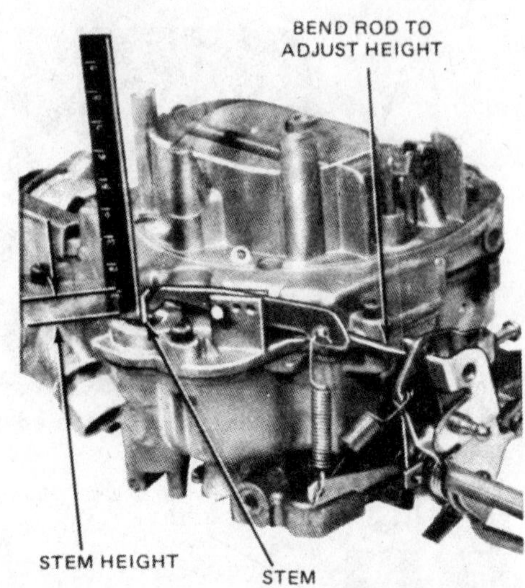

Accelerator pump stroke adjustment—Autolite 4300 4-bbl

To check that the shaft pin is located in the specified piston hole, remove the carburetor air horn and invert it. Disconnect the accelerator pump from the operating arm by pressing downward on the spring and sliding the arm out of the pump shaft slot. Disassemble the spring and nylon keeper retaining the adjustment pin. If the pin is not in its specified hole, remove it, reposition the shaft to the correct hole in the piston assembly and reinstall the pin. Then, slide the nylon retainer over the pin and position the spring on the shaft. Finally, compress the spring on the shaft and install the pump on the pump arm.

NOTE: *Under no circumstances should you adjust the stroke of the accelerator pump by turning the vacuum limiter lever adjusting nut. This adjustment is preset at the factory and modification could result in poor cold driveability.*

ANTI-STALL DASHPOT ADJUSTMENT

All Carburetors

Having made sure that the engine idle speed and mixture are correct and that the engine is at normal operating temperature, loosen the anti-stall dashpot locking nut (see accompanying illustration). With the throttle held closed, depress the plunger with a screwdriver blade and measure the clearance between the throttle lever and the plunger tip. If the clearance is not as specified in the "Carburetor Specifications" chart, turn the dashpot until the proper clearance is obtained between the throttle lever and the plunger tip. After tightening the locking nut, recheck the adjustment.

Model 2700 and 7200-VV (Variable Venturi)

The variable venturi carburetor is similar in appearance to a conventional carburetor, and like a conventional carburetor uses a normal float and fuel bowl system. However, the similarity ends there.

The variable venturi (VV) carburetors are able to vary the area of venturi according to the engine load and speed requirements. In place of the normal choke plate and fixed area venturis, the VV carburetors have a pair of small oblong castings in the top of the upper carburetor body. These castings slide back and forth across the top of the carburetor in response to the air flow requirements of the engine.

Fuel is admitted into the venturi area by means of tapered metering rods that fit into the main jets. These rods are attached to the venturis, and, as the venturis open or close in response to air demand, the fuel needed to maintain the proper mixture increases or decreases as the metering rods slide into the jets. In comparison to a conventional carburetor with fixed venturis and a variable air supply, this system provides a much more precise control of the fuel-air supply during all modes of operation.

The 7200 VV carburetor is the more common of the two VV carburetors. The difference between the 2700VV and the 7200VV is the feedback capability of the 7200 model.

The 7200VV feed-back carburetor varies the air-fuel ratio in response to commands from the EEC module. The air bleed feedback system uses a stepper motor to regulate bleed air admitted into the main fuel metering system in response to a signal from the EEC. The stepper motor governs the metering rods thereby varying the air bleed; the greater the amount of air, the leaner the air-fuel mixture which aids in lower engine emissions.

Since the variable venturi, in both models, keeps air speed constant, separate idle and enrichment systems are not needed in these carburetors.

NOTE: *Any service or troubleshooting on the "VV" carburetors should be performed by qualified mechanics.*

REMOVAL

1. Label and disconnect all hoses attached to the air cleaner. Remove the air cleaner.
2. Remove the throttle cable from the throttle lever. Label and disconnect all vacuum lines, emission hoses, the fuel line and electrical connections to the carburetor. On models with EEC, disconnect the TPS (throttle position sensor) at the harness connecter.
3. Remove the carburetor mounting nuts and remove the carburetor.
4. Remove the mounting gasket/spacer (if equipped) and the lower gasket from the intake manifold. Always use new gaskets when reinstalling.

INSTALLATION

1. Clean the gasket mounting surfaces of the intake manifold, spacer and carburetor.
2. Install the two gaskets with the spacer in between on the intake manifold. Position the carburetor on the intake manifold and connect the spark and EGR lines before bolting the carburetor in position. Connect the TPS harness. Tighten the mounting bolts in stages to prevent damage to the mounting flange of the carburetor.
3. Connect all other lines and hoses removed.
4. Connect the throttle cable. Start the engine and allow it to warm up. Adjust the idle speed.
5. When the carburetor is removed or replaced it is necessary to check or adjust the transmission kickdown or throttle valve lever. Refer to the transmission chapter for procedures.

CURB IDLE SPEED

The VV carburetors may have a vacuum operated throttle modulator (VOTM) (similar to a dashpot) in conjunction with a solenoid, a VOTM alone, or neither of these devices. Vehicles without air conditioning should not be equipped with either a solenoid or a VOTM. Vehicles with air conditioning may have either a solenoid in conjunction with a VOTM or simply the VOTM. On all models equipped with automatic parking brake release, disconnect the vacuum line at the parking brake and plug it.

Vehicles with No Solenoid or VOTM

1. Place the transmission in drive.
2. Turn the throttle stop adjusting screw until the corret idle speed is obtained.
3. Cycle the throttle to check the idle. If the idle falls to within plus or minus 50 rpm of the specified speed, leave it alone.

Vehicles With Both a Solenoid and VOTM

1. Place the transmission in drive, turn the air conditioner on, and make sure the cold enrichment rod is fully seated.
2. Disconnect the electro-magnetic clutch.

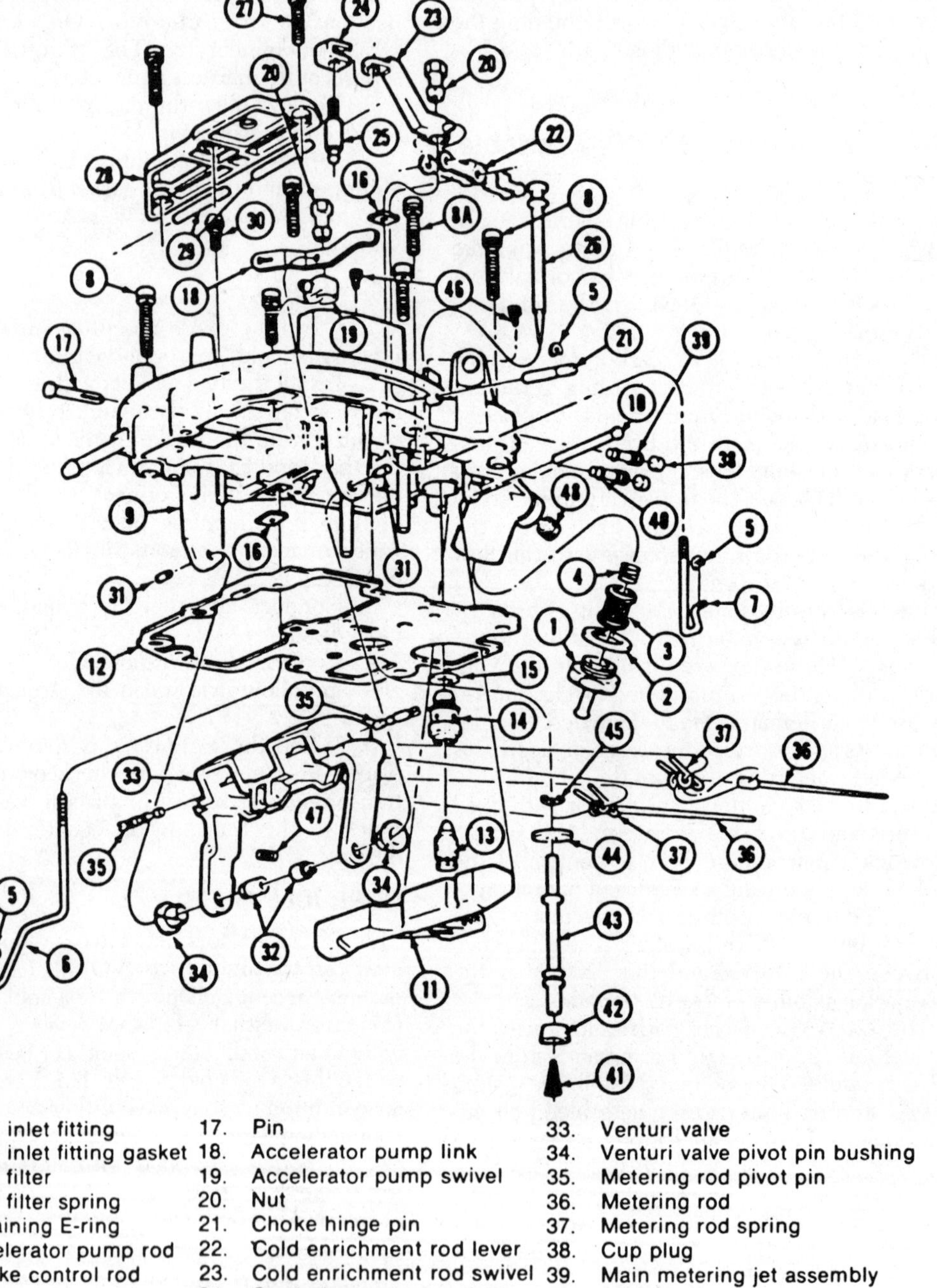

1. Fuel inlet fitting
2. Fuel inlet fitting gasket
3. Fuel filter
4. Fuel filter spring
5. Retaining E-ring
6. Accelerator pump rod
7. Choke control rod
8. Screw
8A. Screw
9. Upper body
10. Float hinge pin
11. Float assembly
12. Float bowl gasket
13. Fuel inlet valve
14. Fuel inlet seat
15. Fuel inlet seat gasket
16. Dust seal
17. Pin
18. Accelerator pump link
19. Accelerator pump swivel
20. Nut
21. Choke hinge pin
22. Cold enrichment rod lever
23. Cold enrichment rod swivel
24. Control vacuum regulator adjusting nut
25. Control vacuum regulator
26. Cold enrichment rod
27. Screw
28. Venturi valve cover plate
29. Roller bearing
30. Venturi air bypass screw
31. Venturi valve pivot plug
32. Venturi valve pivot pin
33. Venturi valve
34. Venturi valve pivot pin bushing
35. Metering rod pivot pin
36. Metering rod
37. Metering rod spring
38. Cup plug
39. Main metering jet assembly
40. O-ring
41. Accelerator pump return spring
42. Accelerator pump cup
43. Accelerator pump plunger
44. Internal vent valve
45. Retaining E-ring
46. Idle trim screw
47. Venturi valve limiter adjusting screw
48. Pipe plug

Typical upper body—VV carburetor (2700VV shown)

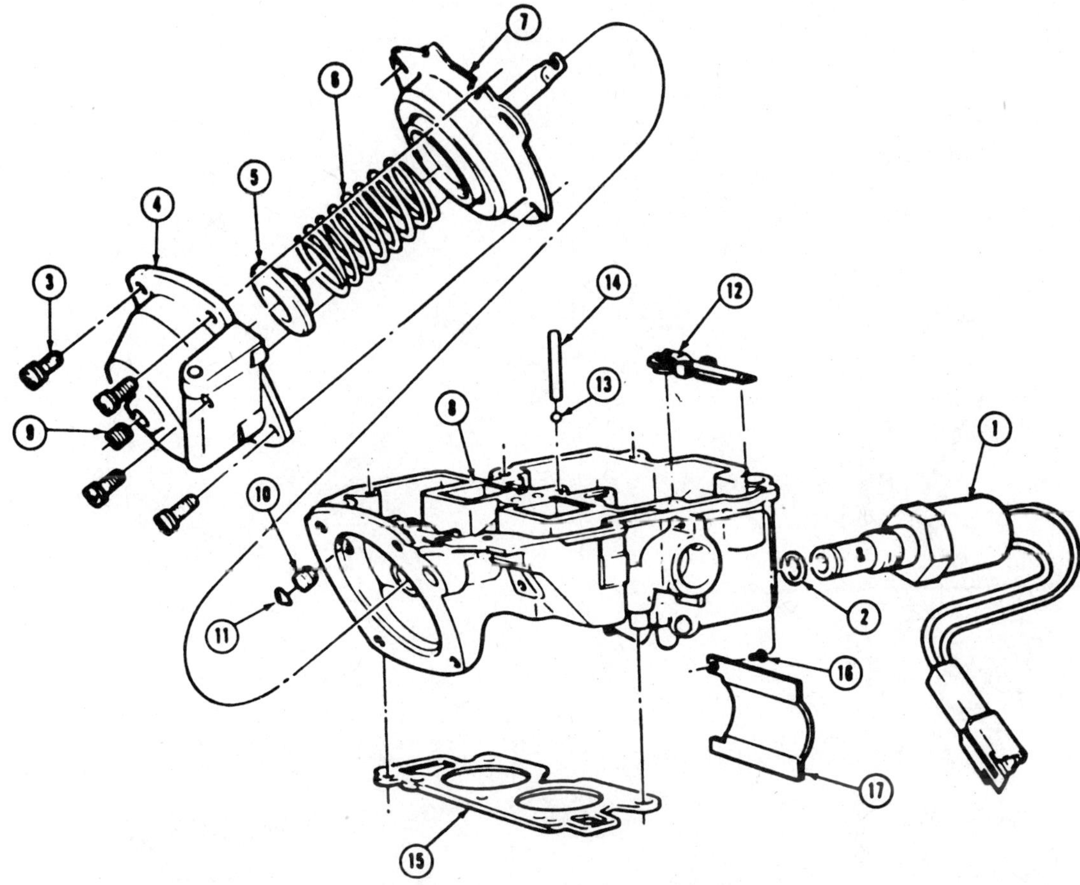

1. Cranking enrichment solenoid
2. O-ring seal
3. Screw
4. Venturi valve diaphragm cover
5. Venturi valve diaphragm spring guide
6. Venturi valve diaphragm spring
7. Venturi valve diaphragm assembly
8. Main body
9. Venturi valve adjusting screw
10. Wide open stop screw
11. Plug expansion
12. Cranking fuel control assembly
13. Accelerator pump check ball
14. Accelerator pump check ball weight
15. Throttle body gasket
16. Screw
17. Choke heat shield

Typical main body—VV carburetor (2700VV shown)

3. Turn the screw at the rear of the solenoid/VOTM to adjust the idle speed.

4. Cycle the throttle to check the repeatability to within plus or minus 50 rpm.

NOTE: *The procedure is the same for a carburetor equipped with only a VOTM.*

CARBURETOR TROUBLESHOOTING

The best way to diagnose a bad carburetor is to eliminate all other possible sources of the problem. If the carburetor is suspected to be the problem, first perform all of the adjustments given in this Section. If this doesn't correct the difficulty, then check the following. Check the ignition system to make sure that the spark plugs, breaker points, and condenser are in good condition and adjusted to the proper specifications. Examine the emission control equipment to make sure that all the vacuum lines are connected and none are blocked or clogged. See the first half of this Chapter. Check the ignition timing adjustment. Check all of the vacuum lines on the engine for loose connections, slips or breaks. Torque the carburetor and intake manifold attaching bolts to the proper specifications. If, after performing all of these checks and adjustments, the problem is still not solved, then you can safely assume that the carburetor is the source of the problem.

OVERHAUL

Efficient carburetion depends greatly on careful cleaning and inspection during overhaul since dirt, gum, water or varnish in or on the carburetor parts are often responsible for poor performance.

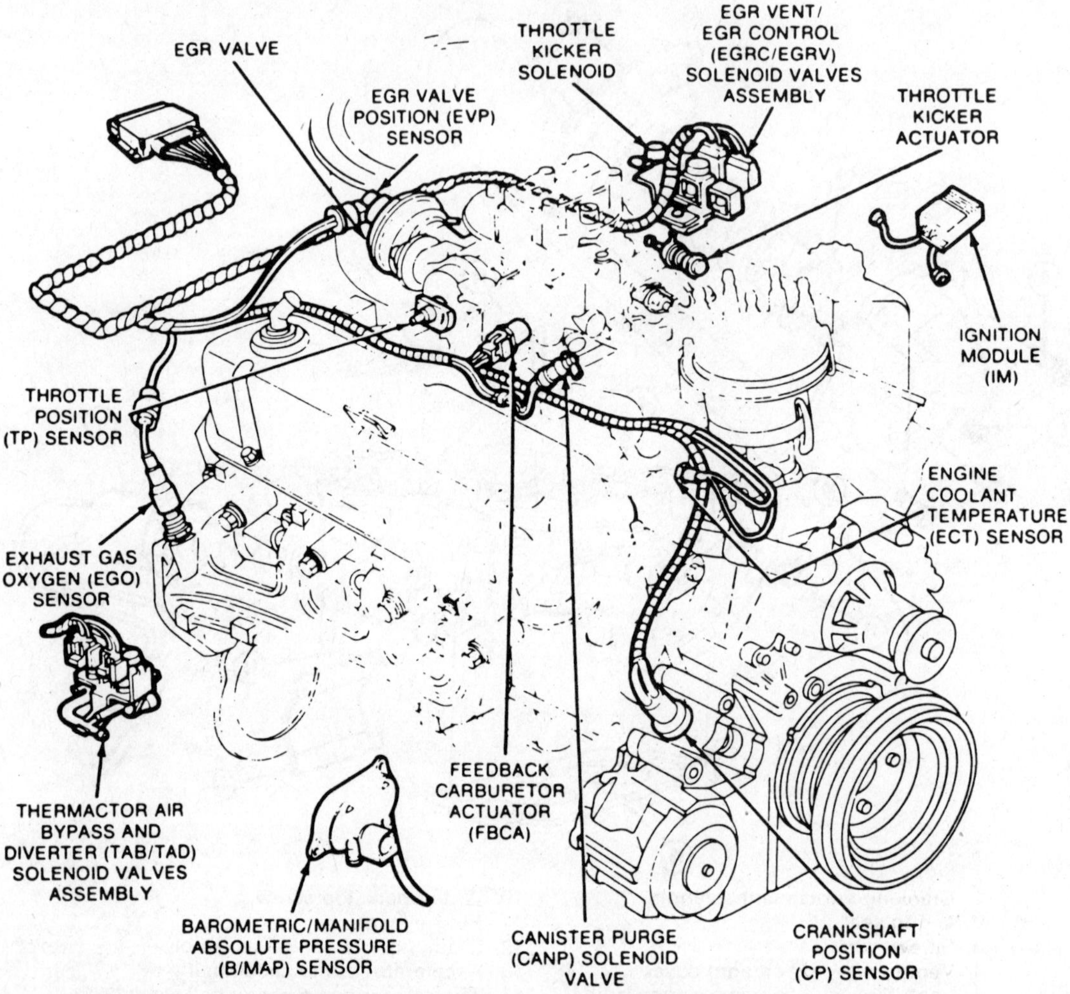

EGR VALVE
EGR VALVE POSITION (EVP) SENSOR
THROTTLE KICKER SOLENOID
EGR VENT/ EGR CONTROL (EGRC/EGRV) SOLENOID VALVES ASSEMBLY
THROTTLE KICKER ACTUATOR
IGNITION MODULE (IM)
THROTTLE POSITION (TP) SENSOR
ENGINE COOLANT TEMPERATURE (ECT) SENSOR
EXHAUST GAS OXYGEN (EGO) SENSOR
FEEDBACK CARBURETOR ACTUATOR (FBCA)
THERMACTOR AIR BYPASS AND DIVERTER (TAB/TAD) SOLENOID VALVES ASSEMBLY
BAROMETRIC/MANIFOLD ABSOLUTE PRESSURE (B/MAP) SENSOR
CANISTER PURGE (CANP) SOLENOID VALVE
CRANKSHAFT POSITION (CP) SENSOR

VV feedback carburetor wiring and vacuum diagram

"C"-CLIP
ACCELERATOR PUMP OPERATING LEVER
THROTTLE LEVER
ACCELERATOR PUMP
VACUUM PISTON LIMITER LEVER
VACUUM PISTON LIMITER LEVER ADJUSTMENT
ACCELERATOR PUMP LINK

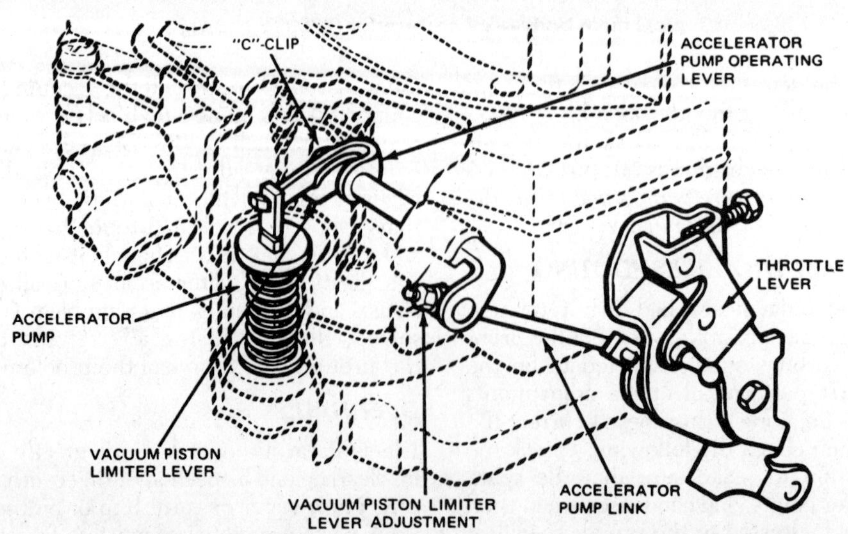

Throttle-to-accelerator pump linkage on the Autolite 4350 4-bbl

Carburetor Specifications

Carter Model YF 1-BBL

Year	Engine No. Cyl Displacement (cu in.)	Carb Tag Number	Float Level (in.)	Main Jet (in.)	Pump Jet (in.)	Choke System: Cap Setting	Choke System: Pull-down (in.)	Choke System: De-choke (in.)	Dashpot Setting (in.)	Fast Idle Cam Kick-down (in.)
1968	6-240	C8UF-G	7/32 ①	0.104	—	—	—	0.280	0.100	—
1969	6-240	C8UF-M	7/32	0.104	—	—	—	0.280	0.100	—
1970	6-240	DOTF-J	7/32	0.101	0.028	Index	0.225	0.280	7/64	—
		DOTF-E	7/32	0.101	0.028	Index	0.225	0.280	Solenoid	—
		DOTF-L	7/32	0.101	0.031	Index	0.225	0.280	Solenoid	—
	6-300	DOTF-K	7/32	0.107	0.028	1 Lean	0.265	0.280	7/64	—
		DOTF-F	7/32	0.107	0.028	1 Lean	0.265	0.280	Solenoid	—
		DOTF-G	7/32	0.107	0.028	Index	0.265	0.280	Solenoid	—
1971	6-240	D1TF-VA	3/8	0.101	0.031	Index	0.230	0.280	Solenoid	0.175
		D1TF-XA	3/8	0.101	0.031	Index	0.230	0.280	NA	0.175
		D1TF-YA	3/8	0.101	0.031	Index	0.230	0.280	7/64	0.175
	6-300	D1TF-ABA	7/32	0.107	0.028	1 Lean	0.260	0.280	7/64	0.175
		D1TF-ZA	7/32	0.107	0.028	1 Lean	0.260	0.280	Solenoid	0.175
		D1TF-AAA	7/32	0.107	0.028	Index	0.260	0.280	Solenoid	0.175
1972	6-240	D2TF-MA	3/8	0.104	0.031	Index	0.230	0.280	Solenoid	0.175
		D2TF-LA	3/8	0.104	0.031	1 Lean	0.230	0.280	Solenoid	0.175
		D2TF-FA	3/8	0.101	0.031	1 Lean	0.230	0.280	Solenoid	0.175
		D2TF-VA	3/8	0.104	0.031	1 Lean	0.230	0.280	Solenoid	0.175
	6-300	D2TF-SA	3/8	0.110	0.031	1 Lean	0.260	0.280	7/64	0.175
1973	6-240	D3TF-TA	3/8	0.104	0.028	Index	0.230	0.280	Solenoid	0.175
		D3TF-KA	3/8	0.098	0.022	1 Lean	0.230	0.280	Solenoid	0.175
		D3TF-AAA	3/8	0.104	0.028	1 Lean	0.230	0.280	Solenoid	0.175
		D3TF-ABA	3/8	0.104	0.028	Index	0.230	0.280	Solenoid	0.175
	6-300	D3TF-LA	3/8	0.101	0.031	1 Rich	0.230	0.280	0.100	0.110
1974	6-240	D4TE-ZA	3/8	0.104	—	1 Lean	0.230	0.280	Solenoid	0.175
	6-300	D4TE-YC	3/8	0.110	—	Index	0.290	0.280	0.100	0.110
1975	6-300	D5TE-ALA	3/8	0.110	—	Index	0.290	0.280	—	0.110
		D5TE-APA	3/8	0.110	—	Index	0.290	0.280	—	0.110
		D5TE-ADA	3/8	0.110	—	Index	0.290	0.280	—	0.110
		D5TE-AKA	3/8	0.110	—	Index	0.290	0.280	—	0.110
		D5TE-AMA	3/8	0.101	—	1 Rich	0.230	0.280	—	0.110
		D5TE-AGA	3/8	0.101	—	1 Rich	0.230	0.280	—	0.110
		D5TE-ANA	3/8	0.101	—	1 Rich	0.230	0.280	—	0.110
1976	6-300	D5TE-ADA	3/8	0.110	—	Index	0.290	0.280	—	0.110
		D5TE-ADB	23/32	0.110	—	Index	0.290	0.280	—	0.110
		D5TE-AKA	3/8	0.110	—	Index	0.290	0.280	—	0.110
		D5TE-AKB	23/32	0.110	—	Index	0.290	0.280	—	0.110
		D5UE-EA	3/8	0.110	—	Index	0.290	0.280	—	0.110

Carburetor Specifications (cont.)

Carter Model YF 1-BBL

Year	Engine No. Cyl Displace-ment (cu in.)	Carb Tag Number	Float Level (in.)	Main Jet (in.)	Pump Jet (in.)	Choke System Cap Setting	Choke System Pull-down (in.)	Choke System De-choke (in.)	Dashpot Setting (in.)	Fast Idle Cam Kick-down (in.)
1976	6-300	D5TE-BSB	23/32	0.107	—	Index	0.290	0.280	—	0.110
		D5TE-CBA	3/8	0.107	—	Index	0.290	0.280	—	0.110
		D5UE-FA	3/8	0.110	—	Index	0.290	0.280	—	0.110
		D5TE-APB	23/32	0.110	—	Index	0.290	0.280	—	0.110
		D5TE-CAB	23/32	0.107	—	Index	0.290	0.280	—	0.110
		D6TE-HA	23/32	0.107	—	Index	0.290	0.280	—	0.110
		D5UE-AAB	23/32	0.107	—	Index	0.290	0.280	—	0.110
		D5UE-HB	23/32	0.110	—	Index	0.290	0.280	—	0.110
		D6TF-DA	23/32	0.107	—	Index	0.290	0.280	—	0.110
		D5UE-GB	23/32	0.110	—	Index	0.290	0.280	—	0.110
		D5TE-AGA	3/8	0.101	—	INR	0.230	0.280	—	0.110
		D5TE-AGB	3/8	0.101	—	INR	0.230	0.280	—	0.110
		D5TE-AFA	3/8	0.104	—	Manual Choke				
		D5TE-AFB	3/8	0.104	—	Manual Choke				
		D5TE-AJA	3/8	0.104	—	Manual Choke				
		D5TE-AJB	3/8	0.104	—	Manual Choke				

① From bead of upper body to lowest surface of float when inverted

Carburetor Specifications (cont.)

Autolite Model 1101A 1-BBL

Year	Engine No. Cyl Displace-ment (cu in.)	Carb Model	Carb Tag Number	Float Level (Dry) (in.)	Main Jet No.	Choke Plate Pull-down (in.)	Anti-Stall Dashpot Clearance	Accelerator Pump Clearance Setting	Accelerator Operating Red Hole Position
1965	6-240	1101A	C5TF-G	1 3/32	69F	0.400	3 1/2	7/32	①
		1101A	C5TF-H	1 3/32	68F	0.400	3 1/2	7/32	①
		1101A	C5TF-1	1 3/32	69F	0.400	3 1/2	7/32	①
		1101A	C5TF-AC	1 3/32	69F	0.400	3 1/2	7/32	①
	6-300	1101A	C5TF-N	1 3/32	69F	0.400	3 1/2	7/32	①
		1101A	C5TF-R	1 3/32	68F	0.400	3 1/2	7/32	①
		1101A	C5TF-M	1 3/32	69F	0.400	3 1/2	7/32	①
1966	6-240	1101A	C5TF-G	1.090	69F	—	3 1/2	0.230	①
		1101A	C5TF-H	1.090	68F	—	3 1/2	0.210	①
		1101A	C5TF-AC	1.090	69F	—	—	0.220	①
		1101A	C5TF-H	—	69F	—	3 1/2	0.210	①
		1101A	C6TF-J	1.202	68F	—	3 1/2	0.210	①

Carburetor Specifications (cont.)

Autolite Model 1101A 1-BBL

Year	Engine No. Cyl Displacement (cu in.)	Carb Model	Carb Tag Number	Float Level (Dry) (in.)	Main Jet No.	Choke Plate Pulldown (in.)	Anti-Stall Dashpot Clearance	Accelerator Pump Clearance Setting	Accelerator Operating Red Hole Position
1966	6-240	1101A	C6TF-E	1.020	69F	—	3½	0.220	①
		1101A	C6TF-M	1.020	69F	—	—	0.220	①
	6-300	1101A	C5TF-N	1.090	69F	—	—	0.230	①
		1101A	C5TF-R	1.090	69F	—	—	0.230	①
		1101A	C6TF-K	1.020	69F	—	—	0.210	①
		1101A	C6TF-L	1.020	68F	—	3½	0.210	①
		1101A	C6TF-D	—	69F	—	—	—	①
		1101A	C6TF-N	1.020	69F	—	—	0.220	①
		1101A	C5TF-AH	1.090	69F	—	—	0.210	①
1967	6-240	1101A	C5TF-G	1 3/32	69F	—	—	0.210	①
		1101A	C6TF-E	1 3/32	69F	—	—	—	①
		1101A	C5TF-AC	1 3/32	69F	—	—	0.220	①
	6-300	1101A	C5TF-N	1 3/32	69F	—	—	0.210	①
		1101A	C6TF-D	1 3/32	69F	—	—	—	—
		1101A	C5TF-AH	1 3/32	69F	—	—	0.220	①
1968	6-240	1101A	C8TF-J	1 3/32	69F	—	—	0.210	Hi
		1101A	C8TF-K	1 3/32	68F	—	3½	0.210	Hi
		1101A	C8TF-C	1 3/32	67F	—	0.100	0.220	—
		1101A	C8TF-M	1 3/32	69F	—	—	0.210	—
		1101A	C8TF-L	1 1/64	69F	—	—	0.210	—
	6-300	1101A	C8TF-R	1 3/32	69F	—	—	0.210	Hi
		1101A	C8TF-S	1 3/32	68F	—	3½	0.210	Hi
		1101A	C8TF-E	1 3/32	69F	—	0.100	0.220	—
		1101A	C8TF-F	1 3/32	68F	—	0.100	0.220	
		1101A	C8TF-T	1 1/64	69F	—	—	0.220	—
		1101A	C8TF-G	1 1/64	68F	—	0.100	0.220	—
		1101A	C8TF-U	1 3/32	69F	—	—	0.220	—
1969	6-240	1101A	C8TF-S	1 3/32	69F	—	—	0.210	Hi
		1101A	C8TF-R	1 3/32	68F	—	3 Turns	0.210	Hi
		1101A	C8TF-L	1 3/32	69F	—	—	0.220	—
		1101A	C8TF-AK	1 3/32	69F	—	—	0.220	—
	6-300	1101A	C8TF-S	1 3/32	69F	—	3½	0.210	Hi
		1101A	C8TF-T	1 3/32	69F	—	—	0.220	—
		1101A	C8TF-U	1 3/32	69F	—	—	0.220	—
		1101A	C9TF-G	1 3/32	71F	—	0.80	0.190	Hi
		1101A	C9TF-H	1 3/32	71F	—	0.80	0.190	—
		1101A	C8TF-F	1 3/32	68F	—	0.100	0.220	—

① 50°F and below position in hole marked "HI"
50°F and above or above altitude position in hole marked "LO"

Carburetor Specifications

Autolite Model 2100A 2-BBL

Year	Engine No. Cyl Displace-ment (cu in.)	Carb Model	Carb Tag Number	Float Level (Wet) (in.)	Idle Jet (in.)	Main Jet No.	Power Jet (in.)	Pump Jet (in.)	Choke System Cap Setting	Pull-down (in.)	Dashpot (in.)	Accelerator Operating Red Hole Position
1965	8-352	2100A	C5TF-B	29/32	—	52F	—	—	—	0.230	—	3
		2100A	C5TF-C	29/32	—	51F	—	—	—	0.230	—	3
		2100A	C5TF-Y	29/32	—	52F	—	—	—	0.230	—	3
		2100A	C5TF-Z	29/32	—	51F	—	—	—	0.230	—	3
1966–67	8-352	2100A	C6TF-B	0.875	—	52F	—	—	—	0.230	—	3
		2100A	C6TF-C	0.875	—	51F	—	—	—	0.230	0.075	3
		2100A	C6TF-T	0.910	—	51F	—	—	—	0.250	0.075	4
		2100A	C6TF-R	0.910	—	51F	—	—	—	0.250	—	4
		2100A	C6TF-S	0.910	—	51F	—	—	—	0.250	—	4

Carburetor Specifications (cont.)

Autolite Model 2100 and 2150 2-BBL

Year	Engine No. Cyl Displace-ment (cu in.)	Carb Model	Carb Tag Number	Float Level (Wet) (in.)	Idle Jet (in.)	Main Jet No.	Power Jet (in.)	Pump Jet (in.)	Choke System Cap Setting	Pull-down (in.)	Dashpot (in.)	Accelerator Operating Rod Hole Position
1970	8-302	2100	DOUF-B	13/16	0.028	48f	0.028	0.028	2 Rich	—	Solenoid	2
		2100	DOUF-C	13/16	0.028	48F	0.028	0.028	Index	0.170	5/64	3
		2100	DOUF-E	13/16	0.028	48F	0.028	0.028	Index	—	Solenoid	2
	8-360, 8-390	2100	DOTF-B	7/8	0.031	55F	0.029	0.031	Index	0.190	1/8	3
		2100	DOTF-N	7/8	0.031	55F	0.029	0.031	Index	0.190	Solenoid	3
		2100	DOTF-C	13/16	0.031	54F	0.031	0.031	Index	0.190	1/8	3
		2100	DOTF-M	13/16	0.031	54F	0.031	0.031	Index	0.190	Solenoid	3
		2100	DOTF-R	13/16	0.031	54F	0.031	0.031	Index	0.190	1/8	3
		2100	DOTF-S	7/8	0.031	55F	0.029	0.031	Index	0.190	1/8	3
1971	8-302	2100	D1TF-AMA	13/16	0.028	47E	0.031	0.031	Index	0.170	Solenoid	2
		2100	D1TF-EA	13/16	0.028	47E	0.032	0.028	Index	0.160	1/8	3
	8-360, 8-390	2100	D1TF-HA	7/8	0.031	55F	0.038	0.031	Index	0.190	1/8	3
		2100	D1TF-ALA	7/8	0.031	55F	0.036	0.031	2 Rich	0.190	1/8	3
		2100	D1TF-NA	13/16	0.031	53F	0.040	0.031	1 Rich	0.190	1/8	3
		2100	D1TF-AKA	13/16	0.031	54F	0.038	0.028	2 Rich	0.170	1/8	3
1972	8-302	2100	D2TF-EA	13/16	0.028	47F	0.033	0.031	2 Rich	0.140	Solenoid	2
		2100	D2TF-CA	13/16	0.028	47F	0.033	0.028	2 Rich	0.140	1/16	3
		2100	D2TF-DB	13/16	0.028	47F	0.034	0.028	2 Rich	0.140	1/16	3
	8-360, 8-390	2100	D2TF-AA	7/8	0.031	54F	0.038	0.031	1 Lean	0.160	1/8	3

Carburetor Specifications (cont.)

Autolite Model 2100 and 2150 2-BBL

Year	Engine No. Cyl Displace-ment (cu in.)	Carb Model	Carb Tag Number	Float Level (Wet) (in.)	Idle Jet (in.)	Main Jet No.	Power Jet (in.)	Pump Jet (in.)	Choke System: Cap Setting	Choke System: Pull-down (in.)	Dashpot (in.)	Accelerator Operating Rod Hole Position
1972	8-326, 8-390	2100	D2TF-AB	7/8	0.031	54F	0.038	0.031	1 Lean	0.160	1/8	3
		2100	D2TF-FC	7/8	0.031	54F	0.038	0.031	1 Lean	0.160	Solenoid	2
		2100	D2TF-AAA	7/8	0.031	54F	0.038	0.031	1 Lean	0.160	Solenoid	2
		2100	D2TF-JA	7/8	0.031	55F	0.038	0.031	2 Rich	0.160	1/8	3
		2100	D2TF-GA	13/16	0.031	53F	0.040	0.031	Index	0.160	1/8	3
		2100	D2TF-KA	13/16	0.031	54F	0.040	0.031	2 Rich	0.160	1/8	3
1973	8-302	2100	NR	13/16	0.028	47F	0.038	0.031	2 Rich	—	Solenoid	2
		2100	D3TF-NA	13/16	0.028	47F	0.038	0.031	2 Rich	—	Solenoid	2
		2100	D3TF-BE	29/36	0.028	47F	0.035	0.031	2 Rich	—	Solenoid	2
	8-360, 8-390	2100	D3TF-DD	7/8	0.031	55F	0.038	0.031	Index	—	Solenoid	3
		2100	D3TF-MC	13/16	0.031	55F	0.038	0.031	Index	—	Solenoid	3
		2100	D3TF-GC	7/8	0.031	55F	0.038	0.031	Index	—	None	3
		2100	D3TF-HC	13/16	0.031	55F	0.038	0.031	Index	—	0.065	3
		2100	D3TF-DE	7/8	0.033	54F	0.038	0.031	Index	—	Solenoid	3
		2100	D3TF-UA	13/16	0.031	53F	0.040	0.031	Index	—	Solenoid	3
		2100	D3TF-MC	13/16	0.033	54F	0.038	0.031	Index	—	Solenoid	3
		2100	D3TF-VA	7/8	0.031	53F	0.040	0.031	Index	—	Solenoid	3
		2100	D3TF-XA	13/16	0.031	53F	0.040	0.031	1 Lean	—	Solenoid	3
1974	8-302	2100	D4TE-EA	13/16	—	47F	—	—	2 Rich	—	—	2
		2100	D4TE-CAA	13/16	—	49F	—	—	2 Rich	—	—	2
		2100	D4TE-LA	13/16	—	48F	—	—	2 Rich	—	—	2
		2100	D4TE-AZA	13/16	—	49F	—	—	2 Rich	—	—	2
	8-360	2100	D4TE-GA	13/16	—	47F	—	—	2 Rich	—	—	3
		2100	D4TE-TA	7/8	—	53F	—	—	Index	—	—	3
		2100	D4TE-BAA	7/8	—	56F	—	—	1 Rich	—	—	3
1975	8-302	2150	D5TE-BHA	7/8	—	52F	—	—	Index	0.135	—	2
		2150	D5TE-LA	7/8	—	52F	—	—	Index	0.135	—	2
		2150	D5TE-PA	7/8	—	52F	—	—	3 Rich	0.160	—	2
	8-360	2150	D5TE-BCA	7/8	—	57F	—	—	2 Rich	0.179	—	3
		2150	D5TE-BCB	7/8	—	58F	—	—	2 Rich	0.179	—	3
		2150	D5TE-BFA	7/8	—	57F	—	—	2 Rich	0.179	—	3
		2150	D5TE-BFB	7/8	—	57F	—	—	2 Rich	0.179	—	3
		2150	D5TE-VA	7/8	—	57F	—	—	2 Rich	0.179	—	3
		2150	D5TE-AUB	7/8	—	57F	—	—	2 Rich	0.179	—	3
		2150	D5TE-BGA	7/8	—	55F	—	—	3 Rich	0.179	—	3
		2150	D5TE-ZA	7/8	—	56F	—	—	3 Rich	0.179	—	3
		2150	D5TE-YD	7/8	—	56F	—	—	3 Rich	0.179	—	3
		2150	D5TE-AAD	7/8	—	56F	—	—	3 Rich	0.179	—	3

Carburetor Specifications (cont.)

Autolite Model 2100 and 2150 2-BBL

Year	Engine No. Cyl Displace-ment (cu in.)	Carb Model	Carb Tag Number	Float Level (Wet) (in.)	Idle Jet (in.)	Main Jet No.	Power Jet (in.)	Pump Jet (in.)	Choke System: Cap Setting	Choke System: Pull-down (in.)	Dashpot (in.)	Accelerator Operating Rod Hole Position
1975	8-390	2150	D5TE-BDA	7/8	—	57F	—	—	2 Rich	0.179	—	3
		2150	D5TE-BDB	7/8	—	57F	—	—	2 Rich	0.179	—	3
		2150	D5TE-BEA	7/8	—	56F	—	—	2 Rich	0.179	—	3
1976	8-302	2150	D5TE-BMA	7/8	—	—	—	—	2R	—	—	3
		2150	D5TE-PA	7/8	—	—	—	—	3R	—	—	2
	8-360	2150	D5TE-ABA	0.810	—	47F	—	—	Manual		—	4
		2150	D5TE-ASA	7/8	—	57F	—	—	Index	0.179	—	4
		2150	D5TE-ATA	7/8	—	57F	—	—	Index	0.179	—	4
		2150	D5TE-BYA	7/8	—	56F	—	—	2NR	0.140	—	3
		2150	D5TE-AAF	7/8	—	55F	—	—	3NR	0.140	—	3
		2150	D5TE-YF	7/8	—	56F	—	—	2NR	0.140	—	3
		2150	D5TE-ZB	7/8	—	56F	—	—	2NR	0.140	—	3
	8-390	2150	D5TE-BEB	7/8	—	56F	—	—	2NR	0.140	—	3

Carburetor Specifications (cont.)

Holley Model 2300 2-BBL

Year	Engine No. Cyl Displace-ment (cu in.)	Carb Model	Carb Tag Number	Float Level (Wet)	Main Metering Jet No.	Power Valve No.	Accelerator Pump Clearance (in.)	Accelerator Pump Operating Rod Hole Position	Fast Idle RPM
1965	8-361	2300	C4TF-BZ	①	60	45	0.015	2	2600
1966–67	8-361	2300	C5TF-AU	①	60	45	—	2	2600
1968	8-361	2300	C7TF-AD	①	61	95	0.015	2	2600
		2300	C8TF-AR	①	60	65	0.015	2	2300 ②
1969	8-361	2300	C8TF-AR	①	60	6–8	0.015	2	2300 ②
		2300	C9HF-B	①	59	3–5	0.015	2	2300 ②

① Lower edge of sight plug ② On high step of cam

Carburator Specifications (cont.)

Holley Model 4150 4-BBL

Year	Engine No. Cyl Displace-ment (cu in.)	Carb Model	Carb Tag Number	Float Level (Wet)	Main Metering Jet No.	Power Valve No.	Accelerator Pump Clearance (in.)	Accelerator Pump Operating Rod Hole Position	Fast Idle RPM
1965	8-391	4150	C4TF-CA	①	51	45	—	—	2600
1966–67	8-391	4150	C5TF-AT	①	52	65	—	2	2600
1968	8-391	4150	C7TF-AE	①	53	95	—	1	—
		4150	C8TF-AS	①	51	65	—	—	—
1969	8-391	4150	C8TF-AS	①	60	—	—	1	2300
		4150	C9HF-C	①	51	—	—	2	2300

① Lower edge of sight plug opening

Carburetor Specifications (cont.)

Autolite Model 4300 and 4350 4-BBL

Year	Engine No. Cyl Displace-ment (cu in.)	Carb Model	Carb Tag Number	Float Level (in.)	Main Metering Jet No.	Choke System: Cap Setting	Choke System: Pull-down (in.)	Choke System: Fast Idle Cam (in.)	Choke System: De-choke (in.)	Accelerator Pump Operating Rod Hole Position
1974	8-460	4300	D4TE-BB	3/4	61F	Index	0.220	0.220	—	1
1975	8-460	4350	D5TE-ARC	15/16	421	Index	0.160	0.170	0.300	1
		4350	D5TE-ARD	1.00	421	Index	0.160	0.170	0.300	1
		4350	D5TE-BBA	15/16	421	Index	0.160	0.170	0.300	1
		4350	D5TE-BBB	59/64	421	Index	0.160	0.170	0.300	1
		4350	D5TE-BBC	1.00	421	Index	0.160	0.170	0.300	1
1976	8-460	4350	D6UE-KA	1.00	421	Index	0.160	0.170	0.300	Inner 2
		4350	D6UE-LA	1.00	421	Index	0.160	0.170	0.300	Inner 2
		4350	D5TE-NA	1.00	421	Index	0.160	0.170	0.300	Inner 2
		4350	D6TE-AU	1.00	421	Index	0.160	0.170	0.300	Inner 2

Carburetor Specifications (cont.)

Holley Model 4160 4-BBl

Year	Engine No. Cyl Displace-ment (cu in.)	Carb Model	Carb Tag Number	Float Level	Main Metering Jet No.	Power Valve No.	Choke System: Cap Setting	Choke System: Pull-down (in.)	Choke System: Fast Idle Cam (in.)	Unloader (in.)
1975	8-390	4160	D5TE-DA	①	652	10	Index	0.180	Top Step	0.315
		4160	D5TE-EA	①	612	18	Index	0.180	—	0.315
		4160	D5TE-FA	①	652	10	Index	0.180	—	0.315
		4160	D5TE-GA	①	612	10	Index	0.180	—	0.315

① See text for procedure

1979–81 Carburetor Specifications

To determine the applicable carburetor specifications listed in the table below, refer to the engine calibration code on the vehicle's underhood sticker. This method is necessary due to the multiplicity of engine setting variations which are required to meet Federal and California emission regulations.

Calibration Number	Choke Plate Pulldown Setting (inches)	Time for Choke Plate to Rotate (come off) (seconds—maximum)	Air Flow (pounds per minute)	Choke Setting	Fast Idle rpm: High Cam	Fast Idle rpm: Kick Down	Curb Idle rpm: ①A/C Off/On	Curb Idle rpm: Non-AC	TSP Off rpm: AC	TSP Off rpm: Non-AC	Timing rpm
9-51G-RO	.230	80	.06	Index	—	1600	700	700	500	500	500
9-51J-RO	.230	80	.06	Index	—	1600	700	700	500	500	500
9-51K-RO	.230	80	.06	Index	—	1600	700	700	500	500	500
9-51L-RO	.230	80	.06	Index	—	1600	700	700	500	500	500
9-51M-RO	.230	80	.06	Index	—	1600	700	700	500	500	500

1979–81 Carburetor Specifications (cont.)

Calibration Number	Choke Plate Pulldown Setting (inches)	Time for Choke Plate to Rotate (come off) (seconds—maximum)	Air Flow (pounds per minute)	Choke Setting	Fast Idle rpm		Curb Idle rpm		TSP Off rpm		Timing rpm
					High Cam	Kick Down	① A/C Off/On	Non-AC	AC	Non-AC	
9-51S-RO	.230	80	.06	Index	—	1600	700	700	500	500	500
9-51T-RO	.230	80	.06	Index	—	1600	700	700	500	500	500
9-52G-RO	.230	80	.06	Index	—	1600	550	550	500	500	500
9-52J-RO	.230	80	.06	Index	—	1600	550	550	500	500	500
9-52L-RO	.230	80	.06	Index	—	1600	550	550	500	500	500
9-52M-RO	.230	80	.06	Index	—	1600	550	550	500	500	500
9-53G-RO	.140	235	.085	3 Rich	2000	—	700	700	—	—	550
9-53H-RO	.140	125	.085	3 Rich	2000	—	700	700	—	—	550
9-54G-RO	.145	150	.079	3 Rich	2000	—	600	600	550	550	550
9-54H-RO	.145	150	.079	3 Rich	2000	—	600	600	550	550	550
9-54J-RO	.145	135	.079	2 Rich	2000	—	600	600	550	550	550
9-54R-RO	.145	135	.079	3 Rich	2000	—	600	600	550	550	550
9-54S-RO	.136	75	.080	1 Rich	2400	—	650	650	550	550	550
9-54T-RO	.145	150	.079	3 Rich	2000	—	600	600	550	550	550
9-54U-RO	.136	75	.080	1 Rich	2400	—	650	650	550	550	550
9-59H-RO	.135	84	.074	Index	2000	—	650	650	—	—	650
9-59J-RO	.145	84	.074	Index	2000	—	650	650	—	—	650
9-59K-RO	.145	84	.074	Index	2000	—	650	650	—	—	650
9-59S-RO	.135	84	.07	Index	2000	—	650	650	—	—	650
9-59T-RO	.150	84	.07	Index	2000	—	650	650	—	—	650
9-60G-RO	.145	84	.079	Index	2000	—	550	550	—	—	500
9-60H-RO	.150	84	.08	Index	2000	—	550	550	—	—	500
9-60J-RO	.140	84	.079	Index	2000	—	550	550	—	—	500
9-60L-RO	.150	84	.08	Index	2000	—	550	550	—	—	500
9-60M-RO	.150	84	.08	Index	2000	—	550	550	—	—	500
9-60S-RO	.150	84	—	3 Rich	2100	—	550	550	—	—	500
9-61G-RO	.145	84	.074	Index	2000	—	650	650	—	—	650
9-61H-RO	.135	84	.076	Index	2000	—	650	650	—	—	650
9-62J-RO	.145	85	.079	Index	1900	—	550	550	—	—	550
9-62M-RO	.145	85	.079	Index	1900	—	550	550	—	—	500
9-63H-RO	.190	77	.06	Index	—	1500	800	800	500	500	500
9-64G-RO	.200	67	.06	Index	2200	—	600	600	500	500	500
9-64H-RO	.200	67	.06	Index	2200	—	600	600	500	500	500
9-64S-RO	.200	67	.06	Index	2200	—	600	600	500	500	500
9-66G-RO	.210	130	.09	5 Rich	—	1600	650 ②	650	800 ③	800	650 TSP Off

① Only for A/C-TSP equipped, A/C compressor electromagnetic clutch de-energized.
② Energize A/C electromagnetic clutch.
③ De-energize A/C electromagnetic clutch.

1982 Carburetor Specifications
Carter YFA

Check the carburetor part number tab to determine which specifications to use for your vehicle

Engine	Part Number	Choke Pulldown Setting	Fast Idle Cam Setting	Dechoke Setting	Choke Plate Come-Off Time	Float Setting (Dry)	Choke Cap Setting	Fast Idle
6-300	E2TE-9510-BZA, BVA	.270	.140	.280	110 sec.	.780	Index	①
	E2TE-9510-AMA E2UE-9510-EA	.230	.140	.280	110 sec.	.780	Index	①
	E2TE-9510-CEA, JA,KA,DA	.320	.140	.330	110 sec.	.780	2NR	①
	E2TE-9510-YA, AAA,MA,ANA	.300	.140	.280	110 sec.	.780	2NR	①
	D5TE-9510-AGB	.230	.110	.280	110 sec.	.875	1NR	①
	D9TE-9510-CA, CB,VB E2TE-9510-ZA EOTE-9510-AMA, AMB,FA,FB	.290	.140	.280	—	.690	Index	①

① Refer to underhood emission sticker

Motorcraft 2150

Engine	Part Number	Choke Pulldown Setting	Fast Idle Cam Setting	Dechoke Setting	Float Level (Wet)	Float Level (Dry)	Accelerator Pump Lever Location	Choke Cap Setting	Fast Idle
8-302	E2TE-9510-AYA, BEA,CJA	.130	V-notch	.200	.810	7/16	#2	V-notch	①
	E2TE-9510-BFA, BAA,BBA	.125	V-notch	.200	.810	7/16	#2	V-notch	①
	E2TEP9510-CKA	.120	V-notch	.200	.810	7/16	#2	V-notch	①
	E2TE-9510-JA	.130	V-notch	.200	.875	31/64	#2	V-notch	①
	E3TE-9510-BPA, BRA	.130	V-notch	.250	.875	31/64	#3	V-notch	①
8-351	E2UE-9510-FA E1UE-9510-JA	.120	V-notch	.200	.875	31/64	#3	V-notch	①
	E1UE-9510-KA	.120	V-notch	.200	.875	31/64	#2	V-notch	①
	E2UE-9510-AAA, ABA,AKA,ANA,HA, RA,SA	.180	V-notch	.250	.875	31/64	#3	V-notch	①
8-400	E2TE-9510-BGA, BHA	.180	V-notch	.250	.875	31/64	#4	V-notch	①
	E2TE-9510-DCA, DBA	.180	V-notch	.250	.875	31/64	#3	V-notch	①
	E2TE-9510-BJA, BKA	.175	V-notch	.250	.875	31/64	#4	V-notch	①
	E2TE-9510-DDA, DEA	.175	V-notch	.250	.875	31/64	#3	V-notch	①

① Refer to underhood emission sticker

Motorcraft 7200

Engine	Part Number	Fast Idle Cam Setting	Float Drop	Float Level (Dry)	Accelerator Pump Lever Lash	Choke Cap Setting	Fast Idle
8-302	All	.355–.365 ②	1.430–1.490	1.010–1.070	.010 ③	Index	①
8-351	All	.355–.365 ②	1.430–1.490	1.010–1.070	.010 ③	Index	①

① Refer to underhood emission sticker
② 2nd highest step
③ Plus one turn counterclockwise

Motorcraft 4180

Engine	Part Number	Choke Pulldown Setting	Dechoke Setting	Fuel Level	Choke Cap Setting	Pump Lever Location
8-460	All	.200–.220	.295–.335	sight plug	2NR	#1

1983 Carburetor Specifications
Carter YFA

Check the carburetor part number tag to determine which specifications to use for your vehicle

Engine	Part Number	Choke Pulldown Setting	Fast Idle Cam Setting	Dechoke Setting	Choke Plate Come-Off Time	Float Setting (Dry)	Choke Cap Setting	Fast Idle
6-300	E3TE-9510-AMA, APA,YA,ASA,AGA, AHA,AJA,AFA,ANA	.270	.140	.280	90–140 sec.	.780	Red	①
	E3TE-9510-BNA, GA,BDA,ZA,ALA, FA,BKA	.320	.140	.330	90–140 sec.	.780	Red	①
	E3TE-9510-ZA, ABA,BRA,AKA	.300	.140	.280	90–140 sec.	.780	White	①
	E3TE-9510-AAA, ARA	.300	.140	.280	90–140 sec.	.780	Red	①
	D5TE-9510-AGB	.230	.110	.280	—	.375	1NR	①
	EOTE-9510-AMB, FB E2TE-9510-ZA	.290	.140	.280	—	.690	Index	①

① Refer to underhood emission sticker

Motorcraft 2150

Engine	Part Number	Choke Pulldown Setting	Fast Idle Cam Setting	Dechoke Setting	Float Level (Wet)	Float Level (Dry)	Accelerator Pump Lever Location	Choke Cap Setting	Fast Idle
8-302	E3TE-9510-AUA	.142	V-notch	.200	.810	7/16	#3	V-notch	①
	E3TE-9510-BHA	.152	V-notch	.200	.810	7/16	#3	V-notch	①
	E3TE-9510-AYA	.137	V-notch	.250	.810	7/16	#4	V-notch	①
	E3TE-9510-AVA, BEA	.149	V-notch	.250	.810	7/16	#3	V-notch	①
	E3TE-9510-BJA	.157	V-notch	.200	.810	7/16	#4	V-notch	①
	E3TE-9510-BLA, BPA	.157	V-notch	.200	.810	7/16	#3	V-notch	①
	E3TE-9510-BMA	.150	V-notch	.200	.810	7/16	#4	V-notch	①
	E3TE-9510-AZA, BAA E2TE-9510-BPA, BRA	.130	V-notch	.250	.875	31/64	#3	V-notch	①
8-351	E3UE-9510-CA E2UE-9510-FA	.120	V-notch	.200	.875	31/64	#3	V-notch	①
	E3UE-9510-BA E2UE-9510-KA	.120	V-notch	.200	.875	31/64	#2	V-notch	①
	E3UE-9510-EA, DA E2UE-9510-ANA, AKA	.180	V-notch	.250	.875	31/64	#3	V-notch	①

① Refer to underhood emission sticker

Motorcraft 7200

Engine	Part Number	Fast Idle Cam Setting	Float Drop	Float Level (Dry)	Accelerator Pump Lever Lash	Choke Cap Setting	Fast Idle
8-351	All	.355–.365 ②	1.43–1.49	1.010–1.070	.010 ③	Index	①

① Refer to underhood emission sticker
② 2nd highest step
③ Plus one turn counterclockwise

Motorcraft 4180

Engine	Part Number	Choke Pulldown Setting	Dechoke Setting	Fuel Level	Choke Cap Setting	Pump Lever Location
8-460	All	.210–.230	.300–.330	sight plug	3NR	#1

1984 Carburetor Specifications
Carter YFA

Check the carburetor part number tag to determine which specifications to use for your vehicle

Engine	Part Number	Choke Pulldown Setting	Fast Idle Cam Setting	Dechoke Setting	Choke Plate Come-Off Time	Float Setting (Dry)	Choke Cap Setting	Fast Idle
6-300	E4TE-9510-VA, HA,FA,UA,AAA, GA,EA,ZA	.360	.140	.330	90–141 sec.	.780	Red	①
	D5TE-9510-AGB	.230	1NR	.280	—	.375	—	①
	D5TE-9510-AMB, FB	.290	Index	.280	—	.690	Index	①

① Refer to underhood emission sticker

Models YF/YFA

(All measurements in inches)

Year	Carburetor Number	Float Level	Float Drop	Choke Unloader Setting	Choke Setting	Dash Pot Plunger	Initial Choke Opening
'85–'86	E5TE-9510 DA	.65	—	.270	Gray ①	—	.320
	VA,UA,TA, BA,RA,SA, JA	.78	—	.330	Red ①	—	.360
	FA	.78	—	.330	Red ①	—	.340
	HA	.78	—	.330	Red ①	—	.320
	DA,MA,CA ②	.78	—	.330	Red ①	—	.360
	D5TE-9510 AGB	⅜	—	.280	—	—	.230
	EOTE-9510 AMB,FB	.69	—	.280	Index	—	.290

① Choke cap index plate color
② Feedback carburetor

Model 2150

(All measurements in inches)

Year	Carburetor Number	Float Level (Dry)	Choke Unloader Setting	Choke Setting	Accelerator Pump Rod Location	Fuel Level (Wet)	Choke Pulldown Setting (Min)
'85–'86	E57E-9510 BA,CA	1/16	.250	3-Rich	4	.810 ④	.136
	E5TE-9510			V-notch	4	.875	.150
	YA	9/32	.220				
	ACA	9/32	.200	3 Rich	4	.875	.150
	AAA	¼	.200	V-notch	4	.810	.155
	PA	¼	.200	3 Rich	4	.810	.152
	E3UE-9510 EA,DA	31/64	.250	V-notch	3	.875	.180

Motorcraft 2150

Engine	Part Number	Choke Pulldown Setting	Fast Idle Cam Setting	Dechoke Setting	Float Level (Wet)	Float Level (Dry)	Accelerator Pump Lever Location	Choke Cap Setting	Fast Idle
8-302	E4TE-9510-AMA	.140	V-notch	.250	.875	31/64	#3	V-notch	①
	E4TE-9510-AEA	.142	V-notch	.250	.875	31/64	#3	V-notch	①
	E4TE-9510-ALA	.125	V-notch	.250	.875	31/64	#3	V-notch	①
	E4TE-9510-APA	.145	V-notch	.250	.875	31/64	#3	V-notch	①
	E4TE-9510-AKA	.137	V-notch	.250	.875	31/64	#3	V-notch	①
	E4TE-9510-AHA	.150	V-notch	.250	.875	31/64	#4	V-notch	①
	E4TE-9510-AJA	.150	V-notch	.250	.875	31/64	#3	V-notch	①
	E4TE-9510-AFA	.144	V-notch	.250	.875	31/64	#3	V-notch	①
	E3TE-9510-BAA, AZA	.130	V-notch	.250	.875	31/64	#3	V-notch	①
8-351	E4TE-9510-ADA	.152	V-notch	.250	.810	7/16	#4	V-notch	①
	E4TE-9510-ACA	.155	V-notch	.250	.810	7/16	#4	V-notch	①
	E3UE-9510-EA, DA	.180	V-notch	.250	.875	31/64	#3	V-notch	①

① Refer to underhood emission sticker

Model 4180C

(All measurements in inches)

Year	Carburetor Number	Fuel Level (Wet)	Choke Pulldown Setting	Choke Unloader Setting	Choke Setting	Pump Lever Location	Enrichment Valve Indent.
'84–'86	E4TE-9510-ARA	①	.185	.300	Index	#1	13
	E3TE-9510 PD	①	.220	.295–.335	3 Rich	#1	8
	TC	①	.210–.230	.300–.330	3 Rich	#1	8
	RD	①	.200	.315	3 Rich	#1	8A
	SC	①	.210–.230	.315	3 Rich	#1	8A

① At bottom of sight plug

Overhaul the carburetor in a clean, dustfree area. Carefully disassemble the carburetor, referring often to the exploded views. Keep all similar and lookalike parts segregated during disassembly and cleaning to avoid accidental interchange during assembly. Make a note of all jet sizes.

When the carburetor is disassembled, wash all parts (except diaphragms, electric choke units, pump plunger and any other plastic, leather, fiber, or rubber parts) in clean carburetor solvent. Do not leave the parts in the solvent any longer than is necessary to sufficiently loosen the dirt and deposits. Excessive cleaning may remove the special finish from the float bowl and choke valve bodies, leaving these parts unfit for service. Rinse all parts in clean solvent and blow them dry with compressed air or allow them to air dry, while resting on clean, lintless paper. Wipe clean all cork, plastic, leather and fiber parts with a clean, lintfree cloth.

Blow out all passages and jets with compressed air and be sure that there are no restrictions or blockages. Never use wire or similar tools to clean jets, fuel passages or air bleeds. Clean all jets and valves separately to avoid accidental interchange.

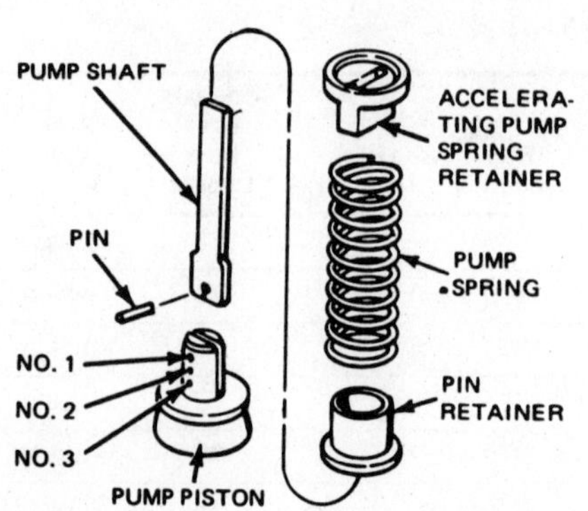

Accelerator pump stroke adjustment—Autolite 4350 4-bbl

Examine all parts for wear or damage. If wear or damage is found, replace the defective parts. Especially, inspect the following:

1. Check the float needle and seat for wear. If wear is found, replace the complete assembly.
2. Check the float hinge pin for wear and the float(s) for dents or distortion. Replace the float if fuel has leaked into it.
3. Check the throttle and choke shaft bores for wear or an out-of-round condition. Damage or wear to the throttle arm, shaft or shaft bore will often require replacement of the throttle body. These parts require a close tolerance of fit; wear may allow air leakage, which could affect starting and idling.

NOTE: *Throttle shafts and bushings are not normally included in overhaul kits. They can be purchased separately.*

4. Inspect the idle mixture adjusting needles for burrs or grooves. Any such condition requires replacement of the needle, since you will not be able to obtain a satisfactory idle.
5. Test the accelerator pump check valves. They should pass air one way, but not the other. Test for proper seating by blowing and sucking on the valve. Replace the valve as necessary. If the valve is satisfactory, wash the valve again to remove moisture.
6. Check the bowl cover for warped surfaces with a straightedge.
7. Closely inspect the valves and seats for wear and damage, replacing as necessary.
8. After the carburetor is assembled, check the choke valve for freedom of operation.

Carburetor overhaul kits are recommended for each overhaul. These kids contain all gaskets and new parts to replace those which deteriorate most rapidly. Failure to replace all of the parts supplied with the kit (especially gaskets) can result in poor performance later.

Most carburetor manufacturers supply overhaul kits of three basic types: minor repair; major repair; and gasket kits.

After cleaning and checking all components, reassemble the carburetor, using new parts and referring to the exploded view. When reassembling, make sure that all screws and jets are right in their seats, but do not overtighten, as the tips will be distorted. Tighten all screws gradually, in rotation. Do not tighten needle valves into their seats; uneven jetting will result. Always use new gaskets. Be sure to adjust the float level.

NOTE: *Most carburetor rebuilding kits contain a sheet of specific instructions pertaining to the carburetor the kit is for.*

Air Intake Throttle Body Fuel Injection

REMOVAL AND INSTALLATION

1. Disconnect the air intake hose.
2. Disconnect the throttle position sensor and air by-pass valve connectors.
3. Remove the four throttle body mounting nuts and carefully separate the air throttle body from the upper intake manifold.
4. Remove and discard the mounting gasket. Clean all mounting surfaces using care not to damage the gasket surfaces of the throttle body and manifold. Do not allow any material to drop into the intake manifold.
5. Install the throttle body in the reverse order of removal. The mounting nuts are tightened to 12–15 ft. lbs.

Fuel Supply Manifold

REMOVAL AND INSTALLATION

1. Remove the gas tank fill cap. Relieve fuel system preessure by locating and disconnecting the electrical connection to either the fuel pump relay, the inertia switch or the in-line high pressure fuel pump. Crank the engine for about ten seconds. If the engine starts, crank for an additional five seconds after the engine stalls. Reconnect the connector. Disconnect the negative battery cable. Remove the upper intake manifold assembly.

NOTE: *Special tool T81P-19623-G or equivalent is necessary to release the garter springs that secure the fuel line/hose connections.*

2. Disconnect the fuel crossover hose from the fuel supply manifold. Disconnect the fuel supply and return line connections at the fuel supply manifold.
3. Remove the two fuel supply manifold retaining bolts. Carefully disengage the manifold from the fuel injectors and remove the manifold.

4. When installing: Make sure the injector caps are clean and free of contamination. Place the fuel supply manifold over each injector and seat the injectors into the manifold. Make sure the caps are seated firmly.

5. Torque the fuel supply manifold retaining bolts to 15–22 ft. lbs. Install the remaining components in the reverse order of removal.

NOTE: *Fuel injectors may be serviced after the fuel supply manifold is removed. Grasp the injector and pull up on it while gently rocking injector from side to side. Inspect the mounting O-rings and replace any that show deterioration.*

DIESEL ENGINE FUEL SYSTEM

Fuel Pump

REMOVAL

1. Loosen the threaded connections with the proper size wrench (a flare nut wrench is preferred) and retighten snugly. *Do not remove the lines at this time.*

2. Loosen the mounting bolts, one to two turns. Apply force with your hand to loosen the fuel pump if the gasket is stuck. Rotate the engine by nudging the starter, until the fuel pump cam lobe is at the low position. At this position, spring tension against the fuel pump bolts will be greatly reduced.

3. Disconnect the fuel supply pump inlet, outlet and fuel return line.

CAUTION: *Use care to prevent combustion of the spilled fuel.*

4. Remove the fuel pump attaching bolts and remove the pump and gasket. Discard the old gasket.

INSTALLATION

1. Remove the remaining fuel pump gasket material from the engine and from the fuel pump if you are reinstalling the old pump. Make sure both mounting surfaces are clean.

2. Install the attaching bolts into the fuel supply pump and install a new gasket on the bolts. Position the fuel pump onto the mounting pad. Turn the attaching bolts alternately and evenly and tighten the bolts to the specifications according to the size bolts used on the pump. See the accompanying standard torque chart for reference.

NOTE: *The cam must be at its low position before attempting to install the fuel supply pump. If it is difficult to start the mounting bolts, remove the pump and reinstall with a lever on the bottom side of the cam.*

3. Install the fuel outlet line. Start the fitting by hand to avoid crossthreading.

4. Install the inlet line and the fuel return line.

5. Start the engine and observe all connections for fuel leaks for two minutes.

6. Stop the engine and check all fuel supply pump fuel line connections. Check for oil leaks at the pump mounting pad.

Glow Plug System

The 6.9L diesel engine utilizes an electric glow plug system to aid in the start of the engine. The function of this stem is to pre-heat the combustion chamber to aid ignition of the fuel.

The system consists of eight glow plugs (one for each cylinder), control switch, power relay, after glow relay, wait lamp latching relay, wait lamp and the eight fusible links located between the harness and the glow plug terminal.

On initial start with cold engine, the glow plug system operates as follows: The glow plug control switch energizes the power relay (which is a magnetic switch) and the power relay contacts close. Battery current energizes the glow plugs. Current to the glow plugs and a wait lamp will be shut off when the glow plugs are

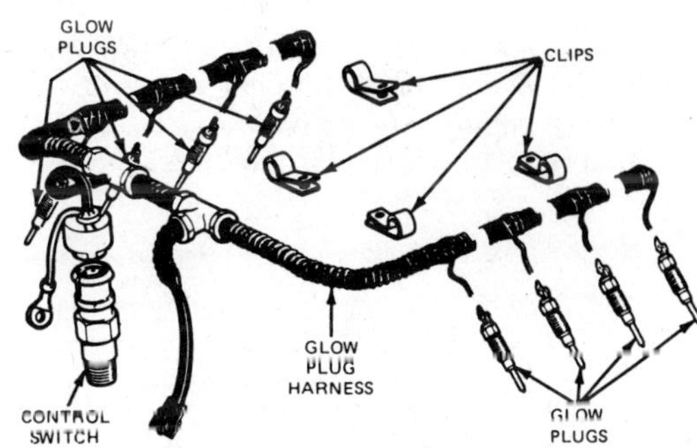

6.9L diesel glow plug system

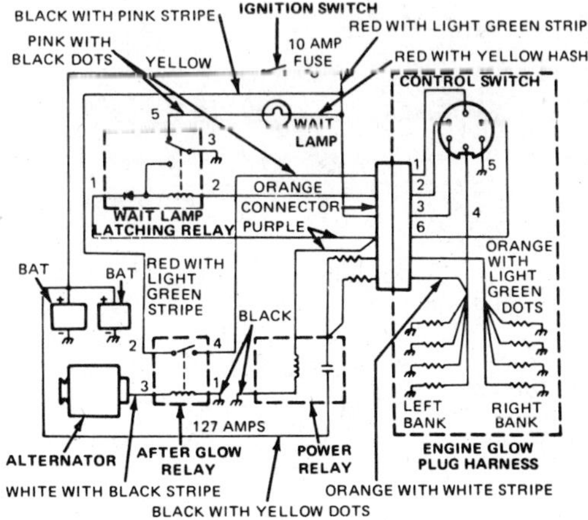

Diesel glow plug wiring schematic

hot enough. This takes from 2 to 10 second after the key is first turned on. When the wait lamp goes off, the engine is ready to start. After the engine is started the glow plugs begin an on-off cycle for about 40 to 90 seconds. This cycle helps to clear start-up smoke. The control switch (the brain of the operation) is threaded into the left cylinder head coolant jacket. The control unit senses engine coolant temperature. Since the control unit senses temperature and glow plug operation the glow plug system will not be activated unless needed. On a restart (warm engine) the glow plug system will not be activated unless the coolant temperature drops below 165°F (91°C).

Since the fast start system utilizes 6 volt glow plugs in a 12 volt system to achieve rapid heating of the glow plug, a cycling device is required in the circuit.

CAUTION: *Never bypass the power relay of the glow plug system. Constant battery current (12 volts) to glow plugs will cause them to overheat and fail.*

Injection Nozzles

REMOVAL

NOTE: *Before removing the nozzle assemblies, clean the exterior of each nozzle assembly and the surrounding area with clean fuel oil or solvent to prevent entry of dirt into the engine when nozzle assemblies are removed. Also, clean the fuel inlet and fuel leak-off piping connections. Blow dry with compressed air.*

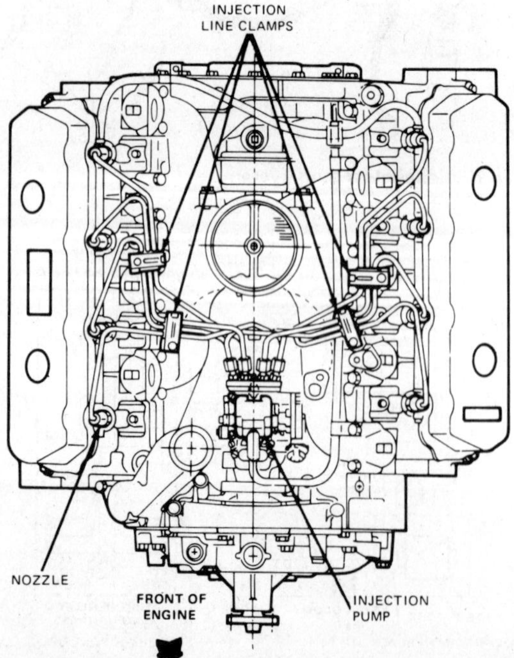

Injection line clamps, Diesel V8. Injectors also shown

1. Remove the fuel line retaining clamp(s) from the nozzle lines that are to be removed.
2. Disconnect the nozzle fuel inlet (high pressure) and fuel leak-off tees from each nozzle assembly and position out of the way. Cover the open ends of the fuel inlet and outlet or nozzles with protective caps, to prevent dirt from entering.
3. Remove the injection nozzles by turning them counterclockwise. Pull the nozzle assembly with the copper washer attached from the engine. Cover the nozzle fuel opening and spray tip, with plastic caps, to prevent the entry of dirt.

   NOTE: *Remove the copper injector nozzle gasket from the nozzle bore with special tool, T71P-19703-C, or equivalent, whenever the gasket does not come out with the nozzle.*
4. Place the nozzle assemblies in a fabricated holder as they are removed from the heads. The holder should be marked with numbers corresponding to the cylinder numbering of the engine. This will allow for re-installation of the nozzle in the same ports from which they were removed.

INSTALLATION

1. Thoroughly clean the nozzle bore in cylinder head before reinserting the nozzle assembly with nozzle seat cleaner, special tool T83T-9527-A or equivalent. *Make certain that no small particles of metal or carbon remain on the seating surface.* Blow out the particles with compressed air.
2. Remove the protective cap and install a new copper gasket on the nozzle assembly, with a small dab of grease.

   NOTE: *Anti-seize compound or equivalent should be used on nozzle threads to aid in installation and future removal.*
3. Install the nozzle assembly into the cylinder head nozzle bore.
4. Tighten the nozzle assembly to 33 ft. lbs.
5. Remove the protective caps from nozzle assemblies and fuel lines.
6. Install the leak-off tees to the nozzle assemblies.

   NOTE: *Install two new 0-ring seals for each fuel return tee.*
7. Connect the high pressure fuel line and tighten, using a flare nut wrench.
8. Install the fuel line retainer clamps.
9. Start the engine and check for leaks.

Injecton Pump

NOTE: *Before removing any fuel lines, clean exterior with clean fuel oil or solvent to pre-*

vent entry of dirt into engine when fuel lines are removed.

CAUTION: *Do not wash or steam clean engine while engine is running. Serious damage to injection pump could occur.*

REMOVAL

1. Disconnect battery ground cables from both batteries.
2. Remove the engine oil filler neck.
3. Remove the bolts attaching injection pump to drive gear.
4. Disconnect the electrical connectors to injection pump.
5. Disconnect the accelerator cable and speed control cable from throttle lever, if so equipped.
6. Remove the air cleaner and install clean rags to prevent dirt from entering the intake manifold.
7. Remove the accelerator cable bracket, with cables attached, from the intake manifold and position out of the way.

NOTE: *All fuel lines and fittings must be capped using Fuel System Protective Cap Set T83T-9395-A or equivalent, to prevent fuel contamination.*

8. Remove the fuel filter-to-injection pump fuel line and cap fittings.
9. Remove and cap the injection pump inlet elbow and the injection pump fitting adapter.

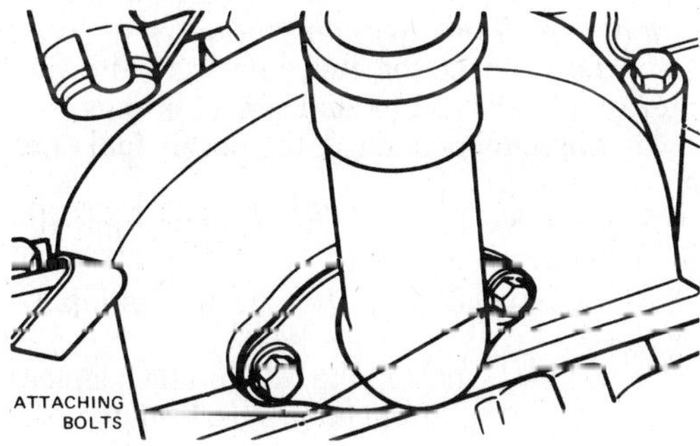

Diesel oil filler neck removal

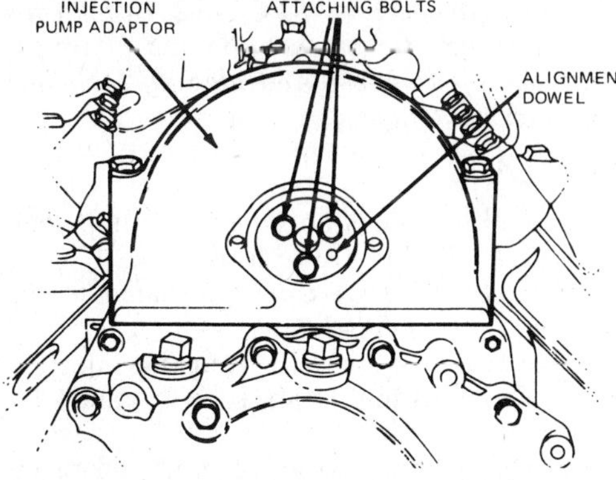

Diesel injection pump drive gear attaching bolts

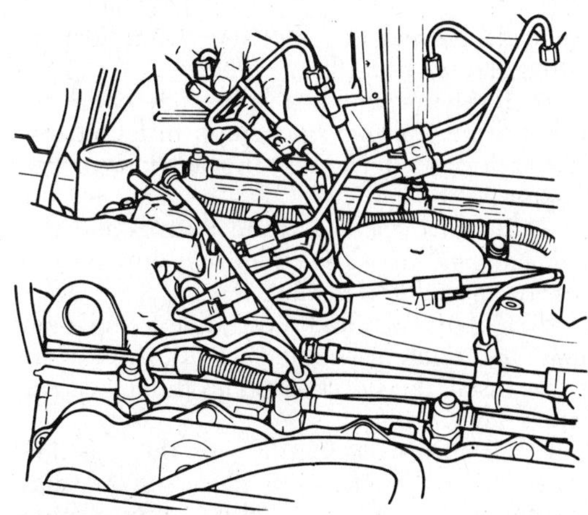
Diesel injection pump removal. Be careful not to crimp or bend the fuel lines

10. Remove the fuel return line on injection pump, rotate out of the way, and cap all fittings.

NOTE: *It is not necessary to remove injection lines from injection pump to remove injection pump. If lines are to be removed, loosen injection line fittings at injection pump before removing it from engine.*

11. Remove the fuel injection lines from the nozzles and cap lines and nozzles.
12. Remove the three nuts attaching the injection pump to injection pump adapter using Tool T83T-9000-B.
13. If the injection pump is to be replaced, loosen the injection line retaining clips and the injection nozzle fuel lines with Tool T83T-9396-A and cap all fittings at this time with protective cap set T83T-9395-A or equivalent. Do not install the injection nozzle fuel lines until the new pump is installed in engine.
14. Lift the injection pump, with the nozzle lines attached, up and out of the engine compartment.

CAUTION: *Do not carry injection pump by injection nozzle fuel lines as this could cause lines to bend or crimp.*

INSTALLATION

1. Install a new O-ring on the drive gear end of the injection pump.
2. Move the injection pump down and into position.
3. Position the alignment dowel on injection pump into the alignment hole on drive gear.
4. Install the bolts attaching the injection pump to drive gear and tighten.
5. Install the nuts attaching injection pump to adapter. Align scribe lines on the injection

pump flange and the injection pump adapter and tighten to 14 ft. lbs.

6. If the injection nozzle fuel lines were removed from the injection pump install at this time, refer to Fuel Lines—Installation, in this chapter.

7. Remove the caps from nozzles and the fuel lines and install the fuel line nuts on the nozzles and tighten to 22 ft. lbs.

8. Connect the fuel return line to injection pump and tighten the nuts.

9. Install the injection pump fitting adapter with a new O-ring.

10. Clean the old sealant from the injection pump elbow threads, using clean solvent, and dry thoroughly. Apply a light coating of pipe sealant on the elbow threads.

11. Install the elbow in the injection pump adapter and tighten to a minimum of 6 ft. lbs. Then tighten further, if necessary, to align the elbow with the injection pump fuel inlet line, but do not exceed 360° of rotation or 10 ft. lbs.

12. Remove the caps and connect the fuel filter-to-injection pump fuel line.

13. Install the accelerator cable bracket to the intake manifold.

14. Remove the rags from the intake manifold and install air cleaner.

15. Connect the accelerator and speed control cable, if so equipped, to throttle lever.

16. Install the electrical connectors on injection pump.

17. Clean the injection pump adapter and oil filler neck sealing surfaces.

18. Apply a ⅛ inch bead of RTV sealant on the adapter housing.

19. Install the oil filler neck and tighten the bolts.

20. Connect the battery ground cables to both batteries.

21. Run the engine and check for fuel leaks.

22. If necessary, purge high pressure fuel lines of air by loosening connector one half to one turn and cranking engine until solid fuel, free from bubbles flows from connection.

CAUTION: *Keep eyes and hands away from nozzle spray. Fuel spraying from the nozzle under high pressure can penetrate the skin.*

23. Check and adjust injection pump timing as described in this chapter.

Fuel Lines

REMOVAL

NOTE: *Before removing any fuel lines, clean the exterior with clean fuel oil, or solvent to prevent entry of dirt into fuel system when the fuel lines are removed. Blow dry with compressed air.*

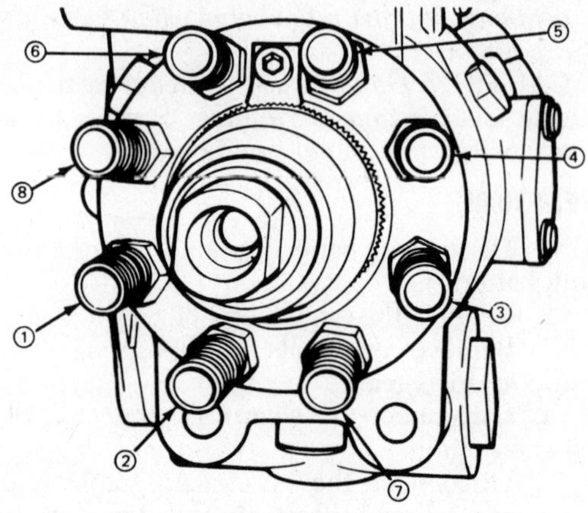

Injection pump cylinder numbering sequence

1. Disconnect the battery ground cables from both batteries.

2. Remove the air cleaner and cap intake manifold opening with clean rags.

3. Disconnect the accelerator cable and speed control cable, if so equipped, from the injection pump.

4. Remove the accelerator cable bracket from the intake manifold and position out of the way with cable(s) attached.

NOTE: *To prevent fuel system contamination, cap all fuel lines and fittings.*

5. Disconnect the fuel line from the fuel filter to injection pump and cap all fittings.

6. Disconnect and cap the nozzle fuel lines at nozzles.

7. Remove the fuel line clamps from the fuel lines to be removed.

8. Remove and cap the injection pump inlet elbow.

9. Remove and cap the inlet fitting adapter.

10. Remove the injection nozzle lines, one at a time, from injection pump using Tool T83T-9396-A.

NOTE: *Fuel lines must be removed following this sequence; 5-6-4-8-3-1-7-2. Install caps on each end of each fuel line and pump fitting as it is removed and identify each fuel line accordingly.*

INSTALLATION

1. Install fuel lines on injection pump, one at a time, and tighten to 22 ft. lbs.

NOTE: *Fuel lines must be installed in the sequence: 2-7-1-3-8-4-6-5.*

2. Clean the old sealant from the injection pump elbow, using clean solvent, and dry thoroughly.

3. Apply a light coating of pipe sealant on the elbow threads.

55 WAYS TO IMPROVE FUEL ECONOMY

CHILTON'S FUEL ECONOMY & TUNE-UP TIPS

Tune-up • Spark Plug Diagnosis • Emission Controls

Fuel System • Cooling System • Tires and Wheels

General Maintenance

CHILTON'S FUEL ECONOMY & TUNE-UP TIPS

Fuel economy is important to everyone, no matter what kind of vehicle you drive. The maintenance-minded motorist can save both money and fuel using these tips and the periodic maintenance and tune-up procedures in this Repair and Tune-Up Guide.

There are more than 130,000,000 cars and trucks registered for private use in the United States. Each travels an average of 10-12,000 miles per year, and, and in total they consume close to 70 billion gallons of fuel each year. This represents nearly ⅔ of the oil imported by the United States each year. The Federal government's goal is to reduce consumption 10% by 1985. A variety of methods are either already in use or under serious consideration, and they all affect you driving and the cars you will drive. In addition to "down-sizing", the auto industry is using or investigating the use of electronic fuel delivery, electronic engine controls and alternative engines for use in smaller and lighter vehicles, among other alternatives to meet the federally mandated Corporate Average Fuel Economy (CAFE) of 27.5 mpg by 1985. The government, for its part, is considering rationing, mandatory driving curtailments and tax increases on motor vehicle fuel in an effort to reduce consumption. The government's goal of a 10% reduction could be realized — and further government regulation avoided — if every private vehicle could use just 1 less gallon of fuel per week.

How Much Can You Save?

Tests have proven that almost anyone can make at least a 10% reduction in fuel consumption through regular maintenance and tune-ups.. When a major manufacturer of spark plugs sur-

TUNE-UP

1. Check the cylinder compression to be sure the engine will really benefit from a tune-up and that it is capable of producing good fuel economy. A tune-up will be wasted on an engine in poor mechanical condition.

2. Replace spark plugs regularly. New spark plugs alone can increase fuel economy 3%.

3. Be sure the spark plugs are the correct type (heat range) for your vehicle. See the Tune-Up Specifications.

Heat range refers to the spark plug's ability to conduct heat away from the firing end. It must conduct the heat away in an even pattern to avoid becoming a source of pre-ignition, yet it must also operate hot enough to burn off conductive deposits that could cause misfiring.

The heat range is usually indicated by a number on the spark plug, part of the manufacturer's designation for each individual spark plug. The numbers in bold-face indicate the heat range in each manufacturer's identification system.

Manufacturer	**Typical Designation**
AC	R **45** TS
Bosch (old)	WA **145** T30
Bosch (new)	HR **8** Y
Champion	RBL **15** Y
Fram/Autolite	41**5**
Mopar	P-**62** PR
Motorcraft	BRF-**4**2
NGK	BP **5** ES-15
Nippondenso	W **16** EP
Prestolite	14GR **5** 2A

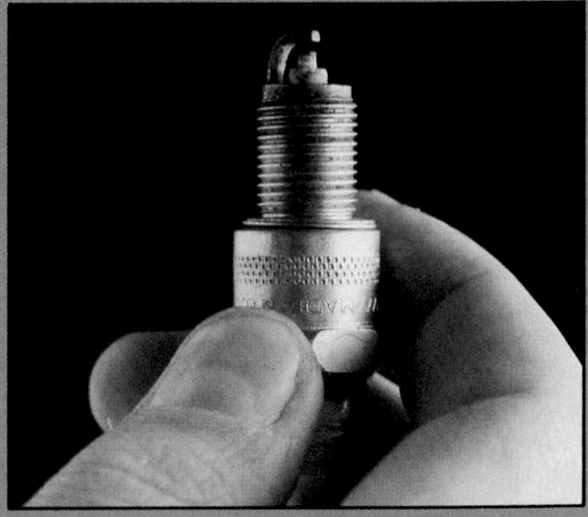

Periodically, check the spark plugs to be sure they are firing efficiently. They are excellent indicators of the internal condition of your engine.

On AC, Bosch (new), Champion, Fram/Autolite, Mopar, Motorcraft and Prestolite, a higher number indicates a hotter plug. On Bosch (old), NGK and Nippondenso, a higher number indicates a colder plug.

4. Make sure the spark plugs are properly gapped. See the Tune-Up Specifications in this book.

5. Be sure the spark plugs are firing efficiently. The illustrations on the next 2 pages show you how to "read" the firing end of the spark plug.

6. Check the ignition timing and set it to specifications. Tests show that almost all cars have incorrect ignition timing by more than 2°.

veyed over 6,000 cars nationwide, they found that a tune-up, on cars that needed one, increased fuel economy over 11%. Replacing worn plugs alone, accounted for a 3% increase. The same test also revealed that 8 out of every 10 vehicles will have some maintenance deficiency that will directly affect fuel economy, emissions or performance. Most of this mileage-robbing neglect could be prevented with regular maintenance.

Modern engines require that all of the functioning systems operate properly for maximum efficiency. A malfunction anywhere wastes fuel. You can keep your vehicle running as efficiently and economically as possible, by being aware of your vehicle's operating and performance characteristics. If your vehicle suddenly develops performance or fuel economy problems it could be due to one or more of the following:

PROBLEM	POSSIBLE CAUSE
Engine Idles Rough	Ignition timing, idle mixture, vacuum leak or something amiss in the emission control system.
Hesitates on Acceleration	Dirty carburetor or fuel filter, improper accelerator pump setting, ignition timing or fouled spark plugs.
Starts Hard or Fails to Start	Worn spark plugs, improperly set automatic choke, ice (or water) in fuel system.
Stalls Frequently	Automatic choke improperly adjusted and possible dirty air filter or fuel filter.
Performs Sluggishly	Worn spark plugs, dirty fuel or air filter, ignition timing or automatic choke out of adjustment.

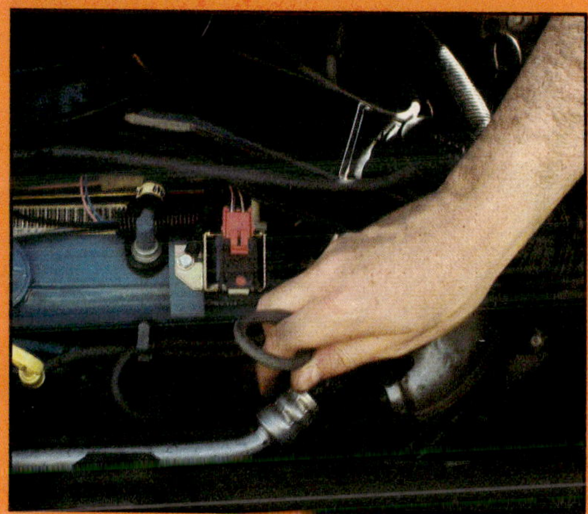

Check spark plug wires on conventional point type ignition for cracks by bending them in a loop around your finger.

Be sure that spark plug wires leading to adjacent cylinders do not run too close together. (Photo courtesy Champion Spark Plug Co.)

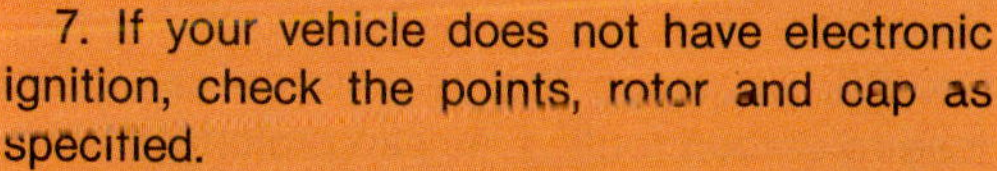

7. If your vehicle does not have electronic ignition, check the points, rotor and cap as specified.

8. Check the spark plug wires (used with conventional point-type ignitions) for cracks and burned or broken insulation by bending them in a loop around your finger. Cracked wires decrease fuel efficiency by failing to deliver full voltage to the spark plugs. One misfiring spark plug can cost you as much as 2 mpg.

9. Check the routing of the plug wires. Misfiring can be the result of spark plug leads to adjacent cylinders running parallel to each other and too close together. One wire tends to pick up voltage from the other causing it to fire "out of time".

10. Check all electrical and ignition circuits for voltage drop and resistance.

11. Check the distributor mechanical and/or vacuum advance mechanisms for proper functioning. The vacuum advance can be checked by twisting the distributor plate in the opposite direction of rotation. It should spring back when released.

12. Check and adjust the valve clearance on engines with mechanical lifters. The clearance should be slightly loose rather than too tight.

SPARK PLUG DIAGNOSIS

Normal

APPEARANCE: This plug is typical of one operating normally. The insulator nose varies from a light tan to grayish color with slight electrode wear. The presence of slight deposits is normal on used plugs and will have no adverse effect on engine performance. The spark plug heat range is correct for the engine and the engine is running normally.
CAUSE: Properly running engine.
RECOMMENDATION: Before reinstalling this plug, the electrodes should be cleaned and filed square. Set the gap to specifications. If the plug has been in service for more than 10-12,000 miles, the entire set should probably be replaced with a fresh set of the same heat range.

Incorrect Heat Range

APPEARANCE: The effects of high temperature on a spark plug are indicated by clean white, often blistered insulator. This can also be accompanied by excessive wear of the electrode, and the absence of deposits.
CAUSE: Check for the correct spark plug heat range. A plug which is too hot for the engine can result in overheating. A car operated mostly at high speeds can require a colder plug. Also check ignition timing, cooling system level, fuel mixture and leaking intake manifold.
RECOMMENDATION: If all ignition and engine adjustments are known to be correct, and no other malfunction exists, install spark plugs one heat range colder.

Photos Courtesy Fram Corporation

Oil Deposits

APPEARANCE: The firing end of the plug is covered with a wet, oily coating.
CAUSE: The problem is poor oil control. On high mileage engines, oil is leaking past the rings or valve guides into the combustion chamber. A common cause is also a plugged PCV valve, and a ruptured fuel pump diaphragm can also cause this condition. Oil fouled plugs such as these are often found in new or recently overhauled engines, before normal oil control is achieved, and can be cleaned and reinstalled.
RECOMMENDATION: A hotter spark plug may temporarily relieve the problem, but the engine is probably in need of work.

Carbon Deposits

APPEARANCE: Carbon fouling is easily identified by the presence of dry, soft, black, sooty deposits.
CAUSE: Changing the heat range can often lead to carbon fouling, as can prolonged slow, stop-and-start driving. If the heat range is correct, carbon fouling can be attributed to a rich fuel mixture, sticking choke, clogged air cleaner, worn breaker points, retarded timing or low compression. If only one or two plugs are carbon fouled, check for corroded or cracked wires on the affected plugs. Also look for cracks in the distributor cap between the towers of affected cylinders.
RECOMMENDATION: After the problem is corrected, these plugs can be cleaned and reinstalled if not worn severely.

MMT Fouled

APPEARANCE: Spark plugs fouled by MMT (Methycyclopentadienyl Maganese Tricarbonyl) have reddish, rusty appearance on the insulator and side electrode.
CAUSE: MMT is an anti-knock additive in gasoline used to replace lead. During the combustion process, the MMT leaves a reddish deposit on the insulator and side electrode.
RECOMMENDATION: No engine malfunction is indicated and the deposits will not affect plug performance any more than lead deposits (see Ash Deposits). MMT fouled plugs can be cleaned, regapped and reinstalled.

High Speed Glazing

APPEARANCE: Glazing appears as shiny coating on the plug, either yellow or tan in color.
CAUSE: During hard, fast acceleration, plug temperatures rise suddenly. Deposits from normal combustion have no chance to fluff-off; instead, they melt on the insulator forming an electrically conductive coating which causes misfiring.
RECOMMENDATION: Glazed plugs are not easily cleaned. They should be replaced with a fresh set of plugs of the correct heat range. If the condition recurs, using plugs with a heat range one step colder may cure the problem.

Ash (Lead) Deposits

APPEARANCE: Ash deposits are characterized by light brown or white colored deposits crusted on the side or center electrodes. In some cases it may give the plug a rusty appearance.
CAUSE: Ash deposits are normally derived from oil or fuel additives burned during normal combustion. Normally they are harmless, though excessive amounts can cause misfiring. If deposits are excessive in short mileage, the valve guides may be worn.
RECOMMENDATION: Ash-fouled plugs can be cleaned, gapped and reinstalled.

Detonation

APPEARANCE: Detonation is usually characterized by a broken plug insulator.
CAUSE: A portion of the fuel charge will begin to burn spontaneously, from the increased heat following ignition. The explosion that results applies extreme pressure to engine components, frequently damaging spark plugs and pistons.

Detonation can result by over-advanced ignition timing, inferior gasoline (low octane) lean air/fuel mixture, poor carburetion, engine lugging or an increase in compression ratio due to combustion chamber deposits or engine modification.
RECOMMENDATION: Replace the plugs after correcting the problem.

Photos Courtesy Champion Spark Plug Co.

EMISSION CONTROLS

13. Be aware of the general condition of the emission control system. It contributes to reduced pollution and should be serviced regularly to maintain efficient engine operation.

14. Check all vacuum lines for dried, cracked or brittle conditions. Something as simple as a leaking vacuum hose can cause poor performance and loss of economy.

15. Avoid tampering with the emission control system. Attempting to improve fuel econ-

FUEL SYSTEM

Check the air filter with a light behind it. If you can see light through the filter it can be reused.

Extremely clogged filters should be discarded and replaced with a new one.

18. Replace the air filter regularly. A dirty air filter richens the air/fuel mixture and can increase fuel consumption as much as 10%. Tests show that ⅓ of all vehicles have air filters in need of replacement.

19. Replace the fuel filter at least as often as recommended.

20. Set the idle speed and carburetor mixture to specifications.

21. Check the automatic choke. A sticking or malfunctioning choke wastes gas.

22. During the summer months, adjust the automatic choke for a leaner mixture which will produce faster engine warm-ups.

COOLING SYSTEM

29. Be sure all accessory drive belts are in good condition. Check for cracks or wear.

30. Adjust all accessory drive belts to proper tension.

31. Check all hoses for swollen areas, worn spots, or loose clamps.

32. Check coolant level in the radiator or expansion tank.

33. Be sure the thermostat is operating properly. A stuck thermostat delays engine warm-up and a cold engine uses nearly twice as much fuel as a warm engine.

34. Drain and replace the engine coolant at least as often as recommended. Rust and scale

TIRES & WHEELS

38. Check the tire pressure often with a pencil type gauge. Tests by a major tire manufacturer show that 90% of all vehicles have at least 1 tire improperly inflated. Better mileage can be achieved by over-inflating tires, but never exceed the maximum inflation pressure on the side of the tire.

39. If possible, install radial tires. Radial tires deliver as much as ½ mpg more than bias belted tires.

40. Avoid installing super-wide tires. They only create extra rolling resistance and decrease fuel mileage. Stick to the manufacturer's recommendations.

41. Have the wheels properly balanced.

omy by tampering with emission controls is more likely to worsen fuel economy than improve it. Emission control changes on modern engines are not readily reversible.

16. Clean (or replace) the EGR valve and lines as recommended.

17. Be sure that all vacuum lines and hoses are reconnected properly after working under the hood. An unconnected or misrouted vacuum line can wreak havoc with engine performance.

23. Check for fuel leaks at the carburetor, fuel pump, fuel lines and fuel tank. Be sure all lines and connections are tight.

24. Periodically check the tightness of the carburetor and intake manifold attaching nuts and bolts. These are a common place for vacuum leaks to occur.

25. Clean the carburetor periodically and lubricate the linkage.

26. The condition of the tailpipe can be an excellent indicator of proper engine combustion. After a long drive at highway speeds, the inside of the tailpipe should be a light grey in color. Black or soot on the insides indicates an overly rich mixture.

27. Check the fuel pump pressure. The fuel pump may be supplying more fuel than the engine needs.

28. Use the proper grade of gasoline for your engine. Don't try to compensate for knocking or "pinging" by advancing the ignition timing. This practice will only increase plug temperature and the chances of detonation or pre-ignition with relatively little performance gain.

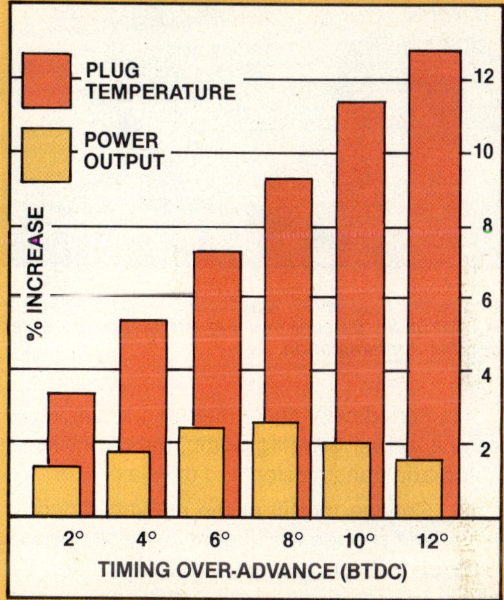

Increasing ignition timing past the specified setting results in a drastic increase in spark plug temperature with increased chance of detonation or preignition. Performance increase is considerably less. (Photo courtesy Champion Spark Plug Co.)

that form in the engine should be flushed out to allow the engine to operate at peak efficiency.

35. Clean the radiator of debris that can decrease cooling efficiency.

36. Install a flex-type or electric cooling fan, if you don't have a clutch type fan. Flex fans use curved plastic blades to push more air at low speeds when more cooling is needed; at high speeds the blades flatten out for less resistance. Electric fans only run when the engine temperature reaches a predetermined level.

37. Check the radiator cap for a worn or cracked gasket. If the cap does not seal properly, the cooling system will not function properly.

42. Be sure the front end is correctly aligned. A misaligned front end actually has wheels going in differed directions. The increased drag can reduce fuel economy by .3 mpg.

43. Correctly adjust the wheel bearings. Wheel bearings that are adjusted too tight increase rolling resistance.

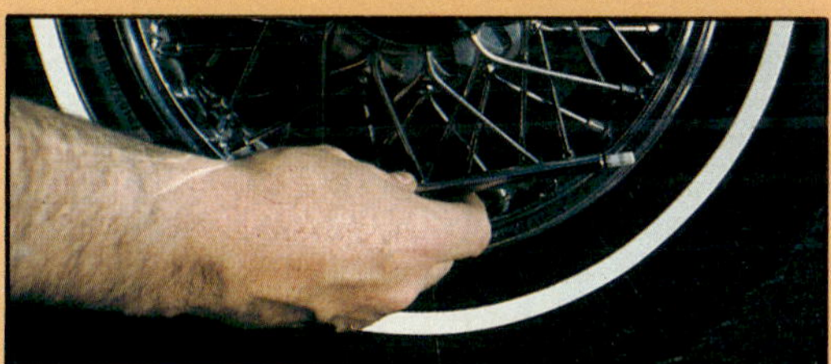

Check tire pressures regularly with a reliable pocket type gauge. Be sure to check the pressure on a cold tire.

GENERAL MAINTENANCE

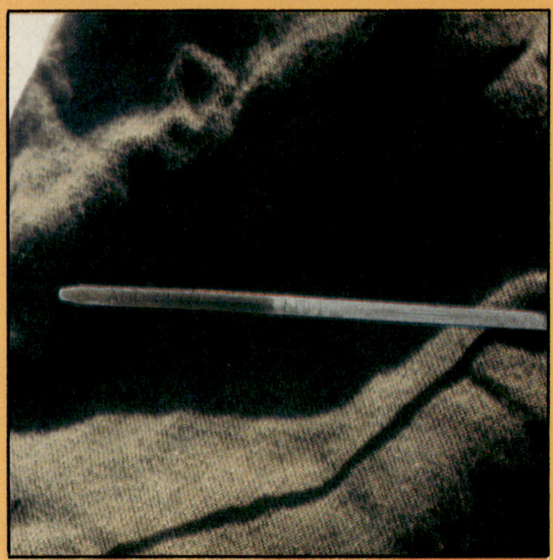

Check the fluid levels (particularly engine oil) on a regular basis. Be sure to check the oil for grit, water or other contamination.

A vacuum gauge is another excellent indicator of internal engine condition and can also be installed in the dash as a mileage indicator.

44. Periodically check the fluid levels in the engine, power steering pump, master cylinder, automatic transmission and drive axle.

45. Change the oil at the recommended interval and change the filter at every oil change. Dirty oil is thick and causes extra friction between moving parts, cutting efficiency and increasing wear. A worn engine requires more frequent tune-ups and gets progressively worse fuel economy. In general, use the lightest viscosity oil for the driving conditions you will encounter.

46. Use the recommended viscosity fluids in the transmission and axle.

47. Be sure the battery is fully charged for fast starts. A slow starting engine wastes fuel.

48. Be sure battery terminals are clean and tight.

49. Check the battery electrolyte level and add distilled water if necessary.

50. Check the exhaust system for crushed pipes, blockages and leaks.

51. Adjust the brakes. Dragging brakes or brakes that are not releasing create increased drag on the engine.

52. Install a vacuum gauge or miles-per-gallon gauge. These gauges visually indicate engine vacuum in the intake manifold. High vacuum = good mileage and low vacuum = poorer mileage. The gauge can also be an excellent indicator of internal engine conditions.

53. Be sure the clutch is properly adjusted. A slipping clutch wastes fuel.

54. Check and periodically lubricate the heat control valve in the exhaust manifold. A sticking or inoperative valve prevents engine warm-up and wastes gas.

55. Keep accurate records to check fuel economy over a period of time. A sudden drop in fuel economy may signal a need for tune-up or other maintenance.

Diesel Injection Timing

STATIC TIMING

1. Break the torque of the injection pump mounting nuts (keeping the nuts snug).

2. Rotate the injection pump using Tool T83-9000-C or equivalent to bring the mark on the pump into alignment with the mark on pump mounting adapter.

3. Visually recheck the alignment of the timing marks and tighten injection pump mounting nuts.

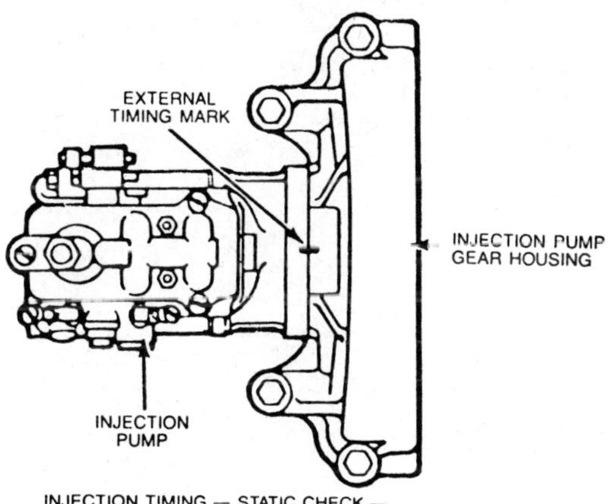

Diesel injection pump static timing marks

DYNAMIC TIMING

1. Bring the engine up to normal operating temperature.

2. Stop the engine and install a dynamic timing meter, Rotunda ® 78-0100 or equivalent, by placing the magnetic probe pick-up into the probe hole.

3. Remove the No. 1 glow plug wire and remove the glow plug, install the luminosity probe and tighten to 12 ft. lbs. Install the photocell over the probe.

4. Connect a dynamic timing meter to the battery and adjust the offset of the meter.

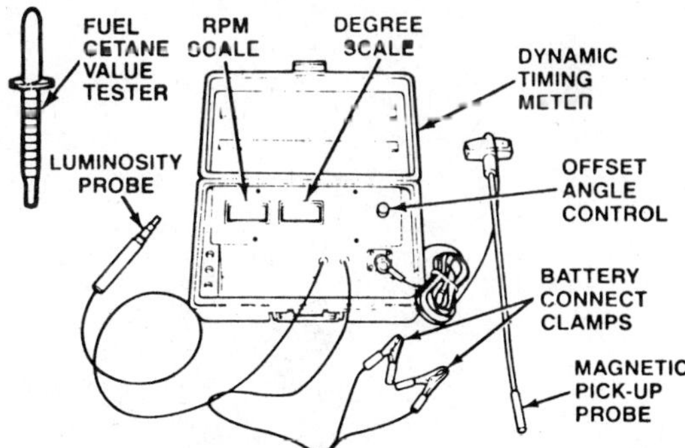

Rotunda® dynamic timing meter used for diesel injection timing. Cetane tester, magnetic pick-up probe and luminosity probe also shown

V8 diesel magnetic pick-up probe hole location

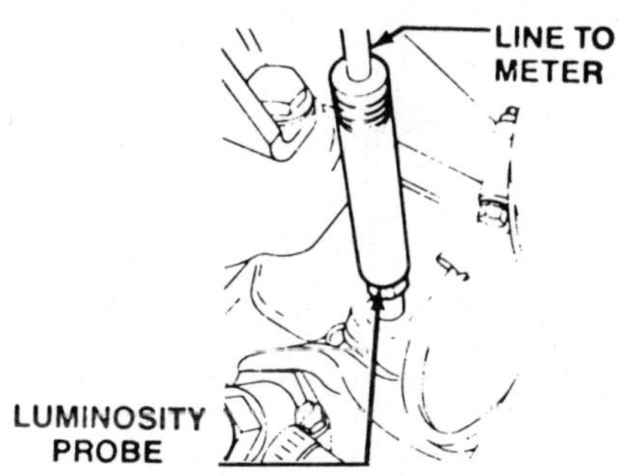

Luminosity probe used for diesel injection timing

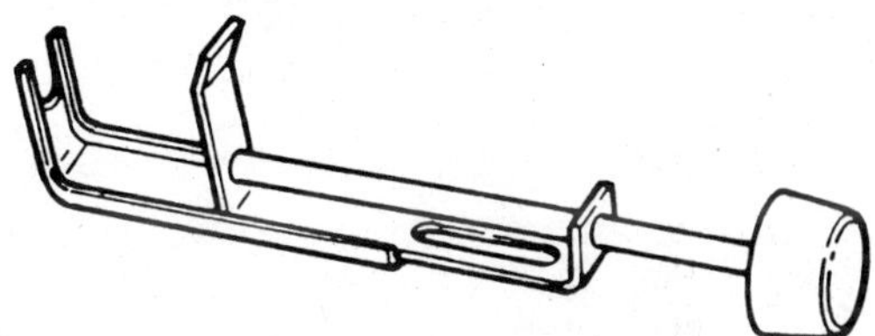

Rotunda® diesel throttle control tool

5. Set the transmission in neutral and raise the rear wheels off the ground. Using Rotunda ® 14-0302, throttle control, set the engine speed to 1400 rpm with no accessory load. Observe the injection timing on the dynamic timing meter.

NOTE: *Obtain a fuel sample from the vehicle and check the cetane value using the tester supplied with the Ford special tools 78-0100 or equivalent. Refer to the dynamic timing chart to find the correct timing in degrees.*

6. If the dynamic timing is not within ±2° of specification, then the injection pump timing will require adjustment.

Dynamic Timing Specifications

	Altitude	
Fuel Cetane Value	**0-3000 Ft ①**	**Above 3000 Ft ①**
38–42	6° ATDC	7° ATDC
43–46	5° ATDC	6° ATDC
47–50	4° ATDC	5° ATDC

① Installation of resetting tolerance for dynamic timing is ± 1°. Service limit is ± 2°.

7. Turn the engine off. Note the timing mark alignment. Loosen the injection pump-to-adapter nuts.

8. Rotate the injection pump clockwise (when viewed from the front of the engine) to retard and counterclockwise to advance timing. Two degrees of dynamic timing is approximately .030 in. (.75 mm) of timing mark movement.

9. Start the engine and recheck the timing. If the timing is not within ±1° of specification, repeat steps 7 through 9.

10. Turn off the engine. Remove the dynamic timing equipment. Lightly coat the glow

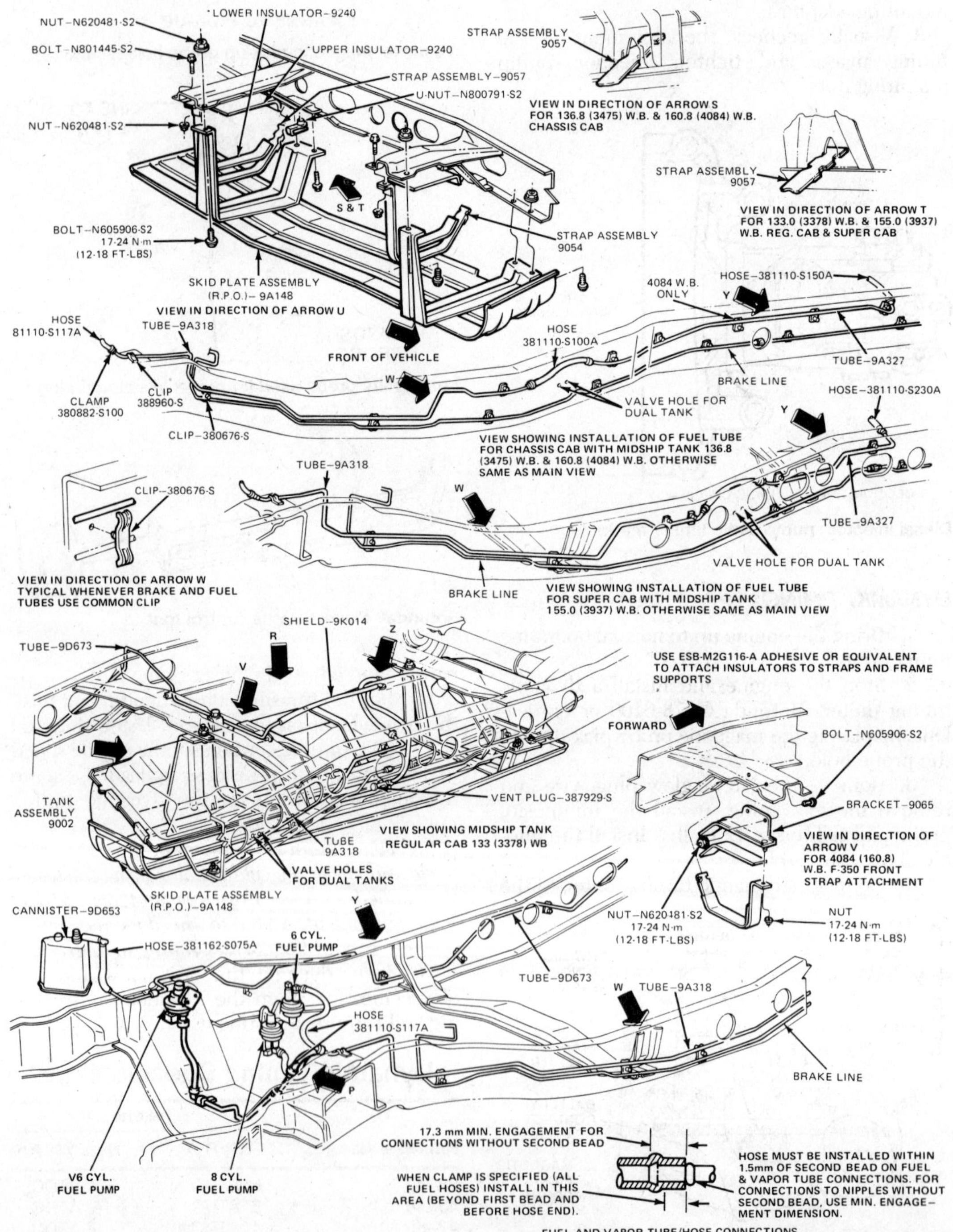

Late-model F-100 through F-350 midships fuel tank installation showing fuel lines, gasoline engine models. Earlier models vary slightly

plug threads with anti-seize compound, install the glow plug and tighten to 12 ft. lbs. Connect the glow plug wires.

Fuel Tank

REMOVAL AND INSTALLATION

In-Cab Fuel Tank

1. Siphon the fuel from the tank into a suitable container through the filler neck.
2. Move the seat to the full forward position and tilt the seat forward.
3. Disconnect the fuel gauge sending unit wire and fuel line from the tank. Disconnect the vapor vent chamber and vapor lines of the fuel evaporative emission control system.
4. Loosen the filler neck hose clamp at the tank end of the hose, and pull the filler neck away from the tank.
5. Remove the fuel tank retaining nuts and bolts and lift the tank out of the cab. If the tank is being replaced, remove the fuel gauge sending unit and install it in the new tank.
6. Install the fuel tank in the reverse order of removal.

In-Frame Fuel Tank

1. Drain the fuel from the tank into a suitable container by either removing the drain plug, if so equipped, or siphoning through the filler cap opening.
2. Disconnect the fuel gauge sending unit wire and fuel outlet line.
3. Disconnect the air relief tube from the filler neck and fuel tank.
4. Loosen the filler neck hose clamp at the fuel tank and pull the filler neck away from the tank.
5. Remove the retaining strap mounting nuts and bolts and lower the tank to the floor.
6. If a new tank is being installed, change over the fuel gauge sending unit to the new tank.
7. Install the fuel tank in the reverse order of removal.

Behind-The-Axle Fuel Tank.

1. Raise the rear of the truck.
2. Disconnect the negative battery cable.
3. Disconnect the fuel gauge sending unit wire at the fuel tank.

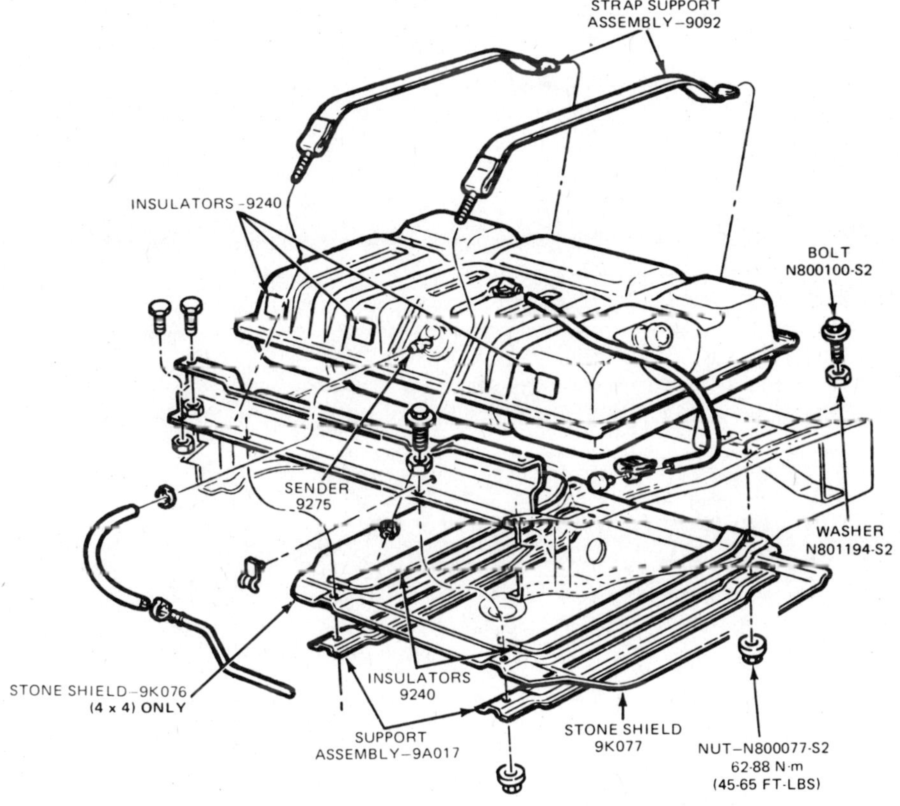

Typical aft fuel tank installation, gasoline-engined models

4. Remove the fuel drain plug or siphon the fuel from the tank into a suitable container.

5. Loosen the fuel line hose clamps, slide the clamps forward and disconnect the fuel line at the fuel gauge sending unit.

6. If the sending unit is to be removed, turn the unit retaining ring counterclockwise and remove the sending unit, retaining ring and gasket. Discard the gasket.

7. Loosen the clamps on the fuel filler pipe and vent hose as necessary and disconnect the filler pipe hose and vent hose from the tank.

8. If the tank is the metal type, support the tank and remove the bolts attaching the tank supports to the frame. Carefully lower the tank and disconnect the vent tube from the vapor emission control valve in the top of the tank. Finish removing the filler pipe and filler pipe vent hose if not possible previously. Remove the tank from under the vehicle.

9. If the tank is the plastic type, support the tank and remove the bolts attaching the combination skid plate and tank support to the frame. Carefully lower the tank and disconnect the vent tube from the vapor emisson control valve in the top of the tank. Finish removing the filler pipe and filler pipe vent hose if it was not possible previously. Remove the skid plate and tank from under the vehicle. Remove the skid plate from the tank.

10. Install the tank in the reverse order of removal.

Chassis Electrical

5

HEATER

Blower

1965–77

Removal and Installation

1. Disconnect the electrical connectors and the ground wire from the top of the heater.
2. Remove the screws retaining the motor to the plenum chamber and remove the motor assembly.
3. Loosen the blower wheel allen screw and remove the wheel.
4. Remove the motor from the mounting plate.
5. Install the motor to the mounting plate.
6. Install the blower wheel.
7. Position the motor to the plenum chamber. Install the retaining screws.
8. Connect the electrical lead and the ground wire.
9. Check the operation of the blower motor.

1978–79 STANDARD HEATER, WITHOUT AIR CONDITIONING

Removal

1. Disconnect the temperature and function control Bowden cables from the heater housing. This must be done to prevent damage to the cables.
2. Disconnect the wires from the blower resistor.
3. Remove five screws attaching the air inlet (vent) duct to the heater housing.
4. Disconnect the blower wires.
5. Drain the radiator and remove the heater hoses from the heater core.
6. Remove three heater stud retaining nuts and remove heater.
7. Remove gasket between the heater hose ends and the dash panel at core tubes.
8. Remove two screws and two nuts attaching blower to heater.
9. Remove blower fan from motor shaft, and remove motor from mounting plate.

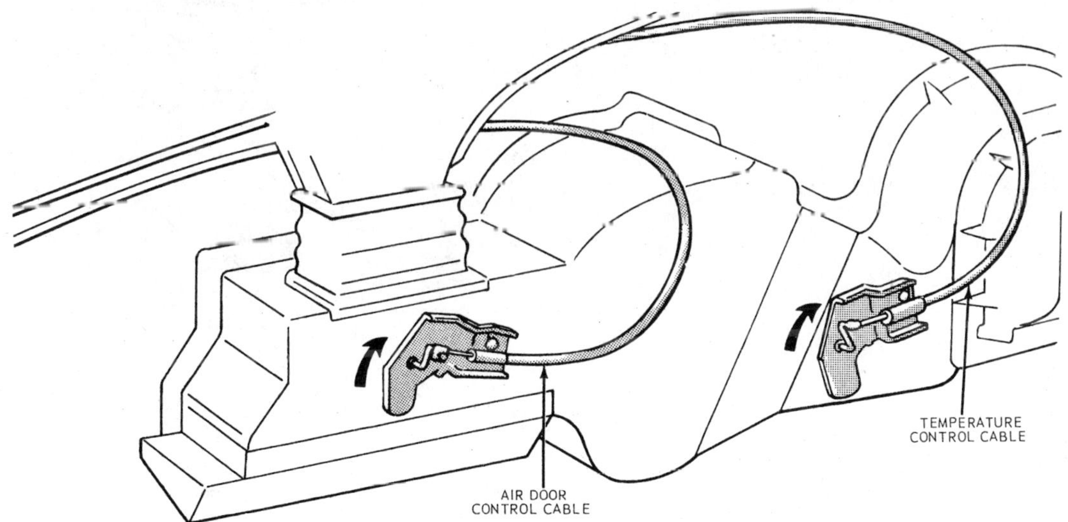

Heater control cable attachment—1974 F-100 through F-350

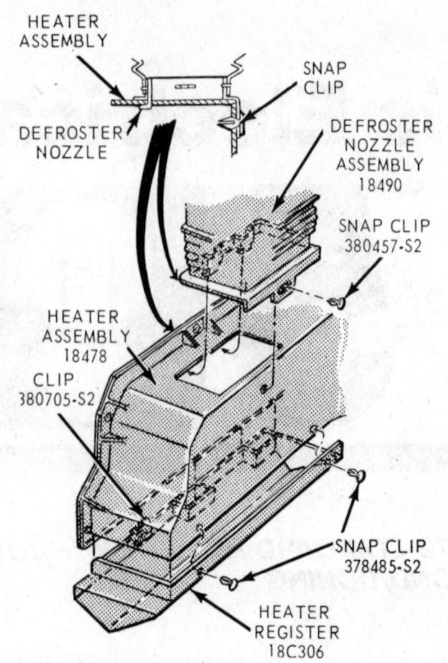

1974 defroster duct attachment at heater plenum, F-100 through F-350

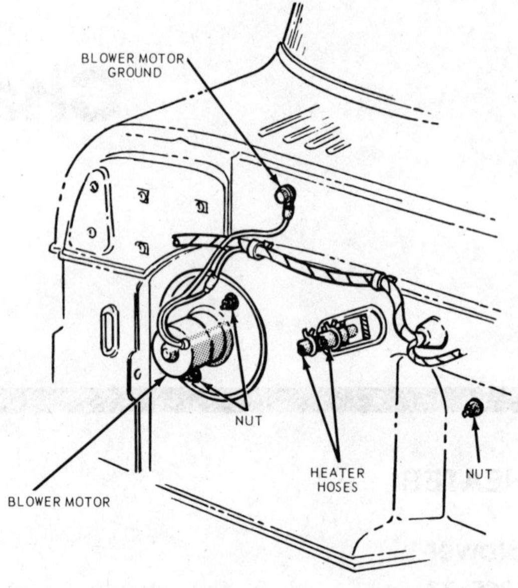

Heater attaching stud locations, mid-'70s F-100 through F-350 shown

Installation

1. Install new motor on mounting plate and install blower fan on motor shaft.
2. Install blower and motor in heater.
3. Position heater assembly in vehicle and install three stud retaining nuts.
4. Connect heater hoses to heater core and fill radiator.
5. Connect blower motor wires.
6. Place defroster nozzle on heater so that the defroster and heater openings are in the up position and there is no air leak around the seal.
7. Install air inlet (vent) duct to heater. Push duct firmly against seal on side cowl and tighten five attaching screws.
8. Connect wires to blower motor resistor.
9. Connect temperature and function control cables to heater, and adjust the cables.
10. Re-install gasket between the heater hose ends and the dash panel at core ends.
11. Fill cooling system.

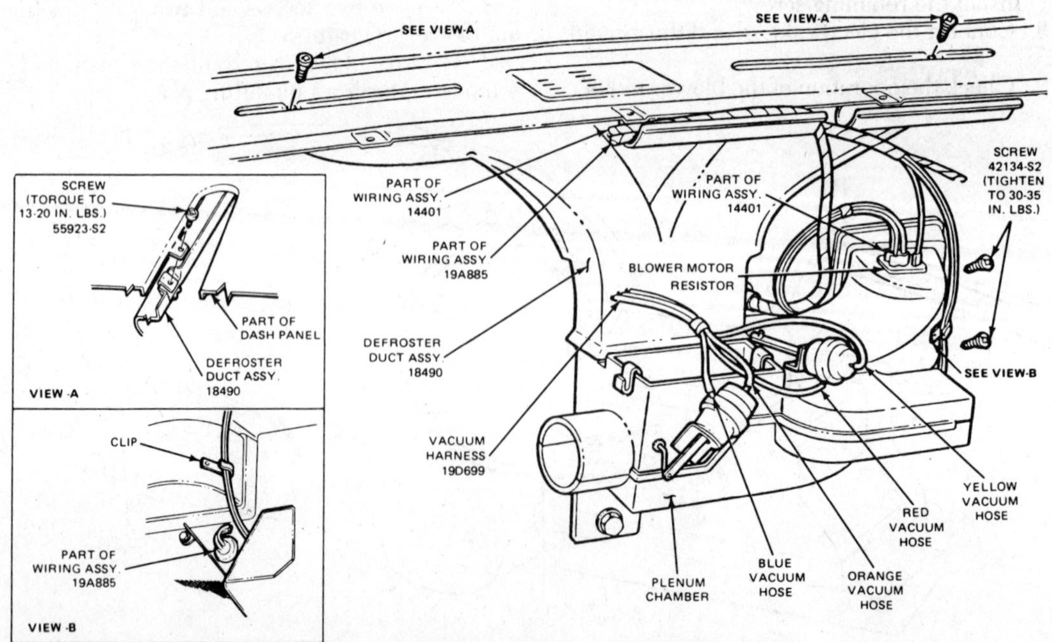

Plenum chamber and nozzle assembly, 1978–79

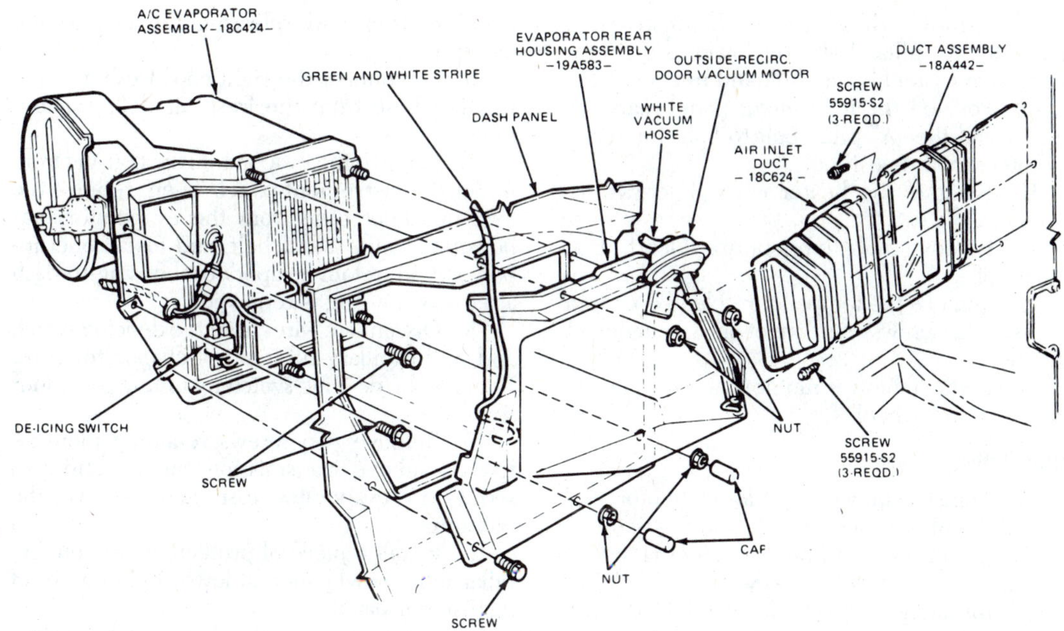

Evaporator rear housing, 1978–79

1978–79 DELUXE HI-LO HEATER, WITHOUT AIR CONDITIONING

Removal

1. Disconnect the battery cable, remove the carburetor air cleaner and partially drain the coolant system.
2. Remove the heater hoses from the heater core.
3. Remove the glove box liner and remove the register duct by pulling from the instrument panel register and releasing the clip at the plenum.
4. Disconnect the right cowl outside air inlet vacuum hose from the outside-recirculating door vacuum motor.
5. Remove the rear housing from under the instrument panel. Remove the outside air inlet duct from the rear housing (4 nuts and 1 bolt) and install one upper nut to retain heater housing-to-dash after rear housing is removed.
6. Remove two screws retaining plenum-to-dash (above transmission tunnel) and two screws to heater housing and remove the plenum.
7. Install a piece of protective tape on "A" pillar inner cowl panel, at lower right corner of instrument panel.

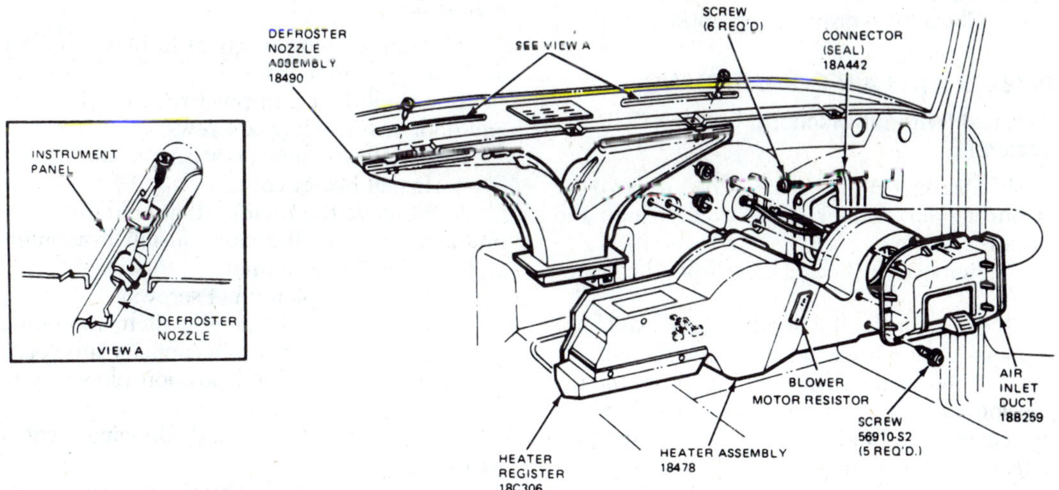

1973–79 heater installation

8. Remove the lower right instrument panel-to-"A" pillar bolt and lower the center instrument panel brace, bolt and nut.

9. Position the instrument panel rearward and install the "A" pillar bolt to hold the panel in the rearward position.

10. Remove the heater core (3 screws retaining 2 plates).

11. Remove the temperature blend door (snaps off).

12. Remove the temperature blend door arm support (2 screws) and pivot arm retainer (1 screw).

13. Remove blower motor (2 screws) and remove blower wheel.

Installation

1. Transfer blower to blower motor and panel assembly.

2. Install door arm pivot retainer (1 screw) and door arm support (2 screws).

3. Install the temperature blend door (snaps on).

4. Install heater core.

5. Install the plenum (4 screws).

6. Connect blower wires.

7. Remove heater housing upper retaining nut and install the heater outlet (4 nuts and 1 bolt). Position the air inlet duct.

8. Connect the white vacuum hose to the outside-recirculating door vacuum motor.

9. Reposition the instrument panel, install the retaining bolts and remove the protective tape at the "A" pillar inner cowl panel, lower right corner of instrument panel.

10. Install the right register duct assembly and install the glove box liner.

11. Connect heater hoses to the heater core assembly.

12. Fill cooling system, install the air cleaner and connect the battery cable to the battery.

13. Check blower motor operation.

1978–79 WITH AIR CONDITIONING

Removal (Without Discharging the A/C System)

1. Disconnect the battery cable, remove the carburetor air cleaner and partially drain the coolant system.

2. Remove the heater hoses from the heater core.

3. From under the hood, remove A/C hose support bracket from the cowl (one screw).

4. Remove the insulation tape from the expansion valve and sensing bulb. Then remove the cover plate and seal from the evaporator housing at the expansion valve (two screws).

5. Remove the glove box liner and remove the A/C duct by pulling from the instrument panel register and releasing the clip at the plenum.

6. Disconnect the right cowl fresh air inlet vacuum hose from the fresh air door vacuum motor.

7. Remove the evaporator rear housing from under the instrument panel. Then, remove the fresh air inlet tube from the evaporator rear housing (4 nuts and 1 bolt) and install one upper nut to retain evaporator housing-to-dash after rear housing is removed.

8. Disconnect wires from the de-icing switch and pull capillary tube out of evaporator core. Remove the de-icing switch mounting plate (four screws).

9. Remove two screws retaining plenum-to-dash (above transmission tunnel) and two screws to evaporator case and remove the plenum.

10. Install a piece of protective tape on "A" pillar inner cowl panel, at lower right corner of instrument panel.

11. Then, remove the lower right instrument panel-to-"A" pillar bolt and lower the center instrument panel brace, bolt and nut.

12. Position the instrument panel rearward and install the "A" pillar bolt to hold the panel in the rearward position.

13. Remove four evaporator retaining screws.

14. Position the evaporator away from the case and secure it rearward and upward. Remove evaporator sealing grommet.

15. Remove heater core (3 screws retaining 2 plates).

16. Remove A/C-heat door (snaps off).

17. Remove A/C-heat door arm support (2 screws) and pivot arm retainer (1 screw).

18. Remove blower motor (2 screws) and remove blower wheel.

Installation

1. Transfer blower wheel to blower motor and panel assembly.

2. Install door arm pivot retainer (1 screw) and door arm support (2 screws).

3. Install A/C-heat door (snaps on).

4. Install heater core.

5. Remove the retainer that held the evaporator away from the case, install evaporator and tube sealing grommet.

6. Install the plenum (4 screws).

7. Install the de-icing switch mounting plate, install de-icing switch capillary tube back into evaporator core and position blower wire grommet.

8. Connect blower and de-icing switch wires.

9. Remove upper evaporator case regaining nut and install the evaporator outlet (4 nuts

and 1 bolt). Then, position the air inlet bellows.

10. Connect the right cowl fresh air inlet vacuum hose to the fresh air door vacuum motor.

11. Reposition the instrument panel, install the retaining bolts and remove the protective tape at the "A" pillar inner cowl panel, lower right corner of instrument panel.

12. Install the right A/C duct assembly and install the glove box liner.

13. Install seal cover plate to the evaporator case at the expansion valve.

14. Install insulation tape over the expansion valve and sensing bulb.

15. Install the A/C hose support bracket-to-cowl.

16. Connect heater hoses to the heater core assembly.

17. Fill cooling system, install the carburetor air cleaner and connect the battery cable to the battery.

18. Check blower motor operation.

1980–81 COMFORT VENT HEATERS, WITHOUT AIR CONDITIONING

Removal

1. Disconnect the motor wires at the hard shell connectors.
2. Disconnect the blower motor air cooling tube from the motor.
3. Remove four (4) blower motor mounting plate attaching screws and remove the motor and wheel assembly from the blower housing.
4. Remove the hub clamp spring from the blower wheel hub and the retainer from the motor shaft. Then, remove the blower wheel from the motor shaft.

Installation

1. Position the blower wheel on the blower motor shaft. Then, install a new hub clamp spring on the blower hub as shown. The hub clamp spring is included with a new blower wheel but not with the blower motor.
2. Install a new flange gasket on the blower motor flange.
3. Position the blower motor and wheel assembly in the blower housing and install the four (4) attaching screws.

   NOTE: *The wire clamp should be installed under the screw closest to the resistor assembly.*
4. Cement the blower motor air tube on the nipple of the blower housing with RTV silicone adhesive.
5. Connect the blower motor wires at the hard shell connectors.
6. Check the blower motor for proper operation.

1980–AND LATER STANDARD & HIGH OUTPUT HEATERS, WITHOUT AIR CONDITIONING

Removal

1. Disconnect the motor wire at the hard shell connector and the ground wire at the ground screw.
2. Remove four (4) screws attaching the blower motor and wheel to the heater case.
3. Remove the blower motor and wheel from the heater case.
4. Remove the blower wheel hub clamp spring and the tab lock washer from the motor shaft. Then, pull the blower wheel from the motor shaft.

Installation

1. Install the blower wheel on the blower motor shaft.
2. Install the hub clamp spring on the blower hub.
3. Position the blower motor and wheel to the heater case, and install the four (4) attaching screws.
4. Connect the blower motor wires and check the blower motor for proper operation.

1980 AND LATER WITH AIR CONDITIONING

Removal (Without Discharging the A/C System)

1. Disconnect the motor wires at the hard shell connectors.
2. Disconnect the blower motor air cooling tube from the motor.
3. Remove four (4) blower motor mounting plate attaching screws and remove the motor and wheel assembly from the blower housing.
4. Remove the hub clamp spring from the blower wheel hub and the retainer from the motor shaft. Then, remove the blower wheel from the motor shaft.

Installation

1. Position the blower wheel on the blower motor shaft to the dimension shown. Then, install a new hub clamp spring on the blower hub as shown. The hub clamp spring is included with a new blower wheel but not with the blower motor.
2. Install a new flange gasket on the blower motor flange.
3. Position the blower motor and wheel assembly in the blower housing and install the four (4) attaching screws. Note: the wire clamp

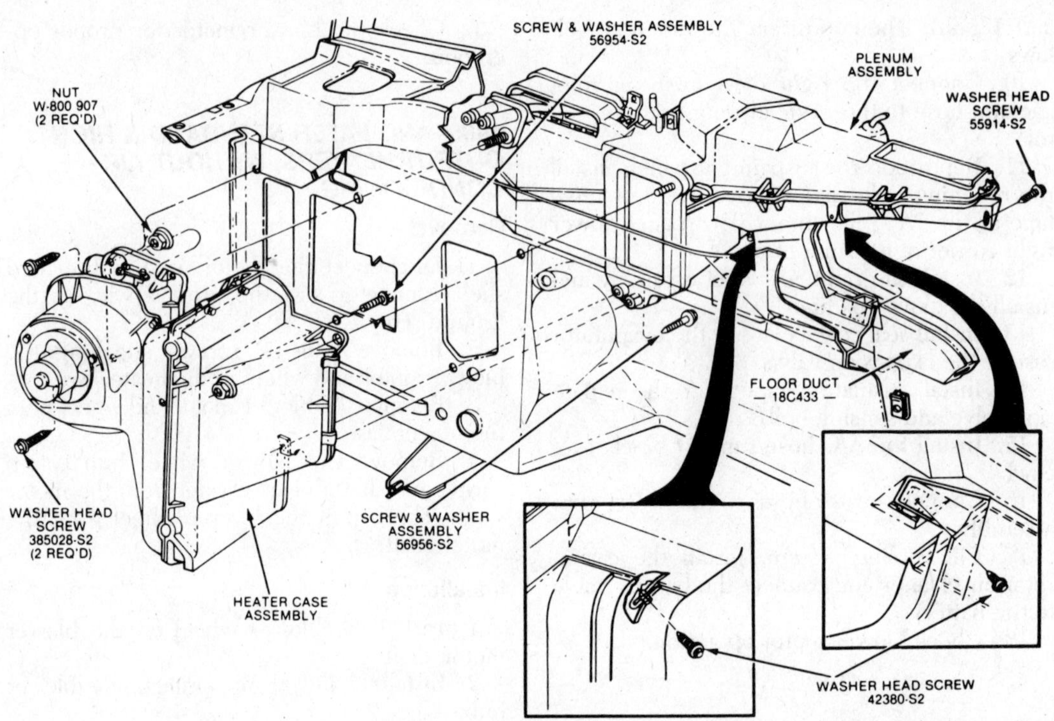

Heater case and plenum assemblies, 1980–81

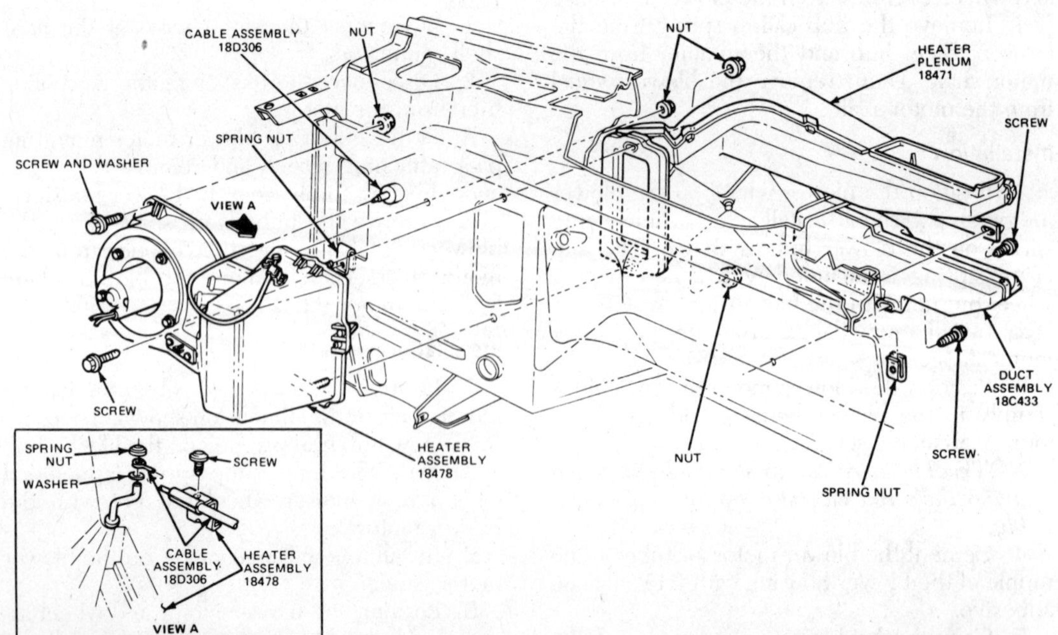

Heater case and plenum assemblies, 1980 and later standard and high output units without A/C

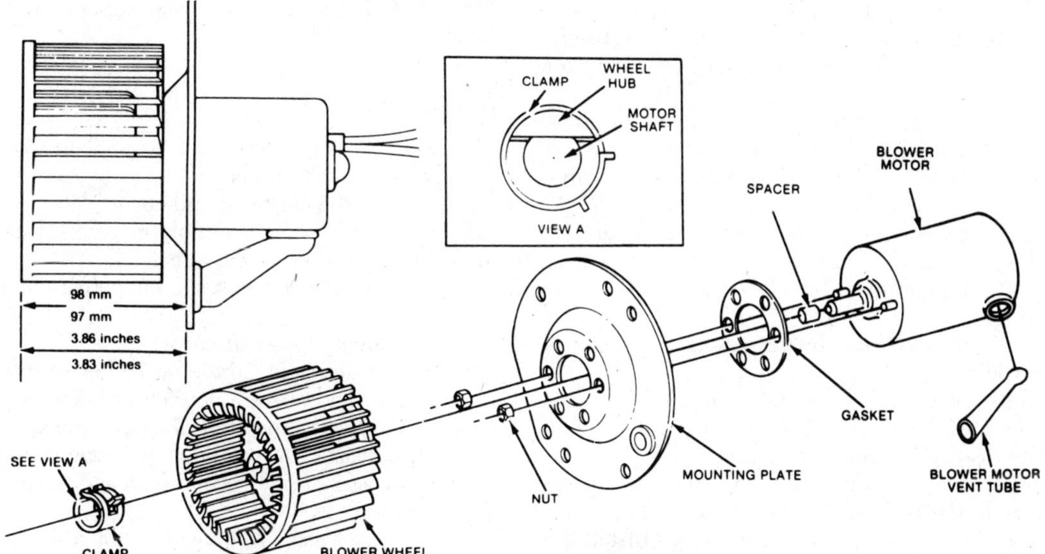

Blower motor and wheel, 1980 and later without A/C

should be installed under the screw closest to the resistor assembly.

4. Cement the blower motor air tube on the nipple of the blower housing with RTV silicone adhesive.
5. Connect the blower motor wires at the hard shell connectors.
6. Check the blower motor for proper operation.

Heater Core

1965–77

Removal and Installation

1. Drain the cooling system.
2. Disconnect the two heater hoses at the heater and remove the rubber pads from the core.

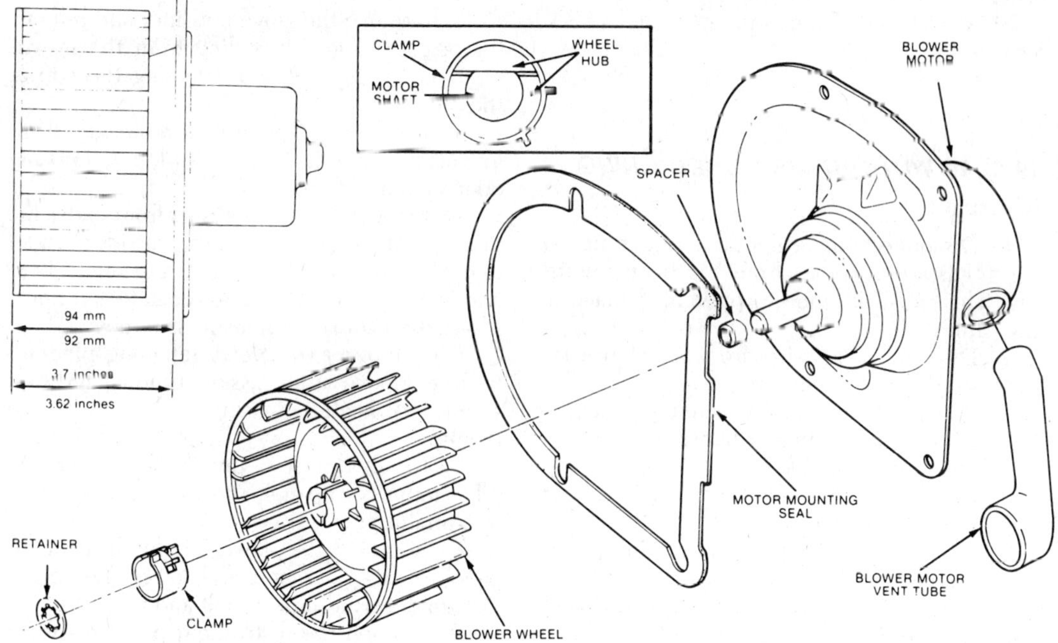

Blower motor and wheel, 1980 and later with A/C

3. Remove the nuts and star washers retaining the heater assembly to the dash panel.
4. Disconnect the right and left defroster hoses at the plenum.
5. Disconnect the fresh air inlet at the cowl. Rest the heater on the floor.
6. Disconnect the heat/defrost door cable at the door crank arm.
7. Disconnect the outside air door cable at the crank arm.
8. Disconnect the electrical wires at the connector.
9. Remove the heater assembly from the vehicle.
10. Remove the screws retaining the rear cover. Remove the clip retaining the core in the case and remove the core.
11. Transfer the seals from the old heater core to the new heater core.
12. Position the core in the case. Install the retaining clip. Position the cover and install the retaining screws.
13. Position the heater assembly on the floor in the vehicle. Connect the wire connectors.
14. Connect and adjust the outside air door control cable.
15. Connect and adjust the heat/defrost door control cable.
16. Position the heater assembly to the dash and install the nuts and washers.
17. Position the heater core pads over the core and connect both hoses.
18. Connect the defroster hoses and fresh air intake.
19. Fill the cooling system with the proper coolant mixture.
20. Check the heater operation and check for leaks.

1978–79 WITHOUT AIR CONDITIONING

Removal

1. Disconnect the temperature and function control Bowden cables from the heater housing. This must be done to prevent damage to the cables.
2. Disconnect the wires from the blower resistor.
3. Remove five screws attaching the air inlet (vent) duct to the heater housing.
4. Disconnect the blower wires.
5. Drain the radiator and remove the heater hoses from the heater core.
6. Remove three heater stud retaining nuts and remove heater.
7. Remove gasket between the heater hose ends and the dash panel at core tubes.
8. Remove heater core cover and gasket (four screws).
9. Pull heater core and lower support from heater.

Installation

1. Install foam gaskets on heater core and install in heater assembly.
2. Install the core seal and cover plate.
3. Position heater assembly in vehicle and install three stud retaining nuts.
4. Connect heater hoses to heater core and fill radiator.
5. Connect blower motor wires.
6. Place defroster nozzle on heater so that the defroster and heater openings are in the up position and there is no air leak around the seal.
7. Install air inlet (vent) duct to heater. Push duct firmly against seal on side cowl and tighten five attaching screws.
8. Connect wires to blower motor resistor.
9. Connect temperature and function control cables to heater, and adjust the cables.
10. Re-install gasket between the heater hose ends and the dash panel at core ends.
11. Fill Cooling System.

1978–79 DELUXE HI-LO HEATER, WITHOUT AIR CONDITIONING

Removal

1. Disconnect the battery cable, remove the carburetor air cleaner and partially drain the coolant system.
2. Remove the heater hoses from the heater core.
3. Remove the glove box liner and remove the register duct by pulling from the instrument panel register and releasing the clip at the plenum.
4. Disconnect the right cowl outside air inlet vacuum hose from the outside-recirculating door vacuum motor.
5. Remove the rear housing from under the instrument panel. Remove the outside air inlet duct from the rear housing (4 nuts and 1 bolt) and install one upper nut to retain heater housing-to-dash after rear housing is removed.
6. Remove two screws retaining plenum-to-dash (above transmission tunnel) and two screws to heater housing and remove the plenum.
7. Install a piece of protective tape on "A" pillar inner cowl panel, at lower right corner of instrument panel.
8. Remove the lower right instrument panel-to-"A" pillar bolt and lower the center instrument panel brace, bolt and nut.
9. Position the instrument panel rearward and install the "A" pillar bolt to hold the panel in the rearward position.

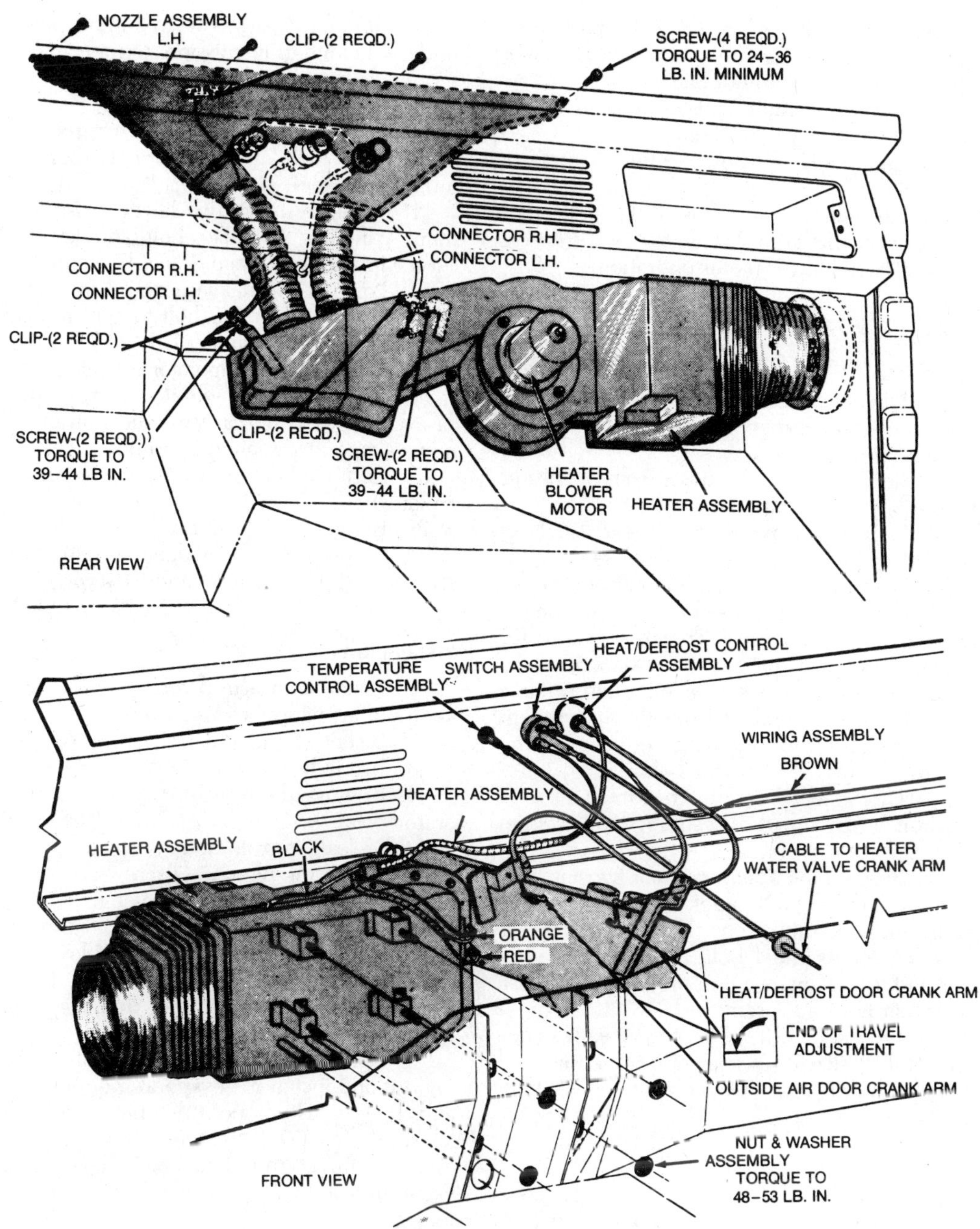

Heater assembly, 1966–77

10. Remove heater core (3 screws retaining 2 plates).
11. Remove the temperature blend door (snaps off).
12. Remove the temperature blend door arm support (2 screws) and pivot arm retainer (1 screw).
13. Remove blower motor (2 screws) and remove blower wheel.

Installation

1. Transfer blower wheel to blower motor and panel assembly.
2. Install door arm pivot retainer (1 screw) and door arm support (2 screws).
3. Install the temperature blend door (snaps on).
4. Install heater core.
5. Install the plenum (4 screws).
6. Connect blower wires.
7. Remove heater housing upper retaining nut and install the heater outlet (4 nuts and 1 bolt). Position the air inlet duct.
8. Connect the white vacuum hose to the outside-recirculating door vacuum motor.
9. Reposition the instrument panel, install

the retaining bolts and remove the protective tape at the "A" pillar inner cowl panel, lower right corner of instrument panel.

10. Install the right register duct assembly and install the glove box liner.

11. Connect heater hoses to the heater core assembly.

12. Fill cooling system, install the air cleaner and connect the battery cable to the battery.

13. Check blower motor operation.

1978–79 WITH AIR CONDITIONING

Removal (Without Discharging A/C System)

1. Disconnect the battery cable, remove the carburetor air cleaner and partially drain the coolant system.

2. Remove the heater hoses from the heater core.

3. From under the hood, remove A/C hose support bracket from the cowl (one screw).

4. Remove the insulation tape from the expansion valve and sensing bulb. Then remove the cover plate and seal from the evaporator housing at the expansion valve (two screws).

5. Remove the glove box liner and remove the A/C duct by pulling from the instrument panel register and releasing the clip at the plenum.

6. Disconnect the right cowl fresh air inlet vacuum hose from the fresh air door vacuum motor.

7. Remove the evaporator rear housing from under the instrument panel. Then, remove the fresh air inlet tube from the evaporator rear housing (4 nuts and 1 bolt) and install one upper nut to retain evaporator housing-to-dash after rear housing is removed.

8. Disconnect wires from the de-icing switch and pull capillary tube out of evaporator core. Remove the de-icing switch mounting plate (four screws).

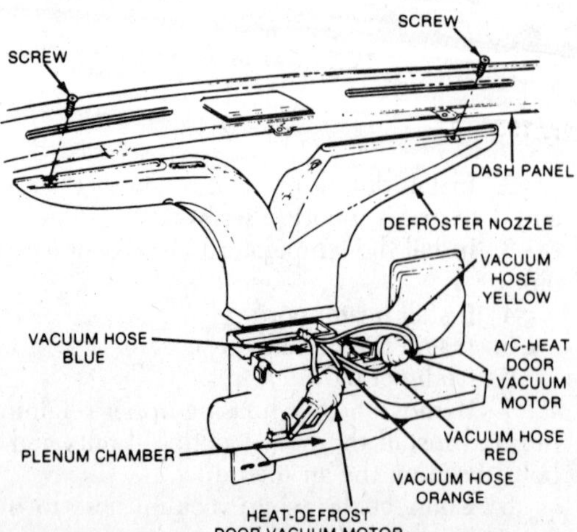

A/C-heater control connections, 1978–79

9. Remove two screws retaining plenum-to-dash (above transmission tunnel) and two screws to evaporator case and remove the plenum.

10. Install a piece of protective tape on "A" pillar inner cowl panel, at lower right corner of intrument panel.

11. Then, remove the lower right instrument panel-to-"A" pillar bolt and lower the center instrument panel brace, bolt and nut.

12. Position the instrument panel rearward and install the "A" pillar bolt to hold the panel in the rearward position.

13. Remove four evaporator retaining screws.

14. Position the evaporator away from the case and secure it rearward the upward. Remove evaporator sealing grommet.

15. Remove heater core (3 screws retaining 2 plates).

16. Remove A/C-heat door (snaps off).

17. Remove A/C-heat door arm support (2 screws) and pivot arm retainer (1 screw).

Installation

1. Install door arm pivot retainer (1 screw) and door arm support (2 screws).

2. Install A/C-heat door (snaps on).

3. Install heater core.

4. Remove the retainer that held the evaporator away from the case, install evaporator and tube sealing grommet.

5. Install the plenum (4 screws).

6. Install the de-icing switch mounting plate, install de-icing switch capillary tube back into evaporator core and position blower wire grommet.

7. Connect blower and de-icing switch wires.

8. Remove upper evaporator case retaining nut and install the evaporator outlet (4 nuts and 1 bolt). Then, position the air inlet bellows.

9. Connect the right cowl fresh air inlet vacuum hose to the fresh air door vacuum motor.

10. Reposition the instrument panel, install the retaining bolts and remove the protective tape at the "A" pillar inner cowl panel, lower right corner of instrument panel.

11. Install the right A/C duct assembly and install the glove box liner.

12. Install seal and cover plate to the evaporator case at the expansion valve.

13. Install insulation tape over the expansion valve and sensing bulb.

14. Install the A/C hose support bracket-to-cowl.

15. Connect heater hoses to the heater core assembly.

16. Fill cooling system, install the carbu-

retor air cleaner and connect the battery cable to the battery.

17. Check blower motor operation.

1980–81 COMFORT VENT HEATERS, WITHOUT AIR CONDITIONING

Removal

1. Disconnect the heater hoses from the heater core tubes and plug the hoses with suitable ⅝ inch plugs.
2. Remove the glove compartment liner.
3. Remove two (2) spring clips attaching the heater core cover to the plenum along the top edge of the heater core cover.
4. Remove eight (8) screws attaching the heater core cover to the plenum and remove the cover.
5. Remove the heater core from the plenum taking care not to spill coolant from the core.

Installation

1. Install the heater core in the plenum.
2. Install the heater core cover (eight (8) screws and two (2) spring clips along the top edge of the cover).
3. Install the glove compartment liner.
4. Connect the heater hoses to the heater core. Tighten the hose clamps.
5. Add coolant to raise the coolant level to specification.
6. Check the system for proper operation and for coolant leaks.

1980–81 STANDARD & HIGH OUTPUT HEATERS, WITHOUT AIR CONDITIONING

Removal

1. Disconnect the temperature cable from the temperature blend door and the mounting bracket on top of the heater case.
2. Disconnect the wires from the blower motor resistor and the blower motor.
3. Disconnect the heater hoses from the heater core and plug the hoses with suitable ⅝ inch plugs.
4. Working under the instrument panel, remove two (2) nuts retaining te left end of the heater case and the right end of the plenum to the dash panel.
5. In the engine compartment, remove one (1) screw attaching the top center of te heater case to the dash panel.
6. Remove two (2) screws attaching the right

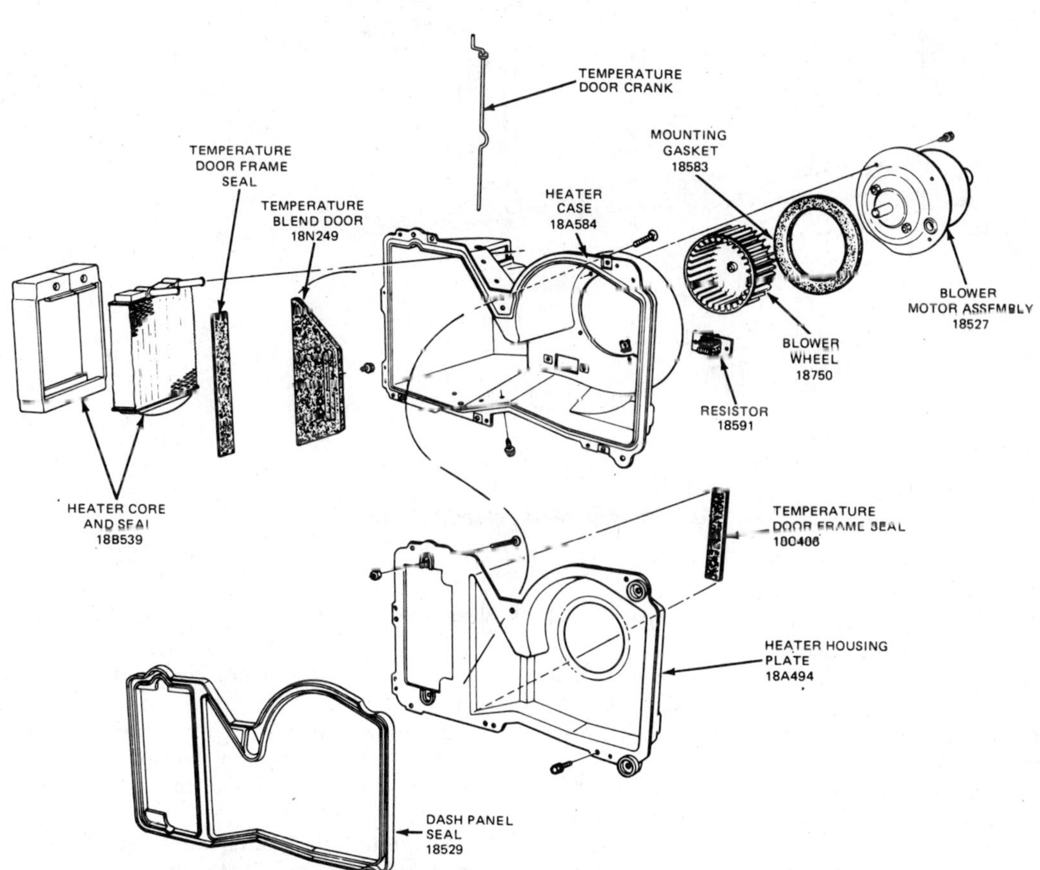

Heater case assembly showing core and blower, 1980 and later shown

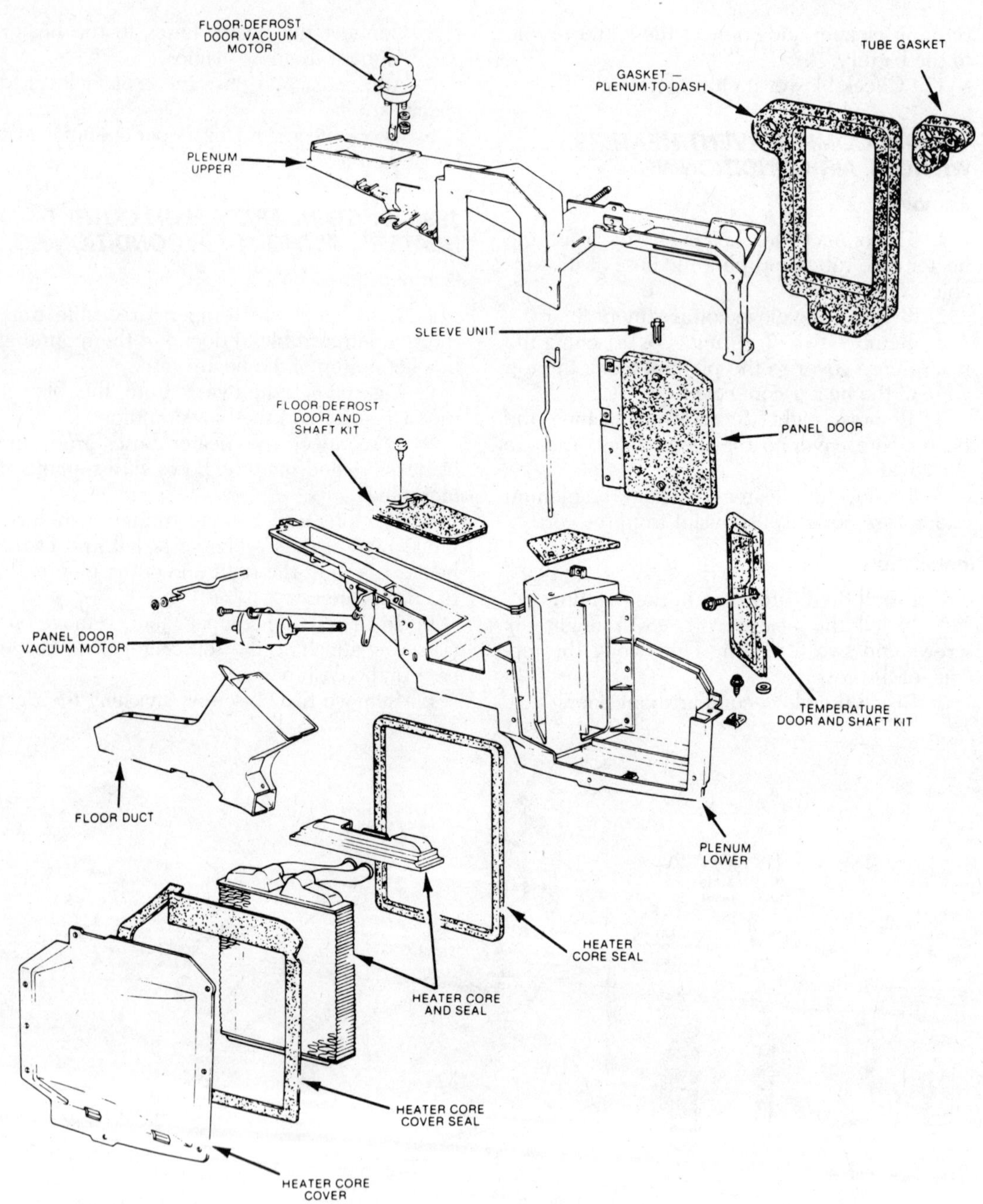

Comfort Vent heater plenum, 1980–81

end of the heater case to the dash panel, and remove the heater case from the vehicle.

7. Remove nine (9) screws and one (1) bolt and nut attaching the heater housing plate to the heater case, and remove the heater housing plate.

8. Remove three (3) screws attaching the heater core frame to the heater case and remove the frame.

9. Remove the heater core and seal from the heater case.

Installation

1. Position the heater core and seal in the heater case.

2. Install the heater core frame (3 screws).

3. Position the heater housing plate on the heater case and install the nine (9) screws and one (1) bolt and nut.

4. Position the heater case to the dash panel and install the three (3) attaching screws.

5. Working in the passenger compart-

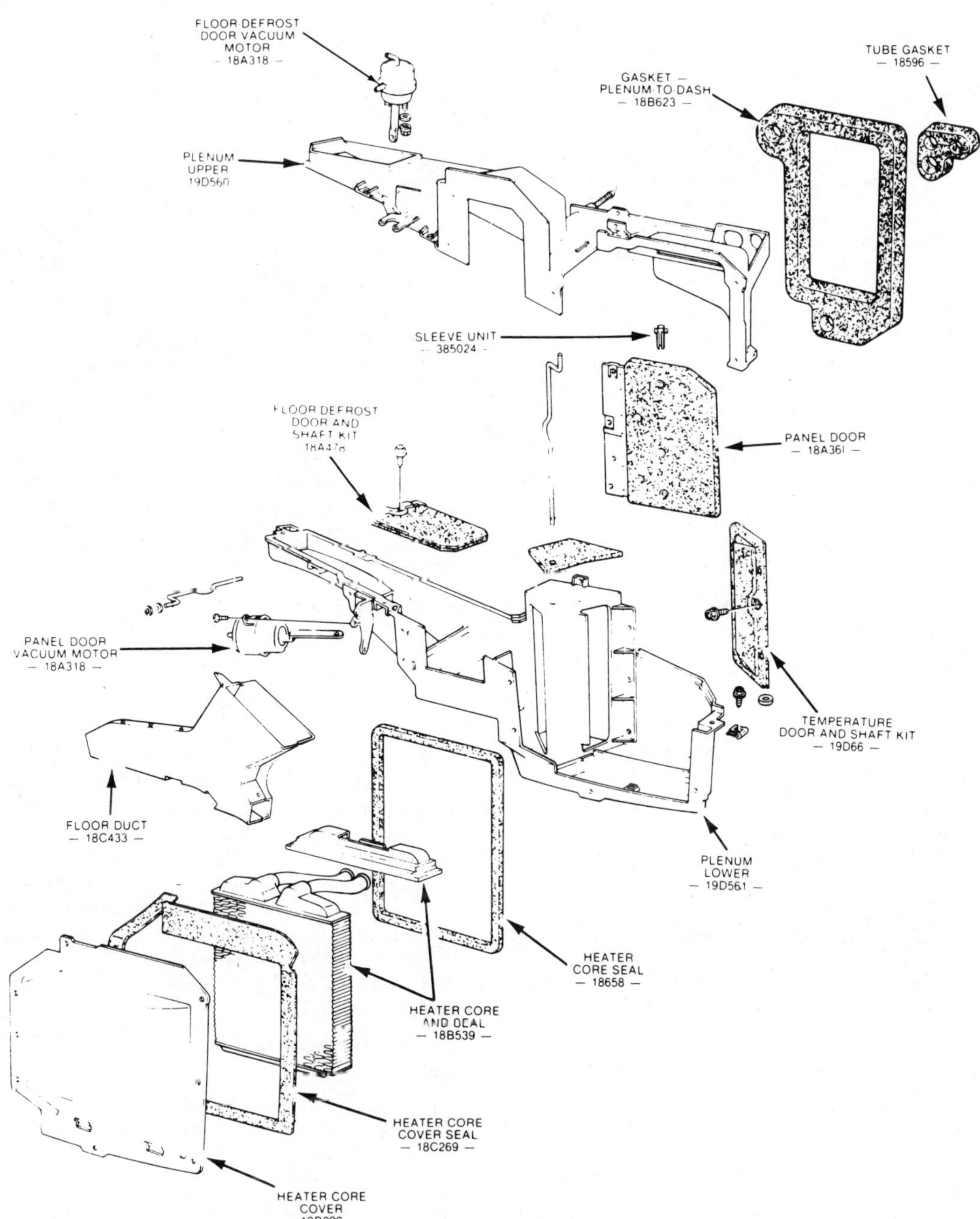

Manual A/C—heater plenum, 1980 and later

ment, install two (2) nuts to retain the heater case and plenum right end to the dash panel.

6. Connect the heater hoses to the heater core. Tighten the hose clamps.

7. Connect the wires to the blower motor resistor assembly.

8. Connect the blower motor wires.

9. Positin (slide) the self-adjusting clip on the temperature cable to a position approximately one (1) inch from the cable end loop.

10. Snap the temperature cable on the cable mounting bracket of the heater case. Then, position the self-adjusting clip on the door crank arm.

11. Adjust the temperature cable.

12. Check the system for proper operation.

1982 AND LATER STANDARD & HIGH OUTPUT HEATERS, WITHOUT AIR CONDITIONING

Removal

1. Disconnect the temperature cable from the temperature blend door and the mounting bracket on top of the heater case.

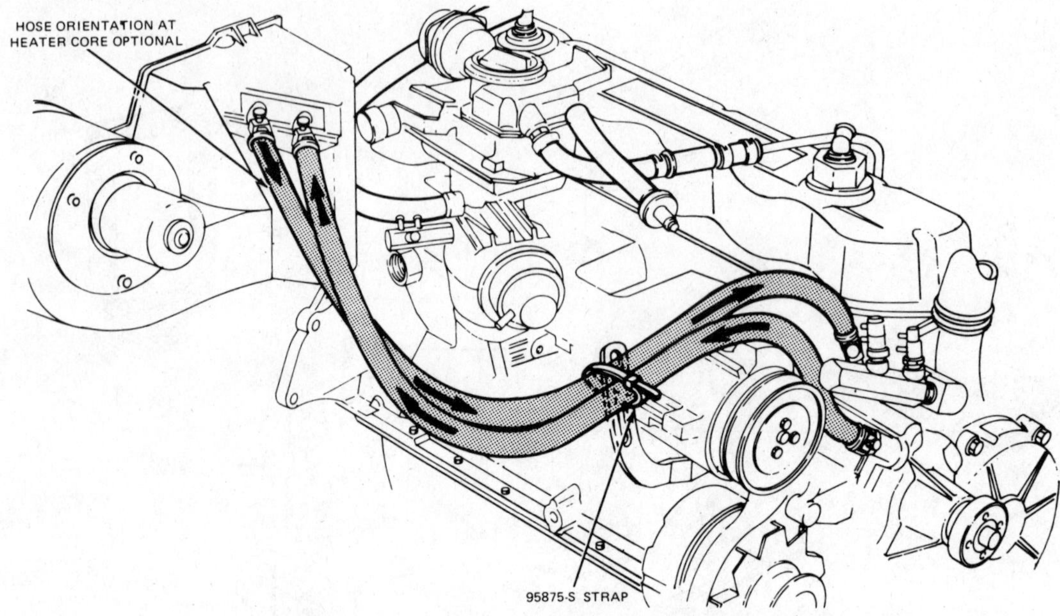

Heater hose connections, inline six cylinder models

2. Disconnect the wires from the blower motor resistor and the blower motor.
3. Disconnect the heater hoses from the heater core and plug the hoses with suitable ⅝ inch plugs.
4. Working under the instrument panel, remove three nuts retaining the left end of the heater case and the right end of the plenum to the dash panel.
5. Remove two screws attaching the right end of the heater case to the dash panel, and remove the heater case from the vehicle.
6. Remove eleven screws and one bolt and nut attaching the heater housing plate to the heater case, and remove the heater housing plate.
7. Remove the heater core and seal from the heater case.

Installation

1. Position the heater core and seal in the heater case.
2. Position the heater housing plate on the heater case and install the eleven screws and one bolt and nut.
3. Position the heater case to the dash panel and install the two attaching screws.
4. Working in the passenger compartment, install three nuts to retain the heater case and plenum right end to the dash panel.
5. Connect the heater hoses to the heater core. Tighten the hose clamps.
6. Connect the wires to the blower motor resistor assembly.
7. Connect the wire harness connector to the blower motor.
8. Position the temperature cable pigtail on the temperature door crank arm with the pigtail up. Be sure a flat washer is placed under the pigtail. Then, install a new pushnut to retain the pigtail on the crank arm.
9. Position the temperature cable flag to the mounting bracket and install the attaching screw.
10. Check the system for proper operation.

1980 AND LATER WITH AIR CONDITIONING

Removal (Without Discharging the A/C System)

1. Disconnect the heater hoses from the heater core tubes and plug the hoses with suitable ⅝ inch plugs.
2. Remove the glove compartment liner.
3. Remove eight (8) screws attaching the heater core cover to the plenum and remove the cover.
4. Remove the heater core from the plenum taking care not to spill coolant from the core.

Installation

1. Install the heater core in the plenum.
2. Install the heater core cover (eight screws).
3. Install the glove compartment liner.
4. Connect the heater hoses to the heater core. Tighten the hose clamps.
5. Add coolant to raise the coolant level to specification.

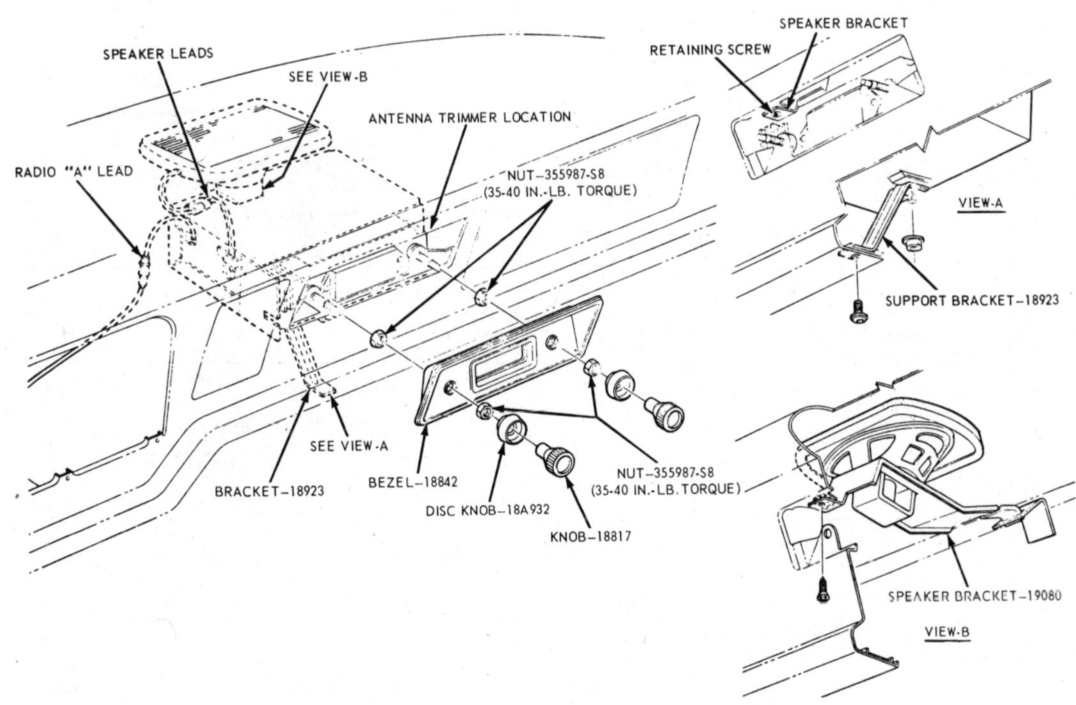

Typical 1965–74 F-100 through F-350 radio installation

RADIO

REMOVAL AND INSTALLATION

1965–77

1. Disconnect the radio lead wire at the receptacle on the fuse panel.
2. Disconnect the speaker leads at the receptacle on the underside of the radio chassis.
3. Disconnect the antenna lead at the receptacle on the right side of the radio chassis.
4. Remove (pull) the volume control and the manual tuning control knobs from the shafts.
5. Remove the screws that retain the dial assembly to the instrument panel and remove the dial assembly.
6. Remove the retaining nuts and the retaining plate that secure the radio to the instrument panel.
7. Remove the radio bottom support bracket retaining screw and remove the radio assembly from the instrument panel.

To install the radio:

8. Position the radio to the inner side of the instrument panel, and install the right and left support bracket to the radio retaining nuts.

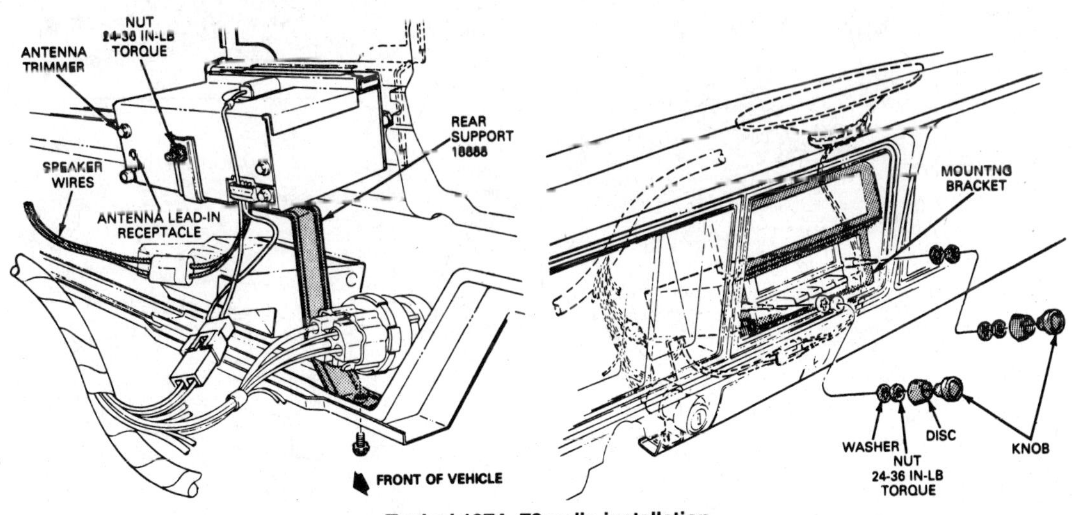

Typical 1974–78 radio installation

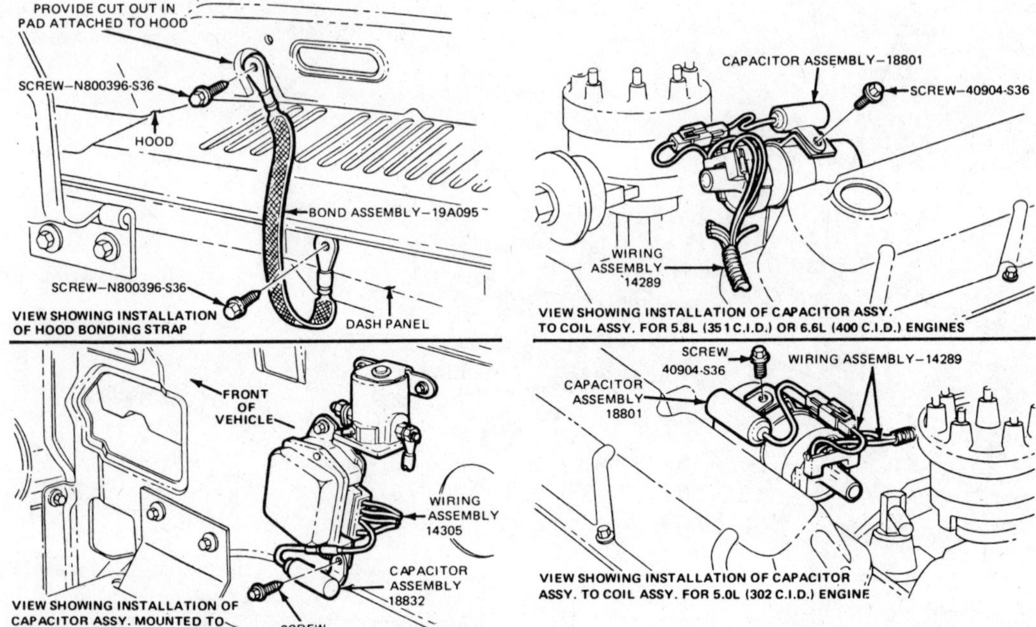

Typical radio supression equipment, pickups. These, along with the spark plug wires and radio itself, are the areas to check when radio reception becomes poor

9. Position the retaining plate to the outer side of the instrument panel over the pilot light and control shafts, and install the retaining nuts.
10. Position the dial assembly, install the retaining screw and seat the knobs on the control shafts.
11. Connect the speaker leads, the antenna lead, and the radio power lead wire at the fuse panel.
12. Calibrate the dial pointer with the tuner by rotating the tuning knob until the dial pointer reaches the end of its travel at the right side of the dial.
13. Check the operation of the radio and adjust the antenna trimmer.

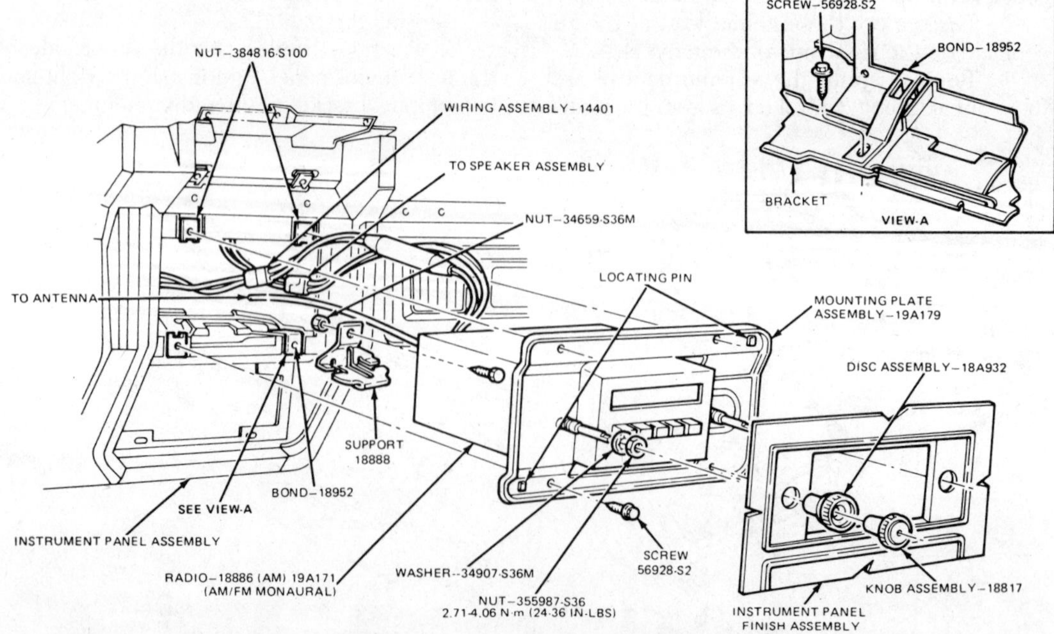

Typical 1979 and later radio installation

1978–84

1. Disconnect the battery ground cable.
2. On 1978–79 models, remove the ash tray and bracket.
3. Disconnect the antenna, speakers and radio lead.
4. Remove the bolt attaching the radio rear support to the lower edge of the instrument panel.
5. On 1978 models equipped with air conditioning, disconnect the left A/C duct hose from the A/C plenum.
6. Remove the knobs and discs from the radio control shafts.
7. Remove the retaining nuts from the control shafts and remove the bezel.
8. Remove the nuts and washers from the control shafts and remove the radio from the panel.
9. Installation is the reverse of removal.

WINDSHIELD WIPERS

Motor

REMOVAL AND INSTALLATION

Vacuum Type

1. Pull the wiper arm and blade assembly off the motor pivot shaft. Remove the grommet from the shaft with a puller.
2. If the vehicle has a padded header, loosen the set screw in the windshield wiper switch knob and remove the knob. Remove the header pad assembly.
3. Disconnect the vacuum hoses to the motor. Remove the screws retaining the motor to the header and remove the motor.
4. Position the new motor to the header and install the retaining screws. Connect the vacuum hoses.
5. Tap the grommet in place around the motor pivot shaft and stake it. Install the wiper arm and blade assembly.
6. Install the padded header assembly and windshield wiper switch knob, if so equipped.
7. Check the operation of the wiper motor and adjust the blade parking position if necessary.

Electric Type up to 1977

1. The motor is mounted on the left side of the windshield header. To remove the motor it will be necessary to first remove the cover and disconnect the linkage arm and pivot shaft assembly from the motor driving arm by removing the retaining clip.
2. Disconnect the motor electrical leads at the multiple connector. Remove the two bolts and nuts that attach the motor mounting bracket to the windshield header, and remove the bracket and motor assembly.
3. Install the windshield wiper motor in the reverse order of removal. When installing the motor, tighten the motor bracket-to-windshield header bolts to 48–72 in. lbs. and the nuts to 20–30 in. lbs.

1978–79

1. Disconnect the battery ground cable.
2. Remove the radio.
3. Remove the engine components attached to the lower wiper bracket bolt, if so equipped.
4. Remove the wiper motor bracket attaching bolts.
5. Disconnect the wiper motor wires. Then, disconnect the wiper arm linkage from the motor shaft.
6. Connect the linkage to motor and install motor bracket attaching bolts. Tighten bolts to 8–12 ft. lbs., and install engine components to lower bracket bolts.
7. Connect wiper motor wires.
8. Install radio.
9. Connect battery cable and check wiper motor operation.

1980 and Later

1. Disconnect the battery ground cable.
2. Remove both wiper arm and blade assemblies.
3. Remove the cowl grille attaching screws and lift the cowl grille slightly.
4. Disconnect the washer nozzle hose and remove the cowl grille assembly.
5. Remove the wiper linkage clip from the motor output arm.
6. Disconnect the wiper motor's wiring connector.
7. Remove the wiper motor's three attaching screws and remove the motor.
8. Install the motor and attach the three attaching screws. Tighten to 60–85 in. lbs.
9. Connect wiper motor's wiring connector.
10. Install wiper linkage clip to the motor's output arm.
11. Connect the washer nozzle hose and install the cowl assembly and attaching screws.
12. Install both wiper arm assemblies.
13. Connect battery ground cable.

Linkage

1965–77

REMOVAL AND INSTALLATION (ELECTRIC TYPE ONLY)

1. Remove the windshield wiper arm and blade assemblies from their pivot shafts.

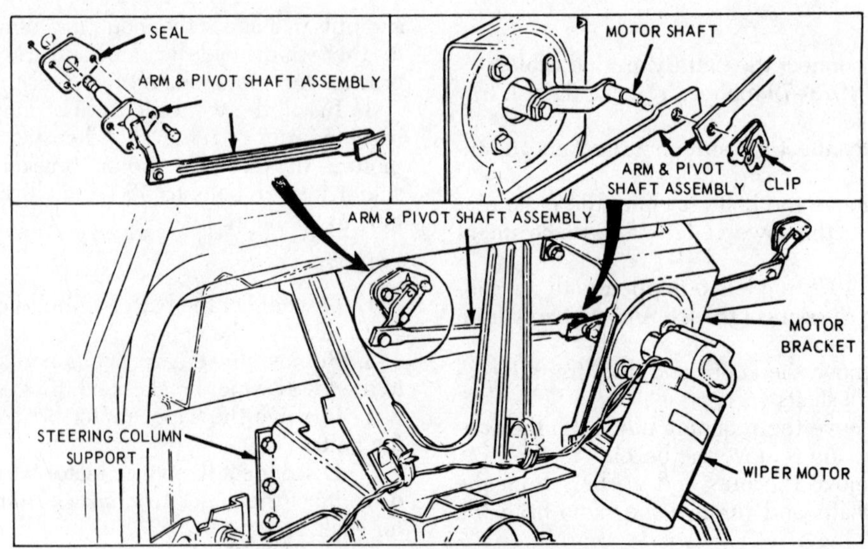

1973–79 wiper motor installation

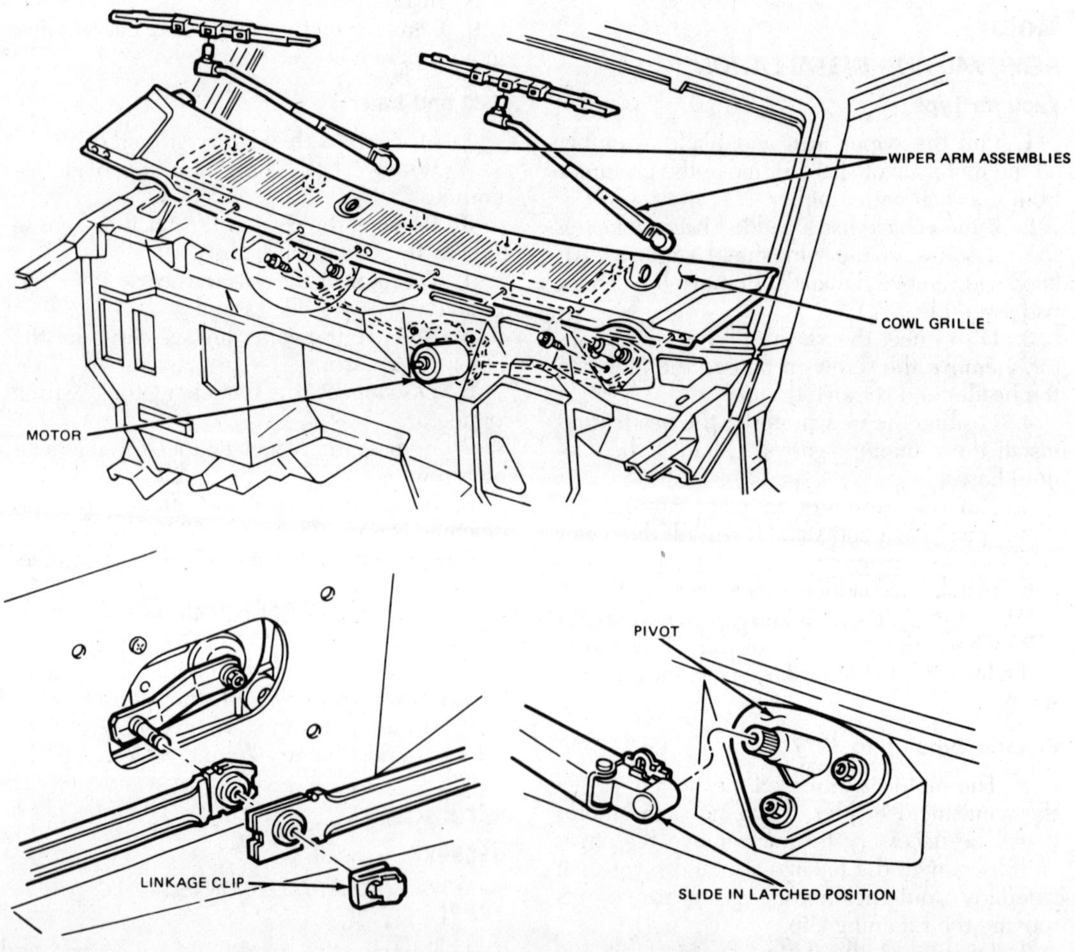

1980 and later wiper motor installation

2. Disconnect the linkage arm from the motor drive arm by removing the retaining clip.
3. The right and left pivot shaft assemblies are each retained to the windshield header by two mounting screws and a nut. Remove these mounting screws and the nut, and remove the pivot shafts and linkage as an assembly.
4. Install the linkage in the reverse order of removal.

1978–79

REMOVAL

1. Open the hood and disconnect the battery ground cable. Remove the arm and blade assemblies from the pivot shafts.
2. Reach under the instrument panel and disconnect the speedometer cable from the rear of the instrument cluster.
3. Remove the instrument cluster bezel.
4. Loosen the three bolts retaining the wiper motor bracket to the cowl. This will allow access between the cowl panel and the link assembly.
5. Remove the clip retaining the motor drive arm to the link assemblies.
6. Through the cluster bezel opening, remove the retaining bolts from the left pivot assembly. Remove the left pivot and link assembly from under the instrument panel.
7. Remove the glove box assembly.
8. Remove the three bolts retaining the right pivot and link assembly to the cowl panel.
9. Disconnect the right link assembly from the drive arm and remove the right pivot and link assembly.

INSTALLATION

1. Place gaskets on the pivot shafts and position the shafts to the cowl panel and install the retaining bolts.
2. Install the glove box assembly.
3. Position the link assemblies to the motor drive arm and install the retaining clip.
4. Tighten the bolts retaining the motor bracket to the cowl and then re-install engine components to lower bracket bolt.
5. Install the wiper arm and blade assemblies.
6. Position and install the instrument cluster bezel.
7. Connect the speedometer cable.
8. Connect the battery ground cable and close the hood and check the operation of the wipers.

1980–84

REMOVAL

1. Disconnect the battery ground cable.
2. Remove both wiper arm assemblies.
3. Remove the cowl grille attaching screws and lift the cowl grille slightly.
4. Disconnect the washer nozzle hose and remove the cowl grille assembly.
5. Remove the wiper linkage clip from the motor output arm and pull the linkage from the output arm.
6. Remove the pivot body to cowl screws and remove the linkage and pivot shaft assembly (three screws on each side). The left and right pivots and linkage are independent and can be serviced separately.

INSTALLATION

1. Attach the linkage and pivot shaft assembly to cowl with attaching screws.
2. Replace the linkage to the output arm and attach the linkage clip.
3. Connect the washer nozzle and cowl grilled assembly.
4. Attach cowl grille attaching screws.
5. Replace both wiper arm assemblies.
6. Connect battery ground cable.

Wiper Arm Assembly Removal

1965–79

Bend the arm backwards at the joint next to the pivot. Now, pull the arm straight off the splined pivot shaft. To replace the arm, hold it in the bent position and slide it on the pivot.

1980 and Later

Raise the blade end of the arm off of the windshield and move the slide latch away from the pivot shaft. This will unlock the wiper arm from the pivot shaft and hold the blade end of the arm off of the glass at the same time. The wiper arm can now be pulled off of the pivot shaft without the aid of any tools.

Blade Assembly to Wiper Arm

1978–79

Wiper blades are used from two different manufacturers.

Trico and Anco blades come in two types. With a bayonet type, the blade saddle slides over the end of the arm and is engaged by a locking stud. With the bottom type, a screw and nut is used to retain the blade on the arm.

BAYONET TYPE

To remove an Anco type blade, press down on the arm to unlatch the top stud. Depress the tab on the saddle and pull the blade from the arm.

To remove a Trico type blade, press inward on the tab and pull the blade from the arm.

To install a new blade assembly, slide the

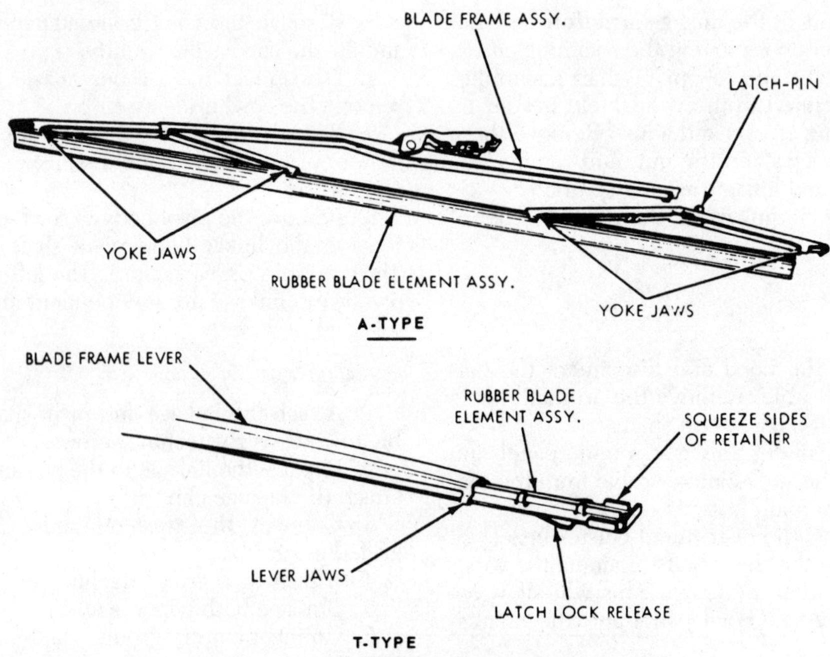

Anco (A) and Trico (T) type wiper blade installation

blade saddle over the end of the wiper arm so that the locking stud snaps into place.

SIDE SADDLE PIN TYPE

To remove a pin type Trico-type blade, insert an appropriate tool into the spring release opening of the blade saddle, depress the spring clip and pull the blade from the arm.

To install, push the blade saddle on to the pin, so that the spring clip engages the pin. Be sure the blade is securely attached to the arm.

1980 and Later

1. Cycle arm and blade assembly to a position on the windshield where removal of blade assembly can be performed without difficulty. Turn ignition key off at desired position.

2. With blade assembly resting on windshield, grasp either end of the wiper blade frame and pull away from windshield, then pull blade assembly from pin.

NOTE: *Rubber element extends past frame. To prevent damage to the blade element, be*

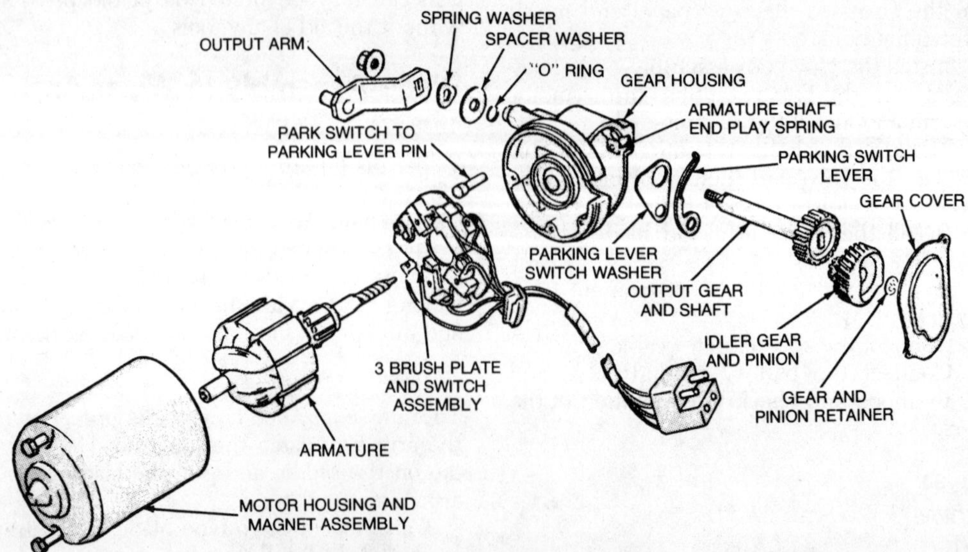

1966–77 wiper motor and transmission

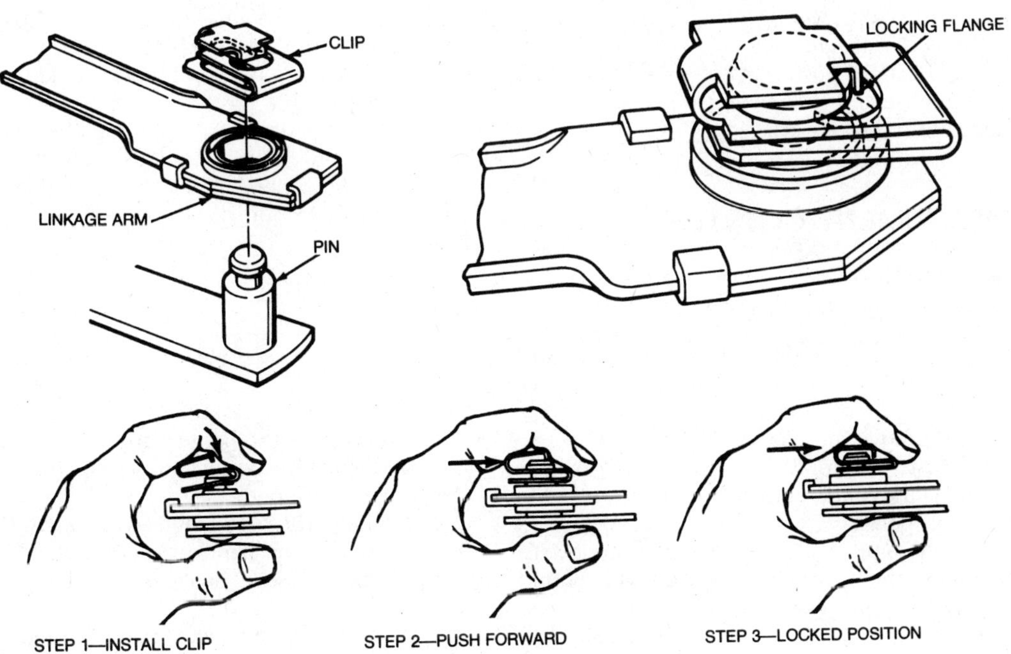

Installing the wiper arm connecting clip

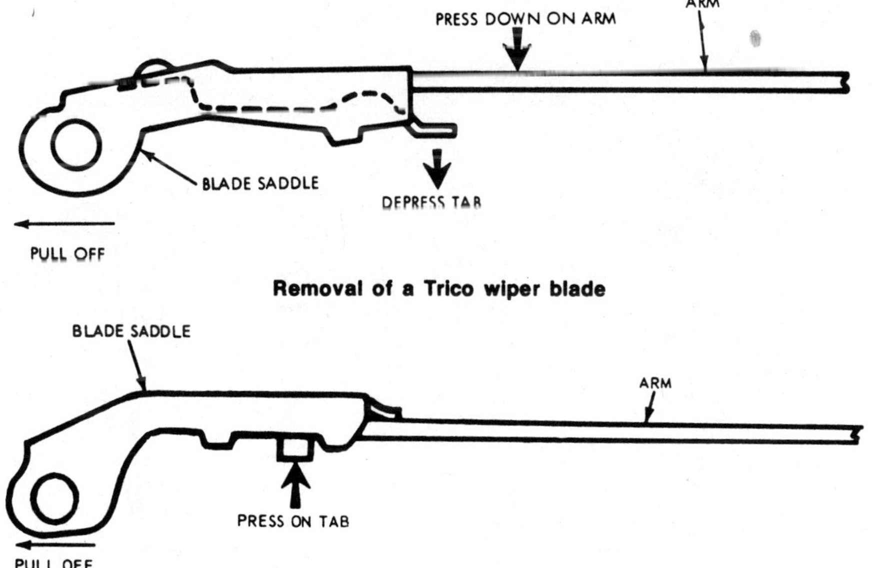

Removal of a Trico wiper blade

Anco-type wiper arm removal

sure to grasp blade frame and not the end of the blade element.

3. To install, push blade assembly onto pin until fully seated. Be sure blade is securely attached to the wiper arm.

INSTRUMENT CLUSTER

1965–77

REMOVAL AND INSTALLATION

1. Disconnect the battery ground cable and disconnect the speedometer cable from the back of the speedometer head.
2. Remove the screws retaining the instrument cluster assembly to the instrument panel.
3. Remove the cluster from behind the instrument panel.
4. Disconnect the feed wires to the instruments and the instrument voltage regulator and remove the light sockets from the cluster back, noting their positions. Remove the two clips that retain the wiring harness to the cluster back and pull the harness away from the cluster. Remove the instrument cluster assembly.

To install the instrument cluster:

5. Mount the wiring harness to the lower edge of the cluster back by installing the two retaining clips.
6. Connect the instrument voltage regulator and the instrument wires to the cluster assembly and install the light sockets. Be sure that the ammeter wire is routed through the ammeter loop of the charge indicator correctly to prevent reverse gauge indications.
7. Connect the speedometer cable and tighten the nut.
8. Carefully move the instrument cluster into position from behind the instrument panel, guiding all wiring and cables into position to prevent damage. Be careful not to kink the speedometer cable.
9. Install the screws retaining the instrument cluster to the instrument panel.
10. Connect the battery ground cable and check the operation of all gauges, lights and signals.

1978–79

REMOVAL

1. Disconnect the battery ground cable.
2. Remove the radio knobs from the radio shafts (if so equipped).
3. Remove the fuel gauge switch knob (if so equipped), heater control knobs and wiper-washer knob. Use a hook-shaped tool to release each knob lock tab.
4. Remove the knob and shaft from the light switch.
5. Remove one nut and washer from each radio control shaft, and remove the radio bezel.
6. Remove the cluster trim cover. The attaching screws are located as follows: four screws along top of bezel; one screw between the lights and wiper-washer switch, and two screws below the radio. Then, disconnect the A/C duct (if so equipped), and illumination light from the bezel. The illumination light is located between the lights and wiper-washer switches. Remove four cluster attaching screws, disconnect the speedometer cable and wire connector from the printed circuit, and remove the cluster.

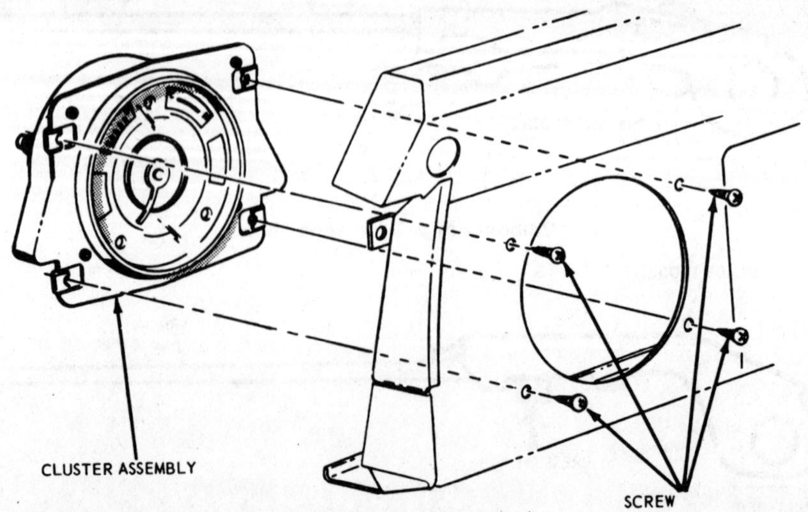

1966–77 instrument cluster

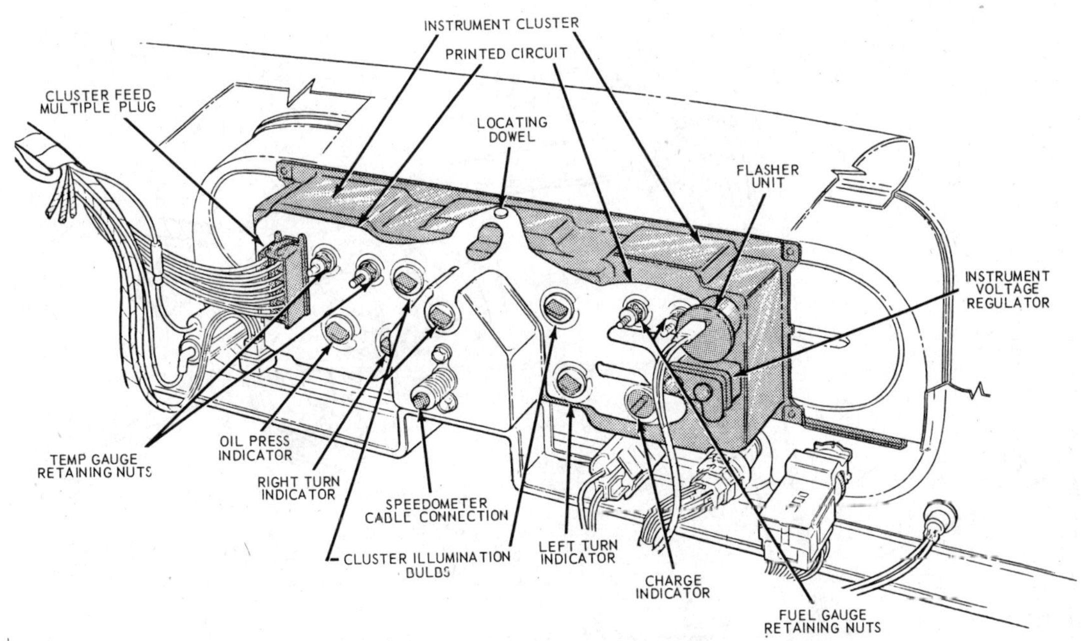

Rear view of 1974 instrument cluster, typical of early-to-mid '70s pickups

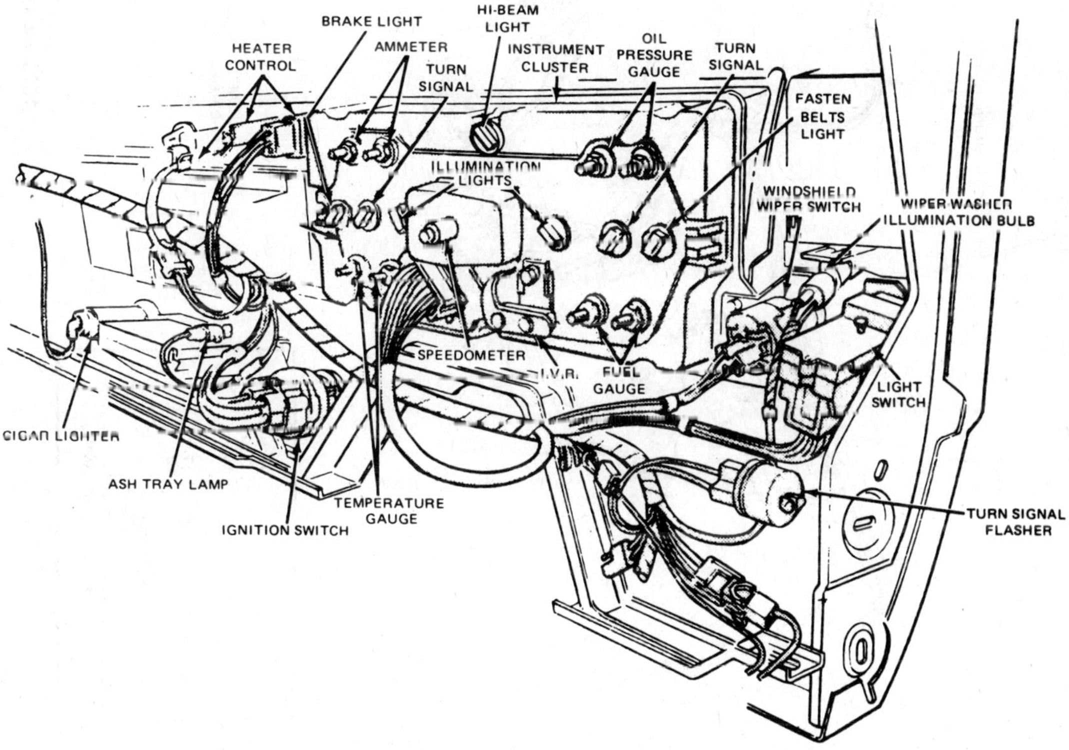

1978–79 instrument cluster rear view

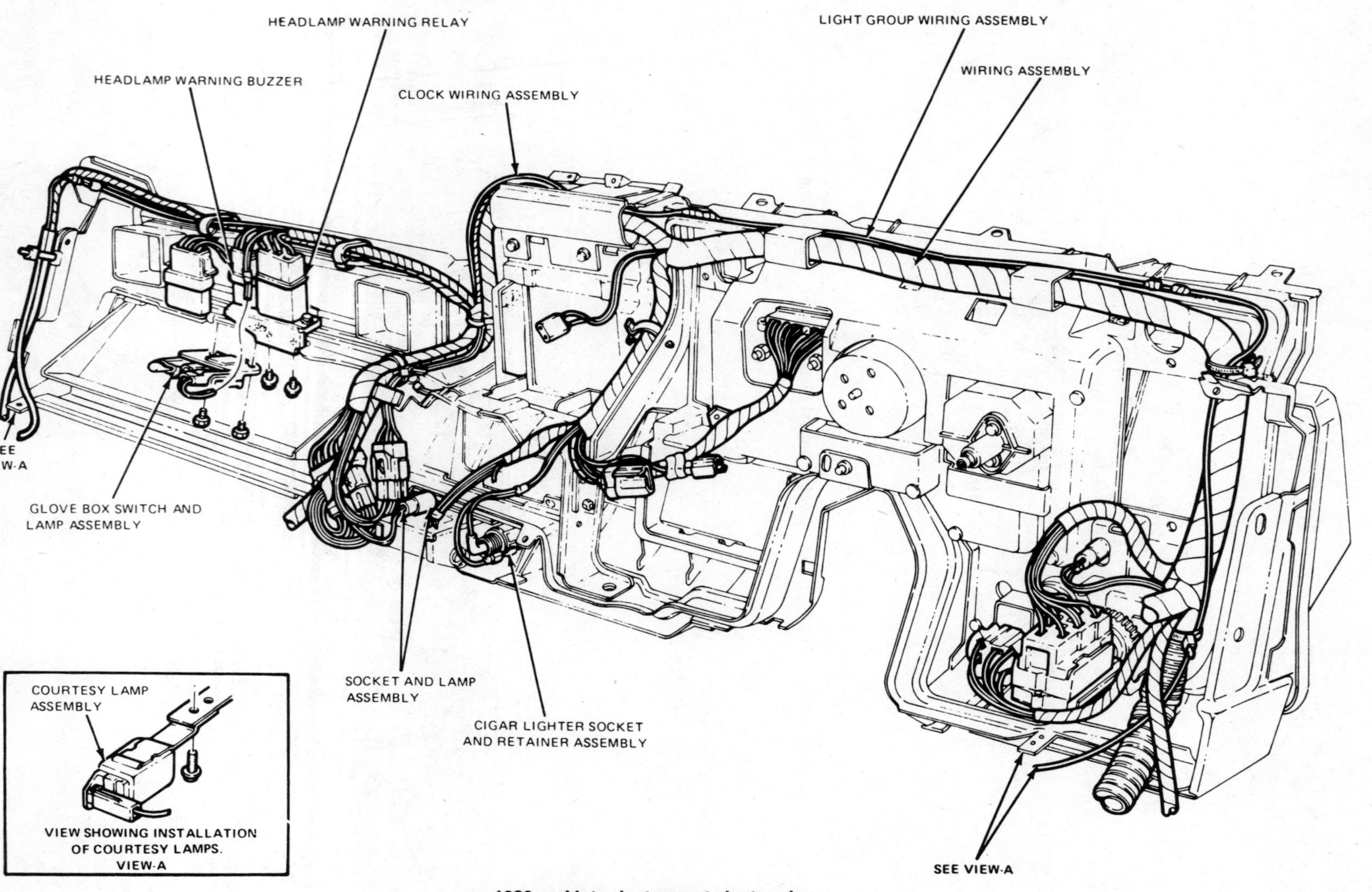

1980 and later instrument cluster view

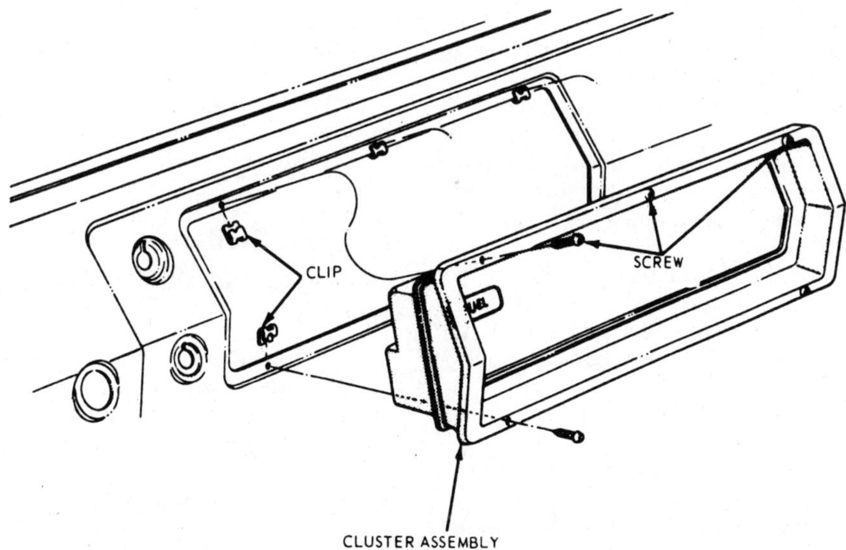

Instrument cluster bezel installation, typical of 1965–72 models

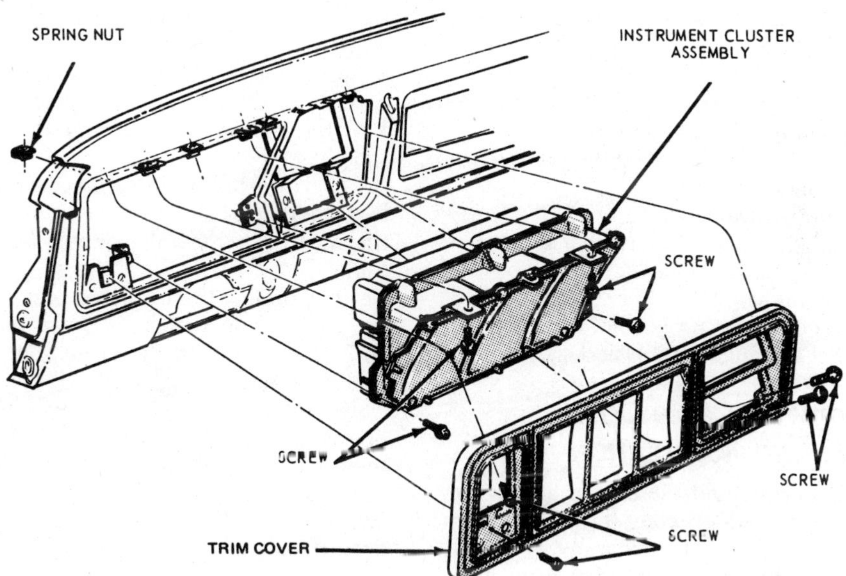

Typical 1973 and later instrument cluster and bezel removal and installation

INSTALLATION

1. Position cluster to opening and connect the multiple connector and the speedometer cable. Connect the A/C duct and A/C illumination light (if so equipped) and install the four cluster retaining screws.
2. Install the trim cover.
3. Install the radio bezel (if so equipped).
4. Install the light switch knob and shaft.
5. Install the heater control knobs and the wiper-washer control knobs.
6. Install the radio knobs, (if so equipped).
7. Connect the battery cable, and check the operation of all gauges, lights and signals.

1980 and Later

REMOVAL

1. Disconnect the battery ground cable.
2. Remove the fuel gauge switch knob (if so equipped), and wiper-washer knob. Use a hook tool to release each knob lock tab.
3. Remove the knob from the headlamp and windshield wiper switch. Remove the fog lamp switch knob, if so equipped.

4. Remove steering column shroud. Care must be taken not to damage transmission control selector indicator (PRNDL) cable on vehicles equipped with automatic transmission.

5. On vehicles equipped with automatic transmission, remove loop on indicator cable assembly from retainer pin. Remove bracket screw from cable bracket and slide bracket out of slot in tube.

6. Remove the cluster trim cover. Remove four cluster attaching screws, disconnect the speedometer cable, wire connector from the printed circuit, 4 x 4 indicator light and remove the cluster.

INSTALLATION

1. Position cluster to opening and connect the multiple connector, the speedometer cable and 4 x 4 indicator light. Install the four cluster retaining screws.
2. If so equipped, place loop on transmission indicator cable assembly over retainer on column.
3. Position the tab on steering column bracket into slot on column. Align and attach screw.
4. Place transmission selector lever on steering column into "D" position.
5. Adjust slotted bracket so the pin is within the letter band.
6. Install the trim cover.
7. Install the headlamp switch knob. If so equipped, install the fog lamp switch.
8. Install the wiper-washer control knobs.
9. Connect the battery cable, and check the operation of all gauges, lights and signals.

Speedometer Cable Core

REMOVAL AND INSTALLATION

1. Reach up behind the cluster and disconnect the cable by depressing the quick disconnect tab and pulling the cable away.
2. Remove the cable from the casing. If the cable is broken, raise the vehicle on a hoist and disconnect the cable from the transmission.
3. Remove the cable from the casing.
4. To remove the casing from the vehicle, pull it through the floor pan.

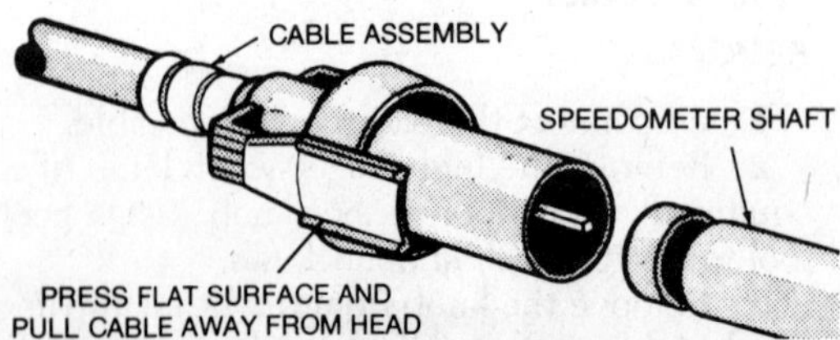

Speedometer cable quick-disconnect

5. To replace the cable, slide the new cable into the casing and connect it at the transmission.
6. Route the cable through the floor pan and position the grommet in its groove in the floor.
7. Push the cable onto the speedometer head.

Ignition Switch

REMOVAL AND INSTALLATION

1965–79

1. Disconnect the battery ground cable.
2. Turn the ignition key to Accessories and slightly depress the release pin in the face of the lock cylinder.
3. Turn the key counterclockwise and pull the key and lock assembly out of the switch.
4. From under the instrument panel, press in on the rear of the switch ⅛ turn counterclockwise.
5. Remove the bezel and switch. Remove the retainer and spring.
6. Remove the nut from the back of the switch.
7. Remove the accessory and gauge feed wires from the accessory terminal of the switch. Pull the insulated plug from the rear of the switch.
8. To install: insert a screwdriver into the lock opening of the switch and turn the slot in the switch to the full counterclockwise position.
9. Connect the insulated plug and wires to the back of the switch. Connect the accessory and gauge wires to the switch and install the retaining nut.
10. Place the bezel and switch in the switch opening, press the switch toward the instrument panel and rotate it ⅛ turn to lock it.
11. Position the spring and retainer on the switch with the open face of the retainer away from the switch. Place the switch in the opening.
12. Press the switch toward the instrument panel and install the bezel.
13. Place the key in the cylinder and turn the key to the accessory position. Place the lock and key in the switch, depress the release pin slightly, and turn the key counterclockwise. Push the new lock cylinder into the switch. Turn the key to check the operation.
14. Connect the battery.

1980 and Later

REMOVAL

1. Disconnect the battery ground cable.
2. Remove steering colum shroud and lower the steering column.

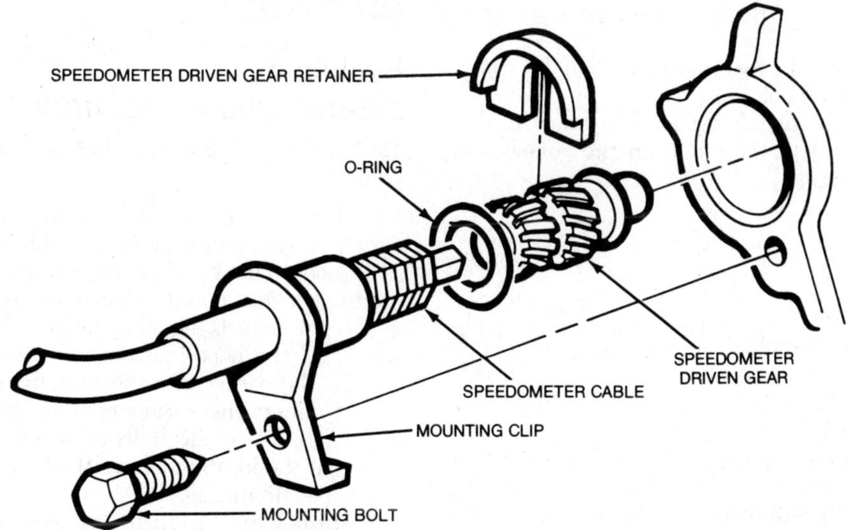

Speedometer driven gear to-transmission installation, all models similar

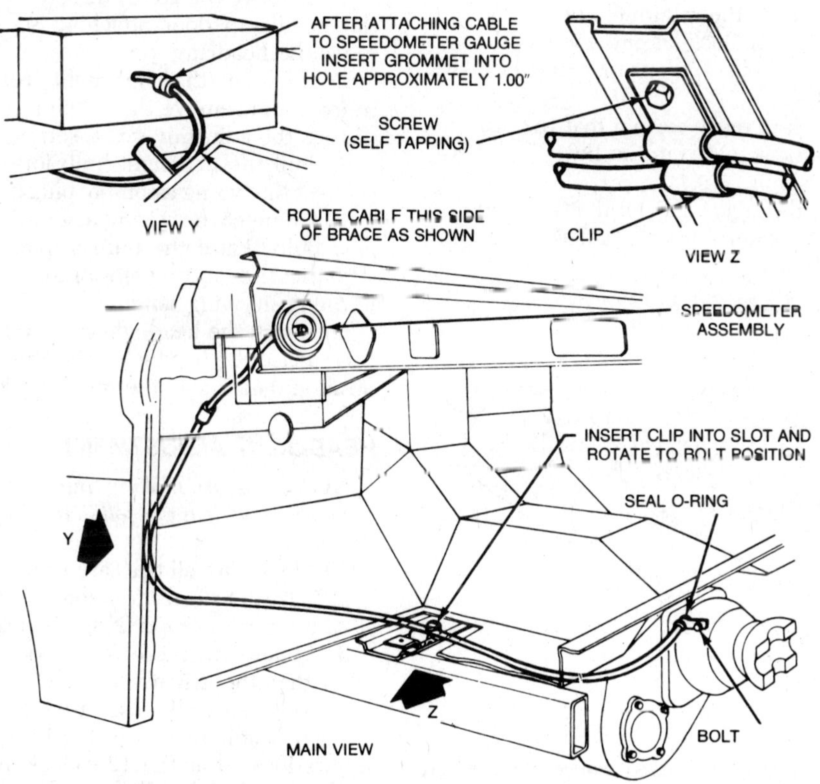

Speedometer cable installation, 4×4 model shown

3. Disconnect the switch wiring at the multiple plug.
4. Remove the two nuts that retain the switch to the steering column.
5. Lift the switch vertically upward to disengage the actuator rod from the switch and remove switch.

INSTALLATION

1. When installing the ignition switch, both the locking mechanism at the top of the column and the switch itself must be in LOCK position for correct adjustment.

To hold the mechanical parts of the column in LOCK position, move the shift lever into PARK (with automatic transmissions) or REVERSE (with manual transmissions), turn the key to LOCK position, and remove the key. New replacement switches, when received, are already pinned in LOCK position by a metal shipping pin inserted in a locking hole on the side of the switch.

2. Engage the actuator rod in the switch.
3. Position the switch on the column and install the retaining nuts, but do not tighten them.
4. Move the switch up and down along the column to locate the mid-position of rod lash, and then tighten the retaining nuts.
5. Remove the locking pin, connect the battery cable, and check for proper start in PARK or NEUTRAL.

Also check to make certain that the start circuit cannot be actuated in the DRIVE and REVERSE position.

6. Raise the steering column into position at instrument panel. Install steering column shroud.

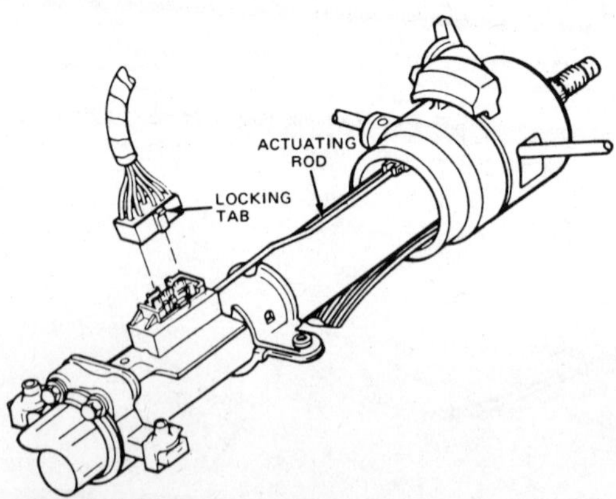

Blade-type connector ignition switch on steering column, 1980 and later models

LIGHTING

Headlights

REMOVAL AND INSTALLATION

1965–77 and 1978 Except Ranger and XLT Options

1. Remove the screws retaining the headlight trim ring and remove the trim ring.
2. Loosen the headlight retaining ring screws, rotate the ring counterclockwise and remove it. Do not disturb the adjusting screw settings.
3. Pull the headlight bulb forward and disconnect the wiring assembly plug from the hub.
4. Connect the wiring assembly plug to the new bulb. Place the bulb in position, making sure that the locating tabs of the bulb are fitted in the positioning slots.
5. Install the headlight retaining ring, slipping the ring tabs over the screws and rotating the ring clockwise as far as possible. Tighten the screws.
6. Place the headlight trim ring into position, and install the retaining screws.
7. Check the operation of the headlight.

1978 Ranger and XLT Option and All 1979 and Later Models

1. Remove the attaching screws and remove the headlamp door attaching screws and remove the headlamp door.
2. Remove the headlight retaining ring screws, and remove the retaining ring. Do not disturb the adjusting screw settings.
3. Pull the headlight bulb forward and disconnect the wiring assembly plug from the bulb.
4. Connect the wiring assembly plug to the new bulb. Place the bulb in position, making sure that the locating tabs of the bulb are fitted in the positioning slots.
5. Install the headlight retaining ring.
6. Place the headlight trim ring or door into position, and install the retaining screws.

HEADLIGHT ADJUSTMENT

NOTE: *Before making any headlight adjustments, perform the following steps for preparation:*

1. Make sure all tires are properly inflated.
2. Take into consideration any faulty wheel alignment or improper rear axle tracking.
3. Make sure there is no load in the truck other than the driver.
4. Make sure all lenses are clean.

Each headlight is adjusted by means of two screws located at the 12 o'clock and 9 o'clock positions on the headlight underneath the trim

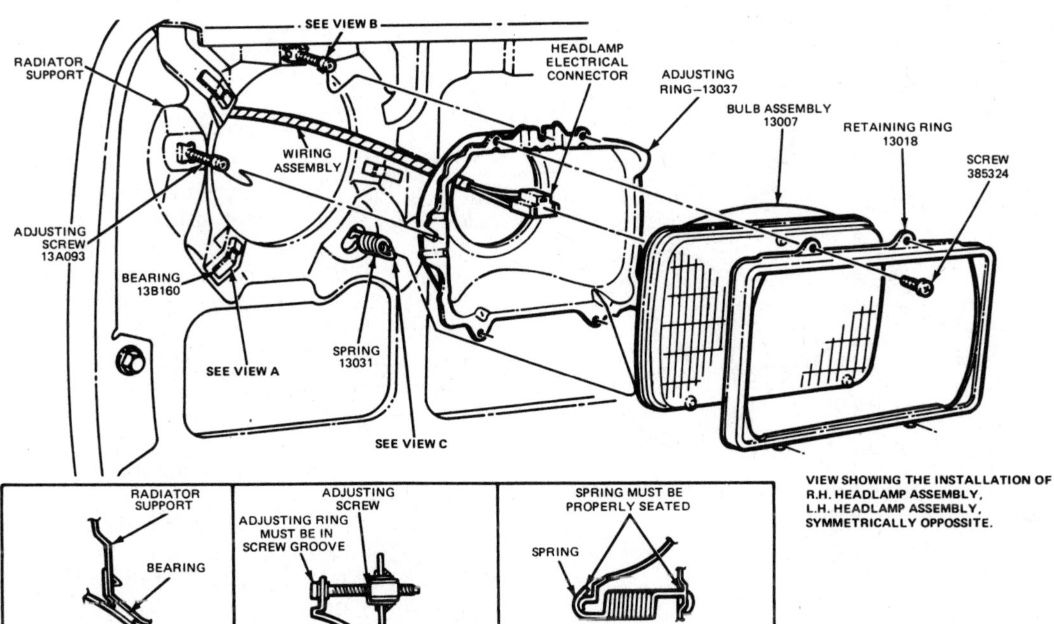

Headlight mounting: round headlights similar

Headlight aiming screws. Round headlight models similar

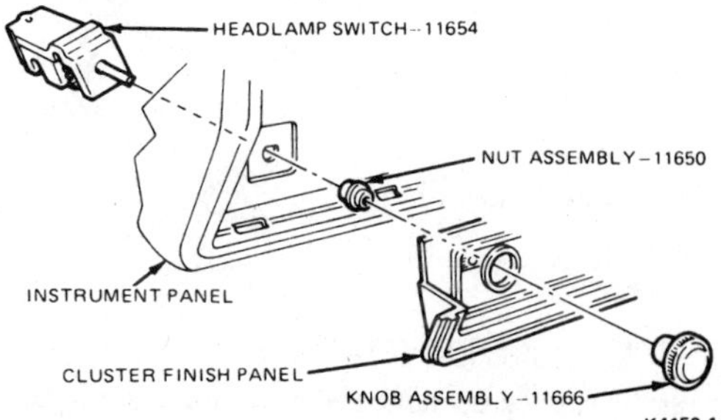

Typical headlight switch installation

ring. Always bring each beam into final position by turning the adjusting screws clockwise so that the headlight will be held against the tension springs when the operation is completed.

Back-Up Light Switch

REMOVAL AND INSTALLATION

A faulty back-up light switch is usually the cause of the back-up lights not working properly. The switch can be found in either of two locations on the 1965 through 1984 models. Earlier models have their switches mounted in the engine compartment on a bracket secured to the front end of the steering column by a clamp. To remove the switch, place the transmission shift lever in some gear other than reverse, and disconnect the two connectors from the switch terminals. Remove the switch retaining clip. To install, reverse this procedure.

To adjust the steering column-mounted switch, loosen the screw on the bracket clamp and move the bracket and switch so that the steering column switch lever will actuate the switch in reverse, but not in neutral. Tighten the clamp screw.

On later models, the back-up light switch is mounted on the transmission extension housing. This switch is not adjustable. To remove, place the transmission shift lever in any gear but neutral, and disconnect the electrical connector from the switch. Remove the switch as-

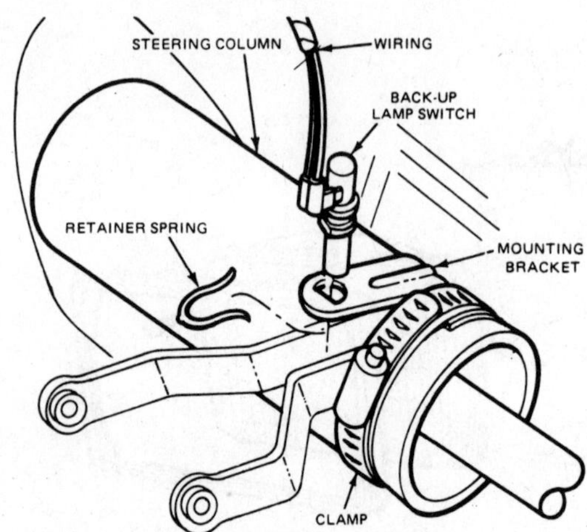

Early-type back-up light switch mounted on engine compartment side of steering wheel

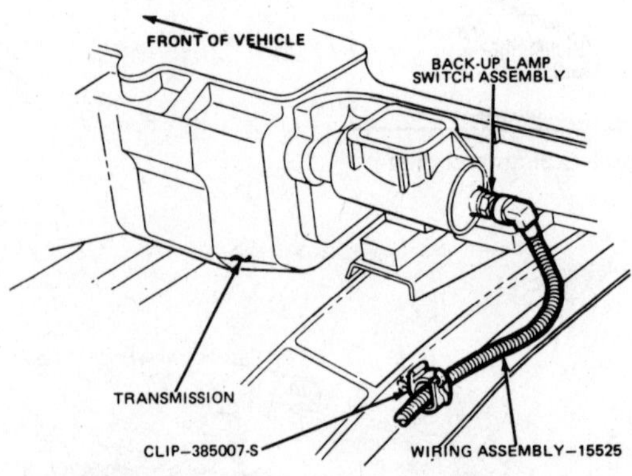

Later-type back-up light switch mounted on transmission

sembly from the transmission and install a new switch in the reverse order of removal.

CIRCUIT PROTECTION

Turn Signal and Hazard Flasher Locations

The turn signal flasher unit is mounted in a clip on the left side of the instrument panel brace, between the top of the instrument cluster and the steering column. The 1978–81 turn signal flasher unit is attached to the left side cowl.

The 1965–77 hazard flasher unit is clipped to the rear of the hazard flasher switch. The 1978–81 hazard flasher unit is taped to the wiring harness.

Both the turn signal flasher and the hazard warning flasher are mounted on the fuse panel on the 1982–84 pickups. The turn signal flasher is mounted on the front of the fuse panel, and the hazard warning flasher is mounted on the rear of the fuse panel.

Fuse Link

The fuse link is a short length of special, Hypalon (high temperature) insulated wire, integral with the engine compartment wiring harness and should not be confused with standard wire. It is several wire gauges smaller than the circuit which it protects. Under no circumstances should a fuse link replacement repair be made using a length of standard wire cut from bulk stock or from another wiring harness.

To repair any blown fuse link use the following procedure:

1. Determine which circuit is damaged, its location and the cause of the open fuse link. If the damaged fuse link is one of three fed by a common No. 10 or 12 gauge feed wire, determine the specific affected circuit.
2. Disconnect the negative battery cable.
3. Cut the damaged fuse link from the wiring harness and discard it. If the fuse link is one of three circuits fed by a single feed wire, cut it out of the harness at each splice end and discard it.
4. Identify and procure the proper fuse link and butt connectors for attaching the fuse link to the harness.
5. To repair any fuse link in a 3-link group with one feed:
   a. After cutting the open link out of the harness, cut each of the remaining undamaged fuse links close to the feed wire weld.
   b. Strip approximately ½ inch of insulation from the detached ends of the two good fuse links. Then insert two wire ends into one end of a butt connector and carefully push one stripped end of the replacement fuse link into the same end of the butt connector and crimp all three firmly together.

   NOTE: *Care must be taken when fitting the three fuse links into the butt connector as the internal diameter is a snug fit for three wires. Make sure to use a proper crimping tool. Pliers, side cutters, etc. will not apply the proper crimp to retain the wires and withstand a pull test.*

   c. After crimping the butt connector to the three fuse links, cut the weld portion from the feed wire and strip approximately ½ inch of insulation from the cut end. Insert the stripped end into the open end of the butt connector and crimp very firmly.
   d. To attach the remaining end of the replacement fuse link, strip approximately ½ inch of insulation from the wire end of the

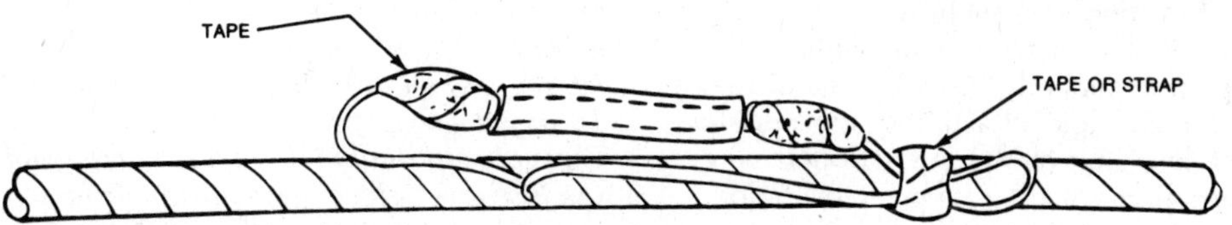

TYPICAL REPAIR USING THE SPECIAL #17 GA. (9.00" LONG-YELLOW) FUSE LINK REQUIRED FOR THE AIR/COND. CIRCUITS (2) #687E and #261A LOCATED IN THE ENGINE COMPARTMENT

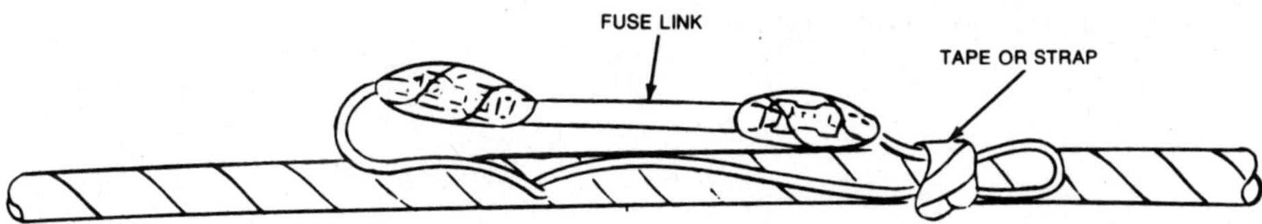

TYPICAL REPAIR FOR ANY IN-LINE FUSE LINK USING THE SPECIFIED GAUGE FUSE LINK FOR THE SPECIFIC CIRCUIT

TYPICAL REPAIR USING THE EYELET TERMINAL FUSE LINK OF THE SPECIFIED GAUGE FOR ATTACHMENT TO A CIRCUIT WIRE END

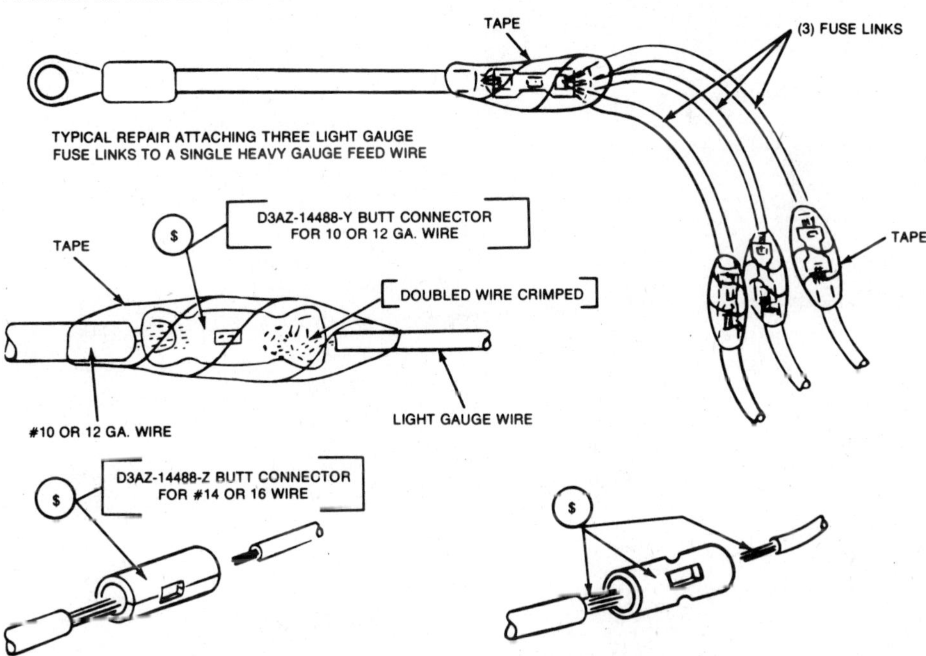

General fuse link repair procedure

circuit from which the blown fuse link was removed, and firmly crimp a butt connector or equivalent to the stripped wire. Then, insert the end of the replacement link into the other end of the butt connector and crimp firmly.

e. Using rosin core solder with a consistency of 60 percent tin and 40 percent lead, solder the connectors and the wires at the repairs and insulate with electrical tape.

6. To replace any fuse link on a single circuit in a harness, cut out the damaged portion, strip approximately ½ inch of insulation from the two wire ends and attach the appropriate replacement fuse link to the stripped wire ends with two proper size butt connectors. Solder the

connectors and wires and insulate with tape.

7. To repair any fuse link which has an eyelet terminal on one end such as the charging circuit, cut off the open fuse link behind the weld, strip approximately ½ inch of insulation from the cut end and attach the appropriate new eyelet fuse link to the cut stripped wire with an appropriate size butt connector. Solder the connectors and wires at the repair and insulate with tape.

8. Connect the negative battery cable to the battery and test the system for proper operation.

NOTE: *Do not mistake a resistor wire for a fuse link. The resistor wire is generally longer and has print stating, "Resistor: don't cut or splice."*

NOTE: *When attaching a single No. 16, 17, 18 or 20 gauge fuse link to a heavy gauge wire, always double the stripped wire end of the fuse link before inserting and crimping it into the butt connector for positive wire retention.*

Clutch and Transmission

6

MANUAL TRANSMISSION

Identification

Ford pick-ups have used eight manual transmissions since 1965. The transmission identification letter is located on a metal tag or plate attached to the case or it is stamped directly on the transmission case. To identify your transmission find out the letter code and refer to the Transmission Code Chart in the Serial Number Identification section of Chapter 1. Also refer to the Transmission and Transfer Case Capacities Chart for complete model application.

LINKAGE ADJUSTMENT

Ford 3.03 and Warner T-85N, T-87, T-89

1. Place the shifter in the Neutral position and insert a gauge pin (3⁄16 in. diameter) through the steering column shift levers and the locating hole in the spacer.
2. If the shift rods at the transmission are equipped with threaded sleeves, adjust the sleeves so that they enter the shift levers on the transmission easily with the shift levers in the Neutral position. Now lengthen the rods seven turns of the sleeves and insert them into the shift levers.
3. If the shift rods are slotted, loosen the attaching nut, make sure that the transmission shift levers are in the Neutral position, then retighten the attaching nuts.
4. Remove the gauge pin and check the operation of the shift linkage.

Ford Four-Speed Overdrive

1. Attach the shift rods to the levers.
2. Rotate the output shaft to determine that the transmission is in neutral.
3. Insert an alignment pin into the shift control assembly alignment hole.
4. Attach the slotted end of the shift rods over the flats of the studs in the shift control assembly.
5. Install the lock nuts and remove the alignment pin.

REMOVAL AND INSTALLATION

Ford 3.03 and Warner T-85N, T-87, T-89

1. Raise the vehicle and support it with jackstands. Support the engine with a jack and a block of wood placed under the oil pan.
2. Drain the lubricant out of the transmission by removing the drain plug if so equipped, or removing the lower extension housing-to-transmission bolt.
3. Position a transmission jack under the transmission.
4. Disconnect the gearshift linkage at the transmission.
5. On the Warner T-85N model, disconnect the solenoid and governor wires at the connectors near the solenoid. Remove the overdrive wiring harness from its clip on the transmission. Disconnect the overdrive cable.
6. If the vehicle has 4WD, remove the transfer case shift lever bracket from the transmission.
7. Disconnect the speedometer cable.
8. Disconnect the driveshaft from the differential and transmission and remove it from the vehicle.
9. Raise the transmission if necessary and remove the rear support.
10. Remove the transmission-to-flywheel housing attaching bolts.
11. Move the transmission to the rear until the input shaft clears the flywheel housing and lower the transmission out and from under the vehicle.

    NOTE: *Do not depress the clutch pedal while the transmission is removed.*

12. Before installing the transmission, apply a light film of grease to the release bearing in

ner hub surface, the release lever fulcrum and fork, and the front bearing retainer of the transmission. Do not apply excessive grease because it will fly off due to centrifugal force and contaminate the clutch disc.

13. Install the transmission in the reverse order of removal. It may be necessary to turn the output shaft with the transmission in gear to align the input shaft splines with the splines in the clutch disc. Fill the transmission with lubricant and adjust the shift linkage.

Warner T-18 4-Speed

1. Disconnect the back-up light switch at the rear of the gearshift housing cover.
2. Remove the rubber boot, floor mat, and the body floor pan cover. Remove the gearshift lever. Remove the weather pad.
3. Raise the vehicle and support it with jackstands. Position a transmission jack under the transmission and disconnect the speedometer cable.
4. Disconnect the driveshaft from the transmission and wire it up to one side.
5. Remove the rear transmission support.
6. Remove the transmission attaching bolts.
7. Move the transmission to the rear until the input shaft clears the flywheel housing and lower the transmission.
8. Before installing the transmission, apply a light film of grease to the inner hub surface of the clutch release bearing, the release lever fulcrum and the front bearing retainer of the transmission. Do not apply excessive grease because it will fly off onto the clutch disc.
9. Install the transmission in the reverse order of removal. It may be necessary to turn the output shaft with the transmission in gear to align the input shaft splines with the splines in the clutch disc. Fill the transmission with lubricant if it was drained.

New Process 435 4-Speed

1. Remove the rubber boot and floor mat.
2. Remove the floor pan, transmission cover plate, and weather pad. It may be necessary to remove the seat assembly.
3. Disconnect the back-up light switch located in the rear of the gearshift housing cover.
4. Raise the vehicle and place jackstands under the frame to support it. Place a transmission jack under the transmission and disconnect the speedometer cable.
5. Disconnect the parking brake lever from its linkage and remove the gearshift housing.
6. Disconnect the driveshaft.
7. Remove the transmission rear support.
8. Remove the transmission-to-flywheel housing attaching bolts, slide the transmission rearward until the input shaft clears the flywheel housing and lower it out from under the truck.
9. Before installing the transmission, apply a light film of grease to the inner hub surface of the clutch release bearing, release lever fulcrum and fork, and the front bearing retainer of the transmission. Do not apply excessive grease because if will fly off and contaminate the clutch disc.
10. Install the transmission in the reverse order of removal. It may be necessary to turn the output shaft with the transmission in gear to align the input shaft splines with the splines in the clutch disc. The front bearing retainer is installed through the clutch release bearing.

Ford Four-Speed Overdrive

1. Raise the truck and support it on jackstands.
2. Mark the driveshaft so that it can be installed in the same position.
3. Disconnect the driveshaft at the rear U-joint and slide it off the transmission output shaft.
4. Disconnect the speedometer cable from the transmission.
5. Remove the shift rods from the levers and the shift control from the extension housing.
6. Support the engine and remove the extension housing-to-crossmember bolts.
7. Support the transmission on a jack and unbolt it from the engine.
8. Move the transmission and jack rearward until clear. If necessary, lower the engine enough for clearance.
9. Installation is the reverse of removal. It is a good idea to install and snug-down the upper transmission-to-engine bolts first, then the lower. For linkage adjustment, see the beginning of this chapter. Check the fluid level.

Single Rail Four-Speed Overdrive

1. Raise the vehicle on a hoist and remove the lubricant.
2. Mark the driveshaft so that it can be installed in the same position then disconnect the drive shaft from the rear U-joint flange. Slide the driveshaft off the transmission output shaft.
3. Disconnect the speedometer cable from the extension housing.
4. Remove the three screws securing the shift tower to the turret assembly.
5. Remove the shift tower from the turret assembly.
6. Support the engine with a transmission jack and remove the bolts which attach the rear extension housing to the engine.
7. Raise the rear of the engine high enough to remove the weight from the crossmember.
8. Remove the bolts retaining the cross-

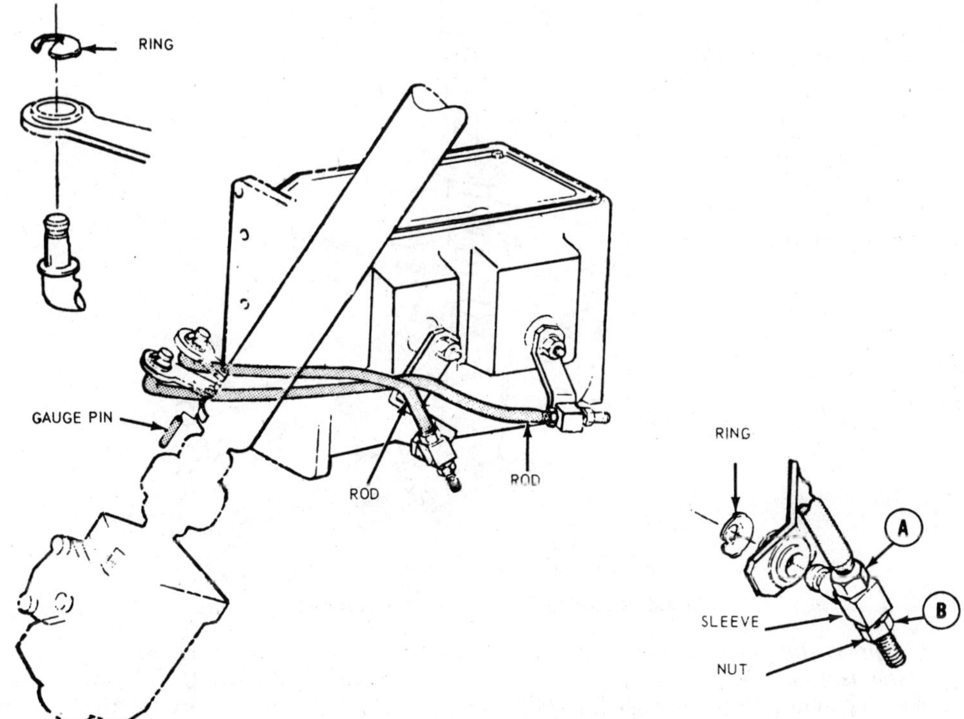

Three-speed manual transmission shift linkage adjustment—threaded sleeves

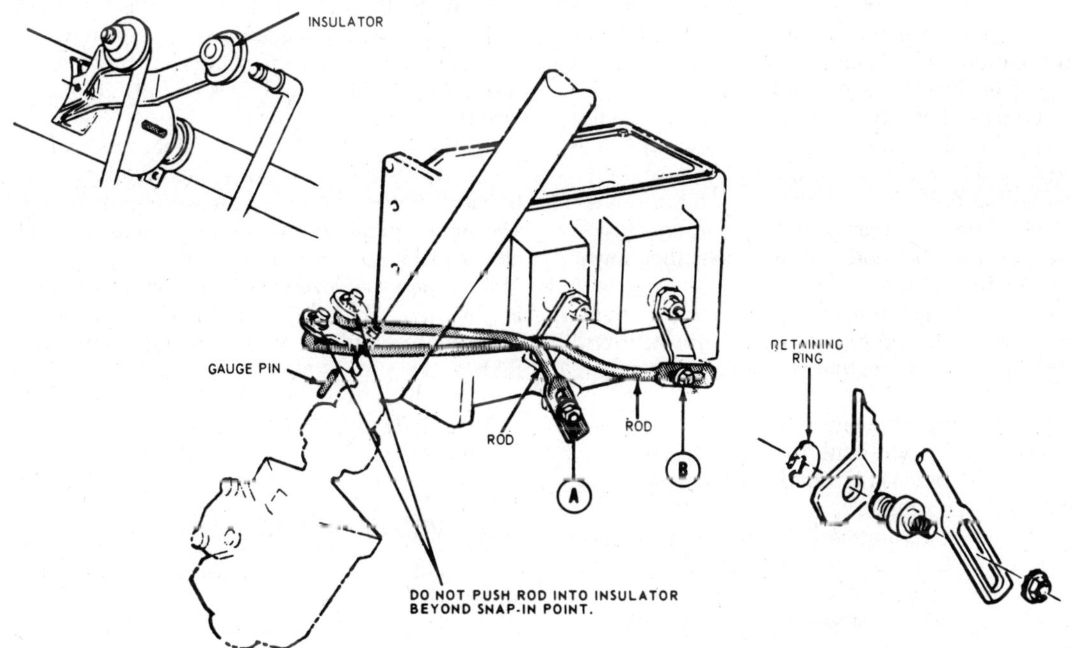

Three-speed manual transmission shift linkage adjustment—slotted rods

member to the frame side supports and remove the crossmember.

9. Support the transmission on a jack and remove the bolts that attach the transmission to the fly wheel housing.

10. Move the transmission and jack rearward until the transmission input shaft clears the flywheel housing.

NOTE: *If necessary lower the engine enough to obtain clearance for transmisson removal.*

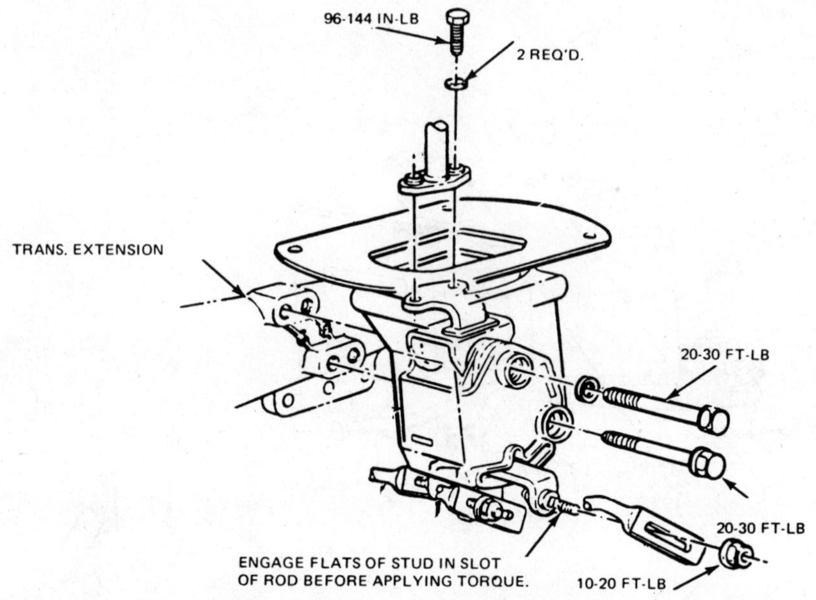

Shifter details for four-speed overdrive

Do not depress the clutch pedal while the transmission is removed.

11. Before installing the transmission install two guide pins in the flywheel housing lower mounting bolt holes.

12. Move the transmission forward on the guide pins until the input shaft splines enter the clutch hub splines and the case is positioned against the flywheel housing.

13. Install the two upper transmission to flywheel housing mounting bolts snug, and then remove the two guide pins. Install the two lower mounting bolts.

14. Raise the rear of the engine and install the crossmember and attaching bolts then lower the engine.

15. With the transmission extension housing resting on the engine rear support, install the transmission extension housing attaching bolts.

16. Position the shift tower to the extension housing and secure with the three screws.

17. Reconnect the speedometer cable to the extension housing.

18. Slide the forward end of the driveshaft over the transmission output shaft. Connect the driveshaft to the rear U-joint flange.

19. Fill with transmission lubricant and lower the vehicle.

MECHANICAL CLUTCH

All Models Except 1983 and Later Diesels, 1984 And Later Gas Engines

PEDAL AND LINKAGE ADJUSTMENT

1. Measure the clutch pedal free-play by depressing the pedal slowly until the freeplay between the release bearing assembly and the pressure plate is removed. Note this measurement. The difference between this measurement and when the pedal is not depressed is the free-play measurement.

2. If the free-play measurement is less than ¾ in., the clutch linkage must be adjusted.

3. Loosen the two jam nuts on the release rod under the truck and back off both nuts several turns.

4. Loosen or tighten the first jam nut (nearest the release lever) against the bullet (rod extension) until a free-play measurement of ¾–1½ in. is obtained. A free-play measurement closer to 1½ in. is more desirable.

5. When the correct free-play measurement is obtained, hold the first jam nut in position and securely tighten the other nut against the first.

6. Recheck the free-play adjustment.

NOTE: *Total pedal travel is fixed and is not adjustable.*

REMOVAL AND INSTALLATION

1. Disconnect the release lever retracting spring and pushrod assembly.

2. Remove the transmission.

3. If the clutch housing does not have a dust cover, remove the starter. Remove the flywheel housing attaching bolts and remove the housing.

4. If the flywheel housing does have a dust cover, remove the cover and then remove the release lever and bearing from the clutch housing.

5. Mark the pressure plate and cover as-

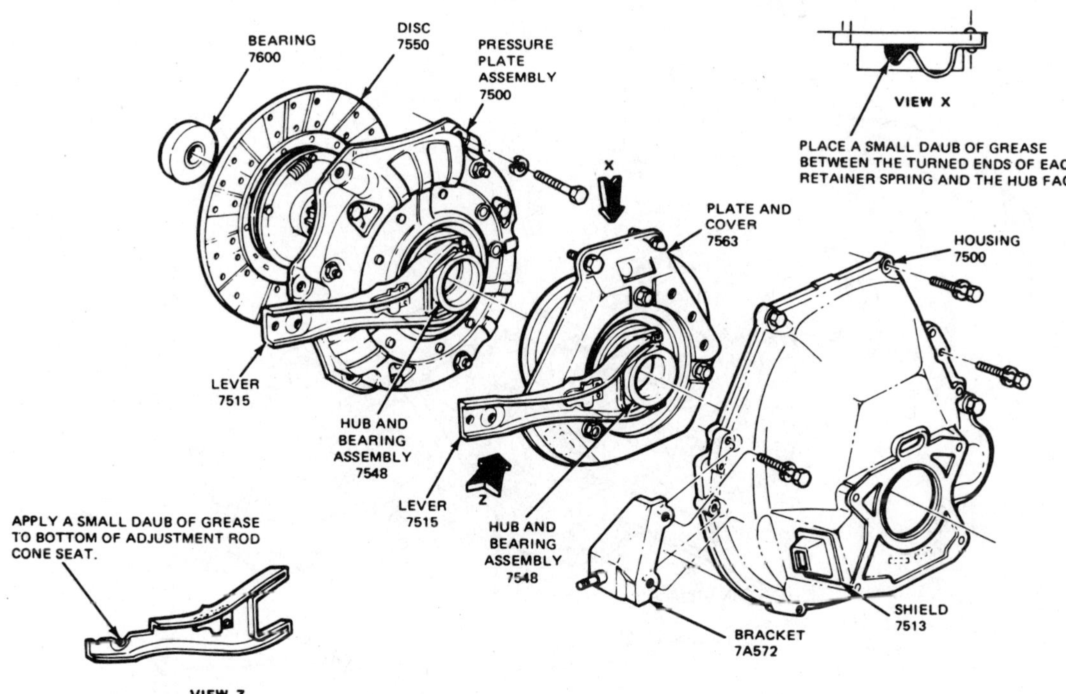

351 and 400 V8 clutch installation

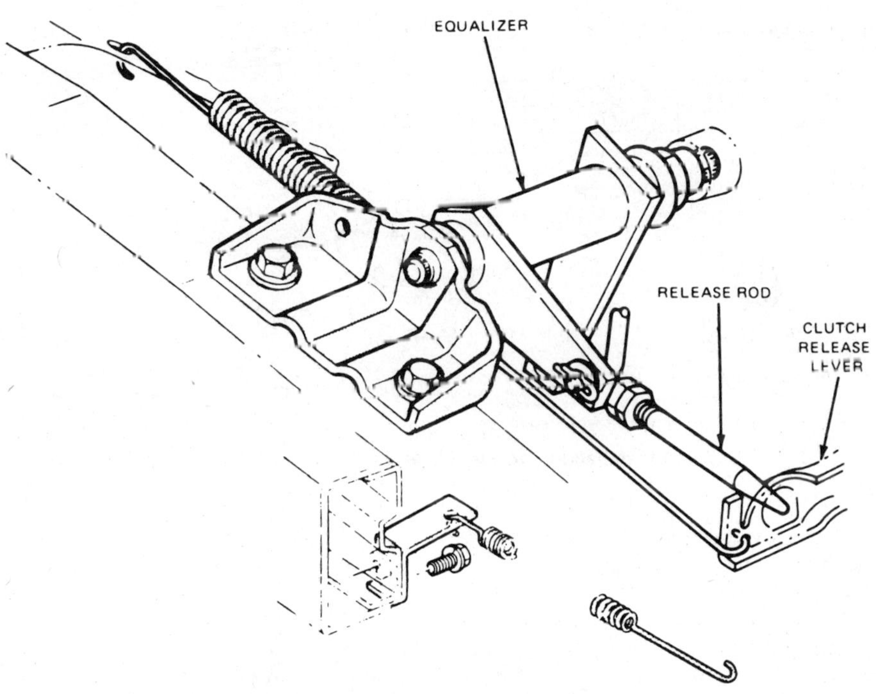

1978–79 clutch pedal free travel adjustment

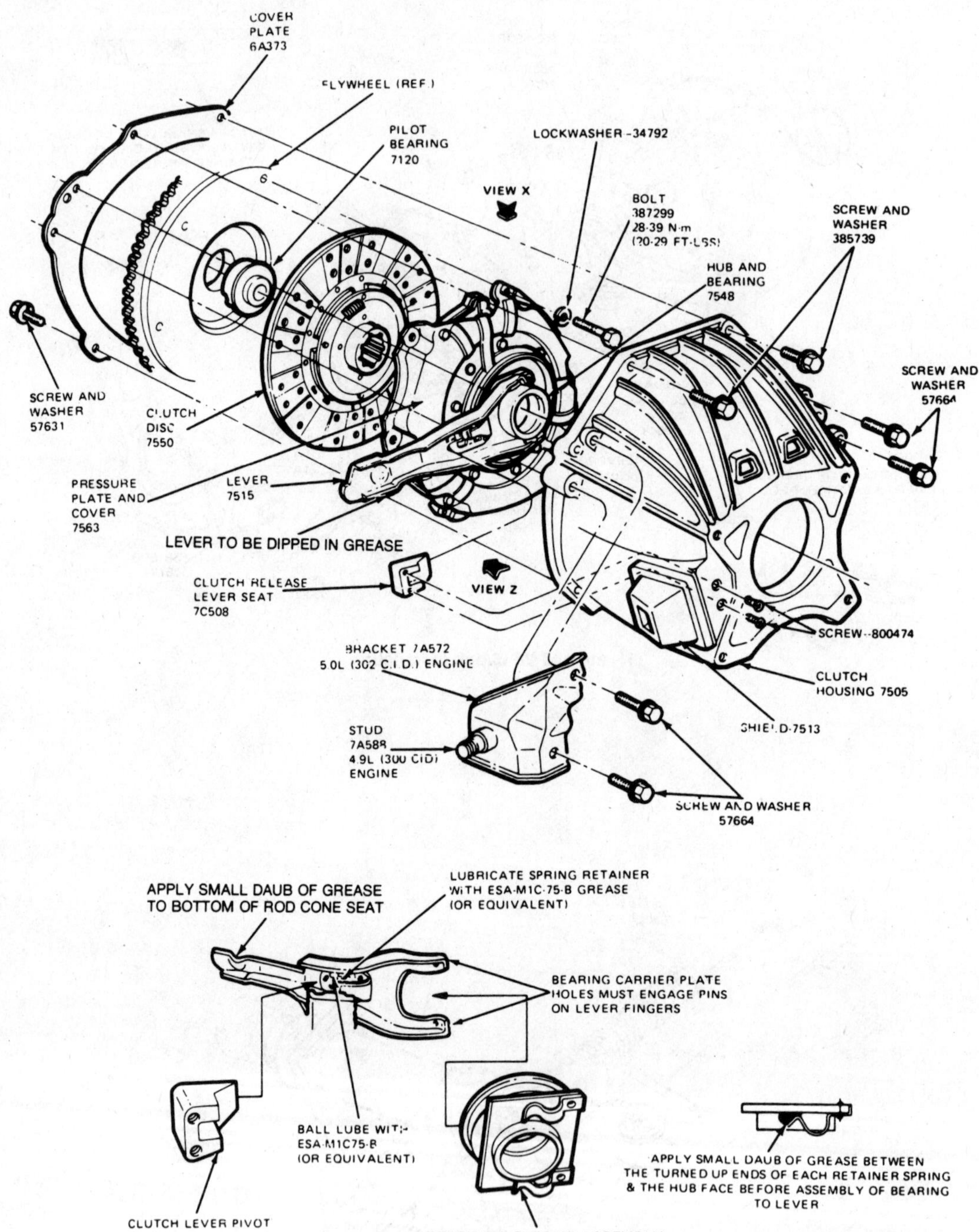

Clutch installation, 1980 and later 300 six and 302/351W V8s

sembly and the flywheel so that they can be reinstalled in the same relative position.

6. Loosen the pressure plate and cover attaching bolts evenly in a staggered sequence a turn at a time until the pressure plate springs are relieved of their tension. Remove the attaching bolts.

7. Remove the pressure plate and cover assembly and the clutch disc from the flywheel.

8. Position the clutch disc on the flywheel so that an aligning tool or spare transmission mainshaft can enter the clutch pilot bearing and align the disc.

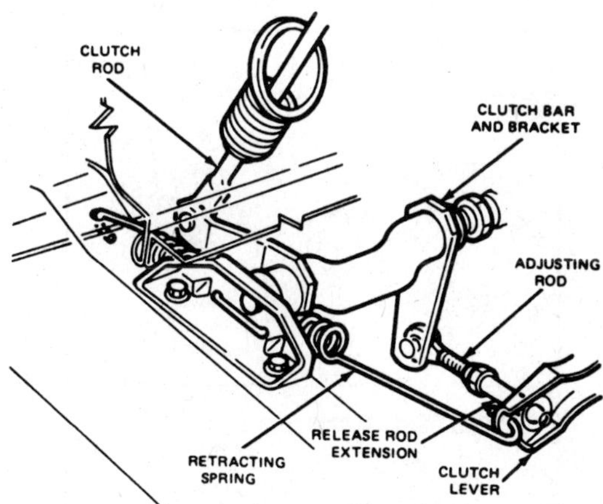

Clutch pedal free play adjustment, 1980 and later

9. When reinstalling the original pressure plate and cover assembly, align the assembly and flywheel according to the marks made during removal. Position the pressure plate and cover assembly on the flywheel, align the pressure plate and disc, and install the retaining bolts. Tighten the bolts in an alternating sequence a few turns at a time until 15–20 ft. lbs. is reached.

10. Remove the tool used to align the clutch disc.

11. With the clutch fully released, apply a light coat of grease on the sides of the driving lugs.

12. Position the clutch release bearing and the bearing hub on the release lever. Install the release lever on the fulcrum in the flywheel housing. Apply a light coating of grease to the release lever fingers and the fulcrum. Fill the groove of the release bearing hub with grease.

13. If the flywheel housing has been removed, position it against the rear engine cover plate and install the attaching bolts and tighten them to 40–50 ft. lbs.

14. Install the starter motor.

15. Install the transmission.

16. Connect the release lever retracting spring and install the dust cover, if so equipped.

17. Adjust the clutch linkage.

HYDRAULIC CLUTCH

1983 and Later Diesels, 1984 and Later Gasoline Engines

The hydraulic clutch system operates much like a hydraulic brake system. When you push down (disengage) the clutch pedal, the mechanical clutch pedal movement is converted into hydraulic fluid movement, which is then converted back into mechanical movement by the slave cylinder to actuate the clutch release lever.

The system consists of a combination clutch fluid reservoir/master cylinder assembly, a slave cylinder mounted on the bellhousing, and connecting tubing.

Fluid level is checked at the master cylinder reservoir. The hydraulic clutch system continually remains in adjustment, like a hydraulic disc brake system, so no clutch linkage or pedal adjustment is necessary.

Hydraulic System

REMOVAL

NOTE: *The clutch hydraulic system is serviced as a complete assembly and is pre-filled and bled. Individual components are not available.*

CAUTION: *Prior to any vehicle service that requires removal of the slave cylinder, such as transmission and/or clutch housing removal, the clutch master cylinder pushrod must be disconnected from the clutch pedal. Failure to do this may damage the slave cylinder if the clutch pedal is depressed while the slave cylinder is disconnected.*

1. From inside the truck cab, remove the cotter pin retaining the clutch master cylinder pushrod to the clutch pedal lever. Disconnect the pushrod and remove the bushing.

2. Remove the two nuts retaining the clutch reservoir and master cylinder assembly to the firewall.

3. From the engine compartment, remove the clutch reservoir and master cylinder assembly from the firewall. Note here how the clutch tubing routes to the slave cylinder.

4. Push the clutch slave cylinder rearward to disengage the two retaining tabs of the release cylinder from the retainer bracket, and from the recess in the bell housing lugs. Slide the cylinder outward to remove. Disengage the pushrod from the release lever as the slave cylinder is removed.

5. Remove the clutch hydraulic system from the truck.

INSTALLATION

1. Position the clutch pedal reservoir and master cylinder assembly into the firewall from inside the cab, and install the two nuts and tighten.

2. Route the clutch tubing and slave cylinder to the bell housing, taking care that the nylon lines are kept away from any hot exhaust sytem components.

3. Install the slave cylinder by pushing the slave cylinder pushrod into the cylinder. Engage the pushrod into the release lever and slide

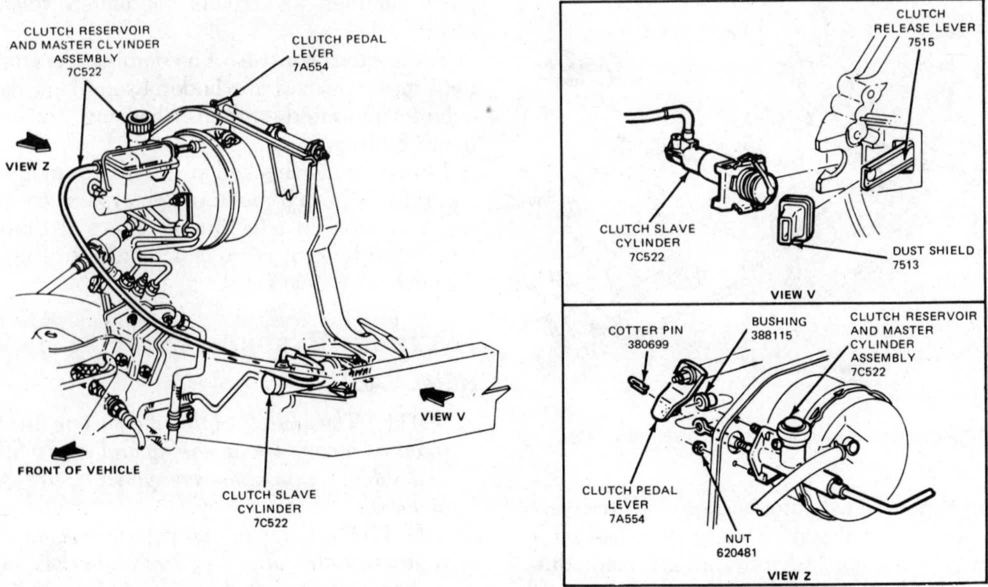

Hydraulic clutch assembly, all 1983 and later V8 diesels and 1984 and later gasoline-engined models

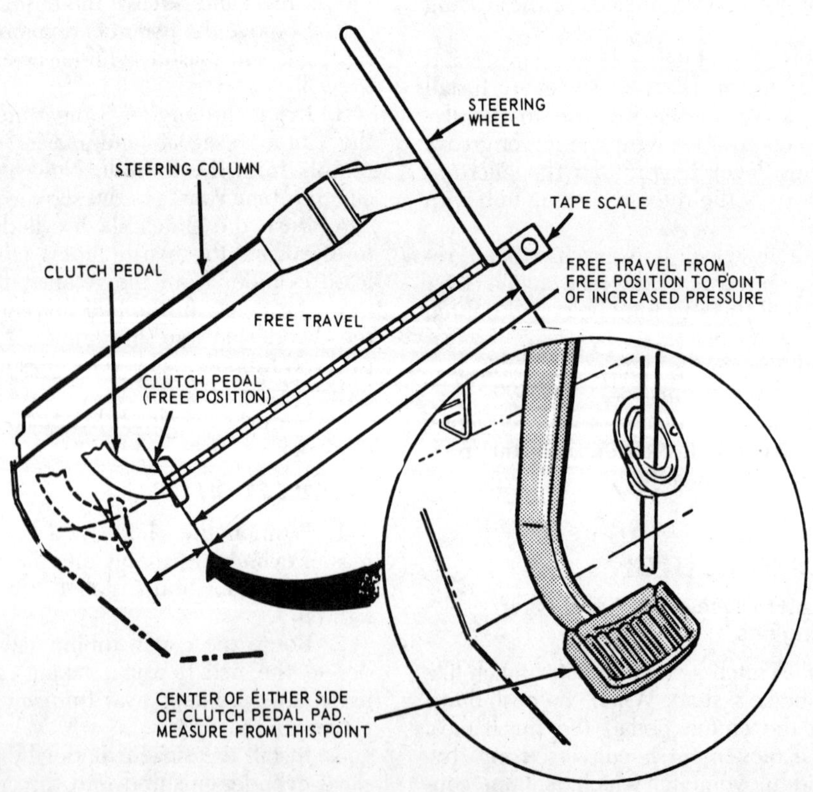

Measuring clutch pedal free-play

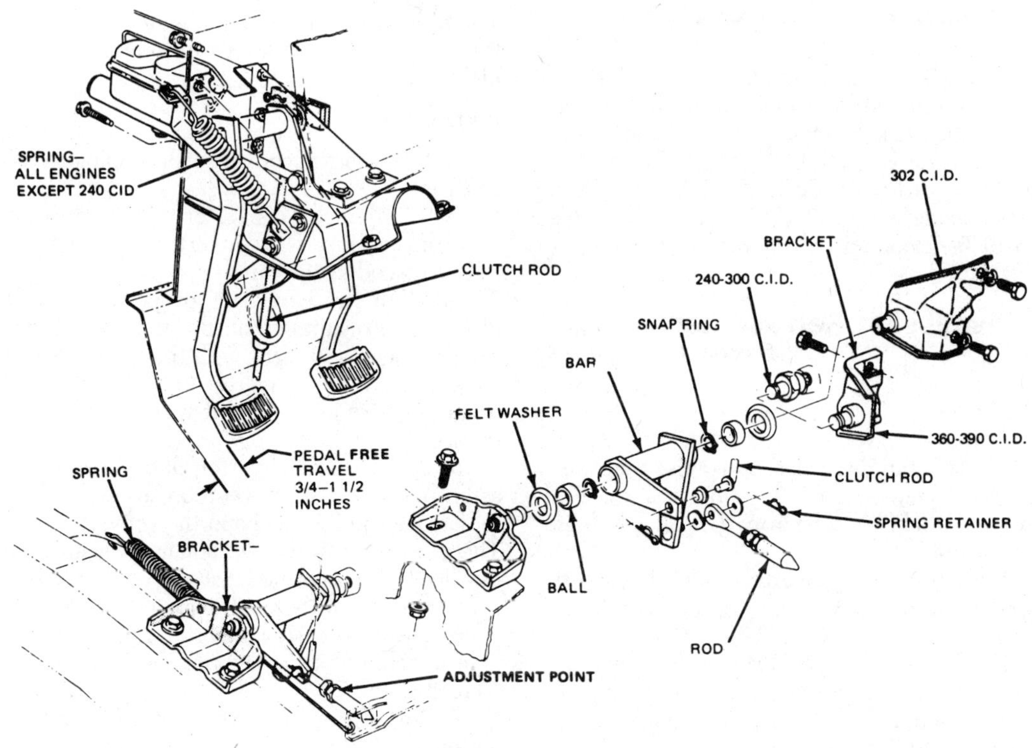

Clutch linkage and adjustment point

the slave cylinder into the bell housing lugs. Seat the cylinder into the recess in the lugs.

NOTE: *When installing a new hydraulic system, you'll notice that the slave cylinder contains a shipping strap that prepositions the pushrod for installation, and also provides a bearing insert. Following installation of the new slave cylinder, the first actuation of the clutch pedal will break the shipping strap and give normal clutch action.*

4. Clean the master cylinder pushrod bearing and apply a light film of SAE 30 engine oil.

5. From inside the cab, install the bushing on the clutch pedal lever. Connect the clutch master cylinder pushrod to the clutch pedal lever and install the cotter pin.

6. Check the clutch reservoir and add fluid if required. Depress the clutch pedal at least ten times to verify smooth operation and proper clutch release.

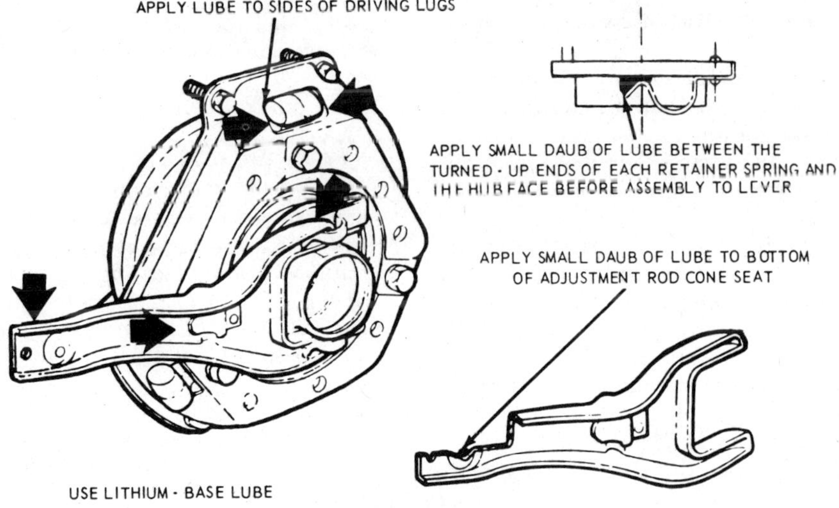

Clutch lubrication points

AUTOMATIC TRANSMISSION

On 1973–84 models, transmission identification may be made by referring to the Vehicle Certification Label on the driver's side door post. The C4 code is G, the C5 code is W, the automatic overdrive code is T, FMX code is J, and C6 code is P until 1982, then K 1983–84. On 1970–72 models, check the fluid pan.

Transmission Replacement

C4, C5

REMOVAL

1. Raise the vehicle on a hoist.
2. Place the drain pan under the transmission fluid pan on pan fill transmissions. Remove the fluid filler tube from the pan and drain the transmission fluid.
3. Remove the converter drain plug access cover from the lower end of the converter housing.
4. Remove the converter-to-flywheel attaching nuts. Place a wrench on the crankshaft pulley attaching bolt to turn the converter to gain access to the nuts.
5. With the wrench on the crankshaft pulley attaching bolt, turn the converter to gain access to the converter drain plug and remove the plug. Place a drain pan under the converter to catch the fluid. With fluid drained, reinstall the plug.
6. Remove the driveshaft.
7. Disconnect the oil cooler lines from the transmission.
8. Disconnect the manual and downshift linkage rods from the transmission control levers.
9. Remove the speedometer gear from the extension housing.
10. Disconnect the back-up switch wires from the retaining clips and retainer.
11. Disconnect the starter cable. Remove the three starter-to-converter housing attaching bolts and remove the starter.
12. Remove the vacuum line hose from the transmission vacuum unit. Disconnect the vacuum line from the retaining clip.
13. Position the transmission jack to support the transmission. Install the safety chain to hold the transmission on the jack.
14. Remove the two engine rear support crossmember-to-frame attaching bolts.
15. Remove the two engine rear support-to-extension housing attaching bolts.
16. Raise the transmission and remove the rear support. Remove the six converter housing-to-engine attaching bolts.
17. Move the converter and transmission assembly away from the engine. Lower the transmission and remove it from under the vehicle.

INSTALLATION

1. Tighten the converter drain plug to 15–28 ft. lbs.
2. Position the converter on the transmission making sure the converter drive flats are fully engaged in the pump gear.
3. With the converter properly installed, place the transmission on the jack. Secure the transmission to the jack with the safety chain.
4. Rotate the converter until the studs and drain plug are in alignment with their holes in the flywheel.
5. Move the converter and transmission assembly forward into position, using care not to damage the flywheel and the converter pilot. The converter must rest squarely against the flywheel. This indicates that the converter pilot is not binding in the engine crankshaft.
6. Install the six converter housing-to-engine attaching bolts. Tighten the bolts to 40–50 ft. lbs.
7. Install the converter-to-flywheel attaching nuts. Tighten the nuts to 20–34 ft. lbs. Remove the safety chain from the transmission.
8. Install the rear support. Install the rear support-to-extension housing attaching bolts. Tighten the bolts.
9. Position the starter into the converter housing and install the three attaching bolts. Tighten the bolts to 20–30 ft. lbs. Install the starter cable.
10. Remove the transmission jack.
11. Connect the transmission filler tube to the transmission pan. Connect the oil cooler lines to the transmission.
12. Attach the back-up switch wires to the connector clip.
13. Install the speedometer driven gear in the extension housing. Tighten the attaching bolt.
14. Connect the transmission linkage rods to the transmission control levers.

    NOTE: *When making transmission control attachments, new retaining rings and grommets should always be used. Attach the shift rod to the steering column shift lever. Align the flats of the adjusting stud with the flats of the rod slot and insert the stud through the rod. Assemble the adjusting stud nut and washer to a loose fit. Perform a linkage adjustment.*
15. Install the driveshaft.
16. Install the vacuum line in the retaining clip. Connect the vacuum line to the diaphragm unit.
17. At the front lower area of the converter

housing, install the lower cover and the control lever dust shield. Install the attaching bolts. Tighten the bolts.

18. Secure the fluid filler tube to the pan. Tighten the fitting to 32–42 ft. lbs.

19. Lower the vehicle.

20. Fill the transmission to the proper level.

21. Raise the vehicle and check for transmission fluid leakage. Lower the vehicle and adjust the throttle and manual linkage.

C6 and FMX

REMOVAL

1. Drive the vehicle on a hoist, but do not raise at this time.

2. Remove the two upper converter housing-to-engine bolts.

3. Remove the bolt securing the fluid filler tube to the engine cylinder head.

4. Raise the vehicle on a hoist or stands.

5. Place the drain pan under the transmission fluid pan. Starting at the rear of the pan and working toward the front, loosen the attaching bolts and allow the fluid to drain. Finally remove all of the pan attaching bolts except two at the front, to allow the fluid to further drain. With fluid drained, install two bolts on the rear side of the pan to temporarily hold it in place.

6. Remove the converter drain plug access cover from the lower end of the converter housing.

7. Remove the converter-to-flywheel attaching nuts. Place a wrench on the crankshaft pulley attaching bolt to turn the converter to gain access to the nuts.

8. With the wrench on the crankshaft pulley attaching bolt, turn the converter to gain access to the converter drain plug. Place a drain pan under the converter to catch the fluid and remove the plug. After the fluid has been drained, re-install the plug.

9. Disconnect the driveshaft from the rear axle and slide shaft rearward from the transmission. Install a seal installation tool in the extension housing to prevent fluid leakage.

10. Disconnect the speedometer cable from the extension housing.

11. Disconnect the downshift and manual linkage rods from the levers at the transmission.

12. Disconnect the oil cooler lines from the transmission.

13. Remove the vacuum hose from the vacuum diaphragm unit. Remove the vacuum line retaining clip.

14. Disconnect the cable from the terminal on the starter motor. Remove the three attaching bolts and remove the starter motor.

15. On F-150—F-350 (4 x 4) remove the transfer case.

16. Remove the two engine rear support and insulator assembly-to-attaching bolts.

17. Remove the two engine rear support and insulator assembly-to-extension housing attaching bolts.

18. Remove the six bolts securing the No. 2 crossmember to the frame side rails.

19. Raise the transmission with a transmission jack and remove both crossmembers.

20. Secure the transmission to the jack with the safety chain.

21. Remove the remaining converter housing-to-engine attaching bolts.

22. Move the transmission away from the engine. Lower the jack and remove the converter and transmission assembly from under the vehicle.

INSTALLATION

1. Tighten the converter drain plug.

2. Position the converter on the transmission making sure the converter drive flats are fully engaged in the pump gear.

3. With the converter properly installed, place the transmission on the jack. Secure the transmission to the jack with the chain.

4. Rotate the converter until the studs and drain plug are in alignment with their holes in the flywheel.

5. Move the converter and transmission assembly forward into position, using care not to damage the flywheel and the converter pilot. The converter must rest squarely against the flywheel. This indicates that the converter pilot is not binding in the engine crankshaft

6. Install and tighten the converter housing-to-engine attaching bolts.

7. Remove the transmission jack safety chain from around the transmission.

8. Position the No. 2 crossmember to the frame side rails. Install and tighten the attaching bolts.

9. Install transfer case on F-150—F-250 (4 x 4).

10. Position the engine rear support and insulator assembly above the crossmember. Install the rear support and insulator assembly-to-extension housing mounting bolts and tighten the bolts.

11. Lower the transmission and remove the jack.

12. Secure the engine rear support and insulator assembly to the crossmember with the attaching bolts and tighten them.

13. Connect the vacuum line to the vacuum diaphragm making sure that the line is in the retaining clip.

14. Connect the oil cooler lines to the transmission.

15. Connect the downshift and manual linkage rods to their respective levers on the transmission.

16. Connect the speedometer cable to the extension housing.

17. Secure the starter motor in place with the attaching bolts. Connect the cable to the terminal on the starter.

18. Install a new O-ring on the lower end of the transmission filler tube and insert the tube in the case.

19. Secure the converter-to-flywheel attaching nuts and tighten them.

20. Install the converter housing access cover and secure it with the attaching bolts.

21. Connect the driveshaft.

22. Adjust the shift linkage as required.

23. Lower the vehicle. Then install the two upper converter housing-to-engine bolts and tighten them.

24. Position the transmission fluid filler tube to the cylinder head and secure with the attaching bolt.

25. Make sure the drain pan is securely attached, and fill the transmission to the correct level with the specified fluid.

Automatic Overdrive

REMOVAL

1. Raise the vehicle on a hoist or stands.

2. Place the drain pan under the transmission fluid pan. Starting at the rear of the pan and working toward the front, loosen the attaching bolts and allow the fluid to drain. Finally remove all of the pan attaching bolts except two at the front, to allow the fluid to further drain. With fluid drained, install two bolts on the rear side of the pan to temporarily hold it in place.

3. Remove the converter drain plug access cover from the lower end of the converter housing.

4. Remove the converter-to-flywheel attaching nuts. Place a wrench on the crankshaft pulley attaching bolt to turn the converter to gain access to the nuts.

5. Place a drain pan under the converter to catch the fluid. With the wrench on the crankshaft pulley attaching bolt, turn the converter to gain access to the converter drain plug and remove the plug. After the fluid has been drained, reinstall the plug.

6. Disconnect the driveshaft from the rear axle and slide shaft rearward from the transmission. Install a seal installation tool in the extension housing to prevent fluid leakage.

7. Disconnect the cable from the terminal on the starter motor. Remove the three attaching bolts and remove the starter motor. Disconnect the neutral start switch wires at the plug connector.

8. Remove the rear mount-to-crossmember attaching bolts and the two crossmember-to-frame attaching bolts.

9. Remove the two engine rear support-to-extension housing attaching bolts.

10. Disconnect the TV linkage rod from the transmission TV lever. Disconnect the manual rod from the transmission manual lever at the transmission.

11. Remove the two bolts securing the bellcrank bracket to the converter housing.

12. Raise the transmission with a transmission jack to provide clearance to remove the crossmember. Remove the rear mount from the crossmember and remove the crossmember from the side supports.

13. Lower the transmission to gain access to the oil cooler lines.

14. Disconnect each oil line from the fittings on the transmission.

15. Disconnect the speedometer cable from the extension housing.

16. Remove the bolt that secures the transmission fluid filler tube to the cylinder block. Lift the filler tube and the dipstick from the transmission.

17. Secure the transmission to the jack with the chain.

18. Remove the converter housing-to-cylinder block attaching bolts.

19. Carefully move the transmission and converter assembly away from the engine and, at the same time, lower the jack to clear the underside of the vehicle.

20. Remove the converter and mount the transmission in a holding fixture.

INSTALLATION

1. Tighten the converter drain plug.

2. Position the converter on the transmission, making sure the converter drive flats are fully engaged in the pump gear by rotating the converter.

3. With the converter properly installed, place the transmission on the jack. Secure the transmission to the jack with a chain.

4. Rotate the converter until the studs and drain plug are in alignment with the holes in the flywheel.

5. Move the converter and transmission assembly forward into position, using care not to damage the flywheel and the converter pilot. The converter must rest squarely against the flywheel. This indicates that the converter pilot is not binding in the engine crankshaft.

6. Install and tighten the converter hous-

ing-to-engine attaching bolts to 40–50 ft. lb.

7. Remove the safety chain from around the transmission.

8. Install a new O-ring on the lower end of the transmission filler tube. Insert the tube in the transmission case and secure the tube to the engine with the attaching bolt.

9. Connect the speedometer cable to the extension housing.

10. Connect the oil cooler lines to the right side of transmission case.

11. Position the crossmember on the side supports. Position the rear mount on the crossmember and install the attaching bolt and nut.

12. Secure the engine rear support to the extension housing and tighten the bolts to 16–20 ft. lb.

13. Lower the transmission and remove the jack.

Pan

REMOVAL AND INSTALLATION

C4, C5

NOTE: *The torque converter on all of the transmissions has a drain plug. If the converter is drained, refill the C4 with 5 qts of fluid and the C6 and FMX models with 8 qts of fluid.*

1. Raise the vehicle so that the transmission oil pan is readily accessible.

2. Disconnect the fluid filler tube from the pan and allow the fluid to drain into an appropriate container.

NOTE: *It is not recommended that the drained fluid be used over again; refill the transmission with new fluid. However, in an emergency situation, the old fluid can be reused. The old fluid should be strained through a #100 screen or a fine mesh cloth before being reinstalled.*

3. Remove the transmission oil pan attaching bolts, pan and gasket.

To install the transmission oil pan:

4. Clean the transmission oil pan and transmission mating surfaces.

5. Install the transmission oil pan in the reverse order of removal, torquing the attaching bolts to 12–16 ft. lbs. and using a new gasket. Fill the transmission with 3 qts of the correct type fluid, check the operation of the transmission and check for leakage.

C6, FMX, and AOD

1. Raise the truck on a hoist or jackstands.

2. Place a drain pan under the transmission.

3. Loosen the pan attaching bolts and drain the fluid from the transmission.

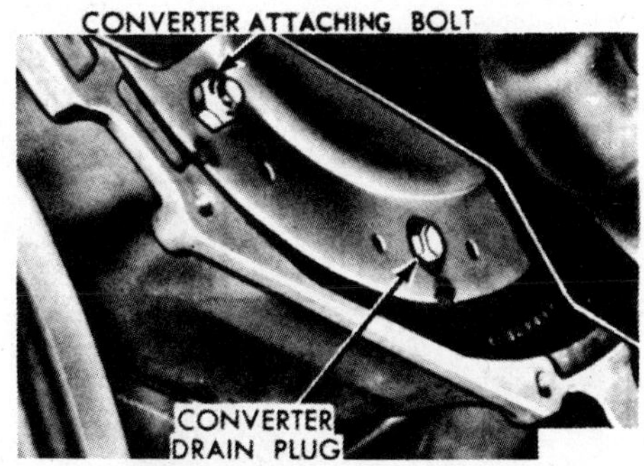

Torque converter drain plug location—typical

4. When the fluid has drained to the level of the pan flange, remove the remaining pan bolts working from the rear and both sides of the pan to allow it to drop and drain slowly.

5. When all of the fluid has drained, remove the pan and clean it thoroughly. Discard the pan gasket.

6. Place a new gasket on the pan, and install the pan on the transmission. Tighten the attaching bolts to 12–16 ft. lbs.

7. Add three quarts of fluid to the transmission through the filler tube.

Filter Service

1. Remove the transmission oil pan and gasket.

2. Remove the screws holding the fine mesh screen to the lower valve body.

NOTE: *Be careful not to lose the throttle pressure limit valve and spring when separating the oil screen from the valve body on a C4.*

3. Install the new filter screen and transmission oil pan gasket in the reverse order of removal.

Adjustments

FRONT BAND ADJUSTMENT

FMX

1. Remove the transmission oil pan.

2. Loosen the front servo adjusting screw locknut.

3. Pull back on the actuating rod, and insert a ¼ in. spacer between the adjusting screw and the servo piston stem.

4. Tighten the adjusting screw to 10 in. lbs.

5. Remove the spacer and tighten the adjusting screw an additional ¾ turn.

6. Hold the adjusting screw stationary and tighten the locknut. Tighten the locknut to 20–25 ft. lbs.

7. Install the oil pan and a new gasket in the reverse order of removal.

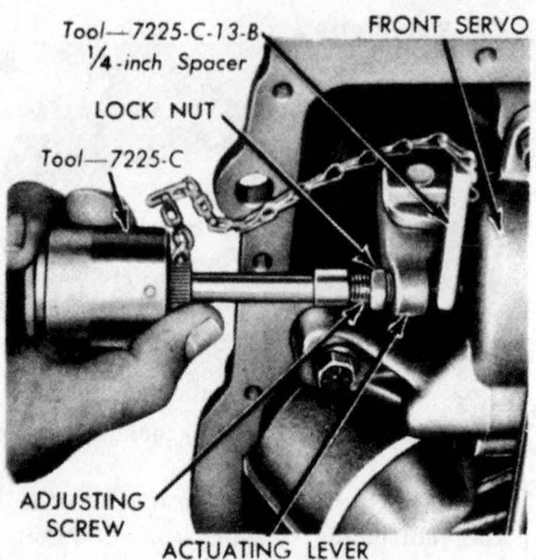

Front band adjustment on an FMX

Adjusting the intermediate band on a C6

INTERMEDIATE BAND ADJUSTMENT

C4, C5 and C6

1. Raise the truck on a hoist or jackstands.
2. Clean all dirt away from the band adjusting screw. Remove and discard the locknut.
3. Install a new locknut and tighten the adjusting screw to 10 ft. lbs.
4. On the C4 transmission, back off the adjusting screw *exactly 1¾ turns.* On the C5, back off the adjusting screw *exactly 4¼ turns.* On a C6 transmission, back off the adjusting screw *exactly 1½ turns.*
5. Hold the adjusting screw from turning and tighten the locknut to 35–45 ft. lbs.
6. Remove the jackstands and lower the vehicle.

LOW-REVERSE BAND ADJUSTMENT

C4, C5

1. Clean all dirt from around the band adjusting screw and remove and discard the locknut.
2. Install a new locknut on the adjusting screw. Using a torque wrench, tighten the adjusting screw to 10 ft. lbs.
3. Back off the adjusting screw *exactly 3 full turns.*
4. Hold the adjusting screw steady and tighten the locknut to 35–45 ft. lbs.

REAR BAND ADJUSTMENT

FMX

1. Remove all dirt away from the adjusting screw threads then oil the threads.
2. Loosen the rear band adjusting screw locknut.
3. Tighten the adjusting screw to 10 ft. lbs.
4. Back off the adjusting screw *exactly 1½ turns.*

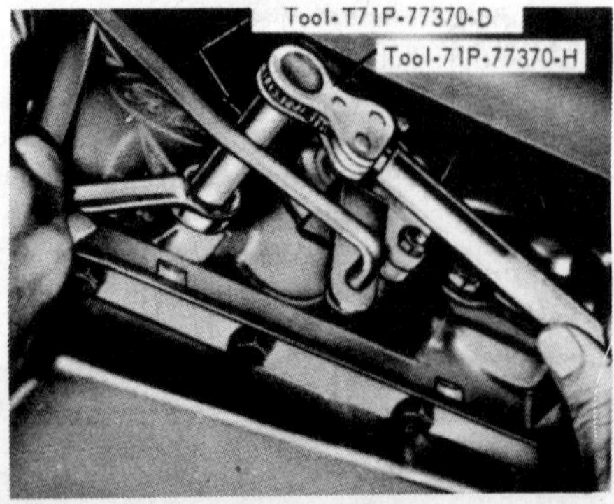

Adjusting the intermediate band on a C4 or C5

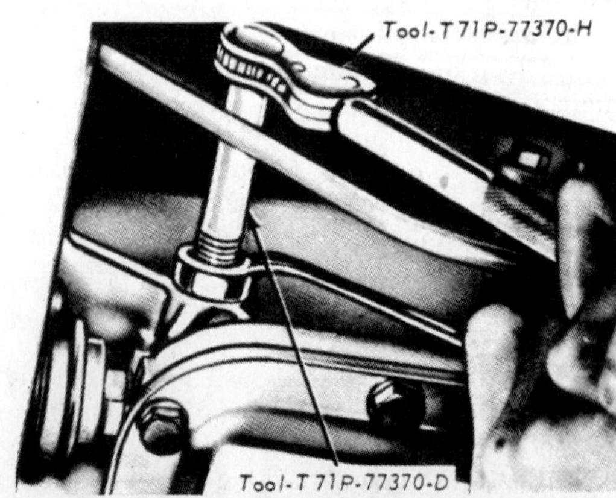

Adjusting the low-reverse band on a C4 or C5

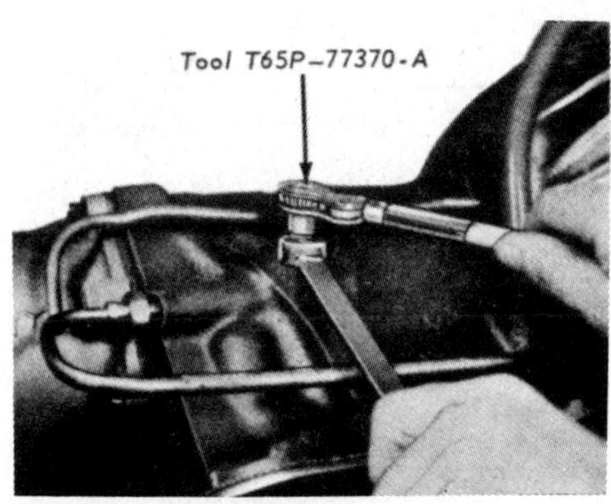

Adjusting the rear band on a FMX

5. Hold the adjusting screw stationary and tighten the adjusting screw locknut to 35–40 ft. lbs.

6. Reinstall the oil pan and a new gasket.

SHIFT LINKAGE ADJUSTMENT

1965–67

1. Disconnect the upper end of the manual shift rod from the selector lever.

2. Position the selector lever so that the pointer is down against the steering column stop in the D1 position.

3. Shift the manual lever on the transmission to the second position from the bottom.

4. Rotate the adjusting sleeve on the manual shift rod until the pin can be easily inserted in the lever.

5. Lock the adjusting sleeve in place and connect the rod to the selector lever.

6. Check the pointer alignment for all positions of the selector lever.

1968–69

1. Disconnect the lower end of the manual shift rod from the transmission manual lever.

2. Position the selector lever so that the pointer is against the steering column stop in the D position.

3. Shift the manual lever on the transmission to the D position, third from the rear.

4. Adjust the length of the shift rod until the end can easily be inserted in the manual lever.

5. Connect the shift rod to the manual lever

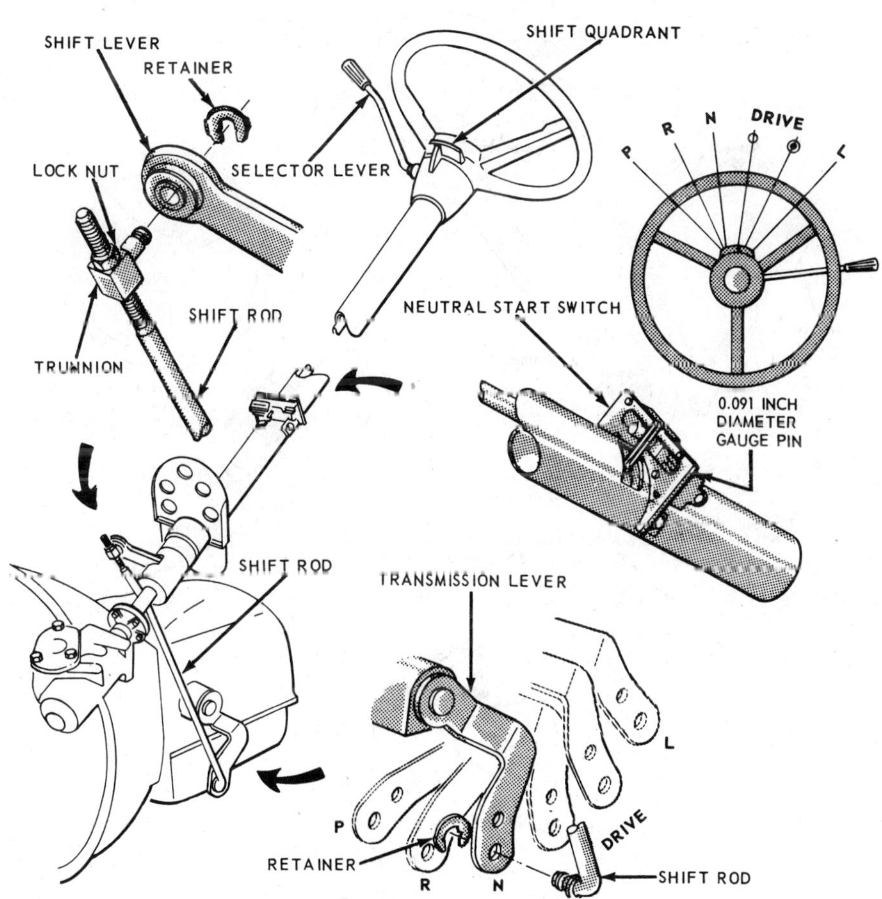

Automatic transmission shift linkage adjustment—1965–67

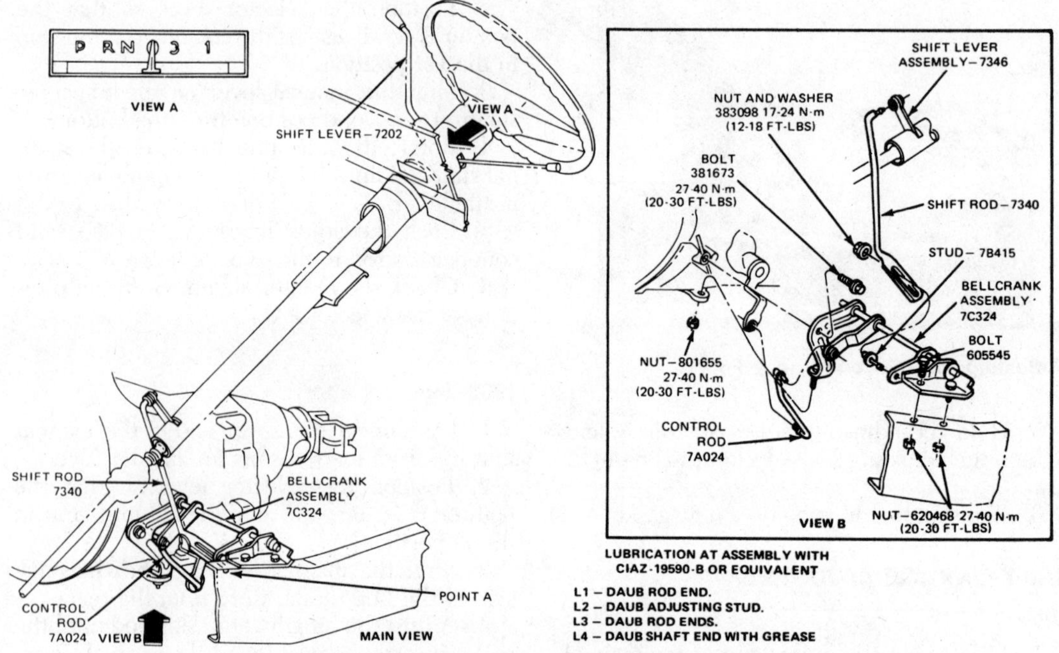

Automatic overdrive shift linkage adjustment

SHIFT LEVER
RETAINER
GROMMET
SELECTOR LEVER
SHIFT QUADRANT
P R N D 2 1
LOCK NUT
SHIFT ROD
TRUNNION
NEUTRAL START SWITCH
0.091 INCH DIAMETER GAUGE PIN
SHIFT ROD
TRANSMISSION LEVER
1
2
P
RETAINER
R
N
D
SHIFT ROD
GROMMET

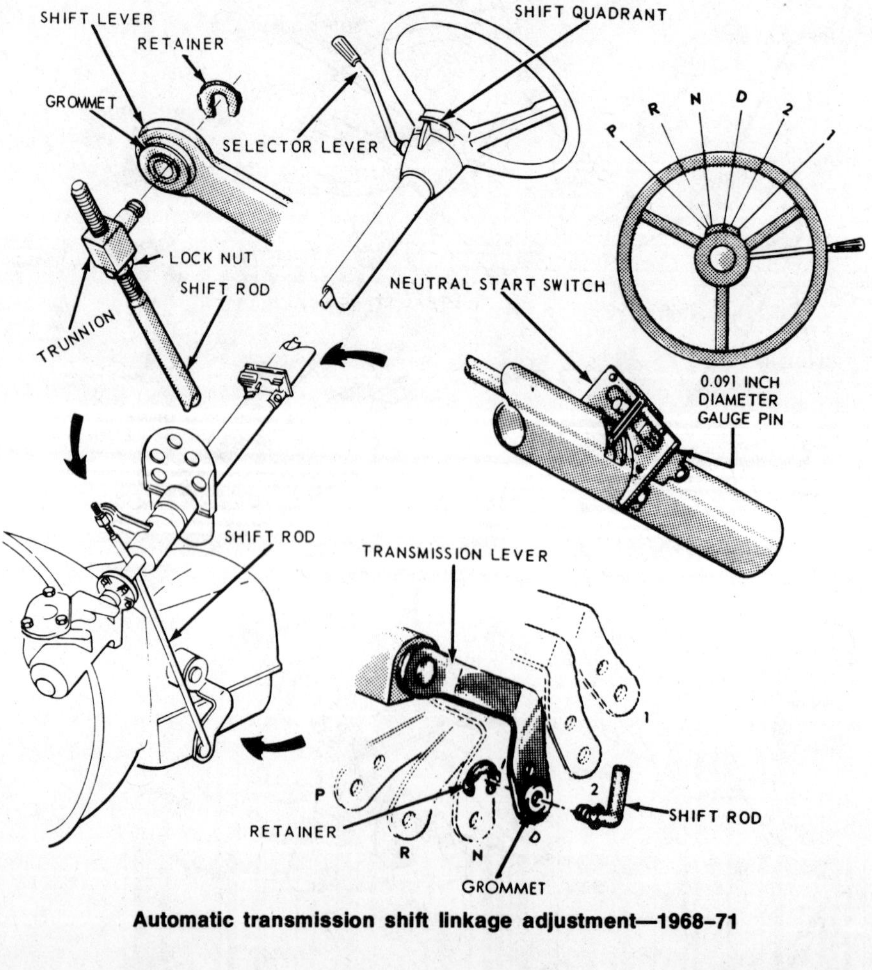

Automatic transmission shift linkage adjustment—1968–71

and tighten the lock nut at the steering column end.

6. Shift into all positions and make sure that the manual lever at the transmission is in the full in all gear ranges. Readjust the manual shift rod one turn at a time, if required.

1970–71

1. With the engine stopped, place the transmission selector lever in the D (Drive) position. Have an assistant hold the selector lever against the D position stop.
2. Remove and discard the shift rod trunnion retainer at the steering column shift lever.
3. Remove the grommet from the shift lever by cutting it off with a sharp knife. The grommet must be replaced each time the shift rod is removed.
4. Install a new grommet in the shift lever.
5. Position the selector in the D position.
6. Shift the manual lever on the transmission to the D position, third from the rear.
7. Adjust the length of the shift rod until the trunnion end can be inserted into the column shift lever easily. Then, lengthen the rod by seven turns of the trunnion.
8. Connect the shift rod trunnion to the column shift lever and secure it with a new retainer ring. Be sure that the inner shoulder of the grommet is properly seated in the wide groove of the trunnion.
9. Tighten the trunnion locknut.
10. Operate the shift lever in all positions to make sure that the lever at the transmission is in the full detent in all the gear positions.

1972

1. With the engine stopped, place the transmission selector lever in the D position against the D stop.
2. Shift the manual lever at the transmission into the D position, second detent position from the rear.
3. With the transmission manual lever in the D position, connect the trunnion to the manual lever.
4. Turn the nuts on each side of the trunnion against the face of the trunnion fingertight.
5. While holding the upper nut stationary, tighten the lower nut to 12–18 ft. lbs.

1973 and Later

1. With the engine stopped, place the transmission selector lever at the steering column in the D position against the D stop.
2. Loosen the shift rod adjusting nut at the transmission lever.
3. Shift the manual lever at the transmission to the D position, two detents from the rear. On an F-100 with 4WD, move the bellcrank lever.
4. With the selector lever and transmission manual lever in the D position, tighten the adjusting nut to 12–18 ft. lbs. Do not allow the rod or shift lever to move while tightening the nut.
5. Check the operation of the shift linkage.

THROTTLE VALVE LINKAGE ADJUSTMENT

Automatic Overdrive

ADJUSTMENT AT THE CARBURETOR

The TV control linkage may be adjusted at the carburetor using the following procedure:

1. Check that engine idle speed is set at specification.
2. De-cam the fast idle cam on the carburetor so that the throttle lever is at its idle stop. Place shift lever in N (neutral), set park brake (engine off).
3. Backout linkage lever adjusting screw all the way (screw end is flush with lever face).
4. Turn in adjusting screw until a thin shim (.005 inch max.) or peice of writing paper fits snugly between end of screw and Throttle Lever. To eliminate effect of friction, push linkage lever forward (tending to close gap) and release before checking clearance between end of screw and throttle lever. Do not apply any load on levers with tools or hands while checking gap.
5. Turn in adjusting screw an additional four turns. (Four turns are preferred. Two turns minimum is permissible if screw travel is limited).
6. If it is not possible to turn in adjusting screw at least two additional turns or if there was insufficient screw adjusting capacity to obtain an initial gap in Step 2 above, refer to Linkage Adjustment at Transmission.

Whenever it is required to adjust idle speed by more than 50 rpm, the adjustment screw on the linkage lever at the carburetor should also be readjusted as shown:

Idle Speed Change/Turns on Linkage Lever Adjustment Screw

- Less than 50 rpm/No change required
- 50 to 100 rpm increase/1½ turns out
- 50 to 100 rpm decrease/1½ turns in
- 100 to 150 rpm increase/2½ turns out
- 100 to 150 rpm decrease/2½ turns in

After making any idle speed adjustments, always verify the linkage lever and throttle lever

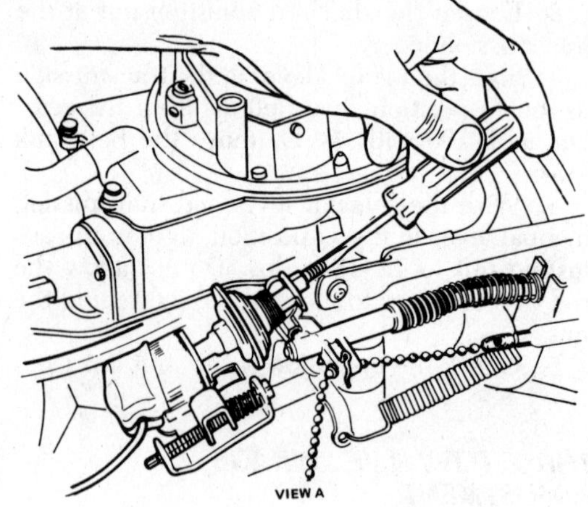

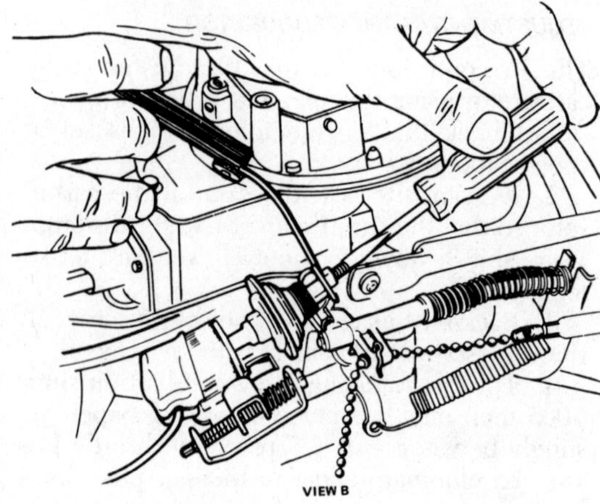

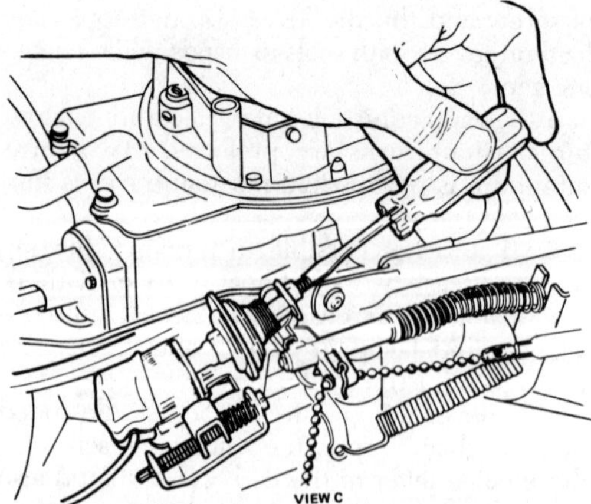

Automatic overdrive throttle linkage adjustment

are in contact with the throttle lever at its idle stop and the shift lever is in N (neutral).

ADJUSTMENT AT TRANSMISSION

The linkage lever adjustment screw has limited adjustment capability. It is is not possible to adjust the TV linkage using this screw, the length of the TV control rod assembly must be readjusted using the following procedure. This procedure must also be followed whenever a new TV control rod assembly is installed.

This procedure requires placing the vehicle on jackstands to give access to the linkage components at the transmission TV control lever.

1. Set the engine curb idle speed to specification.
2. With engine off, de-cam the fast idle cam on the carburetor so that the throttle lever is against the idle stop. Place shift lever in Neutral and set park brake (engine off).
3. Set the linkage lever adjustment screw at its approximately mid-range.
4. If a new TV control rod assembly is being installed, connect the rod to the linkage lever at the carburetor.

CAUTION: *The following steps involve working in proximity to the exhaust system. Allow the exhaust system to cool before proceeding.*

5. Raise the vehicle on the hoist.
6. Using a 13 mm box end wrench, loosen the bolt on the sliding trunnion block on the TV control rod assembly. Remove any corrosion from the control rod and free-up the trunnion block so that it slides freely on the control rod. Insert pin into transmission lever grommet.
7. Push up on the lower end of the control rod to insure that the linkage lever at carburetor is firmly against the throttle lever. Release force on rod. Rod must stay up.
8. Push the TV control lever on the transmission up against its internal stop with a firm force (approximately 5 pounds) and tighten the bolt on the trunnion block. Do not relax force on lever until nut is tightened.
9. Lower the vehicle and verify that the throttle lever is still against the idle stop. If not, repeat steps 2 through 9.

NEUTRAL SAFETY SWITCH ADJUSTMENT

1. Hold the steering column transmission selector lever against the Neutral stop.
2. Move the sliding block assembly on the neutral switch to the neutral position and insert a 0.091 in. gauge pin in the alignment hole on the terminal side of the switch.
3. Move the switch assembly housing so that the sliding block contacts the actuating pin lever. Secure the switch to the outer tube of the steering column and remove the gauge pin.
4. Check the operation of the switch. The engine should only start in Neutral and Park.

BOTTOM VIEW OF SWITCH

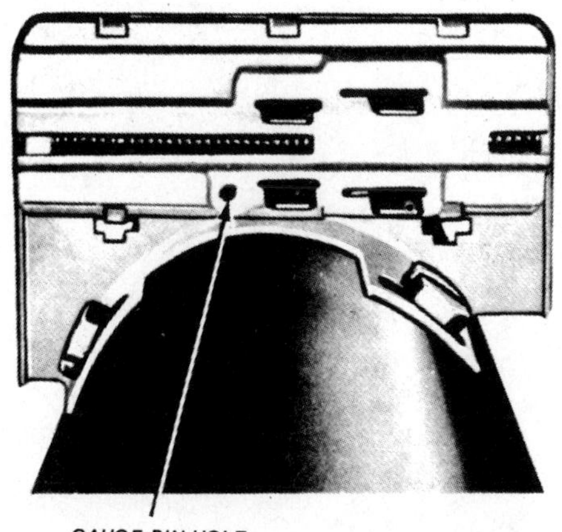

View of the neutral safety switch adjustment gauge pin hole

THROTTLE KICK-DOWN LINKAGE ADJUSTMENT

1. Move the carburetor throttle linkage to the wide open position.
2. Insert a 0.060 in. thick spacer between the throttle lever and the kickdown adjusting screw.
3. Rotate the transmission kick-down lever until the lever engages the transmission internal stop. Do not use the kick-down rod to turn the transmission lever.
4. Turn the adjusting screw until it contacts the 0.060 in. spacer.
5. Remove the spacer.

TRANSFER CASE

The transfer case transmits power from the engine and transmission to the front and rear axles. The front output shaft provides an attachment point for a front driveshaft which drives a front drive axle much like a conventional rear axle.

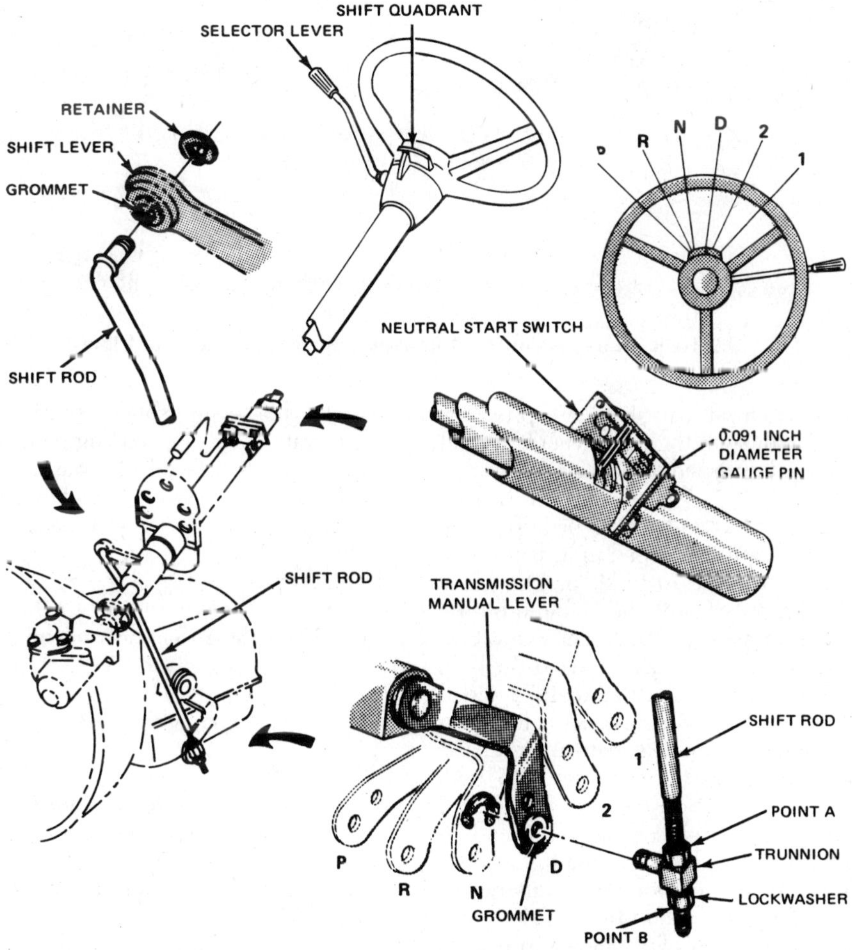

Automatic transmission shift linkage adjustment—1972

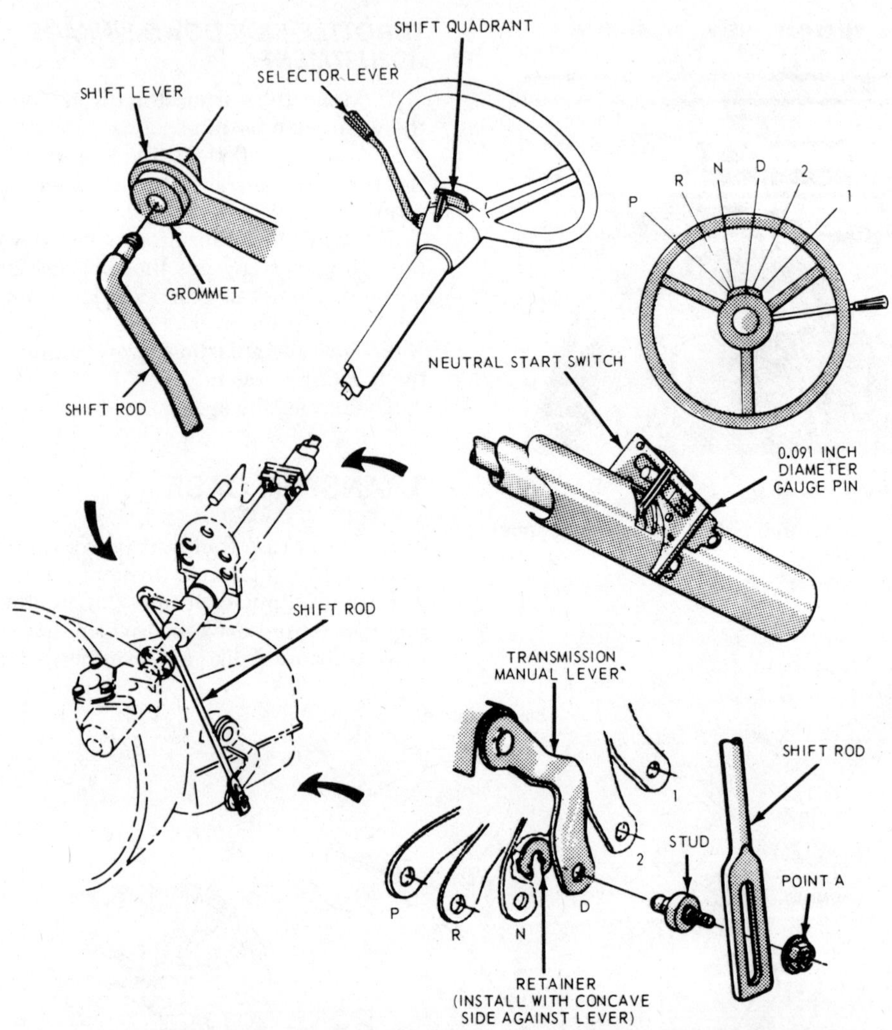

Automatic transmission shift linkage adjustment—1973 and later

The ends of the front axle shafts are provided with universal joints at the front wheels so that the wheels can be turned for steering.

From 1970 to 1978, six transfer cases have been used on F-100 and F-250 pickups. The Dana Model 21, a single-speed unit, is used on the F-100 only from 1970 to 1975. The Dana Model 24 is a 2-speed unit and is found on the F-250 only from 1970 to 1973. The New Process Model 205 transfer case is used on both the F-100 and F-250 from 1972 to 1978 and is a 2-speed unit with a constant-mesh helical gear train. 1979 and later models feature either the New Process 208 or the Borg-Warner 1345, both part-time units. The New Process Model 203 transfer case was introduced on F-100 and F-250 models in 1975 and features full-time 4WD. This transfer case incorporates a differential which is similar in operation to the axle differentials, and compensates for different speeds of the front and rear axles resulting from varying speeds while turning and operating over different terrains, thus permitting continuous 4WD on dry, hard-surfaced highways. Drive to the front axle is by a chain instead of gears.

The Dana 24 and New Process 205 transfer cases are quite similar in external appearance. To differentiate between the two, check the rear of the unit. The rear output shaft exits from the left side on the 205 and from the right side on the 24.

REMOVAL AND INSTALLATION

Dana Model 21

1. Raise the vehicle on a hoist.
2. Disconnect the front and rear driveshafts at the transfer case.
3. Disconnect the shift rod from the transfer case shift lever arm.
4. Remove the bolts and nuts which attach the transfer case to the transmission extension

housing and remove the transfer case from under the truck.

5. Install the transfer case in the reverse order of removal, using a new gasket between the transfer case and the transmission extension housing.

Dana Model 24

1. Drain the transfer case, and disconnect the rear axle driveshaft from the flange at the transfer case.
2. Disconnect the front wheel driveshaft and the transmission output shaft at the transfer case.
3. Disconnect the shift selector rod and the speedometer cable at the transfer case.
4. Place a transmission jack under the transfer case and secure it with a chain.
5. Remove the transfer case mounting bolts.
6. Remove the transfer case from under the vehicle.
7. Install the transfer case in the reverse order of removal, and fill it with lubricant.

New Process Model 205

1. Drain the transfer case and disconnect the rear axle driveshaft from the flange at the transfer case.
2. Disconnect the front wheel driveshaft and the transmission output shaft at the transfer case if on an F-250. On an F-100, disconnect the front wheel driveshaft and remove the bolts attaching the transmission adapter to the transfer case.
3. Disconnect the shift selector rod and the speedometer cable at the transfer case.
4. Place a transmission jack under the transfer case and secure it with a chain.
5. Remove the transfer case mounting bolts and remove the unit from under the vehicle.
6. Install the transfer case in the reverse order of removal.

New Process Model 203 1975–77

1. Drain the transfer case by removing the power take-off lower bolts and the front output rear cover lower bolts.
2. Disconnect the front axle driveshaft from the flange at the transfer case.
3. Disconnect the shift rods from the transfer case.
4. Disconnect the speedometer cable and lockout light switch wire from the transfer case rear output shaft housing.
5. On F-250 pick-ups, disconnect the front input and output shafts from the transfer case flanges. On F-100, 150 trucks, remove the transfer case-to-transmission adapter attaching bolts. Disconnect the rear axle driveshaft at the transfer case flange.
6. Position a transmission jack under the transfer case and secure it with a chain.
7. Remove the transfer case mounting bolts and remove the unit from the vehicle. On F-250 models, remove the stabilizer bar-to-transfer case attaching bolt before lowering the case.
8. Install the transfer case in the reverse order or removal.

1978–79

1. Drain the transfer case by removing the power take-off lower bolts and the front output rear cover lower bolts.
2. Disconnect the front axle drive shaft from the flange of the transfer case.
3. Disconnect the shift rods from the transfer case.
4. Disconnect the speedometer cable and lockout lamp switch wire from the transfer case rear output shaft housing.
5. Remove the bolts which attach the transfer case to the transmission adapter. Disconnect the rear axle drive shaft at the transfer case flange.
6. Position a transmission jack under the transfer case and secure it to the jack.
7. Remove the transfer case mounting bolts and remove the transfer case.
8. Install the transfer case in the reverse order of removal.

New Process Model 208

1. Raise the vehicle on a hoist and drain the fluid from the transfer case.
2. Disconnect the four wheel drive indicator switch wire connector at the transfer case.
3. Disconnect the speedometer driven gear from the transfer case rear bearing retainer.
4. Remove the nut retaining the transmission shift lever assembly to the transfer case.
5. Remove the skid plate from the frame, if so equipped.
6. Remove the heat shield from the frame.
7. Support the transfer case with a transmission jack or equivalent.
8. Disconnect the front driveshaft from the front output shaft yoke.
9. Disconnect the rear driveshaft from the rear output shaft yoke.
10. Remove the bolts retaining the transfer case to the transmission adapter.
11. Lower the transfer case from the vehicle.
12. When installing place a new gasket between the transfer case and the adapter.
13. Raise the transfer case with a transmission jack so the transmission output shaft aligns with the splined transfer case input shaft.
14. Install the bolts retaining the case to the adapter.

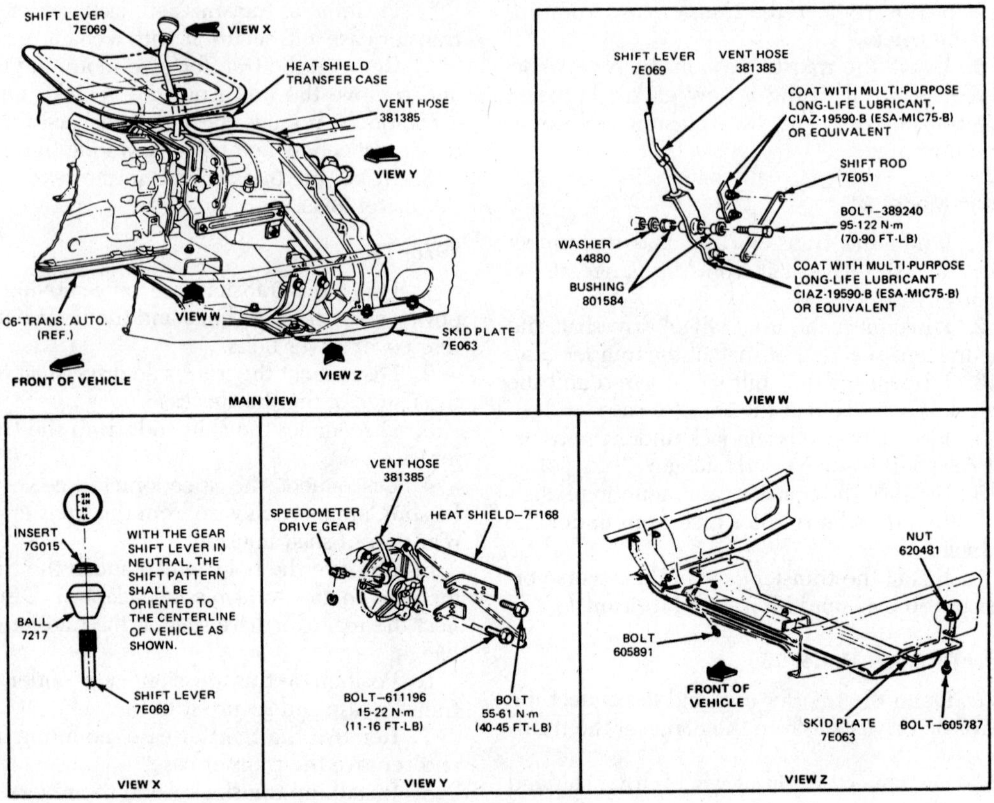

New Process 208 transfer case installation, automatic and four-speed transmissions

15. Connect the rear driveshaft to the rear output shaft yoke.
16. Connect the front driveshaft to the front output yoke.
17. Remove the transmission jack from the transfer case.
18. Position the heat shield to the frame crossmember and mounting lug to the transfer case and install and tighten the bolts and screw.
19. Install the skid plate to the frame.
20. Install the shift lever to the transfer case and tighten the retaining nut.
21. Install the speedometer driven gear to the transfer case.
22. Connect the four wheel drive indicator switch wire to the transfer case.
23. Install the drain plug. Remove the filler plug and install six pints of Dexron II or equivalent type transmission fluid.
24. Lower the vehicle.

Borg-Warner Model 1345

1. Raise the vehicle on a hoist.
2. Drain the fluid from the transfer case.
3. Disconnect the four wheel drive indicator switch wire connector at the transfer case.
4. Remove the skid plate from the frame, if so equipped.
5. Disconnect the front driveshaft from the front output yoke.
6. Disconnect the rear driveshaft from the rear output shaft yoke.
7. Disconnect the speedometer driven gear from the transfer case rear bearing retainer.
8. Remove the retaining rings and shift rod from the transfer case shift lever.
9. Disconnect the vent hose from the transfer case.
10. Remove the heat shield from the frame.
11. Support the transfer case with a transmission jack.
12. Remove the bolts retaining the transfer case to the transmission adapter.
13. Lower the transfer case from the vehicle.
14. When installing place a new gasket between the transfer case and the adapter.
15. Raise the transfer case with the transmission jack so that the transmission output shaft aligns with the splined transfer case input shaft. Install the bolts retaining the transfer case to the adapter.
16. Remove the transmission jack from the transfer case.
17. Connect the rear driveshaft to the rear output shaft yoke.

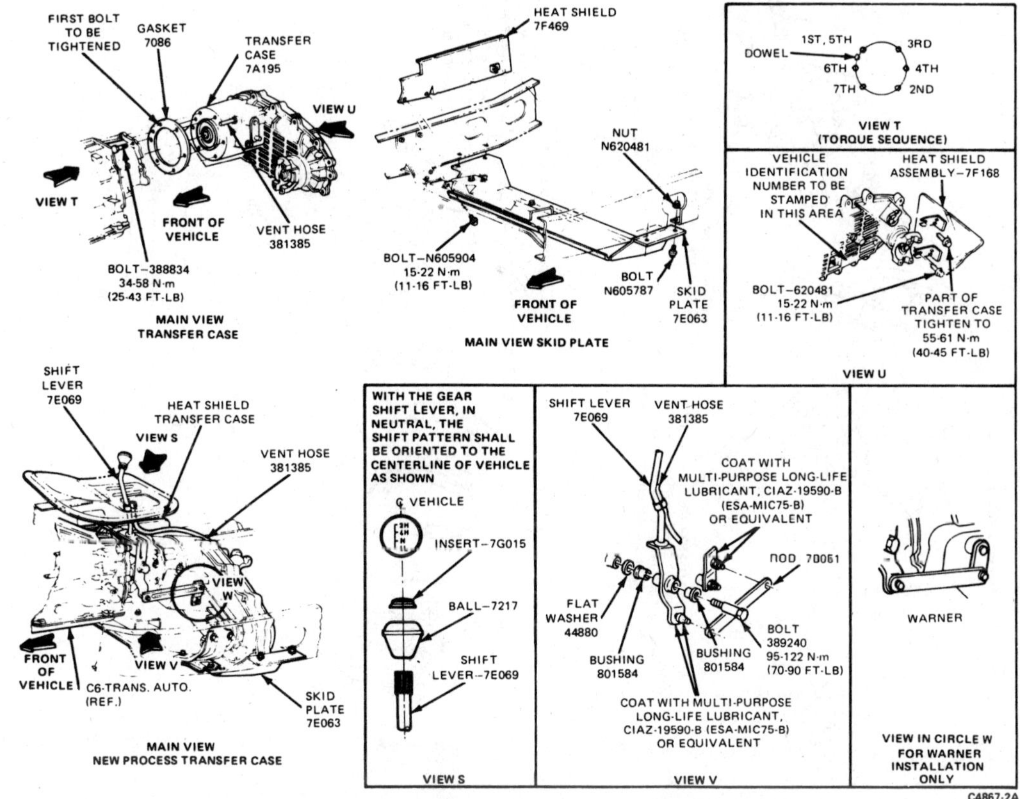

Borg-Warner 1345 transfer case and skid plate installation

18. Install the shift lever to the transfer case and install the retaining nut.
19. Connect the speedometer driven gear to the transfer case.
20. Connect the four wheel drive indicator switch wire connector at the transfer case.
21. Connect the front driveshaft to the front output yoke.
22. Position the heat shield to the frame crossmember and the mounting lug on the transfer case. Install and tighten the retaining bolts.
23. Install the skid plate to the frame.
24. Install the drain plug. Remove the filler plug and install six pints of Dexron II type transmission fluid or equivalent.
25. Lower the vehicle.

TRANSFER CASE SHIFT LINKAGE ADJUSTMENT

New Process Model 205

MANUL TRANSMISSION

Adjust the length of the shift rod between the transfer case and the shift lever with the lever in 4WD-Low so that the distance between the rear face of the transmission and the shift lever-to-rod clevis pin is 3.94 to 3.82 in.

AUTOMATIC TRANSMISSION

Adjust the length of the shift rod between the transfer case and the shift lever with the lever in 4WD-Low so that the distance between the upper surface of the automatic transmission extension housing and the upper horizontal edge of the shift lever is 0.640 to 0.600 in.

New Process 203 Full-Time 4WD

1975–76 F-100, F-150

1. Place the shift lever in the Low position.
2. Remove the adjusting stud nuts from the shift rods under the truck.
3. Disconnect the front driveshaft at the transfer case.
4. Remove the transfer case shifter.
5. Unsnap the top snap of the splash boot, peel the boot back and install a new adjustment pin in the rear of the shifter bracket. The pin is 1.5 in. long, ¼ in. in diameter and must be of breakable material. The pin cannot be reached once the shifter is installed.
6. Reinstall the shifter, tightening the rear bolt to 12–17 ft. lbs. and the front bolt to 70–90 ft. lbs.
7. Move the lower lever on the transfer case completely forward and the upper lever completely rearward.

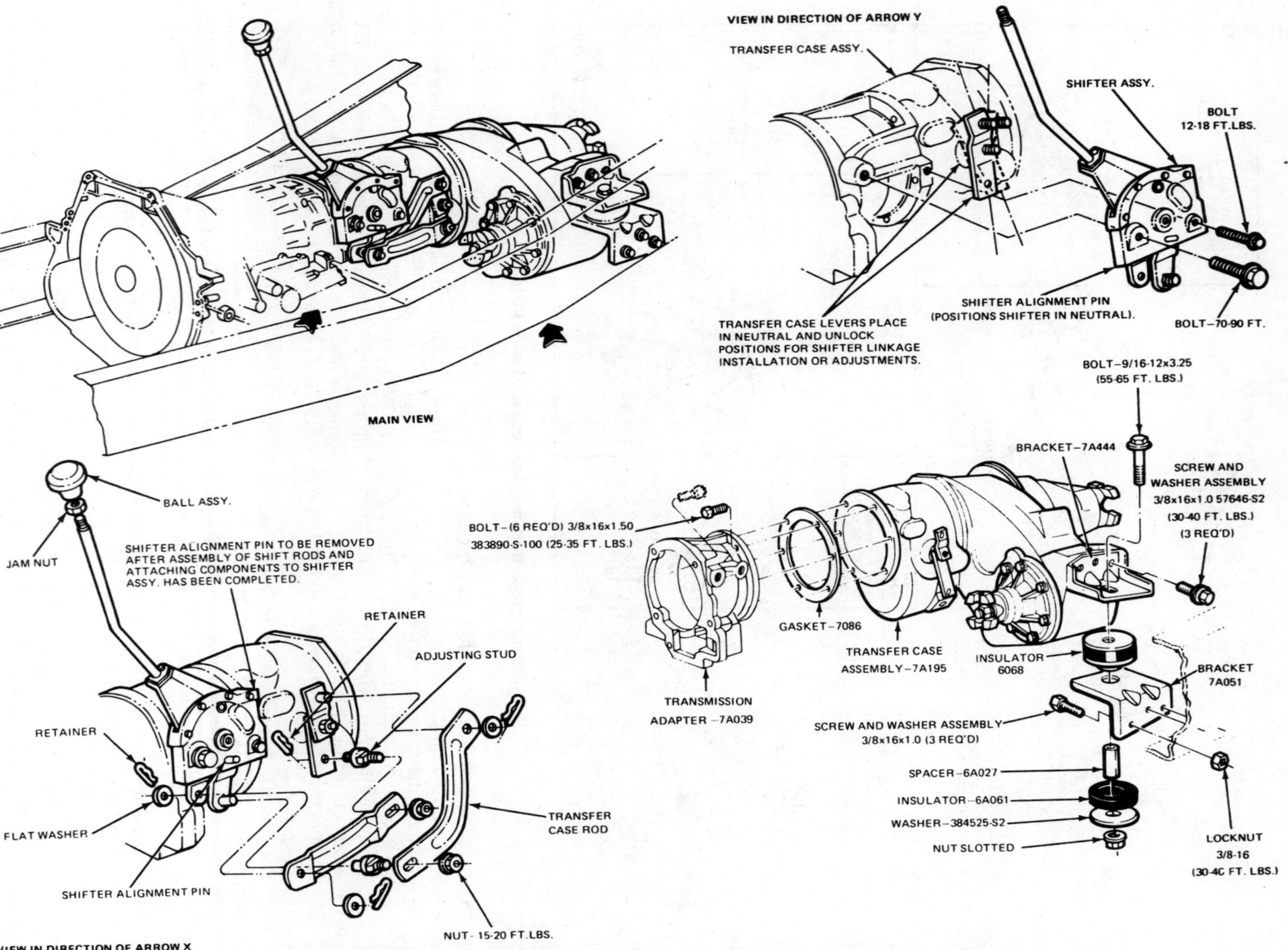

Installation of the New Process model 203 transfer case—F-150-250—1978 and later

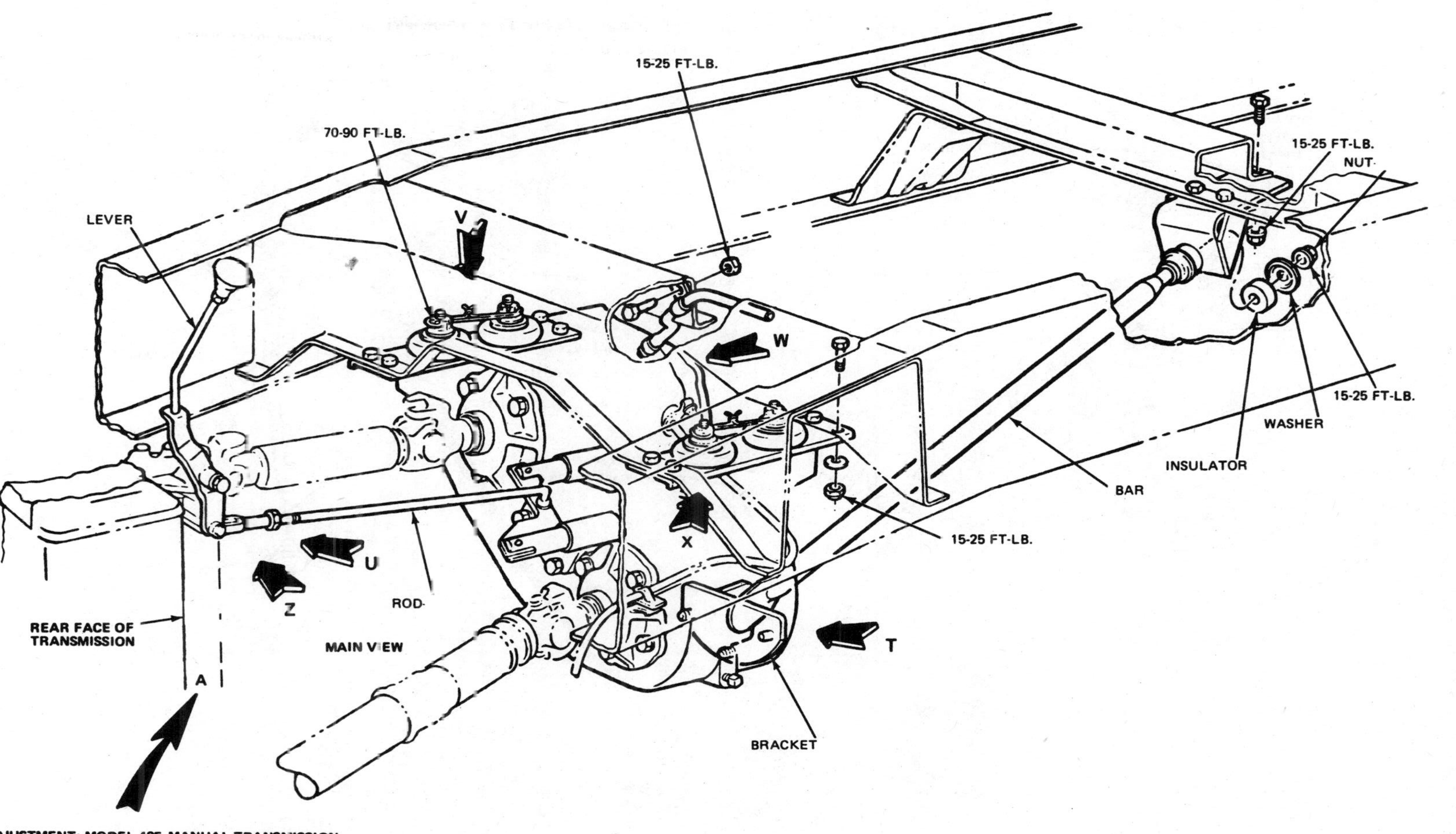

Installation of the New Process model 205 transfer case showing the adjustment of the shift linkage with a manual transmission

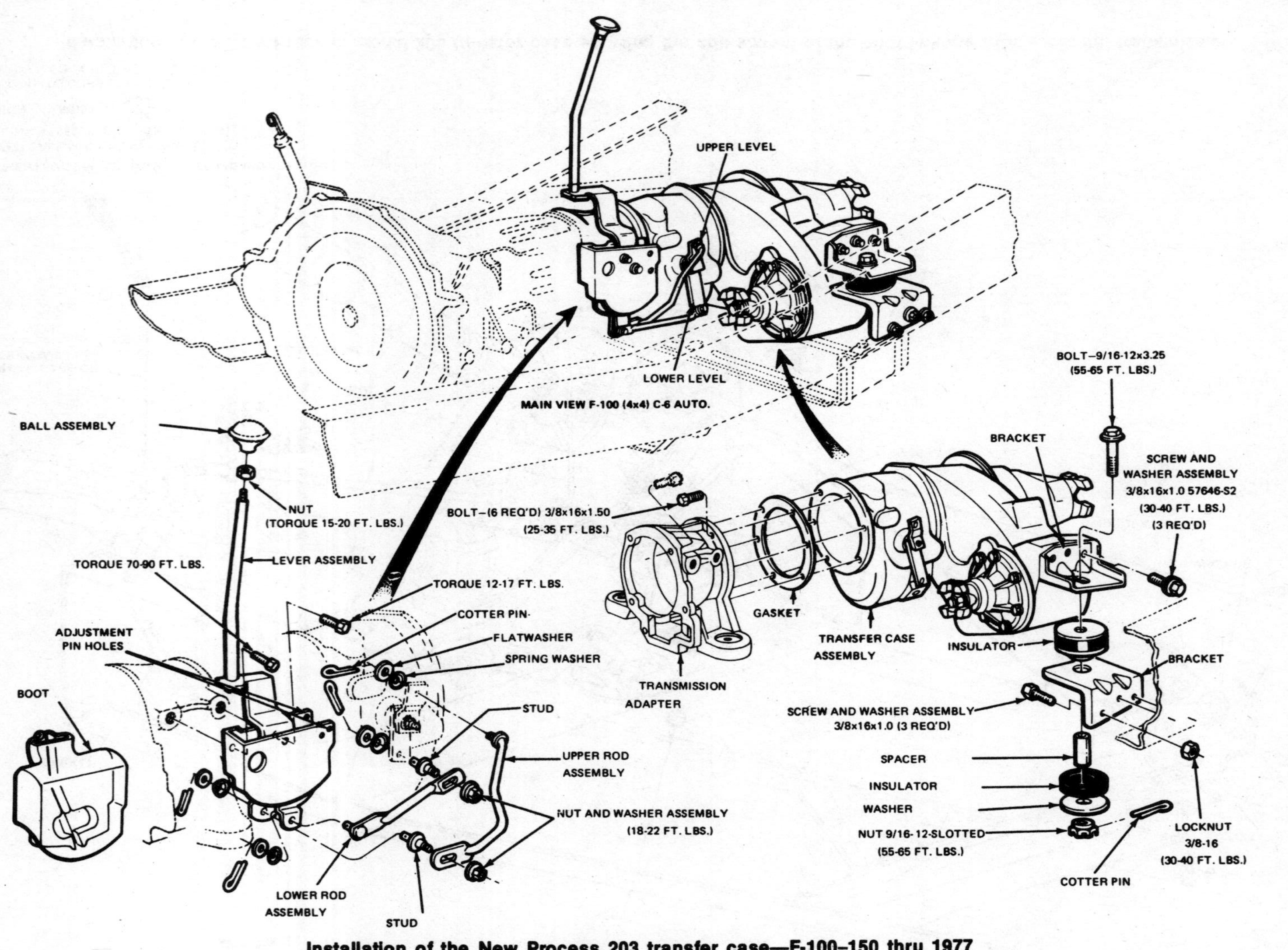

Installation of the New Process 203 transfer case—F-100–150 thru 1977

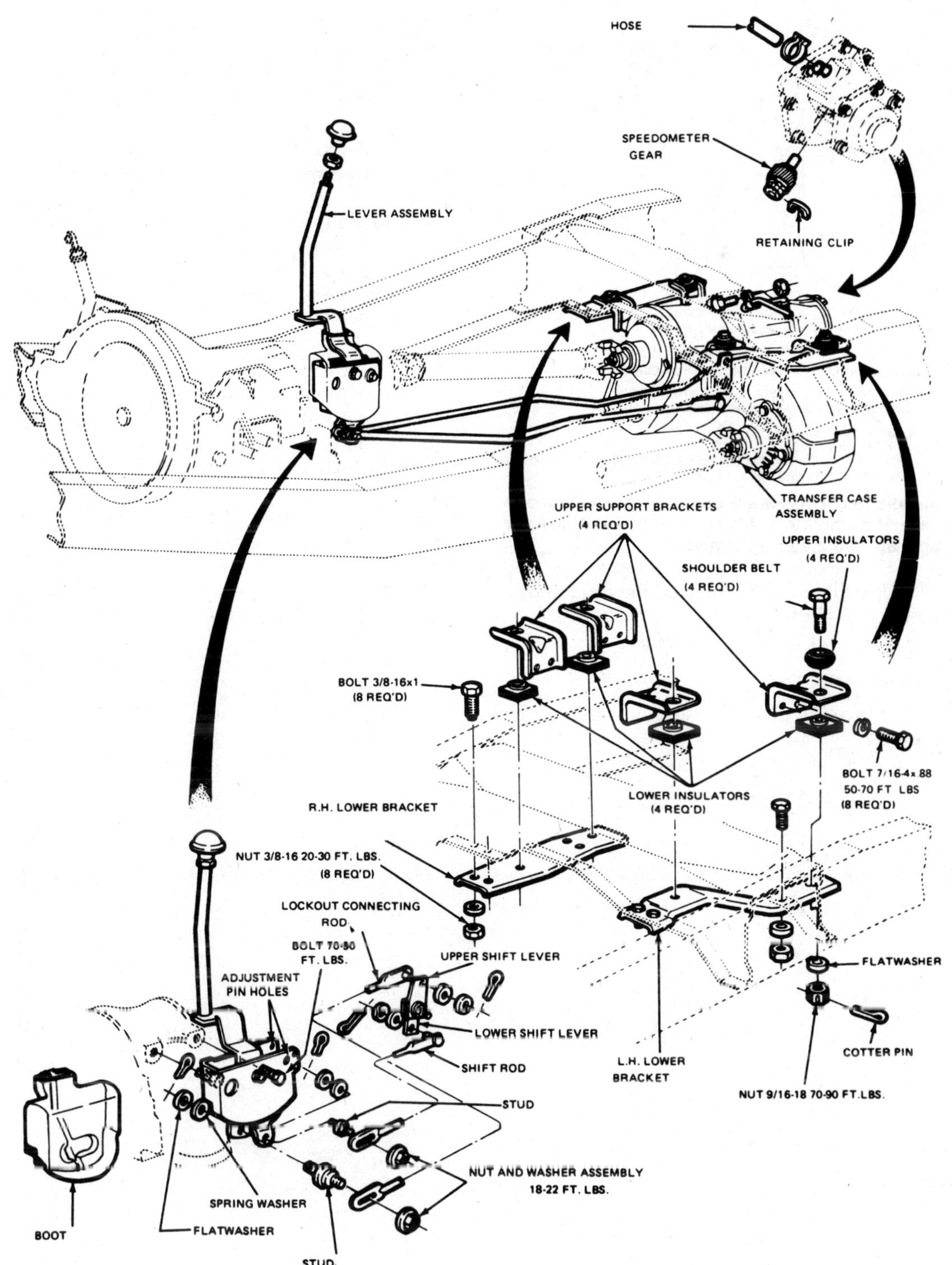

Installation of the New Process 203 transfer case—F-250 thru 1977

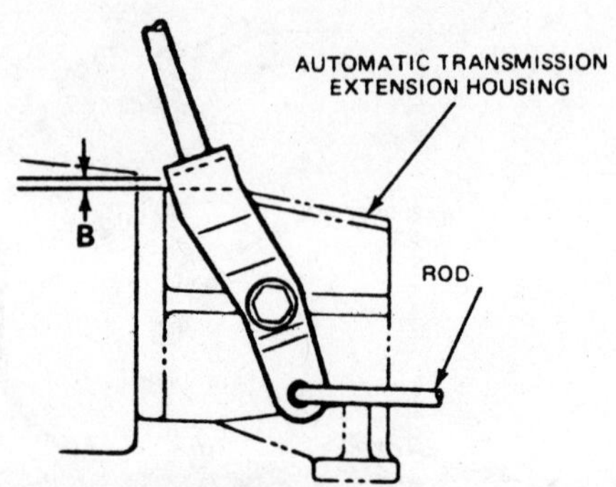

VIEW IN DIRECTION OF ARROW

ADJUSTMENT (AUTOMATIC TRANSMISSION)

TRANSFER CASE MUST BE IN 4 WHEEL LOW (CROSS LINK ASSEMBLY ALL THE WAY IN)

DIMENSION "B" MUST BE .64/.60

ADJUST ROD (7B051) TO CORRECT LENGTH AND TIGHTEN LOCK NUT AT CLEVIS

Installation of the New Process model 205 transfer case showing the adjustment of the shift linkage with an automatic transmission

8. Install new adjusting stud nuts and tighten them to 20–25 ft. lbs.
9. Connect the front driveshaft.

1975–76 F-250

1. Move the transfer case shifter to the Low position.
2. Loosen the adjusting stud nuts.
3. Unsnap the top splash boot snap and peel the boot back. Install a new adjustment pin in the rear of the shifter bracket. The pin is the same size as previously mentioned for the F-100 and F-150. If the pin is made of steel, it must be removed after tightening the adjusting studs.
4. Move the lower lever on the transfer case completely forward and the upper lever completely rearward.
5. Install new adjusting nuts and tighten them to 15–20 ft. lbs.

1977–82

1. Place the shift in the neutral position.
2. Remove the two adjusting stud nuts.
3. Install a 0.025 inch diameter alignment pin (1.25 inches) long through the shifter assembly.
4. Align the bottom transfer case lever (Lock lever) by rotating clockwise to the forward position.
5. Align the top transfer case lever (Range lever) by placing in the middle or neutral position.
6. Re-position the two shift rods and tighten the adjusting stud nuts to 15–20 ft. lbs.
7. Remove the alignment pin from the shifter assembly.

Drive Train

7

DRIVELINE

Driveshaft

REMOVAL AND INSTALLATION

4WD

1. To remove the rear driveshaft, disconnect the double Cardan joint from the flange at the transfer case and the single U-joint from the flange at the rear axle. Remove the driveshaft.

2. To remove the front driveshaft, disconnect the double Cardan joint from the flange at the transfer case and the single U-joint from the front axle. Remove the driveshaft.

3. Installation is the reverse of removal. Torque driveshaft-to-transfer case bolts to 20–25 ft. lbs.; driveshaft to axle bolts to 8–15 ft. lb.

Driveshaft and U-Joints

REMOVAL AND INSTALLATION

2WD

1. Unscrew the nuts attaching the U-bolts to the flange at the rear axle. Remove the U-bolts and allow the rear of the driveshaft to drop down. Slide the front of the driveshaft out of the rear of the transmission, transfer case, or the center support bearing. Remove the driveshaft from the vehicle.

2. On those vehicles equipped with two driveshafts and a center support bearing, unscrew the attaching bolts holding the center support bearing to the frame. If equipped with a sliding yoke at the transmission, slide the coupling shaft out of the rear of the extension housing. Otherwise, remove the nuts from the U-bolts holding the front of the coupling shaft to the flange on the rear of the transmission while supporting the center bearing. Remove the U-bolts from the front flange and remove the coupling shaft assembly together with the center support bearing.

3. Install the driveshaft(s) in the reverse order of removal.

NOTE: *All U-joints on two-piece driveshafts must be on the same horizontal plane when installed.*

U-JOINT OVERHAUL

1. Remove the driveshaft from the vehicle and place it in a vise, being careful not to damage it.

2. Remove the snap-rings which retain the bearings in the flange and in the driveshaft.

3. Remove the driveshaft tube from the vise and position the U-joint in the vise with a socket smaller than the bearing cap on one side and a socket larger than the bearing cap on the other side.

4. Slowly tighten the jaws of the vise so that the smaller socket forces the U joint spider and the opposite bearing into the larger socket.

5. Remove the other side of the spider in the same manner (if applicable) and remove the spider assembly from the driveshaft. Discard the spider assemblies.

6. Clean all foreign matter from the yoke areas at the end of the driveshaft(s).

7. Start the new spider and one of the bearing cap assemblies into a yoke by position ing the yoke in a vise with the spider positioned in place with one of the bearing cap assemblies positioned over one of the holes in the yoke. Slowly close the vise, pressing the bearing cap assembly in the yoke. Press the cap in far enough so that the retaining snap-ring can be installed. Use the smaller socket to recess the bearing cap.

8. Open the vise and position the opposite bearing cap assembly over the proper hole in the yoke with the socket that is smaller than the diameter of the bearing cap located on the cap. Slowly close the vise, pressing the bearing

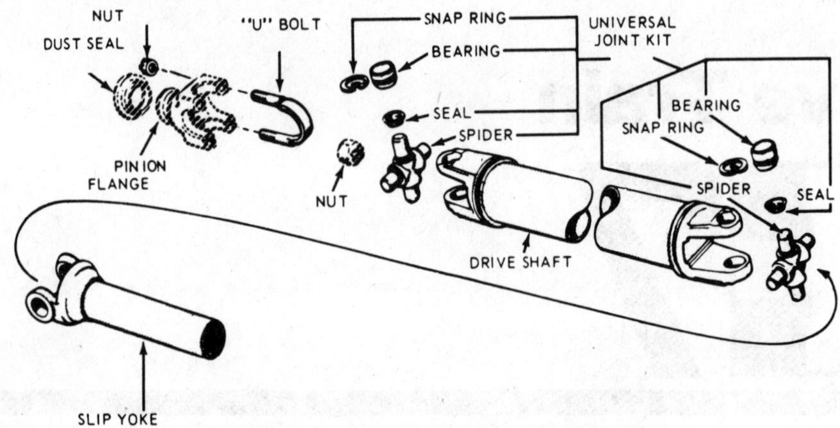

One-piece driveshaft with a slip yoke

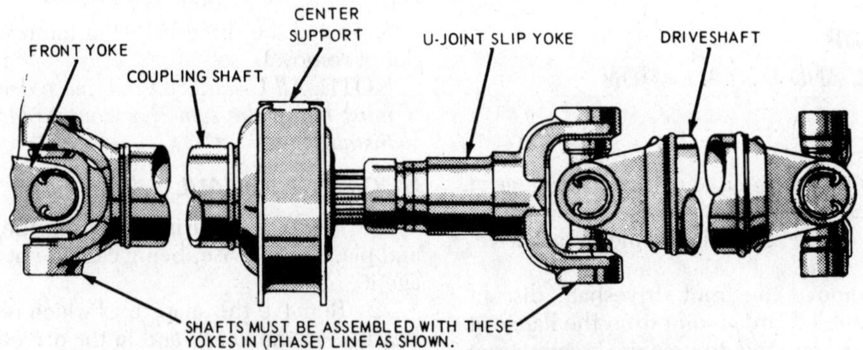

Two-piece driveshaft with a slip yoke at the transmission end

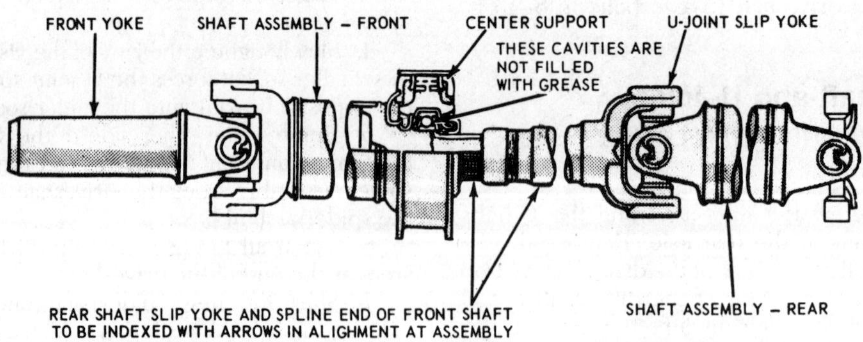

Two-piece driveshaft with a fixed yoke at the transmission end

cap into the hole in the yoke with the socket. Make sure that the spider assembly is in line with the bearing cap as it is pressed in. Press the bearing cap in far enough so that the retaining snap-ring can be installed.

9. Install all remaining U-joints in the same manner.

10. Install the driveshaft and grease the new U-joints.

CENTER BEARING REMOVAL AND INSTALLATION

1. Remove the driveshafts.
2. Remove the two center support bearing attaching bolts and remove the assembly from the vehicle.
3. Do not immerse the sealed bearing in any type of cleaning fluid. Wipe the bearing and

cushion clean with a cloth dampened with cleaning fluid.

4. Check the bearing for wear or rough action by rotating the inner race while holding the outer race. If wear or roughness is evident, replace the bearing.

Examine the rubber cushion for evidence of hardening, cracking, or deterioration. Replace it if it is damaged in any way.

5. Place the bearing in the rubber support and the rubber support in the U-shaped support and install the bearing in the reverse order of removal.

FRONT DRIVE AXLE

Identification

Axle identification and ratio can be determined from the I.D. tag located under one of the bolts on the differential carrier housing. See the drive axle section of the Capacities Chart in Chapter 1 for complete model application.

FREE-RUNNING HUB REMOVAL AND INSTALLATION

See Chapter 1 under "Wheel Bearings—4 x 4" for removal and installation procedures.

AXLE SHAFT REMOVAL AND INSTALLATION

F-100-150

1. Raise vehicle on a hoist.
2. Remove front hub grease cap. Remove driving hub retaining snap-ring, then slide splined driving hub from between axle shaft and wheel hub.
3. Remove driving hub spring.

NOTE. *If equipped with free-wheeling hubs, see hub removal.*

4. Remove lock nut, washer, and wheel bearing adjusting nut from spindle. Remove wheel, hub and drum as an assembly. The wheel outer bearing will be forced off the spindle at the same time. Remove wheel inner bearing cone.
5. Remove capscrews that attach brake backing plate and spindle to steering knuckle. Remove brake backing plate and secure it to one side. Carefully remove the spindle.
6. Pull shaft assembly from axle housing, working universal joint through bore in steering knuckle.
7. To install reverse the removal procedure.

F-250 1971–75

1. Raise the vehicle and support it with jackstands placed under the frame side rails.
2. Remove the front wheel free-running hub. Remove the hub and brake drum.
3. Place a drain pan under the steering knuckle assembly.
4. Remove the capscrews which hold the brake backing plate and spindle to the steering knuckle. Remove the backing plate and spindle. Support the brake backing plate with a piece of wire so that the tension is removed from the brake fluid hose.
5. Slide the axle shaft out through the opening in the steering knuckle.
6. Installation is the reverse of removal.

F-250-350 1976–79

1. Raise and support the front of the truck.
2. Remove the wheel.
3. Remove the caliper from the rotor and suspend it from the frame.
4. Remove the dust cap, cotter pin, nut, washer and outer bearing and remove the rotor from the spindle.
5. Remove the inner bearing cone and seal.
6. Remove the axle shaft, working the U-joint through the bore of the steering knuckle. Be careful not to damage the seal.
7. Installation is the reverse of removal.

F-150, F-250, F-350 1980 and Later

1. Remove the axle shaft assembly as described in Front Wheel Spindle Removal and Installation located in Chapter 8. Remove the axle bearing as follows:
2. Remove the stub assembly by removing the three bolts attaching the retainer plate to the carrier housing.
3. Place the axle shaft in a vise and drill a ¼" hole in the outside of the bearing retaining ring to a depth of ¾ of the thickness of the ring.
4. Place a chisel across the hole and strike sharply with a hammer to remove the retaining ring. ,Replace the bearing retaining ring upon assembly.
5. Press the bearing from the axle shaft using special tools Axle Bearing Remover No. T80T-4000M and Sleeve No. T80T-4000L.
6. Remove the seal and retainer plate from the stub shaft.
7. To install place the new seal and retainer plate on the shaft.
8. Place the bearing on the shaft with the large radius on the inner race facing the yoke end of the shaft.
9. Press the bearing onto the shaft using an Axle Bearing Replacer No. T80T-4000-N and a Pinion Bearing Cone Remover No. T71P-4621-B. A 0.0015 inch feeler gauge should not fit between the bearing seat and the bearing.
10. Using the same special tools in step 9 press the bearing retainer ring onto the stub

shaft. A 0.0015 inch feeler gauge should not fit between the ring and the bearing. There must be one point between the bearing and the ring where the feeler gauge cannot enter. If the feeler gauge enters completely around the circumferences press the retainer further onto the shaft.

11. Push the seal and retainer plate away from the bearing to form a space between the seal and the bearing. Fill the space with the proper bearing grease and wrap tape around the space.

12. Pull the seal towards the bearing until it contacts the inner race and forces the grease between the rollers and cup. Remove the tape.

13. Install the stub shaft in the carrier and install the three retainer bolts. Tighten to 35 ft. lbs.

14. Install the right hand axle shaft assembly into the slip yoke.

15. Install the spindle as described in Chapter 8.

Axle Shaft Bearing—Models with Dana 44IFS, 44IFS-HD, or 50IFS Axles

This procedure requires the use of special tools.

Removal

1. Remove the axle shaft assembly as described in this part under Axle Shaft and Steering Knuckle.

2. Remove the stub assembly by removing 3 bolts attaching retainer plate to carrier housing.

3. Place the axle shaft in a vise and drill a 6.35 mm (¼ inch) hole in the outside of the Bearing retaining ring to a depth ¾ the thickness of the ring.

NOTE: *Do not drill through the ring because this will damage the axle shaft.*

4. With a chisel placed across the hole, strike sharply with a hammer to remove the retaining ring. Replace bearing retaining ring upon assembly.

5. Press the bearing from the axle shaft with the special tools T80 axle bearing remover T80T-4000-M and sleeve T80T-4000-L.

NOTE: *Do not use a torch to aid in bearing removal or the stub shaft will be damaged.*

6. Remove the seal and retainer plate from the stub shaft. Discard seal and replace with new seal upon assembly.

Installation

1. Inspect the retainer plate and stub shaft for distortion, nicks or burrs. Replace if necessary.

2. Install retainer plate and new seal on shaft. Coat oil seal with ESA-M175B or equivalent.

3. Place the bearing on the shaft. The large radius on the inner race must face the yoke end of the shaft.

4. Use axle bearing replacer T80T-4000-N and pinion bearing cone remover T71P-4621-B to press the bearing onto the shaft until completely seated. A 0.038 mm (0.0015 inch) feeler gauge should not fit between the bearing seat and bearing.

5. Use axle bearing replacer T80T-4000-N and pinion bearing cone remover T71P-4621-B to press the bearing retainer ring onto the stub shaft. Press the bearing retainer ring until completely seated. A 0.038 mm (0.0015 inch) feeler gauge should not fit between the ring and bearing. There must be one point between the bearing and ring where the feeler gauge cannot enter. If feeler gauge enters completely around the circumference press the retainer further onto the shaft.

6. Push the seal and retainer plate away from the bearing to form a space between the seal and bearing. Fill the space with wheel bearing grease meeting Ford specification ESA-MIC75B or equivalent.

7. With the space filled with grease, wrap tape around the space.

8. Pull the seal towards the bearing until it contacts the inner race. This will force grease between the rollers and cup. Remove tape.

NOTE: *If grease is not visible on the small end of the rollers, repeat steps 6 through 8 until grease is visible. Install the slip yoke and U-joint to stub shaft.*

8. Install the stub shaft in the carrier and install 3 retainer bolts. Torque to 30–40 ft. lbs. Install right hand axle shaft assembly into slip yoke.

10. Install splash shield and spindle.

AXLE SHAFT U-JOINT OVERHAUL

Follow the procedures outlined under Axle Shaft Removal and Installation to gain access to the U-joints. Overhaul them as described under U-Joints.

BALL JOINT REPLACEMENT

NOTE: *A combination ball joint puller/press and a special spanner wrench are needed for this job. If these aren't available the job should not be attempted.*

1. Follow the procedures under Axle Shaft Removal.

2. Disconnect the connecting rod end from the knuckle.

3. Remove the cotter pin from the upper ball socket and loosen the upper and lower ball socket nuts. Discard the nut from the lower ball socket after the knuckle breaks loose from the yoke.

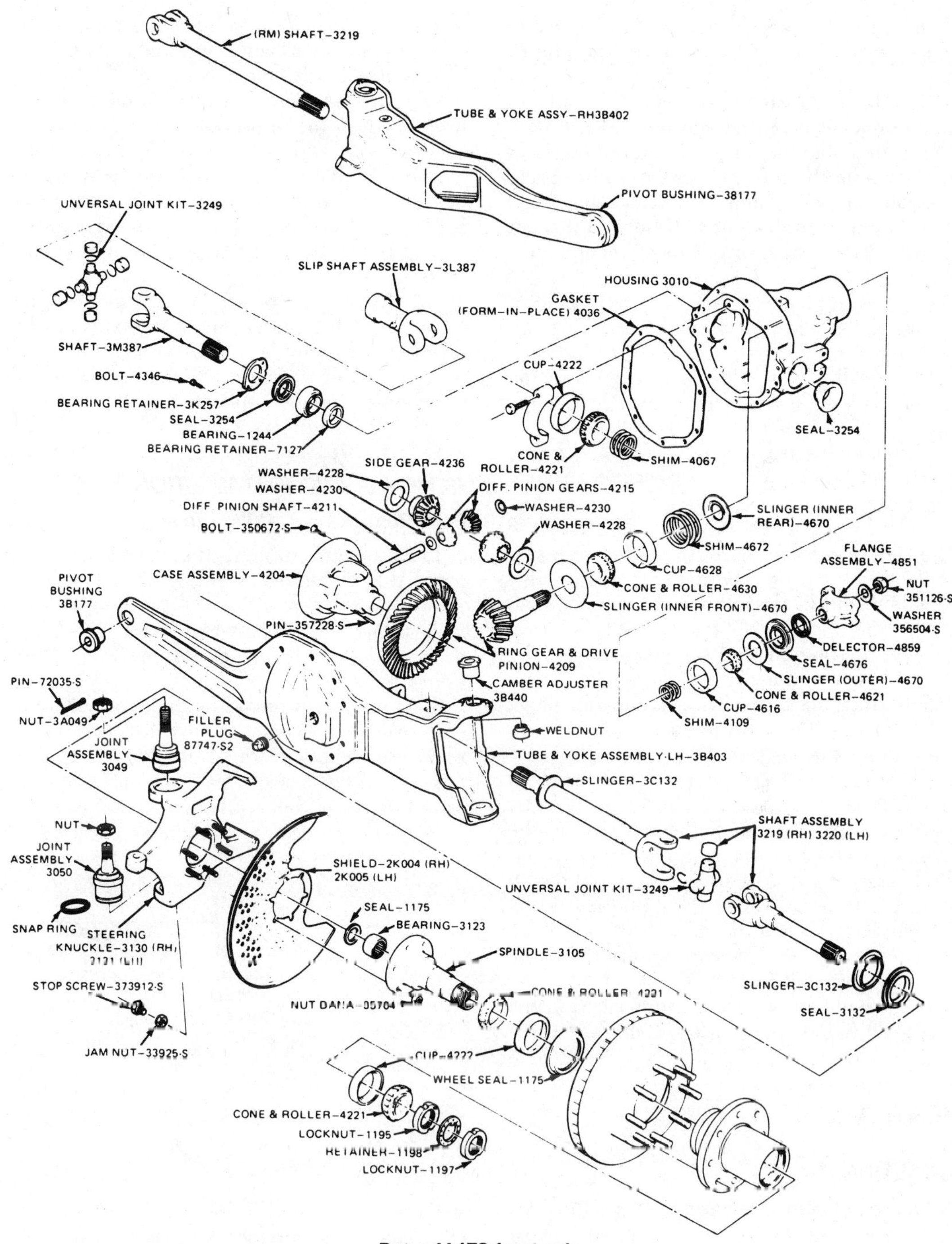

Dana 44-IFS front axle

4. Remove the knuckle from the yoke. If the upper socket remains in the yoke, remove it by hitting the top of the stud with a soft-faced hammer. Discard the socket and adjusting sleeve.

5. Remove the bottom socket with a ball joint puller (available at most auto parts stores) after first removing the snap ring.

For installation:

6. Place the knuckle in a vise and assemble the bottom socket. Place the new socket into the knuckle making sure it isn't cocked, place the driver over the socket, place the forcing screw into the socket and force the socket into the knuckle.

7. Make sure that the socket shoulder is

seated against the knuckle. Use a .0015 in. feeler gauge between the socket seat and the knuckle.

8. The gauge should not enter the area of minimum contact. Install the snap ring.

9. Assemble the top socket into the knuckle. Assemble the holding plate onto the backing plate screw. Tighten the nuts snugly. Place a new socket into the knuckle. Be sure it is not cocked. Place a driver over the socket and force the socket assembly into the knuckle. Using a .0015 in. gauge, check the fit at the shoulder. The gauge should not enter the area of minimum wrench.

10. Install a new adjusting sleeve into the top of the yoke leaving about two threads exposed.

11. Assemble the knuckle and yoke. Install a new nut on the bottom socket and make it finger tight.

12. Place a wrench and step plate over the adjusting sleeve and install the puller so that it grasps the step plate. Tighten the forcing screw to pull the knuckle assembly into the yoke. With torque still applied, tighten the nut to 70–90 ft. lb. If the bottom stud should turn with the nut, add more torque to the puller forcing screw. Remove the puller, step plate and holding plate.

13. Tighten the adjusting sleeve to 40 ft. lb. and remove the wrench.

14. Install the top socket nut and torque it to 100 ft. lb. Line up the cotter pin hole by tightening, *not loosening*, the nut. Install the cotter pin and test the steering effort with a spring scale attached to the knuckle. Pull should not exceed 26 ft. lb. If it does, the ball joints will have to be replaced.

15. Connect the steering linkage to the knuckle. Torque it to 40 ft. lb.

16. Install the axle shaft as described in the Axle Shaft Removal and Installation procedure.

REAR AXLE

Identification

Two types of rear axles are used on Ford F-100, F-150, 250 and F-350 pick-ups: the Dana integral carrier full-floating rear axle used on all three models; and the Ford removable carrier semi-floating rear axle used on F-100 and F-150 models.

On a full-floating rear axle, the weight of the vehicle is supported by the axle housing. The axle shafts can be removed without disturbing the wheel bearings. On a semi-floating axle, the outboard end of the axle shaft is supported by the bearing which is mounted in a recess in the end of the axle housing.

The axle shaft on a full-floating rear axle is held in place by a flange and bolts attaching it to the hub on the outboard side. The hub is held to the rear spindle by nuts which are also used to adjust the preload of the rear axle bearings.

The axle shaft on a semi-floating rear axle is held in position by a bearing retainer plate and the bearing assembly which is pressed onto the outer ends of the axle shaft and set in the outer ends of the axle housing.

Axle Identification and Ratio are found on an I.D. tag located under one of the bolts on the differential housing. Also refer to the Drive Axle Section of the Capacities Chart in Chapter 1 for complete model application.

Axle Shaft

REMOVAL AND INSTALLATION

Ford Removable Carrier Type

1. Raise and support the vehicle and remove the wheel/tire assembly from the brake drum.

2. Remove the nuts which secure the brake drum to the axle flange, then remove the drum from the flange.

3. Working through the hole provided in each axle shaft flange, remove the nuts which secure the wheel bearing retainer plate.

4. Using an axle puller, pull the axle shaft assembly out of the axle housing.

NOTE: *The brake backing plate must not be*

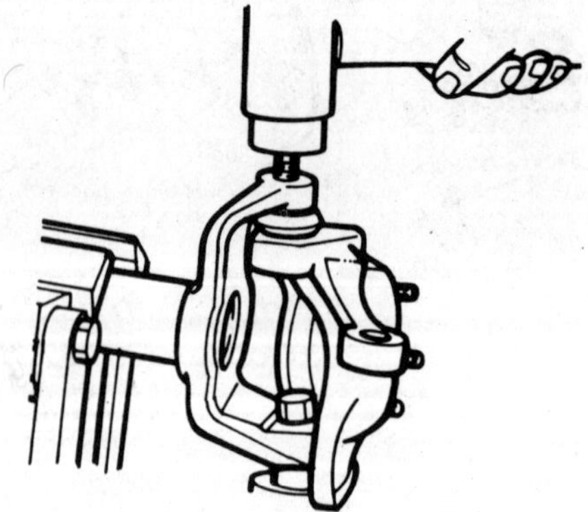

Four-wheel drive steering knuckle removal

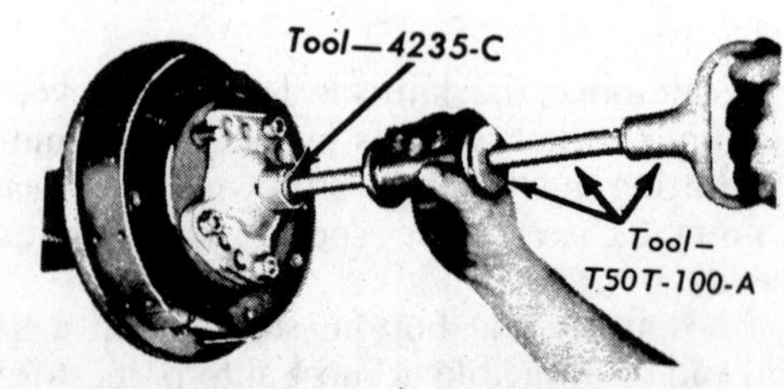

Removing the axle shaft with a puller

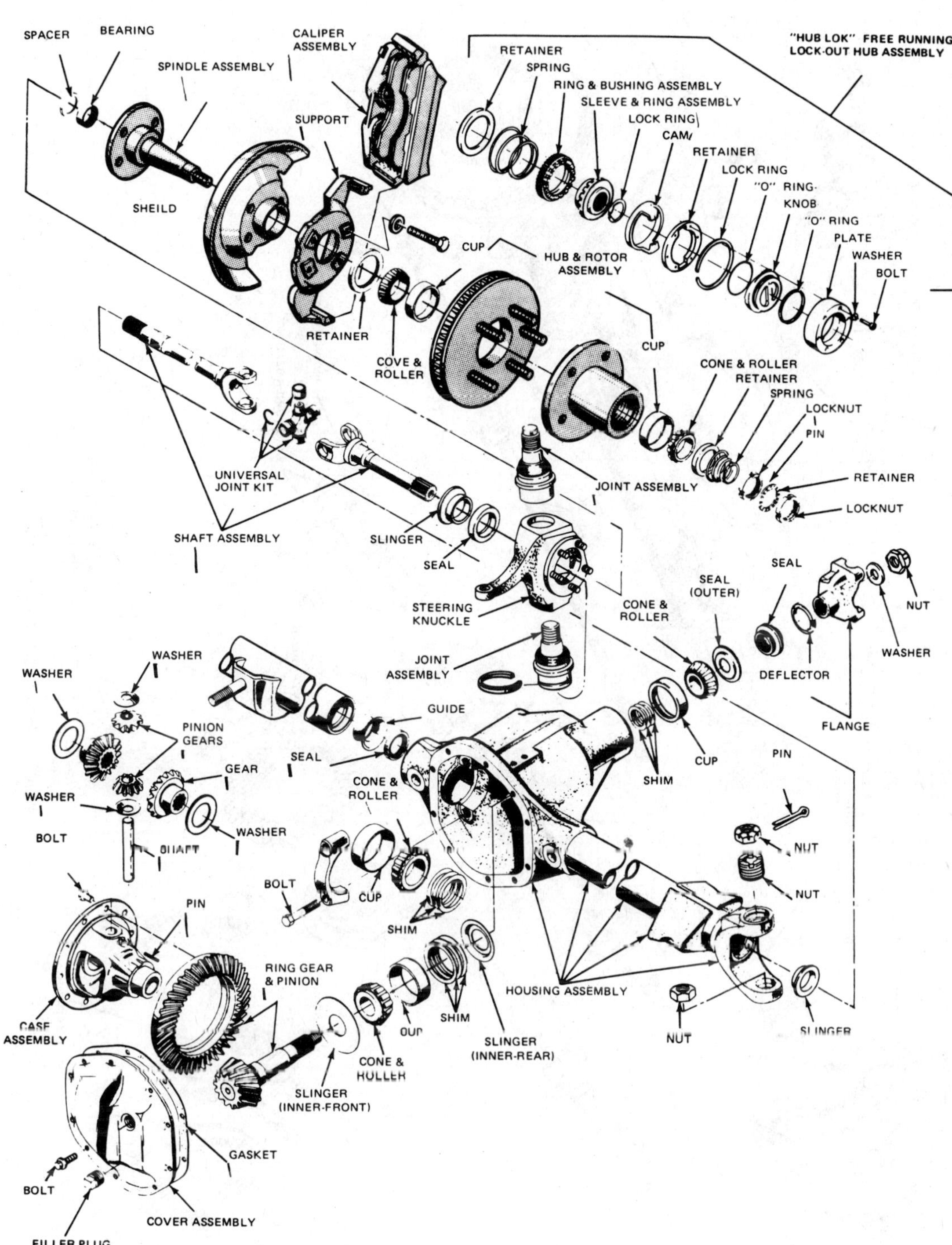

Dana 44F and 44-7F front drive axle—exploded view

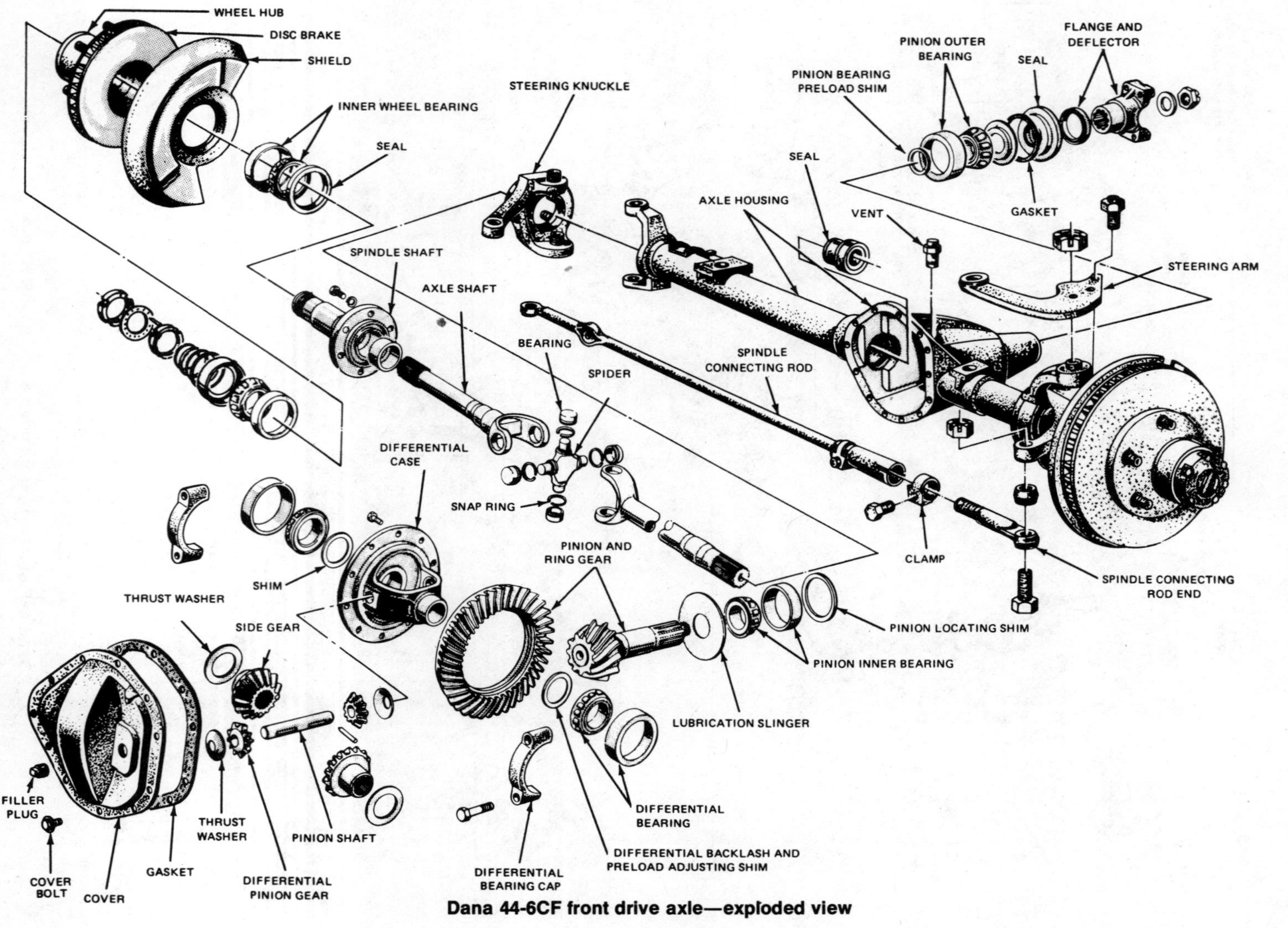

Dana 44-6CF front drive axle—exploded view

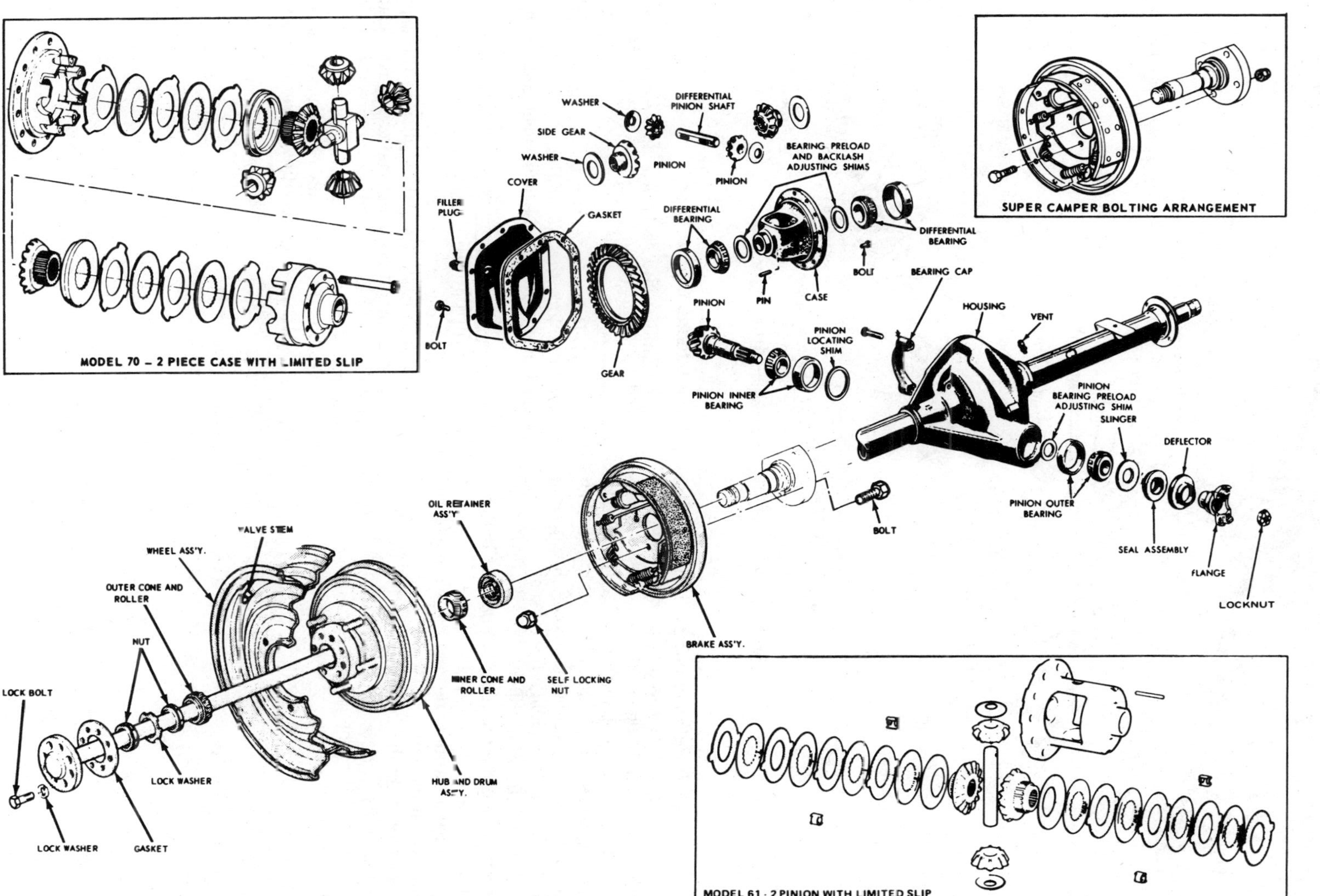

Exploded view of a Dana integral carrier type axle

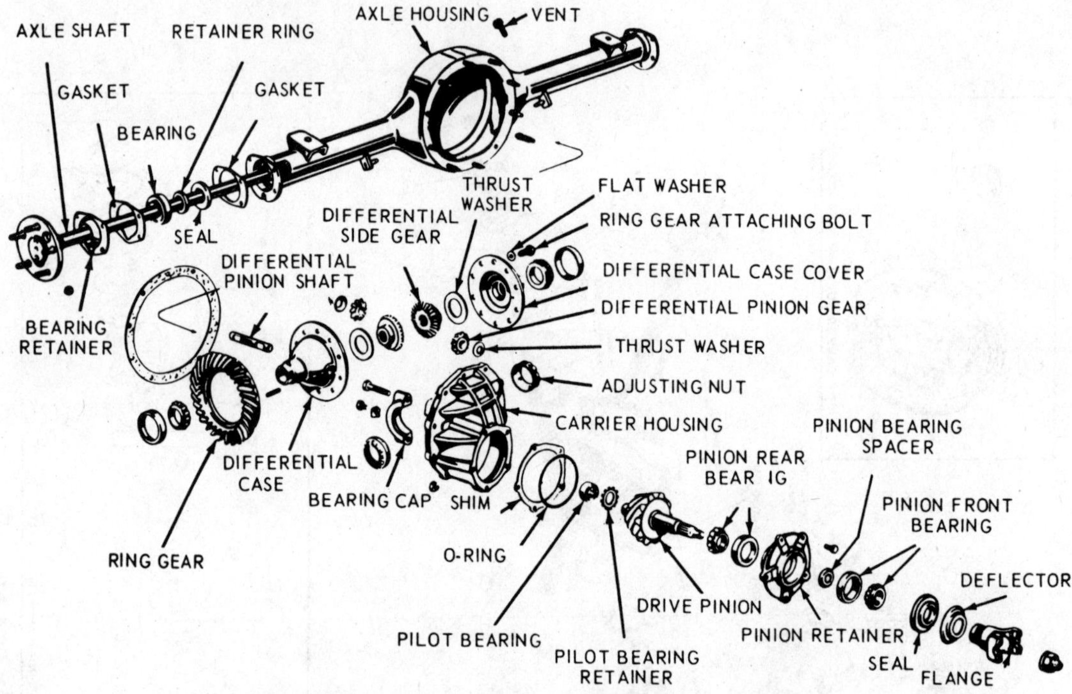

Exploded view of a Ford removable-carrier type axle

dislodged. Install one nut to hold the plate in place after the axle shaft is removed.

To replace the axle shaft:

5. Remove the one nut which holds the brake backing plate and carefully slide the axle shaft into the housing, so that the rough forgings on the shaft will not damage the oil seal.
6. Start the axle splines into the side gear and push the shaft in until the bearing bottoms in the housing.
7. Install the bearing retainer plate and the nuts which secure it.
8. Install the brake drum and the drum attaching nuts.
9. Install the wheel/tire assembly and lower the vehicle.

Dana Integral Carrier Type

1. Remove the lockbolts and lockwashers which hold the axle flange to the hub and drum assembly.

NOTE: *It is not necessary to raise the vehicle to remove the axle shafts.*

2. Carefully slide the axle shaft out of the axle housing.
3. Clean the mating surfaces of the axle flange and the hub and drum assembly.
4. Position a new gasket on the axle flange and carefully slide the axle shaft into the axle housing. When the splined end of the axle shaft reaches the side gear, gently rotate the shaft until it is inserted into the side gear.
5. Position the gasket between the axle flange and the hub and drum and install the lockbolts and lockwashers.

Suspension and Steering

8

FRONT SUSPENSION

Trucks with 2WD use two I-beam type front axles; one for each wheel. One end of each axle is attached to the spindle and a radius arm, and the other end is attached to a frame pivot bracket on the opposite side of the truck.

The suspension of an F-100 and F-150 4WD consists of a driving axle attached to the frame with two coil springs, two radius arms, and a track bar.

The front suspension on an F-250 and 350 4WD consists of a driving axle attached to the frame with two semi-elliptic leaf springs. Each spring is clamped to the axle with two U-bolts. The front of the spring rests in a front shackle bracket and the rear is attached to a frame bracket.

Springs

REMOVAL AND INSTALLATION

2WD

1. Raise the front of the vehicle and place jackstands under the frame and a jack under the axle.
2. Disconnect the shock absorber from the lower bracket.
3. Remove one bolt and nut and remove the rebound bracket.
4. Remove the two spring upper retainer attaching bolts from the top of the spring upper seat and remove the retainer.
5. Remove the nut attaching the spring lower retainer to the lower seat and axle and remove the retainer.
6. Lower the axle and remove the spring.
7. Place the spring in position and raise the front axle.
8. Position the spring lower retainer over the stud and lower seat, and install the two attaching bolts.
9. Position the upper retainer over the spring coil and against the spring upper seat, and install the two attaching bolts.
10. Tighten the upper and lower retainer attaching nuts and bolts to 15–25 ft. lbs.
11. Connect the shock absorber to the lower bracket and install the rebound bracket.
12. Remove the jack and safety stands.

4WD—F-100, F-150 Thru 1979

1. Raise the vehicle until the tires are a few inches off the ground and place jackstands under the frame side rails. Position a hydraulic floor jack under the center of the front axle housing.
2. Remove the shock absorber-to-lower bracket attaching bolt and nut.
3. Remove the spring lower retainer attaching bolts from the inside of the spring coil.
4. Lower the axle enough to relieve tension from the spring.
5. Remove the spring upper retainer attaching bolts and nuts and remove the upper retainer.
6. Remove the spring, lower retainer and the lower seat from the front spring.
7. Position the upper retainer over the spring coil and loosely install the attaching bolts and nuts.
8. Position the spring lower seat, and the lower retainer to the frame spring pocket and the radius arm.
9. Raise the axle up into position and install the two lower retainer attaching bolts and tighten them.
10. Tighten the upper retainer attaching bolts.
11. Position the shock absorber to the lower bracket and install the attaching bolt and nut.
12. Remove the jack stands and lower the vehicle.

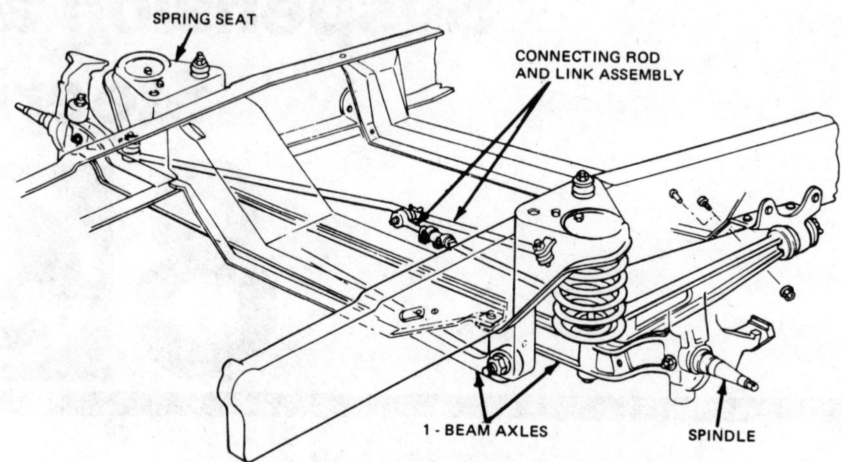

Twin I-beam suspension (forged axle shown)—2WD

4WD—F-250–F-350 Thru 1979

1. Raise the vehicle until the weight is off the front spring with the wheels still touching the floor.
2. Disconnect the lower end of the shock absorber from the axle. Remove the U-bolts and spacer.
3. Remove the nut from the shackle bolt retaining spring at the front and drive the shackle bolt out with a drift.
4. Remove the nuts and shackle bar at the rear shackle bracket. Drive out the two shackle bolts and remove the spring.
5. Position the spring on the spring seat cap and install the shackle bolts through the shackle bracket and spring.
6. Install the shackle bar and nuts on the shackle bolts and tighten them to 90–130 ft. lbs.
7. Position the front of the spring to allow the front shackle bolts to be installed. Tighten the nut to 90–130 ft. lbs.
8. Position the U-bolt spacer and place the U-bolts in position through the holes in the spring seat cap. Install the U-bolt nuts, but do not tighten them yet.
9. Connect the lower end of the shock absorber to the axle.
10. Lower the vehicle and tighten the U-bolt nuts to 100–135 ft. lbs.

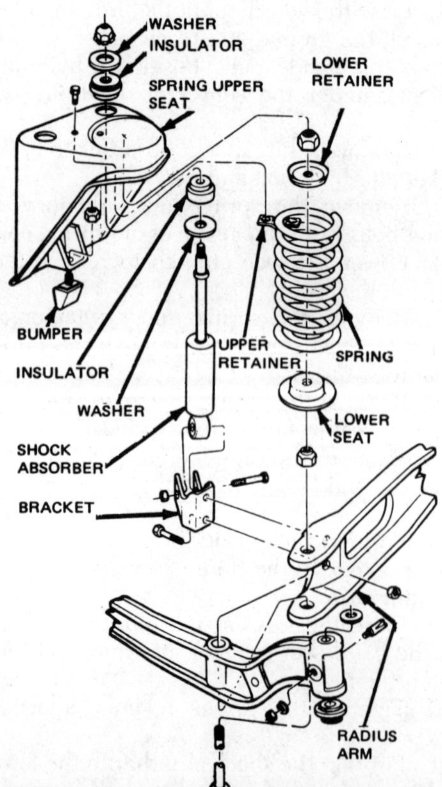

Exploded view of the front spring assembly and shock absorber for 2WD Ford pick-ups—typical

4WD—F-150 1980 and Later

1. Raise the vehicle and remove the shock absorber lower attaching bolt and nut.

NOTE: *Refer to Jacking and Hoisting in Chapter 1 for the proper lifting procedures.*

2. Remove the spring lower retainer nuts from inside of the spring coil.
3. Remove the upper spring retainer by removing the attaching screw.
4. Position safety stands under the frame side rails and lower the axle enough to relieve tension from the spring.

NOTE: *The axle must be supported on the jack throughout spring removal, and must not be permitted to hang from the brake hose. If the length of the brake hose does not provide sufficient clearance it may be necessary to remove and support the brake caliper.*

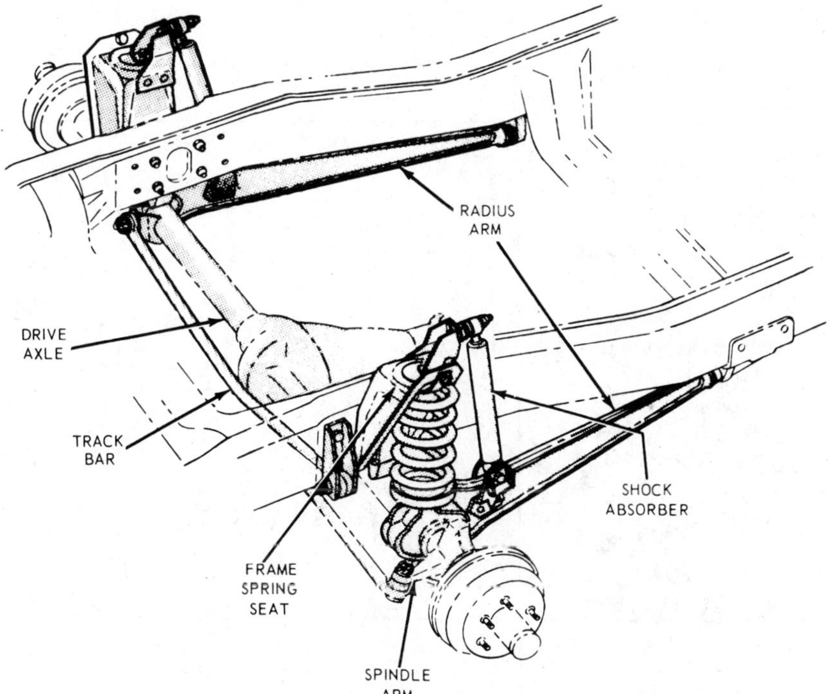

Front suspension—F-100–150 4WD thru 1979

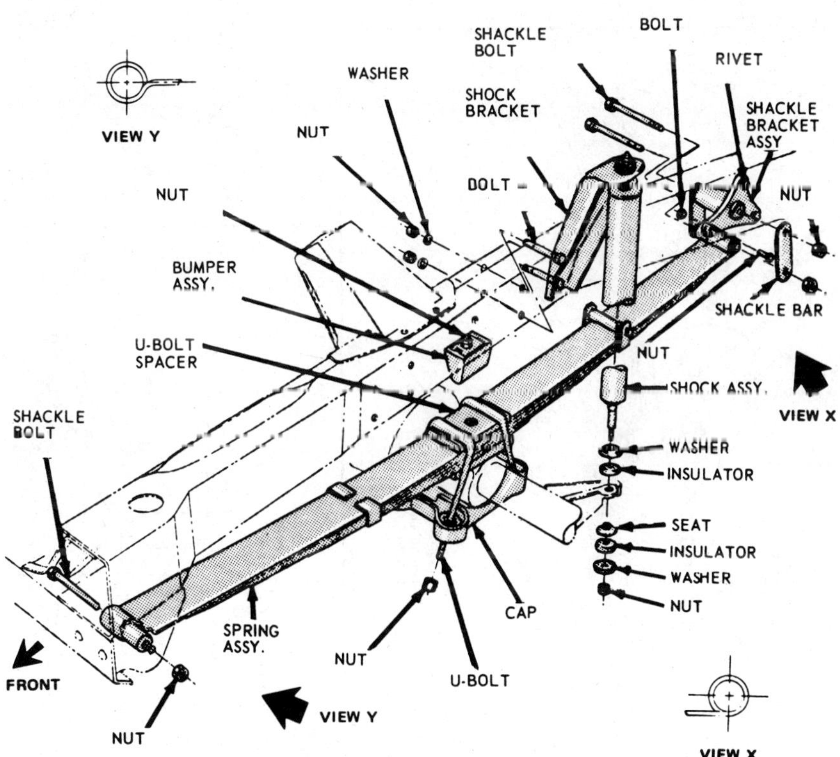

Front suspension—F-250–350 4WD thru 1979

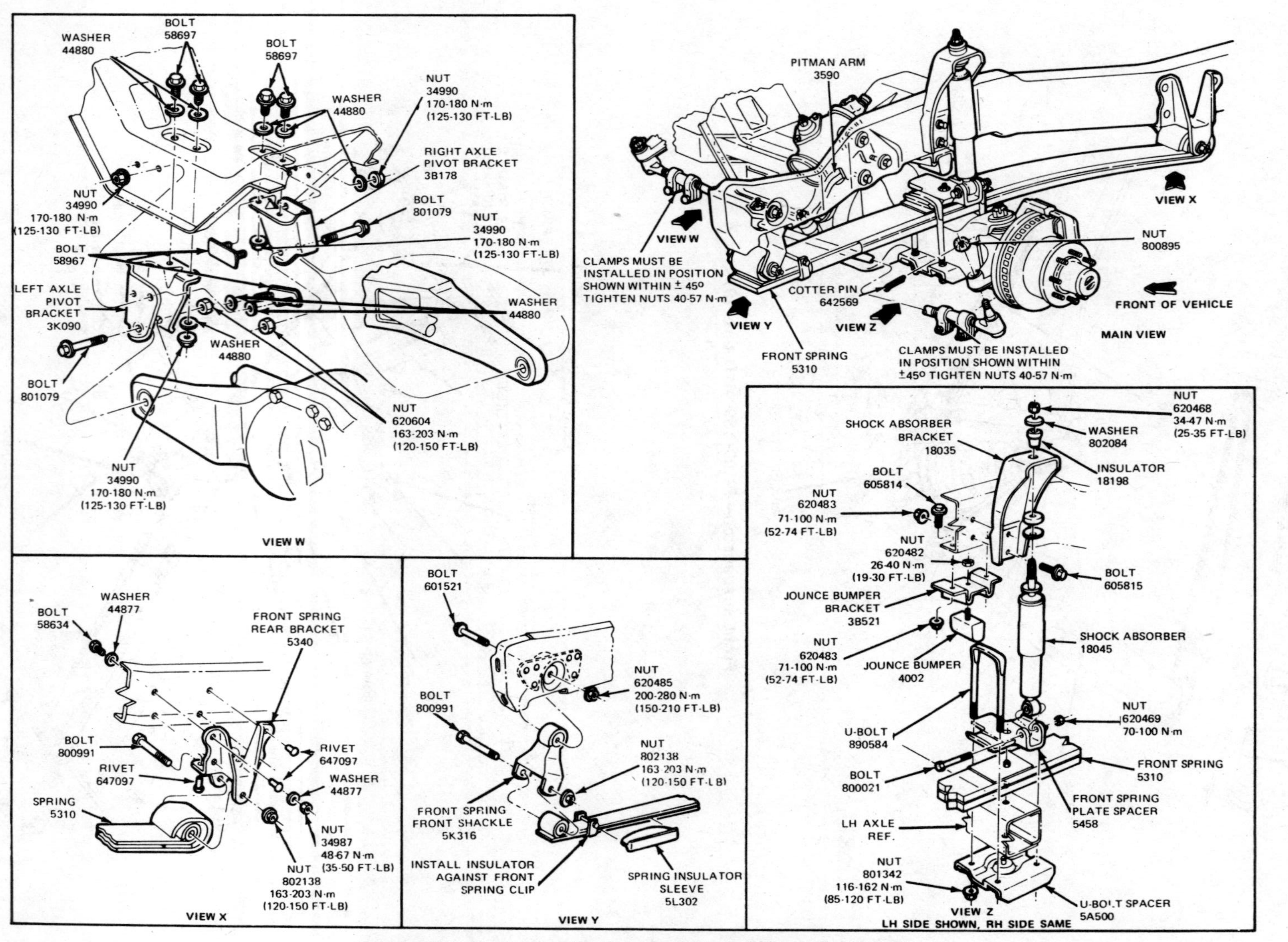

1980 and later leaf spring front suspension, F-250/F-350 with 4WD

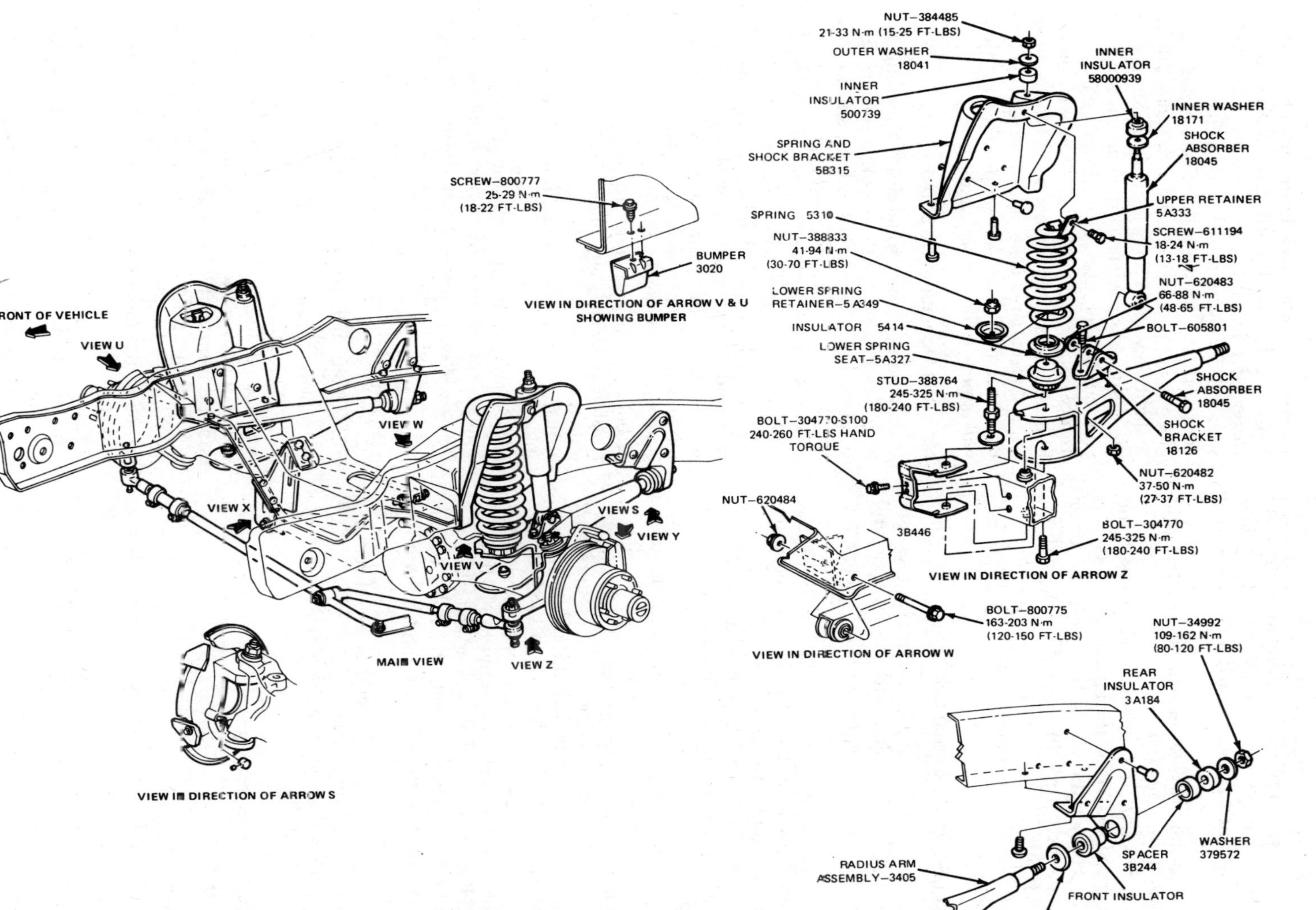

1980 and later F-150 4×4 front suspension

5. Remove the spring lower retainer and lower the spring from the vehicle.

6. To install place the spring in position and slowly raise the front axle. Make sure the springs are positioned correctly in the upper spring seats.

7. Install the lower spring retainer and torque the nut to 50 ft. lbs.

8. Position the upper retainer over the spring coil and install the attaching screws.

9. Position the shock absorber to the lower bracket and torque the attaching bolt and nut to 53 ft. lbs.

10. Remove the safety stands and lower the vehicle.

4WD—F-250, F350 1980 and Later

1. Raise the vehicle frame until the weight is off the front spring with the wheels still touching the floor. Support the axle to prevent rotation.

2. Disconnect the lower end of the shock absorber from the U-bolt spacer. Remove the U-bolts, U-bolt cap and spacer.

3. Remove the nut from the hanger bolt retaining the spring at the rear and drive out the hanger bolt.

4. Remove the nut connecting the front shackle and spring eye and drive out the shackle bolt and remove the spring.

5. To install position the spring on the spring seat. Install the shackle bolt through the shackle and spring. Torque the nuts to 135 ft. lbs.

6. Position the rear of the spring and install the hanger bolt. Torque the nut to 175 ft. lbs.

7. Position the U-bolt spacer and place the U-bolts in position through the holes in the spring seat cap. Install but do not tighten the U-bolt nuts.

8. Connect the lower end of the shock absorber to the U-bolt spacer.

9. Lower the vehicle and tighten the U-bolt nuts to 100 ft. lbs.

Shock Absorbers

TESTING

Bounce Test

Each shock absorber can be tested by bouncing the corner of the truck until maximum up and down movement is obtained. Let go of the truck. It should stop bouncing in 1–2 bounces. If not, the shock should be inspected for damage and possibly replaced.

Inspect the Shock Mounts

Check the shock mountings for worn or defective grommets, loose mounting nuts, interference or missing bump stops. If no apparent defects are noted, continue testing.

Inspecting Shocks for Leaks

Disconnect each shock lower mount and pull down on the shock until it is fully extended. Inspect for leaks in the seal area. Shock absorber fluid is very thin and has a characteristic odor and dark brown color. Don't confuse the glossy paint on some shocks with leaking fluid. A slight trace of fluid is a normal condition; they are designed to seep a certain amount of fluid past the seals for lubrication. If you are in doubt as to whether the fluid on the shock is coming from the shock itself or from some other source, wipe the seal area clean and manually operate the shock (see the following procedure). Fluid will appear if the unit is leaking.

Manually Operating the Shocks

It may be necessary to fabricate a holding fixture for certain types of shock absorbers. If a suspected problem is in the front shocks, disconnect both front shock lower mountings.

NOTE: *When manually operating air shocks, the air line must be disconnected at the shock.*

Grip the lower end of the shock and pull down (rebound stroke) and then push up (compression stroke). The control arms will limit the movement of front shocks during the compression stroke. Compare the rebound resistance of both shocks and compare the compression resistance. Usually any shock showing a noticeable difference will be the one at fault.

If the shock has internal noises, extend the shock fully than exert an extra pull. If a small additional movement is felt, this usually means a loose piston and the shock should be replaced. Other noises that are cause for replacing shocks are a squeal after a full stroke in both directions, a clicking noise on fast reverse and a lag at reversal near mid-stroke.

REMOVAL AND INSTALLATION

To replace the front shock absorber, remove the self-locking nut, steel washer, and rubber bushings at the upper end of the shock absorber. Remove the bolt and nut at the lower end and remove the shock absorber.

When installing a new shock absorber, use new rubber bushings. Position the shock absorber on the mounting brackets with the stud end at the top.

Install the rubber bushing, steel washer and self-locking nut at the upper end, and the bolt and nut at the lower end. Tighten the upper end to 15–25 ft. lbs. and the lower end to 40–60 ft. lbs.

Twin I-Beam Front Suspension

NOTE: *Front drive axle procedures are found in Chapter 7.*

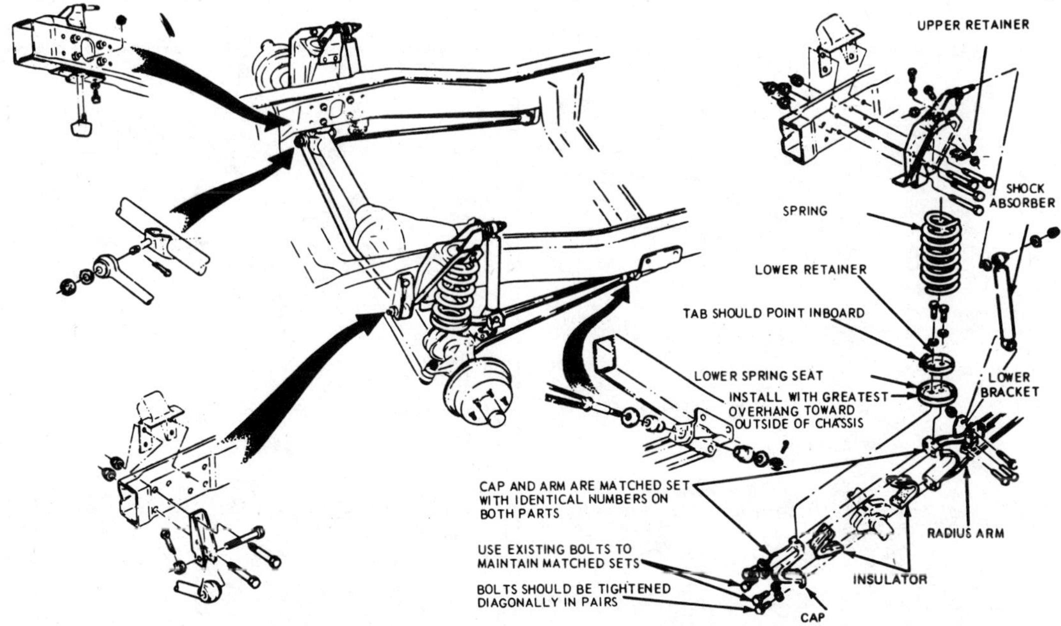

Exploded view of the front spring assembly and shock absorber—F-100–150 4WD—typical

Front Wheel Spindle 2WD

REMOVAL AND INSTALLATION

NOTE: *There are two basic types of front axle spindle mounting on the 2WD Ford pickups. Some later light-duty F-100 and F-150 models utilize a stamped I-beam; on these trucks the spindle assemblies are mounted on ball joints on the top and bottom of axle ends. On the heavier-duty F-250 and F-350 models, the front axles are forged; the spindles on these axles are attached via kingpins ("spindle bolts" in the text and illustrations).*

There are two basic ways to identify a kingpin system over a ball joint system. If the axle ends are solid steel with a true "I-beam" cross section, you have a kingpin system. The stamped axles are a much wider boxed-section towards their ends and are actually fabricated from stamped sheet steel. The second method of identification is by turning the wheels to full-lock in one direction. Inspect the inside of the spindle assembly where it attaches to the axle. You can see the kingpin running between the upper and lower spindle bushings the length of the spindle assembly, whereas the stamped axles have a ball joint on the top and bottom. See the accompanying illustrations.

F-250/F-350 with Forged I-Beam Axles (Kingpins)

1. Raise the front of the truck until the front wheel clears the ground and place jackstands under the frame.

2. Remove the wheel and tire, and remove the hub, brake drum, and wheel bearings as an assembly. Back off the brake adjustment, if necessary.

3. On a truck with drum brakes, remove the brake backing plate and spindle-to-spindle arm attaching bolt. Remove the spinddle arm and the brake backing plate from the spindle. Support the brake backing plate so as not to damage the hose.

4. On a truck with disc brakes, remove the caliper key retaining screw. Drive out the caliper support key and spring with brass drift and hammer. Remove the caliper from the spindle by pushing the caliper downward against the spindle assembly and rotating the upper end of the caliper upward and out of the spindle assembly. It is not necessary to disconnect the brake fluid hose. Wire the caliper to a suspension part to remove the weight of the caliper from the hose. Disconnect the steering linkage from the spindle arm.

5. Disconnect the steering linkage from the integral spindle and spindle arm.

6. Remove the nut and lockwasher from the locking pin, and remove the locking pin.

7. Remove the upper and lower spindle bolt plugs, and drive the spindle bolt out from the top of the axle. Remove the spindle and bearing. Knock out the seal.

8. Make sure that the spindle bolt hole in the axle is free of nicks, burrs, and dirt. Install a new seal and coat the spindle bolt bushings and bolt hole with oil.

9. Place the spindle in position on the axle.

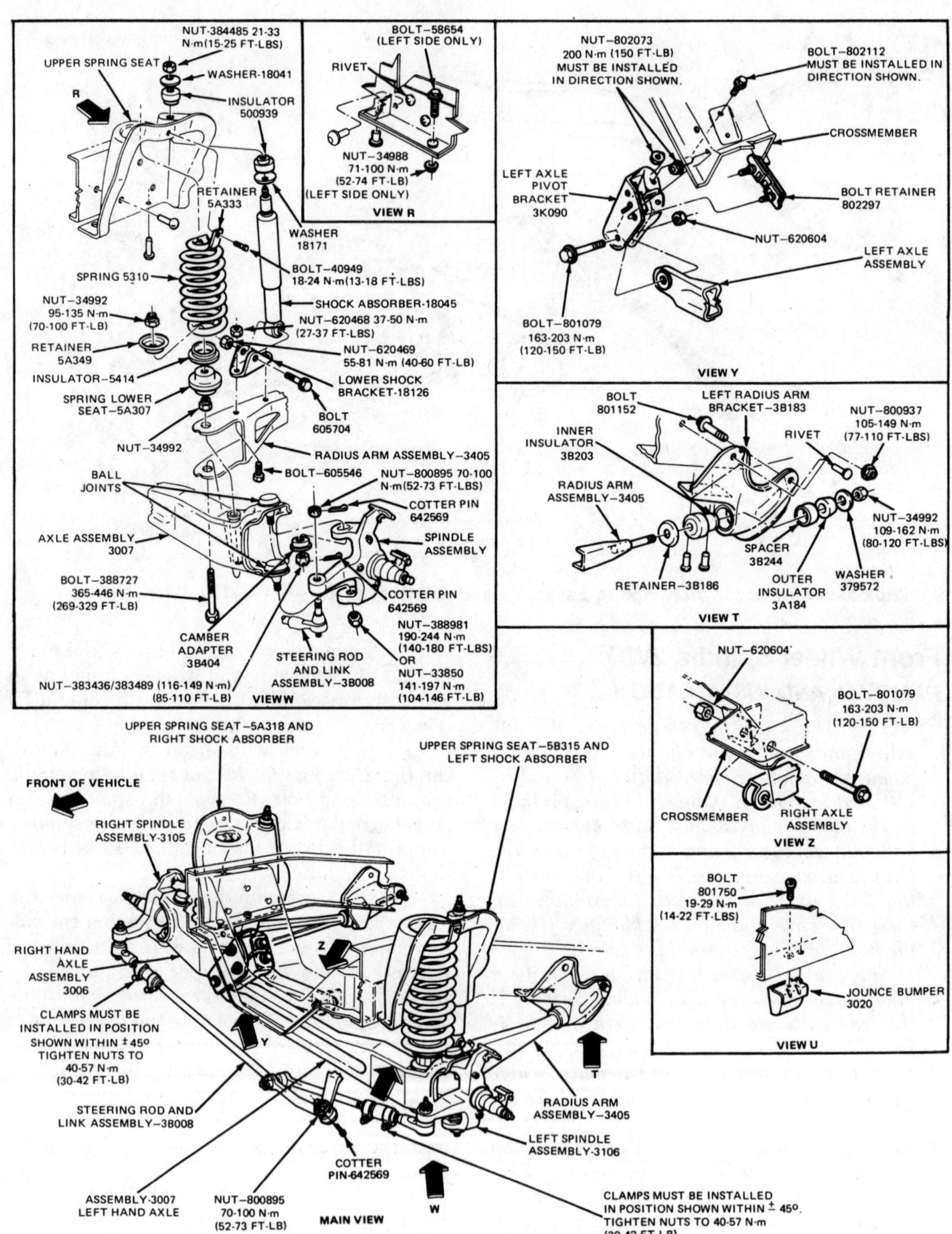

F-100/F-150 stamped front axle. View "W" shows ball joint spindle mounting

10. Pack the spindle thrust bearing with chassis lubricant and insert the bearing into the spindle with the open end of the bearing seal facing down into the spindle.

11. Install the spindle pin in the spindle with the locking pin notch in the spindle bolt aligned with the locking pin hole in the axle. Drive the spindle bolt through the axle from the top side until the spindle bolt locking pin notch is aligned with the locking pin hole in the axle.

12. Install a new locking pin. Install the locking pin lockwasher and nut. Tighten the nut to 40–55 ft. lbs. Install the spindle bolt plugs at the top and bottom of the spindle bolt.

13. On trucks with drum brakes, install the brake backing plate and spindle arm. Tighten

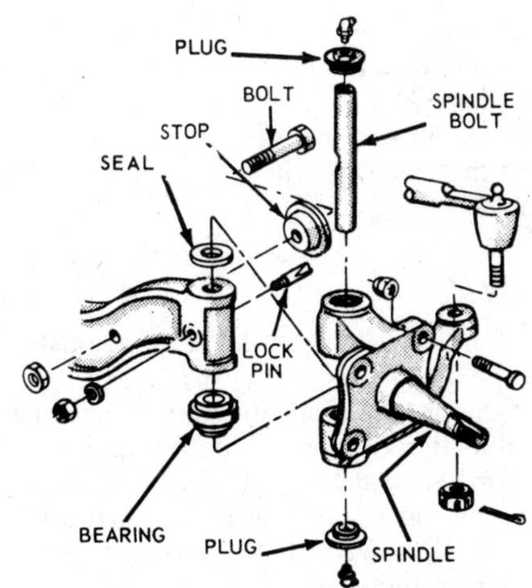

Spindle installation on heavy-duty 2WD F-250

the backing plate and spindle-to-spindle arm bolt and nut to 30–50 ft. lbs. Advance the castellated nut as required for installation of the cotter pin.

14. On trucks with disc brakes, position the caliper on the spindle assembly. Be careful to prevent tearing or cutting of the piston boot as the caliper is slipped over the inner brake pad. Use a screwdriver or brake adjusting tool to hold the upper machined surface of the caliper against the surface of the spindle. Install the caliper support spring and key. Drive the key and spring into position with a soft hammer. Install the key retaining screw and tighten it to 12–18 ft. lbs. Connect the steering linkage to the spindle and tighten the nut to 50–70 ft. lbs., advancing the nut as necessary to install the cotter pin.

15. Install the wheel, hub and drum assembly, and adjust the wheel bearing.

16. Grease the spindle assembly with a grease gun.

17. Check and adjust, if necessary, the toe-in adjustment.

F-100 and F-150 with Stamped Front Axle (Ball Joints)

1. Jack up the front of the truck and safely support it with jackstands.
2. Remove the wheel and tire assembly.
3. Remove the front brake caliper assembly and hold it out of the way with a piece of wire. *Do not disconnect the brake line.*
4. Remove the brake rotor from the spindle.
5. Remove the inner bearing cone and seal. Discard the seal, as you'll be fitting a new one during installation.
6. Remove the brake dust shield.

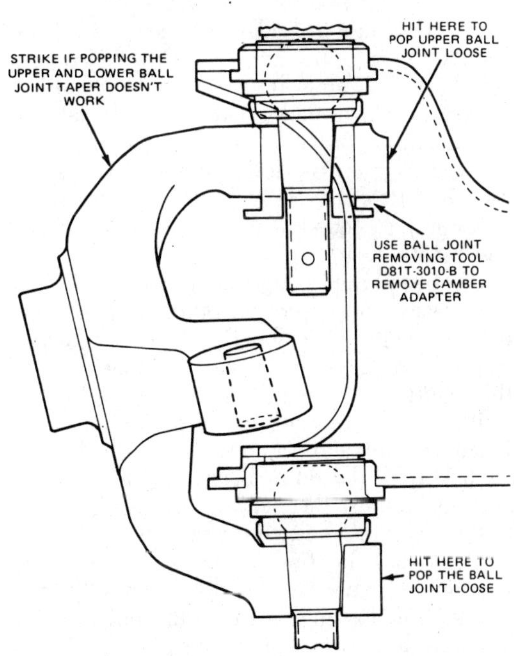

Spindle removal, 2WD F-100/F-150 with ball-joint type stamped front axles

7. Disconnect the steering linkage from the spindle arm using a tie-rod removal tool.
8. Remove the cotter pins and nuts from the upper and lower ball joint studs. Discard the cotter pins, as new ones should be installed during reassembly.
9. Strike the inside area or the spindle as shown in the illustration to pop the ball joints loose from the spindle.

CAUTION: *Do not use a forked ball joint removal tool to separate the ball joints as this will damage the seal and ball joint socket.*

10. Remove the spindle.
11. Before reassembly, note that new cotter pins should be used on the ball joints, and that new bearing seal(s) should also be used. Also, make sure the upper and lower ball joint seals are in place.
12. Place the spindle over the ball joints.
13. Install the nut on the lower ball joint stud and partially tighten to 30 ft. lbs. Turn the castellated nut until you are able to install the cotter pin.

NOTE: *If the lower ball stud turns while the nut is being tightened, push the spindle up against the ball stud.*

14. Install the camber adapter in the upper spindle over the upper ball joint stud. Be sure the adapter is aligned properly.

NOTE: *If camber adjustment is necessary, special adapters must be installed.*

15. Install the nut on the upper ball joint stud. Hold the camber adapter with a wrench to keep the ball stud from turning. If the ball

stud turns, tap the adapter deeper into the spindle. Tighten the nut to 85–110 ft. lbs. and continue tightening the castellated nut until it lines up with the hole in the stud. Install the cotter pin.

16. Retighten the lower nut to 104–146 ft. lbs. on F-100s with 4650 lb. GVW; tighten the lower nut to 140–180 ft. lbs. on other F-100 and F-150s.

17. Install the brake dust shield.

18. Pack the inner and outer bearing cone with a quality wheel bearing grease by hand, working the grease through the cage behind the rollers.

19. Install the inner bearing cone and seal. Install the hub and rotor on the spindle.

20. Install the outer bearing cone, washer, and nut. Adjust the bearing end-play and install the nut retainer, cotter pin and dust cap.

21. Install the brake caliper. Connect the steering linkage to the spindle. Tighten the nut to 52–73 ft. lbs. and advance the nut as far as you have to to install the cotter pin.

22. Install the wheel and tire assembly. Lower the truck and adjust toe-in if necessary.

Upper and Lower Ball Joints

INSPECTION

F-100 and F-150 (2WD) with Stamped Front Axles

1. Before any inspection of the ball joints, make sure the front wheel bearings are properly packed and adjusted.

2. Jack up the front of the truck and safely support it with jackstands, placing the stands under the I-beam axle beneath the spring as shown in the accompanying illustration.

3. Have a helper grab the lower edge of the tire and move the wheel assembly in and out.

4. While the wheel is being moved, observe the lower spindle arm and the lower part of the axle jaw (the end of the axle to which the spindle assembly attaches). If there is 1/32 in. or greater movement between the lower part of the axle jaw and the lower spindle arm, the lower ball joint must be replaced.

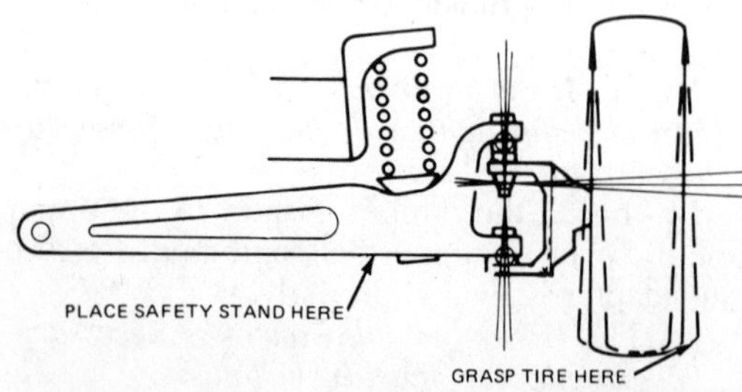

Check ball joint wear by pulling in and out on either the bottom of the tire (to check lower ball joints) or the top of the tire (to check the upper joints)

5. To check upper ball joints, grab the upper edge of the tire and move the wheel in and out. If there is 1/32 in. or greater movement between the upper spindle arm and the upper part of the axle jaw, the upper ball joint must be replaced.

REMOVAL

1. Remove the spindle as previously described.

2. Remove the snap-ring from the ball joints. Assemble the C-frame assembly and receiver cup (Ford special tool or equivalent shown in illustration) on upper ball joint. Turn the forcing screw clockwise until the ball joint is removed from the axle.

3. Repeat step 2 on the lower ball joint.

NOTE: *The upper ball joint must always be removed first. DO NOT heat the ball joint or axle!*

INSTALLATION

NOTE: *The lower ball joint must be installed first.*

1. To install the lower ball joint, assemble the C-frame ball joint tool and turn the forcing screw clockwise until the ball joint is seated. DO NOT heat the ball joint to aid in installation!

2. Install the snap-ring onto the ball joint.

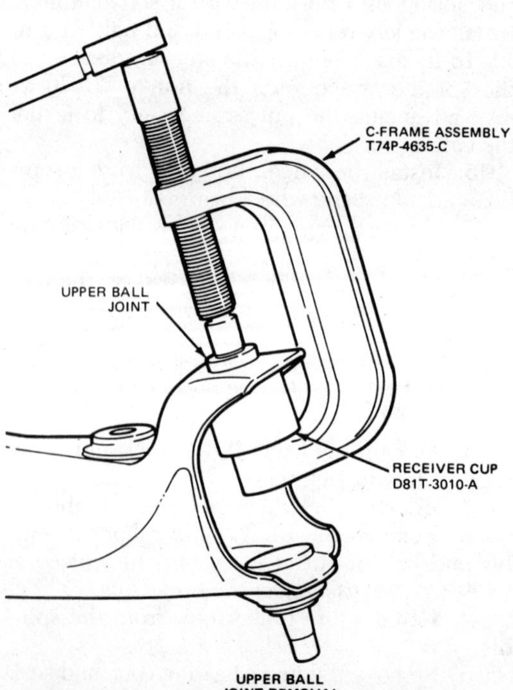

Upper ball joint removal; lower ball joint removal similar

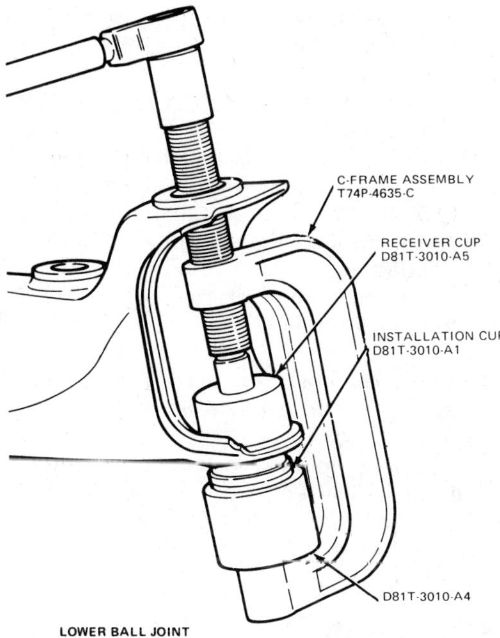

F-100/F-150 lower ball joint installation; upper joint similar

3. Install the upper ball joint in the same manner as the lower ball joint.
4. Install the spindle assembly.

Front Wheel Spindle 4WD 1980 and Later

NOTE: *This procedure also includes bearing and seal replacement and repacking.*

1. Raise the vehicle and install safety stands.
2. If equipped with manual locking hubs remove the hubs as follows:
   a. Remove the six socket head bolts from the cap assembly and separate the cap assembly from the body.
   b. Remove the snap ring from the end of the axle shaft.
   c. Remove the lock ring seated in the groove of the wheel hub and slide the body assembly out of the wheel hub.
3. If equipped with automatic locking hubs remove the hubs as follows:
   a. Remove the bolts and remove the hub cap assembly from the spindle.
   b. Remove the bolt from the end of the shaft.
   c. Remove the lock ring seated in the groove of the wheel hub.
   d. Remove the body assembly from the spindle. Use a puller if necessary.
   e. Unscrew all three set screws in the spindle locknut until the heads are flush with the edge of the locknut.
   f. Remove the outer spindle locknut with tool T80T-4000-V, Automatic Hub Locknut Wrench.
4. Remove the front hub grease cap and driving hub snap ring.
5. Remove the splined driving hub and the pressure spring. Slightly pry off if necessary.
6. Remove the wheel bearing locknut, lock ring and adjusting nut using special tool T59T-1197-B or equivalent.
7. Remove the hub and disc assembly. The

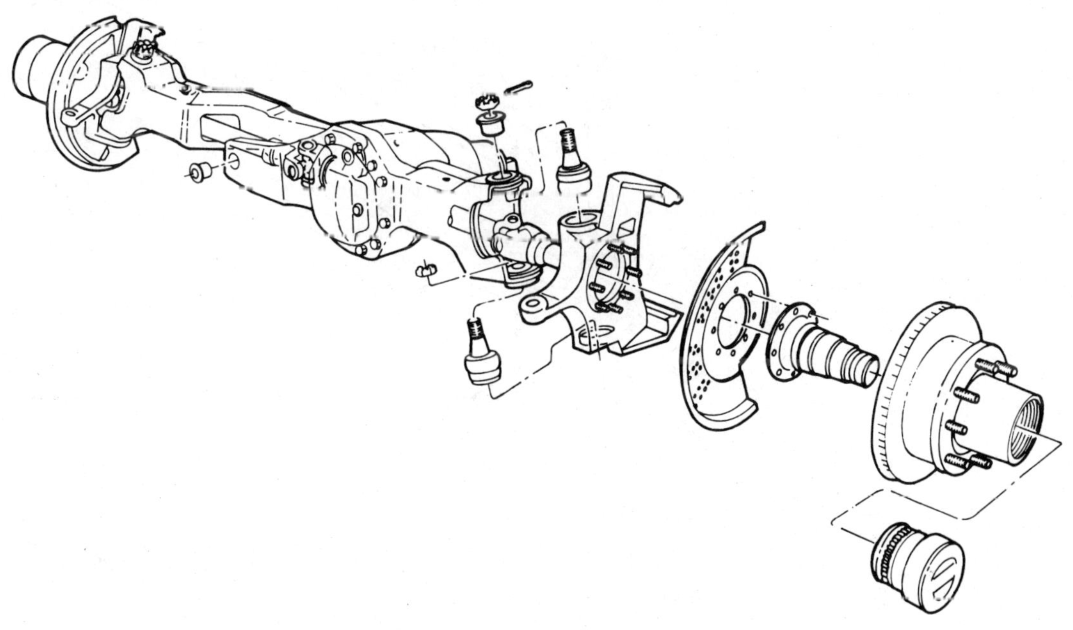

1980–82 4-WD knuckle and spindle

outer wheel bearing and spring retainer will slide out as the hub is removed.

8. Remove the spindle nuts and remove the spindle, splash shield and axle shaft assembly.

NOTE: *It may be necessary to break the spindle loose with a plastic hammer.*

9. Clean all old grease from the needle bearings and wipe clean the spindle face that mates with the spindle bore seal.

10. Remove the spindle bore seal, V-seal, and thrust washer from the outer axle shaft. Clean and replace if necessary.

11. Using Multi-Purpose Lubricant Ford ESA-M1C75-B or equivalent, thoroughly lubricate the needle bearing and pack the spindle face that mates with the spindle bore seal.

12. Position the V-seal in the spindle bore next to the needle bearing. Assemble the spindle bore seal on the axle shaft.

13. Assemble the spindle with the axle shaft on the knuckle studs and tighten the retaining nuts to 75 ft. lbs.

14. Carefully drive the inner bearing cone and grease seal out of the hub using tool T77F-1102-A or equivalent.

15. Inspect the inner bearing cups and if necessary remove with a drift.

NOTE: *If new cups are installed, install new bearings.*

16. Lubricate the bearings with the lubricant specified earlier and clean all old grease from the hub. Pack the cones and rollers with lubricant. Try to pack as much as possible between the rollers and the cages.

17. Position the inner bearing cone and roller in the inner cup and install the grease retainer.

18. Install the hub and disc assembly on the spindle.

19. Install the outer bearing cone and roller, and the adjusting nut.

20. Using tool T59T-1197-B or equivalent and a torque wrench tighten the bearing adjusting nut to 50 ft. lbs. while rotating the wheel back and forth. Back off the adjusting nut no more than 90 degrees.

21. Assemble the lock ring by turning the nut to the nearest hole and inserting the dowel pin.

NOTE: *The dowel pin must seat in the lock ring hole for proper bearing adjustment and wheel retention.*

22. Install the outer lock nut and tighten to 65 ft. lbs. Final end play on the wheel and spindle should be 0.001–0.006 inch.

23. Adjust the brake if necessary and lower the vehicle.

Radius Arm

REMOVAL AND INSTALLATION

All Except 1980–and Later F-150 with 4WD

1. Raise the front of the vehicle and place safety stands under the frame and a jack under the wheel or axle.

2. Disconnect the shock absorber from the radius arm bracket.

3. Remove the two spring upper retainer attaching bolts from the top of the spring upper seat and remove the retainer.

4. Remove the nut which attaches the spring

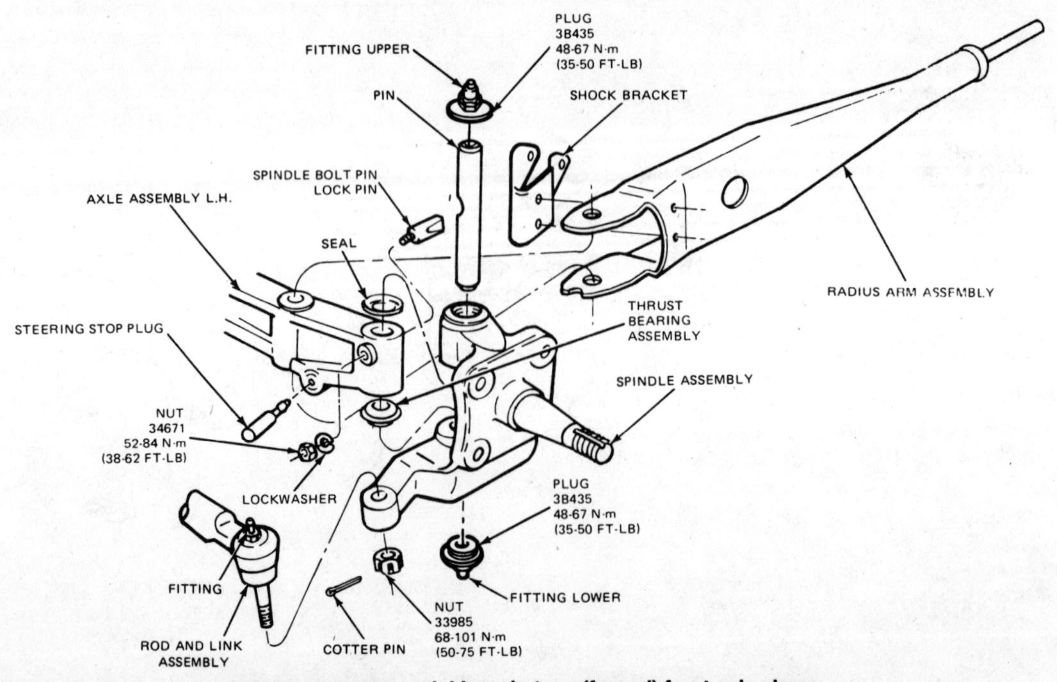

Radius arm removal, king-pin type (forged) front axle shown

lower retainer to the lower seat and axle and remove the retainer.

5. Lower the axle and remove the spring.

6. Disconnect the steering rod from the spindle arm.

7. Remove the spring lower seat and shim from the radius arm. Then, remove the bolt and nut which attach the radius arm to the axle.

8. Remove the cotter pin, nut and washer from the radius arm rear attachment.

9. Remove the bushing from the radius arm and remove the radius arm from the vehicle.

10. Remove the inner bushing from the radius arm.

11. Position the radius arm to the axle and install the bolt and nut finger-tight.

12. Install the inner bushing on the radius arm and position the arm to the frame bracket.

13. Install the bushing, washer, and attaching nut. Tighten the nut and install the cotter pin.

14. Connect the steering rod to the spindle arm and install the attaching nut. Tighten the radius arm-to-axle attaching bolt and nut.

F-150 4WD—1980–and Later

1. Raise the vehicle and position safety stands under the frame side rails.

2. Remove the shock absorber lower attaching bolt and nut and pull the shock absorber free of the radius arm.

3. Remove the lower spring retaining bolt from the inside of the spring coil.

4. Remove the nut attaching the radius arm to the frame bracket and remove the radius arm rear insulator. Lower the axle and allow the axle to move forward.

NOTE: *The axle must be supported on the jack throughout spring removal, and must not be permitted to hang from the brake hose. If the length of the brake hose does not provide sufficient clearance it may be necessary to remove and support the brake caliper.*

5. Remove the bolt and stud attaching the radius arm to the axle.

6. Move the axle forward and remove the radius arm from the axle. Then, pull the radius arm from the frame bracket.

7. Installation is the reverse of removal. Install new bolts and the stud type bolt which attach the radius arm to the axle and tighten to 210 ft. lbs. Tighten the radius arm rear attaching nut to 100 ft. lbs.

Front End Alignment

Proper alignment of the front wheels must be maintained in order to ensure ease of steering and satisfactory tire life.

The most important factors of front wheel alignment are wheel camber, axle caster, and wheel toe-in.

Wheel toe-in is the distance by which the wheels are closer together at the front than at the rear.

Wheel camber is the amount the top of the wheels incline in or out from the vertical.

From axle caster is the amount in degrees that the top of the steering pivot pins are tilted toward the rear of the vehicle. Positive caster is inclination of the top of the pivot pin toward the rear of the vehicle.

These points should be checked at regular intervals, particularly when the front axle has been subjected to a heavy impact. When checking wheel alignment, it is important that wheel bearings and knuckle bearings be in proper adjustment. Loose bearings will affect instrument readings when checking the camber and toe-in.

If you start to notice abnormal tire wear patterns and handling characteristics (steering wheel is hard to return to the straightahead position after negotiating a turn), then front end misalignment can be suspected. However, toe-in alignment maladjustment, rather than caster or camber, is more likely to be the cause of excessive or uneven tire wear on vehicles with twin "I"-beam front axles. Seldom is it necessary to correct caster or camber. Hard steering wheel return after turning a corner is, however, a characteristic of improper caster angle. Nevertheless, the toe-in alignment should be checked before the caster and camber angles after making the following checks:

1. Check the air pressure in all the tires. Make sure that the pressures agree with those specified for the tires and vehicle model being checked.

2. Raise the front of the vehicle off the ground. Grasp each front tire at the front and rear, and push the wheel inward and outward. If any free-play is noticed between the brake drum and the brake backing plate, adjust the wheel bearings.

NOTE: *There is supposed to be a very, very small amount of free-play present where the wheel bearings are concerned. Replace the bearings if they are worn or damaged.*

3. Check all steering linkage for wear or maladjustment. Adjust and/or replace all worn parts.

4. Check the torque on the steering gear mounting bolts and tighten as necessary.

5. Rotate each front wheel slowly, and observe the amount of lateral or side run-out. If the wheel run-out exceeds ⅛ in., replace the wheel or install the wheel on the rear.

6. Inspect the radius arms to be sure that they are not bent or damaged. Inspect the bushings at the radius arm-to-axle attachment

and radius arm-to-frame attachment points for wear or looseness. Repair or replace parts as required.

CASTER

1965–72 F-100–250 (2WD)
1967–72 F-350

The caster on these models can be adjusted by twisting the axle beam outboard of the radius arm (strut) attachment, however this procedure can only be accomplished with the use of a variety of special tools and it is recommended that it be taken to a qualified shop for adjustment.

1965–77 F-250 (4WD)
1965–66 F-350

The caster angle is controlled by the angle of the front spring pads. The caster angle can be adjusted by installing tapered wedges between the springs and the spring pads. Only one wedge per side should be used.

1965–72 F-100 (4WD)
1973–77 All Models Exc. F-250 (4WD)
1978–and Later Models

The caster angles are designed into the front axle and cannot be adjusted.

CAMBER

1965–72 F-100, F-250, F-350 (2WD)

The camber on these models can be increased or decreased by bending the axle beam, however this procedure can only be accomplished with the use of a variety of special tools and it is recommended that it be taken to a qualified shop for adjustment.

1965–72 F-100–250 (4WD)
1973–and Later Models

The camber angles are designed into the front axle and cannot be adjusted.

TOE-IN ADJUSTMENT

All Models

Toe-in can be measured by either a front end alignment machine or by the following method:

With the front wheels in the straightahead position, measure the distance between the extreme front and the extreme rear of the front wheels. In other words, measure the distance across the undercarriage of the vehicle between the two front edges and the two rear edges of the two front wheels. Both of these measurements (front and rear of the two wheels) must be taken at an equal distance from the floor and at the approximate centerline of the spindle. The difference between these two distances is the amount that the wheels toe-in or toe-out. The wheels should always be adjusted to toe-in according to specifications.

1. Loosen the clamp bolts at each end of the left tie-rod, seen from the front of the vehicle. Rotate the connecting rod tube until the correct toe-in is obtained, then tighten the clamp bolts.

2. Recheck the toe-in to make sure that no changes occurred when the bolts were tightened.

NOTE: *The clamps should be positioned 3/16 in. from the end of the rod with the clamp*

Wheel Alignment Specifications

Year	Model	Caster		Camber		Toe-in (in.)	Steering Axis Inclination (deg)
		Range (deg)	Preferred Setting (deg)	Range (deg)	Preferred Setting (deg)		
1965	F-100, 250, 2WD	4¼ to 5¾	5	2/8 to 1	5/8	1/8	—
	F-100, 250 4WD	3¼ to 4¾	4	2/8 to 1	5/8	1/8	7½
	F-350	3½ to 4½	4	½ to 1½	1	1/16	4
1966	F-100, 250 2WD	4¼ to 5¾	5	0 to ¾	5/8	1/8	4
	F-100, 4WD	—	—	—	—	1/8	—
	F-250 4WD	3½ to 4½	4	—	—	1/8	—
	F-350	3½ to 4½	4	1/8 to 5/8	3/8	1/8	4 5/8
1967	F-100, 250 2WD	3 1/8 to 4¾	4	½ to 1½	1	1/8	4
	F-100 4WD	—	—	—	—	1/8	—
	F-250 4WD	3½ to 4½	4	—	—	1/8	—
	F-350	4¼ to 5¾	5	0 to 1	½	1/8	4

Wheel Alignment Specifications (cont.)

		Caster		Camber			
Year	Model	Range (deg)	Preferred Setting (deg)	Range (deg)	Preferred Setting (deg)	Toe-in (in.)	Steering Axis Inclination (deg)
1968	F-100, 250 2WD	3¼ to 4¾	4	½ to 1½	1	⅛	4
	F-100 4WD	2¾ to 4¼	3½	1 to 2	1	⅛	8½
	F-250 4WD	3½ to 4½	4	1 to 2	1½	⅛	7½
	F-350	4¼ to 5¾	5	0 to 1	½	⅛	4
1969	F-100, 250 2WD	3¼ to 4¾	4	½ to 1½	1	⅛	4
	F-100 4WD	2¾ to 4¼	3½	1 to 2	1½	⅛	8½
	F-250 4WD	3½ to 4½	4	1 to 2	1½	⅛	7½
	F-350	4¼ to 5¾	5	0 to 1	½	⅛	4
1970–71	F-100, 150 2WD	½ to 5½	3	½ to 2½	1	3/32	—
	F-100, 150 4WD	1¾ to 3¾	2½	½ to 2½	1½	⅛	8½
	F-250 2WD	½ to 5½	3	½ to 2½	1	3/32	—
	F-250 4WD	3½ to 4½	4	1 to 2	1½	⅛	7½
	F-350	½ to 5½	3	0 to 3	—	⅛	4
1972–73	F-100, 150 2WD	½ to 5½	3	½ to 2½	1	3/32	—
	F-100, 150 4WD	1¾ to 3¾	2¼	½ to 2½	1½	⅛	8½
	F-250 2WD	½ to 5½	3	½ to 2½	1	5/32	—
	F-250 4WD	3½ to 4½	4	1 to 2	1½	⅛	7½
	F-350	3½ to 8½	—	0 to 3	—	3/32	—
1974–75	F-100, 250 2WD	½ to 8½	4½	½ to 2½	1	3/32	7½
	F-250 4WD	3½ to 4½	4	1 to 2	1½	⅛	7½
	F-100, 150 4WD	2¾ to 4½	3½	1 to 2	1½	5/32	8½
	F-350	½ to 8½	—	0 to 3	—	3/32	—
1976	F-100, 250 2WD	½ to 8½	4½	½ to 2½	1	3/32	7½
	F-250 4WD	3½ to 4½	4	1 to 2	1½	⅛	7½
	F-100, 150 4WD	2¾ to 4½	3½	1 to 2	1½	5/32	8½
	F-350	½ to 8½	—	0 to 3	—	⅛	—
1977	F-100, 150, 250 2WD, 6200–6900 GVW	4 to 9	6½	1 to 3	1	3/32	—
	F-250 Supercab 2WD; F-250 7800–8000 GVW	3¼ to 8½	5⅞	0 to 3¼	1⅝	3/32	—
	F-250 Crewcab; F-250 Supercab 8100 GVW	3¼ to 9	6⅛	0 to 3¾	1⅛	3/32	—
	F-150 4WD	2¾ to 4¼	3½	1 to 2	1½	5/32	8½
	F-250 4WD	3 to 5	4	½ to 1½	1	5/32	7½
	F-350	3¼ to 9	—	0 to 3¾	—	⅛	—
1978	F-150 4WD	4¼ to 5½	3½	1 to 2	1½	3/32	8½
	F-250 4WD	2⅛ to 5	4	½ to 1½	1	5/32	8½
1979	F-150 4WD	6½ to 9½	3½	1 to 3	1½	3/32	8½
	F-150 Supercab 4WD F-250, 350 4WD	2½ to 5½	4	0 to 3	1½	3/32	8½

Wheel Alignment Specifications

1978 F-100 To F-350 Two Wheel Drive

Ride Height		F-100/150/250 6200–6900 GVW * ② Regular Cab				F-250 7800–8000 GVW Regular Cab * ② 6350–7800 Super Cab				F-350 (All) * ② F-250 8100 GVW Super Cab F-250 Super Cab w/RPO Suspension			
		Camber		Caster		Camber		Caster		Camber		Caster	
At Least	Not More Than	Min ①	Max	Min ①	Max	Min ①	Max	Min ①	Max	Min ①	Max	Min ①	Max
2.75	3.00	−1°	+½°	8¼°	9⅝°	−½°	+1°	7⅝°	8⅞°	−⅜°	−¼°	9¾°	10⅞°
3.00	3.25	−½°	+1°	7¾°	9°	−¼°	+1½°	6⅞°	8⅜°	−1°	+⅝°	9°	10¼°
3.25	3.50	−¼°	+1½°	7°	8¾°	0°	+1¾°	5⅜°	7¾°	−½°	+1°	8¼°	9⅝°
3.50	3.75	0°	+1¾°	6¼°	7⅜°	+½°	+2¼°	5¾°	7°	−¼°	+1½°	7⅝°	8⅝°
3.75	4.00	+½°	+2¼°	5¾°	7°	+¾°	+2½°	5°	6½°	0°	+1¾°	6⅞°	8⅜°
4.00	4.25	+¾°	+2½°	5°	6½°	+1¼°	+3°	4½°	5⅞°	+½°	+2¼°	6⅜°	7¼°
4.25	4.50	+1¼°	+3°	4½°	5⅞°	+1¾°	+3¼°	3⅞°	5⅛°	+¾°	+2½°	5¾°	7°
4.50	4.75	+1⅝°	+3¼°	3¾°	5°	+2°	+3½°	3⅛°	4½°	+1¼°	+3°	5⅛°	6½°
4.75	5.00	+2°	+3¾°	3⅛°	4½°	+2⅜°	+4⅛°	2½°	4°	+1¾°	+3¼°	4½°	5⅞°
5.00	5.25	+2⅜°	+4⅛°	2½°	4°	+2¾°	+4½°	2°	3¼°	+2°	+3¼°	3⅞°	5⅛°

① All vehicles with normal operating attitudes.
② Toe-in range for these vehicles is 1/32″ out to 7/32″ in (3/32″ nominal).
③ Toe range for these vehicles is 5/32″ in (1/32″ nominal).
* NOTE: Toe-in should be checked using a trammel bar with frictionless plates.

Wheel Alignment Specifications (cont.)

1979 F-100 To F-350 Two Wheel Drive

Model Axle Part # Ride Height		F-250 R/C (7700–7900) F-250 S/C (6300–7800) ① ②				F-350 All ② F-250 S/C (3100) F-250 S/C RPO Suspension ① ②			
		Camber		Caster		Camber		Caster	
At Least	Not More Than	Min ①	Max	Min ①	Max	Min ①	Max	Min ①	Max
2.75	3.00	−1⅞	−¼	7¾	9	−2⅛	−⅝	9⅝	11
3.00	3.25	−1½	+⅛	7	8⅜	−1¾	−¼	8⅞	10⅜
3.25	3.50	−1⅛	+½	6⅜	7¾	−1⅜	+⅛	8⅜	9¾
3.50	3.75	−¾	+⅞	5⅞	7⅛	−1⅛	+½	7¾	9
3.75	4.00	−⅜	+1¼	5⅛	6½	−¾	+¾	7	8⅜
4.00	4.25	0	+1⅝	4½	5⅞	−¼	+1¼	6⅜	7¾
4.25	4.50	⅜	+2	3⅞	5¼	0	+1⅝	5¾	7⅛
4.50	4.75	⅞	2½	3¼	4⅝	+⅜	+2	5⅛	6½
4.75	5.00	1¼	2¾	2⅝	4	+¾	+2⅜	4½	5⅞
5.00	5.25	1⅝	3⅛	2	3⅜	+1¼	+2¾	3⅞	5¼
5.25	5.50	—	—	—	—	—	—	—	—

① All vehicles with normal operating altitudes.
② Toe setting is 3/32 inch in.
③ Toe setting is 1/32 inch in.

Wheel Alignment Specifications

F-100 to F-350 Two Wheel Drive

Ride Height (in.)		F-100, 150				F-250, 350			
		Camber (deg)		Caster		Camber (deg)		Caster (deg)	
At Least	Not More Than	Min	Max	Min	Max	Min	Max	Min	Max
2¼	2¾	−3	−½	+6	+10	−1½	+1	+4¾	+8
2¾	3¼	−2	+½	+5	+9	−¾	+1¾	+3¾	+7
3¼	3½	−1¼	+1¼	+4	+8	+¼	+2¾	+2¾	+6
3½	4	−¼	+2¼	+3	+7	+1	+3½	+1¾	+5
4	4¼	+½	+3	+2	+6	+2	+4½	+¾	+4
4¼	4¾	+1½	+4	+1	+5	—	—	—	—

Wheel Alignment Specifications

F-150, 250, 350 Four Wheel Drive

Ride Height (in.)		F-150				F-250, 350			
		Camber (deg)		Caster (deg)		Camber (deg)		Caster (deg)	
At Least	Not More Than	Min	Max	Min	Max	Min	Max	Min	Max
2¾	3¼	−2½	−¼	+6	+9	—	—	—	—
3¼	3½	−1¾	+½	+5	+8	—	—	—	—
3½	4	−¾	+1½	+4	+7	—	—	—	—
4	4¼	0	+2¼	+3	+6	—	—	—	—
4¼	4¾	+1	+3¼	+2	+5	—	—	—	—
4¾	5	+1¾	+4	+1	+4	−2¾	−¼	+3	+5
5	5½	—	—	—	—	−1¾	+¾	+3⅛	+5⅛
5½	6	—	—	—	—	−¾	+1¾	+3⅛	+5⅛
6	6¼	—	—	—	—	+¼	+2¾	+3¼	+5¼
6¼	6¾	—	—	—	—	+1¼	+4	+3⅜	+5⅜
6¾	7	—	—	—	—	+2½	+5	+3½	+5½

bolts in a vertical position in front of the tube, with the nut down.

REAR SUSPENSION

Semi-elliptic, leaf-type springs are used at the rear axle. The front end of the spring is attached to a spring bracket on the frame side member. The rear end of the spring is attached to a bracket on the frame side member with a shackle. Each spring is attached to the axle with two U-bolts. A spacer is located between the spring and the axle on some applications to obtain a level ride position.

Springs

REMOVAL AND INSTALLATION

2WD

1. Raise the vehicle by the frame until the weight is off the rear spring with the tires still on the floor.
2. Remove the nuts from the spring U-bolts and drive the U-bolts from the U-bolt plate. Remove the auxiliary spring and spacer, if so equipped.
3. Remove the spring-to-bracket nut and bolt at the front of the spring.
4. Remove the upper and lower shackle nuts and bolts at the rear of the spring and remove

the spring and shackle assembly from the rear shackle bracket.

5. Remove the bushings in the spring or shackle, if they are worn or damaged, and install new ones.

6. Position the spring in the shackle and install the upper shackle-to-spring nut and bolt with the bolt head facing outward.

7. Position the front end of the spring in the bracket and install the nut and bolt.

8. Position the shackle in the rear bracket and install the nut and bolt.

9. Position the spring on top of the axle with the spring center bolt centered in the hole provided in the seat. Install the auxiliary spring and spacer, if so equipped.

10. Install the spring U-bolts, plate, and nuts.

11. Lower the vehicle and tighten the attaching hardware as follows: U-bolt nuts, ½ in.—45–70 ft. lbs.; 9⁄16 in.—85–115 ft. lbs.; front spring hanger, 9⁄16 in.—75–105 ft. lbs.; ⅝ in.—150–190 ft. lbs.; rear spring hanger—75–105 ft. lbs.

4WD

1. Raise the truck by the frame until the weight is off the rear springs and the wheels are still touching the ground.

2. Remove the nuts from the spring U-bolts and drive the U-bolts out of the spring seat cap. Remove the spring cap. Remove the auxiliary spring and spacer, if so equipped.

3. Remove the shackle pin lockbolts from each end of the spring. Insert a drift in the hole provided in the frame from the inner side and drive the shackle pin out of each spring bracket.

4. Remove the spring and shackle from the truck. Remove the spring-to-axle spacer.

5. Drive the remaining shackle pin out of the rear spring eye and remove the shackle from the spring.

6. After checking and replacing worn or damaged bushings, nuts and bolts, and broken or weak springs, position the shackle to the rear spring eye.

7. Install the shackle pin through the shackle and spring eye with the lubrication fitting on the shackle pin facing outboard.

8. Align the shackle pin lockbolt groove with the lockbolt hole in the shackle, and install the lockbolt, washer, and nut.

9. Position the spring on the axle with the spring center bolt in the hole provided in the axle spring seat or spacer. Install the spacer between the spring seat and the spring. Make sure that the spacer dowel is positioned in the pilot hole of the axle spring seat.

10. Install the shackle pin through the shackle and rear bracket. The lubrication fitting on the shackle pin faces outboard. Align the pin groove with the lock bolt hole in the bracket and install the lockbolt, washer, and nut.

11. Install the shackle pin at the front bracket and spring eye in the same manner as above.

12. Install the auxiliary spring and spacer, if so equipped. Place the spring cap on top of the spring at the center bolt and place the spring U-bolts over the spring assembly and axle.

13. Position the spring seat cap, and install the nuts on the spring U-bolts.

14. Lower the truck to the ground and tighten the attaching hardware.

Shock Absorbers

TESTING

Check, inspect, and test the rear shock absorbers in the same manner as outlined for the front shock absorbers.

REMOVAL AND INSTALLATION

To replace the rear shock absorber, remove the self-locking nut, steel washer, and rubber bushings at the upper and lower ends and remove the shock abosrber.

When a new shock absorber is installed, use new rubber bushings. Position the shock on the mounting brackets with the large hole at the top.

Install the rubber bushings, steel washer, and self-locking nut. Tighten the nut until it rests against the shoulder of the stud. If air is suspected in the shock absorber, hold the unit upside down and expand and collapse it several times.

STEERING

Steering Wheel

REMOVAL AND INSTALLATION

1965–74

1. Remove the horn button or ring by pressing it down and turning it counterclockwise or remove the screws behind the trim pad and remove the pad.

2. Remove the steering wheel nut.

3. Make sure that the wheels are in the straight-ahead position and mark the steering wheel and steering column so that the steering wheel can be reassembled in the same position from which it is removed.

4. Remove the steering wheel with a puller.

5. Install the steering wheel in the reverse order of removal.

1975 and Later

1. Set the front wheels in the straight ahead position and make chalk marks on the column

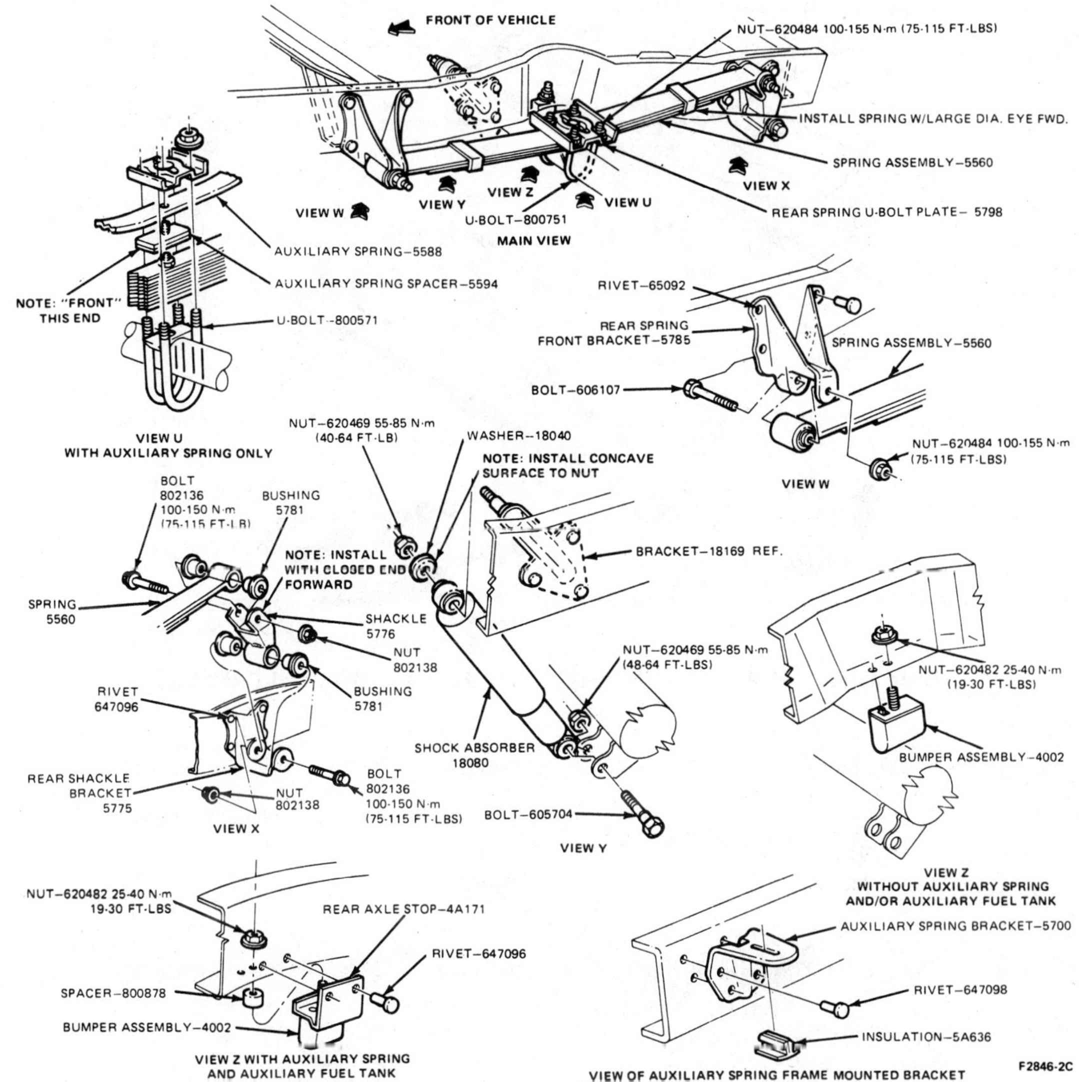

F-100/F-150 rear leaf spring and shock absorber mounting

and steering wheel hub for alignment purposes during installation.

2. Disconnect the negative battery cable.

3. Remove the one screw from the underside of each steering wheel spoke, and lift the horn switch assembly (steering wheel pad) from the steering wheel. On vehicles equipped with the sport steering wheel option, pry the button cover off with a screwdriver.

4. Disconnect the horn switch wires at the connector and remove the switch assembly.

5. Remove the steering wheel retaining nut and remove the steering wheel with a puller.

6. Install the steering wheel in the reverse order of removal.

Turn Signal Switch

REMOVAL AND INSTALLATION

1. Disconnect the battery ground cable.

2. Remove the steering wheel.

3. Remove the turn signal lever by removing the retaining screw (1965–67) or unscrewing it (1968 and later) from the steering column.

4. Disconnect the turn indicator switch wiring connector plug by lifting up the tabs on the side of the plug and pulling it apart.

5. Remove the switch assembly attaching screws.

6. Record the color code and location of each

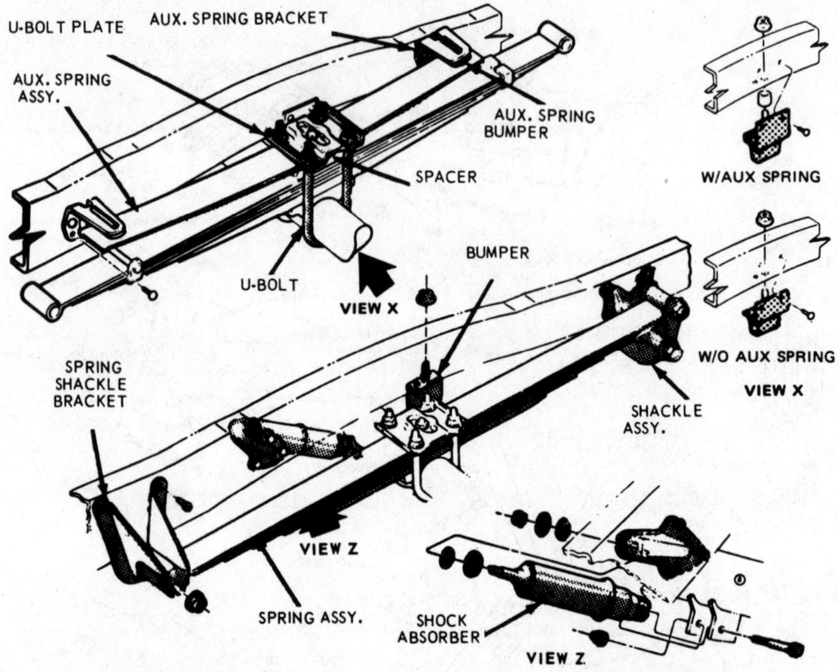

Rear spring installation on the F-100, F-150 2WD and 4WD, and F-250 2WD

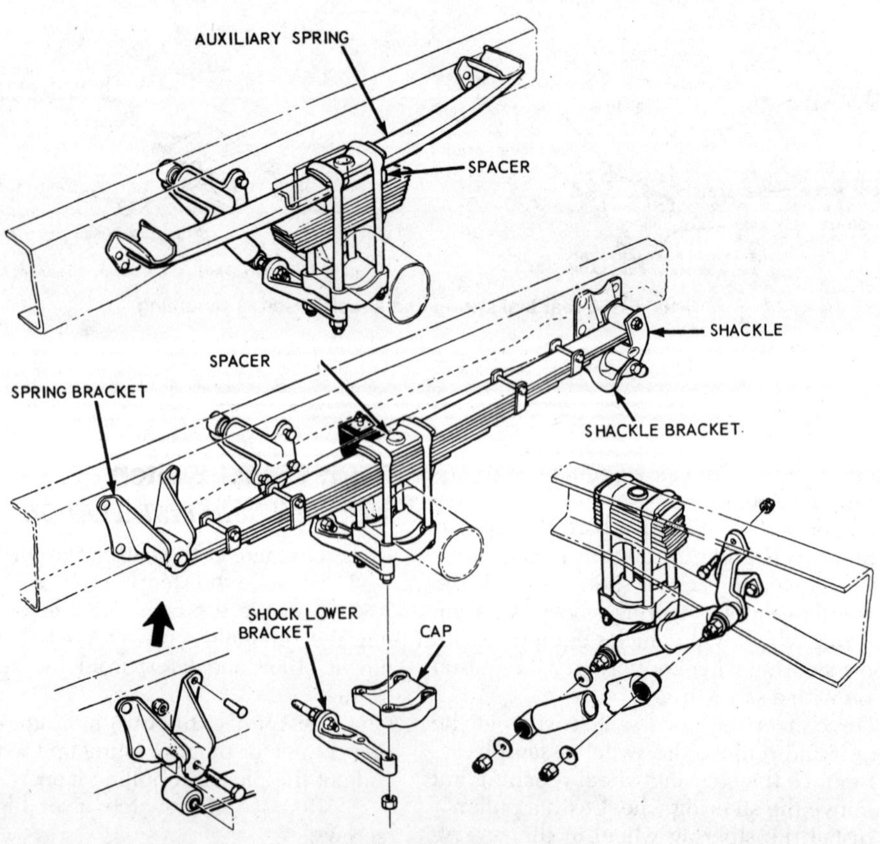

Rear spring installation—F-350

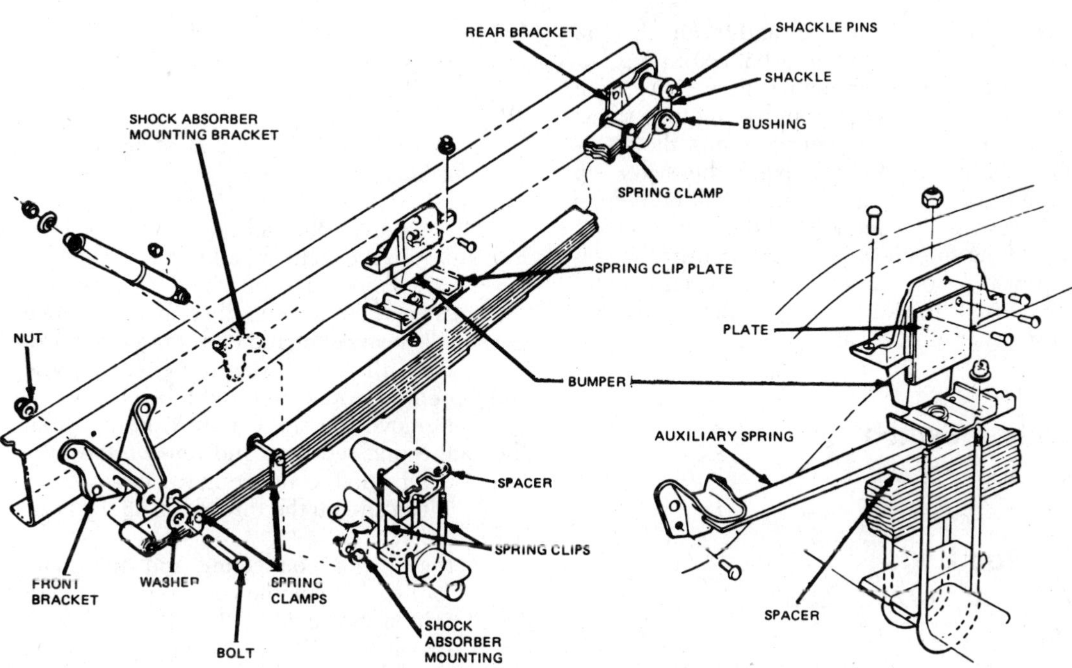

Rear spring installation on F-250 4WD

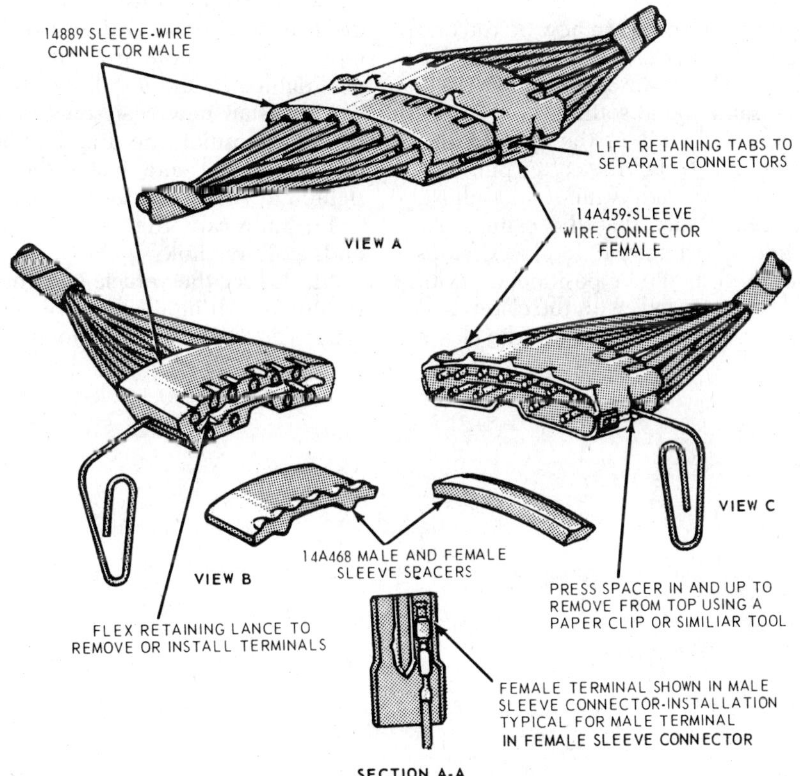

Wire connector disassembly

wire and remove the wires and terminals from the steering column wiring connector plug.

7. Remove the protective wire cover from the wiring harness and remove the turn signal switch and wires through the top of the steering column. Before removing the wires up through the steering column, it will be helpful to tie a wire or string around the wires to have something to pull the wire back down the column with when reinstalling the switch.

8. Install the turn signal switch in the reverse order of removal.

Ignition Switch

See Chapter 5.

Tie Rod Ends

REMOVAL AND INSTALLATION

2WD

Replace the tie rod ends if the ball is excessively loose.

1. Remove the cotter pin and nut from the tie rod end ball stud.
2. Remove the ball stud from the spindle arm.
3. Loosen the clamp bolt, and turn the rod end out of the tie rod.
4. Lubricate the threads of a new tie rod end and turn it into the tie rod about the same distance as the old rod end was installed. This will give about the same toe-in setting.
5. Install the ball stud in the spindle arm and tighten the nut. Install the cotter pin.
6. Check the toe-in adjustment and adjust, if necessary. Make sure that the clamps are tightened after adjusting the toe-in. Clamps which are not fixed should be positioned 3/16 in. from the end of the tie rod, with the clamp bolt at right angles to the slot in the rod. The clamp bolt must be vertical with the head up and the clamp facing forward.

4WD

1. Raise the vehicle on a hoist and disconnect the drag link from the spindle connecting rod end.
2. Disconnect the right spindle connecting rod end from the right spindle arm.
3. Disconnect the left spindle connecting rod ends from the left spindle arm and remove the spindle connecting rod ends from the truck.
4. Place the connecting rod ends in a vise and loosen the connecting rod tube clamps.
5. Remove the short (right) rod end from the connecting rod tube and remove the tube from the long (left) connecting rod end.
6. Clean and oil the threads on all the parts to be reused.
7. Install the connecting rod tube and clamps on the left spindle connecting rod end. Don't tighten the clamps yet.
8. Install the right connecting rod end in the tube and remove the assembly from the vise.
9. Install new dust seals on the left spindle connecting rod end and position the end on the left spindle arm.
10. Install the connecting rod end attaching nut, tighten it, and install the cotter pin.
11. Install new dust seals on the right spindle connecting rod end and position the end on the right spindle arm. Install the attaching nut, tighten it, and install the cotter pin.
12. Install new seals on the drag link ball stud and position the drag link on the spindle connecting rod end. Install the attaching nut, tighten it, and install the cotter pin.
13. Lubricate the spindle connecting rod ends and drag link.
14. Lower the vehicle and check and adjust the toe-in setting. Tighten the connecting rod clamps after adjusting the toe-in.

Brakes

9

BRAKE SYSTEM

NOTE: *Clean, high-quality brake fluid is essential to the safe and proper operation of the brake system. You should always buy the highest quality brake fluid that is available. If the brake fluid becomes contaminated, drain and flush the system and fill the master cylinder with new fluid.*

NOTE: *Never reuse any brake fluid. Any brake fluid that is removed from the system should be discarded.*

Adjustment

The drum brakes are self-adjusting and require a manual adjustment only after the brake shoes have been relined, replaced, or when the length of the adjusting screw has been changed while performing some other service operation, as, i.e., taking off the self-adjusters and putting on manual ones.

To adjust the brakes, follow the procedure given below:

1. Raise the vehicle and support it with safety stands.
2. Remove the rubber plug from the adjusting slot on the backing plate.
3. Insert a brake adjusting spoon into the slot and engage the lowest possible tooth on the starwheel. Move the end of the brake spoon downward to move the starwheel upward and expand the adjusting screw. Repeat this operation until the brakes lock the wheel.

NOTE: *Step 4 applies only to vehicles equipped with self-adjusters.*

4. Insert a small screwdriver or piece of firm wire (coathanger wire) into the adjusting slot and push the automatic adjusting lever out and free of the starwheel on the adjusting screw and hold it there.
5. Engage the topmost tooth possible on the starwheel with the brake adjusting spoon. Move the end of the adjusting spoon upward to move the adjusting screw starwheel downward and contract the adjusting screw. Back off the adjusting screw starwheel until the wheel spins freely with a minimum of drag. Keep track of the number of turns that the starwheel is backed off, or the number of strokes taken with the brake adjusting spoon.
6. Repeat this operation for the other side. When backing off the brakes on the other side, the starwheel adjuster must be backed off the same number of turns to prevent side-to-side brake pull.
7. Repat this operation on the other set of brakes (front or rear).
8. When all four brakes are adjusted, on vehicles equipped with self-adjusting brakes, make several stops while backing the vehicle, to equalize the brakes at all of the wheels. On vehicles not equipped with self-adjusters, make a few low-speed stops while going forward to check for brake pull. If the front end of the car has a tendency to pull to one side when the brakes are applied, back off the adjustment of the brake assembly on the side the vehicle pulls to.
9. Remove the safety stands and lower the vehicle. Road test the vehicle.

NOTE: *Disc brakes cannot be adjusted.*

Master Cylinder

REMOVAL AND INSTALLATION

1. Disconnect the wires from the stoplight switch.
2. Disconnect the hydraulic system brake lines at the master cylinder.
3. Remove the shoulder bolt and nut retaining the pushrod to the brake pedal. Remove the pushrod bushing.
4. Slide the master cylinder pushrod off the brake pedal pin. Remove the bushings and

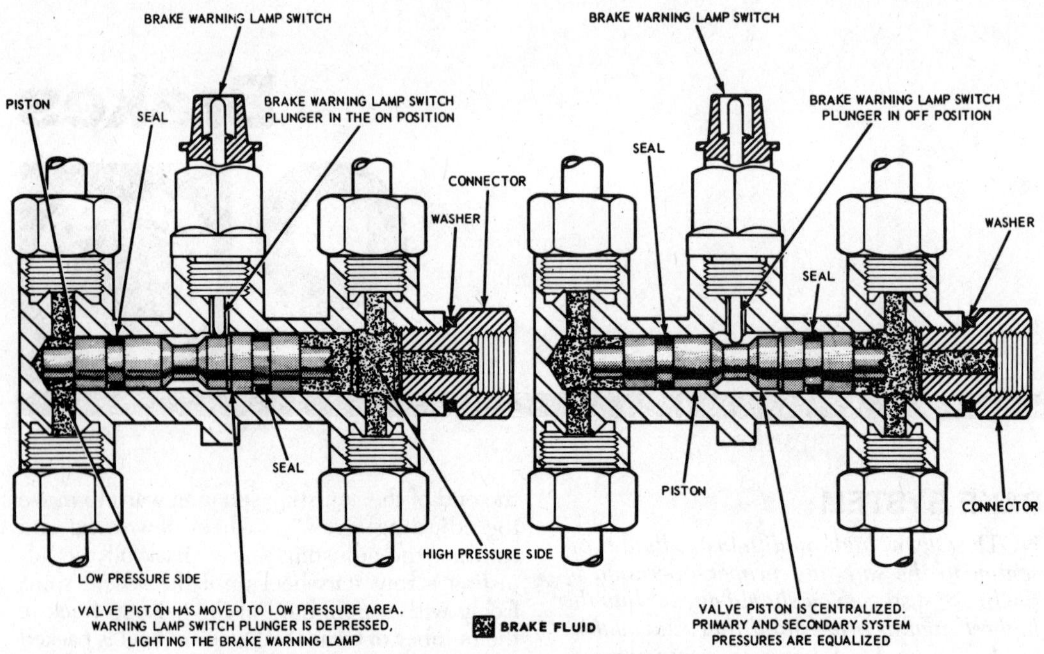

Cutaway view of the operation of the pressure differential valve

washers. Remove the stop-light switch and the rubber boot.

5. Remove the master cylinder retaining bolts and remove the master cylinder.

To install the master cylinder:

6. Position the master cylinder assembly on the dash panel and install the retaining bolts.

7. Connect the hydraulic brake system lines to the master cylinder.

8. Install the stop light switch and rubber boot.

9. Lubricate the pushrod and bushing. Insert the bushing in the pushrod and install the shoulder bolt which secures the pushrod to the brake pedal.

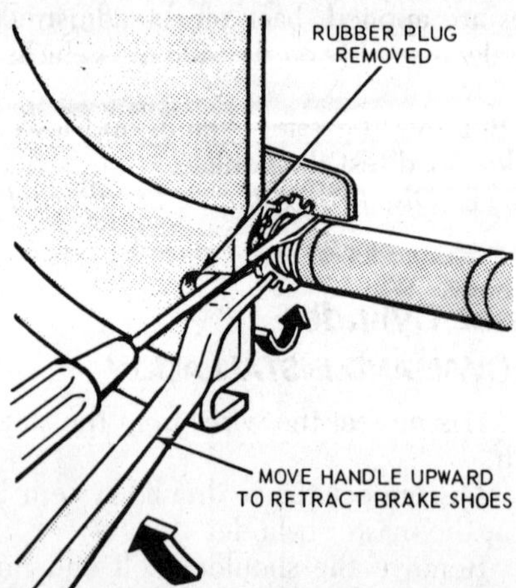

Positioning and operation of the brake adjusting tools during the adjustment procedure on F-100 and F-250 light duty models—backing off the brakes

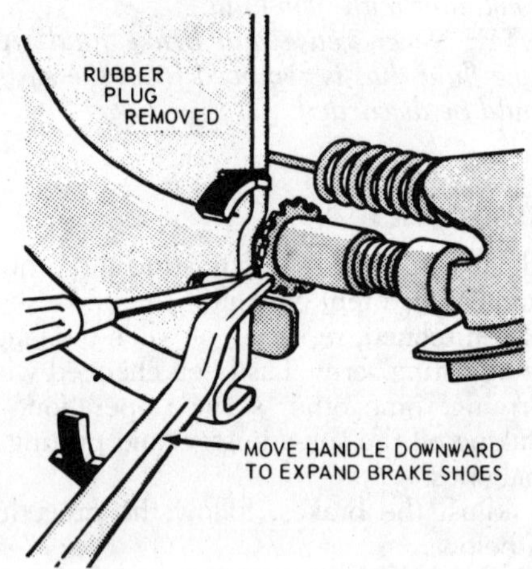

Positioning and operation of the brake adjusting tools during the adjustment procedure on the F-250–350 heavy duty models—expanding the brakes

10. Connect the stoplight switch wires to the switch.

11. Bleed the hydraulic brake system.

NOTE: *The preceding procedure applies to trucks equipped with non-power brakes. To remove the master cylinder from trucks equipped with power brakes, expel any vacuum from the booster by pressing down on the brake pedal several times, disconnect the hydraulic lines, remove the master cylinder-to-booster attaching nuts and lockwasher, and remove the master cylinder from the vehicle.*

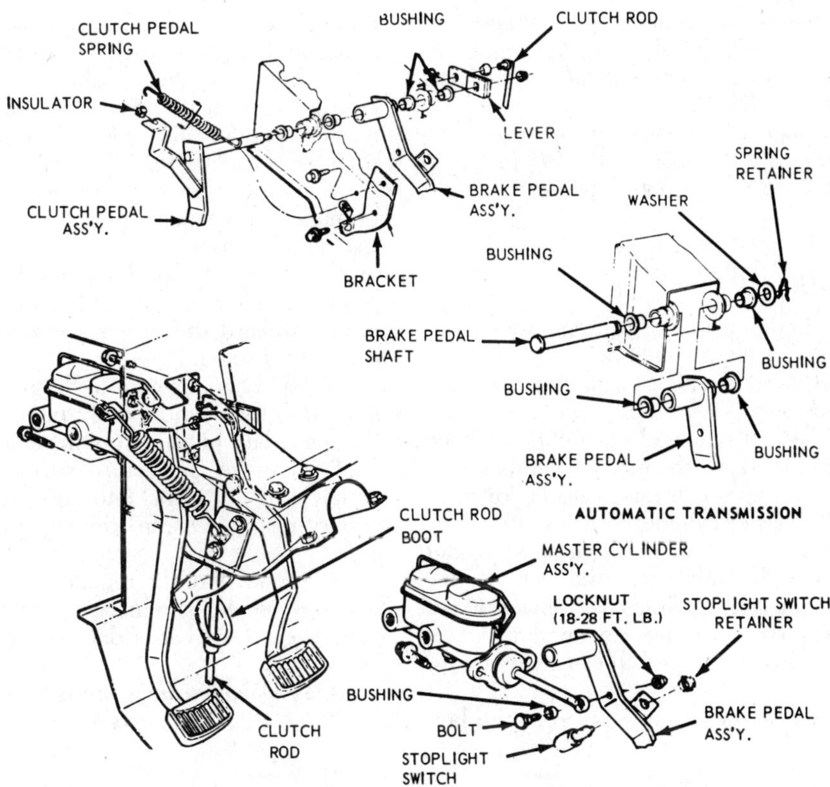

Master cylinder and brake pedal installation—non-power brakes—1967 and later

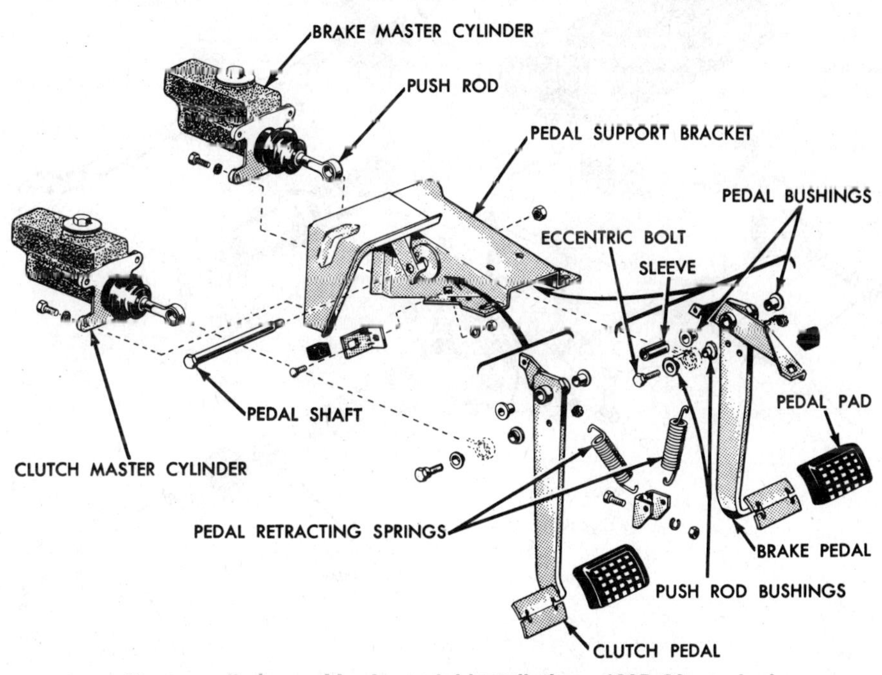

Master cylinder and brake pedal installation—1965–66—typical

Install the master cylinder in the reverse order of removal, and bleed the hydraulic system of air. The pushrod should extend past the face of the booster:

- *Through 1976: .880–.895 in.*
- *1977–82 F-100-250: .931–.946 in.*
- *1977–82 F-350: .980–.995 in.*

OVERHAUL

The most important thing to remember when rebuilding the master cylinder is cleanliness. Work in clean surroundings with clean tools and clean cloths or paper for drying purposes. Have plenty of clean alcohol and brake fluid on hand to clean and lubricate the internal components. There are service repair kits available for overhauling the master cylinder.

1. Clean the outside of the master cylinder and remove the filler cap and gasket (diaphragm). Pour out any fluid that remains in the cylinder reservoir. Do not use any fluids other than brake fluid or alcohol to clean the master cylinder.
2. Unscrew the piston stop from the bottom of the cylinder body. Remove the O-ring seal from the piston stop. Discard the seal.
3. Remove the pushrod boot, if so equipped, from the groove at the rear of the master cylinder and slide the boot away from the rear of the master cylinder.
4. Remove the snap-ring which retains the primary and secondary piston assemblies within the cylinder body.
5. Remove the pushrod (if so equipped) and primary piston assembly from the master cylinder. Discard the piston assembly, including the boot (if so equipped).
6. Apply an air hose to the rear brake outlet port of the cylinder body and carefully blow the secondary piston out of the cylinder body.
7. Remove the return spring, spring retainer, cup protector, and cups from the secondary piston. Discard the cup protector and cups.
8. Clean all of the remaining parts in clean isopropyl alcohol and inspect the parts for chipping, excessive wear or damage. Replace them as required.

NOTE: *When using a master cylinder repair kit, install all the parts supplied in the kit.*

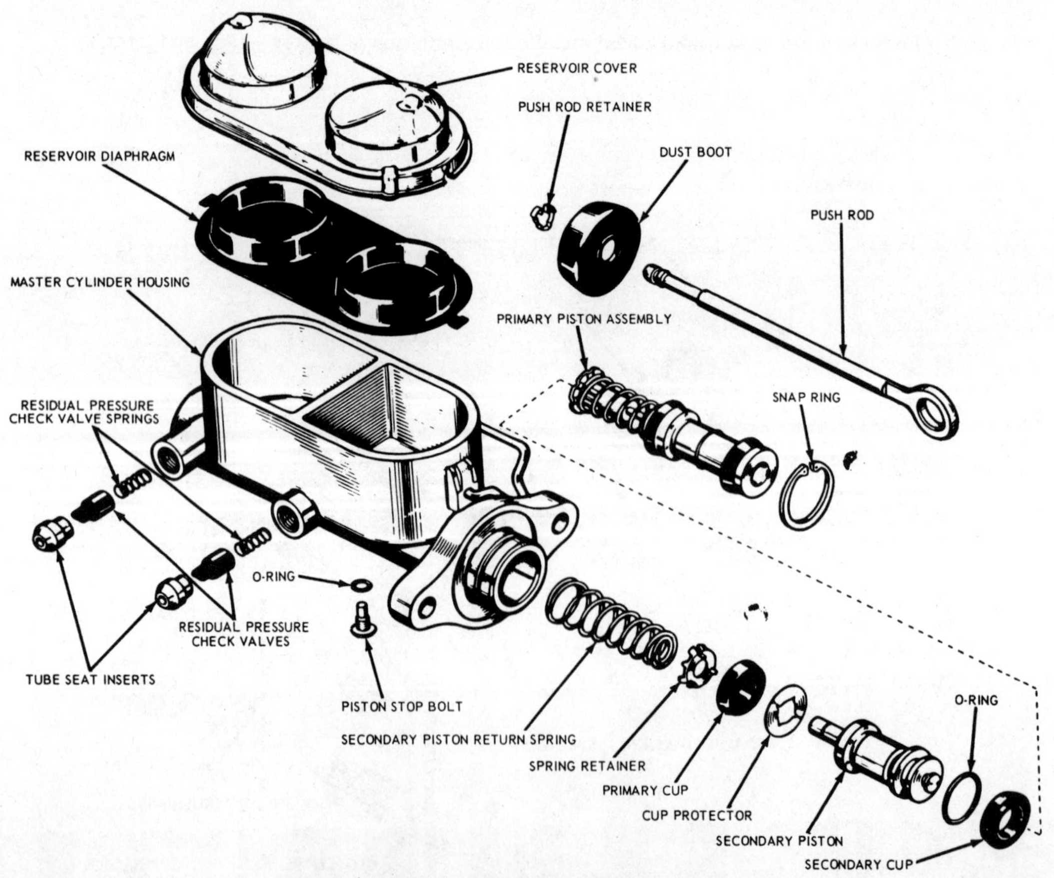

Exploded view of master cylinder—1967 and later

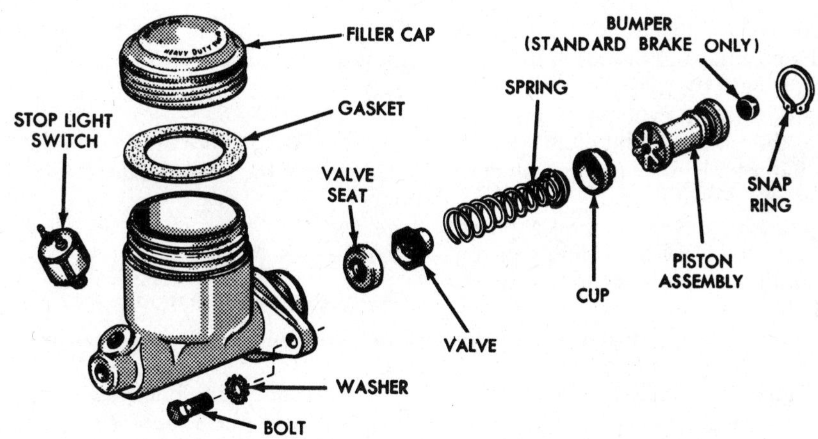

Exploded view of master cylinder—F-100–250—1965–66

9. Check all recesses, openings and internal passages to be sure that they are open and free from foreign matter. Use compressed air to blow out dirt and cleaning solvent remaining after the parts have been cleaned in the alcohol. Place all the parts on a clean pan, lint-free cloth, or paper to dry.

10. Dip all the parts, except the cylinder body, in clean brake fluid.

11. Assemble the two secondary cups, back-to-back, in the grooves near the end of the secondary piston.

12. Install the secondary piston assembly in the master cylinder.

13. Install a new O-ring on the piston stop, and insert the stop in the cylinder body.

14. Position the boot, snap-ring and push-rod retainer on the pushrod. Make sure that the pushrod retainer is seated securely on the ball end of the rod. Seat the pushrod in the primary piston assembly.

15. Install the primary piston assembly in the master cylinder. Push the primary piston inward and tighten the secondary piston stop to

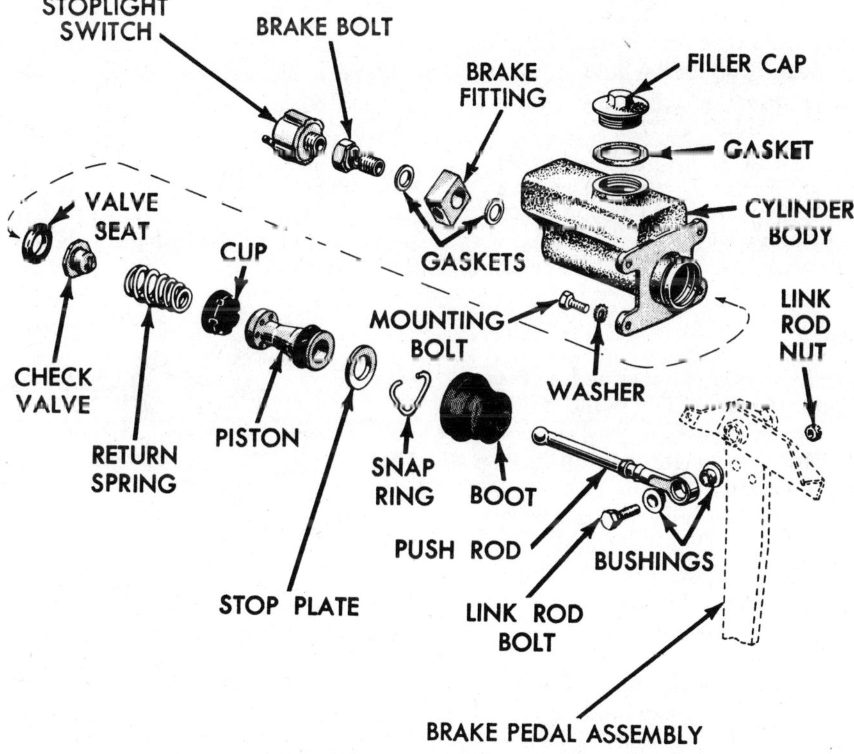

Exploded view of master cylinder—F-350—1965–66

retain the secondary piston in the bore.

16. Press the pushrod and pistons inward and install the snap-ring in the cylinder body.

17. Before the master cylinder is installed on the vehicle, the unit must be bled: support the master cylinder body in a vise, and fill both fluid reservoirs with brake fluid.

18. Loosely install plugs in the front and rear brake outlet bores. Depress the primary piston several times until air bubbles cease to appear in the brake fluid.

19. Tighten the plugs and attempt to depress the piston. The piston travel should be restricted after all air is expelled.

20. Remove the plugs. Install the cover and gasket (diaphragm) assembly, and make sure that the cover retainer is tightened securely.

21. Install the master cylinder in the vehicle and bleed the hydraulic system.

1965–66 F-100–250

1. Remove the master cylinder and pour out any brake fluid that may remain in the cylinder and reservoir.
2. Remove the stop light switch if it is mounted on the master cylinder.
3. Remove the bolt type fitting from the forward end of the cylinder.
4. Remove the snap ring from the bore at the rear end of the cylinder, and remove the piston, cup, spring and valve seat.
5. Remove the rubber bumper from the piston.
6. Dip all parts except the master cylinder body in clean heavy duty brake fluid.
7. Install the brake fitting bolt on the forward end of the cylinder.
8. Attach the stop light switch if it mounts on the master cylinder.
9. Install the valve seat, valve, spring, cup, piston in the cylinder bore.
10. Install the snap ring in the rear end of the bore.

1965–66 F-350

1. Remove the master cylinder and pour out any brake fluid that may remain in the cylinder and reservoir.
2. Remove the stop light switch if it is mounted on the master cylinder.
3. Remove the brake bolt, fitting and gaskets from the forward end of the cylinder.
4. Remove the snap ring from the bore at the rear end of the cylinder and remove the stop plate, piston, cup, spring, check valve and seat from the bore.
4. Dip all parts except the master cylinder body in clean heavy duty brake fluid.
5. Install the brake fitting, bolt and new gaskets on the forward end of the cylinder.
6. If the stop light switch attaches to the master cylinder attach the switch to the brake bolt.
7. Install the valve seat, valve, spring, cup, piston and stop plate in the cylinder bore.
8. Install the snap ring in the rear end of the bore.

Pressure Differential Valve

Removal and Installation

1. Disconnect the electrical leads from the valve.
2. Disconnect the brake lines from the valve.
3. Remove the differential valve attaching screw holding the valve in place and remove the valve from the truck.
4. Install the valve in the reverse order of removal. If a new differential valve is being installed, remove the brake system warning light switch from the old valve and install it in the new one.

CENTRALIZING THE PRESSURE DIFFERENTIAL VALVE

After any repair or bleeding of the primary (front brake) or secondary (rear brake) system, the dual-brake system warning light will usually remain illuminated due to the pressure differential valve remaining in the off-center position.

To centralize the pressure differential valve and turn off the warning light after the systems have been bled, follow the procedure below.

1. Turn the ignition switch to the ACC or ON position.
2. Check the fluid level in the master cylinder reservoirs and fill them to within 1/4 in. of the top with brake fluid, as necessary.
3. Depress the brake pedal and the piston should center itself causing the brake warning light to go out.

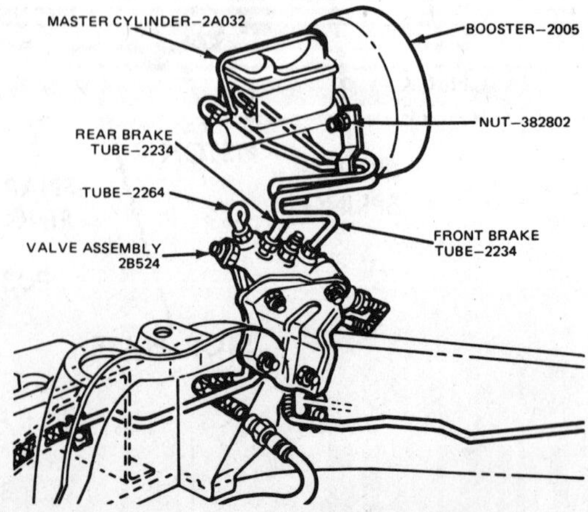

Brake proportioning valve assembly location

4. Turn the ignition switch to the OFF position.
5. Before driving the vehicle, check the operation of the brakes and be sure that a firm pedal is obtained.

Brake Booster Vacuum Pump

DIESEL MODELS

Unlike gasoline engines, diesel engines have little vacuum available to power brake booster systems. The 6.9L V8 diesel available in 1983 and later Ford pick-ups is thus equipped with a vacuum pump, which is driven by a single belt off of the alternator. This pump is located on the top right side of the engine.

Diesel pick-ups are also equipped with a low vacuum indicator switch which actuates the BRAKE warning lamp when available vacuum is below a certain level. The switch senses vacuum through a fitting in the vacuum manifold that intercepts the vacuum flow from the pump. The low vacuum switch is mounted on the right side of the engine compartment, adjacent to the vacuum pump on F-250 and F-350 models.

NOTE: *The vacuum pump cannot be disassembled. It is only serviced as a unit (the pulley is separate).*

REMOVAL AND INSTALLATION

1. Remove the hose clamp and disconnect the pump from the hose on the manifold vacuum outlet fitting.
2. Loosen the vacuum pump adjustment bolt and the pivot bolt. Slide the pump downward and remove the drive belt from the pulley.
3. Remove the pivot and adjustment bolts and the bolts retaining the pump to the adjustment plate. Remove the vacuum pump and adjustment plate.
4. To install, install the pump-to-adjustment plate bolts and tighten to 11–18 ft. lbs. Position the pump and plate on the vacuum pump bracket and loosely install the pivot and adjustment bolts.
5. Connect the hose from the manifold vacuum outlet fitting to the pump and install the hose clamp.
6. Install the drive belt on the pulley. Place a ⅜ in. drive breaker bar or ratchet into the slot on the vacuum pump adjustment plate. Lift up on the assembly until the proper belt tension is obtained. Tighten the pivot and adjustment bolts to 11–18 ft. lbs.
7. Start the engine and make sure the brake system functions properly.

NOTE: *The BRAKE light will glow until brake vacuum builds up to the normal level.*

Bleeding the Brakes

When any part of the hydraulic system has been disconnected for repair or replacement, air may get into the lines and cause spongy pedal action (because air can be compressed and brake fluid cannot). To correct this condition, it is necessary to bleed the hydraulic system after it has been properly connected to be sure that all

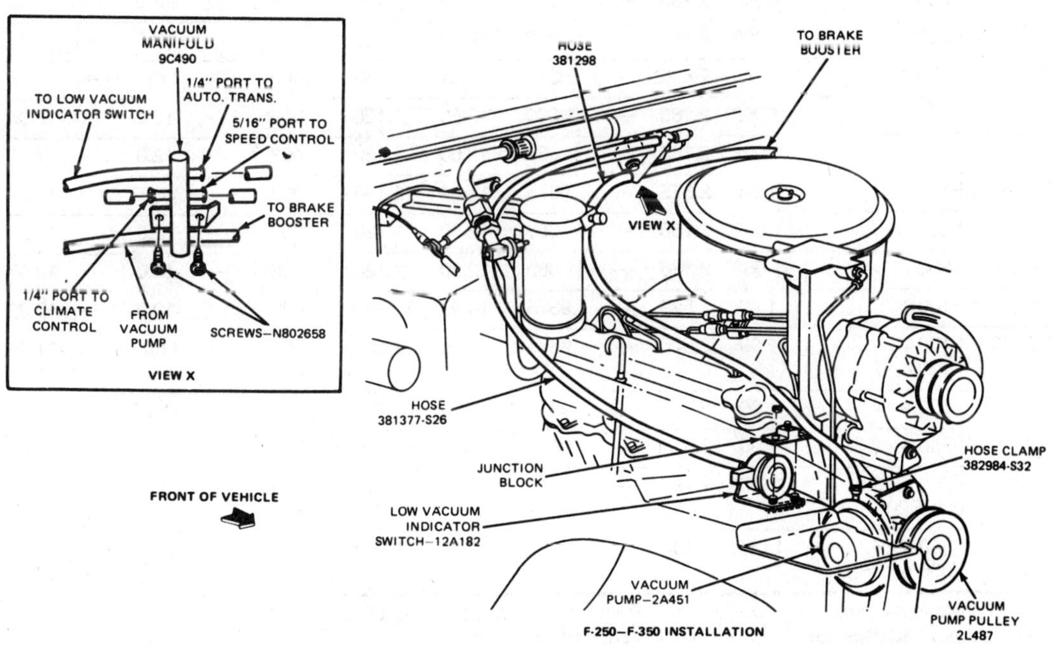

Brake booster pump and low-vacuum indicator switch, 6.9L diesel models

air is expelled from the brake cylinders and lines.

When bleeding the brake system, bleed one brake cylinder at a time, beginning at the cylinder with the longest hydraulic line (farthest from the master cylinder) first. Keep the master cylinder reservoir filled with brake fluid during the bleeding operation. Never use brake fluid that has been drained from the hydraulic system, no matter how clean it is.

It will be necessary to centralize the pressure differential valve after a brake system failure has been corrected and the hydraulic system has been bled.

The primary and secondary hydraulic brake systems are individual systems and are bled separately. During the entire bleeding operation, *do not allow the reservoir to run dry*. Keep the master cylinder reservoirs filled with brake fluid.

1. Clean all dirt from around the master cylinder fill cap, remove the cap and fill the master cylinder with brake fluid until the level is within ¼ in. of the top edge of the reservoir.
2. Clean off the bleeder screws at all 4 wheel cylinders. The bleeder screws are located on the inside of the brake backing plate, on the backside of the wheel cylinders or calipers.
3. Attach a length of rubber hose over the nozzle of the bleeder screw at the wheel to be done first. Place the other end of the hose in a glass jar, submerged in brake fluid.
4. Open the bleeder screw valve ½–¾ turn.
5. Have an assistant slowly depress the brake pedal. Close the bleeder screw valve and tell your assistant to allow the brake pedal to return slowly. Continue this pumping action to force any air out of the system. When bubbles cease to appear at the end of the bleeder hose, close the bleeder valve and remove the hose.
6. Check the master cylinder fluid level and add fluid accordingly. Do this after bleeding each wheel.
7. Repeat the bleeding operation at the remaining 3 wheels, ending with the one closest to the master cylinder. Fill the master cylinder reservoir.

DISC BRAKES

To determine whether your truck has floating or sliding caliper disc brakes, remove the front wheel. The floating caliper unit is operated by two pistons per caliper. The caliper is mounted

Brake Specifications

Year	Model	Master Cylinder Bore	Caliper Bore	Wheel Cylinder Bore Front	Wheel Cylinder Bore Rear	Rotor Diameter	Rotor Minimum Thickness	Rotor Maximum Run-out	Brake Drum Diameter Front	Brake Drum Diameter Rear	Machined Oversize Front	Machined Oversize Rear
'77	F100, 150	1.00	2.875	—	.9375	11.54	1.180	.003	—	11.03	—	11.09
	F250	1.062	2.180	—	1.000	12.50	1.120	.003	—	12.0	—	12.06
	F350	1.062	2.180	—	1.062	12.50	1.120	.003	—	12.0	—	12.06
'78	F100, 150	1.00	2.875	—	.9375	11.54	1.180	.003	—	11.03	—	11.09
	F250	1.062	2.180	—	1.000	12.50	1.120	.003	—	12.0	—	12.06
	F350	1.062	2.180	—	1.062	12.50	1.120	.003	—	12.0	—	12.06
'79–'80	F100, 150	1.00	2.875	—	.9375	11.54	1.180	.003	—	11.03	—	11.09
	F250	1.062	2.180	—	1.000	12.50	1.120	.003	—	12.0	—	12.06
	F350	1.062	2.180	—	1.062	12.50	1.120	.003	—	12.0	—	12.06
'81	F100 ①	1.00	2.599	—	.9375	10.97	1.120 ⑤	.003	—	10.0	—	10.09
'82–'86	F100 ②, F150 4×2	1.00	2.875	—	.9375	11.65	1.120	.003	—	11.03	—	11.09
	F150 4×4	1.00	2.875	—	.9375	11.65	1.120	.003	—	11.03	—	11.09
	F250 4×2 ③	1.00	2.875	—	.9375	12.59	1.120	.003	—	12.0	—	12.06
	F250 Super cab, F200 ④ 4×2	1.062	2.180	—	1.062 ⑥	12.56	1.180	.003	—	12.0	—	12.06
	F350 4×4, F350 4×4	1.062	2.180	—	1.062 ⑥	12.48	1.180	.003	—	12.0	—	12.06

① w/std payload package
② exc. std payload package
③ Regular cab w/payload under 8500 lb.
④ Regular cab w/payload over 8500 lb.
⑤ 1982: .810 or LD models
⑥ '83 and later: 1.00

on a support, and the support and shield are mounted directly to the spindle. There are two types of sliding calipers, the LD sliding caliper and the HD Rail slider caliper. The LD sliding caliper unit is operated by one piston per caliper. The caliper and steering arm are cast as one piece and combined with the spindle stem to form an integral spindle assembly. The HD slider caliper unit contains two pistons on the same side of the rotor. The caliper slides on the support assembly and is retained by a key and spring.

Disc Brake Pads

INSPECTION

Remove the brake pads as described below and measure the thickness of the lining. If the lining at any point on the pad assembly is less than 0.210 in. thick (above the backing plate or rivets), or there is evidence of the lining being contaminated by brake fluid or oil, replace the brake pads.

REMOVAL AND INSTALLATION

Floating Caliper

1. Remove the tire and wheel assembly.
2. Remove the brake pad mounting pins, anti-rattle springs, and then lift out the brake pads.
3. Before installing the new brake pads, remove the master cylinder cover, and loosen the piston housing-to-caliper mounting bolts enough to allow installation of the new (thicker) brake pads. Do not move the pistons.
4. Install the new pads. Install the mounting pins and anti-rattle spring.

   NOTE: *Make sure that the spring tangs engage the holes in the brake pad plates.*
5. Tighten the brake pad mounting pins to 17–23 ft. lbs.
6. Tighten the piston-to-housing mounting bolts to reset the pistons in the cylinders.

   NOTE: *Make sure that you keep the cylinder housing square with the caliper.*
7. Tighten the piston housing-to-caliper mounting bolts to 155–185 ft. lbs.
8. Install the wheel and tire assembly.
9. Check the level in the master cylinder. It is normal for the brake fluid level to rise with the replacement of worn front brake pads with new ones. If the fluid level was added to before the old pads were replaced, the master cylinder may overflow. Adjust the level of the brake fluid in the master cylinder reservoir to within ¼ in. from the top of the filler neck as necessary.

LD Sliding Caliper (Single Piston)

1. To avoid overflowing of the master cylinder when the caliper pistons are pressed into the caliper cylinder bores, siphon or dip some brake fluid out of the larger reservoir.
2. Jack up the front of the truck and remove the wheels.
3. Place an 8 in. C-clamp on the caliper and tighten the clamp to bottom the caliper piston in the cylinder bore. Remove the C-clamp.
4. Remove the caliper support key retaining screw.
5. Drive out the caliper support key and support spring with a drift and hammer.
6. Remove the caliper from the spindle assembly by pushing it downward against the spindle assembly, and rotating the upper end upward and out of the spindle assembly. Lay the caliper on the tie-rod.

   NOTE: *Do not allow the caliper to hand by the brake hose.*
7. Remove the outer brake pad from the caliper. It may be necessary to tap the pad loose from the caliper.
8. Remove the inner pad from the spindle assembly. Remove the brake pad anti-rattle clip from the lower pad abutment surface of the spindle assembly.
9. Thoroughly clean the areas of the caliper and spindle assembly which contact each other during the sliding action of the caliper.
10. Place a new anti-rattle clip in the lower pad abutment in the spindle assembly. Make sure that the tabs on the clip are positioned correctly and the loop-type spring is away from the rotor.
11. Place the lower end of the inner brake pad in the spindle assembly pad abutment, against the anti-rattle clip, and slide the upper end of the pad into position. Be sure that the clip is still in position.
12. Check and make sure that the caliper piston is fully bottomed in the cylinder bore. Use a large C-clamp to bottom the piston, if necessary.

    NOTE: *The replacement outer brake pads differ slightly from the original equipment. The replacement brake pads have tabs on the flange at the lower edge of the pad plate and the distance between the upper tabs and the lower flange is reduced to provide a slip-on interference fit.*
13. Position the outer brake pad on the caliper, and press the pad tabs into place with your fingers. If the pad cannot be pressed into place by hand, use a C-clamp. Be careful not to damage the lining with the clamp.
14. Position the caliper on the spindle as-

sembly by pivoting the caliper around the spindle upper mounting surface. Be careful not to tear or cut the piston boot as it slips over the inner brake pad.

15. Hold the upper machined surface of the caliper against the surface of the spindle assembly with a brake adjusting tool or screwdriver and install a new caliper support spring and key. Drive the key and spring assembly into position and install the key retaining screw. Tighten the screw to 12–20 ft. lbs.

16. After the new brake pads and wheel assemblies have been installed on both front wheels, lower the truck, and check the master cylinder reservoirs. Adjust the level of brake fluid in the master cylinder as necessary.

17. Depress the brake pedal firmly several times to seat the brake pad linings against the rotors. Do not move the truck until the pedal is firm.

Rail Slider Sliding Caliper (Two Piston)

1. Raise and secure the vehicle. Remove the wheel and tire assembly.
2. Disconnect the brake hose from the caliper and plug the hose and inlet port.
3. Remove the key retaining screw.
4. Using a brass rod and light hammer drive out the key and spring.
5. Remove the caliper from its support assembly by rotating the key and spring end out and away from the rotor. Slide the opposite end of the caliper clear of the slide in the support and off the rotor. Lay the caliper on the tie rod or axle.
6. Remove the caliper brake shoe anti-rattle spring and the inner and outer shoe and lining assemblies.
7. Thoroughly clean the areas of the caliper and support that contact during the sliding action of the caliper.
8. Place a C-clamp on the caliper housing midway between the piston bores, and using the old inner shoe and lining over the pistons, tighten the clamp to bottom of the caliper pistons in the cylinder bores. Remove the clamp and inner shoe lining assembly.
9. Before installation check to be sure that the caliper pistons are fully bottomed in the cylinder bores.
10. Install a new inner and outer shoe and lining assemblies and install the anti-rattle spring.
11. Place the caliper rail into the slide on the support and rotate the caliper into the rotor.
12. Position the key and spring between the caliper and support assembly and start in by hand. Note that the spring is between the key and caliper and that the spring tangs overlap the ends of the key. Use a break adjusting tool or screwdriver to hold up the caliper against the support assembly.
13. Using a hammer, drive the key and spring into position aligning the correct notch with the existing hole in the support.
14. Secure the key to the support with the key retaining screw. Tigthen the screw to 20 ft. lbs.
15. Place new copper washer on the brake hose fitting and connect to the caliper inlet port.
16. Bleed the system, lower the vehicle, and refill the master cylinder if necessary.

Disc Brake Calipers

REMOVAL AND INSTALLATION

Floating Caliper

1. Raise the front of the truck and support it.
2. Remove the wheel and tire assembly.
3. Disconnect the brake hose from the caliper.
4. Remove the pins and nuts retaining the caliper assembly to the anchor plate, and remove the caliper from the vehicle.
5. Place the caliper assembly on the anchor plate and install the retaining pins and nuts. Apply a light coat of chassis grease on the pins before installing them. Tighten the nuts to 17–23 ft. lbs.
6. Connect the brake hose to the caliper. It is advised that a new copper washer be used.
7. Install the wheel and tire assembly.
8. Bleed the brake hydraulic system and lower the vehicle.

Sliding Caliper

1. Raise the front of the truck and support it. Remove the wheel and tire assembly.
2. Disconnect the brake hose from the caliper.
3. Remove and install the caliper and the brake pads as outlined under "Disc Brake Pad Removal and Installation."
4. Connect the brake fluid hose to the caliper. It is recommended that a new copper washer be used at the connection of the brake hose and caliper.
5. Bleed the brake system and install the wheel and tire assembly. Lower the truck.

OVERHAUL

Floating Caliper

NOTE: *If the caliper assembly is leaking brake fluid, replace the piston assemblies. If the cylinder bores are scored, corroded or excessively worn, and the leaking cannot be stopped by replacing the pistons, replace the*

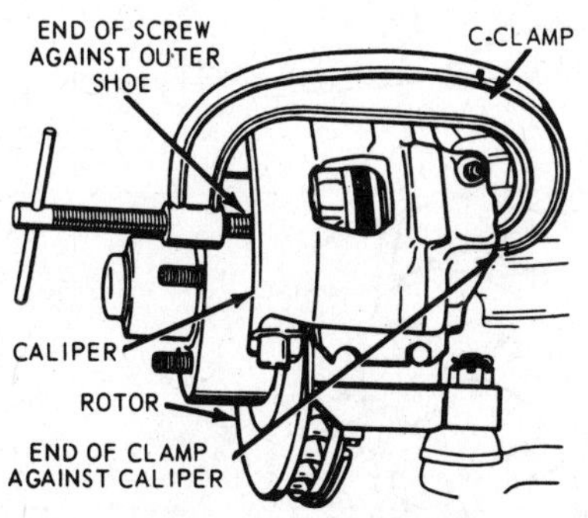

Bottom the piston in the cylinder bore with a C-clamp

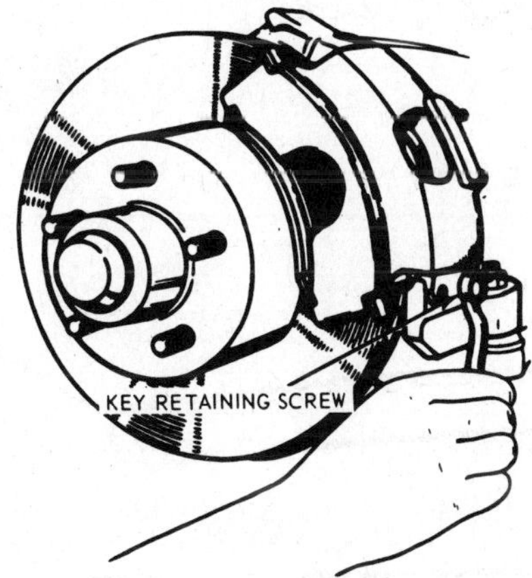

Removing the caliper support key retaining screw

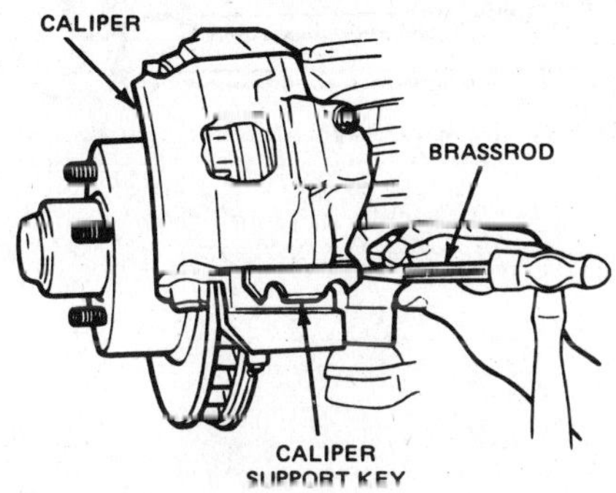

Driving out the caliper support key with a drift

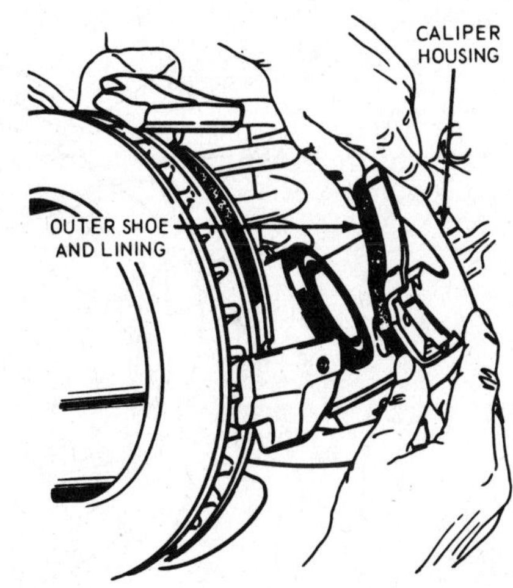

Removing the outer brake pad

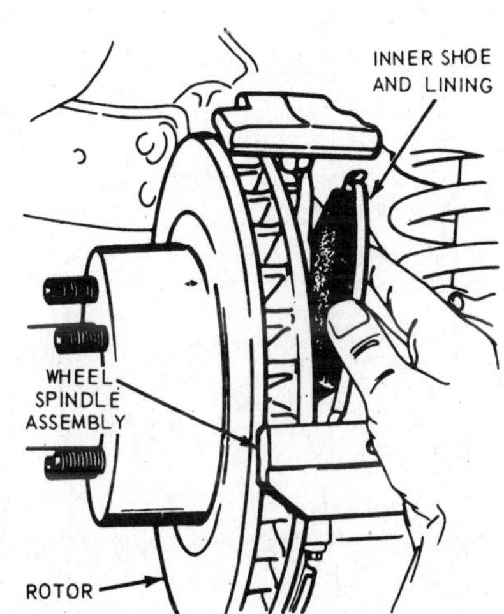

Removing the inner brake pad

piston housing. Do not hone the cylinder bores. There are no oversize pistons available for oversize bores.

1. Remove the caliper assembly from the truck and secure it in a vise.
2. Remove the brake pads from the caliper.
3. Place a 1⅛ in. thick block of wood between the caliper and the pistons and apply low air pressure to the brake fluid inlet. This should force the pistons out of the bores to the block of wood.
4. Remove the block of wood and remove the pistons.
5. Remove the bolts which attach the caliper to the cylinder housing and separate the caliper from the housing.
6. Remove and discard the piston seals.
7. Lubricate the new piston seals with clean brake fluid and install them in the seal grooves in the cylinder bores.
8. Apply a film of clean brake fluid to the cylinder bores.
9. Lubricate the retaining lips of the dust boots with clean brake fluid and install them in the boot retaining grooves in the cylinder bores.
10. Apply a film of clean brake fluid to the piston.
11. Insert the pistons into the dust boots and start them into the cylinders by hand until they

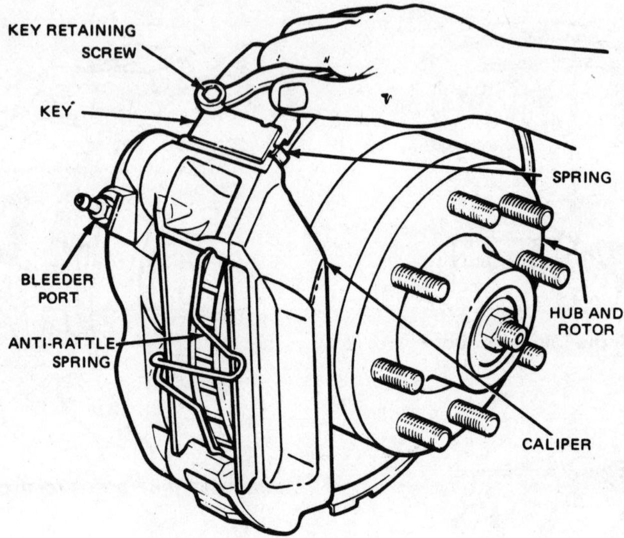

Removing the key retaining screw

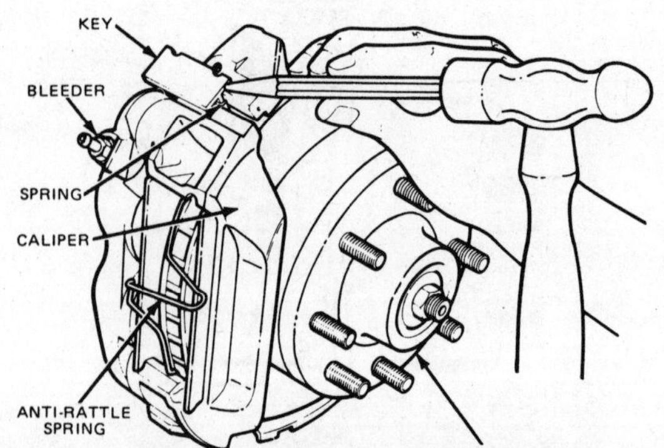

Removing the key and spring

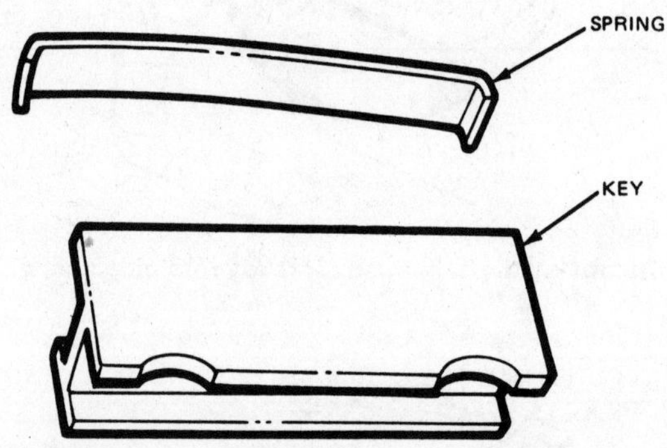

Caliper spring and key

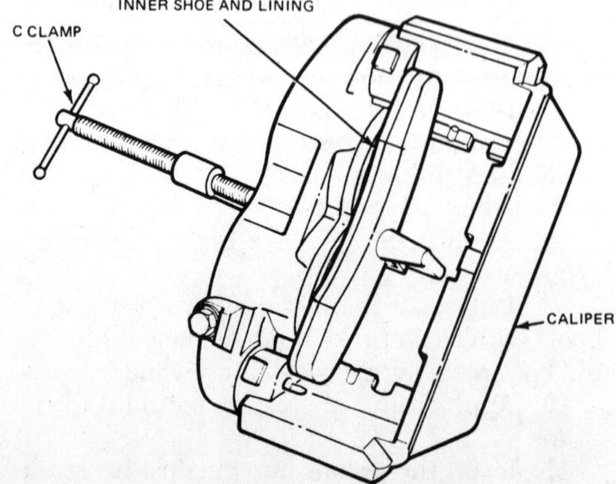

Using the C-clamp to bottom the caliper pistons

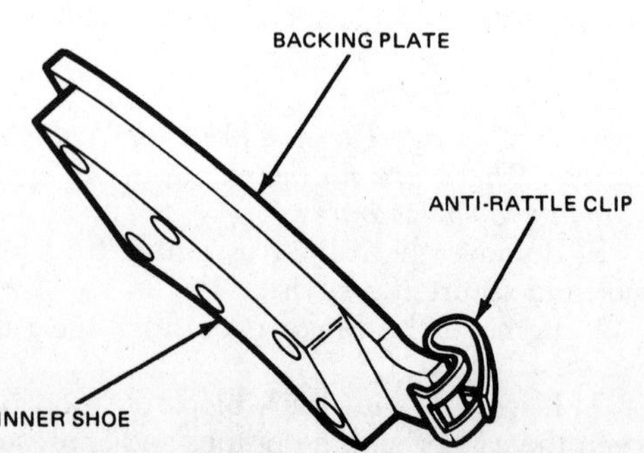

Anti-rattle clip installation on brake shoe

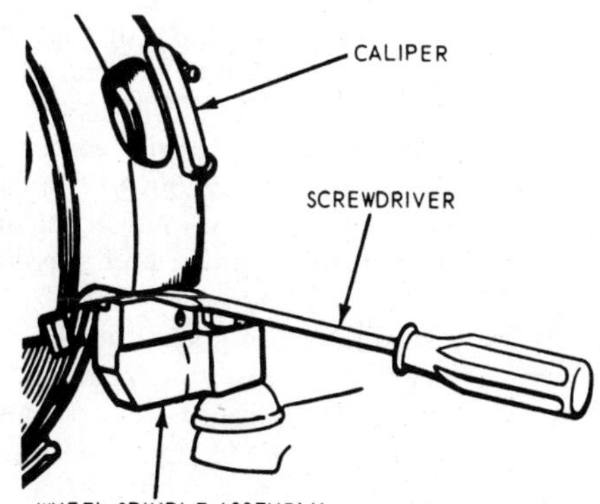

Holding the upper machined surface of the caliper against the surface of the spindle assembly in preparation for installing the caliper support spring and key

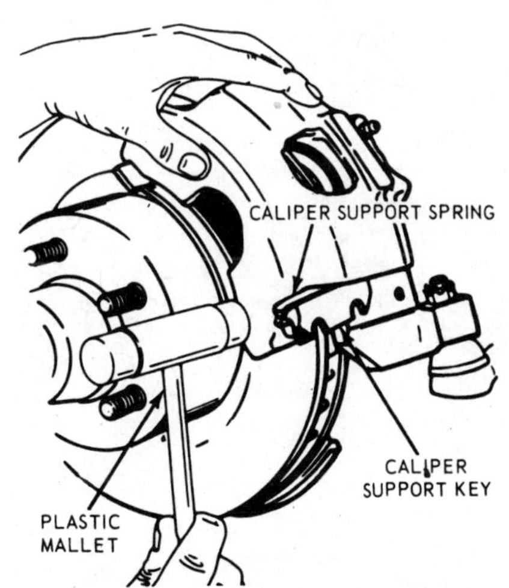

Installation of the caliper support spring and key

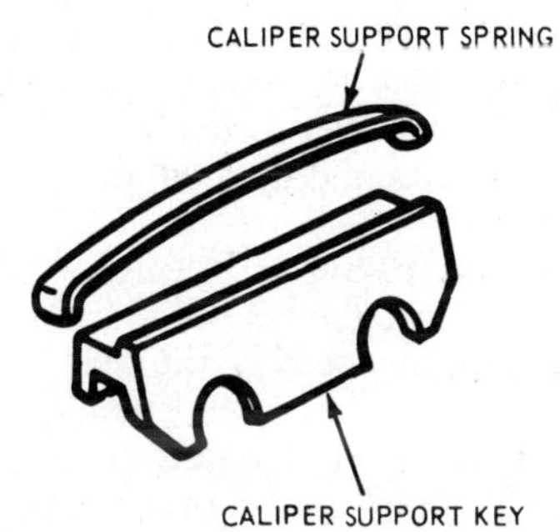

Assembly of the caliper spring and key

are past the piston seals. Be careful not to damage or dislodge the seal.

12. Place a block of wood over one piston and press the piston into the cylinder, being careful not to cock the piston in the cylinder bore. Install the second piston in the same manner.

13. Install the brake pads.

14. Place the piston housing on the caliper and install the piston housing-to-caliper mounting bolts and washers. Tighten them to 155–185 ft. lbs.

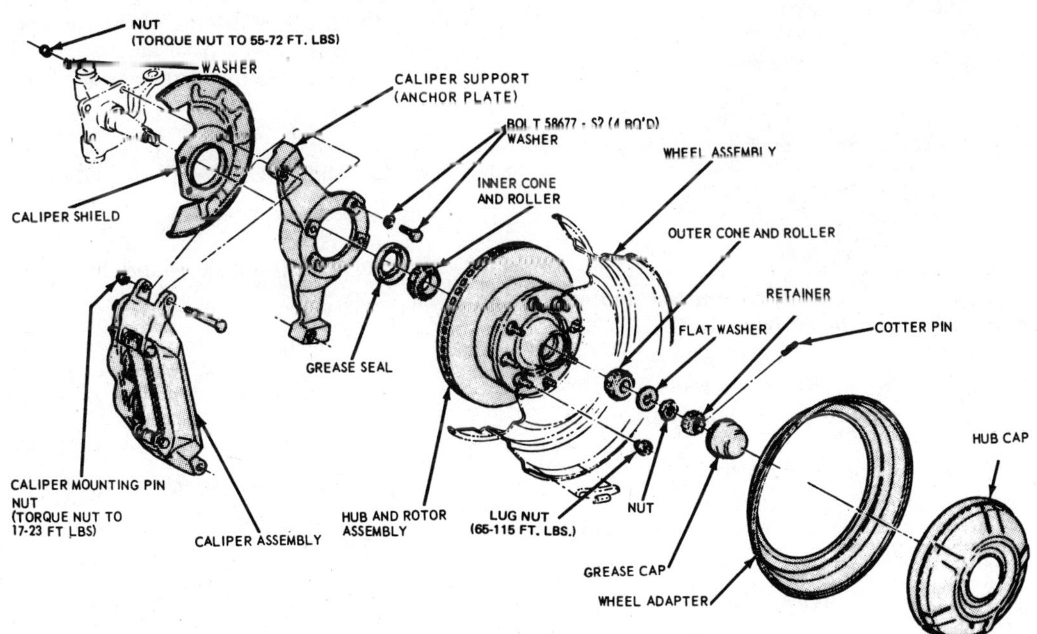

Exploded view of the floating caliper assembly

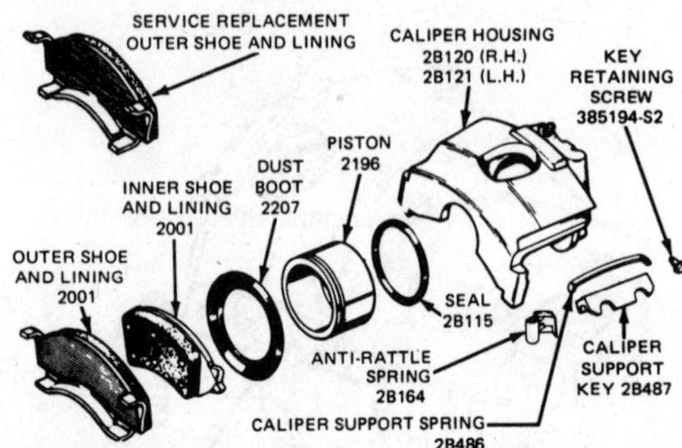

Sliding caliper assembly

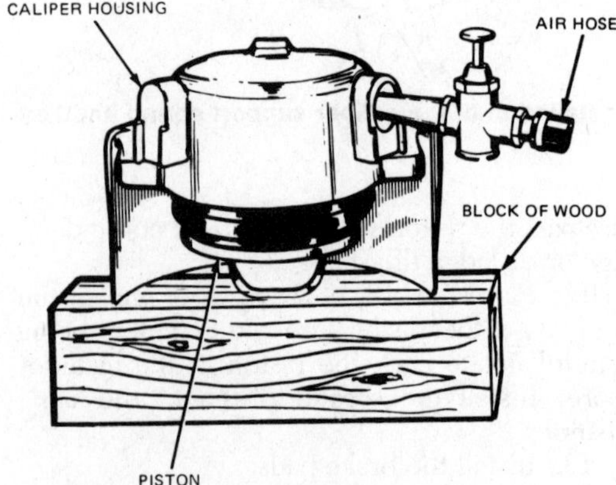

Carefully blow out the brake pistons with compressed air. Use low air pressure

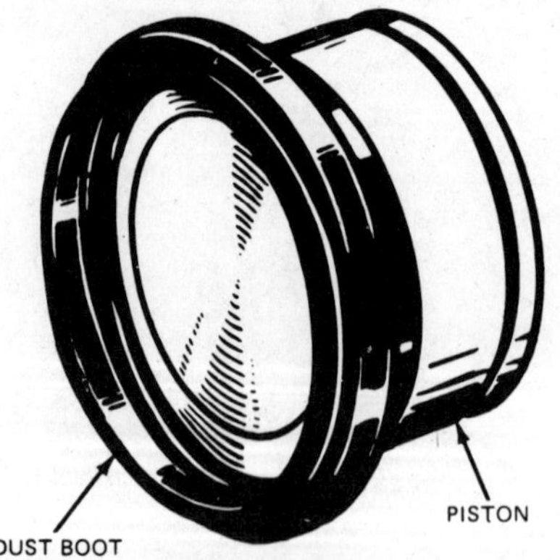

When assembling, use new dust boots and lubricate the pistons with clean brake fluid

15. Position the caliper assembly on the support and install all the retaining pins and nuts.

16. Install the brake fluid hose, bleed the brake hydraulic system, and center the pressure differential valve. Do not drive the truck until a firm brake pedal is obtained.

LD Sliding Caliper (Single Piston)

1. Clean the outside of the caliper in alcohol after removing it from the vehicle and removing the brake pads.

2. Roll some thick shop cloths or rags and place them between the piston and the outer legs of the caliper.

3. Apply compressed air to the caliper inlet port until the piston comes out of the caliper bore. Use low air pressure to avoid having the piston pop out too rapidly and possibly causing injury.

4. If the piston becomes cocked in the cylinder bore and will not come out, remove the air pressure and tap the piston with a soft hammer to try and straighten it. Do not use a sharp tool or pry the piston out of the bore. Reapply the air pressure.

5. Remove the boot from the piston and seal from the caliper cylinder bore.

6. Clean the piston and caliper in alcohol.

7. Lubricate the piston seal with clean brake fluid, and position the seal in the groove in the cylinder bore.

8. Coat the outside of the piston and both of the beads of the dust boot with clean brake fluid. Insert the piston through the dust boot until the boot is around the bottom (closed end) of the piston.

9. Hold the piston and dust boot directly above the caliper cylinder bore, and use your fingers to work the bead of the dust boot into the groove near the top of the cylinder bore.

10. After the bead is seated in the groove, press straight down on the piston until it bottoms in the bore. Be careful not to cock the piston in the bore. Use a C-clamp with a block of wood inserted between the clamp and the piston to bottom the piston, if necessary.

11. Install the brake pads and install the caliper. Bleed the brake hydraulic system and recenter the pressure differential valve. Do not drive the vehicle until a firm brake pedal is obtained.

HD Rail Slider Sliding Caliper (Two Piston)

1. Disconnect and plug the flexible brake hose.

2. Remove the front shoe and lining assemblies.

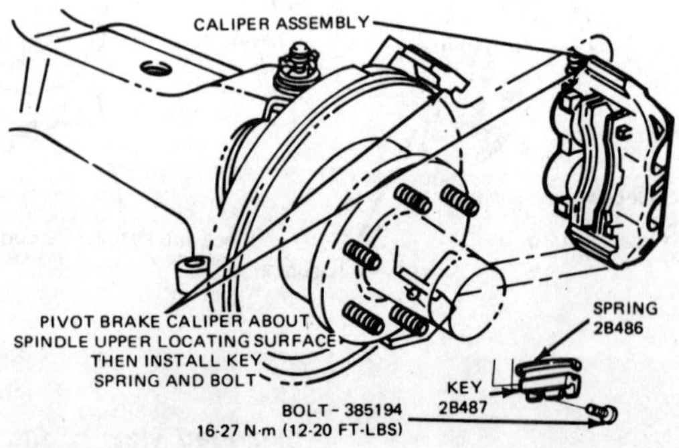

F-250/F-350 caliper installation

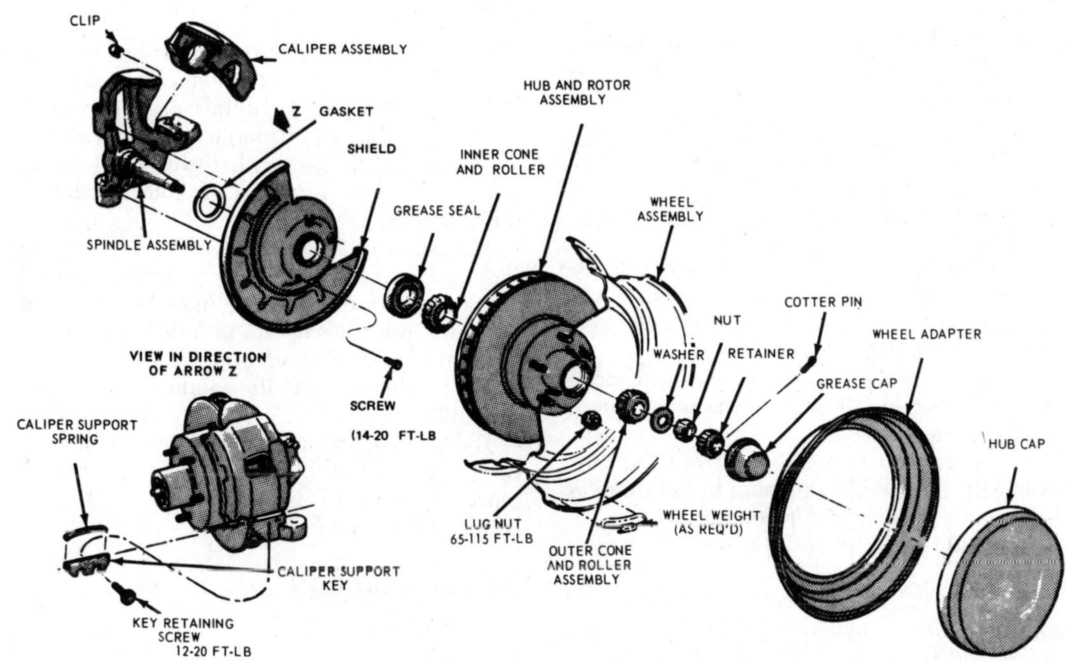

Exploded view of the sliding caliper assembly

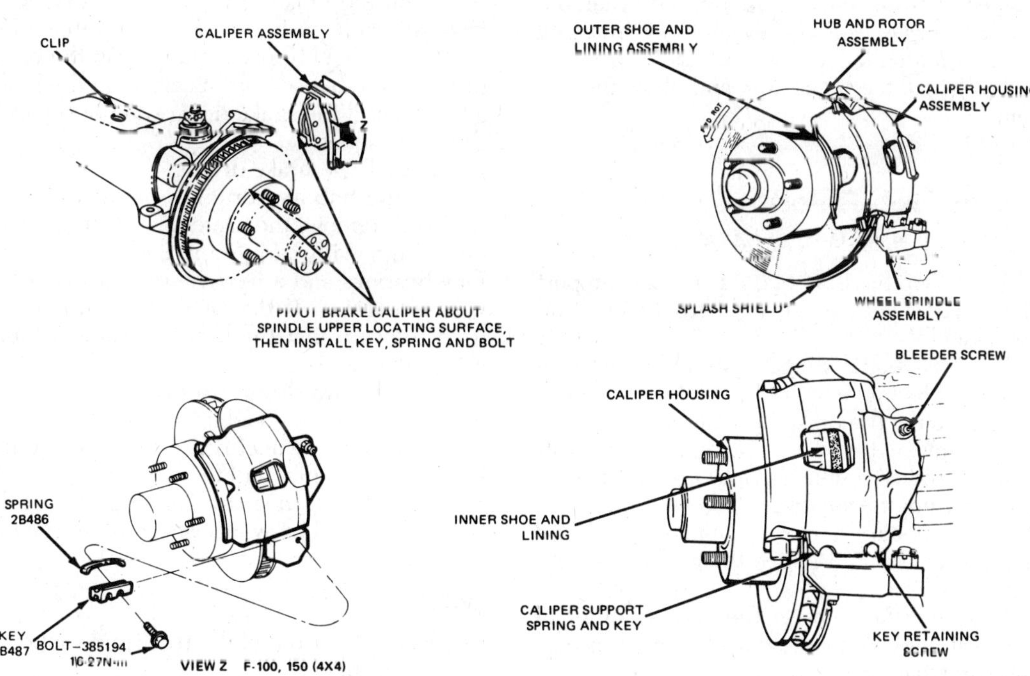

4WD F-150 sliding caliper mounting

3. Drain the fluid from the cylinders.
4. Secure the caliper in a vise and place a block of wood between the caliper bridge and the cylinders.
5. Apply low pressure air to the brake hose inlet and the pistons will be forced out to the wood block.
6. Remove the block of wood and remove the pistons.
7. Remove the bolts and washers that attach the caliper to the cylinder housing and separate the caliper from the housing.
8. Remove the piston seals.
9. Lubricate the new piston seals with clean brake fluid and install them in the seal grooves in the cylinder bores.
10. Lubricate the retaining lips of the dust boots with clean brake fluid and install them in the grooves of the cylinder bores.
11. Apply a film of clean brake fluid to the pistons.
12. Insert the pistons into the dust boots and start them into the cylinders by hand until they are beyond the piston seals. Be careful not to dislodge or damage the piston seal.
13. Place a block of wood over one piston and press the piston into the cylinder. Be careful not to cock the piston in the cylinder bore.
14. Install the second piston in the same manner.
15. Attach the piston housing to the caliper and tighten the mounting bolts to 155–185 ft. lbs.
16. Install the brake shoe assemblies and antirattle clip in the caliper assembly. Place the caliper assembly on the support and install the caliper support spring, key and key retaining screw. Tighten the screw to 12–20 ft. lbs.
17. Install the brake hose and bleed the system.

Brake Disc (Rotor)

REMOVAL AND INSTALLATION

1. Jack up the front of the truck and support it with jackstands. Remove the front wheel and tire assembly.
2. Remove the caliper assembly and support it to the frame with a piece of wire without disconnecting the brake fluid hose.
3. Remove the dust cap, cotter pin, nut, washer, and the outer bearing. Remove the rotor/hub from the spindle.
4. If necessary, remove the inner grease seal and inner bearing. Replace the grease seal with a new one.
5. Install the rotor in the reverse order of removal, and adjust the wheel bearing as outlined in Chapter 1.

INSPECTION

If the rotor is deeply scarred or has shallow cracks, it may be refinished on a disc brake rotor lathe. Also, if the lateral run-out exceeds 0.010 in. within a 6 in. radius when measured with a dial indicator, with the stylus 1 in. in from the edge of the rotor, the rotor should be refinished or replaced.

A maximum of 0.020 in. of material may be removed equally from each friction surface of the rotor. If the damage cannot be corrected when the rotor has been machined to the minimum thickness shown on the rotor (0.940 in.—floating caliper; 1.20 in.—sliding caliper), it should be replaced.

The finished braking surfaces of the rotor must be parallel within 0.007 in. and lateral run-out must not be more than 0.003 in. on the inboard surface in a 5 in. radius.

Wheel Bearings

See Chapter 1 for wheel bearing service.

FRONT DRUM BRAKES

Brake Drums

REMOVAL AND INSTALLATION

2WD

1. Raise the vehicle until the tire clears the floor.
2. Remove the wheel cover or hub cap and the wheel bearing dust cap. Remove the cotter pin, nut lock, nut and washer.
3. Pull the brake drum approximately 2 in. forward, then push it back into position. Remove the wheel bearing and pull off the brake drum and hub assembly. Back off on the brake adjustment if the brake drum will not slip over the brake shoes.

To install the brake drums:

4. If the hub and drum assembly are to be replaced, remove the protective coating from a new drum with carburetor degreaser. Install new bearings and a new grease seal. Pack the wheel bearings. If the original drum is being used, be sure that the hub is clean and lubricated adequately.
5. Install the drum assembly, outer wheel bearing, washer, and adjusting nut.
6. Adjust the wheel bearing, install the nut lock and cotter pin, and the grease cap.
7. Install the wheel and hub cap. Adjust the brake shoes if they were backed off to remove the drum.

4WD

1. Raise the front of the truck and support it with jackstands.

2. Loosen the brake shoe adjustment.
3. Remove the hub dust cap.
4. On an F-100, F-150 only (standard), remove the hub retaining snap-ring, and slide the splined driving hub from between the axle shaft and the wheel hub. Remove the driving hub spacer and spring.
5. If the vehicle is equipped with free-wheeling hubs, remove the hub assembly as described in Chapter 1.
6. Remove the locknut, nut lock, the wheel bearing adjusting nut from the steering spindle. Remove the wheel, hub and drum as an assembly. The outer wheel bearing will be forced off the spindle at the same time. Remove the inner wheel bearing.
7. Remove the front wheel-to-hub retaining nuts and remove the wheel and tire as an assembly from the hub and drum.
8. Remove the brake drum retaining bolts and nuts and remove the brake drum from the hub.
9. Install the brake drums in the reverse order of removal and adjust the wheel bearings and brake shoes.

INSPECTION

After the brake drum has been removed from the vehicle, it should be inspected for runout, severe scoring, cracks, and the proper inside diameter.

Minor scores on a brake drum can be removed with fine emery cloth, provided that all grit is removed from the drum before it is installed on the vehicle.

A badly scored, rough, or out-of-round (runout) drum can be ground or turned on a brake drum lathe. Do not remove any more material from the drum than is necessary to provide a smooth surface for the brake shoe to contact. The maximum diameter of the braking surface is shown on the inside of each brake drum. Brake drums that exceed the maximum braking surface diameter shown on the brake drum, either through wear or refinishing, must be replaced. This is because after the outside wall of the brake drum reaches a certain thickness (thinner than the original thickness) the drum loses its ability to dissipate the heat created by the friction between the brake drum and the brake shoes, when the brakes are applied. Also, the brake drum will have more tendency to warp and/or crack.

The maximum braking surface diameter specification, which is shown on each drum, allows for a 0.060 in. machining cut over the original nominal drum diameter plus 0.030 in. additional wear before reaching the diameter where the drum must be discarded. Use a brake drum micrometer to measure the insider diameter of the brake drums.

Brake Shoes

INSPECTION

Remove the brake drum and inspect the brake drum linings for wear or damage which could affect brake operation, i.e., severely cracked or chipped lining, grease or brake fluid soaked lining, or brake lining which is severely gouged or grooved due to the entrance of dirt or sand. Replace any brake lining observed as above or that is worn to within 1/32 in. of any rivet head or brake shoe.

REMOVAL AND INSTALLATION

F-100, F-150, F-250 Light-Duty

1. Raise and support the vehicle and remove the wheel and brake drum from the wheel to be worked on.

NOTE: *If you have never replaced the brakes on a car before and you are not too familiar with the procedures involved, only disassemble and assemble one side at a time, leaving the other side intact as a reference during reassembly.*

2. Install a clamp over the ends of the wheel cylinder to prevent the pistons of the wheel cylinder from coming out, causing loss of fluid and much grief.
3. Contract the brake shoes by pulling the self-adjusting lever away from the starwheel adjustment screw and turn the starwheel up and back until the pivot nut is drawn onto the starwheel as far as it will come.
4. Pull the adjusting lever, cable and au-

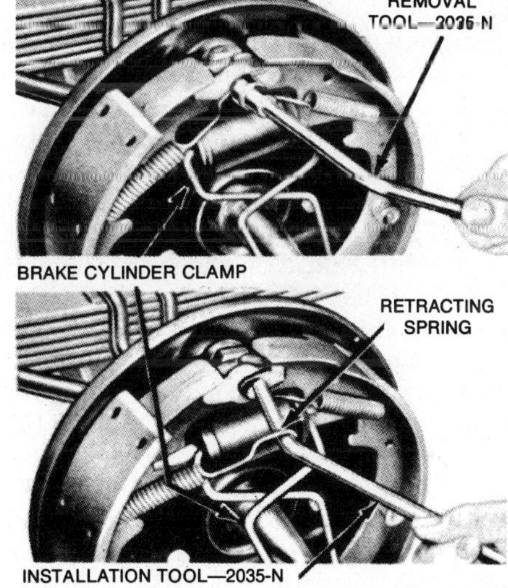

Removing and installing the brake shoe retracting springs

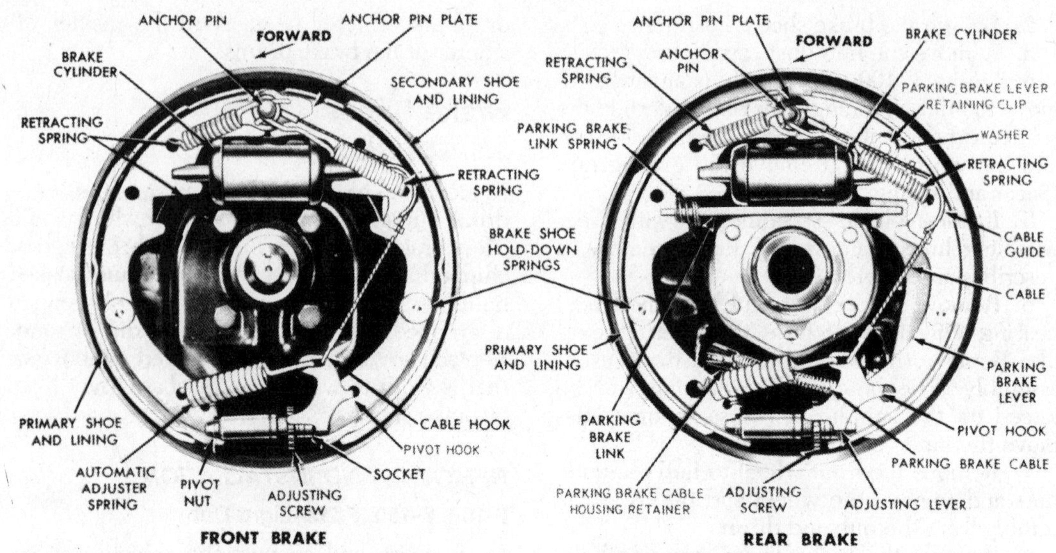

Front and rear drum brakes on F-100 and F-250 light-duty

tomatic adjuster spring down and toward the rear to unhook the pivot hook from the large hole in the secondary shoe web. Do not attempt to pry the pivot hook from the hole.

5. Remove the automatic adjuster spring and the adjusting lever.

6. Remove the secondary shoe-to-anchor spring with a brake tool. (Brake tools are very common implements and are available at auto parts stores). Remove the primary shoe-to-anchor spring and unhook the cable anchor. Remove the anchor pin plate.

7. Remove the cable guide from the secondary shoe.

8. Remove the shoe hold-down springs, shoes, adjusting screw, pivot nut, and socket. Note the color of each holddown spring for assembly. To remove the hold-down springs, reach behind the brake backing plate and place one finger on the end of one of the brake hold-down spring mounting pins. Using a pair of pliers, grasp the washer-type retainer on top of the hold-down spring that corresponds to the pin which you are holding. Push down on the pliers and turn them 90° to align the slot in the washer with the head on the spring mounting pin. Remove the spring and washer retainer and repeat this operation on the holddown spring on the other shoe.

9. On rear brakes, remove the parking brake link and spring. Disconnect the parking brake cable from the parking brake lever.

10. After removing the rear brake secondary shoe, disassemble the parking brake lever from the shoe by removing the retaining clip and spring washer.

To assemble and install the brake shoes:

11. On rear brakes, assemble the parking brake lever to the secondary shoe and secure it with the spring washer and retaining clip.

12. Apply a *light* coating of Lubriplate® at the points where the brake shoes contact the backing plate.

13. Position the brake shoes on the backing plate, and install the hold-down spring pins, springs, and spring washer-type retainers. On the rear brake, install the parking brake link, spring and washer. Connect the parking brake cable to the parking brake lever.

14. Install the anchor pin plate, and place the cable anchor over the anchor pin with the crimped side toward the backing plate.

15. Install the primary shoe-to-anchor spring with the brake tool.

16. Install the cable guide on the secondary

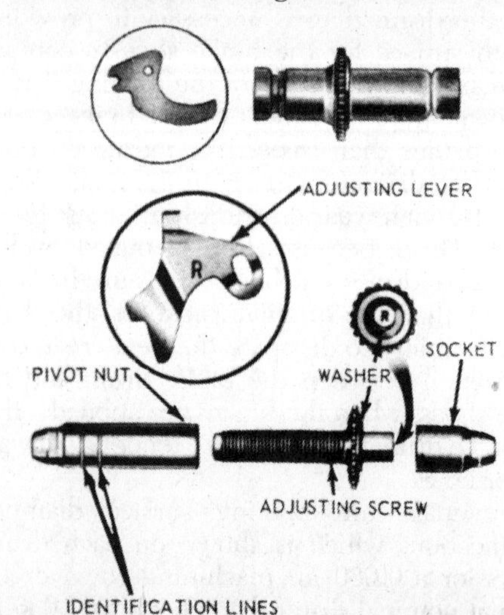

Identification of the adjusting screws and self-adjusting lever components

shoe web with the flanged holes fitted into the hole in the secondary shoe web. Thread the cable around the cable guide groove.

17. Install the secondary shoe-to-anchor (long) spring. Be sure that the cable end is not cocked or binding on the anchor pin when installed. All of the parts should be flat on the anchor pin. Remove the wheel cylinder piston clamp.

18. Apply Lubriplate® to the threads and the socket end of the adjusting starwheel screw. Turn the adjusting screw into the adjusting pivot nut to the limit of the threads and then back off ½ turn.

NOTE: *Interchanging the brake shoe adjusting screw assemblies from one side of the vehicle to the other would cause the brake shoes to retract rather than expand each time the automatic adjusting mechanism is operated. To prevent this, the socket end of the adjusting screw is stamped with an "R" or an "L" for RIGHT or LEFT. The adjusting pivot nuts can be distinguished by the number of lines machined around the body of the nut; one line indicates lefthand nut and two lines indicate a righthand nut.*

19. Place the adjusting socket on the screw and install this assembly between the shoe ends with the adjusting screw nearest to the secondary shoe.

20. Place the cable hook into the hole in the adjusting lever from the backing plate side. The adjusting levers are stamped with an "R" (right) or an "L" (left) to indicate their installation on the right or left-hand brake assembly.

21. Position the hooked end of the adjuster spring in the primary shoe web and connect the loop end of the spring to the adjuster lever hole.

22. Pull the adjuster lever, cable and automatic adjuster spring down toward the rear to engage the pivot hook in the large hole in the secondary shoe web.

23. After installation, check the action of the adjuster by pulling the section of the cable between the cable guide and the adjusting lever toward the secondary shoe web far enough to lift the lever past a tooth on the adjusting screw starwheel. The lever should snap into position behind the next tooth, and release of the cable should cause the adjuster spring to return the lever to its original position. This return action of the lever will turn the adjusting screw starwheel one tooth. The lever should contact the adjusting screw starwheel one tooth above the centerline of the adjusting screw.

If the automatic adjusting mechanism does not perform properly, check the following:

1. Check the cable and fittings. The cable ends should fill or extend slightly beyond the crimped section of the fittings. If this is not the case, replace the cable.

2. Check the cable guide for damage. The cable groove should be parallel to the shoe web, and the body of the guide should lie flat against the web. Replace the cable guide if this is not so.

3. Check the pivot hook on the lever. The hook surfaces should be square with the body on the lever for proper pivoting. Repair or replace the hook as necessary.

4. Make sure that the adjusting screw starwheel is properly seated in the notch in the shoe web.

F-250, F-350 Heavy-Duty

1. Raise and support the vehicle.
2. Remove the wheel and drum.
3. On a front wheel, remove the spring clip retainer fastening the adjustment cable anchor fitting to the brake anchor pin. On a rear wheel, remove the parking brake lever assembly retaining nut from behind the backing plate and remove the parking brake lever assembly.

NOTE: *From this point on, the removal of the front and rear brakes is the same.*

4. Remove the adjusting cable assembly from the anchor pin, cable guide, and adjusting lever.
5. Remove the brake shoe retracting springs.
6. Remove the brake shoe hold-down spring from each shoe.
7. Remove the brake shoes and adjusting screw assembly.
8. Disassemble the adjusting screw assembly.

To install the brake shoes:

9. Clean the ledge pads on the backing plate. Apply a light coat of Lubriplate® to the ledge pads (where the brake shoes rub the backing plate).
10. Apply Lubriplate® to the adjusting screw assembly and the hold-down and retracting spring contacts on the brake shoes.
11. Install the upper retracting spring on the primary and secondary shoes and position the shoe assembly on the backing plate with the wheel cylinder pushrods in the shoe slots.
12. Install the brake shoe hold-down springs.
13. Install the brake shoe adjustment screw assembly with the slot in the head of the adjusting screw toward the primary shoe, lower retracting spring, adjusting lever spring, adjusting lever assembly, and connect the adjusting cable to the adjusting lever. Position the cable in the cable guide and install the cable anchor fitting on the anchor pin.
14. Install the adjusting screw assemblies in the same locations from which they were re-

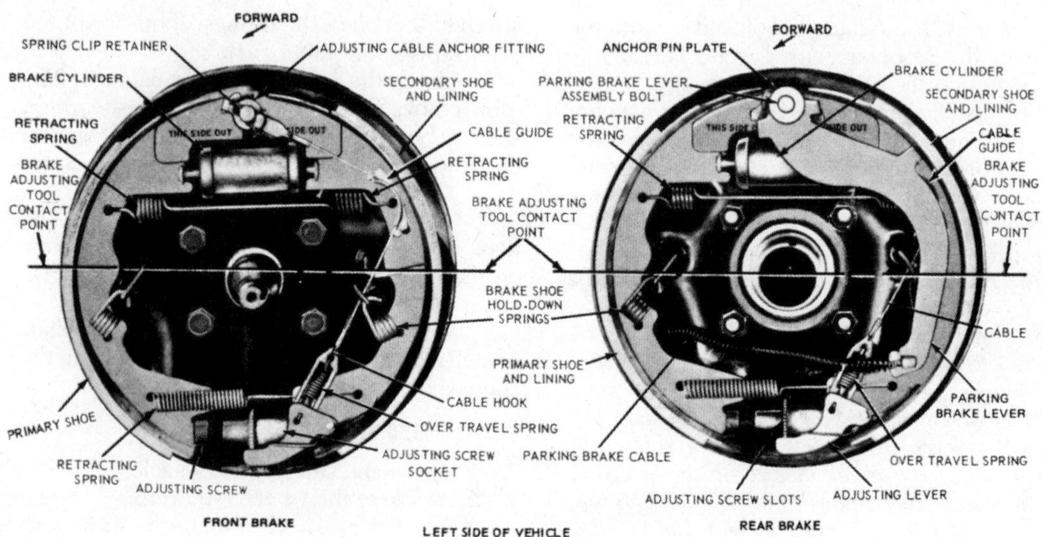

Front and rear drum brakes—F-250–350 heavy-duty

moved. Interchanging the brake shoe adjusting screws from one side of the vehicle to the other will cause the brake shoes to retract rather than expand each time the automatic adjusting mechanism is operated. To prevent incorrect installation, the socket end of each adjusting screw is stamped with an R or an L to indicate their installation on the right or left-side of the vehicle. The adjusting pivot nuts can be distinguished by the number of lines machined around the body of the nut. Two lines indicate a right-hand nut; one line indicates a left-hand nut.

15. On a rear wheel, install the parking brake assembly in the anchor pin and secure with the retaining nut behind the backing plate.

16. Adjust the brakes before installing the brake drums and wheels. Install the brake drums and wheels.

17. Lower the vehicle and road test the brakes. New brakes may pull to one side or the other before they are seated. Continued pulling or erratic braking should not occur.

Wheel Cylinders

OVERHAUL

Wheel cylinder rebuilding kits are available for reconditioning the wheel cylinders. The kits usually contain new cup springs, cylinder cups, and in some cases, new boots. The most important factor to keep in mind when rebuilding wheel cylinders is cleanliness. Keep all dirt away from the wheel cylinders when you are reassembling them.

1. To remove the wheel cylinder, jack up the vehicle and remove the wheel, hub, and drum.

2. Disconnect the brake line at the fitting on the brake backing plate.

3. Remove the brake assemblies.

4. Remove the screws which hold the wheel cylinder to the backing plate and remove the wheel cylinder from the vehicle.

5. Remove the rubber dust covers on the ends of the cylinder. Remove the pistons and piston cups and the spring. Remove the bleeder screw and make sure that it is not plugged.

6. Discard all of the parts which the rebuilding kit will replace.

7. Examine the inside of the cylinder. If it is severely rusted, pitted or scratched, then the cylinder must be replaced as the piston cups won't be able to seal against the walls of the cylinder.

8. Using a wheel cylinder hone or emery cloth and crocus cloth, polish the inside of the cylinder. The purpose of this is to put a new surface on the inside of the cylinder. Keep the inside of the cylinder coated with brake fluid while honing. If crocus cloth is being used, rotate the cloth around the inside of the wheel cylinder; not in and out.

9. Wash out the cylinder with clean brake fluid after honing.

10. When reassembling the cylinder, dip all

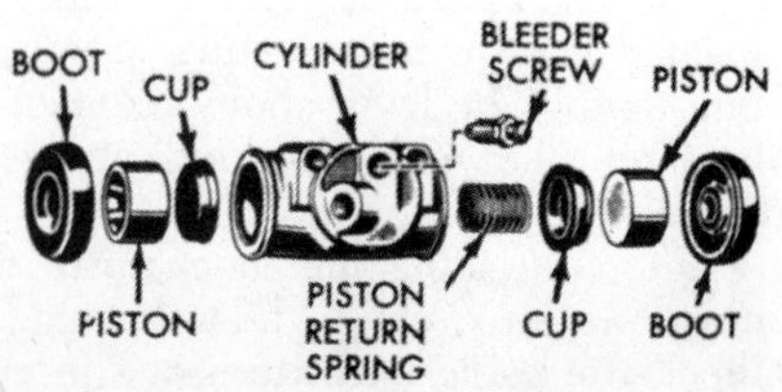

Exploded view of the wheel cylinder

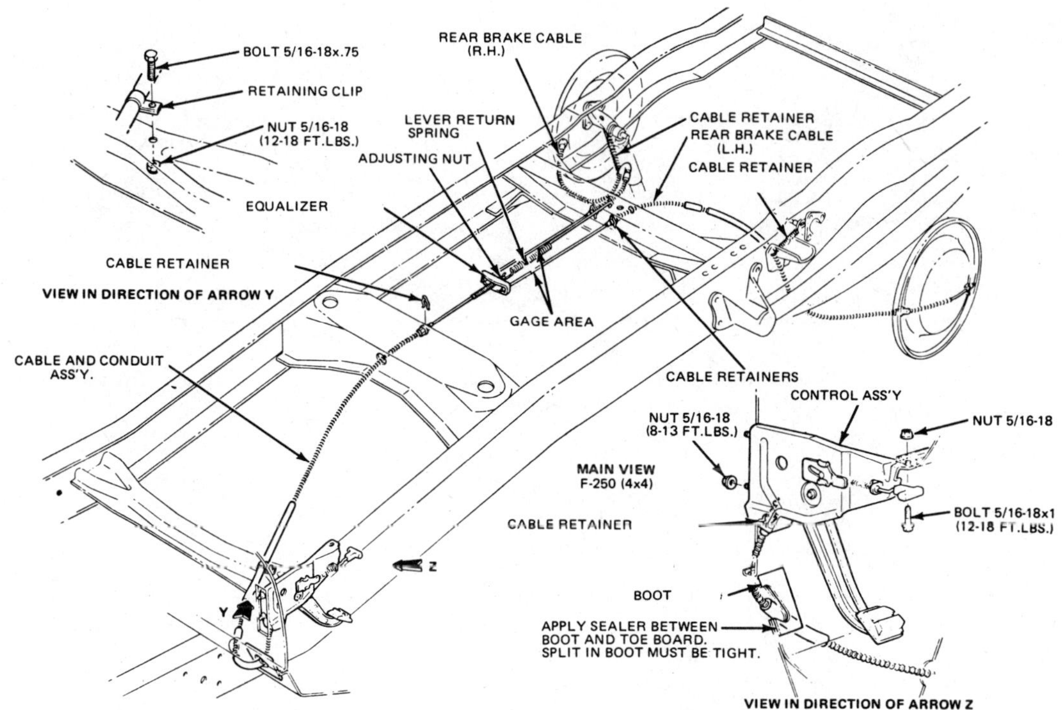

Parking brake cable routing—F-250 4WD

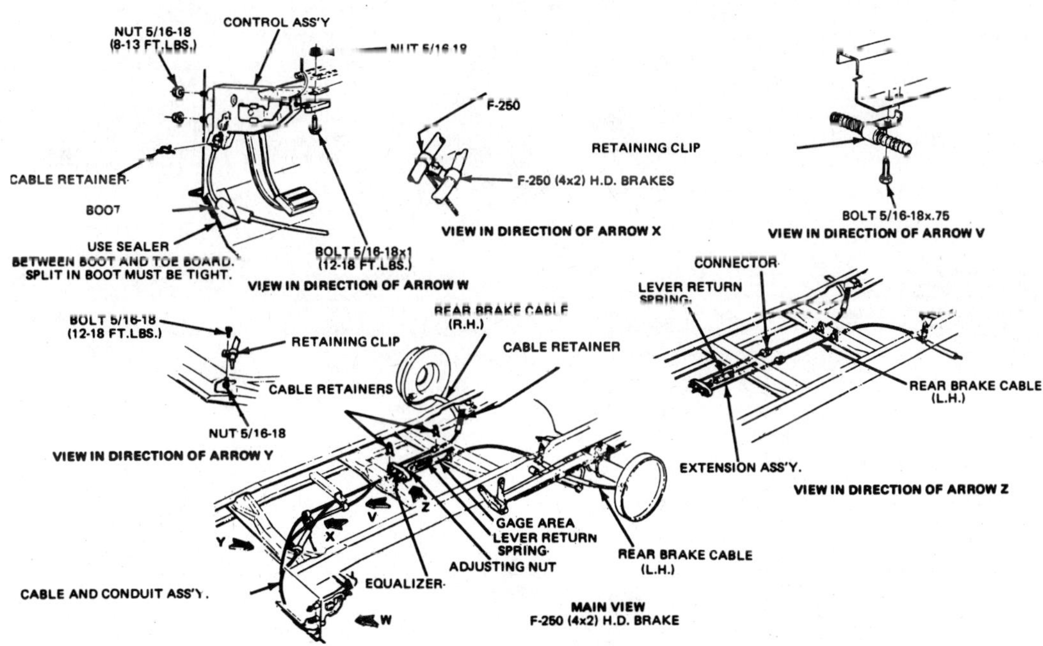

Parking brake cable routing—F-250–350 2WD heavy-duty

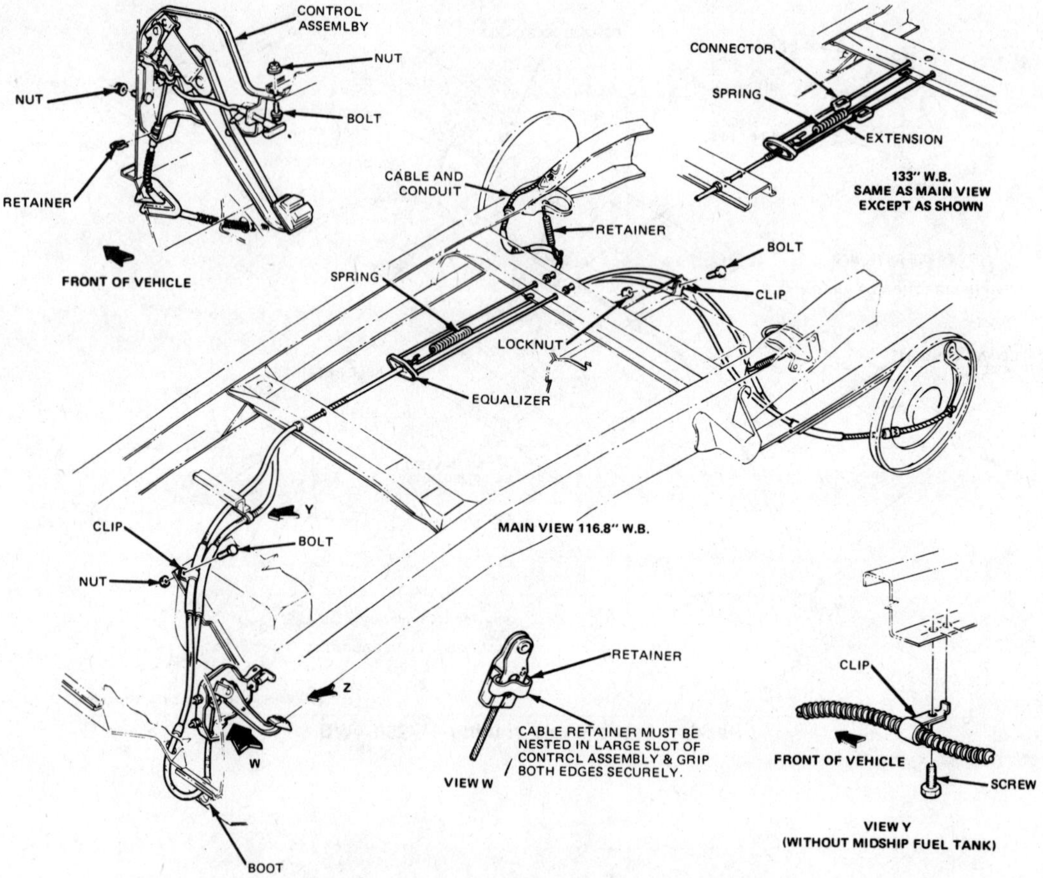

Parking brake cable routing—F-100–150 2WD, F-150 4WD

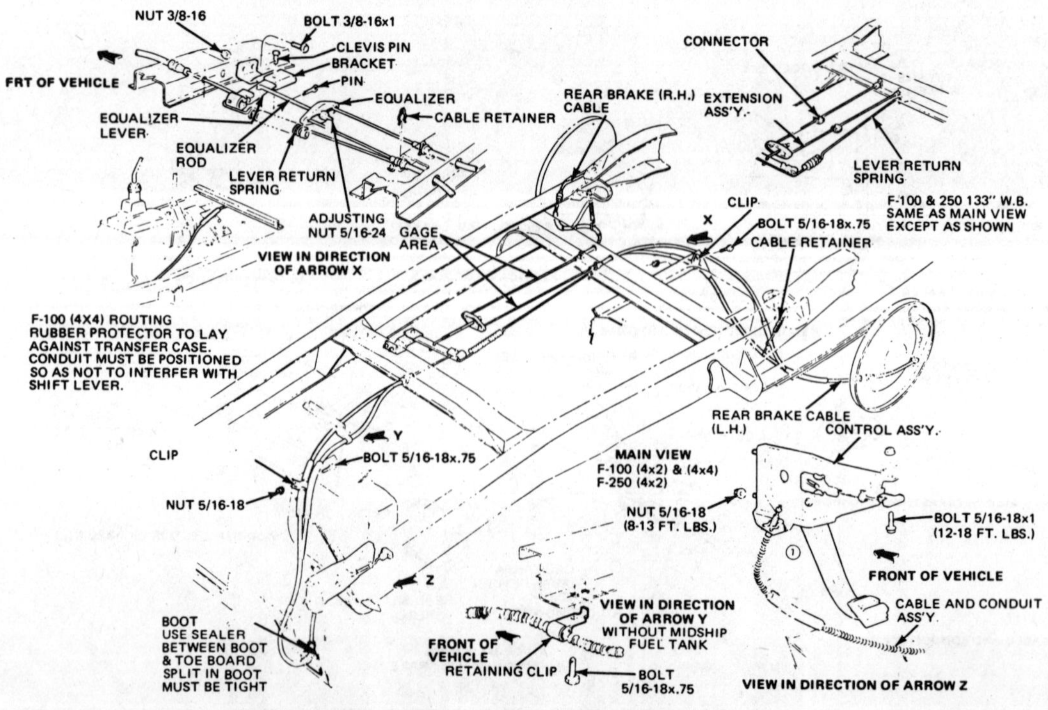

Parking cable routing—F-100, F-150, F-250 light-duty

of the parts in clean brake fluid. Assemble the wheel cylinder in the reverse order of removal and disassembly.

Wheel Bearings

See Chapter 1 for wheel bearing service.

REAR DRUM BRAKES

Brake Drums

INSPECTION

Use the same procedure for inspecting the rear brake drums as is outlined for the front brake drums.

REMOVAL AND INSTALLATION

F-100, F-150, and F-250 Light-Duty

1. Raise the vehicle so that the wheel to be worked on is clear of the floor and install jackstands under the vehicle.
2. Remove the hub cap and the wheel/tire assembly. Remove the three retaining nuts and remove the brake drum. It may be necessary to back off the brake shoe adjustment in order to remove the brake drum. This is because the drum might be grooved or worn from being in service for an extended period of time.
3. Before installing a new brake drum, be sure to remove any protective coating with carburetor degreaser.
4. Install the brake drum in the reverse order of removal and adjust the brakes.

F-250, F-350 Heavy-Duty

1. Raise the vehicle and install jackstands.
2. Remove the wheel/tire assembly. Loosen the rear brake shoe adjustment.
3. Remove the rear axle retaining bolts and lockwashers, axle shaft, and gasket.
4. Remove the wheel bearing locknut, lockwasher, and adjusting nut.
5. Remove the hub and drum assembly from the axle.
6. Remove the brake drum-to-hub retaining screws, bolts, or bolts and nuts. Remove the brake drum from the hub.

To install the rear brake drum:

7. Place the drum on the hub and attach it to the hub with the attaching nuts and bolts.
8. Place the hub and drum assembly on the axle and start the adjusting nut.
9. Adjust the wheel bearing nut and install the wheel bearing lockwasher and locknut.
10. Install the axle shaft with a new gasket and install the axle retaining bolts and lockwashers.
11. Install the wheel/tire assembly and adjust the brake shoes. Remove the jackstands and lower the vehicle.

Brake Shoes

REMOVAL AND INSTALLATION

See the procedure given for removal and installation of the front drum brake shoes.

Wheel Cylinders

OVERHAUL

Remove and overhaul the rear wheel cylinders in the same manner as is outlined for the front wheel cylinders.

Parking Brake

ADJUSTMENT

1. Adjust the rear brakes as outlined in the beginning of this chapter.
2. Push down on the parking brake pedal two ratchet clicks.
3. Loosen the locknut at the cable equalizer under the vehicle.
4. Tighten the adjusting nut against the equalizer until there is noticeable drag of the brakes when the rear wheels are turned forward.
5. Retighten the locknut against the equalizer.
6. Release the parking brake foot pedal fully. There should be no brake drag with the foot pedal released. If drag is present, back off the cable equalizer adjustment as necessary.

Troubleshooting 10

This section is designed to aid in the quick, accurate diagnosis of automotive problems. While automotive repairs can be made by many people, accurate troubleshooting is a rare skill for the amateur and professional alike.

In its simplest state, troubleshooting is an exercise in logic. It is essential to realize that an automobile is really composed of a series of systems. Some of these systems are interrelated; others are not. Automobiles operate within a framework of logical rules and physical laws, and the key to troubleshooting is a good understanding of all the automotive systems.

This section breaks the car or truck down into its component systems, allowing the problem to be isolated. The charts and diagnostic road maps list the most common problems and the most probable causes of trouble. Obviously it would be impossible to list every possible problem that could happen along with every possible cause, but it will locate MOST problems and eliminate a lot of unnecessary guesswork. The systematic format will locate problems within a given system, but, because many automotive systems are interrelated, the solution to your particular problem may be found in a number of systems on the car or truck.

USING THE TROUBLESHOOTING CHARTS

This book contains all of the specific information that the average do-it-yourself mechanic needs to repair and maintain his or her car or truck. The troubleshooting charts are designed to be used in conjunction with the specific procedures and information in the text. For instance, troubleshooting a point-type ignition system is fairly standard for all models, but you may be directed to the text to find procedures for troubleshooting an individual type of electronic ignition. You will also have to refer to the specification charts throughout the book for specifications applicable to your car or truck.

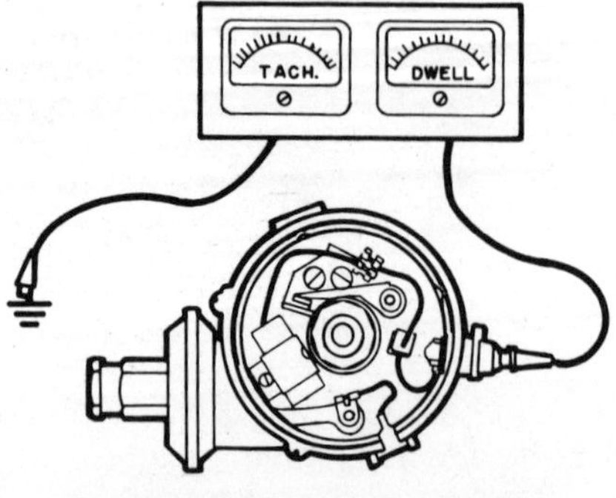

Tach-dwell hooked-up to distributor

TOOLS AND EQUIPMENT

The tools illustrated in Chapter 1 (plus two more diagnostic pieces) will be adequate to troubleshoot most problems. The two other tools needed are a voltmeter and an ohmmeter. These can be purchased separately or in combination, known as a VOM meter.

In the event that other tools are required, they will be noted in the procedures.

Troubleshooting Engine Problems

See Chapters 2, 3, 4 for more information and service procedures.

Index to Systems

System	To Test	Group
Battery	Engine need not be running	1
Starting system	Engine need not be running	2
Primary electrical system	Engine need not be running	3
Secondary electrical system	Engine need not be running	4
Fuel system	Engine need not be running	5
Engine compression	Engine need not be running	6
Engine vacuum	Engine must be running	7
Secondary electrical system	Engine must be running	8
Valve train	Engine must be running	9
Exhaust system	Engine must be running	10
Cooling system	Engine must be running	11
Engine lubrication	Engine must be running	12

Index to Problems

Problem: Symptom	Begin at Specific Diagnosis, Number
Engine Won't Start:	
Starter doesn't turn	1.1, 2.1
Starter turns, engine doesn't	2.1
Starter turns engine very slowly	1.1, 2.4
Starter turns engine normally	3.1, 4.1
Starter turns engine very quickly	6.1
Engine fires intermittently	4.1
Engine fires consistently	5.1, 6.1
Engine Runs Poorly:	
Hard starting	3.1, 4.1, 5.1, 8.1
Rough idle	4.1, 5.1, 8.1
Stalling	3.1, 4.1, 5.1, 8.1
Engine dies at high speeds	4.1, 5.1
Hesitation (on acceleration from standing stop)	5.1, 8.1
Poor pickup	4.1, 5.1, 8.1
Lack of power	3.1, 4.1, 5.1, 8.1
Backfire through the carburetor	4.1, 8.1, 9.1
Backfire through the exhaust	4.1, 8.1, 9.1
Blue exhaust gases	6.1, 7.1
Black exhaust gases	5.1
Running on (after the ignition is shut off)	3.1, 8.1
Susceptible to moisture	4.1
Engine misfires under load	4.1, 7.1, 8.4, 9.1
Engine misfires at speed	4.1, 8.4
Engine misfires at idle	3.1, 4.1, 5.1, 7.1, 8.4

Sample Section

Test and Procedure	Results and Indications	Proceed to
4.1—Check for spark: Hold each spark plug wire approximately ¼" from ground with gloves or a heavy, dry rag. Crank the engine and observe the spark.	→ If no spark is evident:	→ **4.2**
	→ If spark is good in some cases:	→ **4.3**
	→ If spark is good in all cases:	→ **4.6**

Specific Diagnosis

This section is arranged so that following each test, instructions are given to proceed to another, until a problem is diagnosed.

Section 1—Battery

Test and Procedure	*Results and Indications*	*Proceed to*
1.1—Inspect the battery visually for case condition (corrosion, cracks) and water level.	If case is cracked, replace battery:	**1.4**
	If the case is intact, remove corrosion with a solution of baking soda and water (**CAUTION:** ***do not get the solution into the battery***), and fill with water:	**1.2**
Inspect the battery case		
1.2—Check the battery cable connections: Insert a screwdriver between the battery post and the cable clamp. Turn the headlights on high beam, and observe them as the screwdriver is gently twisted to ensure good metal to metal contact.	If the lights brighten, remove and clean the clamp and post; coat the post with petroleum jelly, install and tighten the clamp:	**1.4**
	If no improvement is noted:	**1.3**
TESTING BATTERY CABLE CONNECTIONS USING A SCREWDRIVER		
1.3—Test the state of charge of the battery using an individual cell tester or hydrometer.	If indicated, charge the battery. **NOTE:** ***If no obvious reason exists for the low state of charge (i.e., battery age, prolonged storage), proceed to:***	**1.4**

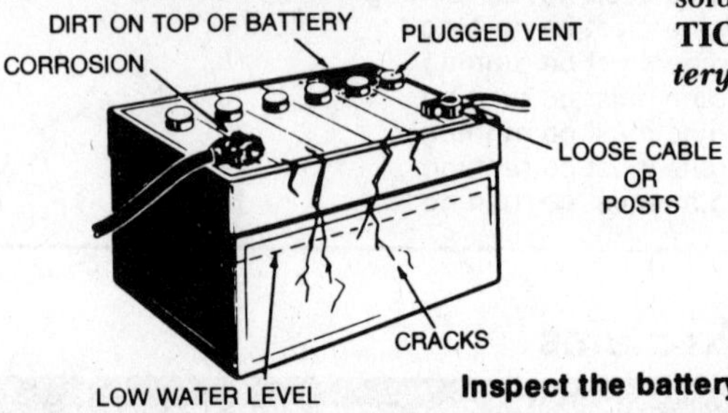

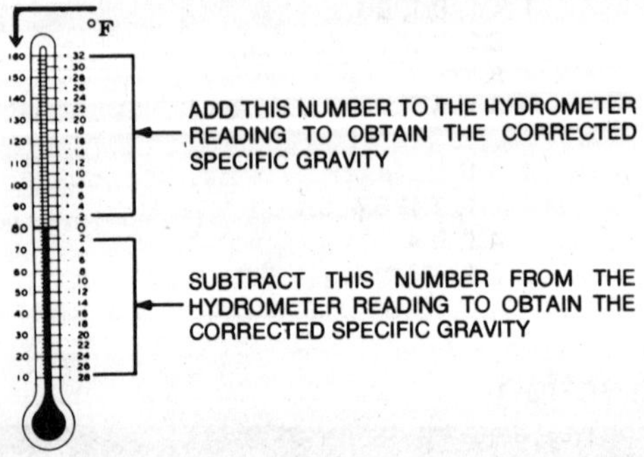

ADD THIS NUMBER TO THE HYDROMETER READING TO OBTAIN THE CORRECTED SPECIFIC GRAVITY

SUBTRACT THIS NUMBER FROM THE HYDROMETER READING TO OBTAIN THE CORRECTED SPECIFIC GRAVITY

Specific Gravity (@ 80° F.)

Minimum	*Battery Charge*
1.260	100% Charged
1.230	75% Charged
1.200	50% Charged
1.170	25% Charged
1.140	Very Little Power Left
1.110	Completely Discharged

The effects of temperature on battery specific gravity (left) and amount of battery charge in relation to specific gravity (right)

1.4—Visually inspect battery cables for cracking, bad connection to ground, or bad connection to starter.	If necessary, tighten connections or replace the cables:	**2.1**

Section 2—Starting System

See Chapter 3 for service procedures

Test and Procedure	*Results and Indications*	*Proceed to*
Note: Tests in Group 2 are performed with coil high tension lead disconnected to prevent accidental starting.		
2.1—Test the starter motor and solenoid: Connect a jumper from the battery post of the solenoid (or relay) to the starter post of the solenoid (or relay).	If starter turns the engine normally:	**2.2**
	If the starter buzzes, or turns the engine very slowly:	**2.4**
	If no response, replace the solenoid (or relay).	**3.1**
	If the starter turns, but the engine doesn't, ensure that the flywheel ring gear is intact. If the gear is undamaged, replace the starter drive.	**3.1**
2.2—Determine whether ignition override switches are functioning properly (clutch start switch, neutral safety switch), by connecting a jumper across the switch(es), and turning the ignition switch to "start".	If starter operates, adjust or replace switch:	**3.1**
	If the starter doesn't operate:	**2.3**
2.3—Check the ignition switch "start" position: Connect a 12V test lamp or voltmeter between the starter post of the solenoid (or relay) and ground. Turn the ignition switch to the "start" position, and jiggle the key.	If the lamp doesn't light or the meter needle doesn't move when the switch is turned, check the ignition switch for loose connections, cracked insulation, or broken wires. Repair or replace as necessary:	**3.1**
	If the lamp flickers or needle moves when the key is jiggled, replace the ignition switch.	**3.3**

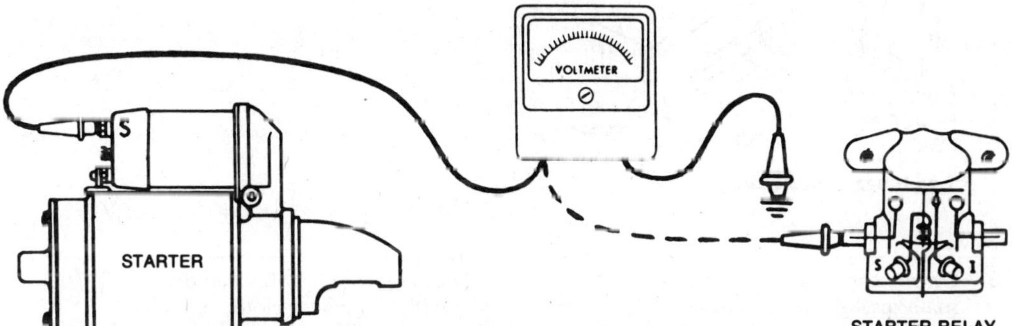

Checking the ignition switch "start" position

2.4—Remove and bench test the starter, according to specifications in the engine electrical section.	If the starter does not meet specifications, repair or replace as needed:	**3.1**
	If the starter is operating properly:	**2.5**
2.5—Determine whether the engine can turn freely: Remove the spark plugs, and check for water in the cylinders. Check for water on the dipstick, or oil in the radiator. Attempt to turn the engine using an 18" flex drive and socket on the crankshaft pulley nut or bolt.	If the engine will turn freely only with the spark plugs out, and hydrostatic lock (water in the cylinders) is ruled out, check valve timing:	**9.2**
	If engine will not turn freely, and it is known that the clutch and transmission are free, the engine must be disassembled for further evaluation:	**Chapter 3**

Section 3—Primary Electrical System

Test and Procedure	Results and Indications	Proceed to
3.1—Check the ignition switch "on" position: Connect a jumper wire between the distributor side of the coil and ground, and a 12V test lamp between the switch side of the coil and ground. Remove the high tension lead from the coil. Turn the ignition switch on and jiggle the key.	If the lamp lights:	**3.2**
	If the lamp flickers when the key is jiggled, replace the ignition switch:	**3.3**
	If the lamp doesn't light, check for loose or open connections. If none are found, remove the ignition switch and check for continuity. If the switch is faulty, replace it:	**3.3**

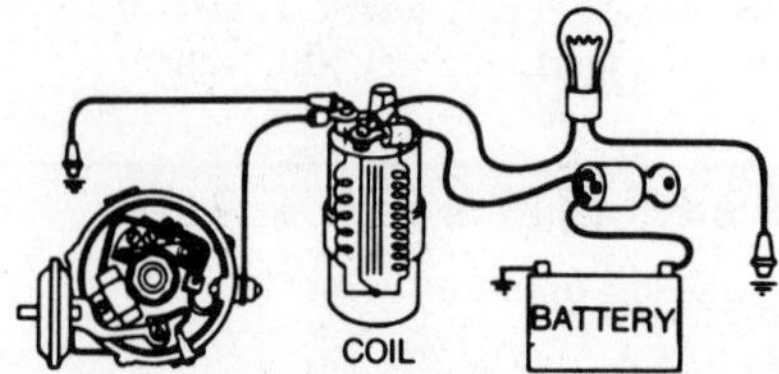

Checking the ignition switch "on" position

Test and Procedure	Results and Indications	Proceed to
3.2—Check the ballast resistor or resistance wire for an open circuit, using an ohmmeter. See Chapter 3 for specific tests.	Replace the resistor or resistance wire if the resistance is zero. **NOTE:** ***Some ignition systems have no ballast resistor.***	**3.3**

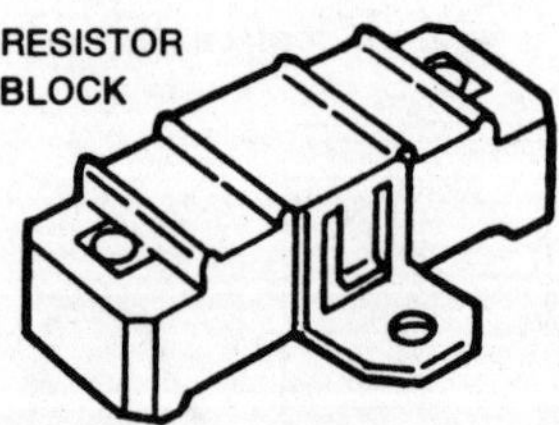

Two types of resistors

Test and Procedure	Results and Indications	Proceed to
3.3—On point-type ignition systems, visually inspect the breaker points for burning, pitting or excessive wear. Gray coloring of the point contact surfaces is normal. Rotate the crankshaft until the contact heel rests on a high point of the distributor cam and adjust the point gap to specifications. On electronic ignition models, remove the distributor cap and visually inspect the armature. Ensure that the armature pin is in place, and that the armature is on tight and rotates when the engine is cranked. Make sure there are no cracks, chips or rounded edges on the armature.	If the breaker points are intact, clean the contact surfaces with fine emery cloth, and adjust the point gap to specifications. If the points are worn, replace them. On electronic systems, replace any parts which appear defective. If condition persists:	**3.4**

Test and Procedure	*Results and Indications*	*Proceed to*
3.4—On point-type ignition systems, connect a dwell-meter between the distributor primary lead and ground. Crank the engine and observe the point dwell angle. On electronic ignition systems, conduct a stator (magnetic pickup assembly) test. See Chapter 3.	On point-type systems, adjust the dwell angle if necessary. **NOTE:** ***Increasing the point gap decreases the dwell angle and vice-versa.***	**3.6**
	If the dwell meter shows little or no reading;	**3.5**
	On electronic ignition systems, if the stator is bad, replace the stator. If the stator is good, proceed to the other tests in Chapter 3.	

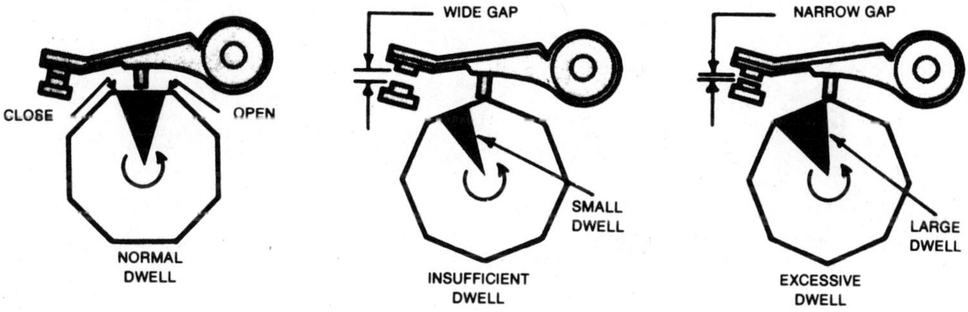

Dwell is a function of point gap

3.5—On the point-type ignition systems, check the condenser for short: connect an ohmeter across the condenser body and the pigtail lead.	If any reading other than infinite is noted, replace the condenser	**3.6**

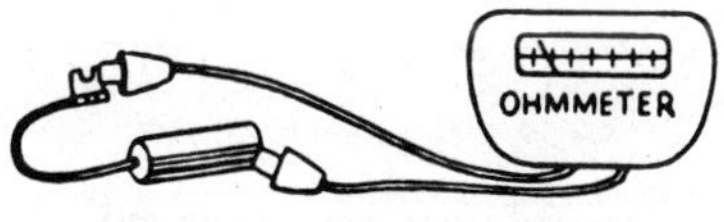

Checking the condenser for short

3.6—Test the coil primary resistance: On point-type ignition systems, connect an ohmmeter across the coil primary terminals, and read the resistance on the low scale. Note whether an external ballast resistor or resistance wire is used. On electronic ignition systems, test the coil primary resistance as in Chapter 3.	Point-type ignition coils utilizing ballast resistors or resistance wires should have approximately 1.0 ohms resistance. Coils with internal resistors should have approximately 4.0 ohms resistance. If values far from the above are noted, replace the coil.	**4.1**

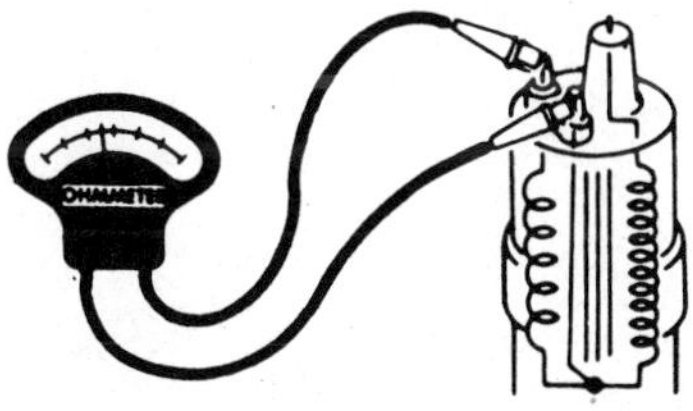

Check the coil primary resistance

Section 4—Secondary Electrical System

See Chapters 2–3 for service procedures

Test and Procedure	Results and Indications	Proceed to
4.1—Check for spark: Hold each spark plug wire approximately ¼″ from ground with gloves or a heavy, dry rag. Crank the engine, and observe the spark.	If no spark is evident:	**4.2**
	If spark is good in some cylinders:	**4.3**
	If spark is good in all cylinders:	**4.6**
Check for spark at the plugs		
4.2—Check for spark at the coil high tension lead: Remove the coil high tension lead from the distributor and position it approximately ¼″ from ground. Crank the engine and observe spark. **CAUTION:** ***This test should not be performed on engines equipped with electronic ignition.***	If the spark is good and consistent:	**4.3**
	If the spark is good but intermittent, test the primary electrical system starting at 3.3:	**3.3**
	If the spark is weak or non-existent, replace the coil high tension lead, clean and tighten all connections and retest. If no improvement is noted:	**4.4**
4.3—Visually inspect the distributor cap and rotor for burned or corroded contacts, cracks, carbon tracks, or moisture. Also check the fit of the rotor on the distributor shaft (where applicable).	If moisture is present, dry thoroughly, and retest per 4.1:	**4.1**
	If burned or excessively corroded contacts, cracks, or carbon tracks are noted, replace the defective part(s) and retest per 4.1:	**4.1**
	If the rotor and cap appear intact, or are only slightly corroded, clean the contacts thoroughly (including the cap towers and spark plug wire ends) and retest per 4.1:	
	If the spark is good in all cases:	**4.6**
	If the spark is poor in all cases:	**4.5**

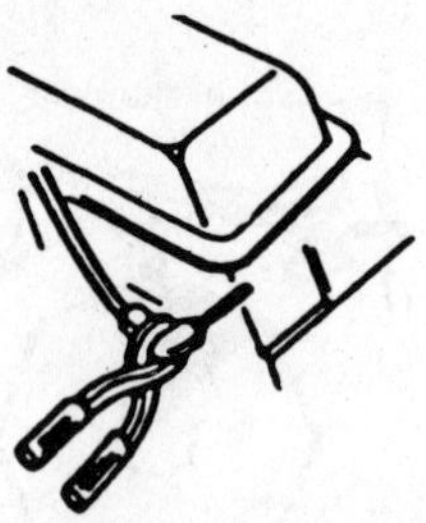

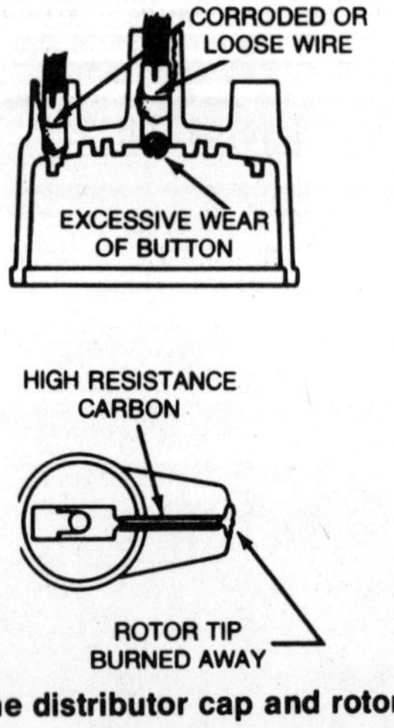

Inspect the distributor cap and rotor

Test and Procedure	Results and Indications	Proceed to
4.4—Check the coil secondary resistance: On point-type systems connect an ohmmeter across the distributor side of the coil and the coil tower. Read the resistance on the high scale of the ohmmeter. On electronic ignition systems, see Chapter 3 for specific tests.	The resistance of a satisfactory coil should be between 4,000 and 10,000 ohms. If resistance is considerably higher (i.e., 40,000 ohms) replace the coil and retest per 4.1. **NOTE:** ***This does not apply to high performance coils.***	

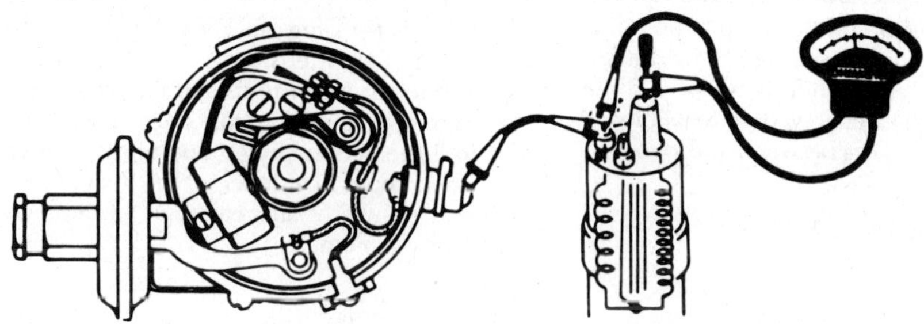

Testing the coil secondary resistance

Test and Procedure	Results and Indications	Proceed to
4.5—Visually inspect the spark plug wires for cracking or brittleness. Ensure that no two wires are positioned so as to cause induction firing (adjacent and parallel). Remove each wire, one by one, and check resistance with an ohmmeter.	Replace any cracked or brittle wires. If any of the wires are defective, replace the entire set. Replace any wires with excessive resistance (over 8000 Ω per foot for suppression wire), and separate any wires that might cause induction firing.	**4.6**

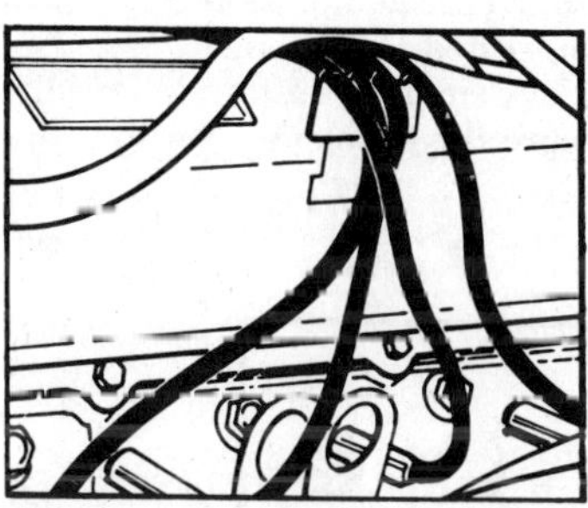

Misfiring can be the result of spark plug leads to adjacent, consecutively firing cylinders running parallel and too close together

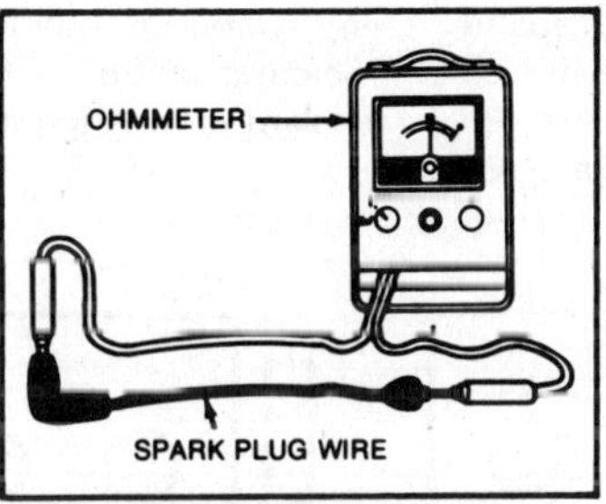

On point-type ignition systems, check the spark plug wires as shown. On electronic ignitions, do not remove the wire from the distributor cap terminal; instead, test through the cap

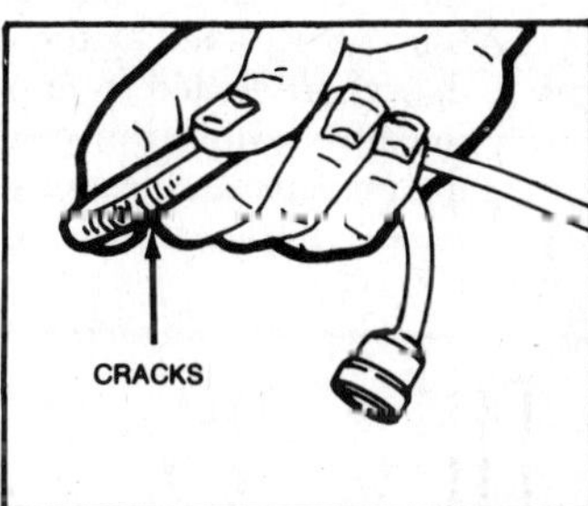

Spark plug wires can be checked visually by bending them in a loop over your finger. This will reveal any cracks, burned or broken insulation. Any wire with cracked insulation should be replaced

Test and Procedure	Results and Indications	Proceed to
4.6—Remove the spark plugs, noting the cylinders from which they were removed, and evaluate according to the color photos in the middle of this book.	See following.	**See following.**

Test and Procedure	Results and Indications	Proceed to
4.7—Examine the location of all the plugs.	The following diagrams illustrate some of the conditions that the location of plugs will reveal.	**4.8**

Two adjacent plugs are fouled in a 6-cylinder engine, 4-cylinder engine or either bank of a V-8. This is probably due to a blown head gasket between the two cylinders

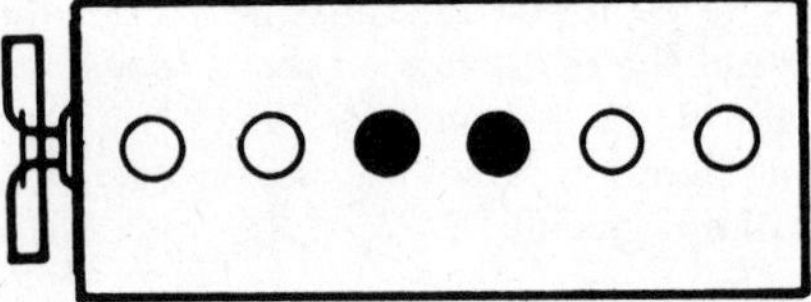

The two center plugs in a 6-cylinder engine are fouled. Raw fuel may be "boiled" out of the carburetor into the intake manifold after the engine is shut-off. Stop-start driving can also foul the center plugs, due to overly rich mixture. Proper float level, a new float needle and seat or use of an insulating spacer may help this problem

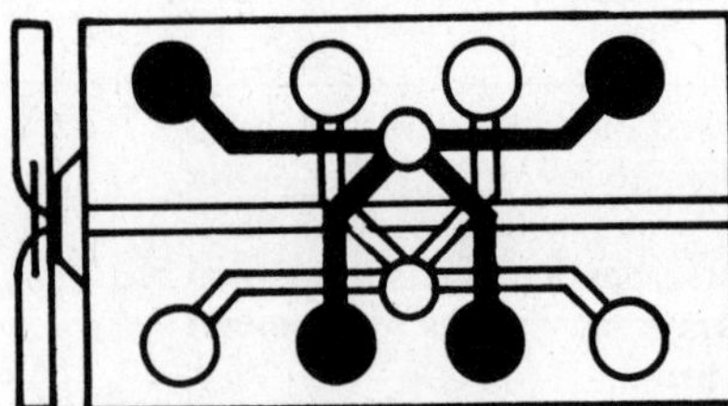

An unbalanced carburetor is indicated. Following the fuel flow on this particular design shows that the cylinders fed by the right-hand barrel are fouled from overly rich mixture, while the cylinders fed by the left-hand barrel are normal

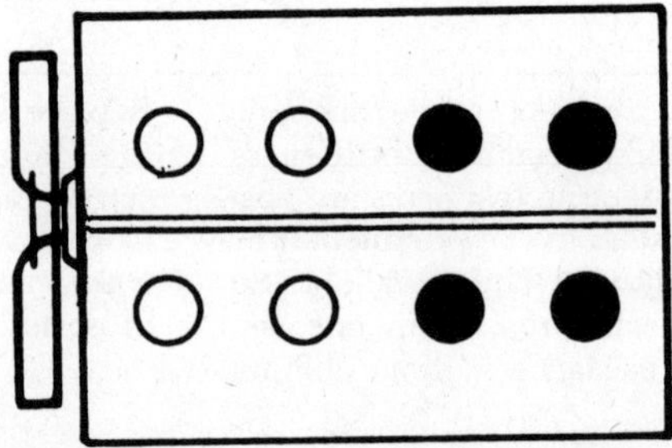

If the four rear plugs are overheated, a cooling system problem is suggested. A thorough cleaning of the cooling system may restore coolant circulation and cure the problem

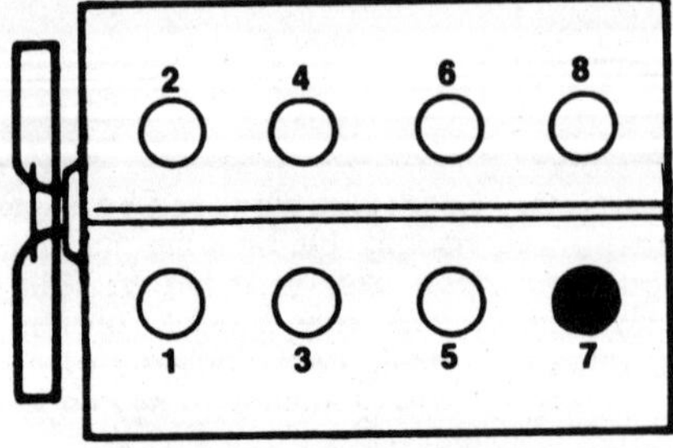

Finding one plug overheated may indicate an intake manifold leak near the affected cylinder. If the overheated plug is the second of two adjacent, consecutively firing plugs, it could be the result of ignition cross-firing. Separating the leads to these two plugs will eliminate cross-fire

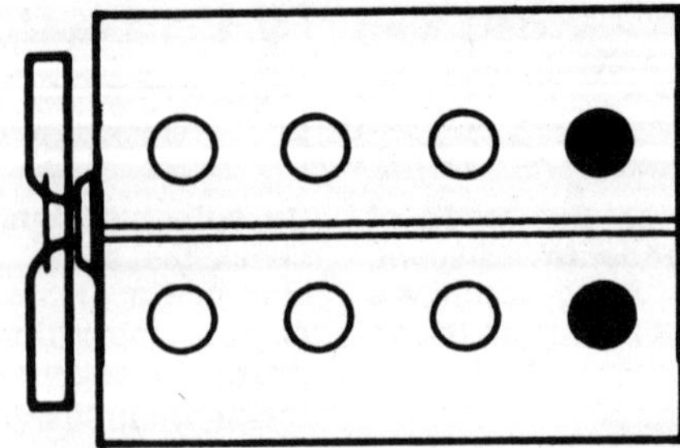

Occasionally, the two rear plugs in large, lightly used V-8's will become oil fouled. High oil consumption and smoky exhaust may also be noticed. It is probably due to plugged oil drain holes in the rear of the cylinder head, causing oil to be sucked in around the valve stems. This usually occurs in the rear cylinders first, because the engine slants that way

EASY STEP-BY-STEP TIPS FROM PROS

CHILTON'S
AUTO BODY REPAIR TIPS

Tools and Materials • Step-by-Step Illustrated Procedures
How To Repair Dents, Scratches and Rust Holes
Spray Painting and Refinishing Tips

With a little practice, basic body repair procedures can be mastered by any do-it-yourself mechanic. The step-by-step repairs shown here can be applied to almost any type of auto body repair.

TOOLS & MATERIALS

You may already have basic tools, such as hammers and electric drills. Other tools unique to body repair — body hammers, grinding attachments, sanding blocks, dent puller, half-round plastic file and plastic spreaders — are relatively inexpensive and can be obtained wherever auto parts or auto body repair parts are sold. Portable air compressors and paint spray guns can be purchased or rented.

Auto Body Repair Kits

The best and most often used products are available to the do-it-yourselfer in kit form, from major manufacturers of auto body repair products. The same manufacturers also merchandise the individual products for use by pros.

Kits are available to make a wide variety of repairs, including holes, dents and scratches and fiberglass, and offer the advantage of buying the materials you'll need for the job. There is little waste or chance of materials going bad from not being used. Many kits may also contain basic body-working tools such as body files, sanding blocks and spreaders. Check the contents of the kit before buying your tools.

BODY REPAIR TIPS

Safety

Many of the products associated with auto body repair and refinishing contain toxic chemicals. Read all labels before opening containers and store them in a safe place and manner.

- Wear eye protection (safety goggles) when using power tools or when performing any operation that involves the removal of any type of material.
- Wear lung protection (disposable mask or respirator) when grinding, sanding or painting.

Sanding

1 Sand off paint before using a dent puller. When using a non-adhesive sanding disc, cover the back of the disc with an overlapping layer or two of masking tape and trim the edges. The disc will last considerably longer.

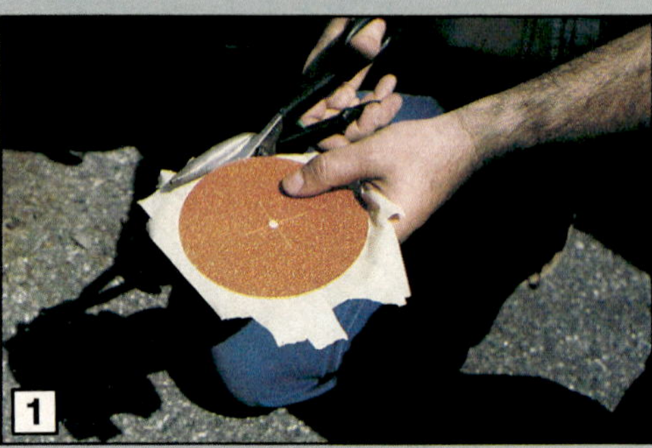
1

2 Use the circular motion of the sanding disc to grind *into* the edge of the repair. Grinding or sanding away from the jagged edge will only tear the sandpaper.

3 Use the palm of your hand flat on the panel to detect high and low spots. Do not use your fingertips. Slide your hand slowly back and forth.

3

WORKING WITH BODY FILLER

Mixing The Filler

Cleanliness and proper mixing and application are extremely important. Use a clean piece of plastic or glass or a disposable artist's palette to mix body filler.

1 Allow plenty of time and follow directions. No useful purpose will be served by adding more hardener to make it cure (set-up) faster. Less hardener means more curing time, but the mixture dries harder; more hardener means less curing time but a softer mixture.

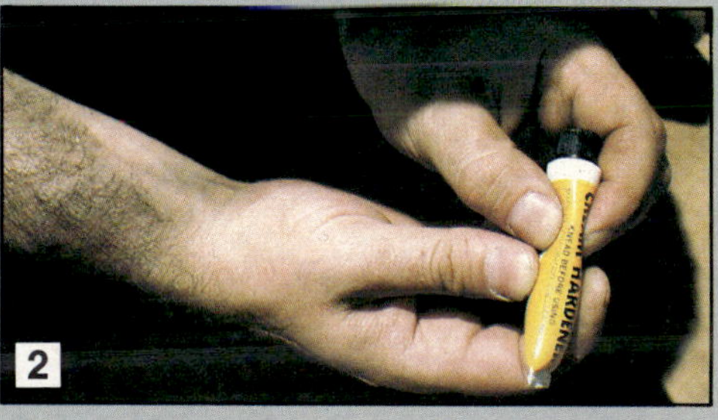

2

2 Both the hardener and the filler should be thoroughly kneaded or stirred before mixing. Hardener should be a solid paste and dispense like thin toothpaste. Body filler should be smooth, and free of lumps or thick spots.

Getting the proper amount of hardener in the filler is the trickiest part of preparing the filler. Use the same amount of hardener in cold or warm weather. For contour filler (thick coats), a bead of hardener twice the diameter of the filler is about right. There's about a 15% margin on either side, but, if in doubt use less hardener.

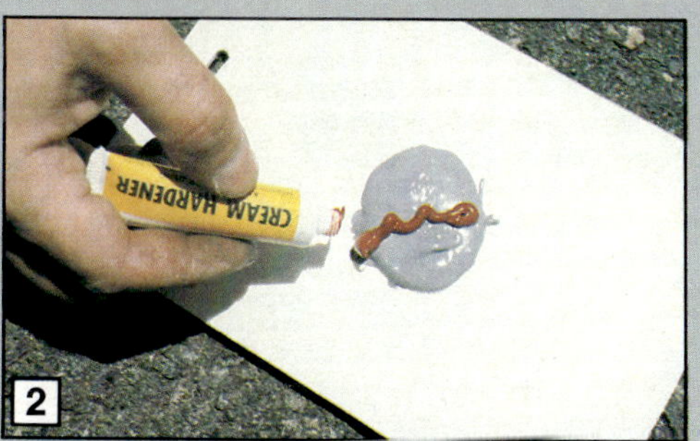

2

2

3 Mix the body filler and hardener by wiping across the mixing surface, picking the mixture up and wiping it again. Colder weather requires longer mixing times. Do not mix in a circular motion; this will trap air bubbles which will become holes in the cured filler.

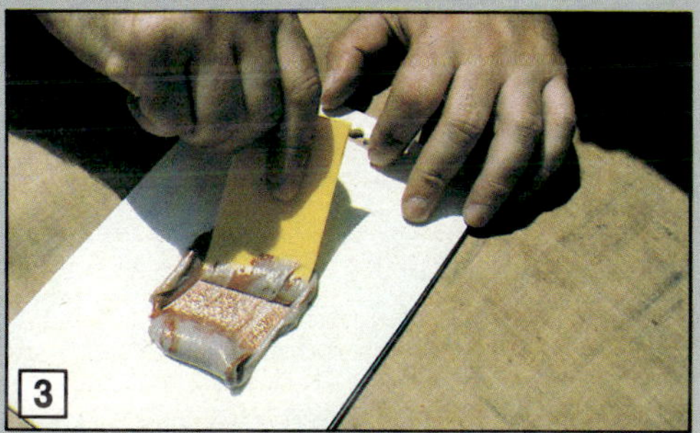

3

Applying The Filler

1 For best results, filler should not be applied over 1/4" thick.

Apply the filler in several coats. Build it up to above the level of the repair surface so that it can be sanded or grated down.

The first coat of filler must be pressed on with a firm wiping motion.

Apply the filler in one direction only. Working the filler back and forth will either pull it off the metal or trap air bubbles.

REPAIRING DENTS

Before you start, take a few minutes to study the damaged area. Try to visualize the shape of the panel before it was damaged. If the damage is on the left fender, look at the right fender and use it as a guide. If there is access to the panel from behind, you can reshape it with a body hammer. If not, you'll have to use a dent puller. Go slowly and work the metal a little at a time. Get the panel as straight as possible before applying filler.

1 This dent is typical of one that can be pulled out or hammered out from behind. Remove the headlight cover, headlight assembly and turn signal housing.

2 Drill a series of holes ½ the size of the end of the dent puller along the stress line. Make some trial pulls and assess the results. If necessary, drill more holes and try again. Do not hurry.

3 If possible, use a body hammer and block to shape the metal back to its original contours. Get the metal back as close to its original shape as possible. Don't depend on body filler to fill dents.

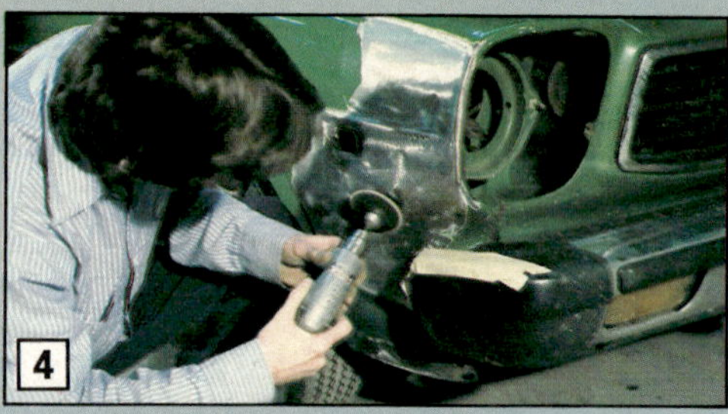

4 Using an 80-grit grinding disc on an electric drill, grind the paint from the surrounding area down to bare metal. Use a new grinding pad to prevent heat buildup that will warp metal.

5 The area should look like this when you're finished grinding. Knock the drill holes in and tape over small openings to keep plastic filler out.

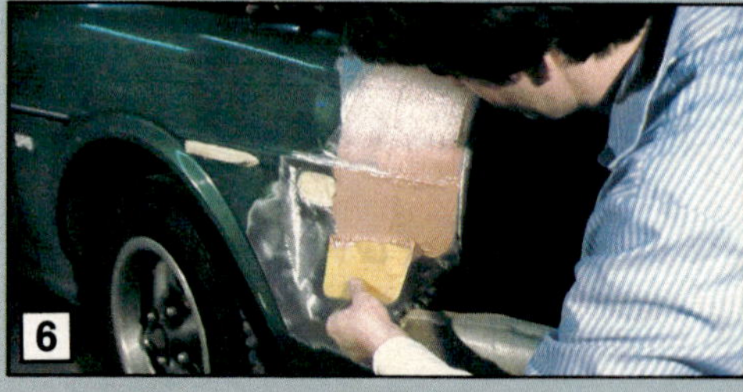

6 Mix the body filler (see Body Repair Tips). Spread the body filler evenly over the entire area (see Body Repair Tips). Be sure to cover the area completely.

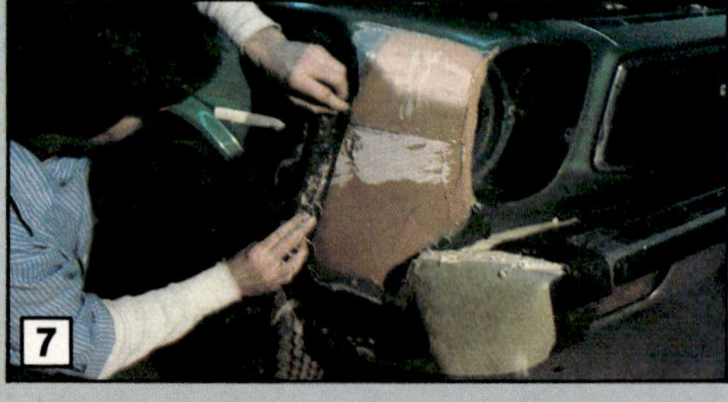

7 Let the body filler dry until the surface can just be scratched with your fingernail. Knock the high spots from the body filler with a body file ("Cheesegrater"). Check frequently with the palm of your hand for high and low spots.

8 Check to be sure that trim pieces that will be installed later will fit exactly. Sand the area with 40-grit paper.

9 If you wind up with low spots, you may have to apply another layer of filler.

10 Knock the high spots off with 40-grit paper. When you are satisfied with the contours of the repair, apply a thin coat of filler to cover pin holes and scratches.

11 Block sand the area with 40-grit paper to a smooth finish. Pay particular attention to body lines and ridges that must be well-defined.

12 Sand the area with 400 paper and then finish with a scuff pad. The finished repair is ready for priming and painting (see Painting Tips).

Materials and photos courtesy of Ritt Jones Auto Body, Prospect Park, PA.

REPAIRING RUST HOLES

There are many ways to repair rust holes. The fiberglass cloth kit shown here is one of the most cost efficient for the owner because it provides a strong repair that resists cracking and moisture and is relatively easy to use. It can be used on large and small holes (with or without backing) and can be applied over contoured areas. Remember, however, that short of replacing an entire panel, no repair is a guarantee that the rust will not return.

1 Remove any trim that will be in the way. Clean away all loose debris. Cut away all the rusted metal. But be sure to leave enough metal to retain the contour or body shape.

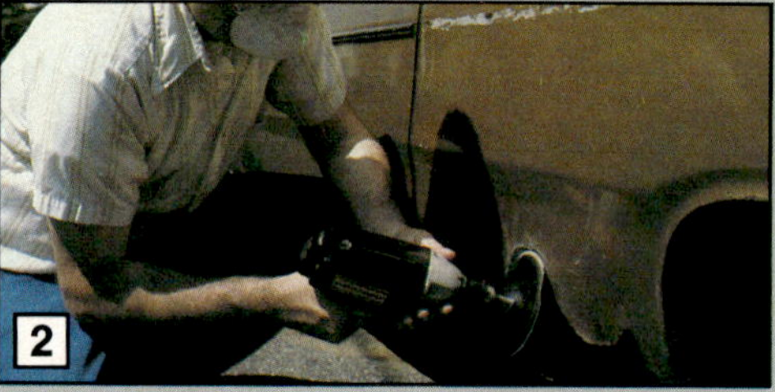

2 Grind away all traces of rust with a 24-grit grinding disc. Be sure to grind back 3-4 inches from the edge of the hole down to bare metal and be sure all traces of paint, primer and rust are removed.

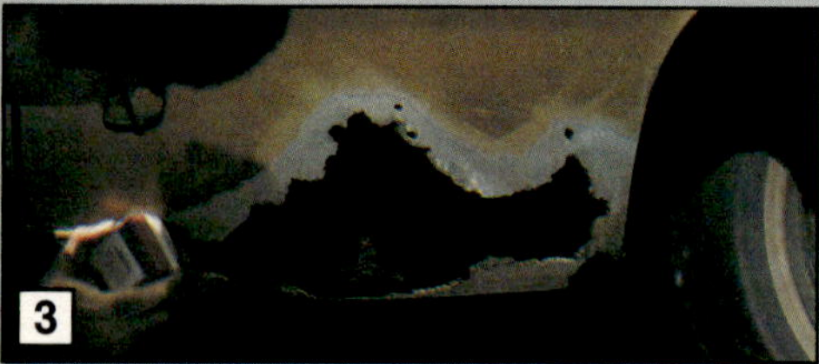

3 Block sand the area with 80 or 100 grit sandpaper to get a clear, shiny surface and feathered paint edge. Tap the edges of the hole inward with a ball peen hammer.

4 If you are going to use release film, cut a piece about 2-3″ larger than the area you have sanded. Place the film over the repair and mark the sanded area on the film. Avoid any unnecessary wrinkling of the film.

5 Cut 2 pieces of fiberglass matte to match the shape of the repair. One piece should be about 1″ smaller than the sanded area and the second piece should be 1″ smaller than the first. Mix enough filler and hardener to saturate the fiberglass material (see Body Repair Tips).

6 Lay the release sheet on a flat surface and spread an even layer of filler, large enough to cover the repair. Lay the smaller piece of fiberglass cloth in the center of the sheet and spread another layer of filler over the fiberglass cloth. Repeat the operation for the larger piece of cloth.

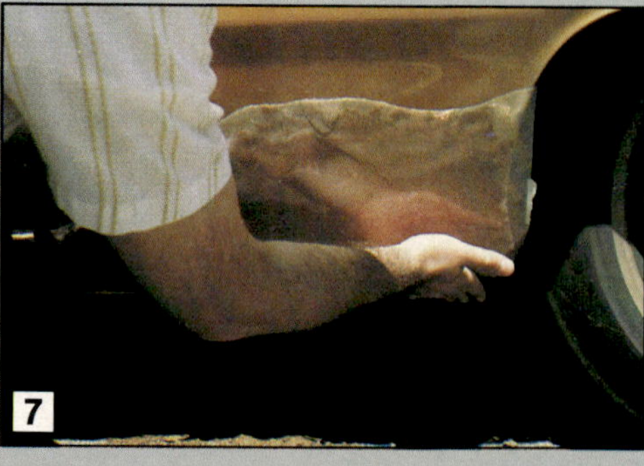

7 Place the repair material over the repair area, with the release film facing outward. Use a spreader and work from the center outward to smooth the material, following the body contours. Be sure to remove all air bubbles.

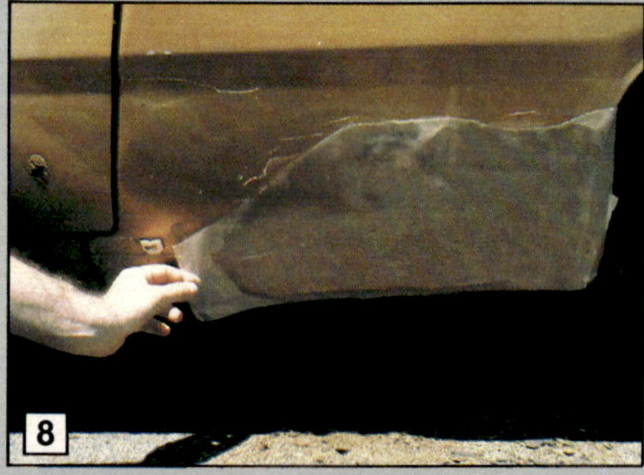

8 Wait until the repair has dried tack-free and peel off the release sheet. The ideal working temperature is 60°-90° F. Cooler or warmer temperatures or high humidity may require additional curing time. Wait longer, if in doubt.

9

9 Sand and feather-edge the entire area. The initial sanding can be done with a sanding disc on an electric drill if care is used. Finish the sanding with a block sander. Low spots can be filled with body filler; this may require several applications.

10

10 When the filler can just be scratched with a fingernail, knock the high spots down with a body file and smooth the entire area with 80-grit. Feather the filled areas into the surrounding areas.

11

11 When the area is sanded smooth, mix some topcoat and hardener and apply it directly with a spreader. This will give a smooth finish and prevent the glass matte from showing through the paint.

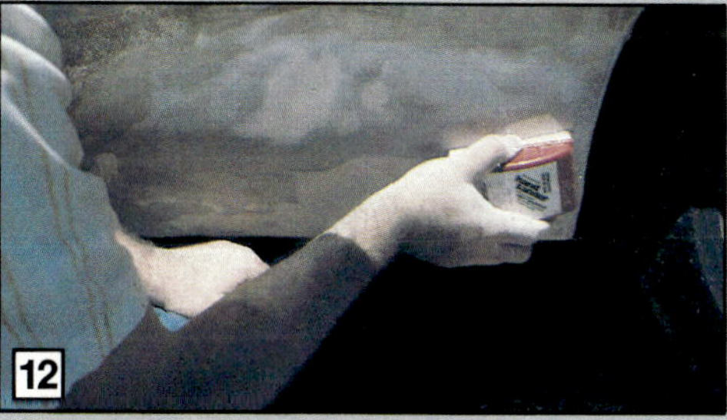

12

12 Block sand the topcoat smooth with finishing sandpaper (200 grit), and 400 grit. The repair is ready for masking, priming and painting (see Painting Tips).

Materials and photos courtesy Marson Corporation, Chelsea, Massachusetts

PAINTING TIPS

Preparation

1 SANDING — Use a 400 or 600 grit wet or dry sandpaper. Wet-sand the area with a 1/4 sheet of sandpaper soaked in clean water. Keep the paper wet while sanding. Sand the area until the repaired area tapers into the original finish.

2 CLEANING — Wash the area to be painted thoroughly with water and a clean rag. Rinse it thoroughly and wipe the surface dry until you're sure it's completely free of dirt, dust, fingerprints, wax, detergent or other foreign matter.

3 MASKING — Protect any areas you don't want to overspray by covering them with masking tape and newspaper. Be careful not get fingerprints on the area to be painted.

4 PRIMING — All exposed metal should be primed before painting. Primer protects the metal and provides an excellent surface for paint adhesion. When the primer is dry, wet sand the area again with 600 grit wet-sandpaper. Clean the area again after sanding.

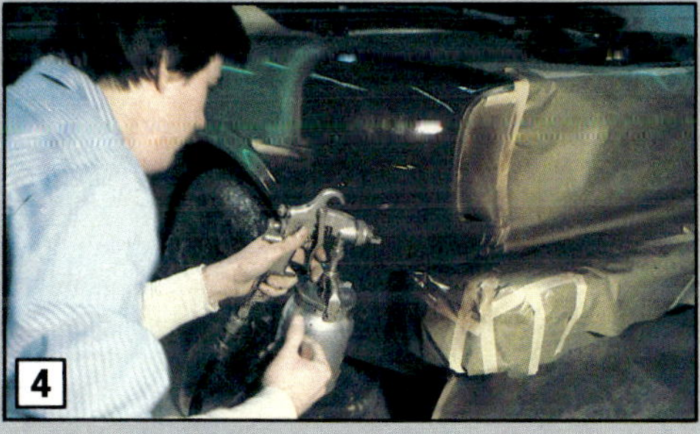

4

Painting Techniques

Paint applied from either a spray gun or a spray can (for small areas) will provide good results. Experiment on an old piece of metal to get the right combination before you begin painting.

SPRAYING VISCOSITY (SPRAY GUN ONLY) — Paint should be thinned to spraying viscosity according to the directions on the can. Use only the recommended thinner or reducer and the same amount of reduction regardless of temperature.

AIR PRESSURE (SPRAY GUN ONLY) — This is extremely important. Be sure you are using the proper recommended pressure.

TEMPERATURE — The surface to be painted should be approximately the same temperature as the surrounding air. Applying warm paint to a cold surface, or vice versa, will completely upset the paint characteristics.

THICKNESS — Spray with smooth strokes. In general, the thicker the coat of paint, the longer the drying time. Apply several thin coats about 30 seconds apart. The paint should remain wet long enough to flow out and no longer; heavier coats will only produce sags or wrinkles. Spray a light (fog) coat, followed by heavier color coats.

DISTANCE — The ideal spraying distance is 8″-12″ from the gun or can to the surface. Shorter distances will produce ripples, while greater distances will result in orange peel, dry film and poor color match and loss of material due to overspray.

OVERLAPPING — The gun or can should be kept at right angles to the surface at all times. Work to a wet edge at an even speed, using a 50% overlap and direct the center of the spray at the lower or nearest edge of the previous stroke.

RUBBING OUT (BLENDING) FRESH PAINT — Let the paint dry thoroughly. Runs or imperfections can be sanded out, primed and repainted.

Don't be in too big a hurry to remove the masking. This only produces paint ridges. When the finish has dried for at least a week, apply a small amount of fine grade rubbing compound with a clean, wet cloth. Use lots of water and blend the new paint with the surrounding area.

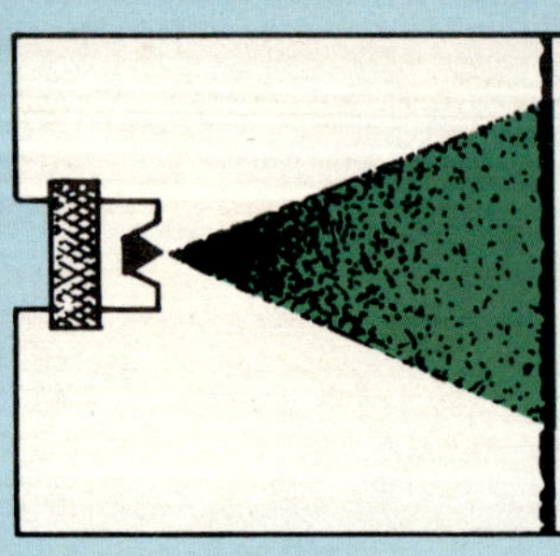

WRONG

Thin coat. Stroke too fast, not enough overlap, gun too far away.

CORRECT

Medium coat. Proper distance, good stroke, proper overlap.

WRONG

Heavy coat. Stroke too slow, too much overlap, gun too close.

Test and Procedure	Results and Indications	Proceed to
4.8—Determine the static ignition timing. Using the crankshaft pulley timing marks as a guide, locate top dead center on the compression stroke of the number one cylinder.	The rotor should be pointing toward the No. 1 tower in the distributor cap, and, on electronic ignitions, the armature spoke for that cylinder should be lined up with the stator.	4.8
4.9—Check coil polarity: Connect a voltmeter negative lead to the coil high tension lead, and the positive lead to ground (**NOTE:** ***Reverse the hook-up for positive ground systems***). Crank the engine momentarily.	If the voltmeter reads up-scale, the polarity is correct:	5.1
	If the voltmeter reads down-scale, reverse the coil polarity (switch the primary leads):	5.1
	Checking coil polarity	

Section 5—Fuel System

See Chapter 4 for service procedures

Test and Procedure	Results and Indications	Proceed to
5.1—Determine that the air filter is functioning efficiently: Hold paper elements up to a strong light, and attempt to see light through the filter.	Clean permanent air filters in solvent (or manufacturer's recommendation), and allow to dry. Replace paper elements through which light cannot be seen:	5.2
5.2—Determine whether a flooding condition exists: Flooding is identified by a strong gasoline odor, and excessive gasoline present in the throttle bore(s) of the carburetor.	If flooding is not evident:	5.3
	If flooding is evident, permit the gasoline to dry for a few moments and restart. If flooding doesn't recur:	5.7
	If flooding is persistent:	5.5
	If the engine floods repeatedly, check the choke butterfly flap	
5.3—Check that fuel is reaching the carburetor: Detach the fuel line at the carburetor inlet. Hold the end of the line in a cup (not styrofoam), and crank the engine.	If fuel flows smoothly:	5.7
	If fuel doesn't flow (**NOTE:** ***Make sure that there is fuel in the tank***), or flows erratically:	5.4

Check the fuel pump by disconnecting the output line (fuel pump-to-carburetor) at the carburetor and operating the starter briefly

Test and Procedure	Results and Indications	Proceed to
5.4—Test the fuel pump: Disconnect all fuel lines from the fuel pump. Hold a finger over the input fitting, crank the engine (with electric pump, turn the ignition or pump on); and feel for suction.	If suction is evident, blow out the fuel line to the tank with low pressure compressed air until bubbling is heard from the fuel filler neck. Also blow out the carburetor fuel line (both ends disconnected):	**5.7**
	If no suction is evident, replace or repair the fuel pump: **NOTE:** ***Repeated oil fouling of the spark plugs, or a no-start condition, could be the result of a ruptured vacuum booster pump diaphragm, through which oil or gasoline is being drawn into the intake manifold (where applicable).***	**5.7**
5.5—Occasionally, small specks of dirt will clog the small jets and orifices in the carburetor. With the engine cold, hold a flat piece of wood or similar material over the carburetor, where possible, and crank the engine.	If the engine starts, but runs roughly the engine is probably not run enough. If the engine won't start:	**5.9**
5.6—Check the needle and seat: Tap the carburetor in the area of the needle and seat.	If flooding stops, a gasoline additive (e.g., Gumout) will often cure the problem:	**5.7**
	If flooding continues, check the fuel pump for excessive pressure at the carburetor (according to specifications). If the pressure is normal, the needle and seat must be removed and checked, and/or the float level adjusted:	**5.7**
5.7—Test the accelerator pump by looking into the throttle bores while operating the throttle. **Check for gas at the carburetor by looking down the carburetor throat while someone moves the accelerator**	If the accelerator pump appears to be operating normally:	**5.8**
	If the accelerator pump is not operating, the pump must be reconditioned. Where possible, service the pump with the carburetor(s) installed on the engine. If necessary, remove the carburetor. Prior to removal:	**5.8**
5.8—Determine whether the carburetor main fuel system is functioning: Spray a commercial starting fluid into the carburetor while attempting to start the engine.	If the engine starts, runs for a few seconds, and dies:	**5.9**
	If the engine doesn't start:	**6.1**

Test and Procedure	Results and Indications	Proceed to
5.9—Uncommon fuel system malfunctions: See below:	If the problem is solved:	6.1
	If the problem remains, remove and recondition the carburetor.	

Condition	Indication	Test	Prevailing Weather Conditions	Remedy
Vapor lock	Engine will not restart shortly after running.	Cool the components of the fuel system until the engine starts. Vapor lock can be cured faster by draping a wet cloth over a mechanical fuel pump.	Hot to very hot	Ensure that the exhaust manifold heat control valve is operating. Check with the vehicle manufacturer for the recommended solution to vapor lock on the model in question.
Carburetor icing	Engine will not idle, stalls at low speeds.	Visually inspect the throttle plate area of the throttle bores for frost.	High humidity, 32–40° F.	Ensure that the exhaust manifold heat control valve is operating, and that the intake manifold heat riser is not blocked.
Water in the fuel	Engine sputters and stalls; may not start.	Pump a small amount of fuel into a glass jar. Allow to stand, and inspect for droplets or a layer of water.	High humidity, extreme temperature changes.	For droplets, use one or two cans of commercial gas line anti-freeze. For a layer of water, the tank must be drained, and the fuel lines blown out with compressed air.

Section 6—Engine Compression

See Chapter 3 for service procedures

Test and Procedure	Results and Indications	Proceed to
6.1—Test engine compression: Remove all spark plugs. Block the throttle wide open. Insert a compression gauge into a spark plug port, crank the engine to obtain the maximum reading, and record.	If compression is within limits on all cylinders:	7.1
	If gauge reading is extremely low on all cylinders:	6.2
	If gauge reading is low on one or two cylinders: (If gauge readings are identical and low on two or more adjacent cylinders, the head gasket must be replaced.)	6.2

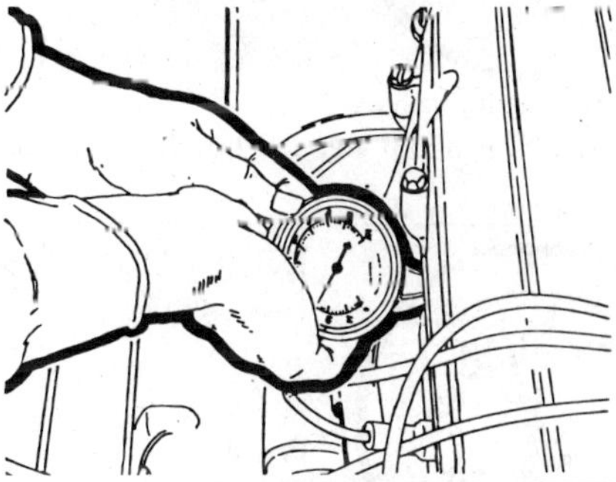

Checking compression

Test and Procedure	Results and Indications	Proceed to
6.2—Test engine compression (wet): Squirt approximately 30 cc. of engine oil into each cylinder, and retest per 6.1.	If the readings improve, worn or cracked rings or broken pistons are indicated:	See Chapter 3
	If the readings do not improve, burned or excessively carboned valves or a jumped timing chain are indicated: **NOTE:** ***A jumped timing chain is often indicated by difficult cranking.***	7.1

Section 7—Engine Vacuum

See Chapter 3 for service procedures

Test and Procedure	Results and Indications	Proceed to
7.1—Attach a vacuum gauge to the intake manifold beyond the throttle plate. Start the engine, and observe the action of the needle over the range of engine speeds.	See below.	**See below**

INDICATION: normal engine in good condition

Proceed to: 8.1

Normal engine

Gauge reading: steady, from 17–22 in./Hg.

INDICATION: sticking valves or ignition miss

Proceed to: 9.1, 8.3

Sticking valves

Gauge reading: intermittent fluctuation at idle

INDICATION: late ignition or valve timing, low compression, stuck throttle valve, leaking carburetor or manifold gasket

Proceed to: 6.1

Incorrect valve timing

Gauge reading: low (10–15 in./Hg) but steady

INDICATION: improper carburetor adjustment or minor intake leak.

Proceed to: 7.2

Carburetor requires adjustment

Gauge reading: drifting needle

INDICATION: ignition miss, blown cylinder head gasket, leaking valve or weak valve spring

Proceed to: 8.3, 6.1

Blown head gasket

Gauge reading: needle fluctuates as engine speed increases

INDICATION: burnt valve or faulty valve clearance. Needle will fall when defective valve operates

Proceed to: 9.1

Burnt or leaking valves

Gauge reading: steady needle, but drops regularly

INDICATION: choked muffler, excessive back pressure in system

Proceed to: 10.1

Clogged exhaust system

Gauge reading: gradual drop in reading at idle

INDICATION: worn valve guides

Proceed to: 9.1

Worn valve guides

Gauge reading: needle vibrates excessively at idle, but steadies as engine speed increases

White pointer = steady gauge hand

Black pointer = fluctuating gauge hand

Test and Procedure	Results and Indications	Proceed to
7.2—Attach a vacuum gauge per 7.1, and test for an intake manifold leak. Squirt a small amount of oil around the intake manifold gaskets, carburetor gaskets, plugs and fittings. Observe the action of the vacuum gauge.	If the reading improves, replace the indicated gasket, or seal the indicated fitting or plug:	**8.1**
	If the reading remains low:	**7.3**
7.3—Test all vacuum hoses and accessories for leaks as described in 7.2. Also check the carburetor body (dashpots, automatic choke mechanism, throttle shafts) for leaks in the same manner.	If the reading improves, service or replace the offending part(s):	**8.1**
	If the reading remains low:	**6.1**

Section 8—Secondary Electrical System

See Chapter 2 for service procedures

Test and Procedure	Results and Indications	Proceed to
8.1—Remove the distributor cap and check to make sure that the rotor turns when the engine is cranked. Visually inspect the distributor components.	Clean, tighten or replace any components which appear defective.	**8.2**
8.2—Connect a timing light (per manufacturer's recommendation) and check the dynamic ignition timing. Disconnect and plug the vacuum hose(s) to the distributor if specified, start the engine, and observe the timing marks at the specified engine speed.	If the timing is not correct, adjust to specifications by rotating the distributor in the engine: (Advance timing by rotating distributor opposite normal direction of rotor rotation, retard timing by rotating distributor in same direction as rotor rotation.)	**8.3**
8.3—Check the operation of the distributor advance mechanism(s): To test the mechanical advance, disconnect the vacuum lines from the distributor advance unit and observe the timing marks with a timing light as the engine speed is increased from idle. If the mark moves smoothly, without hesitation, it may be assumed that the mechanical advance is functioning properly. To test vacuum advance and/or retard systems, alternately crimp and release the vacuum line, and observe the timing mark for movement. If movement is noted, the system is operating.	If the systems are functioning:	**0.4**
	If the systems are not functioning, remove the distributor, and test on a distributor tester:	**8.4**
8.4—Locate an ignition miss: With the engine running, remove each spark plug wire, one at a time, until one is found that doesn't cause the engine to roughen and slow down.	When the missing cylinder is identified:	**4.1**

Section 9—Valve Train

See Chapter 3 for service procedures

Test and Procedure	*Results and Indications*	*Proceed to*
9.1—Evaluate the valve train: Remove the valve cover, and ensure that the valves are adjusted to specifications. A mechanic's stethoscope may be used to aid in the diagnosis of the valve train. By pushing the probe on or near push rods or rockers, valve noise often can be isolated. A timing light also may be used to diagnose valve problems. Connect the light according to manufacturer's recommendations, and start the engine. Vary the firing moment of the light by increasing the engine speed (and therefore the ignition advance), and moving the trigger from cylinder to cylinder. Observe the movement of each valve.	Sticking valves or erratic valve train motion can be observed with the timing light. The cylinder head must be disassembled for repairs.	**See Chapter 3**
9.2—Check the valve timing: Locate top dead center of the No. 1 piston, and install a degree wheel or tape on the crankshaft pulley or damper with zero corresponding to an index mark on the engine. Rotate the crankshaft in its direction of rotation, and observe the opening of the No. 1 cylinder intake valve. The opening should correspond with the correct mark on the degree wheel according to specifications.	If the timing is not correct, the timing cover must be removed for further investigation.	**See Chapter 3**

Section 10—Exhaust System

Test and Procedure	*Results and Indications*	*Proceed to*
10.1—Determine whether the exhaust manifold heat control valve is operating: Operate the valve by hand to determine whether it is free to move. If the valve is free, run the engine to operating temperature and observe the action of the valve, to ensure that it is opening.	If the valve sticks, spray it with a suitable solvent, open and close the valve to free it, and retest.	
	If the valve functions properly:	**10.2**
	If the valve does not free, or does not operate, replace the valve:	**10.2**
10.2—Ensure that there are no exhaust restrictions: Visually inspect the exhaust system for kinks, dents, or crushing. Also note that gases are flowing freely from the tailpipe at all engine speeds, indicating no restriction in the muffler or resonator.	Replace any damaged portion of the system:	**11.1**

Section 11—Cooling System

See Chapter 3 for service procedures

Test and Procedure	*Results and Indications*	*Proceed to*
11.1—Visually inspect the fan belt for glazing, cracks, and fraying, and replace if necessary. Tighten the belt so that the longest span has approximately ½″ play at its midpoint under thumb pressure (see Chapter 1).	Replace or tighten the fan belt as necessary: 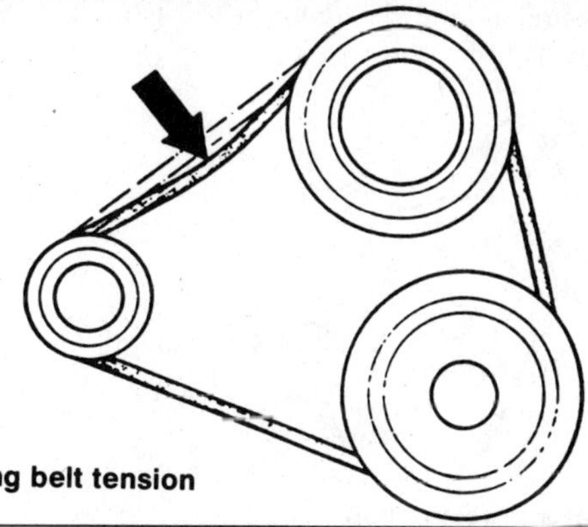 **Checking belt tension**	**11.2**
11.2—Check the fluid level of the cooling system.	If full or slightly low, fill as necessary:	**11.5**
	If extremely low:	**11.3**
11.3—Visually inspect the external portions of the cooling system (radiator, radiator hoses, thermostat elbow, water pump seals, heater hoses, etc.) for leaks. If none are found, pressurize the cooling system to 14–15 psi.	If cooling system holds the pressure:	**11.5**
	If cooling system loses pressure rapidly, reinspect external parts of the system for leaks under pressure. If none are found, check dipstick for coolant in crankcase. If no coolant is present, but pressure loss continues:	**11.4**
	If coolant is evident in crankcase, remove cylinder head(s), and check gasket(s). If gaskets are intact, block and cylinder head(s) should be checked for cracks or holes. If the gasket(s) is blown, replace, and purge the crankcase of coolant:	**12.6**
	NOTE: ***Occasionally, due to atmospheric and driving conditions, condensation of water can occur in the crankcase. This causes the oil to appear milky white. To remedy, run the engine until hot, and change the oil and oil filter.***	
11.4—Check for combustion leaks into the cooling system: Pressurize the cooling system as above. Start the engine, and observe the pressure gauge. If the needle fluctuates, remove each spark plug wire, one at a time, noting which cylinder(s) reduce or eliminate the fluctuation. **Pressurizing the cooling system**	Cylinders which reduce or eliminate the fluctuation, when the spark plug wire is removed, are leaking into the cooling system. Replace the head gasket on the affected cylinder bank(s). 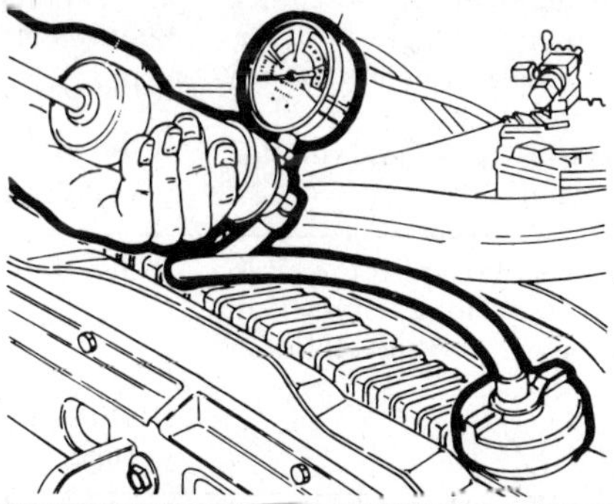	

Test and Procedure	Results and Indications	Proceed to
11.5—Check the radiator pressure cap: Attach a radiator pressure tester to the radiator cap (wet the seal prior to installation). Quickly pump up the pressure, noting the point at which the cap releases.	If the cap releases within ± 1 psi of the specified rating, it is operating properly:	**11.6**
	If the cap releases at more than ± 1 psi of the specified rating, it should be replaced:	**11.6**

Checking radiator pressure cap

Test and Procedure	Results and Indications	Proceed to
11.6—Test the thermostat: Start the engine cold, remove the radiator cap, and insert a thermometer into the radiator. Allow the engine to idle. After a short while, there will be a sudden, rapid increase in coolant temperature. The temperature at which this sharp rise stops is the thermostat opening temperature.	If the thermostat opens at or about the specified temperature:	**11.7**
	If the temperature doesn't increase: (If the temperature increases slowly and gradually, replace the thermostat.)	**11.7**
11.7—Check the water pump: Remove the thermostat elbow and the thermostat, disconnect the coil high tension lead (to prevent starting), and crank the engine momentarily.	If coolant flows, replace the thermostat and retest per 11.6:	**11.6**
	If coolant doesn't flow, reverse flush the cooling system to alleviate any blockage that might exist. If system is not blocked, and coolant will not flow, replace the water pump.	

Section 12—Lubrication

See Chapter 3 for service procedures

Test and Procedure	Results and Indications	Proceed to
12.1—Check the oil pressure gauge or warning light: If the gauge shows low pressure, or the light is on for no obvious reason, remove the oil pressure sender. Install an accurate oil pressure gauge and run the engine momentarily.	If oil pressure builds normally, run engine for a few moments to determine that it is functioning normally, and replace the sender.	—
	If the pressure remains low:	**12.2**
	If the pressure surges:	**12.3**
	If the oil pressure is zero:	**12.3**
12.2—Visually inspect the oil: If the oil is watery or very thin, milky, or foamy, replace the oil and oil filter.	If the oil is normal:	**12.3**
	If after replacing oil the pressure remains low:	**12.3**
	If after replacing oil the pressure becomes normal:	—

Test and Procedure	*Results and Indications*	*Proceed to*
12.3—Inspect the oil pressure relief valve and spring, to ensure that it is not sticking or stuck. Remove and thoroughly clean the valve, spring, and the valve body.	If the oil pressure improves: If no improvement is noted:	— **12.4**
12.4—Check to ensure that the oil pump is not cavitating (sucking air instead of oil): See that the crankcase is neither over nor underfull, and that the pickup in the sump is in the proper position and free from sludge.	Fill or drain the crankcase to the proper capacity, and clean the pickup screen in solvent if necessary. If no improvement is noted:	**12.5**
12.5—Inspect the oil pump drive and the oil pump:	If the pump drive or the oil pump appear to be defective, service as necessary and retest per 12.1:	**12.1**
	If the pump drive and pump appear to be operating normally, the engine should be disassembled to determine where blockage exists:	**See Chapter 3**
12.6—Purge the engine of ethylene glycol coolant: Completely drain the crankcase and the oil filter. Obtain a commercial butyl cellosolve base solvent, designated for this purpose, and follow the instructions precisely. Following this, install a new oil filter and refill the crankcase with the proper weight oil. The next oil and filter change should follow shortly thereafter (1000 miles).		

TROUBLESHOOTING EMISSION CONTROL SYSTEMS

See Chapter 4 for procedures applicable to individual emission control systems used on specific combinations of engine/transmission/model.

TROUBLESHOOTING THE CARBURETOR

See Chapter 4 for service procedures

Carburetor problems cannot be effectively isolated unless all other engine systems (particularly ignition and emission) are functioning properly and the engine is properly tuned.

Condition	Possible Cause
Engine cranks, but does not start	1. Improper starting procedure 2. No fuel in tank 3. Clogged fuel line or filter 4. Defective fuel pump 5. Choke valve not closing properly 6. Engine flooded 7. Choke valve not unloading 8. Throttle linkage not making full travel 9. Stuck needle or float 10. Leaking float needle or seat 11. Improper float adjustment
Engine stalls	1. Improperly adjusted idle speed or mixture **Engine hot** 2. Improperly adjusted dashpot 3. Defective or improperly adjusted solenoid 4. Incorrect fuel level in fuel bowl 5. Fuel pump pressure too high 6. Leaking float needle seat 7. Secondary throttle valve stuck open 8. Air or fuel leaks 9. Idle air bleeds plugged or missing 10. Idle passages plugged **Engine Cold** 11. Incorrectly adjusted choke 12. Improperly adjusted fast idle speed 13. Air leaks 14. Plugged idle or idle air passages 15. Stuck choke valve or binding linkage 16. Stuck secondary throttle valves 17. Engine flooding—high fuel level 18. Leaking or misaligned float
Engine hesitates on acceleration	1. Clogged fuel filter 2. Leaking fuel pump diaphragm 3. Low fuel pump pressure 4. Secondary throttle valves stuck, bent or misadjusted 5. Sticking or binding air valve 6. Defective accelerator pump 7. Vacuum leaks 8. Clogged air filter 9. Incorrect choke adjustment (engine cold)
Engine feels sluggish or flat on acceleration	1. Improperly adjusted idle speed or mixture 2. Clogged fuel filter 3. Defective accelerator pump 4. Dirty, plugged or incorrect main metering jets 5. Bent or sticking main metering rods 6. Sticking throttle valves 7. Stuck heat riser 8. Binding or stuck air valve 9. Dirty, plugged or incorrect secondary jets 10. Bent or sticking secondary metering rods. 11. Throttle body or manifold heat passages plugged 12. Improperly adjusted choke or choke vacuum break.
Carburetor floods	1. Defective fuel pump. Pressure too high. 2. Stuck choke valve 3. Dirty, worn or damaged float or needle valve/seat 4. Incorrect float/fuel level 5. Leaking float bowl

Condition	Possible Cause
Engine idles roughly and stalls	1. Incorrect idle speed 2. Clogged fuel filter 3. Dirt in fuel system or carburetor 4. Loose carburetor screws or attaching bolts 5. Broken carburetor gaskets 6. Air leaks 7. Dirty carburetor 8. Worn idle mixture needles 9. Throttle valves stuck open 10. Incorrectly adjusted float or fuel level 11. Clogged air filter
Engine runs unevenly or surges	1. Defective fuel pump 2. Dirty or clogged fuel filter 3. Plugged, loose or incorrect main metering jets or rods 4. Air leaks 5. Bent or sticking main metering rods 6. Stuck power piston 7. Incorrect float adjustment 8. Incorrect idle speed or mixture 9. Dirty or plugged idle system passages 10. Hard, brittle or broken gaskets 11. Loose attaching or mounting screws 12. Stuck or misaligned secondary throttle valves
Poor fuel economy	1. Poor driving habits 2. Stuck choke valve 3. Binding choke linkage 4. Stuck heat riser 5. Incorrect idle mixture 6. Defective accelerator pump 7. Air leaks 8. Plugged, loose or incorrect main metering jets 9. Improperly adjusted float or fuel level 10. Bent, misaligned or fuel-clogged float 11. Leaking float needle seat 12. Fuel leak 13. Accelerator pump discharge ball not seating properly 14. Incorrect main jets
Engine lacks high speed performance or power	1. Incorrect throttle linkage adjustment 2. Stuck or binding power piston 3. Defective accelerator pump 4. Air leaks 5. Incorrect float setting or fuel level 6. Dirty, plugged, worn or incorrect main metering jets or rods 7. Binding or sticking air valve 8. Brittle or cracked gaskets 9. Bent, incorrect or improperly adjusted secondary metering rods 10. Clogged fuel filter 11. Clogged air filter 12. Defective fuel pump

TROUBLESHOOTING FUEL INJECTION PROBLEMS

Each fuel injection system has its own unique components and test procedures, for which it is impossible to generalize. Refer to Chapter 4 of this Repair & Tune-Up Guide for specific test and repair procedures, if the vehicle is equipped with fuel injection.

TROUBLESHOOTING ELECTRICAL PROBLEMS

See Chapter 5 for service procedures

For any electrical system to operate, it must make a complete circuit. This simply means that the power flow from the battery must make a complete circle. When an electrical component is operating, power flows from the battery to the component, passes through the component causing it to perform its function (lighting a light bulb), and then returns to the battery through the ground of the circuit. This ground is usually (but not always) the metal part of the car or truck on which the electrical component is mounted.

Perhaps the easiest way to visualize this is to think of connecting a light bulb with two wires attached to it to the battery. If one of the two wires attached to the light bulb were attached to the negative post of the battery and the other were attached to the positive post of the battery, you would have a complete circuit. Current from the battery would flow to the light bulb, causing it to light, and return to the negative post of the battery.

The normal automotive circuit differs from this simple example in two ways. First, instead of having a return wire from the bulb to the battery, the light bulb returns the current to the battery through the chassis of the vehicle. Since the negative battery cable is attached to the chassis and the chassis is made of electrically conductive metal, the chassis of the vehicle can serve as a ground wire to complete the circuit. Secondly, most automotive circuits contain switches to turn components on and off as required.

Every complete circuit from a power source must include a component which is using the power from the power source. If you were to disconnect the light bulb from the wires and touch the two wires together (don't do this) the power supply wire to the component would be grounded before the normal ground connection for the circuit.

Because grounding a wire from a power source makes a complete circuit—less the required component to use the power—this phenomenon is called a short circuit. Common causes are: broken insulation (exposing the metal wire to a metal part of the car or truck), or a shorted switch.

Some electrical components which require a large amount of current to operate also have a relay in their circuit. Since these circuits carry a large amount of current, the thickness of the wire in the circuit (gauge size) is also greater. If this large wire were connected from the component to the control switch on the instrument panel, and then back to the component, a voltage drop would occur in the circuit. To prevent this potential drop in voltage, an electromagnetic switch (relay) is used. The large wires in the circuit are connected from the battery to one side of the relay, and from the opposite side of the relay to the component. The relay is normally open, preventing current from passing through the circuit. An additional, smaller, wire is connected from the relay to the control switch for the circuit. When the control switch is turned on, it grounds the smaller wire from the relay and completes the circuit. This closes the relay and allows current to flow from the battery to the component. The horn, headlight, and starter circuits are three which use relays.

It is possible for larger surges of current to pass through the electrical system of your car or truck. If this surge of current were to reach an electrical component, it could burn it out. To prevent this, fuses, circuit breakers or fusible links are connected into the current supply wires of most of the major electrical systems. When an electrical current of excessive power passes through the component's fuse, the fuse blows out and breaks the circuit, saving the component from destruction.

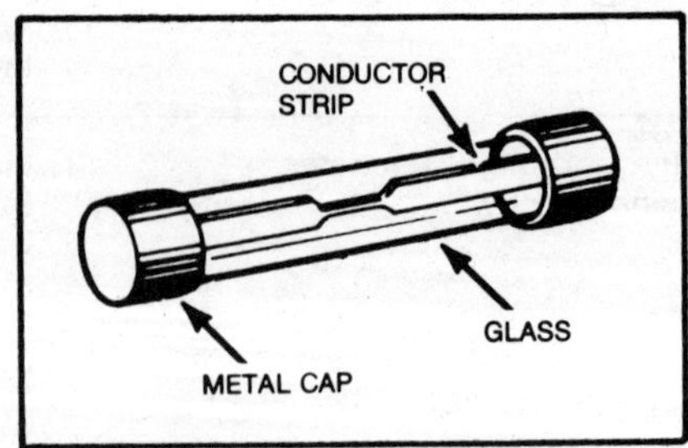

Typical automotive fuse

A circuit breaker is basically a self-repairing fuse. The circuit breaker opens the circuit the same way a fuse does. However, when either the short is removed from the circuit or the surge subsides, the circuit breaker resets itself and does not have to be replaced as a fuse does.

A fuse link is a wire that acts as a fuse. It is normally connected between the starter relay and the main wiring harness. This connection is usually under the hood. The fuse link (if installed) protects all the

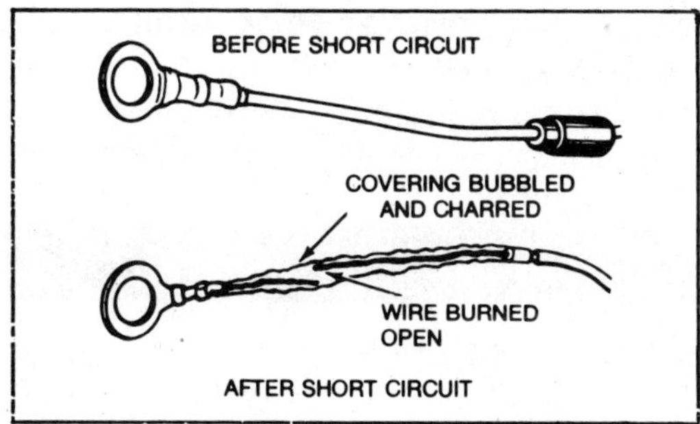

Most fusible links show a charred, melted insulation when they burn out

chassis electrical components, and is the probable cause of trouble when none of the electrical components function, unless the battery is disconnected or dead.

Electrical problems generally fall into one of three areas:

1. The component that is not functioning is not receiving current.
2. The component itself is not functioning.
3. The component is not properly grounded.

The electrical system can be checked with a test light and a jumper wire. A test light is a device that looks like a pointed screwdriver with a wire attached to it and has a light bulb in its handle. A jumper wire is a piece of insulated wire with an alligator clip attached to each end.

If a component is not working, you must follow a systematic plan to determine which of the three causes is the villain.

1. Turn on the switch that controls the inoperable component.
2. Disconnect the power supply wire from the component.
3. Attach the ground wire on the test light to a good metal ground.
4. Touch the probe end of the test light to the end of the power supply wire that was disconnected from the component. If the component is receiving current, the test light will go on.

NOTE: ***Some components work only when the ignition switch is turned on.***

If the test light does not go on, then the problem is in the circuit between the battery and the component. This includes all the switches, fuses, and relays in the system. Follow the wire that runs back to the battery. The problem is an open circuit between the

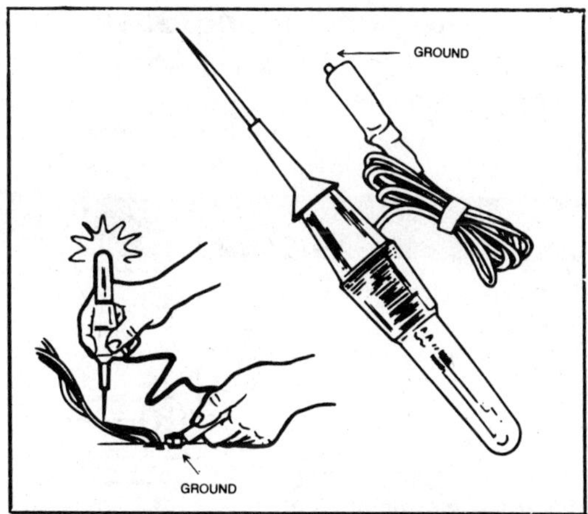

The test light will show the presence of current when touched to a hot wire and grounded at the other end

battery and the component. If the fuse is blown and, when replaced, immediately blows again, there is a short circuit in the system which must be located and repaired. If there is a switch in the system, bypass it with a jumper wire. This is done by connecting one end of the jumper wire to the power supply wire into the switch and the other end of the jumper wire to the wire coming out of the switch. If the test light lights with the jumper wire installed, the switch or whatever was bypassed is defective.

NOTE: ***Never substitute the jumper wire for the component, since it is required to use the power from the power source.***

5. If the bulb in the test light goes on, then the current is getting to the component that is not working. This eliminates the first of the three possible causes. Connect the power supply wire and connect a jumper wire from the component to a good metal ground. Do this with the switch which controls the component turned on, and also the ignition switch turned on if it is required for the component to work. If the component works with the jumper wire installed, then it has a bad ground. This is usually caused by the metal area on which the component mounts to the chassis being coated with some type of foreign matter.
6. If neither test located the source of the trouble, then the component itself is defective. Remember that for any electrical system to work, all connections must be clean and tight.

Troubleshooting Basic Turn Signal and Flasher Problems

See Chapter 5 for service procedures

Most problems in the turn signals or flasher system can be reduced to defective flashers or bulbs, which are easily replaced. Occasionally, the turn signal switch will prove defective.

F = Front R = Rear ● = Lights off ○ = Lights on

Condition		Possible Cause
Turn signals light, but do not flash	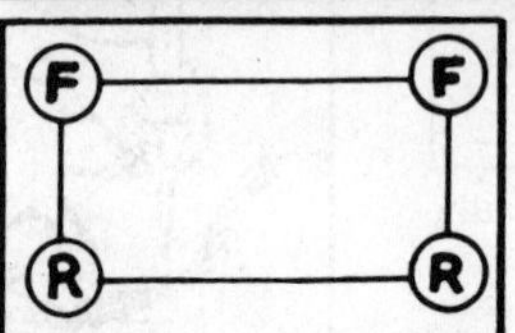	Defective flasher
No turn signals light on either side	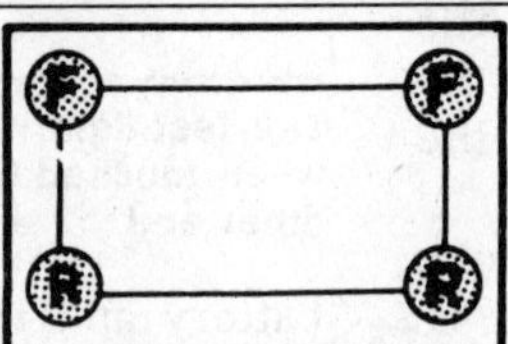	Blown fuse. Replace if defective. Defective flasher. Check by substitution. Open circuit, short circuit or poor ground.
Both turn signals on one side don't work	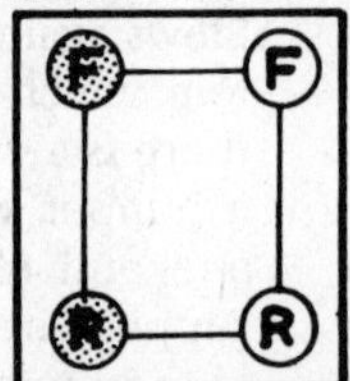	Bad bulbs. Bad ground in both (or either) housings.
One turn signal light on one side doesn't work	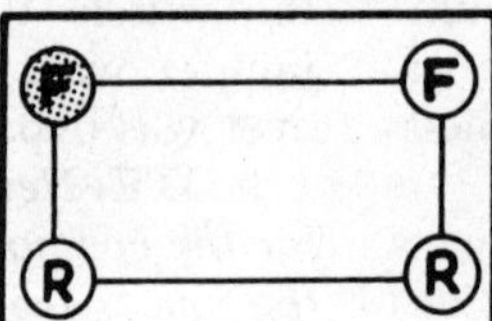	Defective bulb. Corrosion in socket. Clean contacts. Poor ground at socket.
Turn signal flashes too fast or too slowly	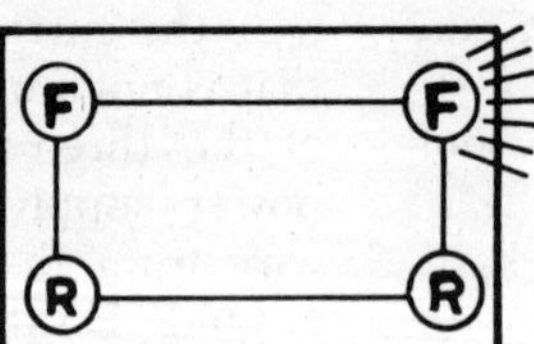	Check any bulb on the side flashing too fast. A heavy-duty bulb is probably installed in place of a regular bulb. Check the bulb flashing too slowly. A standard bulb was probably installed in place of a heavy-duty bulb. Loose connections or corrosion at the bulb socket.
Indicator lights don't work in either direction	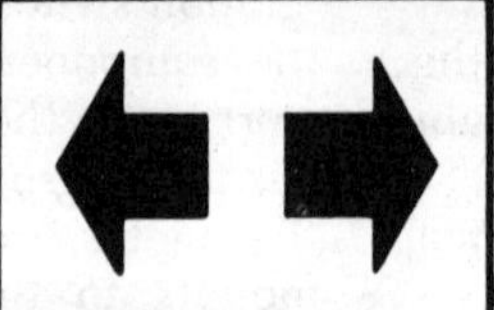	Check if the turn signals are working. Check the dash indicator lights. Check the flasher by substitution.
One indicator light doesn't light	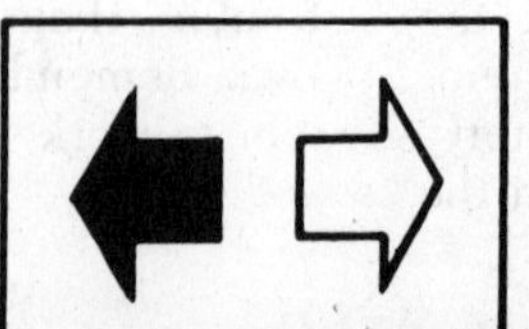	On systems with one dash indicator: See if the lights work on the same side. Often the filaments have been reversed in systems combining stoplights with taillights and turn signals. Check the flasher by substitution. On systems with two indicators: Check the bulbs on the same side. Check the indicator light bulb. Check the flasher by substitution.

Troubleshooting Lighting Problems

See Chapter 5 for service procedures

Condition	Possible Cause
One or more lights don't work, but others do	1. Defective bulb(s) 2. Blown fuse(s) 3. Dirty fuse clips or light sockets 4. Poor ground circuit
Lights burn out quickly	1. Incorrect voltage regulator setting or defective regulator 2. Poor battery/alternator connections
Lights go dim	1. Low/discharged battery 2. Alternator not charging 3. Corroded sockets or connections 4. Low voltage output
Lights flicker	1. Loose connection 2. Poor ground. (Run ground wire from light housing to frame) 3. Circuit breaker operating (short circuit)
Lights "flare"—Some flare is normal on acceleration—If excessive, see "Lights Burn Out Quickly"	High voltage setting
Lights glare—approaching drivers are blinded	1. Lights adjusted too high 2. Rear springs or shocks sagging 3. Rear tires soft

Troubleshooting Dash Gauge Problems

Most problems can be traced to a defective sending unit or faulty wiring. Occasionally, the gauge itself is at fault. See Chapter 5 for service procedures.

Condition	Possible Cause
COOLANT TEMPERATURE GAUGE	
Gauge reads erratically or not at all	1. Loose or dirty connections 2. Defective sending unit 3. Defective gauge. To test a bi-metal gauge, remove the wire from the sending unit. Ground the wire for an instant. If the gauge registers, replace the sending unit. To test a magnetic gauge, disconnect the wire at the sending unit. With ignition ON gauge should register COLD. Ground the wire; gauge should register HOT.
AMMETER GAUGE—TURN HEADLIGHTS ON (DO NOT START ENGINE). NOTE REACTION	
Ammeter shows charge Ammeter shows discharge Ammeter does not move	1. Connections reversed on gauge 2. Ammeter is OK 3. Loose connections or faulty wiring 4. Defective gauge

Condition	Possible Cause
OIL PRESSURE GAUGE	
Gauge does not register or is inaccurate	1. On mechanical gauge, Bourdon tube may be bent or kinked. 2. Low oil pressure. Remove sending unit. Idle the engine briefly. If no oil flows from sending unit hole, problem is in engine. 3. Defective gauge. Remove the wire from the sending unit and ground it for an instant with the ignition ON. A good gauge will go to the top of the scale. 4. Defective wiring. Check the wiring to the gauge. If it's OK and the gauge doesn't register when grounded, replace the gauge. 5. Defective sending unit.
ALL GAUGES	
All gauges do not operate	1. Blown fuse 2. Defective instrument regulator
All gauges read low or erratically	3. Defective or dirty instrument voltage regulator
All gauges pegged	4. Loss of ground between instrument voltage regulator and frame 5. Defective instrument regulator
WARNING LIGHTS	
Light(s) do not come on when ignition is ON, but engine is not started	1. Defective bulb 2. Defective wire 3. Defective sending unit. Disconnect the wire from the sending unit and ground it. Replace the sending unit if the light comes on with the ignition ON.
Light comes on with engine running	4. Problem in individual system 5. Defective sending unit

Troubleshooting Clutch Problems

It is false economy to replace individual clutch components. The pressure plate, clutch plate and throwout bearing should be replaced as a set, and the flywheel face inspected, whenever the clutch is overhauled. See Chapter 6 for service procedures.

Condition	Possible Cause
Clutch chatter	1. Grease on driven plate (disc) facing 2. Binding clutch linkage or cable 3. Loose, damaged facings on driven plate (disc) 4. Engine mounts loose 5. Incorrect height adjustment of pressure plate release levers 6. Clutch housing or housing to transmission adapter misalignment 7. Loose driven plate hub
Clutch grabbing	1. Oil, grease on driven plate (disc) facing 2. Broken pressure plate 3. Warped or binding driven plate. Driven plate binding on clutch shaft
Clutch slips	1. Lack of lubrication in clutch linkage or cable (linkage or cable binds, causes incomplete engagement) 2. Incorrect pedal, or linkage adjustment 3. Broken pressure plate springs 4. Weak pressure plate springs 5. Grease on driven plate facings (disc)

Troubleshooting Clutch Problems (cont.)

Condition	Possible Cause
Incomplete clutch release	1. Incorrect pedal or linkage adjustment or linkage or cable binding 2. Incorrect height adjustment on pressure plate release levers 3. Loose, broken facings on driven plate (disc) 4. Bent, dished, warped driven plate caused by overheating
Grinding, whirring grating noise when pedal is depressed	1. Worn or defective throwout bearing 2. Starter drive teeth contacting flywheel ring gear teeth. Look for milled or polished teeth on ring gear.
Squeal, howl, trumpeting noise when pedal is being released (occurs during first inch to inch and one-half of pedal travel)	Pilot bushing worn or lack of lubricant. If bushing appears OK, polish bushing with emery cloth, soak lube wick in oil, lube bushing with oil, apply film of chassis grease to clutch shaft pilot hub, reassemble. NOTE: Bushing wear may be due to misalignment of clutch housing or housing to transmission adapter
Vibration or clutch pedal pulsation with clutch disengaged (pedal fully depressed)	1. Worn or defective engine transmission mounts 2. Flywheel run out. (Flywheel run out at face not to exceed 0.005") 3. Damaged or defective clutch components

Troubleshooting Manual Transmission Problems

See Chapter 6 for service procedures

Condition	Possible Cause
Transmission jumps out of gear	1. Misalignment of transmission case or clutch housing. 2. Worn pilot bearing in crankshaft. 3. Bent transmission shaft. 4. Worn high speed sliding gear. 5. Worn teeth or end-play in clutch shaft. 6. Insufficient spring tension on shifter rail plunger. 7. Bent or loose shifter fork. 8. Gears not engaging completely. 9. Loose or worn bearings on clutch shaft or mainshaft. 10. Worn gear teeth. 11. Worn or damaged detent balls.
Transmission sticks in gear	1. Clutch not releasing fully. 2. Burred or battered tooth on clutch shaft, or sliding sleeve. 3. Burred or battered transmission mainshaft. 4. Frozen synchronizing clutch. 5. Stuck shifter rail plunger. 6. Gearshift lever twisting and binding shifter rail. 7. Battered teeth on high speed sliding gear or on sleeve. 8. Improper lubrication, or lack of lubrication. 9. Corroded transmission parts. 10. Defective mainshaft pilot bearing. 11. Locked gear bearings will give same effect as stuck in gear.
Transmission gears will not synchronize	1. Binding pilot bearing on mainshaft, will synchronize in high gear only. 2. Clutch not releasing fully. 3. Detent spring weak or broken. 4. Weak or broken springs under balls in sliding gear sleeve. 5. Binding bearing on clutch shaft, or binding countershaft. 6. Binding pilot bearing in crankshaft. 7. Badly worn gear teeth. 8. Improper lubrication. 9. Constant mesh gear not turning freely on transmission mainshaft. Will synchronize in that gear only.

Condition	Possible Cause
Gears spinning when shifting into gear from neutral	1. Clutch not releasing fully. 2. In some cases an extremely light lubricant in transmission will cause gears to continue to spin for a short time after clutch is released. 3. Binding pilot bearing in crankshaft.
Transmission noisy in all gears	1. Insufficient lubricant, or improper lubricant. 2. Worn countergear bearings. 3. Worn or damaged main drive gear or countergear. 4. Damaged main drive gear or mainshaft bearings. 5. Worn or damaged countergear anti-lash plate.
Transmission noisy in neutral only	1. Damaged main drive gear bearing. 2. Damaged or loose mainshaft pilot bearing. 3. Worn or damaged countergear anti-lash plate. 4. Worn countergear bearings.
Transmission noisy in one gear only	1. Damaged or worn constant mesh gears. 2. Worn or damaged countergear bearings. 3. Damaged or worn synchronizer.
Transmission noisy in reverse only	1. Worn or damaged reverse idler gear or idler bushing. 2. Worn or damaged mainshaft reverse gear. 3. Worn or damaged reverse countergear. 4. Damaged shift mechanism.

TROUBLESHOOTING AUTOMATIC TRANSMISSION PROBLEMS

Keeping alert to changes in the operating characteristics of the transmission (changing shift points, noises, etc.) can prevent small problems from becoming large ones. If the problem cannot be traced to loose bolts, fluid level, misadjusted linkage, clogged filters or similar problems, you should probably seek professional service.

Transmission Fluid Indications

The appearance and odor of the transmission fluid can give valuable clues to the overall condition of the transmission. Always note the appearance of the fluid when you check the fluid level or change the fluid. Rub a small amount of fluid between your fingers to feel for grit and smell the fluid on the dipstick.

If the fluid appears:	It indicates:
Clear and red colored	Normal operation
Discolored (extremely dark red or brownish) or smells burned	Band or clutch pack failure, usually caused by an overheated transmission. Hauling very heavy loads with insufficient power or failure to change the fluid often result in overheating. Do not confuse this appearance with newer fluids that have a darker red color and a strong odor (though not a burned odor).
Foamy or aerated (light in color and full of bubbles)	1. The level is too high (gear train is churning oil) 2. An internal air leak (air is mixing with the fluid). Have the transmission checked professionally.
Solid residue in the fluid	Defective bands, clutch pack or bearings. Bits of band material or metal abrasives are clinging to the dipstick. Have the transmission checked professionally.
Varnish coating on the dipstick	The transmission fluid is overheating

TROUBLESHOOTING DRIVE AXLE PROBLEMS

First, determine when the noise is most noticeable.

Drive Noise: Produced under vehicle acceleration.

Coast Noise: Produced while coasting with a closed throttle.

Float Noise: Occurs while maintaining constant speed (just enough to keep speed constant) on a level road.

External Noise Elimination

It is advisable to make a thorough road test to determine whether the noise originates in the rear axle or whether it originates from the tires, engine, transmission, wheel bearings or road surface. Noise originating from other places cannot be corrected by servicing the rear axle.

ROAD NOISE

Brick or rough surfaced concrete roads produce noises that seem to come from the rear axle. Road noise is usually identical in Drive or Coast and driving on a different type of road will tell whether the road is the problem.

TIRE NOISE

Tire noise can be mistaken as rear axle noise, even though the tires on the front are at fault. Snow tread and mud tread tires or tires worn unevenly will frequently cause vibrations which seem to originate elsewhere; *temporarily, and for test purposes only*, inflate the tires to 40–50 lbs. This will significantly alter the noise produced by the tires, but will not alter noise from the rear axle. Noises from the rear axle will normally cease at speeds below 30 mph on coast, while tire noise will continue at lower tone as speed is decreased. The rear axle noise will usually change from drive conditions to coast conditions, while tire noise will not. Do not forget to lower the tire pressure to normal after the test is complete.

ENGINE/TRANSMISSION NOISE

Determine at what speed the noise is most pronounced, then stop in a quiet place. With the transmission in Neutral, run the engine through speeds corresponding to road speeds where the noise was noticed. Noises produced with the vehicle standing still are coming from the engine or transmission.

FRONT WHEEL BEARINGS

Front wheel bearing noises, sometimes confused with rear axle noises, will not change when comparing drive and coast conditions. While holding the speed steady, lightly apply the footbrake. This will often cause wheel bearing noise to lessen, as some of the weight is taken off the bearing. Front wheel bearings are easily checked by jacking up the wheels and spinning the wheels. Shaking the wheels will also determine if the wheel bearings are excessively loose.

REAR AXLE NOISES

Eliminating other possible sources can narrow the cause to the rear axle, which normally produces noise from worn gears or bearings. Gear noises tend to peak in a narrow speed range, while bearing noises will usually vary in pitch with engine speeds.

Noise Diagnosis

The Noise Is:	Most Probably Produced By:
1. Identical under Drive or Coast	Road surface, tires or front wheel bearings
2. Different depending on road surface	Road surface or tires
3. Lower as speed is lowered	Tires
4. Similar when standing or moving	Engine or transmission
5. A vibration	Unbalanced tires, rear wheel bearing, unbalanced driveshaft or worn U-joint
6. A knock or click about every two tire revolutions	Rear wheel bearing
7. Most pronounced on turns	Damaged differential gears
8. A steady low-pitched whirring or scraping, starting at low speeds	Damaged or worn pinion bearing
9. A chattering vibration on turns	Wrong differential lubricant or worn clutch plates (limited slip rear axle)
10. Noticed only in Drive, Coast or Float conditions	Worn ring gear and/or pinion gear

Troubleshooting Steering & Suspension Problems

Condition	Possible Cause
Hard steering (wheel is hard to turn)	1. Improper tire pressure 2. Loose or glazed pump drive belt 3. Low or incorrect fluid 4. Loose, bent or poorly lubricated front end parts 5. Improper front end alignment (excessive caster) 6. Bind in steering column or linkage 7. Kinked hydraulic hose 8. Air in hydraulic system 9. Low pump output or leaks in system 10. Obstruction in lines 11. Pump valves sticking or out of adjustment 12. Incorrect wheel alignment
Loose steering (too much play in steering wheel)	1. Loose wheel bearings 2. Faulty shocks 3. Worn linkage or suspension components 4. Loose steering gear mounting or linkage points 5. Steering mechanism worn or improperly adjusted 6. Valve spool improperly adjusted 7. Worn ball joints, tie-rod ends, etc.
Veers or wanders (pulls to one side with hands off steering wheel)	1. Improper tire pressure 2. Improper front end alignment 3. Dragging or improperly adjusted brakes 4. Bent frame 5. Improper rear end alignment 6. Faulty shocks or springs 7. Loose or bent front end components 8. Play in Pitman arm 9. Steering gear mountings loose 10. Loose wheel bearings 11. Binding Pitman arm 12. Spool valve sticking or improperly adjusted 13. Worn ball joints
Wheel oscillation or vibration transmitted through steering wheel	1. Low or uneven tire pressure 2. Loose wheel bearings 3. Improper front end alignment 4. Bent spindle 5. Worn, bent or broken front end components 6. Tires out of round or out of balance 7. Excessive lateral runout in disc brake rotor 8. Loose or bent shock absorber or strut
Noises (see also "Troubleshooting Drive Axle Problems")	1. Loose belts 2. Low fluid, air in system 3. Foreign matter in system 4. Improper lubrication 5. Interference or chafing in linkage 6. Steering gear mountings loose 7. Incorrect adjustment or wear in gear box 8. Faulty valves or wear in pump 9. Kinked hydraulic lines 10. Worn wheel bearings
Poor return of steering	1. Over-inflated tires 2. Improperly aligned front end (excessive caster) 3. Binding in steering column 4. No lubrication in front end 5. Steering gear adjusted too tight
Uneven tire wear (see "How To Read Tire Wear")	1. Incorrect tire pressure 2. Improperly aligned front end 3. Tires out-of-balance 4. Bent or worn suspension parts

HOW TO READ TIRE WEAR

The way your tires wear is a good indicator of other parts of the suspension. Abnormal wear patterns are often caused by the need for simple tire maintenance, or for front end alignment.

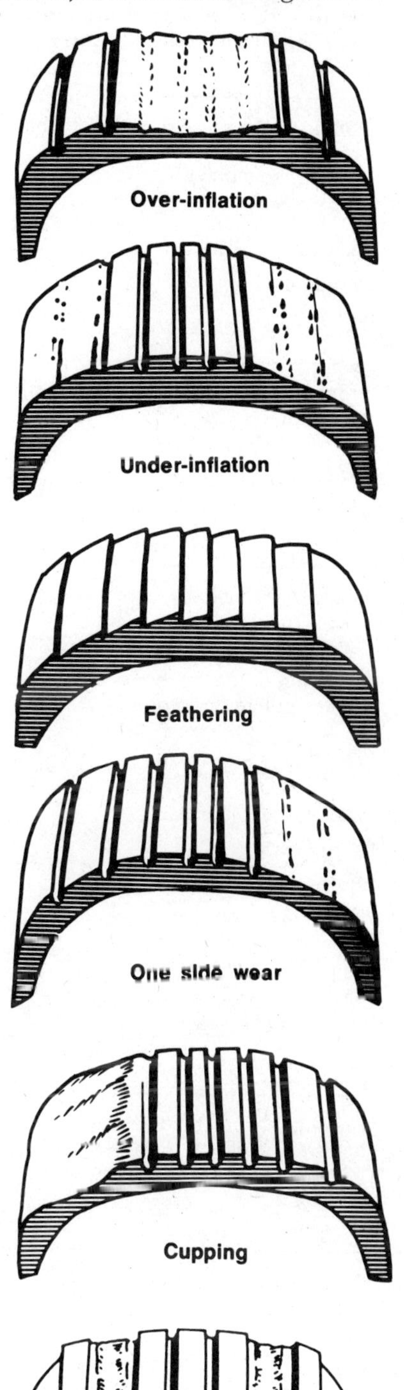

Excessive wear at the center of the tread indicates that the air pressure in the tire is consistently too high. The tire is riding on the center of the tread and wearing it prematurely. Occasionally, this wear pattern can result from outrageously wide tires on narrow rims. The cure for this is to replace either the tires or the wheels.

This type of wear usually results from consistent under-inflation. When a tire is under-inflated, there is too much contact with the road by the outer treads, which wear prematurely. When this type of wear occurs, and the tire pressure is known to be consistently correct, a bent or worn steering component or the need for wheel alignment could be indicated.

Feathering is a condition when the edge of each tread rib develops a slightly rounded edge on one side and a sharp edge on the other. By running your hand over the tire, you can usually feel the sharper edges before you'll be able to see them. The most common causes of feathering are incorrect toe-in setting or deteriorated bushings in the front suspension.

When an inner or outer rib wears faster than the rest of the tire, the need for wheel alignment is indicated. There is excessive camber in the front suspension, causing the wheel to lean too much putting excessive load on one side of the tire. Misalignment could also be due to sagging springs, worn ball joints, or worn control arm bushings. Be sure the vehicle is loaded the way it's normally driven when you have the wheels aligned.

Cups or scalloped dips appearing around the edge of the tread almost always indicate worn (sometimes bent) suspension parts. Adjustment of wheel alignment alone will seldom cure the problem. Any worn component that connects the wheel to the suspension can cause this type of wear. Occasionally, wheels that are out of balance will wear like this, but wheel imbalance usually shows up as bald spots between the outside edges and center of the tread.

Second-rib wear is usually found only in radial tires, and appears where the steel belts end in relation to the tread. It can be kept to a minimum by paying careful attention to tire pressure and frequently rotating the tires. This is often considered normal wear but excessive amounts indicate that the tires are too wide for the wheels.

Troubleshooting Disc Brake Problems

Condition	Possible Cause
Noise—groan—brake noise emanating when slowly releasing brakes (creep-groan)	Not detrimental to function of disc brakes—no corrective action required. (This noise may be eliminated by slightly increasing or decreasing brake pedal efforts.)
Rattle—brake noise or rattle emanating at low speeds on rough roads, (front wheels only).	1. Shoe anti-rattle spring missing or not properly positioned. 2. Excessive clearance between shoe and caliper. 3. Soft or broken caliper seals. 4. Deformed or misaligned disc. 5. Loose caliper.
Scraping	1. Mounting bolts too long. 2. Loose wheel bearings. 3. Bent, loose, or misaligned splash shield.
Front brakes heat up during driving and fail to release	1. Operator riding brake pedal. 2. Stop light switch improperly adjusted. 3. Sticking pedal linkage. 4. Frozen or seized piston. 5. Residual pressure valve in master cylinder. 6. Power brake malfunction. 7. Proportioning valve malfunction.
Leaky brake caliper	1. Damaged or worn caliper piston seal. 2. Scores or corrosion on surface of cylinder bore.
Grabbing or uneven brake action—Brakes pull to one side	1. Causes listed under "Brakes Pull". 2. Power brake malfunction. 3. Low fluid level in master cylinder. 4. Air in hydraulic system. 5. Brake fluid, oil or grease on linings. 6. Unmatched linings. 7. Distorted brake pads. 8. Frozen or seized pistons. 9. Incorrect tire pressure. 10. Front end out of alignment. 11. Broken rear spring. 12. Brake caliper pistons sticking. 13. Restricted hose or line. 14. Caliper not in proper alignment to braking disc. 15. Stuck or malfunctioning metering valve. 16. Soft or broken caliper seals. 17. Loose caliper.
Brake pedal can be depressed without braking effect	1. Air in hydraulic system or improper bleeding procedure. 2. Leak past primary cup in master cylinder. 3. Leak in system. 4. Rear brakes out of adjustment. 5. Bleeder screw open.
Excessive pedal travel	1. Air, leak, or insufficient fluid in system or caliper. 2. Warped or excessively tapered shoe and lining assembly. 3. Excessive disc runout. 4. Rear brake adjustment required. 5. Loose wheel bearing adjustment. 6. Damaged caliper piston seal. 7. Improper brake fluid (boil). 8. Power brake malfunction. 9. Weak or soft hoses.

Troubleshooting Disc Brake Problems (cont.)

Condition	*Possible Cause*
Brake roughness or chatter (pedal pumping)	1. Excessive thickness variation of braking disc. 2. Excessive lateral runout of braking disc. 3. Rear brake drums out-of-round. 4. Excessive front bearing clearance.
Excessive pedal effort	1. Brake fluid, oil or grease on linings. 2. Incorrect lining. 3. Frozen or seized pistons. 4. Power brake malfunction. 5. Kinked or collapsed hose or line. 6. Stuck metering valve. 7. Scored caliper or master cylinder bore. 8. Seized caliper pistons.
Brake pedal fades (pedal travel increases with foot on brake)	1. Rough master cylinder or caliper bore. 2. Loose or broken hydraulic lines/connections. 3. Air in hydraulic system. 4. Fluid level low. 5. Weak or soft hoses. 6. Inferior quality brake shoes or fluid. 7. Worn master cylinder piston cups or seals.

Troubleshooting Drum Brakes

Condition	*Possible Cause*
Pedal goes to floor	1. Fluid low in reservoir. 2. Air in hydraulic system. 3. Improperly adjusted brake. 4. Leaking wheel cylinders. 5. Loose or broken brake lines. 6. Leaking or worn master cylinder. 7. Excessively worn brake lining.
Spongy brake pedal	1. Air in hydraulic system. 2. Improper brake fluid (low boiling point). 3. Excessively worn or cracked brake drums. 4. Broken pedal pivot bushing.
Brakes pulling	1. Contaminated lining. 2. Front end out of alignment. 3. Incorrect brake adjustment. 4. Unmatched brake lining. 5. Brake drums out of round. 6. Brake shoes distorted. 7. Restricted brake hose or line. 8. Broken rear spring. 9. Worn brake linings. 10. Uneven lining wear. 11. Glazed brake lining. 12. Excessive brake lining dust. 13. Heat spotted brake drums. 14. Weak brake return springs. 15. Faulty automatic adjusters. 16. Low or incorrect tire pressure.

Condition	Possible Cause
Squealing brakes	1. Glazed brake lining. 2. Saturated brake lining. 3. Weak or broken brake shoe retaining spring. 4. Broken or weak brake shoe return spring. 5. Incorrect brake lining. 6. Distorted brake shoes. 7. Bent support plate. 8. Dust in brakes or scored brake drums. 9. Linings worn below limit. 10. Uneven brake lining wear. 11. Heat spotted brake drums.
Chirping brakes	1. Out of round drum or eccentric axle flange pilot.
Dragging brakes	1. Incorrect wheel or parking brake adjustment. 2. Parking brakes engaged or improperly adjusted. 3. Weak or broken brake shoe return spring. 4. Brake pedal binding. 5. Master cylinder cup sticking. 6. Obstructed master cylinder relief port. 7. Saturated brake lining. 8. Bent or out of round brake drum. 9. Contaminated or improper brake fluid. 10. Sticking wheel cylinder pistons. 11. Driver riding brake pedal. 12. Defective proportioning valve. 13. Insufficient brake shoe lubricant.
Hard pedal	1. Brake booster inoperative. 2. Incorrect brake lining. 3. Restricted brake line or hose. 4. Frozen brake pedal linkage. 5. Stuck wheel cylinder. 6. Binding pedal linkage. 7. Faulty proportioning valve.
Wheel locks	1. Contaminated brake lining. 2. Loose or torn brake lining. 3. Wheel cylinder cups sticking. 4. Incorrect wheel bearing adjustment. 5. Faulty proportioning valve.
Brakes fade (high speed)	1. Incorrect lining. 2. Overheated brake drums. 3. Incorrect brake fluid (low boiling temperature). 4. Saturated brake lining. 5. Leak in hydraulic system. 6. Faulty automatic adjusters.
Pedal pulsates	1. Bent or out of round brake drum.
Brake chatter and shoe knock	1. Out of round brake drum. 2. Loose support plate. 3. Bent support plate. 4. Distorted brake shoes. 5. Machine grooves in contact face of brake drum (Shoe Knock). 6. Contaminated brake lining. 7. Missing or loose components. 8. Incorrect lining material. 9. Out-of-round brake drums. 10. Heat spotted or scored brake drums. 11. Out-of-balance wheels.

Troubleshooting Drum Brakes (cont.)

Condition	*Possible Cause*
Brakes do not self adjust	1. Adjuster screw frozen in thread. 2. Adjuster screw corroded at thrust washer. 3. Adjuster lever does not engage star wheel. 4. Adjuster installed on wrong wheel.
Brake light glows	1. Leak in the hydraulic system. 2. Air in the system. 3. Improperly adjusted master cylinder pushrod. 4. Uneven lining wear. 5. Failure to center combination valve or proportioning valve.

Mechanic's Data

General Conversion Table

Multiply By	To Convert	To	
	LENGTH		
2.54	Inches	Centimeters	.3937
25.4	Inches	Millimeters	.03937
30.48	Feet	Centimeters	.0328
.304	Feet	Meters	3.28
.914	Yards	Meters	1.094
1.609	Miles	Kilometers	.621
	VOLUME		
.473	Pints	Liters	2.11
.946	Quarts	Liters	1.06
3.785	Gallons	Liters	.264
.016	Cubic inches	Liters	61.02
16.39	Cubic inches	Cubic cms.	.061
28.3	Cubic feet	Liters	.0353
	MASS (Weight)		
28.35	Ounces	Grams	.035
.4536	Pounds	Kilograms	2.20
—	To obtain	From	Multiply by

Multiply By	To Convert	To	
	AREA		
.645	Square inches	Square cms.	.155
.836	Square yds.	Square meters	1.196
	FORCE		
4.448	Pounds	Newtons	.225
.138	Ft./lbs.	Kilogram/meters	7.23
1.36	Ft./lbs.	Newton-meters	.737
.112	In./lbs.	Newton-meters	8.844
	PRESSURE		
.068	Psi	Atmospheres	14.7
6.89	Psi	Kilopascals	.145
	OTHER		
1.104	Horsepower (DIN)	Horsepower (SAE)	.9861
.746	Horsepower (SAE)	Kilowatts (KW)	1.34
1.60	Mph	Km/h	.625
.425	Mpg	Km/1	2.35
—	To obtain	From	Multiply by

Tap Drill Sizes

National Coarse or U.S.S.

Screw & Tap Size	Threads Per Inch	Use Drill Number
No. 5	40	39
No. 6	32	36
No. 8	32	29
No. 10	24	25
No. 12	24	17
1/4	20	8
5/16	18	F
3/8	16	5/16
7/16	14	U
1/2	13	27/64
9/16	12	31/64
5/8	11	17/32
3/4	10	21/32
7/8	9	49/64

National Coarse or U.S.S.

Screw & Tap Size	Threads Per Inch	Use Drill Number
1	8	7/8
1 1/8	7	63/64
1 1/4	7	1 7/64
1 1/2	6	1 11/32

National Fine or S.A.E.

Screw & Tap Size	Threads Per Inch	Use Drill Number
No. 5	44	37
No. 6	40	33
No. 8	36	29
No. 10	32	21

National Fine or S.A.E.

Screw & Tap Size	Threads Per Inch	Use Drill Number
No. 12	28	15
1/4	28	3
6/16	24	1
3/8	24	Q
7/16	20	W
1/2	20	29/64
9/16	18	33/64
5/8	18	37/64
3/4	16	11/16
7/8	14	13/16
1 1/8	12	1 3/64
1 1/4	12	1 11/64
1 1/2	12	1 27/64

Index

Wiring Diagrams from

CHILTON BOOK COMPANY

Wiring diagrams for all vehicles covered by this book are now available from Chilton Book Co., for only $5.00 per wiring diagram.

Please send me the wiring diagram for the vehicle(s) listed below.

YEAR	MAKE	MODEL	ENGINE	PRICE

Sub-Total	
PA Residents add 6% sales tax (30¢ per wiring diagram)	
TOTAL ENCLOSED (Check or Money Order). DO NOT SEND CASH!	

IMPORTANT!

This is your mailing label. Print clearly or type. All orders will be shipped postpaid by third class mail. Please allow 4-5 weeks for delivery.

Radnor, Pennsylvania 19089

SHIP TO:

Name ______________________________

Street Address ______________________________

City ____________________ State __________ Zip __________

Mail this page to: CHILTON BOOK COMPANY
Dept WD
201 King of Prussia Road
Radnor, PA 19089-0230